2003
CHILDREN'S WRITER'S & ILLUSTRATOR'S

800+ EDITORS AND ART DIRECTORS WHO WANT YOUR WORK *MARKET*

EDITOR **ALICE POPE**

ASSISTANT EDITOR **MONA MICHAEL**

WRITER'S DIGEST BOOKS
CINCINNATI, OH

Editorial Director, Annuals Department: Barbara Kuroff
Writer's Digest Books websites: www.writersdigest.com, www.writersmarket.com

International Standard Serial Number 0897-9790
International Standard Book Number 1-58297-148-X

Cover illustration by Linda Howard Bittner

Attention Booksellers: This is an annual directory of F&W Publications.
Return deadline for this edition is January 15, 2004.

Contents

Page 86

MARKETS

Page 229

RESOURCES

Page 137

From the Editor

It's terrible to move when you're a book person. I moved into a new house recently, and toted several dozen boxes of (mostly children's) books. As I sweated and strained my back, I swore out loud (no one was home but the cat, so I guess I was talking to the bookstore gods) that I would never, ever, ever bring another book into my house. And I stuck to that . . . for about a day.

Less than 24 hours after my grand proclamation, *Because of Winn-Dixie* arrived in my office.

I had just gotten Lisa Rondinelli Albert's article The Writer's Menu for Success: Crafting Stories Readers Crave (page 41). Lisa quotes Candlewick editor Kara LaReau about what drew her in to read beyond the first page of Kate DiCamillo's Newbery Honor Book: "Never mind the first page—I think the first sentence of *Winn-Dixie* speaks for itself! How could anyone not want to read on?"

When I read that, I put down the article and picked up *Because of Winn-Dixie*. I read the first line. And I was hooked. I could have taken the rest of my workday and kept reading (I love my job), but I really wanted to hear that line out loud.

Eventually 5 o'clock rolled around. I grabbed *Winn-Dixie*, sped home, and read the line aloud. Then I read it out loud a few more times. That night, I began reading *Winn-Dixie* aloud to my (almost) husband. (He'll be my husband by the time you read this.) Reading to him was an excuse, really. I just wanted to hear it. Kate DiCamillo's language deserves as much. (See her Insider Report on page 122.)

In my interview with Newbery Honor winner Jennifer L. Holm (page 144), she says, "I was a huge reader when I was young. One of our neighbors said recently his clearest memory of me as a kid was raking the lawn one-handed while I read a book with the other!" Books are still a passion for Jenni. "Reading is my favorite thing in life. Literally," she says.

Linda Sue Park (featured in the 2002 *Children's Writer's & Illustrator's Market*), Newbery Medal winner in 2002 and a prolific reader since childhood, talked about her father's influence on her reading life in her Newbery acceptance speech. "He took me to the library. Every two weeks without fail, he spent an hour each Saturday morning choosing books for my siblings and me." Linda Sue quotes Stephen King's *On Writing* on her website: "If you don't have time to read, you don't have the time (or the tools) to write. Simple as that."

Because of Winn-Dixie author Kate DiCamillo said in an interview on teenreads.com: "Every well-written book is a light for me. When you write, you use other writers and their books as guides in the wilderness. I am deeply appreciative of all those writers who work hard to tell their stories right and true, thereby showing me the way to tell my own stories."

It's no coincidence these award-winning authors are also avid readers. If you're a writer, you owe it to yourself to hit the stores, hit the libraries, read, and allow other writers to be your "guides in the wilderness." You could start with *Because of Winn-Dixie*. (By now, you must be curious about the first line.) Don't be afraid to read it out loud to yourself and listen to its sound. Read your own work out loud, even if only to the cat. Someday other writers will do the same with your published work. And the next time you relocate, you can always hire movers.

© 2001 Chris Sheban

Alice Pope
cwim@fwpubs.com

Just Getting Started? Some Quick Tips

If you're new to the world of children's publishing, buying *Children's Writer's & Illustrator's Market* may have been one of the first steps in your journey to publication. What follows is a list of suggestions and resources that can help make that journey a smooth and swift one:

1. Make the most of *Children's Writer's & Illustrator's Market*. Be sure to read How to Use This Book to Sell Your Work on page 4 for tips on reading the listings and using the indexes. Also be sure to take advantage of the articles and interviews in the book. The insights of the authors, illustrators, editors and agents we've interviewed will inform and inspire you.

2. Join the Society of Children's Books Writers and Illustrators. SCBWI, more than 17,000 members strong, is an organization for those interested in writing and illustrating for children from the beginner to the professional level. They offer members a slew of information and support through publications, a recently redesigned website, and a host of Regional Advisors overseeing chapters in almost every state in the U.S. and in a growing number of locations around the globe (including France, Canada, Japan and Australia). SCBWI puts on a number of conferences, workshops and events on the regional and national level (many listed in the Conferences & Workshops section of this book). For more information contact SCBWI, 8271 Beverly Blvd., Los Angeles CA 90048, (323)782-1010, or visit their website: www.scbwi.org.

3. Read newsletters. Newsletters, such as *Children's Book Insider*, *Children's Writer* and the SCBWI *Bulletin*, offer updates and new information about publishers on a timely basis and are relatively inexpensive. Many local chapters of SCBWI offer regional newsletters as well. (See Helpful Books & Publications on page 345 for contact information on the newsletters listed above and others. For information on regional SCBWI newsletters, visit www.scbwi.org and click on "Publications.")

4. Read trade and review publications. Magazines like *Publishers Weekly* (which offers two special issues each year devoted to children's publishing available on newsstands), *The Horn Book*, *Riverbank Review* and *Booklinks* offer news, articles, reviews of newly-published titles and ads featuring upcoming and current releases. Referring to them will help you get a feel for what's happening in children's publishing.

5. Read guidelines. Most publishers and magazines offer writer's and artist's guidelines which provide detailed information on needs and submission requirements, and some magazines offer theme lists for upcoming issues. Many publishers and magazines state the availability of guidelines within their listings. Send a self-addressed, stamped envelope (SASE) to publishers who offer guidelines. You'll often find submission information on publishers' and magazines' websites.

6. Look at publishers' catalogs. Perusing publishers' catalogs can give you a feel for their line of books and help you decide where your work might fit in. Send for catalogs with a SASE if they are available (often stated within listings). Visit publishers' websites which often contain their full catalogs. You can also ask librarians to look at catalogs they have on hand. You can even search Amazon.com (www.amazon.com) by publisher and year. (Click on "book search" then "publisher, date" and plug in, for example, "Atheneum" under "publisher" and "2002" under year. You'll get a list of all the Atheneum titles published in 2002 which you can peruse.)

7. Visit bookstores. It's not only informative to spend time in bookstores—it's fun, too! Frequently visit the children's section of your local bookstore (whether a chain or an independent) to see the latest from a variety of publishers and the most current issues of children's magazines. Look for books in the genre you're writing or with illustrations similar in style to yours, and spend some time studying them. It's also wise to get to know your local booksellers—they can tell you what's new in the store and provide insight into what kids and adults are buying.

8. Read, read, read! While you're at that bookstore, pick up a few things, or keep a list of the books that interest you and check them out of your library. Read and study the latest releases, the award winners, and the classics. You'll learn from other writers, get ideas and get a feel for what's being published. Think about what works and doesn't work in a story. Pay attention to how plots are constructed and how characters are developed or the rhythm and pacing of picture book text. It's certainly enjoyable research!

9. Take advantage of Internet resources. There are innumerable sources of information available on the Internet about writing for children (and anything else you could possibly think of). It's also a great resource for getting (and staying) in touch with other writers and illustrators through listservs and e-mail, and can serve as a vehicle for self-promotion. (Visit some authors' and illustators' web pages for ideas. See Useful Online Resources on page 348 for a list of helpful websites.)

10. Consider attending a conference. If time and finances allow, attending a conference is a great way to meet peers and network with professionals in the field of children's publishing. As mentioned above, SCBWI offers conferences in various locations year round (see www.scbwi. org and click on "Events" for a full calendar of conferences). General writers' conferences often offer specialized sessions just for those interested in children's writing. Many conferences offer optional manuscript and portfolio critiques as well, giving you a chance for feedback from seasoned professionals. (See No More Piranhas! Editors' Thoughts on Conferences on page 75 and Need Information? Inspiration? Validation? Try a Conference on page 73.)

11. Network, network, network! Don't work in a vacuum. You can meet other writers and illustrators through a number of the things listed above—SCBWI, conferences, online. Attend local meetings for writers and illustrators whenever you can. Befriend other writers in your area (SCBWI offers members a roster broken down by state)—share guidelines, share subscriptions, be conference buddies and roommates, join a critique group or writing group, exchange information and offer support. Get online—sign on to listservs, post on message boards, visit chatrooms. (America Online offers them. Also, visit author Verla Kay's website, www.verlakay.com, for information on weekly workshops. See Useful Online Resources on page 348 for more information.) Exchange addresses, phone numbers and e-mail addresses with writers or illustrators you meet at events. And at conferences don't be afraid to talk to people, ask strangers to join you for lunch, approach speakers and introduce yourself, chat in elevators and hallways. Remember, you're not alone.

12. Perfect your craft and don't submit until your work is its best. It's often been said that a writer should try to write every day. Great manuscripts don't happen overnight—there's time, research and revision involved. As you visit bookstores and study what others have written and illustrated, really step back and look at your own work and ask yourself—honestly—*How does my work measure up? Is it ready for editors or art directors to see?* If it's not, keep working. You may want to ask a writer's group for constructive comments, or get a professional manuscript or portfolio critique.

13. Be patient, learn from rejection and don't give up! Thousands of manuscripts land on editors' desks; thousands of illustration samples line art directors' file drawers. There are so many factors that come into play when evaluating submissions. Keep in mind that you might not hear back from publishers promptly. Persistence and patience are important qualities in writers and illustrators working for publication. Keep at it—it will come. It can take a while, but when you get that first book contract or first assignment, you'll know it was worth the wait. (Read First Books on page 95 for proof.)

How to Use This Book to Sell Your Work

As a writer, illustrator or photographer first picking up *Children's Writer's & Illustrator's Market*, you may not know quite how to start using the book. Your impulse may be to flip through the book and quickly make a mailing list, then submit to everyone in hopes that someone will take interest in your work. Well, there's more to it. Finding the right market takes time and research. The more you know about a company that interests you, the better chance you have of getting work accepted.

We've made your job a little easier by putting a wealth of information at your fingertips. Besides providing listings, this directory includes a number of tools to help you determine which markets are the best ones for your work. By using these tools, as well as researching on your own, you raise your odds of being published.

USING THE INDEXES

This book lists hundreds of potential buyers of freelance material. To learn which companies want the type of material you're interested in submitting, start with the indexes.

The Age-Level Index

Age groups are broken down into these categories in the Age-Level Index:
- **Picture books** or **picture-oriented material** are written and illustrated for preschoolers to 8-year-olds.
- **Young readers** are for 5- to 8-year-olds.
- **Middle readers** are for 9- to 11-year-olds.
- **Young adults** are for ages 12 and up.

Age breakdowns may vary slightly from publisher to publisher, but using them as general guidelines will help you target appropriate markets. For example, if you've written an article about trends in teen fashion, check the Magazines Age-Level Index under the Young Adult subheading. Using this list, you'll quickly find the listings for young adult magazines.

The Subject Index

But let's narrow the search further. Take your list of young adult magazines, turn to the Subject Index, and find the Fashion subheading. Then highlight the names that appear on both lists (Young Adult and Fashion). Now you have a smaller list of all the magazines that would be interested in your teen fashion article. Read through those listings and decide which ones sound best for your work.

Illustrators and photographers can use the Subject Index as well. If you specialize in painting animals, for instance, consider sending samples to book and magazine publishers listed under Animals and, perhaps, Nature/Environment. Illustrators can simply send general examples of their style (in the form of tearsheets or postcards) to art directors to keep on file. The indexes may be more helpful to artists sending manuscripts/illustration packages. Always read the listings for the potential markets to see the type of work art directors prefer and what type of samples they'll keep on file, and send for art or photo guidelines if they're available.

The Poetry Index

This index lists book publishers and magazines interested in submissions from poets. Always send for writer's guidelines from publishers and magazines that interest you.

The Photography Index

You'll find lists of book and magazine publishers, as well as greeting card, puzzle and game manufacturers, that buy photos from freelancers in the Photography Index. Copy the lists and read the listings for specific needs. Send for photo guidelines if they're offered.

USING THE LISTINGS

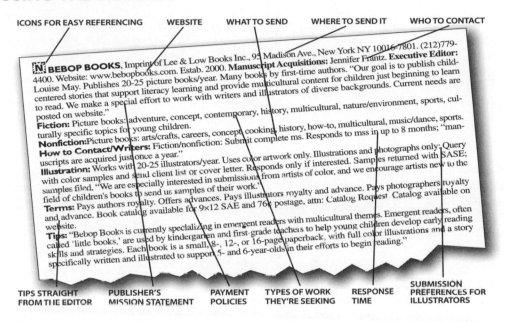

ICONS FOR EASY REFERENCING   WEBSITE   WHAT TO SEND   WHERE TO SEND IT   WHO TO CONTACT

TIPS STRAIGHT FROM THE EDITOR   PUBLISHER'S MISSION STATEMENT   PAYMENT POLICIES   TYPES OF WORK THEY'RE SEEKING   RESPONSE TIME   SUBMISSION PREFERENCES FOR ILLUSTRATORS

Many listings begin with one or more symbols. (Refer to the inside covers of the book for quick reference.) Here's what each icon stands for:

- **N** indicates a listing is new to this edition.
- indicates a listing is Canadian.
- indicates a company publishes educational material.
- indicates an electronic publisher of publication.
- indicates a listing is a book packager or producer.
- indicates a change to a company's mailing address since last year's edition.
- **A** indicates a publisher only accepts submissions through agents.
- indicates a company's publications have received awards recently.

In the Book Publishers section, you'll find contact names after **Manuscript Acquisitions** and **Art Acquisitions**. Contact names in Magazines follow boldface titles such as **Fiction Editor**, **Articles Editor** or **Art Director**. Following contact information in many of these listings are mission statements. Read these to get a general idea of the aim of certain publishers and magazines to help you decide whether to explore them further.

The subheadings under each listing contain more specific information about what a company needs. In Book Publishers and Magazines, for example, you'll find such things as age levels and subjects needed under the **Fiction** and **Nonfiction** subheads. Here's an example from a listing in the Book Publishers section:

Fiction: Picture books: adventure, animal, contemporary, fantasy, humor. Young readers: animal, contemporary, humor, sports, suspense/mystery. Middle readers: adventure, humor, sports. Young adults: humor, problem novels.

Also check the listings for information on how to submit your work and response time. In Book Publishers and Magazines, writers will find this information under the How to Contact/ Writers subhead:

How to Contact/Writers: Query with outline/synopsis and 2 sample chapters. Responds to queries in 6 weeks.

For information on submission procedures and formats, turn to Before Your First Sale on page 8.

Also look for information regarding payment and rights purchased. Some markets pay on acceptance, others on publication. Some pay a flat rate for manuscripts and artwork, others pay advances and royalties. Knowing how a market operates will keep you from being shocked when you discover your paycheck won't arrive until your manuscript is published—a year after it was accepted. This information is found under **Terms** in Book Publishers, Magazines and Play Publishers. Here's an example from the Magazines section:

Terms: Pays on acceptance. Buys first North American serial rights or reprint rights. Pays $50-100 for stories/articles. Pays illustrators $75-125 for b&w or color inside; $150-200 for color cover.

Under **Tips** you'll find special advice straight from an editor or art director about what their company wants or doesn't want, or other helpful advice:

Tips: "We are looking for picture books centered on a strong, fully-developed protaganist who grows or changes during the course of the story."

Additional information about specific markets in the form of comments from the editors of this book is set off by bullets (•) within listings:

• This publisher accepts only queries and manuscripts submitted by agents.

Many listings indicate whether submission guidelines are available. If a publisher you're interested in offers guidelines, send for them and read them. The same is true with catalogs. Sending for catalogs and seeing and reading about the books a publisher produces gives you a better idea whether your work would fit in. (You should also look at a few of the books in the catalog at a library or bookstore to get a feel for the publisher's material.) Note that a number of publishers offer guidelines and catalogs on their websites.

Especially for artists and photographers

Along with information for writers, listings provide information for photographers and illustrators. Illustrators will find numerous markets that maintain files of samples for possible future assignments. If you're both a writer and illustrator, look for markets that accept manuscript/ illustration packages. You'll find sample illustrations from various publishers sprinkled throughout the listings. These illustrations serve as examples of the kind of art these particular companies buy. Read the captions for additional information about the artwork and the market.

If you're a photographer, after consulting the Photography Index, read the information under the **Photography** subhead within listings to see what format buyers prefer. For example, some want 35mm color transparencies, others want black & white prints. Note the type of photos a buyer wants to purchase and the procedures for submitting. It's not uncommon for a market to want a résumé and promotional literature, as well as tearsheets from previous work. Listings also note whether model releases and/or captions are required.

Especially for young writers

If you're a parent, teacher or student, you may be interested in Young Writer's & Illustrator's Markets. The listings in this section encourage submissions from young writers and artists. Some may require a written statement from a teacher or parent noting the work is original. Also watch for age limits.

Young people should also check Contests & Awards for contests that accept work by young writers and artists. Some of the contests listed are especially for students; others accept both student and adult work. These listings contain the phrase **open to students** in bold. Some listings in Clubs & Organizations and Conferences & Workshops may also be of interest to students. Organizations and conferences which are open to or are especially for students also include **open to students.**

COMMON ABBREVIATIONS

Throughout the listings, the following abbreviations are used:
- **ms** or **mss** stands for manuscript or manuscripts.
- **SASE** refers to a self-addressed, stamped envelope.
- **SAE** refers to a self-addressed envelope.
- **IRC** stands for International Reply Coupon. These are required with SAEs sent to markets in countries other than your own.

Before Your First Sale

If you're just beginning to pursue your career as a children's book writer or illustrator, it's important to learn the proper procedures, formats, and protocol for the publishing industry. This article outlines the basics you need to know before you head to the post office with your submissions.

FINDING THE BEST MARKETS FOR YOUR WORK

Researching publishers well is a basic element of submitting your work successfully. Editors and art directors hate to receive inappropriate submissions—handling them wastes a lot of their time, not to mention your time and money, and they are the main reason some publishers have chosen not to accept material over the transom. By randomly sending out material without knowing a company's needs, you're sure to meet with rejection.

If you're interested in submitting to a particular magazine, write to request a sample copy, or see if it's available in your local library or bookstore. For a book publisher, obtain a book catalog and check a library or bookstore for titles produced by that publisher. Most publishers and magazines have websites that include catalogs or sample articles (websites are given within the listings). Studying such materials carefully will better acquaint you with a publisher's or magazine's writing, illustration and photography styles and formats.

Most of the book publishers and magazines listed in this book (as well as some greeting card and paper product producers) offer some sort of writer's, artist's or photographer's guidelines for a self-addressed, stamped envelope (SASE). Guidelines are also often found on publishers' websites. It's important to read and study guidelines before submitting work. You'll get a better understanding of what a particular publisher wants. You may even decide, after reading the submission guidelines, that your work isn't right for a company you considered.

SUBMITTING YOUR WORK

Throughout the listings you'll read requests for particular elements to include when contacting markets. Here are explanations of some of these important submission components.

Queries, cover letters and proposals

A query letter is a no-more-than-one-page, well-written piece meant to arouse an editor's interest in your work. Many query letters start with leads similar to those of actual manuscripts. In the rest of the letter, briefly outline the work you're proposing and include facts, anecdotes, interviews or other pertinent information that give the editor a feel for the manuscript's premise—entice her to want to know more. End your letter with a straightforward request to write (or submit) the work, and include information on its approximate length, date it could be completed, and whether accompanying photos or artwork are available.

In a query letter, think about presenting your book as a publisher's catalog would present it. Read through a good catalog and examine how the publishers give enticing summaries of their books in a spare amount of words. It's also important that query letters give editors a taste of your writing style. For good advice and samples of queries, cover letters and other correspondence, consult *How to Write Attention-Grabbing Query & Cover Letters*, by John Wood (Writer's Digest Books).

• **Query letters for nonfiction.** Queries are usually required when submitting nonfiction material to a publisher. The goal of a nonfiction query is to convince the editor your idea is perfect for her readership and that you're qualified to do the job. Note any previous writing experience and include published samples to prove your credentials, especially samples related to the subject matter you're querying about.

• **Query letters for fiction.** More and more, queries are being requested for fiction manuscripts. For a fiction query, explain the story's plot, main characters, conflict and resolution. Just as in nonfiction queries, make the editor eager to see more.

• **Cover letters for writers.** Some editors prefer to review complete manuscripts, especially for fiction. In such cases, the cover letter (which should be no longer than one page) serves as your introduction, establishes your credentials as a writer, and gives the editor an overview of the manuscript. If the editor asked for the manuscript because of a query, note this in your cover letter.

• **Cover letters for illustrators and photographers.** For an illustrator or photographer the cover letter serves as an introduction to the art director and establishes professional credentials when submitting samples. Explain what services you can provide as well as what type of follow-up contact you plan to make, if any.

• **Résumés.** Often writers, illustrators and photographers are asked to submit résumés with cover letters and samples. They can be created in a variety of formats, from a single page listing information, to color brochures featuring your work. Keep your résumé brief, and focus on your achievements, including your clients and the work you've done for them, as well as your educational background and any awards you've received. Do not use the same résumé you'd use for a typical job application.

• **Book proposals.** Throughout the listings in the Book Publishers section, publishers refer to submitting a synopsis, outline and sample chapters. Depending on an editor's preference, some or all of these components, along with a cover letter, make up a book proposal. (See The Nonfiction Proposal: Put Your Best Foot Forward on page 66 for a more detailed discussion.)

A *synopsis* summarizes the book, covering the basic plot (including the ending). It should be easy to read and flow well.

An *outline* covers your book chapter by chapter and provides highlights of each. If you're developing an outline for fiction, include major characters, plots and subplots, and book length.

Sample chapters give a more comprehensive idea of your writing skill. Some editors may request the first two or three chapters to determine if she's interested in seeing the whole book.

Manuscript formats

When submitting a complete manuscript, follow some basic guidelines. In the upper-left corner of your title page, type your legal name (not pseudonym), address and phone number. In the upper-right corner, type the approximate word length. All material in the upper corners should be typed single-spaced. Then type the title (centered) almost halfway down that page, the word "by" two spaces under that, and your name or pseudonym two spaces under "by."

The first page should also include the title (centered) one-third of the way down. Two spaces under that type "by" and your name or pseudonym. To begin the body of your manuscript, drop down two double spaces and indent five spaces for each new paragraph. There should be one-inch margins around all sides of a full typewritten page. (Manuscripts with wide margins are more readable and easier to edit.)

Set your computer on double-space for the manuscript body. From page two to the end of the manuscript, include your last name followed by a comma and the title (or key words of the title) in the upper-left corner. The page number should go in the top right corner. Drop down two double spaces to begin the body of each page. If you're submitting a novel, type each chapter title one-third of the way down the page. For more information on manuscript formats, read *Formatting & Submitting Your Manuscript*, by Jack and Glenda Neff, Don Prues, and the editors of *Writer's Market*; or *Manuscript Submission*, by Scott Edelstein (both Writer's Digest Books).

Picture book formats

The majority of editors prefer to see complete manuscripts for picture books. When typing the text of a picture book, don't include page breaks and don't type each page of text on a new sheet of paper. And unless you are an illustrator, don't worry about supplying art. Editors will find their own illustrators for picture books. Most of the time, a writer and an illustrator who work on the same book never meet. The editor acts as a go-between and works with the writer and illustrator throughout the publishing process. (See Picture Books 101: Pay Attention to Structure on page 61.) *How to Write and Sell Children's Picture Books*, by Jean E. Karl (Writer's Digest Books), offers advice on preparing text and marketing your work.

If you're an illustrator who has written your own book, consider creating a dummy or story-board containing both art and text, then submit it along with your complete manuscript and sample pieces of final art (color photocopies or slides—never originals). Publishers interested in picture books specify in their listings what should be submitted. For tips on creating a dummy, refer to *How to Write and Illustrate Children's Books and Get Them Published*, edited by Treld Pelkey Bicknell and Felicity Trotman (North Light Books), or Frieda Gates's book, *How to Write, Illustrate, and Design Children's Books* (Lloyd-Simone Publishing Company).

Writers may also want to learn the art of dummy making to help them through their writing process with things like pacing, rhythm and length. For a great explanation and helpful hints, see *You Can Write Children's Books*, by Tracey E. Dils (Writer's Digest Books).

Mailing submissions

Your main concern when packaging material is to be sure it arrives undamaged. If your manuscript is less than six pages, simply fold it in thirds and send it in a #10 (business-size) envelope. For a SASE, either fold another #10 envelope in thirds or insert a #9 (reply) envelope which fits in a #10 neatly without folding.

Another option is folding your manuscript in half in a 6×9 envelope, with a #9 or #10 SASE enclosed. For larger manuscripts use a 9×12 envelope both for mailing the submission and as a SASE (which can be folded in half). Book manuscripts require sturdy packaging for mailing. Include a self-addressed mailing label and return postage.

If asked to send artwork and photographs, remember they require a bit more care in packaging to guarantee they arrive in good condition. Sandwich illustrations and photos between heavy cardboard that is slightly larger than the work. The cardboard can be secured by rubber bands or with tape. If you tape the cardboard together, check that the artwork doesn't stick to the tape. Be sure your name and address appear on the back of each piece of art or each photo in case the material becomes separated. For the packaging use either a manila envelope, foam-padded envelope, brown paper or a mailer lined with plastic air bubbles. Bind non-joined edges with reinforced mailing tape and affix a typed mailing label or clearly write your address.

Mailing material first class ensures quick delivery. Also, first-class mail is forwarded for one year if the addressee has moved, and can be returned if undeliverable. If you're concerned about your original material safely reaching its destination, consider other mailing options, such as UPS or certified mail. If material needs to reach your editor or art director quickly, use overnight delivery services.

Remember, companies outside your own country can't use your country's postage when returning a manuscript to you. When mailing a submission to another country, include a self-addressed envelope and International Reply Coupons or IRCs. (You'll see this term in many Canadian listings.) Your postmaster can tell you, based on a package's weight, the correct number of IRCs to include to ensure its return.

If it's not necessary for an editor to return your work (such as with photocopies) don't include return postage. You may want to track the status of your submission by enclosing a postage-paid reply postcard with options for the editor to check, such as "Yes, I am interested," "I'll keep the material on file," or "No, the material is not appropriate for my needs at this time."

Some writers, illustrators and photographers simply include a deadline date. If you don't hear from the editor or art director by the specified date, your manuscript, artwork or photos are automatically withdrawn from consideration. Because many publishing houses and companies are overstocked with material, a minimum deadline should be at least three months.

Unless requested, it's never a good idea to use a company's fax number or e-mail address to send manuscript submissions. This can disrupt a company's internal business. Some publishers, however, are open to e-mail submissions. Simon & Schuster imprints recently set up an e-mail for submitting material, for example. Study the Book Publishers listings for specifics.

Keeping submission records

It's important to keep track of the material you submit. When recording each submission, include the date it was sent, the business and contact name, and any enclosures (such as samples of writing, artwork or photography). You can create a record-keeping system of your own or look for record-keeping software in your area computer store.

Keep copies of articles or manuscripts you send together with related correspondence to make follow-up easier. When you sell rights to a manuscript, artwork or photos you can "close" your file on a particular submission by noting the date the material was accepted, what rights were purchased, the publication date and payment.

Often writers, illustrators and photographers fail to follow up on overdue responses. If you don't hear from a publisher within their stated response time, wait another month or so and follow up with a note asking about the status of your submission. Include the title or description, date sent, and a SASE for response. Ask the contact person when she anticipates making a decision. You may refresh the memory of a buyer who temporarily forgot about your submission. At the very least you'll receive a definite "no," and free yourself to send the material to another publisher.

Simultaneous submissions

If you opt for simultaneous (also called "multiple") submissions—sending the same material to several publishers at the same time—be sure to inform each editor to whom you submit that your work is being considered elsewhere. Many editors are reluctant to receive simultaneous submissions but understand that for hopeful writers and illustrators, waiting several months for a response can be frustrating. In some cases, an editor may actually be more inclined to read your manuscript sooner if she knows it's being considered by another publisher. The Society of Children's Book Writers and Illustrators cautions writers against simultaneous submissions. The official recommendation of SCBWI is to submit to one publisher at a time, but wait only three months (note you'll do so in your cover letter). If no response is received, then send a note withdrawing your manuscript from consideration. SCBWI considers simultaneous submissions acceptable only if you have a manuscript dealing with a timely issue.

It's especially important to keep track of simultaneous submissions, so if you get an offer on a manuscript sent to more than one publisher, you can instruct other publishers to withdraw your work from consideration.

AGENTS & ART REPS

Most children's writers, illustrators and photographers, especially those just beginning, are confused about whether to enlist the services of an agent or representative. The decision is strictly one that each writer, illustrator or photographer must make for herself. Some are confident with their own negotiation skills and believe acquiring an agent or rep is not in their best interest. Others feel uncomfortable in the business arena or are not willing to sacrifice valuable creative time for marketing.

About half of children's publishers accept unagented work, so it's possible to break into children's publishing without an agent. Some agents avoid working with children's books because traditionally low advances and trickling royalty payments over long periods of time make children's books less lucrative. Writers targeting magazine markets don't need the services of an agent. In fact, it's practically impossible to find an agent interested in marketing articles and short stories—there simply isn't enough financial incentive.

One benefit of having an agent, though, is it may speed up the process of getting your work reviewed, especially by publishers who don't accept unagented submissions. If an agent has a good reputation and submits your manuscript to an editor, that manuscript will likely bypass the first-read stage (which is done by editorial assistants and junior editors) and end up on the editor's desk sooner.

When agreeing to have a reputable agent represent you, remember that she should be familiar with the needs of the current market and evaluate your manuscript/artwork/photos accordingly. She should also determine the quality of your piece and whether it is saleable. When your manuscript sells, your agent should negotiate a favorable contract and clear up any questions you have about payments.

Keep in mind that however reputable the agent or rep is, she has limitations. Representation does not guarantee sale of your work. It just means an agent or rep sees potential in your writing, art or photos. Though an agent or rep may offer criticism or advice on how to improve your work, she cannot make you a better writer, artist or photographer.

Literary agents typically charge a 15 percent commission from the sale of writing; art and photo representatives usually charge a 25 to 30 percent commission. Such fees are taken from advances and royalty earnings. If your agent sells foreign rights to your work, she will deduct a higher percentage because she will most likely be dealing with an overseas agent with whom she must split the fee.

Be advised that not every agent is open to representing a writer, artist or photographer who lacks an established track record. Just as when approaching a publisher, the manuscript, artwork or photos, and query or cover letter you submit to a potential agent must be attractive and professional looking. Your first impression must be as an organized, articulate person.

For listings of agents and reps, turn to the Agents & Art Reps section. Also refer to *Guide to Literary Agents* for listings of agents and lots more advice on finding and working with agents. For additional listings of art reps, consult *Artist's & Graphic Designer's Market*; and for photo reps, see *Photographer's Market* (all Writer's Digest Books).

The Business of Writing & Illustrating

A career in children's publishing involves more than just writing skills or artistic talent. Successful authors and illustrators must be able to hold their own in negotiations, keep records, understand contract language, grasp copyright law, pay taxes and take care of a number of other business concerns. Although agents and reps, accountants and lawyers, and writers' organizations offer help in sorting out such business issues, it's wise to have a basic understanding of them going in. This article offers just that—basic information. For a more in-depth look at the subjects covered here, check your library or bookstore for books and magazines to help you, some of which are mentioned. We also tell you how to get information on issues like taxes and copyright from the federal government.

CONTRACTS & NEGOTIATION

Before you see your work in print or begin working with an editor or art director on a project, there is negotiation. And whether negotiating a book contract, a magazine article assignment, or an illustration or photo assignment, there are a few things to keep in mind. First, if you find any clauses vague or confusing in a contract, get legal advice. The time and money invested in counseling up front could protect you from problems later. If you have an agent or rep, she will review any contract.

A contract is an agreement between two or more parties that specifies the fees to be paid, services rendered, deadlines, rights purchased and, for artists and photographers, whether original work is returned. Most companies have standard contracts for writers, illustrators and photographers. The specifics (such as royalty rates, advances, delivery dates, etc.) are typed in after negotiations.

Though it's okay to conduct negotiations over the phone, get a written contract once both parties have agreed on terms. Never depend on oral stipulations; written contracts protect both parties from misunderstandings. Watch for clauses that may not be in your best interest, such as "work-for-hire." When you do work-for-hire, you give up all rights to your creations.

Some reputable children's magazines, such as *Highlights for Children* and the Carus Publishing Groups' magazines, buy all rights, and many writers and illustrators believe it's worth the concession in order to break into the field. (See Answers to All Your Questions About All-Rights Contracts on page 20.) However, once you become more established in the field, it's in

---

Contract Help from Organizations

Writers organizations offer a wealth of information to members, including contract advice:

Society of Children's Book Writers and Illustrators members can find information in the SCBWI publication *Answers to Some Questions About Contracts*. Contact SCBWI at 8271 Beverly Blvd., Los Angeles CA 90048, (323)782-1010, or visit their website: www.scbwi.org.

The Authors Guild also offers contract tips. Visit their website, www.authorsguild.org. (Members of the guild can receive a 75-point contract review from the guild's legal staff.) See the website for membership information and application form, or contact The Authors Guild at 31 E. 28th St., 10th Floor, New York NY 10016, (212)563-5904. Fax: (212)564-5363. E-mail: staff@authorsguild.org. Website: www.authorsguild.org.

your best interest to keep rights to your work. (Note: magazines such as *Highlights* may return rights after a specified time period, so ask about this possibility when negotiating.)

When negotiating a book deal, find out whether your contract contains an option clause. This clause requires the author to give the publisher a first look at her next work before offering it to other publishers. Though it's editorial etiquette to give the publisher the first chance at publishing your next work, be wary of statements in the contract that could trap you. Don't allow the publisher to consider the next project for more than 30 days and be specific about what type of work should actually be considered "next work." (For example, if the book under contract is a young adult novel, specify that the publisher will receive an exclusive look at only your next young adult novel.)

(For more information about SCBWI, The Authors Guild, and other organizations, turn to the Clubs & Organizations section.)

Book publishers' payment methods

Book publishers pay authors and artists in royalties, a percentage of either the wholesale or retail price of each book sold. From large publishing houses, the author usually receives an advance issued against future royalties before the book is published. Half of the advance amount is issued upon signing the book contract; the other half is issued when the book is finished. For illustrations, one-third of the advance should be collected upon signing the contract; one-third upon delivery of sketches; and one-third upon delivery of finished art.

After your book has sold enough copies to earn back your advance, you'll start to get royalty checks. Some publishers hold a reserve against returns, which means a percentage of royalties is held back in case books are returned from bookstores. If you have a reserve clause in your contract, find out the exact percentage of total sales that will be withheld and the time period the publisher will hold this money. You should be reimbursed this amount after a reasonable time period, such as a year. Royalty percentages vary with each publisher, but there are standard ranges.

Book publishers' rates

According to the latest figures from the Society of Children's Book Writers and Illustrators, first-time picture book authors can expect advances of $2,000-3,000; first-time picture book illustrators' advances range from $5,000-7,000; text and illustration packages for first-timers can score $6,000-8,000. Rates go up for subsequent books: $3,500-5,000 for picture book text; $7,000-10,000 for picture book illustration; $8,000-10,000 for text and illustration. Experienced authors can expect higher advances. Royalties for picture books are generally about five percent (split between the author and illustrator) but can go as high as ten percent. Those who both write and illustrate a book, of course, receive the full royalty.

Advances for hardcover novels and nonfiction can fetch authors advances of $4,000-6,000 and 10 percent royalties; paperbacks bring in slightly lower advances of $3,000-5,000 and royalties of 6-8 percent.

As you might expect, advance and royalty figures vary from house to house and are affected by the time of year, the state of the economy and other factors. Some smaller houses may not even pay royalties, just flat fees. Educational houses may not offer advances or offer smaller amounts. Religious publishers tend to offer smaller advances than trade publishers. First-time writers and illustrators generally start on the low end of the scale, while established and high-profile writers are paid more.

Pay rates for magazines

For writers, fee structures for magazines are based on a per-word rate or range for a specific article length. Artists and photographers have a few more variables to contend with before contracting their services.

Payment for illustrations and photos can be set by such factors as whether the piece(s) will be black and white or four-color, how many are to be purchased, where the work appears (cover or inside), circulation, and the artist's or photographer's prior experience.

Remaindering

When a book goes out of print, a publisher will sell any existing copies to a wholesaler who, in turn, sells the copies to stores at a discount. When the books are "remaindered" to a wholesaler, they are usually sold at a price just above the cost of printing. When negotiating a contract with a publisher you may want to discuss the possibility of purchasing the remaindered copies before they are sold to a wholesaler, then you can market the copies you purchased and still make a profit.

KNOW YOUR RIGHTS

A copyright is a form of protection provided to creators of original works, published or unpublished. In general, copyright protection ensures the writer, illustrator or photographer the power to decide how her work is used and allows her to receive payment for each use.

Essentially, copyright also encourages the creation of new works by guaranteeing the creator power to sell rights to the work in the marketplace. The copyright holder can print, reprint or copy her work; sell or distribute copies of her work; or prepare derivative works such as plays, collages or recordings. The Copyright Law is designed to protect work (created on or after January 1, 1978) for her lifetime plus 50 years.

If you collaborate with someone else on a written or artistic project, the copyright will last for the lifetime of the last survivor plus 50 years. The creators' heirs may hold a copyright for an additional 50 years. After that, the work becomes public domain. Works created anonymously or under a pseudonym are protected for 100 years, or 75 years after publication. Under work-for-hire agreements, you relinquish your copyright to your "employer."

Copyright notice and registration

Some feel a copyright notice should be included on all work, registered or not. Others feel it is not necessary and a copyright notice will only confuse publishers about whether the material is registered (acquiring rights to previously registered material is a more complicated process).

Although it's not necessary to include a copyright notice on unregistered work, if you don't feel your work is safe without the notice, it is your right to include one. Including a copyright notice—© (year of work, your name)—should help safeguard against plagiarism.

Registration is a legal formality intended to make copyright public record, and can help you win more money in a court case. By registering work within three months of publication or before an infringement occurs, you are eligible to collect statutory damages and attorney's fees. If you register later than three months after publication, you will qualify only for actual damages and profits.

Ideas and concepts are not copyrightable, only expressions of those ideas and concepts. A character type or basic plot outline, for example, is not subject to a copyright infringement lawsuit. Also, titles, names, short phrases or slogans, and lists of contents are not subject to copyright protection, though titles and names may be protected through the Trademark Office.

You can register a group of articles, illustrations or photos if it meets these criteria:
- the group is assembled in order, such as in a notebook;
- the works bear a single title, such as "Works by (your name)";
- it is the work of one writer, artist or photographer;
- the material is the subject of a single claim to copyright.

It's a publisher's responsibility to register your book for copyright. If you've previously registered the same material, you must inform your editor and supply the previous copyright information, otherwise, the publisher can't register the book in its published form.

For more information about the proper way to register works and to order the correct forms, contact the U.S. Copyright Office, (202)707-3000. The forms available are TX for writing (books, articles, etc.); VA for pictures (photographs, illustrations); and PA for plays and music. For information about how to use the copyright forms, request a copy of Circular I on Copyright Basics. All of the forms and circulars are free. Send the completed registration form along with the stated fee and a copy of the work to the Copyright Office.

For specific answers to questions about copyright (but not legal advice), call the Copyright Public Information Office at (202)707-3000 weekdays between 8:30 a.m. and 5 p.m. EST. Forms can also be downloaded from the Library of Congress website: www.loc.gov/copyright. The site also includes a list of frequently asked questions, tips on filling out forms, general copyright information, and links to other sites related to copyright issues. For members of SCBWI, information about copyrights and the law is available in their publication: Copyright Facts for Writers.

The rights publishers buy

The copyright law specifies that a writer, illustrator or photographer generally sells one-time rights to her work unless she and the buyer agree otherwise in writing. Many publications will want more exclusive rights to your work than just one-time usage; some will even require you to sell all rights. Be sure you are monetarily compensated for the additional rights you relinquish. If you must give up all rights to a work, carefully consider the price you're being offered to determine whether you'll be compensated for the loss of other potential sales.

Writers who only give up limited rights to their work can then sell reprint rights to other publications, foreign rights to international publications, or even movie rights, should the opportunity arise. Artists and photographers can sell their work to other markets such as paper product companies who may use an image on a calendar, greeting card or mug. Illustrators and photographers may even sell original work after it has been published. And there are now galleries throughout the U.S. that display and sell the original work of children's illustrators.

Rights acquired through the sale of a book manuscript are explained in each publisher's contract. Take time to read relevant clauses to be sure you understand what rights each contract is specifying before signing. Be sure your contract contains a clause allowing all rights to revert back to you in the event the publisher goes out of business. (You may even want to have the contract reviewed by an agent or an attorney specializing in publishing law.)

The following are the rights you'll most often sell to publishers, periodicals and producers in the marketplace:

First rights. The buyer purchases the rights to use the work for the first time in any medium. All other rights remain with the creator. When material is excerpted from a soon-to-be-published book for use in a newspaper or periodical, first serial rights are also purchased.

One-time rights. The buyer has no guarantee that she is the first to use a piece. One-time permission to run written work, illustrations or photos is acquired, then the rights revert back to the creator.

First North American serial rights. This is similar to first rights, except that companies who distribute both in the U.S. and Canada will stipulate these rights to ensure that another North American company won't come out with simultaneous usage of the same work.

Second serial (reprint) rights. In this case newspapers and magazines are granted the right to reproduce a work that has already appeared in another publication. These rights are also purchased by a newspaper or magazine editor who wants to publish part of a book after the book has been published. The proceeds from reprint rights for a book are often split evenly between the author and his publishing company.

Simultaneous rights. More than one publication buys one-time rights to the same work at the same time. Use of such rights occurs among magazines with circulations that don't overlap, such as many religious publications.

All rights. Just as it sounds, the writer, illustrator or photographer relinquishes all rights to a piece—she no longer has any say in who acquires rights to use it. All rights are purchased by publishers who pay premium usage fees, have an exclusive format, or have other book or magazine interests from which the purchased work can generate more mileage. If a company insists on acquiring all rights to your work, see if you can negotiate for the rights to revert back to you after a reasonable period of time. If they agree to such a proposal, get it in writing.

Note: Writers, illustrators and photographers should be wary of "work-for-hire" arrangements. If you sign an agreement stipulating that your work will be done as work-for-hire, you will not control the copyrights of the completed work—the company that hired you will be the copyright owner.

Foreign serial rights. Be sure before you market to foreign publications that you have sold only North American—not worldwide—serial rights to previous markets. If so, you are free to market to publications that may be interested in material that's appeared in a North American-based periodical.

Syndication rights. This is a division of serial rights. For example, if a syndicate prints portions of a book in installments in its newspapers, it would be syndicating second serial rights. The syndicate would receive a commission and leave the remainder to be split between the author and publisher.

Subsidiary rights. These include serial rights, dramatic rights, book club rights or translation rights. The contract should specify what percentage of profits from sales of these rights go to the author and publisher.

Dramatic, television and motion picture rights. During a specified time the interested party tries to sell a story to a producer or director. Many times options are renewed because the selling process can be lengthy.

Display rights or electronic publishing rights. They're also known as "Data, Storage and Retrieval." Usually listed under subsidiary rights, the marketing of electronic rights in this era of rapidly expanding capabilities and markets for electronic material can be tricky. Display rights can cover text or images to be used in a CD-ROM or online, or may cover use of material in formats not even fully developed yet. If a display rights clause is listed in your contract, try to negotiate its elimination. Otherwise, be sure to pin down which electronic rights are being purchased. Demand the clause be restricted to things designed to be read only. By doing this, you maintain your rights to use your work for things such as games and interactive software.

RUNNING YOUR BUSINESS

An important part of being a freelance writer, illustrator or photographer is running your freelance business. It's imperative to maintain accurate business records to determine if you're making a profit as a freelancer. Keeping correct, organized records will also make your life easier as you approach tax time.

When setting up your system, begin by keeping a bank account and ledger for your business finances apart from your personal finances. Also, if writing, illustration or photography is secondary to another freelance career, keep separate business records for each.

You will likely accumulate some business expenses before showing any profit when you start out as a freelancer. To substantiate your income and expenses to the IRS, keep all invoices, cash receipts, sales slips, bank statements, canceled checks and receipts related to travel expenses and entertaining clients. For entertainment expenditures, record the date, place and purpose of the business meeting as well as gas mileage. Keep records for all purchases, big and small—don't take the small purchases for granted; they can add up to a substantial amount. File all receipts in chronological order. Maintaining a separate file for each month simplifies retrieving records at the end of the year.

Record keeping

When setting up a single-entry bookkeeping system, record income and expenses separately. Use some of the subheads that appear on Schedule C (the form used for recording income from a business) of the 1040 tax form so you can easily transfer information onto the tax form when filing your return. In your ledger include a description of each transaction—the date, source of income (or debts from business purchases), description of what was purchased or sold, the amount of the transaction, and whether payment was by cash, check or credit card.

Don't wait until January 1 to start keeping records. The moment you first make a business-related purchase or sell an article, book manuscript, illustration or photo, begin tracking your profits and losses. If you keep records from January 1 to December 31, you're using a calendar-year accounting period. Any other accounting period is called a fiscal year.

There are two types of accounting methods you can choose from—the cash method and the accrual method. The cash method is used more often: you record income when it is received and expenses when they're disbursed.

Using the accrual method, you report income at the time you earn it rather than when it's actually received. Similarly, expenses are recorded at the time they're incurred rather than when you actually pay them. If you choose this method, keep separate records for "accounts receivable" and "accounts payable."

Satisfying the IRS

To successfully—and legally—work as a freelancer, you must know what income you should report and what deductions you can claim. But before you can do that, you must prove to the IRS you're in business to make a profit, that your writing, illustration or photography is not merely a hobby.

The Tax Reform Act of 1986 says you should show a profit for three years out of a five-year period to attain professional status. The IRS considers these factors as proof of your professionalism:

- accurate financial records;
- a business bank account separate from your personal account;
- proven time devoted to your profession;
- whether it's your main or secondary source of income;
- your history of profits and losses;
- the amount of training you have invested in your field;
- your expertise.

If your business is unincorporated, you'll fill out tax information on Schedule C of Form 1040. If you're unsure of what deductions you can take, request the IRS publication containing this information. Under the Tax Reform Act, only 30 percent of business meals, entertainment and related tips, and parking charges are deductible. Other deductible expenses allowed on Schedule C include: car expenses for business-related trips; professional courses and seminars; depreciation of office equipment, such as a computer; dues and publications; and miscellaneous expenses, such as postage used for business needs.

If you're working out of a home office, a portion of your mortgage interest (or rent), related utilities, property taxes, repair costs and depreciation may he deducted as business expenses—under special circumstances. To learn more about the possibility of home office deductions, consult IRS Publication 587, Business Use of Your Home

The method of paying taxes on income not subject to withholding is called "estimated tax" for individuals. If you expect to owe more than $500 at year's end and if the total amount of income tax that will be withheld during the year will be less than 90% of the tax shown on the current year's return, you'll generally make estimated tax payments. Estimated tax payments are made in four equal installments due on April 15, June 15, September 15 and January 15 (assuming you're a calendar-year taxpayer). For more information, request Publication 533, Self-Employment Tax.

The Internal Revenue Service's website (www.irs.ustreas.gov/) offers tips and instant access to IRS forms and publications.

Social Security tax

Depending on your net income as a freelancer, you may be liable for a Social Security tax. This is a tax designed for those who don't have Social Security withheld from their paychecks. You're liable if your net income is $400 or more per year. Net income is the difference between your income and allowable business deductions. Request Schedule SE, Computation of Social Security Self-Employment Tax, if you qualify.

If completing your income tax return proves to be too complex, consider hiring an accountant (the fee is a deductible business expense) or contact the IRS for assistance (look in the White Pages under U.S. Government—Internal Revenue Service or check their website, www.irs.ustrea s.gov/). In addition to numerous publications to instruct you in various facets of preparing a tax return, the IRS also has walk-in centers in some cities.

Insurance

As a self-employed professional be aware of what health and business insurance coverage is available to you. Unless you're a Canadian who is covered by national health insurance or a full-time freelancer covered by your spouse's policy, health insurance will no doubt be one of your biggest expenses. Under the terms of a 1985 government act (COBRA), if you leave a job with health benefits, you're entitled to continue that coverage for up to 18 months—you pay 100 percent of the premium and sometimes a small administration fee. Eventually, you must search for your own health plan. You may also need disability and life insurance. Disability insurance is offered through many private insurance companies and state governments. This insurance pays a monthly fee that covers living and business expenses during periods of long-term recuperation from a health problem. The amount of money paid is based on the recipient's annual earnings.

Before contacting any insurance representative, talk to other writers, illustrators or photographers to learn which insurance companies they recommend. If you belong to a writers' or artists' organization, ask the organization if it offers insurance coverage for professionals. (SCBWI has a plan available. Look through the Clubs & Organizations section for other groups that may offer coverage.) Group coverage may be more affordable and provide more comprehensive coverage than an individual policy.

Answers to All Your Questions About All-Rights Contracts

BY RITA CAMMARANO

In February of 2002, Carus Publishing Group switched to an all-rights contract for all of its magazines. That included all of the Cobblestone Group magazines purchased by Carus Group in 2000. Fifteen children's magazines in all. Carus isn't the first to have this kind of contract. *Highlights for Children* and the Children's Better Health Institute, to name two, have had all-rights contracts for a long time. What does all-rights mean? What are the disadvantages to such a contract? Are there any advantages? What should I do if I receive an all-rights contract? This article will answer those questions and more.

Carus is the largest children's magazine publisher to use all-rights contracts. This policy change will have a big impact on the industry and especially on the people who write for their magazines. The new policy has left many freelancers upset and despairing of their abilities to continue to generate sufficient income by writing for children's magazines. Just as children's book writers often make more money through school visits and other speaking engagements than from book sales, reprint sales are important income, especially for established magazine writers. All-rights contracts end any further income from a piece.

One of the biggest disadvantages to all-rights contracts is that the payment received by contributors in no way compensates them for the loss of income in giving up those additional rights. Often, payment isn't even upon acceptance. It's upon publication, usually at least a year away with the all-rights publications. With some publications, your piece won't be published for three or four years. Is it worth the time to write a piece to give up all rights for up to 25¢ per word?

What, exactly does all-rights mean?

It means you are conveying your entire copyright, every right you own in that work, to the publisher. You will no longer have any rights in the piece and can't do anything further with it. The publisher can print and reprint the piece on its own websites, use it for promotional or advertising purposes, print it in an anthology or as a book by itself, and can also sell it to other publishers or organizations they choose. They can have it put on microfiche, sell it to other websites, sell it to test and educational companies, and to searchable databases like SIRS and EBSCO among others. There is no limit on their use or income-generating sales of that piece.

More specifically, all-rights includes first North American print rights, second print rights, all reprint rights, electronic rights and foreign rights among others. This includes your rights to the characters in the story, the setting and plot. If you later wish to write another story or a book with any of those characters or setting, for instance, you could have a problem.

The same is true for illustrators. There may be fewer reprint markets for illustrations since they are produced to suit a specific story. Still, if you do become attached to a character so created and wish to use it for something else, if you've sold all rights to it, you're apt to have a problem.

RITA CAMMARANO *is an author and attorney and the editor of the e-newsletter,* The Business Side of Children's Publishing. *Her website is found at www.ritacammarano.smartwriters.com*

Do the ramifications of giving up all-rights differ depending on whether the piece is fiction or nonfiction?

Some publishers argue that all you are selling is the right to a "specific arrangement of words," but admit that if you rearrange the words and sell to a competing market, they will likely not work with you again. Let's take nonfiction first. How much do you have to change and what is a "competing market"? There is no hard and fast rule concerning markets. Certainly, if you sold all-rights to the original piece to a national, monthly children's magazine for 4- to 7-year-olds, then another national, monthly children's magazine targeting that age group would be a competing market. What if everything stays the same, but the target age group is 6- to 10-year-olds? There is overlap and the same families could well subscribe to both publications, so you might well have a problem there as well. Every publisher wants to give their readers something they can't get anywhere else.

Now if one magazine is for high school kids and you rework the piece and sell it to one that targets the preschool crowd, you're in better shape. Many times, it may be less black and white than that. Younger children often read magazines meant for older ones, so a target age group may not accurately reflect the readership of a given publication. The editors themselves know who is their competition. It would be wise to ask them if you have any questions about whether another publication would be considered a competing one.

Even if you sell the second piece to a non-competing publication, you'll need to make sure the pieces aren't too similar. Most nonfiction authors re-slant the piece, or take it from a different angle. Basically, you'll be using the research you did for the first article, but you will write a new article. When you sell all-rights, you give up the opportunity to write once and sell twice or even three or more times. You have to take the time and effort from other projects to change the focus of the piece and rewrite it. That's a considerable time commitment compared to just remarketing an already written piece.

Another nonfiction-oriented difficulty concerns books. If all-rights are sold to a nonfiction article and you'd later like to include part of it in a book, you wouldn't have the right to. This poses an immediate problem for those researching for a nonfiction book and would like to sell a few articles to magazines while they look for a book publisher. Maybe having an article published would even attract a book publisher. That avenue is closed with all-rights contracts. Some of the publishers with all rights contracts said they would most likely provide permission for such a book, but only after the contributor has found a book publisher. Spending several months or years doing research and then finding a publisher when you don't have the rights to some of the material would be a great risk.

Selling all-rights to fiction is another matter and possibly more prohibitive. There is no way to rearrange a story so it will be sufficiently different than originally sold. Just as importantly, when you sell all-rights to a piece of fiction, you arguably give up any rights to your characters, setting, plots and maybe even the title under trademark law. Authors often like a protagonist enough to want to write other stories about that character, or even a book. Similarly, sometimes a minor character from one story cries out for a story of her own. If not a character, you may create a wonderful setting you'd like to use again, especially if it's labor intensive fantasy or sci-fi. All those avenues could be closed to you if you sell all-rights to a story containing them.

It is always possible to ask the magazine publisher to release those rights, but if they will only consider it once a publisher is involved, the risk of losing all of that time and effort is high. Why would a publisher say no? An editor-in-chief of a well-respected children's magazine shed light on this for me: He wants all-rights so he never has to worry about seeing a publication of his associated with anything he doesn't like. Let's say the publication you're contemplating selling all-rights to is for 8- to 12-year-olds. The novel you reuse the story character in is for the same age, but you or the potential book editor decide the protagonist or plot needs to be a little more edgy or needs more romance. Now do you see where the magazine publisher may object? What if your novel ends up a series and your character becomes YA at some point and deals with more mature subject matter? What if the movie poster is a tad risqué? Many of us wish we had such problems, but at least to that one editor-in-chief, you could be on a major talk show one day explaining how it all started with the story in his magazine. It may not mesh with the image they want.

What should you do when faced with an all-rights contract?

Christine Ammer and Carol Busby, a national contract advisor and assistant advisor for the National Writer's Union, respectively, had these suggestions. Basically there are three choices:

1. Sign the standard contract
2. Negotiate changes
3. Walk away

The negotiating strategies are below, and there is no need to be afraid to negotiate. All of the editors I asked said that you would not harm your relationship with them by requesting changes to the contract. Even if you are not currently in the habit of seeking reprint markets for your work, you may want to keep the door open to do so later.

Your copyright is actually a bundle of rights. Instead of allowing them to be lumped together, try to separate them for negotiation purposes. Maybe you can sell first North American print rights and the non-exclusive right to publish it on the magazine's website. Another possibility is to split the proceeds of any reprint sales the publisher brings to you. Either the author could receive a certain dollar amount each time or a certain percentage of the amount received by the publication. Interestingly, none of the publications I've contacted actually contact any place to sell reprints. If someone contacts them, that's when they sell reprints. A good compromise would be allowing those publishers all rights for a limited time such as three to six months, and then have secondary rights such as reprint rights revert to the contributor.

Always read and be certain you understand what you are signing. For instance, it's good to avoid signing off on broad statements along the lines of "any media or devices ever invented now and in the future."

Are there really reprint markets out there?

Yes, there are reprint markets and sometimes writers receive more payment for reprints than the original sale. There are e-zines that accept reprints, as well as some regional publications, and many religious publications. Pieces in religious publications need not always have overt religious content. Most markets that accept reprints only purchase one-time rights. Since their range or target audiences are smaller (especially the print ones), there may be several non-competing ones to sell to. Some freelancers have sold the same pieces six to nine times.

Who do the all-rights publishers sell reprints to and how much do they make?

Right now, with the proliferation of educational testing, it is largely the testing companies approaching publishers for reprints. For the Children's Better Health Institute, those reprint sales comprise around 80 percent of their reprint sales. The other 20 percent are sales to electronic databases such as SIRS and EBSCO. *Highlights for Children* sells reprints to around 5 percent of its pieces and is approached by the same type of reprint markets. Some publishers have their entire magazines reprinted on such databases and that type of arrangement generates less income than selling reprints to individual pieces. For the most part, $50 a published page is a pretty usual fee paid for these reprints.

Are there any advantages for contributors in an all-rights contract?

There aren't any advantages for a contributor, but there are a couple of circumstances under which it may be worthwhile to sign one. The first that comes to mind is for a writer just beginning to write for magazines. Those first couple of good credits are important and you may consider it worth it to sign away all your rights to get them. An instance in which a more seasoned person may be willing to sign an all-rights contract is if a piece has not sold elsewhere and the author does not see reprint possibilities for the piece. In each of these circumstance, you may still try to negotiate, but instead of walking away if the results are unsatisfactory, you may wish to sign.

First you should know that not all-rights contracts are created equal. Research the markets. There are still many children's magazines that do only purchase first or first and second rights and some of them are very good ones. You may want to try those publications first. If you do decide to send work to one of the magazines with all-rights contracts, check those markets, too. Some pay on acceptance rather than publication, some have a shorter lead-time and some both pay on acceptance and pay a little better.

I'm just one person. Is negotiating and walking away from these contracts if necessary going to change anything?

If enough people do it, the answer is yes. Everyone knows *Boys' Life* magazine. They attempted to switch to a contract that included permanent electronic rights in the early 1990s. At that time, the Internet was a vast, unorganized universe requiring a book the size of the *Oxford English Dictionary* to figure out how to find anything. E-rights were not an issue. When the Internet came together and personal computer sales boomed, e-rights became an issue. Contributors balked at giving up their e-rights and *Boys' Life* changed their policy because they valued their relationships with their contributors. Magazines need us as much as we need them. If enough people refuse the all-rights contracts, publishers will have to change their policies or the quality of their publications will suffer.

How is the larger writing community reacting to these issues?

The National Writer's Union (NWU), the Author's Guild, and other organizations are fighting this battle on several different fronts. The NWU, joined by the Society of Children's Book Writers and Illustrators and other organizations won *Tasini v. New York Times*. The case was about publishers posting contributors' works on their websites and selling electronic rights to those pieces to others without the permission of the authors involved. The Supreme Court sided with the writers and that suit and the subsequent ones filed on behalf of the affected writers are still in mediation at this time to work out a settlement. Right now, there is a "Freelance Writers Protection Act" in Congress. Its purpose is to give authors more bargaining power. Although this act is unlikely to pass anytime soon, the intention is to help level the playing field between individual contributors and publishers.

How are children's writers reacting to the new all-rights contracts?

While some children's magazine contributors have decided not to sell to all-rights magazines at all or as a last resort, others plan to attempt to negotiate. Still others I contacted mentioned giving up writing for children's magazines altogether and concentrating on books or magazines for adults. Time will tell whether writers will be able to make sufficient income through freelancing for children's publications. If these policies aren't flexible, it is possible that many writers will switch their emphasis and newer ones may simply never really consider writing for children's magazines at all. Until this year, when new writers posted to listserves asking if someone could support themselves writing for children, the answer was a qualified "yes." Now that so many of the top children's magazines have all-rights policies, that answer may change to "no." If that happens, these magazines and publishers lose just as much as their potential and/or past contributors do. Not to mention the children accustomed to high-quality fiction and articles. Hopefully, we can all work together to arrange terms more equitable for the contributors. It should be possible since both sides have the common goal of providing quality fiction and articles for children.

Children's Writers Quiz: 20 Questions to Test Your Professionalism

BY ROBERT BROWN & SHARENE MARTIN

Everyone wants to write for children . . . everyone! We receive queries from bankers, lawyers, doctors, teachers, judges, ministers, reporters, animators, and adult fiction writers. However, there are only a very few we are able to consider. Why? Because we want to work with authors who are professional, those who invest the time and effort to work at their craft. Unfortunately, too often we get queries from writers whose primary concerns are fame, wealth, and invitations to talk shows, instead of creating quality literature for children.

Are you one of the many overcome by the intoxicating dream of being a world-renowned children's author, or are you a professional craftsman on the road to publication? Take our 20-question quiz to find out whether you know enough about the business of children's literature to make your dream come true.

THE QUESTIONS

1. Your 4,000-word picture book for ages 4-8 about tolerance in the global community has been rejected over and over again. You don't understand why. Could it be . . .?
   A. Four thousand words is too long for a picture book.
   B. The writing is probably too mature for a picture book.
   C. The subject matter is not for your intended audience.
   D. All of the above.
2. Nonfiction and fiction writing are not that different . . . if you can write one, you can write the other.
   True
   False
3. Joining a professional writing organization is a waste of time.
   True
   False
4. Editors and agents have different submissions standards.
   True
   False
5. A good query should contain which of the following?
   A. A brief synopsis of your work

ROBERT BROWN & SHARENE MARTIN *founded Indiana-based Wylie-Merrick Literary Agency in 1999. Martin, who completed a Master's degree in Language Education from Indiana University, specializes in picture books, and middle-grade and young adult novels, both fiction and nonfiction. Also an alumni of Indiana University, Brown, whose degree is in English and communications, prefers to work with young adult and adult fiction. Both enjoy being published authors and bringing together talented writers and editors to produce great children's literature.*

    B. A brief autobiography of the writer
    C. The word count, format, and category (fiction/nonfiction) of the project
    D. All of the above
 6. The average writer should revise his/her project about how many times before a manuscript is ready to submit?
    A. None, it is ready to go upon completion.
    B. More that 1 but less than 3
    C. More than 3
    D. Depends on the project
 7. Writing for children is . . .
    A. Difficult
    B. Fun
    C. Easy, depending on the format
    D. A and B
 8. Editors and agents do not need to hear about how much your relatives, your colleagues, groups of children, or others love your work.
    True
    False
 9. There are no differences between a writer and a professional writer.
    True
    False
10. Your middle-grade novel about going to a pool party is not getting any interest from editors or agents. It might be that . . .
    A. The story of going to a pool party cannot sustain an entire middle grade novel.
    B. You just haven't sent it to the right publisher.
    C. It isn't trendy enough.
11. What is wrong with the following rhyme?
    Freddy thought it was a pain
    that he would not see his friend again.
    A. The name Freddy is probably not attractive to editors.
    B. It does not scan and "again" and "pain" are false rhymes.
    C. Who cares? Rhyme never sells.
12. You should query on _____ project(s) at a time.
    A. All of your
    B. Three
    C. Two
    D. One
13. Your queries are not getting any positive responses. It could be that the editors or agents don't like the idea of the book, or it could be that . . .?
    A. Your experiences being a mother, librarian, grandfather, or teacher are not adequate qualifications to write a children's book.
    B. Your query contains too much hype or is too gimmicky.
    C. Your query relayed your willingness to go on talk shows to promote the movie version of your book, rather than write it.
    D. Your query indicates you are fully prepared to sell it to a software company or theater troupe, as your project could be both.
    E. All of the above.
14. You send to a publisher listed in a writer's magazine; however, the letter is returned unopened. What could have happened?
    A. The publisher went out of business.
    B. The address was wrong in the listing.

C. They don't like you and won't open your query.

D. Either A or B

15. Your agent lands you a contract from a major publishing house. You are . . .

    A. A published author

    B. Still unpublished, but with a great prospect

    C. Nothing, but your agent is very happy for some reason

16. The publishing industry is dominated by about how many publishing conglomerates?

    A. One

    B. Five

    C. Hundreds

       16.a. Name one _____ (extra credit)

17. Your manuscript is rejected with a polite note that the company no longer publishes that type of book. You could have saved time and money if you had done what?

    A. Talked to your friends about the company

    B. Talked to your kids about the company

    C. Researched the company's website and some of the titles on its list

18. On page 1 of your manuscript, you used incorrect grammar. On page 12, you used "accept" instead of "except." On page 19, you spelled "spleen" incorrectly. What message does this send to an agent or editor?

    A. It doesn't matter. Agents and editors will correct your mistakes if they want your work.

    B. You are unprofessional.

    C. You are a creative genius and cannot be bothered with details.

19. Picture book writers should include the names of illustrators in their queries or submitted work.

    True

    False

20. Every writer needs an agent . . .

    A. In all cases

    B. Never

    C. Depends on the project

    D. Only if he/she wants to become famous

THE ANSWERS

1. D—From picture books to young adult novels, each category of children's literature has specific characteristics that set it apart from the others, such as word count, subject matter, and writing style. No matter what format you write in for children, you should understand the differences and similarities between each. See *The Children's Writer's Reference*, by Berthe Amoss and Eric Suben and *You Can Write Children's Books*, by Tracey E. Dils.

2. FALSE—Nonfiction writers who want to switch to writing fiction think it is as simple as writing from the imagination instead of from facts. It isn't. Writing fiction is an entirely different type of craft. More importantly, writing for children in either category is vastly different than writing for adults. Just because you can write emergent reader fiction does not mean you know how to write nonfiction picture book biographies. Know the difference!

3. FALSE—There's some expense involved, but joining a professional organization like the Society of Children's Book Writers and Illustrators (www.scbwi.org) can provide new insights and opportunities. Grants, conferences, discounts, insurance, and professional information are just some of the benefits available to members. It also shows editors and agents you are serious about writing as a business.

4. FALSE—We at Wylie-Merrick look for the same elements as editors do, because they are our customers. We have to know what they want (good writing and professional presenta-

tion!), so we review every submission with that in mind. We will not take on a project that is not ready to be seen by an editor and "get it ready" for submission. It is the writer's job to prepare the manuscript.

5. D—We like a simple, straightforward query, as do most editors. We need to know only the relevant information about the project and the author, no more, no less. As a standard, you should be able to write a one-paragraph synopsis of your project and a one-paragraph description of your qualifications to write it. Anything more than that is not helpful to us.

6. C—This is a tricky question, and most people will say D. However, we don't know any writer who has revised anything less than 3 times. Even manuscripts with only 50-200 words have to be revised several times before they are ready for submission. Nothing is ready for submission on the first draft, so don't send it.

7. D—We wish writing for children were as easy as people seem to think it is; however, it isn't. Anyone who has written for children will tell you how much effort goes into writing, editing, and revising. Writing for children is fun, but it is also time-consuming, arduous, and intense work.

8. TRUE—To be blunt, we don't care. We don't care what other people think of your manuscript because we want to form our own opinions, and, quite honestly, we don't think relatives, friends, and acquaintances can be objective, even those in the publishing world. You can run you work past other people, but their opinions are not the kind of relevant information we want to see in a query.

9. FALSE—It is incredibly frustrating to work in a profession where everyone thinks he/she can do it. If you want to write for children, you need to get experience and education in the field. Professionals invest time and money in preparing for their careers, and professional writers are no different. Writers don't have to have a college degree, but taking even just one course in creative writing can enhance your writing skills 100 percent.

10. A—There are subjects that specific age groups may or may not be interested in, and, for middle-grade readers, going to a pool party probably isn't one of them, at least not for an entire novel.

11. B—Good, structured rhyme does sell, but bad rhyme leaves a terrible impression. Telling a story in rhyme is very difficult because the writer must sustain the story and the rhyme throughout the text. The number of syllables per line must be consistent and the rhymes must be true. Pain and again do not really rhyme, so they are false rhymes. A true rhyme would be bake and cake or jelly and belly. If you have written a story in rhyme, but you have never heard of scanning or false rhyme, you need to research the craft more.

12. D—We prefer to see or represent one project at a time, and most editors do, too. A red flag goes up when we read a query offering us the chance to review ten manuscripts, none of which are published. Usually, these queries outline children's and adult or fiction and nonfiction projects, or worse, all of the above. Writers, in these instances, are saying, "I can do it all!" Unfortunately, those who can do it all, and do it well, are rare. Children's fiction and nonfiction are distinctly different in their characteristics, and, typically, when a writer claims he/she has written in several areas, they rarely understand the differences and similarities in each.

13. E—Any of these items in a query tells us a writer does not understand the business of publishing or the craft of writing. While experience in a child-related occupation or role is helpful, it does not necessarily qualify a person to write for children. Learning the craft requires research, time, and effort. We look for serious writers with realistic professional expectations, who do not depend on hype or gimmicks. Good, solid writing skills and imagination are the elements we seek; nothing else will do. Writers who want to appear on Oprah are in this profession for the wrong reasons, as most children's writers will never make the talk show circuit. Finally, know what market you are writing for. We receive queries for projects that could be picture books or scripts for educational software. If you

don't know what you've written, you are not ready for publication.

14. D—It pays to research publishers or agents before sending your work. This can save you tremendous amounts of time and energy. Sometimes listings are wrong; however, more often than not, in the interim between submission of information and publication of the magazine, the publishing house may have gone out of business or changed its acceptance policies on queries. Do your research, and this will cut down on the number of "dead" submissions you make.

15. B—Until the book is in print, you are an unpublished author. Contracts can be canceled (they have an "out" clause) or your book may never reach publication. It is frustrating, especially for a first-time author, but there are other issues involved over which the publisher and author have little or no control. Signing a contract is a big step, but writers should keep in mind that this does not promise the book will come to fruition.

16. B—There are about five different publishing conglomerates that dominate the industry-Bertelsmann, Viacom, Rupert Murdoch's News Corporation, Holtzbrinck, and Pearson. It seems strange, but if you read through the corporate family trees of publishing houses, you will begin to see how all of them are related. This information can help in your publishing efforts.

17. C—Research is a vital part of placing your work with an agent or editor. The publishing industry can be volatile, so it is imperative that you thoroughly research publishing houses or agents before wasting your time and theirs by submitting work they do not publish or represent.

18. B—Writers, editors, and agents all make mistakes. However, when we review the first ten pages of a novel and find it filled with errors, we know the writer has not revised her work. This is the sure sign of an amateur. We will not work with anyone who doesn't understand that writing is revision.

19. FALSE—We do not need this information. Most picture book editors prefer to choose their own illustrators for the projects they take on.

20. C—It would be nice to say that every writing project needs representation, but is not always true. We sometimes tell writers they would be better off submitting their work to publishers directly without an agent. Why? Certain projects—educational materials, novelty books, short picture books, etc.—don't pay enough. A writer could submit directly to the house and have a better chance of getting published, in addition to making more of a profit.

SCORING

The scoring for this quiz is very simple. If you missed one, you are not yet ready to submit your work. Read more children's books. Do more professional research. Go to conferences and join a critique group if you are a new writer. Most importantly, study the craft of writing for children and polish your work until it is the best it can be.

We wouldn't be surprised if someday we receive a query from the President of the United States himself, because it seems like everyone wants to write for children. However, we would expect him (or at least his cabinet) to be knowledgeable about children's literature and the fundamental concepts of the publishing industry. Invest the time and effort in your writing, and you'll pass any editor's or agent's test with flying colors!

The ABC's of Writing for Children

BY VERLA KAY

Learning to write for children is not easy, and it can take many years, but it is the most rewarding of professions. When you're starting out, there are many aspects of children's writing and publishing that can only be learned through experience, trial and error, or from someone who has already "been there, done that." I learned a lot during my struggle to become published—things that may help you write better, market manuscripts more effectively, and become more professional. So before you set out on a career as a children's writer, take some time to learn your ABC's.

A is for AGENT

An agent can be a wonderful help to you in your career or a terrible stumbling block. Much depends on what you want from your writing career and which agent you get. Many successful children's authors have never had an agent and many others got an agent only after they had several books already under contract and/or published. In children's publishing, having an agent is not a necessity.

B is for BOOK

Everyone knows what a book is. But unless you have browsed through your local bookstore lately, you may not realize just how many different kinds of children's books are on the market today. A children's book can be a Board Book, a Concept Book, a Novelty Book, a Picture Book, a Picture Story Book, an Easy Reader, an Early Chapter Book, a Chapter Book, a Mid-Grade Novel, a Young Adult Novel, a Nonfiction book in any of these categories, or a Poetry Book. You must read books if you are to be a successful author. By reading many different books, you will gain valuable insight into the kinds of children's books being published today, and get a feel for the various categories of children's books.

Picture Books can be anything from totally wordless (normally done by illustrators) to 2,500 words. Picture books for younger children usually range between 200 and 1,000 words.

Chapter Books are for emergent readers who want to read "big kids' books" but are not experienced enough to read long, involved stories. They have about 10 chapters in them.

Mid-Grade books are for ages 8-12. They are usually 100-150 typewritten pages with an average word count of 35,000. Children of this age are interested in everything! They are insatiable readers of almost anything written within the line of their interests and reading levels.

Young Adult (YA) novels are written for ages 12 and up. YA novels are usually longer and have more mature content than Mid-Grade books. They will often be similar in both style and content to an adult novel, except the ages of the protagonists are around 17 and the novel is normally shorter than an adult book. YA books run about 175-200 typewritten pages with an average word count of 45,000.

VERLA KAY *writes highly acclaimed historical picture books in a unique style she calls cryptic rhyme. Her books include* Orphan Train, Homespun Sarah, Broken Feather, Gold Fever, Iron Horses, Covered Wagons Bumpy Trails, *and* Tattered Sails—*which was named a 2001* Child *magazine Best Book of the Year. Learn more about Verla Kay and how to write for children by visiting her award-winning website* www.verlakay.com *(named one of The Best 101 Websites for Writers by* Writer's Digest *in 2000).*

C is for CHARACTER

Strong characters are important in children's writing. Characters in children's stories should normally be young, but most children aren't interested in reading about children younger than themselves, so make your characters a little older than your target audience. Your characters need to have problems to solve in order to keep your story interesting and they must solve their own problems—don't allow an adult to solve their dilemmas for them, and don't have their problems solved with, "It was just a dream." Allow your characters to have flaws and to make mistakes, and the children who read your stories will love them because your characters will feel so real to them.

D is for DO IT!

In order to become a published writer, you must write and submit. Many wonderful writers never become published because they just don't "do it." You must want to do it enough to sacrifice some of your time and energy to become published.

E is for ESCALATION CLAUSE

An escalation clause is part of a publishing contract. It states that if your book sells over X number of copies, you will receive a larger royalty. This is good for a book that sells well—*if* the clause is in that book's contract. Publishers can be very resistant to putting this clause in a contract. To get it, you may have to first sell several books, or engage an agent to negotiate it for you.

F is for FORTUNE

A fortune is something you should not count on if you write for children. While there are a few children's authors who receive large royalties, most authors are lucky if their books even "earn out" their original advance.

The first money you will usually get will be your advance which is money given to you in advance of your book's sales. Most publishers expect your book to bring in enough money during the first year of publication to "pay off" your advance. You will not receive any royalties until your advance has been paid back. (This is called "earning out" your advance.) Any money earned over the advance amount will be sent to you in a royalty check. Royalties are often paid twice a year.

Average advances for first books for children's authors today are between $500 and $5,000, depending on the publishing house and the book. The standard royalty for a hardcover is 10 percent, but picture book authors split their royalty 50/50 with the illustrator, so they only get 5 percent royalty unless they are also the artist.

Many children's authors make most of their money from doing school visits, speeches, and workshops. This can be a very lucrative addition to a writer's income. But the greatest "fortune" is in knowing that *your* book is being read and enjoyed by children.

G is for GALLEYS

Galleys, also sometimes called advance reading copies, are the actual words printed on pages just the way they will be in the final book. Some galleys are bound and even have soft covers. Authors normally see the galleys of their books for proofreading. It is very important to proofread your galleys carefully. Any mistakes that are missed in the galleys will be printed in your book.

H is for HARD WORK

Most writers work very hard to achieve success, but most of them also love what they do so much, they wouldn't trade it for any other career in the world!

Picture book author Verla Kay pays careful attention to her ABC's, XYZ's and everything in between as she labors over every important word in her historical picture books written in her own "cryptic rhyme" style. In one of her latest books from Putnam, *Broken Feather*, illustrated by Stephen Alcorn, Kay sensitively tells the story of a Native American as white men start moving onto Indian land.

I is for ILLUSTRATORS

Illustrators bring books alive. They labor for long hours making covers and insides of books appealing and exciting to children. Most authors do not pick the illustrators for their books, their publishers do. So be careful where you send your manuscript! Often, publishers like to combine an unknown author with a big name illustrator because that gives the sales of the book a "boost."

J is for JOIN

It is vital for an aspiring author to be around other writers. Their shared knowledge will help you learn, their successes will inspire you, their rejections will console you. They will teach you you're not alone and it's not a tragedy to be rejected. Rejection is a common step in the process of becoming a published writer. So join! Join the Society of Children's Book Writers & Illustrators (SCBWI, www.scbwi.org); join a local critique group that meets once a week or once or twice a month; or join an on-line critique group. Join a writer's e-mail group, like the CW (Children's Writers) list (see Resources for Writers & Illustrators on page 35 sidebar). Join other writers who post to online bulletin boards and meet in chat rooms. You will find yourself becoming a better, more professional writer when you join other writers and share experiences.

K is for KILL FEE

A kill fee is something no writer wants to receive. It's an amount of money paid to a writer when publication of a previously accepted manuscript is cancelled.

L is for LINKS

Links are web addresses. There are many wonderful links that will expand your knowledge. Some are websites, some are forums, and some are e-mail lists. Many of them allow you to read messages from other children's writers and post your own messages when you have something to add to a discussion.

M is for MARKETING

Once you have written a wonderful story, the next step is deciding where to send it. Getting a current market guide is absolutely essential for writers. Always use the most current copy; they go out of date very quickly. *Children's Writer's & Illustrator's Market* is considered by most writers to be the best market guide for writers of children's literature.

Read the listings to find publishers looking for manuscripts like yours. When you've located the most likely candidates for your story, send for sample magazines or publishers' catalogs, go to your local library or bookstore and see if they have some you can examine, or visit their websites.

When you get your magazines or catalogs, study them carefully. Does this publisher publish stories similar to yours? Would your story fit into their magazine or on their list? If your story is going to be illustrated, do you like the majority of the illustrations they use? (This is extremely important as you will most likely have no say in the artist or artwork of your story once a publisher has accepted it.)

When you have narrowed your choices down to five or ten publishers, list them in the order in which you plan to submit your story to them. Post your list where you can see it frequently, and send your manuscript to the first publisher on your list. If it comes back rejected, don't hesitate! Look at the rejection for any clues that might help you improve your story, revise it if necessary, then write a new cover letter to the next publisher on your list and send it out again.

N is for NEGOTIATION

You will need to learn to negotiate your own contract if you don't have an agent to do this for you. There's nothing especially hard about it, except remembering to value yourself if you want others to value you. Get a good book on contracts. Study the book and compare the clauses to your contract. Watch out for option clauses that won't allow you to sell another book until after your first book is published! Make the publisher change those clauses to a limited period of time (like three months after you submit the new story.)

Find out if your book will be published in hardcover or paperback. What size will the book be? If it's a picture book, will the publisher show you illustrations at each step of the process? When do they plan to publish your book?

Ask for more free copies of your book and extra promotion attention; you may be pleasantly surprised at what your publisher is willing to do for you. Remember, once they have made an offer on your book, they *want* it. You are in a good (but not spectacular) position to negotiate. They expect you to negotiate your contract and you won't lose your sale by asking for changes as long as you are polite and willing to compromise when necessary.

O is for OPPORTUNITIES

Writers have opportunities every day to improve their craft and become more successful. Opportunities are all around you. They are in books, on television, on the Internet. They are in conferences and workshops, in classes and critique groups. They are at the library, your local schools and in bookstores. Avail yourself of every opportunity that comes your way and you will be amazed at your eventual success.

P is for PLOT

A book without a plot is often called a "mood piece." Most strong stories have strong plots. The best way to learn about plots is to read a lot of other books and analyze them. What makes plots work—or not work? When you have learned what other writers do to make their stories work, you will be well on your way to creating your own wonderfully plotted stories.

Jacket art © 2003 Ted Rand. Reprinted with permission of G.P. Putnam's Sons.

Verla Kay's *Homespun Sarah*, illustrated by Ted Rand, is a glimpse into hard work and simple pleasures of colonial life, as the title character, Sarah, spends her days tending to chores around the house, caring for her younger sister, carding and spinning wool—and waiting patiently for the day the wool will be transformed into a new dress for her.

Q is for QUIT

If you want to see your words in print, don't quit! You need to keep on writing, keep on improving, and keep on submitting if you want to become a published writer. One of my favorite anonymous quotes is: "The main difference between a published writer and an unpublished one is not necessarily the quality of the writing; it's that the published writer never quit."

R is for REVISION

If you want to be a published writer, revise! Not just once or twice, but over and over and over—until every line in your manuscript "sings" to you. When there aren't any "rough spots" left, it's revised enough to send to publishers.

S is for SLUSH PILE

The unsolicited submissions received daily by publishers are often referred to as the "slush pile." Editors have a love/hate relationship with the slush pile. They dread reading through huge stacks of inappropriate manuscripts that abound in slush piles. But they're always hoping to find that one special manuscript that is so wonderful they absolutely have to publish it! The editor wants to find *you*. She wants to publish *you*. She wants to be the one who discovers that great new author. And when she does, her thrill is nearly as great as yours!

T is for TELLING

One of the biggest errors of many new writers is "telling" their story instead of "showing" it. Example:

TELL—Tommy was mad.

SHOW—Tommy threw his truck on the floor and stomped on it.

When shown, not told, it becomes richer, more interesting, and more saleable!

U is for UNSOLICITED

An unsolicited manuscript is one sent to a publisher who has no idea it's coming. The editor has not previously corresponded with you and asked you to send the story. This is a manuscript that comes in "over the transom." It will be placed in the slush pile with other unsolicited manuscripts waiting their turn to be read.

V is for VANITY PUBLISHERS

Avoid these! A vanity publisher will make you feel very "special." They will tell you they absolutely love your book and want to publish it. "Real" publishers do this, too, but there is a big difference between a legitimate publisher and a vanity publisher! Vanity (also called subsidy) publishers require you to put up at least part of the money to publish your own book. This is not good, and you should run, not walk away from any publisher wanting money from you. Most vanity published books are not reviewed by major reviewers. Most vanity books aren't stocked in major bookstore chains. Most vanity books don't get into schools or libraries. Most writers who publish with vanity publishers end up with a garage full of books that can only be sold to their local businesses and to friends and relatives. "Real" publishers will pay you to publish your book. They take all the financial risks. Publishing your book with a vanity publisher will not help your career. (Note: *Children's Writer's & Illustrator's Market* does not include listings of vanity publishers.)

W is for WAITING

And waiting . . . and waiting . . . and waiting . . . and waiting! Whether it's waiting to hear back from a publisher regarding a submission or waiting for a contracted book to be published, working writers get used to waiting.

X MARKS THE SPOT

X is for the mark on a contract that shows you where to sign. Contracts are legal, binding agreements between authors and publishers. Make sure you know and understand what yours says. If you don't know how to read a contract, get help. If you decide to use a local lawyer, make sure you pick one who is very familiar with the publishing world. Some terms in publishing contracts can be negotiated, but many cannot. A lawyer unfamiliar with publishing will not help you by demanding changes a publisher cannot make. You will be bound by the terms of your contract for as long as your book stays in print, so learn all you can about yours and make sure you understand it before you sign it.

Y is for YOUNG READERS

Young readers are who you're writing for. It's very important to remember the main purpose of writing for children (unless you're writing textbook stories) is to give pleasure and fun to young people. It's to allow young readers to wander for a while into a make-believe world you've created just for them; to give them an alternative to computer games and TV; to let them stretch their own thoughts and feel the power of the written word; to make them laugh and cry with your characters; and to open new worlds in their imaginations.

Z is for "Z" END

The end of a story should satisfy and complete what the beginning promised. If a story started out with action or a life/death situation, then the ending must reflect that seriousness and resolve the problems set forth at the beginning. If the book started out lighthearted and funny, then the ending should delight in the same tone of pleasure and fun. Make sure that whatever your ending is, it feels right for your story. Did you tie up the loose ends? Did your main characters solve their own problems? Was there some kind of "twist" or surprise at the end so your reader felt it was worth reading the entire story to get to the ending? Start your story with an exciting, compelling beginning, end it with a wonderful, satisfying, surprising ending and you will have a wonderful story—one that only you could write.

Resources for Writers & Illustrators

To Find an Agent
- Check the Agents & Art Reps section of this book.
- Request SCBWI's list of agents (available to members only).
- Study *Guide to Literary Agents* (Writer's Digest Books).

Books on Writing
- *Formatting & Submitting Your Manuscripts*, by Jack and Glenda Neff, Don Prues, and the editors of *Writer's Market*
- *How to Write & Illustrate Children's Picture Books and Get Them Published*, edited by Treld Pelkey Bicknell & Felicity Trotman
- *Writing with Pictures*, by Uri Shulevitz
- *Writing for Children & Teenagers*, by Lee Wyndham & Arnold Madison
- *Author to Editor: Query Letter Secrets of the Pros*, edited by Linda Arms White (available through the www.write4kids.com)

Helpful Websites
- **www.scbwi.org**
  The recently redesigned website for SCBWI (Society of Children's Book Writers and Illustrators), the most helpful organization for children's writers.
- **www.authorsguild.org**
  Website for the Author's Guild. Writers must be published or have a contract to be published to join. Yearly fees are contingent upon your yearly writing income.
- **www.verlakay.com**
  Verla Kay's Website for Children's Writers features links to other helpful sites, access to a live chat room (#Kidlit Chat Room for children's writers hosts a nightly chat, www.verlakay.com/chat/chat.html), a message board, online workshops, transcripts, and extensive writing information, as well as instruction on how to join the CW List.
- **www.write4kids.com**
  Features tons of information for children's writers, as well as access to the Write4Kids Bulletin Board a.k.a. "Old Yeller," (www.write4kids.com/wwwboard), a very active online bulletin board for messages and discussions.

Don't Put It Off! How to Combat Procrastination

BY ALMA FULLERTON

This article almost consisted of two sentences:

There was supposed to be an article here but the author put off querying it.

Look for it in the 2004 Children's Writer's & Illustrator's Market.

To be totally honest, I waited several months to query this article and almost missed getting it in on time. After that, it was at least another month before I got the go ahead, because a certain editor (no names revealed) put off finalizing layout plans.

What do the editor and I have in common? That dreaded "P" word. You know the one, because chances are, you do it too—*procrastination.*

In fact, whether they're in the top of their field or novices, 90 percent of people in North America tend to procrastinate. If you're in the other 10 percent, pat yourself on the back (and consider walking out of the room backwards because the rest of us "real" people might feel the need to let the door hit you in the backside as you leave).

WHY DO WE PROCRASTINATE?

There are various reasons creative people procrastinate.

Fear of rejection. Other people's responses to your work are not in your control. Fear of rejection can cause anxiety and interfere with your ability to complete a project.

Fear of success. Once you become successful, you want to stay successful. For some people, it may be easier just to fail and have no further expectations placed on them.

Disorganization. With supplies scattered and notes unorganized, you may feel like getting work done is hopeless.

Feelings of being overwhelmed. Having to complete a story or illustrations can be a daunting task.

Perfectionism. Setting standards too high can make you accomplish less.

Lack of time/family obligations. Kids, spouses, parents, out of the home jobs, other obligations can make you put aside working on your writing.

Lack of incentive. When you're only accountable to yourself why should you worry about getting things done?

Creative block. Whether you just can't get going for lack of ideas or whether there's a missing piece you have to find before you move forward, this one is a major problem with creative people.

Self doubt. When you second-guess your ability to produce anything worthwhile you may stop working altogether.

OVERCOMING PROCRASTINATION
Bring on those rejections!

Perhaps you procrastinate because you worry about spending too much time on a project only to have it rejected. If this is your problem, you have to think about the goals you wish to

---

ALMA FULLERTON *lives and writes in Ontario, Canada where she does her best not to put things off.*

Suggested Reading

The Artist's Way—A Spiritual Path to Higher Creativity, by Julia Cameron
Overcoming Procrastination, by Windy D. Dryden
The Courage to Write—How Writers Transcend Fear, by Ralph Keyes
Bird by Bird, by Anne Lamott
The Right to Write, by Julia Cameron
Writing Down the Bones: Freeing the Writer Within, by Natalie Goldberg
Letters to a Fiction Writer, edited by Frederick Busch.

achieve and accept what you must do to meet them. Realize everything worthwhile takes time and effort to achieve. The feeling you get from completing a project can be as satisfying as an acceptance. Yes, your project may be rejected; but then again maybe it won't.

Every writer, illustrator, performer, and editor has at some time in their career been shot down, whether it was just simply one of their ideas or a complete project.

Wear your rejections with pride. They prove you have enough strength to put your work out there. Many people don't have the courage to take that first step.

Don't let rejections give you that "I'll never do this" attitude. Take an, "I'll show them" attitude. Revise the story if need be—but get it back out there.

Create for yourself

An award-winning author once said that winning a major award for a first book is something she wouldn't wish on anyone.

Why? Once you win an award you feel like critics are watching your every move as you write or illustrate, making sure all your books from then on are of award-winning caliber. That can be enough pressure to make anyone stop working.

Think about why you create. Most of us don't create simply because we want to. We create because something deep inside compels us to. We have stories to tell. Non-production can leave a void in your heart. Fill it by writing to satisfy yourself.

Also remember who your audience is. Children will always enjoy good stories and good illustrations. If your book doesn't win an award, so what? I have yet to see a child turn away a book because there was no gold sticker on it.

Get organized

I don't mean you have to go through your pantry and put everything in alphabetical order, or rearrange your sock drawer by color. But make sure everything you need for your projects is within hands-reach. Check your ink cartridge levels and your paper supply. Gather all your notes or any other research you may need and put them together or pin them up on a corkboard. Don't waste valuable time searching or retrieving things.

Don't let things overwhelm you—start small

Break everything up into baby steps. Start by taking ten minutes to work on a project. Revise or write one scene or one chapter at a time. Do touch ups to an illustration. As a large project, your work-in-progress may look impossible, but by breaking it up into a bunch of smaller tasks, it will become more manageable. As you get into a routine of working every day, gradually add onto the amount of time you spend working.

Get all your works-in-progress together. Put them in order of importance or due dates. If they're all equally important, start with the project that has the least amount of work left to be done on it. By the time you get to the largest project the fact that the others are completed should give you the oomph to finish it.

Get over perfectionism

Commit to working towards achievable goals. Achievable: meaning not perfect. Nothing is perfect.

First drafts or rough sketches are a place you can allow yourself to write or draw garbage. Use them to get the story fleshed out.

Use later drafts to fill in any blanks your first draft leaves in the story. Even third or fourth drafts won't be perfect. If they were, we wouldn't need critique groups and editors wouldn't have jobs.

No time? Make time.

Use your lunch hour and coffee breaks to write, or write during slow times on a note pad. Take a small hands-free tape recorder with you while you drive to record notes or ideas for sketches. During your child's soccer practice take story notes or make rough sketches. Keep soap crayons or waterproof paper and a pen in the bathroom for when inspiration hits you while you're in the shower or bath. Have index cards and pens in every room for taking notes.

Use time you'd normally waste for tidying your house. For example, when you use the bathroom, wipe the sink clean. The next time you're in there, clean the toilet. You can also use the time your kids are in the bathtub to clean the bathroom. Throw a load of laundry in the washing machine or do other cleaning chores while you plot out your next chapter so when you finally sit down at your computer you'll be able to use this time to write instead of just thinking about what to write.

My family needs me

Family interruptions or obligations are often used as a way to procrastinate. Yes, your family is very important, but so is your work. The fact that you do it from your home should not change anything; just like any other professional you have to make time for both work and family.

If possible, have your own workspace and keep regular working hours. Let your family know not to interrupt while you're working unless it's an emergency.

Set your baby's swing up beside you while you work. That way the baby can see you and you can still pay attention to him.

Get a toy computer or art supplies so young children can "work" beside you. It's very important for a child's development for her to learn how to entertain herself. It's also good for kids see you at work. This way they learn to value your work.

Give a needy child a time limit. Say, "If you let me write for one hour, I'll play with you for the next hour."

Make play dates with other parents. Send your kids to their house one day. Take their kids the next. This also gives your children an important lesson on how to interact with other people when you are not around.

Pay an older child to babysit while you work or get your spouse to take the kids out for "daddy" or "mommy" time. Take a trip to the library to work and leave the kids with a babysitter.

If you have elderly parents interrupting, try to make them understand that what you do is your job. Keep your own workspace here too. Your parents need to know your working boundaries. Share your work with them. Let them make suggestions. They may see things in a different way than you do and may be able to find the puzzle pieces you're missing.

Start a creative guilt group

Every week I get together with two other creative friends. During our sessions we share what we did the previous week and make a list of things we have to get done during the next week.

We take down each other's lists as well. It makes us feel good to be able to say I accomplished everything I wanted to last week. But if, by the next session, we don't get anything done, we feel guilty. We've all had times where we've rushed to get things done on the day of the meeting just to say we did it.

The key word is "accountability." Make yourself accountable to others; that way you feel you have to get things done.

Jumpstart your brain

Jumpstarting your brain can be as easy as putting on your left sock before your right sock or vice versa in the morning. Any kind of slight change in routine will make your brain work harder than if you do things the same way every morning.

Exercise before you sit down to work, whether it's just a walk with the dog or a 20-minute full-body workout. Physical movement makes the blood flow faster to your brain, making it easier to concentrate.

If you have missing puzzle pieces that are preventing you from moving forward in your project, go out of your way to find them. Read back through past chapters to see if you can find out what's missing. Go to the library to research. If you can, visit the place your story is set, or at least read about it. If you're an illustrator, study samples of what you're trying to illustrate.

Sometimes, thinking about your work-in-progress just before you go to sleep can allow your subconscious to work the story out in your dreams. Keep a pen, flashlight and notepad beside your bed to write notes as soon as you wake up.

To re-energize try taking a day off and do something different. I don't mean you have to jump out of a plane (unless you really want to). Do something pleasant for yourself. Go to the spa for the day, or go to the lake with a net and catch some small sunfish for your home aquarium—anything that you've never done before.

Fill up your inner being so you have the energy to give youself a new perspective when you go back to your work-in-progress. Giving yourself a day off can also reinforce the idea that your writing is an actual job too.

Something as simple as reading a book or magazine can help jumpstart your imagination. If you procrastinate by reading, then read absolutely nothing for a week.

Go to a museum and look at paintings.

Quick Tips

- Know your goals and work towards them.
- Set realistic goals.
- Evaluate your priorities and put them in order.
- Discipline yourself.
- Make work a part of your daily routine.
- Eliminate distraction—lock your office door and put on earphones.
- Remove the computer games from your writing computer.
- Take a break from e-mail lists.
- Reward yourself after completing a task.
- Motivate yourself by giving yourself a deadline or having a competition with another writer to see who can write the most in a day.
- Lay your work-in-progress out on the table where you can always see it.
- Take regular breaks.
- Keep everything you need within hands-reach to avoid wasting time.

Writing exercises can also renew your creativity. Try this: Grab a subject. If you can't think of anything, try whales. Now take five minutes and write or doodle something on that subject. Write the first thing that comes into your head. Allow yourself to write garbage. If you do this every day, eventually you'll have something you can use for a story.

Can I really do this?

Self-doubt is probably the biggest reason people procrastinate. Most creative people are prone to second-guessing themselves. It's as much part of us as the work we do, and that's okay. If we didn't doubt ourselves, we wouldn't search out the critiques or the editing that forces us to improve our work and make our stories great.

Remember, it's okay to doubt your work, but don't doubt yourself as a writer or an illustrator because that's what you are. And no matter what anyone says, that's what you were meant to be.

The Writer's Menu for Success: Crafting Stories Readers Crave

BY LISA RONDINELLI ALBERT

Warm up your word processing program. On a blank screen, add fresh ideas, well-formed characters, clear plot and rich language. Mix with three ounces black ink and serve on two pounds white bond.

If it were that easy, every manuscript submitted would get a contract. The reality is though: Publishers of children's books are extremely selective when adding titles to their lists. Simply having a fresh idea is not enough.

So how can an author stand out in the competitive publishing industry? By preparing your manuscript in the same manner a cook would prepare a five course meal. With the right ingredients, you'll be serving stories readers crave.

BEGINNINGS
Appetizers . . . with a hook

Every manuscript, whether a picture book or novel, must offer the reader a reason to turn the page right from the start. Hook your reader early with an intriguing voice, a charming character, a fresh plot or a combination of these.

Author and book reviewer, Jane Resh Thomas, advises, "As you write, ask yourself, 'So what?' Is what the character does or story says important enough to interest your reader from the beginning?"

A story that grabs its readers on the first page is what authors need to strive for. It's what editors hope to find while reading through their slush piles. This is demonstrated at many workshops held by the Society of Children's Book Writers and Illustrators (www.scbwi.org) through the increasingly popular First Pages segment. Editors who read the opening page of anonymously submitted manuscripts express why they would or would not continue reading.

"A manuscript definitely needs to engage me right from the start and a paragraph, a sentence, even a title can determine a manuscript's fate," says Viking editor, Melanie Cecka. "Uneven writing or bland concepts are usually easy to spot on the first page, but sometimes it doesn't even come to that. The truth is, a manuscript entitled *Charlie the Choosy Chipmunk* or *Little Bobby Learns a Big Lesson* will go straight to my reject pile."

Cecka acknowledges her evaluation system is harsh, but it is necessary. "I've got to be able to weed through the 50 new manuscripts I get each week in order to make a little more time to read the ones that look promising. If the voice or situation isn't engaging pretty quickly, I won't need to read much to make a decision."

Like a good appetizer, a well-written beginning should make your reader hungry for more. There aren't specific rules for writing an attention-getting opening or first page, but most often this is where the hook is.

LISA RONDINELLI ALBERT *is a writer and co-chair for Southeast Wisconsin SCBWI Spring Events. Her novel,* Mercy Lily, *was a finalist in the 2001 SCBWI Work-in-Progress Grant for a Contemporary Novel for Young People and received Honorable Mention in* ByLine Magazine's *First Chapter of a Novel Contest. She lives in Muskego, Wisconsin with her husband and two children.*

Author, Dori Chaconas says, "While it's important that the opening entice the reader, the hook doesn't have to be a pie-in-the-face." Having sold four titles to Melanie Cecka at Viking and one to Abingdon Press, Chaconas advises, "The first page should establish a good voice, and offer a promise of good things to come."

When asked what drew her in to read beyond the first page of Kate DiCamillo's Newbery Honor Book, *Because of Winn-Dixie*, Candlewick editor, Kara LaReau says, "Never mind the first page—I think the first sentence of *Winn-Dixie* speaks for itself! How could anyone not want to read on?" Speaking on submissions in general, LaReau says, "For me, the first page or first chapter doesn't always matter. I usually give myself until page 30 before asking if the story is working, or if there is even a story at all."

Though Melanie Cecka understands the importance of a good beginning, she cautions, "A great first page or sentence hardly makes for a great book. So while it's true that a positive first impression will encourage me to read more, the writing needs to hold up throughout the entire book."

MIDDLES
The main course . . .where the beef is

Now that your story has passed the taste-test and you've whetted your reader's appetite, don't fall short with a bland middle. Keep your promise of good things to come. Create seamless transitions and build tension for a fulfilling, hearty middle.

"The middle seems to give a lot of people difficulty and I don't think there are any instant magic tricks for getting effortlessly from point A to point C," Melanie Cecka says. "For writers of picture books, it's important to remember that the younger the audience, the shorter the attention span. The challenge is making the child want to sit still long enough to reach the end of the book. So a writer needs to build their story in a way that will make kids want to turn the page—that's the internal tension we commonly call the page-turning-appeal."

Dori Chaconas' picture book, *One Little Mouse*, meets the sit-still challenge. On the surface, *One Little Mouse* is a delightful rhyming story that appears to simply follow a little mouse in search of a new home. Looking deeper, however, there is more to this story than an animal looking for a better place to rest his head. Using a counting sequence, Chaconas skillfully keeps the readers attention by offering hope and then new conflict at every page turn as little mouse encounters various woodland animals. Underlying throughout the story are basic animal and habitat facts. Crucial to the plot, the facts are embedded within the inviting text and are not distracting. *One Little Mouse* is a prime example of how even short text requires tension and smooth transitions.

"For longer stories," Cecka says, "people talk a lot about the 'story arc,' which suggests that a story starts with a conflict, then uses rising action to move it to a climax, then draws to a conclusion. By this definition, a story arc would look somewhat like an upside down V. For me, though, I think a novel needs to constantly offer the reader little surprises along the way. So instead of an arc, I think of a stock market chart: over time you would see the line trending up, but there would be smaller peaks and dips."

Staying on task through the middle can be daunting for any writer. There will be days when cleaning your oven with a toothbrush or organizing your junk drawers will seem more appealing than writing. Don't let procrastination get the best of you.

Jane Resh Thomas admits, "When I began my first novel, *Courage at Indian Deep*, I gave myself a lot of excuses of why I couldn't write." Then she gave herself permission to write with one simple statement. "I haven't written hundreds of pages but, I have written two pages hundreds of times." With that in mind, she recommends focusing on voice, character development and style. "Style is the way *you* use language," Resh Thomas says. "That's the art!" She advises not to get caught up in technique as you write toward the end. "Technique is only a bag of tricks. It is secondary and only a way to get you there."

Kate DiCamillo shares that sentiment saying, "The distressing thing about writing is everybody wants a formula and there isn't one. The minute there is a formula, you're in trouble."

Add a large helping of discipline to your writing habit to give it the steam needed to get to the end. DiCamillo writes two pages at a time and she doesn't expect them to be any good. "I'm easy on myself because I'm still figuring what's going on. In the first draft, I don't do anything but get the story down," DiCamillo says. She doesn't think about what an editor wants while she's writing. "I'm only thinking about what the story wants. It seems a mistake for me to write for anyone but me, the characters and the story."

CREATING SIZZLING CHARACTERS

"A well-rounded character is one with a voice and persona that's distinctive and fresh," Cecka says. Knowing that creating a three dimensional character is easier said than done, Cecka recommends authors get to know their characters inside and out. "I want to see a characterization worked out in every facet: from what they look like to how they dress—to how they express themselves in conversation to how they think and act."

To get to the nitty-gritty of your character's personality take advantage of writing a character profile. Include age, gender, date of birth, favorite color, everything and anything you know about your character, even if it's not relevant to your story. Interview your characters using more than simple yes or no questions. Their answers may surprise you.

Kate DiCamillo says, "Having characters speak or show their persistence by invading your thoughts or almost having a physical presence are the things you wait for as an author."

Rob Horton, DiCamillo's main character in *The Tiger Rising*, first appeared in one of her short stories but continued to hang around the house and drove her crazy. "I finally asked him what he wanted, and he told me he knew where there was a tiger."

In addition to chatting with your character, consider finding a likeness of him/her by flipping through magazines or photographs. This will make you aware of the physical qualities your character has.

"Characters should always be more than the role they play," says Melanie Cecka. "The better an author knows his or her characters, the more authentic and original the characters will be."

"A key element in creating a character is figuring out his/her motivation," says Kara LaReau. "If you can discover what your characters want and why they behave the way they do, it will be easier to know where they (and, in turn, your story) are going to go."

Expanding the roles minor characters play can result in a deeper level of intimacy between the main character and the reader.

"In *Because of Winn-Dixie*, the Dewberry boys, Sweetie Pie Thomas and Amanda Wilkinson were mentioned by name only," Kate DiCamillo says, referring to her original submission to Candlewick.

Editor, Kara LaReau advised DiCamillo to expand their roles rather than eliminating them altogether. "Kate and I talked about how India Opal needed more friends her own age to even out her experience in the story. I was fascinated by these names and wanted to meet the characters behind them. I asked Kate if she could work on fleshing them out."

"When Kara suggested bringing those characters to life," DiCamillo says, "I felt I had already baked a cake and frosted it and she was asking me to add three eggs. I thought it would be impossible but I tried, and by doing so, Kara gave me a much better book."

How your characters react to their situations can persuade your readers to follow the story to the end. Characters who have true-to-life emotions involve readers and give them something to relate to.

LaReau points out, "If your readers don't care about (or believe in) your characters, why would they care about how the characters end up?"

ENDINGS
Like dessert . . .they should satisfy

Experiences your characters have in the beginning and middle must serve a purpose. They need to lead your character toward conflict resolution and result in character change and growth.

Melanie Cecka says, "Describing an event is not the same thing as telling a story. So "the king died," is not a story, but "the king died of a broken heart," is. The second example has given the story emotional stakes—and it also asks readers to invest a little bit of themselves in the characters and their purpose. When we talk about wanting to see characters change over the course of a story it's for that reason: to see that the journey the reader takes with the character is rewarded in the end. A great story and a character who grows through his or her experiences can change a reader forever."

When character change evokes an emotional response in the reader, an author has successfully served not only a satisfying conclusion, but also a lasting and memorable book.

In *Because of Winn-Dixie*, Kate DiCamillo skillfully leads readers through India Opal's story of abandonment, loneliness and heartache. Every event Opal experiences, along with each character she meets, fills an empty spot left by her mother and allows her to move forward. Her hurt and confusion grow into hope and acceptance, leaving the reader emotionally content and satisfied with the outcome.

For a complete ending, all the strings that were used to pull the plot along must be tied together. Making sure your reader isn't left with unanswered questions or leftovers can be achieved through revision.

REVISION & POLISHING
Triming the fat & adding spice

"I'm a big fan of outlines, though I don't think you necessarily have to make one *before* you write a story," says Kara LaReau. "It's often helpful to draw one up afterwards, so you can get a good look at how your story is structured, and where the weak points might be (too many characters, too many subplots, etc.). If you look at your outline and see that a certain section is several pages longer than the rest, that might be a good area to pare down."

Putting a story away for several weeks or months can also give authors insight into their work. "Knowing when to step away from your manuscript is also important," LaReau says. "Coming back to your story with a fresh eye can help you to see what's working and what isn't."

When weighing a manuscript for acquisition, LaReau does take revision possibilities into consideration. "It really depends on the story and the author," says LaReau. "If I think the author is capable of the revisions I have in mind, and if the author is willing to take the story in that direction, I have hope."

Melanie Cecka notes there are many different ways an author can approach revision and says, "Three tips I would offer are: 1) Put the manuscript away for as long as it takes to gain a little objectivity on it. 2) Start with the big components of the story first: plot, characterization, voice, and setting. Is the plot wobbly? Are the characterizations fresh and dimensional? Is the voice kid-like or does the author's voice creep in? Is the setting developed enough to support the story being told? 3) Zoom in: polish on a line-by-line or chapter-by-chapter basis."

When working on her picture books and easy readers, Dori Chaconas looks for areas that need more colorful word choices. For her upcoming book, *Cork and Fuzz*, she revised a ho-hum scene by adding specific actions. The original draft simply read:

When Cork pushed, the log began to roll down the bumpy hill.

Using revision, Chaconas created an exciting scene and introduced Fuzz, the possum. Her final version reads:

Corked pushed. The log began to roll.
"Oh-oh! cried the echo.
The log bumped down a hill.
"Ow!"
The log bumped over a rock.
"Ow! OW!"
It bumped into a big thorn bush.
"EE-YOW!"
A fat possum fell out.

Jane Resh Thomas says, "Polishing and revision are different." She suggests writing tight and getting rid of empty verbs. "Eliminate 'have,' 'got,' 'want' and other words or phrases that slow the story or create distance between the character and reader."

"Flabby language makes writing boring to read," Thomas says. In addition to her success as an author and book reviewer, Thomas was the *Star Tribune*'s Children's Literature Columnist for 25 years. She's also served on judging panels for the American Book Award and the National Book Award and has read hundreds of books.

"Read skilled writers' work and highlight internal monologue," Thomas recommends. "Analyze how the writer gets inside the character without the use of tags such as 'like' and 'thought.' "

Remember, the revision process isn't over once you've submitted your manuscript. Changes will still need to be made.

"I don't think any manuscript is 100 percent perfect when it first comes in," says Melanie Cecka. "If I think a story is terrific in concept but somewhat flawed in execution, I might ask an author to try a revision—that's often the make-or-break test an editor gives to a new writer."

Once you've used the menu for success and included these ingredients in your story recipe, editors will be more likely to ask you to pass the revision test. After that accomplishment is made, readers who crave your stories will ask for seconds or thirds.

Dear Writer: When Editorial Letters Invite Revision

BY ESTHER HERSHENHORN

Sometimes, that SASE waiting in your mailbox holds more than your manuscript and a form rejection letter.

Sometimes, that SASE holds an editorial letter—a well-crafted, thoughtfully written, single-spaced response offering words of encouragement and suggestions to consider. The longed-for closing sentence makes a writer's heart thump:

If you're willing to revise, I'd be happy to see this manuscript again.

Most writers (myself included) admit to outright jubilation at receiving such an invitation. Many writers confess, however, (myself included), that after several re-readings of that long-awaited letter, heart thumps give way to panic and self-doubt. "*WHAT?!*" they exclaim. "Impossible!" they whisper.

In truth, the over-worked editor who penned the invitation is acknowledging that "something" in your manuscript touched her—your use of language, a character's voice, the story itself, perhaps your writer's authority. Her comments offer you the chance to see your manuscript *again*, for the better usually, with refracted eyes. *Re-vision*—the act of *seeing again* or *anew*, with fresh, clearer eyes—can insure your story touches readers, too. It's a necessary step in the writing process.

So, what can you do once you accept the invitation, once you're ready and willing to revise your manuscript?

Push aside the fear and move on

Fear can grab the best of writers, making an already challenging task that much more daunting.

Award-winning picture book author Carolyn Crimi honestly admits, "It's just fear that keeps me from seeing things straight when I'm reading an editor's comments. I keep thinking that I'll never be able to do what they ask instead of thinking about how I can make the changes."

Crimi twice revised her picture book *Boris and Bella* for Harcourt Senior Editor Michael Stearns before a contract was offered. Two more revisions followed once the contract was signed.

Crimi's funny story is a love story, except that as Stearns says, "Hugh Grant and Julia Roberts are played by, um, Boris and Bella, and so aren't very attractive." Bella Legrossi is the messiest monster in Booville. Her neighbor, Boris Kleanitoff, is the tidiest. They battle and scheme against each other on a daily basis until in the end they discover they really *do* have a few things in common.

Crimi calls herself the Woody Allen of the children's book world. "I *never* think I'll be able

---

ESTHER HERSHENHORN *authors picture books and middle grade novels, teaches writing for children at Ragdale, Chicago's Newberry Library and the University of Chicago's Writer's Studio and coaches writers to help them tell their stories well. Her latest titles include the novel* The Confe$$ion$ and $ecret$ of Howard J. Fingerhut *(Holiday House 2002) and the picture book* Chicken Soup By Heart *(Simon & Schuster 2002).*

to do the revisions, I *always* worry about them, and I literally have nightmares about blank pieces of paper chasing me."

What kinds of changes did her editor ask for?

Stearns felt the ending was arrived at too quickly and that the middle dragged. He also asked that she add a party scene.

What Crimi found truly liberating was Stearn's push in terms of language and humor. "He wanted more, more, more, instead of 'Eek, stop, enough!' I liked that he believed in me and felt I could do it even when I felt I couldn't."

In fact, Stearns wrote Crimi's agent at the time, after reading the submission:

> . . . it needs to have the language-driven wit amped up a bit. I wouldn't normally ask for a revision of this sort but Carolyn so clearly can pull off this sort of densely funny writing that I feel confident in asking for more.

Stearns suggested more rhymes, more alliterations, more funny spins on the familiar:

> . . . more language effects will make this a joy to read aloud. And it's just not quite at that level yet. And damn it. . . . it can be.

Once Crimi realized she was simply afraid, she allowed herself to wallow in that fear until she was ready to move on. "I asked myself, 'What's the worst thing that can happen if I don't get it right?' It's not as if I was going to be eaten by a shark or catch some rare disease if I submitted a bad story."

Stearns enclosed a printout of his working copy of *Boris and Bella*, along with his first editorial comments. He warned Crimi not to be alarmed by his markings.

> . . . not one of these changes is hard and fast in my mind; more it was just my tinkering with it to smooth troubled bits . . . I'm not dictating changes. I was just tidying up stray threads. You should, however, view the changes as flags that there was something that needed tweaking in those spots, and so I tweaked. If you dislike the tweaks, please just change them back or tweak them in a way that works for you.

Dear Genius—The Letters of Ursula Nordstrom
Collected and edited by Leonard S. Marcus (HarperCollins)

Ursula Nordstrom, editorial director of Harper's Department of Books for Boys and Girls from 1940 to 1973, was arguably the greatest editor of American children's books in the twentieth century. Known as "children's literature's Maxwell Perkins," Nordstrom's editorial acumen and generous heart nurtured such authors and illustrators as Margaret Wise Brown, E.B. White, Mary Rodgers, Meindert deJong, Garth Williams, Louise Fitzhugh, Ruth Krauss, Russell Hoban, Shel Silverstein, Maurice Sendak, Laura Ingalls Wilder, John Steptoe and Kay Thomas.

Fortunately for anyone interested in children's books, Nordstrom was an inveterate letter writer. She enjoyed a prolific correspondence with her authors and illustrators, all of whom she liked to call "Genius." Noted biographer and critic Leonard S. Marcus, culled a representative collection of some 300 letters from HarperCollins' archives that held thousands. Arranged in chronological order, the collection offers readers a behind-the-scenes look at children's book publishing in the twentieth century. As Marcus says himself in his introduction, "Her letters have much to tell about the arts of writing, illustrating, and editing, the social history of the twentieth century and the pivotal role that books, and a love of books, can play in children's lives."

Crimi confesses that what she hates about her editor is, he's always right. Once she added new scenes for *Boris and Bella*, her word count crept up to about 1,000 words. Stearns requested she trim 250 words from her final revision. "He was annoyingly, frustratingly right *again*. Now, after I've put in all the finishing touches on a manuscript, I always trim it down by about a page. Okay, maybe I don't always do that. But I do *think* about doing it."

Boris and Bella displays Crimi's signature humor and exuberant language, found in *Don't Need Friends* (Random House 1999) and *Tessa's Tip-Tapping Toes* (Orchard 2002). The book, illustrated by Gris Grimley, is scheduled for release in Fall 2004.

Consider possibilities you hadn't considered

Writers are often reminded: there's the story and how the writer *chooses* to tell his story. In children's books, fortunately, format choices abound.

Cynthia Leitich Smith's latest early chapter book *Indian Shoes* (HarperCollins 2002), a collection of six short, interrelated stories about a boy and his grandfather, began life in 1997 as a picture book titled *Something Bigger*. Smith submitted the manuscript to then Lodestar editor Rosemary Brosnan. "There was indeed 'something bigger' in this manuscript that sparked my interest," Brosnan shares. "Terrific writing, sympathetic characters, an author with something to say, a portrayal of contemporary Native Americans that I had rarely seen, and a lovely feeling to the manuscript."

Brosnan wasn't sure the manuscript was working as well as it could, though, and told Smith so in a January 15, 1997, letter:

> . . . *I think you have created appealing characters in Grampa Halfmoon and Ray—and even Uncle Leonard. The idea of the sunrise as 'something bigger' is a lovely one. How-*

Reprinted with permission of HarperCollins.

The characters in Cynthia Leitich Smith's *Indian Shoes* first appeared in a picture book manuscript she submitted to editor Rosemary Brosnan. Brosnan liked the story, but at her editorial meeting, one of the other editors suggested it might work better as a chapter book. Eventually, through revisions lead by Brosnan, the material evolved into its published form, a book of short stories focusing on the relationship between a boy and his grandfather. The experience was invaluable to Smith. "The biggest lesson I learned was, never throw away anything. There's no such thing as a dead story. You can always revisit, resurrect, reinvent or integrate."

ever, the story doesn't quite come together yet for me. I found it hard to believe that Ray had never gotten up to see a sunrise before—isn't this something that all children do? . . . Grampa needs to be developed more—perhaps you need to show his humorous or sly side more, so that it's completely believable that he wouldn't say a word to anyone about why he's not bringing back fish anymore.

Brosnan took a pass on *Something Bigger*, then went on to buy Smith's first published book, the picture book *Jingle Dancer*. Brosnan herself moved on to Morrow Junior Books when Lodestar was eliminated. HarperCollins eventually bought Morrow Junior Books *and* Smith's contract for *Jingle Dancer* and published it in 2000. But Ray and Grampa Halfmoon were still speaking to Smith. She wrote a different adventure for the boy and his grandfather, titled it *Indian Shoes* and submitted it as a picture book to Brosnan. Brosnan liked the story but at the editorial meeting, one of the other editors suggested it might work better as a chapter book.

Brosnan agreed and she and Smith went to work. It was Brosnan who suggested that *Something Bigger* would make a great chapter in *Indian Shoes*, as the book focuses on the relationship between a boy and his grandfather. The slightly revised version now appears as "Night Fishing." The picture book *Indian Shoes* was also rewritten as a short story and opens the collection as "Indian Shoes."

The collection's stories feature Ray and Grampa, a mostly consistent setting—Chicago and Indian Country, Oklahoma—and the people who populate their daily lives. However, each story has its own arc and can stand alone.

Smith agreed to the format changes fairly quickly. She admits, though, that she still struggles with the change at times. "It's hard to abandon an original concept, and I so much wanted a picture book to follow *Jingle Dancer*." Both Brosnan and Smith, however, believed that the chapter book audience was under-served, especially with regard to contemporary Native American themes.

Smith realized, too, just how insightful Brosnan's comments about Grampa were. "To me, Grampa was funny. He was wry. He loved his grandson, probably more than anyone or anything in the world. But he also loved life, the joy and humor in it. Not just the big, obvious things, but also the little everyday delights. It didn't come through early on, but it's very clear by the final version."

The experience was invaluable to Smith. "The biggest lesson I learned was, never throw away anything. There's no such thing as a dead story. You can always revisit, resurrect, reinvent or integrate." Smith suggests a writer should ask himself if he really believes his character belongs in children's literature. Then, if possible, find a way to bring him to that world.

Smith acknowledges another lesson: some of the best stories come from small moments made special, rather than big dramatic and life-changing events. "The key is to maintain your place in the character's perspective, to walk in his shoes." Even Indian shoes.

Mine your manuscript and re-imagine

There are story parts that work, and those that don't. Editors praise the former, offering words of encouragement; they illuminate the latter, offering concrete solutions. Often those solutions are in your manuscript, waiting.

Pam Todd was more than happy when her then-Bantam Doubleday Dell editor Karen Wojtyla offered suggestions for fixing those parts that didn't work in her funny, touching middle grade novel *Pig and the Shrink* (BDD 1999). "Pig" is Angelo Pighetti, the fat kid in seventh grader Tucker Harrison's science class, the one who always gets picked on. Tucker needs to dazzle the judges for his school's science fair to gain him admission to the Math and Science Academy. Why not make Pig his science fair project, Tucker thinks. He could help Pig lose weight and also have a living, breathing, successful experiment. One mishap leads to another as Tucker

Illustration © 1999 Jeff Seaver. Reprinted with permission of Delacorte Press.

The early version of Pam Todd's mid-grade novel *Pig and the Shrink* showed promise for editor Karen Wojtyla. However, Wojtyla's July 1998 editorial letter suggested Todd eliminate one character completely as well as expand the roles of some characters and contract the roles of others. "Karen was someone with high standards, an excellent sense of structure, an understanding of what makes fiction work and what child readers are like," says Todd. She now sees walk-on characters in her manuscripts' first drafts with fresh eyes. "I learned to be on the look-out for characters that have potential that hasn't been maximized."

finally learns about individuality, self-respect and about values that can't be measured or weighed.

Wojtyla first saw Todd's manuscript in 1997 when she served as a Committee Judge for SCBWI's Judy Blume Work-in-Progress Grant for a Contemporary Novel. *Pig and the Shrink* won Todd the grant and an eventual phone call from Wojtyla requesting the manuscript once Todd had completed it. Todd sent it to Wojtyla a few months later.

Wojtyla's July 1998 editorial letter suggested Todd eliminate one character completely as well as expand the roles of some characters and contract the roles of others. (Todd later admitted she adored the eliminated character.) Wojtyla wanted to see more of Tucker's science fair project, with scenes that showed his subterfuge and bent for disaster. She also asked that Todd rework the final chapters and adjust the pacing, so they led to a more credible, satisfying resolution.

Wojtyla's letter heartened Todd. "Karen was someone with high standards, an excellent sense of structure, an understanding of what makes fiction work and what child readers are like." Todd appreciated Wojtyla's encouraging and inspiring words, as well as her concrete suggestions as to how things might be re-imagined.

The editorial letter's closing assured Todd she could fix what was fixable.

> *Everything I've said is coming out of material you've written—I'm just trying to pull out and develop the aspects that I think will make this novel richer and funnier and stronger overall.*

Todd found that Wojtyla's words rang true. Her manuscript already had the makings of those new scenes waiting to be written, of those singular characters waiting to be fully realized. That summer, Todd took her children—and her manuscript—to the local pool.

"As the summer wore on," she says, "my characters had become as real to me as the kids splashing about and shouting around me. As long as I had specific scenes in mind, my characters were more than happy to act them out."

While Todd eventually needed to take another pass at the resolution, Wojtyla was more than pleased with Todd's revision.

> *She took my suggestions and then used her own creativity to refashion scenes and characters, all the while keeping true to her characters and maintaining the book's high energy level. Sometimes a writer will take an editor too literally, trying to do exactly what he or she thinks the editor wants, and that can be deadly to the manuscript. It's the writer's creativity and vision that ultimately animate everything.*

Todd says she learned not to write stories with more characters than a Russian novel. "I can see now that it's quite possible for characters to be redundant and it improves the story if you can eliminate or combine them with other characters. Todd now sees walk-on characters in her manuscripts' first drafts with fresh eyes. "I learned to be on the lookout for characters that have potential that hasn't been maximized."

Todd's readers and fans can look forward to a new set of characters in her next book with Wojtyla, the picture book *Eleanor's Music*.

Reimmerse yourself to see your story clearly

Sometimes, a writer can master narrative elements, such as characterization and plot, and still leave the reader wanting for a story.

YA novelist John H. Ritter credits Philomel senior editor Michael Green with helping him find and shape his first published novel, *Choosing Up Sides*. Set in southern Ohio in 1921, it's the story of Luke Bledsoe, a left-handed preacher's boy, forced by his family's religious beliefs to go through life right-handed, until he discovers he could be a great baseball pitcher—but only with his "forbidden" left arm. Ritter's first novel, published in 1998, was named an ALA Best Book for Young Adults and awarded a Bulletin of the Center for Children's Books Blue Ribbon and an IRA Young Adult Readers Choice recognition.

In what Ritter calls "divine kismet," an early and un-agented manuscript submission to

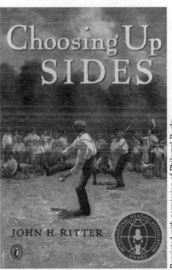

YA novelist John H. Ritter's first novel, *Choosing Up Sides*, set in southern Ohio in 1921, is the story of Luke Bledsoe, a left-handed preacher's boy, forced by his family's religious beliefs to go through life right-handed, until he discovers he could be a great baseball pitcher—but only with his "forbidden" left arm. Ritter credits Philomel senior editor Michael Green with helping him find and shape his first book which was named an ALA Best Book for Young Adults and awarded a Bulletin of the Center for Children's Books Blue Ribbon and an IRA Young Adult Readers Choice recognition.

Philomel eventually found its way to then-associate editor Green's slush pile. Green offered Ritter and his recently-signed-on agent a "warm rejection," inviting Ritter to submit anything else with a younger protagonist. Within a few months, Ritter's agent submitted *Choosing Up Sides*, then titled *Left Out of Heaven*. The second submission drew another warm rejection, although this one was three pages long. Green was enthusiastic about "the intriguing plot and strong narrative voice—two intangibles." Still, Green concluded, "Mr. Ritter has not found his story just yet":

> . . . *It appears, to me, that Mr. Ritter had two approaches to Luke's story: one of baseball as a story catalyst, and one of Huck Finn-like wanderlust as a story catalyst. Instead of choosing one of those and fleshing out a rich story, he tried to weave the two together. The result is that neither steps forward, and the story lacks shape.*

Green suggested Ritter (1) make baseball Luke's vehicle for independence and self-acceptance; and (2) develop Luke as a character more fully, showing the reader Luke's rebellious side:

> . . . *A suppressed passion adds tension, especially when it is a metaphor for rebellion against an over-strict father.*

Green also commented on the story's path to resolution:

> . . . *Running away lacks the dramatic flare of Luke choosing his own path right in Crown Falls, of following his passion right in his father's shadow.*

Ritter and Green eventually went three rounds of revisions before Ritter "found" his powerful story. The manuscript was retitled and a contract was offered. To show his support for Ritter's writing, Green edited the revised manuscripts as if he had already signed them up. Though the final editorial letter was 12-pages long, Ritter never took Green's objections personally.

"Michael and I were always on the same side," Ritter says, "that is, the side of the reader and the story. What we needed to hash out was a unity of vision for the piece." Ritter photocopied Green's editorial letters to share with his small writer's group, so he could determine some degree of consensus *and* so they all could come up with actual solutions. In one instance, Ritter rejected the specifics of a scene Green suggested but embraced the concept, which was to somehow build a love for baseball in a boy who'd never played the game. He went on to create a humorous scene that grounded Luke's eventual change of heart.

Ritter sees revision "as a way to dump all the stupid stuff you put in there before anybody else reads it. And to do that," he says, "you'd better see the story much more clearly before the revision begins or you'll suffer the fate which befalls so many beginning writers—you won't know what to do."

Ritter believes Green's letters helped him to "see the story" with more clarity, as well as give him a greater confidence, through praise, in his ability to paint a scene and to advance the story. Most importantly, Ritter learned to pay attention to the organic nature of a story.

"The story germinates, sprouts, and grows toward its natural bent," Ritter believes. "Certainly a writer prunes and waters as needed, building beauty and strength, but storytelling is not the mere manipulation of characters, facts, and events. True storytelling is the measured introduction of those characters, facts, and events in a natural, credible, and interest-sustaining manner."

Philomel published Ritter's second YA novel *Over the Wall* in 2000. His third YA novel, *Cruz De La Cruz: The Boy Who Saved Baseball (A True Story Based on a Legend)*, appears in 2003.

Celebrate! An editor invited you to revise!

Any writer would be happy to read Michael Stearns closing words to Carolyn Crimi in his first editorial letter concerning her picture book *Boris and Bella*: "I love this story."

Such acknowledgments can fuel several revisions—on both the editor's and writer's parts. Editors invest long hours reading and rereading manuscripts that grab their hearts.

Rosemary Brosnan can spot something promising almost immediately, she says, and Cynthia Leitich Smith's picture book *Something Bigger* met Brosnan's criteria for responding to a manuscript:

> *First of all, the writing must shine and almost lift off the page. Then I need to care about the characters. The author needs to care about them, too, and this will come through when I read the manuscript. The writer must feel passionate about what she or he has to say—I'll be able to see this when I read the manuscript. And, finally, the plot should be compelling. If the author's writing and characters and passion stand out, I can help to shape the plot. But if the author has a good plot and the other ingredients are missing, it's not going to be the kind of book I'll take a chance on.*

Brosnan typically takes time to first read the manuscript in its entirety, then to think and reread, and finally to go about writing the letter. She keeps a pad of paper and a pen (now lighted) by her bedside while she's in the thinking stages of a manuscript, to write down ideas she wakes up with in the night.

Because Pam Todd's middle grade novel was funny, Karen Wojtyla liked *Pig and the Shrink* immediately. She says she never seems to see enough funny manuscripts. She thought Todd portrayed the situation between the two boys with great tenderness as well as humor. Todd struck her as a writer with wit and heart.

> *A manuscript has to stand out in some compelling way; perhaps have an original voice, or a vivid depiction of place or time, or a lyrical mood, or laugh-out-loud humor. And then the whole has to hang together reasonably well, so that the promise of a writer who can shape a novel is there. So often manuscripts begin well and then peter out or fall to pieces, as though the writer has lavished great care on the beginning, but failed to conceptualize the whole, or simply run out of steam.*

Wojtyla commits hours and hours of time to editorial letters in general. She thinks as she reads about what isn't working, making mental notes of places where the writer brought her up short or pulled her out of the narrative. She dips into the manuscript again and again, recalling scenes and characters and how both can be made stronger. Her notes are fragmented at first, but eventually the elements coalesce when she writes the editorial letter.

Michael Green reads a novel twice before writing his editorial letter. During the first read, he waits for the story to draw him in, takes notes, jots down spontaneous reactions that strike him as significant, then moves on to other projects while his questions simmer.

He forms his own vision of the work before he returns to his second reading. The process often takes at least two weeks.

Green thinks a manuscript needs to speak to an editor's heart, head and gut before an editor commits. His heart needs to love the manuscript, which should offer a character, a story arc or a writing voice that draws him in and forces him to turn the page. His head needs to know the story is a wise investment of his time *and* his company's money. His gut needs to know that this is a writer who will be able to raise the story or the writing to a higher level. Green personally needs to affirm at least two of those three conditions before he commits to working with an author.

Green had been a reluctant reader as a boy but has always been a sports fanatic. Ritter's story struck home with him:

> *I recognized that a strong baseball story would appeal to young readers who felt like I once did about books. But a mere play-by-play wouldn't do the trick. John understood this, too; the power of his book lay not with baseball, but with the way he used it to tell a greater story.*

So, celebrate if you're invited to revise. Push aside your fears. Consider the possibilities. Mine your manuscript. Reimmerse yourself. The story that touched you has now touched an editor who is eager to insure your story touches readers.

Some Common Manuscript Problems

In the *Forest for the Trees*, former editor and current agent Betsy Lerner wrote, "Editing is a science and an art. There is a basic architecture to every book. Certain predictable patterns crop up." Karen Wojtyla disagrees with Lerner. "Editing is a craft," she believes, "learned and perfected over time."

Wojtyla and other editors who participated in this article shared several problems that often crop up in manuscripts they see.

- *Rosemary Brosnan*: Wonderful writing piques my interest. And what sometimes happens is that I read a manuscript that is beautifully written but has no plot. This holds true for a novel or a picture book. Or the plot is a tremendous mess. Or the novel is episodic, without a good internal structure or plot that will make young readers turn pages. Or the novel goes along beautifully, but the author is unable to tie together the threads at the end, and it falls apart. These are all common problems.
- *Karen Wojtyla*: The problems I see often are one-dimensional characters, melodramatic plots, a narrative voice that wavers or doesn't stay true, or a manuscript without a solid plot structure that is flat or never builds to climax.
- *Michael Green*: . . . the revelation of an important development without properly setting it up; and resolutions that fall disappointingly flat despite a quality premise. These problems, once pointed out, are always fixable, but it takes a deft touch to work back into a manuscript.

Flipping Pancakes with a Shovel: Writing & Promoting Books for Babies & Toddlers

BY HOPE VESTERGAARD

Arrive at my house unannounced and you might see something strange through the picture window. What's a grown woman doing crawling around the house on her hands and knees?

Research!

Bookshelves loom like skyscrapers when you're thirty inches tall. Imagine flipping pancakes using a shovel. Think about never getting to see all the interesting stuff that happens up on the countertop. These are typical experiences for small children who inhabit a grown-up sized world. In order to write compelling books for babies and toddlers, you need to meet them at their level: talk *with* them rather than *at* them.

To get a good sense of what makes babies and toddlers tick, spend time observing them: at the park, the store, or a child development center. If you're brave (and patient), help out in a classroom or children's library. Take note of interesting situations, phrases, and behaviors. These tidbits may or may not evolve into actual stories, but paying attention to details will breathe authenticity into your writing. My own stories *Wake Up, Mama* and *Driving Daddy* (both Dutton 2003) hatched when I noticed that children would rather climb on their teachers than on the fancy equipment that graces their classrooms and playgrounds.

The most compelling books for young readers feature children just like them. Infants and toddlers are egocentric, and they look for people and problems that are familiar. This is why "perfect" kids are a lot less appealing than imperfect ones like Maurice Sendak's Max or Ian Falconer's Olivia. Much of the conflict in very young picture books centers on developmental challenges: learning to share; separation anxiety; feeling powerless. If your main character waltzes through life without stumbling, she won't be compelling to most kids who "stumble" on a daily, if not hourly, basis. Toddlers' love for the familiar doesn't mean they don't enjoy books about new experiences or cultures, but those stories will be more engaging if they speak to universal themes and struggles.

ARTS & CRAFTS

Well-crafted picture books for babies and toddlers can look deceptively simple, but great ones have all the elements of a classic story: interesting characters, lively language, and a satisfying beginning, middle, and end.

Beginnings must be immediate. Toddlers have short attention spans and only vague concepts of time and place. They live in the here and now, and that's when your story should begin. Young readers find all the setting information they need in the illustration: the story happens

HOPE VESTERGAARD *was an early childhood teacher for eight years and a center director for two. Her first picture book,* Baby Love, *was a fall 2002 release. She's also the author five upcoming picture books, including* Wake Up, Mama!, Driving Daddy, Hillside Lullaby, *and* What Do You Do? *(all with Dutton), as well as* Hello, Snow! *with Melanie Kroupa/FSG. Visit her website: www.hopevestergaard.com.*

inside, or outside. It happens on a farm. Etc. Toddlers also don't need a lot of descriptive information about characters—they glean everything they need to know from the action. We meet Max the Wild Thing in the throes of a tantrum and we immediately know a lot about him. On the first spread of Nancy Shaw's *Sheep in a Jeep* (Houghton Mifflin) we meet the characters and their problem: "Beep! Beep! Sheep in a Jeep on a hill that's steep!" If you get to the crux of your story quickly, even little wigglers will tune in.

Another way to immediately draw the reader into the story is to write intimately. *Do You*

Hope Vestergaard's *Baby Love* (Dutton), illustrated by John Wallace, a collection of playful poems celebrating all kinds of babies and the people who love them, is the first in a string of books for babies and toddlers from the teacher-turned-author. Vestergaard knows, when it comes to writing for babies and toddlers, you can observe a lot just by watching. "My stories *Wake Up, Mama* and *Driving Daddy* (both illustrated by Thierry Courtin Dutton 2003) hatched when I noticed that children would rather climb on their teachers than on the fancy equipment that graces their classrooms and playgrounds."

Know New?, by Jean Marzollo (HarperCollins) speaks directly to the reader in a playful, lyrical voice that is hard to resist: "Do you know knew?/Oh, my, I do!/Brand new, I do." Books that speak directly to the child say, "This is your story, and you are the important person here."

What about the middle of young picture books? Many young picture books do have clear plots or themes, but they tend to be much simpler than those in older books. "Slice of life" stories often depend on patterns for their structure. Repetition is one popular tool. Repeating phrases, incidents, and refrains let children predict what happens next—and thereby feel powerful. Call-and-response books are another kind of repetitive format. In *Brown Bear, Brown Bear*, by Bill Martin Jr. (Henry Holt) a narrator asks each animal (and each reader) what it sees. Children are active learners and active listeners, so stories that require their participation are more likely to hold their interest.

In cumulative stories, each new scene includes a listing of all the events leading up to it, as in the folktale *This is the House that Jack Built*. In Mem Fox's *Harriet, You'll Drive Me Wild* (Harcourt), Harriet's mother corrects young Harriet's missteps with an increasingly impatient refrain. She starts out, "Harriet . . . you'll drive me wild," and adds a line through each of three scenes until she finally loses her temper. The lengthening refrains underscore Harriet's increasingly messy antics and her mother's growing frustration in a great example of format that truly serves the story. Predictable stories also leave room for surprise when the established pattern is broken. The cumulative, rhyming refrain suddenly disappears at the peak of Harriet's mischief: "There was a terrible silence."

Children love rhyme because it's predictable and challenging. Writing in verse provides structure, but it should complement a story rather than prop it up. Rhyme can be very engaging, if done well: it must have flawless meter and true rhymes, in addition to telling a great story. Choppy meter makes a story lurch and stall, rather than sing. A rhyming refrain or internal rhyme in prose (as in, "please don't squeeze") are fun alternatives to stories written entirely in verse. If you want to rhyme well, read all the rhyming texts you can get your hands on, aloud. Have people read your work to you, to see if it scans. Even if your story is prose, it should have rhythm. Make sure that the natural flow of the text suits the story.

Young children enjoy experimenting with speech sounds as they learn to master them. Jane Yolen's *Off We Go!* (Little Brown) is a beautiful example of delicious language: "Dig-deep, diggity deep/Down where day is dark as sleep/Off to Grandma's house I creep/sings Little

---

Online Resources

There's no shortage of wonderful organizations dedicated to promoting literacy in young children. Bookmark these websites to stay in touch with news and conferences about early literacy:

The International Reading Association:
www.reading.org

The National Association for the Education of Young Children:
www.naeyc.org

The National Education Association's "Read Across America" initiative:
www.nea.org/readacross

The National Center for Family Literacy: HeadStart Family Literacy Project:
www.famlit.org/headstart/hsece.html

Zero to Three: National Center for Infants, Toddlers, and Families:
www.zerotothree.org

Mole." Some very young stories take their entire structure from playful language. *Jamberry*, by Bruce Degen, takes the word "berry" and runs with it. There's no particular conflict or plot, just a series of silly vignettes tied together by language play. *Chicka, Chicka, Boom, Boom* (Simon & Schuster), by Bill Martin Jr. and John Archambault is another popular book in this vein. The fact that all of these examples, originally published in hardback, are now available in board book format indicates their appropriateness for babies and toddlers. Use language "flourishes" (see Shoptalk sidebar) judiciously. If they don't enhance the story, they'll distract from it. When a story really works, readers don't notice the techniques that make it sparkle—they're integral to the story itself.

So what about endings? Many popular books for babies and toddlers come full circle: the main character ends in the place where he or she began. The forward motion of the story needs to bring the main character all the way to his destination (a safe place, usually) and not leave the reader wondering if he'll make it okay. Even though Mem Fox's Harriet and her mom have had a row, we see they are fixing things. In *No, David!*, by David Shannon (Blue Sky/Scholastic), mischievous David finally hears the word "yes"—when mom says, "Yes, David, I love you." Hopeful endings are comforting. Depending on the mood of your piece, it may need to wind down or close with a bang, so be sure to choose an ending that serves your story.

REACHING YOUR READERS

So your well-crafted story is finally published. Hurrah! Now you're ready to tackle the P-word: *promotion*. I've heard authors of young picture books complain that they have few opportunities for promotion. Nonsense! Look beyond typical bookstore events and library readings. Your books may not be ideal for elementary school visits, but the early childhood community is a great place to share your work. When teachers like your book they'll use it in the classroom and recommend it to parents. An added bonus is the contact with your audience, which will enhance your future writing.

Start your tour of the early childhood circuit with a center to which you have personal connections—the one your children attended, or a center in your neighborhood. Many early childhood programs offer special events in conjunction with the Month of the Young Child (April) or other seasonal events. When a center contacts you to set up an event, find out who your audience will be. Events for young children generally include an exuberant reading and some related fun: songs, fingerplays, or dances. Parent-centered events tend to be lectures on selecting books for children, reading readiness, or writing. Since many childcare centers have lean budgets, you may need to lower your fee for workshops or sell books at the event as a fundraiser. Whenever you present at a childcare center, be sure they publicize it in their newsletter. Contact a local newspaper to include your event in the community calendar and perhaps do a write-up.

Authors can also do workshops for childcare staff on literacy topics. Teachers need information about hands-on activities to extend learning. They like handouts—reading lists and activity ideas—and they love freebies like bookmarks. Stipends for workshops vary greatly: I've received between $50 and $250 for a two-hour session. Contact your local community college or university to let the education and English departments know that you are available as a guest speaker or lecturer. Register with childcare referral agencies, which provide speaker lists to the early childhood community as well as put on their own events.

Consider submitting a proposal to present at a National Association for the Education of Young Children (NAEYC) or other early childhood conferences. These generally do not pay presenters, but sessions are short and you can arrange to have book signings at vendor booths. Your publisher may even be willing to subsidize your trip—it's worth asking. Many teachers are aspiring authors and they pack into conference sessions on becoming an author. (I did, too.) One big bonus at the national NAEYC conference is the presence of book and magazine publishers. I've met editors at exhibitor booths and conference sessions. Some educational publishers even offer conferees on-the-spot appointments with editors who are seeking submissions.

If you're overwhelmed at the thought of presenting workshops, you can introduce your book to local children and teachers on a smaller scale. Many communities have literacy groups such as the Family Book Club in Ann Arbor, Michigan, which donates new books to low-income families and coordinates reading programs for disadvantaged children. These organizations welcome author visits and are a great destination for authors' surplus books. Think about "adopting" a local childcare center or preschool program. You might donate signed copies of your books and stay in touch with teachers by visiting the classroom for an occasional story hour. Give the center a stack of your promotional postcards or bookmarks for their reception area, and participate in annual picnics or fun days. Besides keeping you in touch with your audience, this kind of relationship is a great way to contribute something meaningful to your community.

STAYING DRY

Doing a book event with children who drool, crawl, and cry is a special kind of challenge. Before you plan your first book event, it's wise to establish some ground rules with your sponsors:

- Children should be accompanied by adults. Make it clear with your host and in your promotional flyers that parents are expected to sit with their children during a reading. Otherwise, they may stroll over to another department or the coffee bar and you will be outnumbered by wigglers.
- Before you begin reading, tell the adults what you need from them: "Please help your children participate or remove them if they are overwhelmed."
- If you plan to sing songs or do fingerplays in a childcare center, send the songs and words ahead of time so the teachers can practice with the children.
- Limit the group size with young children. In a bookstore, several readings with ten children are infinitely more manageable than one reading with thirty. The same goes for community events. If you must do one session, enlist some help for crowd control. Large crowds can be overwhelming for small children (and harried authors).
- Sit where all the children can see you. If no chair is provided, stand up or perch on your knees, or you'll be drowned out by a chorus of "I can't see's!" Expect very young children to fidget, loll, or get up and move around. They are kinetic learners and kinetic listeners.
- Don't read several books at a stretch. Babies and toddlers can't concentrate for more than five minutes or so. Break up your routine with simple songs or fingerplays. Songs that require kids to get up and move are great, as long as you end on a "sit down" note. All told, the performance aspect of an event with babies and toddlers shouldn't last more than 15 or twenty minutes.
- If you use props during your presentation, expect the children to touch them. They can't resist—they haven't learned to delay gratification yet. You can cut simple shapes out of felt for the children to hold—circles for pretend cookies, for example. Don't expect to get them back.
- If a child comes unglued while you're reading, pause so his parent can remove him from the group. Recruit another adult to help you if parents don't get the picture.
- Young children have a hard time with negative phrases. If you say, "No jumping," they have a hard time figuring out what not jumping *is*. It's more effective to say the thing you do want them to do: "Put your feet on the floor."
- Be flexible. If the children aren't interested in your story but they love your songs and fingerplays, go with the flow. You'll all have more fun, and parents will remember you fondly.

My best advice? Honor babies' and toddlers' perspective and experiences in your writing *and* in the presentation of your stories. Whet children's appetites for literature by writing rich stories that they'll want to savor again, and again . . . and again.

Shoptalk

Lovely language can make your story leap off the page. The following books are great examples of some popular "flourishes." (For extra credit, note the other techniques that make these stories so successful!)

Alliteration: using words that begin with similar sounds, as in: "Dustin didn't want to do it." See: *Castles, Caves, and Honeycombs*, by Linda Ashman (Harcourt).

Assonance: using words that have similar vowel sounds, such as "plate" and "bake." See: *Grump*, by Janet S. Wong (McElderry).

Consonance: using words with similar consonant sounds, such as "click," "clack," and "cluck." See: *Tickle Tum!*, by Nancy Van Laan (Atheneum).

Onomatopoeia: sound words that are spelled like they sound, such as "bam," "tinkle," and "crash." See: *All on a Sleepy Night*, by Shutta Crum (Stoddart).

Picture Books 101: Pay Attention to Structure

BY DARCY PATTISON

Short stories and picture books have much in common. Both are short, and both contain a complete story with a beginning, middle and end. But a short story isn't necessarily suited for a picture book. Picture books are short stories molded to a specific structure that includes illustrations on each page. Before we put flesh on the story you're wanting to write, let's look at the skeleton that must hold it up.

PICTURE BOOK STRUCTURE

Picture books are almost always 32 pages. The reasons for this are physical: when printers fold paper, eight pages fold smoothly into what's called a signature, while any more result in a group of pages too thick to bind nicely. In addition, the 32 pages can all be printed on a single sheet of paper, making it cost-effective. In extremely rare cases, picture books may be 16, 24, 40 or 48 pages, all multiples of eight (a signature); but 32 pages is industry standard.

When talking about the page layout, there are two options. First, you can look at each page separately. Second, you can talk about double-page spreads; when a picture book is opened flat, the two facing pages are often illustrated as one. Thus, in a 32-page book, you would have a single page (the right hand side of the book), 15 double-page spreads, and a single page (the left hand side of the book). Decorative end papers, which are glued to the boards, often enclose these.

In those 32 pages, there is usually "front matter" consisting of a title page, a half-title page, and a copyright page. In single pages, this may take 4-5 pages. In double-page spreads, it's the first single page and one or two spreads. The text, then, has 27-28 pages or 14 spreads, plus a last single page.

Concentrating on the skeleton of the picture book may seem boring or unnecessary, but it is one of the two main differences between short stories and picture books. One mistake made by beginners is to have too many or too few pages to fit into this format. Why can't the publisher ignore the standard page limits and just print the size book needed for a particular story? Again, the reasons are physical: the way the paper folds and standard sizes of paper for printing. Tracey Adams, literary agent with McIntosh & Otis, says, "It's definitely easiest to market a picture book meant to be the standard 32 pages."

PICTURE BOOK ILLUSTRATIONS

The second difference between short stories and picture books is the number of illustrations. Magazine stories, for example, may have one or two illustrations for each story. Picture books have an illustration on each page: you must think visually when writing for this genre.

Thinking visually doesn't mean adjectives; illustrators can fill in colors, background, clothing, and other details. Instead, concentrate on verbs; telling your story with pictures requires action.

DARCY PATTISON *dummies her picture book manuscripts in the attic of a 100-year-old Victorian house, which serves as her office. Her next picture book,* The Journey of Oliver K. Woodman, *illustrated by Joe Cepeda (Harcourt) is an April 2003 release. Her children's fantasy novel,* The Wayfinder *(Greenwillow) was published in 2000.*

Unless a description is crucial to the story, cut it. Include actions that move the story along. Thoughts and dialogue may advance the plot, but they can't be illustrated; talking heads make for boring illustrations. Picture book stories find ways to make thoughts concrete. "Visual pacing is needed," Says Francoise Bui, publisher of Random House imprint Doubleday Books. "You can't repeat the same scene over and over. It's too stagnant. The story needs to move to provide the visual variety." Varying the setting is important. For example, if everything takes place in a bedroom, it's hard to provide fourteen or more interesting actions in that setting. It's also important to vary the actions. If every character leaps about, page after page, the illustrations become too repetitive. Of course, you can return to a scene, but add visual variety each time. For example, we see each of the Three Pigs building a house, but the building materials are different: straw, sticks and brick.

Visual pacing also depends on whether the illustrations are single or double-spread. To some extent, the text can set this pace. The amount of text can also speed up or slow down a story. For example, if you want the pace to pick up near the climax, then cut the number of words for these later spreads. If you want a sustained pace that slows near the end—a bedtime book— then word counts should be similar on each page until the end. To slow the pace at the end, you can either add extra words, or use words with long vowels and no plosives (p,b,k,g,t,d).

Think about those page turns, too. Some stories interrupt a sentence with a page turn, which lets the reader anticipate what might be coming next. Rick Walton's book, *Once There was a Bull . . . Frog*, is an excellent example of this. One page reads, "Once there was a bull . . . " Page turn. "Frog. . . ." Children love this invitation to play with the words of the story.

STRUCTURE PLUS STORY

With picture book structure and the importance of illustration possibilities firmly in mind, it's time to turn to your story. First, write a story just as you always do. Unless you are a poet, it's best to write in prose. "Writers tend to think that rhyming texts are easy to write and easy to sell," says Bui. "They are the hardest to write and I reject almost all of them. Beginning

---

Two Tools to Help You Write Picture Books

Because the structure of picture books is so important, you may want to use one of two tools to help you hone your text.

A story board consists of a single page with rectangles drawn to indicate the two-page spreads of a picture book. Draw some indication of what action takes place on each page or spread. Don't be bashful: I use stick figures and no one else would be able to understand them. We're not looking for great art here, but for a way to "see" the entire book at a glance. Look for ways to build in progressions, rhythms, or repetitions, while keeping the illustrations varied and lively.

A dummy book is made by stapling together along the short side sixteen pages of paper. Sue Alexander, author of over twenty picture books including *Behold the Trees* (Scholastic 2001) and *One More Time, Mama* (Cavendish 1997), frequently conducts picture book seminars. She suggests using colored paper to better simulate the idea of colorful illustrations with white sections of text. Cut your printed text into sections and either glue stick or tape into place in the book. Remember that the text will start on either page 4 or 5 because of the front matter. Alexander suggests you ask someone to read it aloud while you listen for rhythm, pacing, and voice. Evaluate how well each page advances the action and provides possible illustrations.

Editors don't want or need to see story boards or dummies. They are trained to think in terms of page divisions and illustrations. These are tools just for writers to use to polish their manuscripts.

writers are better off in prose." Adams agrees: "One of the most common errors is when an author thinks she needs to rhyme and isn't very good at it."

Remember that the audience for picture books is children, so the story should be of interest to them. Unless it is a folk or fairy tale, characters are usually children. Rarely do adult characters or inanimate objects as characters make successful picture books. Bui says, "It's preferable to have a young child as protagonist, or an animal. It needs to be someone the child reader can relate to."

Picture book vocabulary doesn't have to be limited, because usually an adult is reading the story to a child. Likewise, style isn't limited to short, choppy sentences. In fact, the voice of the story is just as important as in any other writing and playing with language is welcomed. Finally, limit the story to 1,000 words or less. "There's a range," Bui says, " from a very simple sparse text, to a longer, more character-driven story. Shorter stories are better received by book buyers.

Successful manuscripts average about four pages (typed, double-spaced, standard formatting)." From an agent's point of view, Adams emphasizes, "I've had the most luck by far licensing picture book manuscripts that are under 1,000 words. Most are actually under 500." Just like a short story, you must introduce a character and his/her problem and provide complications before solving the problem in a satisfying manner that leaves a memorable feeling or thought in the reader's mind. Think about the narrative arc of your story.

Deborah Halverson, Assistant Editor for Harcourt, Inc., points to the narrative arc of *Wilma Unlimited: How Wilma Rudolph Became the World's Fastest Woman*, written by Kathleen Krull, illustrated by David Diaz. Halverson says, "We see Wilma progress from a small girl crippled by polio (she wore a leg brace and was told she'd never walk again) to a record-setting Olympic runner. This is a wonderful example of how picture book biographies can be riveting stories for kids rather than dry recountings of chronological facts. I think the key to the power of this book lies in Krull's decision to let Wilma's growing sense of determination steer the story through the key events on her road to Olympic glory. This is a story about inner strength as much as physical accomplishment." (For more examples see the Strong Narrative Arcs sidebar.) In other words, the "growing sense of determination" creates the narrative arc that builds suspense and interest from the first conflict through the climax.

THE HARD WORK BEGINS

Once I have a story in hand that I think might make a picture book, the real work begins. Now, I must evaluate how well the story fits the structure of picture books and how illustratable the story is. I usually begin by dividing my story into pages, either 28 sections for single pages or 14 for spreads. (This is strictly for myself to edit the story; when I send the manuscript, I don't include these page breaks.) Right away, you may discover your story has too few or too many pages. Revise until you are at least close to this count. There is some flexibility in layout—the illustrator may include a wordless spread, or may decide to put two of your sections onto one page—but you must be close.

Once the page count is close, it's time to evaluate how well the story fits into the story book structure. Each page or spread must do the following:

1. Advance the story.
2. Provide an action for the illustrations.
3. Make the reader want to turn the page.

Overall, the story must move from setting to setting, so the illustrations can be varied. Of course, you can return to a setting, or the rhythm of the story may return to a setting several times. But each repetition must provide a new action or new details for the illustrator.

Inevitably, there are weak pages that need work. Keep reworking the story until it meets the requirements of picture book structure and the need for illustration possibilities. Authors often use story boards or book dummies to help refine the story. (See the Two Tools to Help You Write Picturebooks sidebar.)

Exercise: Thinking in Spreads (With Help from a Sonnet)

You can compare picture book structure to the structure of poetry. For example, sonnets have 14 lines, picture books can have 14 double-page spreads. So, taking a sonnet as an example of structure, you can imitate one of these sonnet structures.

1. The Italian Sonnet consists of an octave (8 lines) and a sestet (6 lines)
   Octave:
   Spreads 1-4 Set up character
   Spreads 5-8 Problem stated
   Sestet:
   Spreads 9-11 Character tries to solve the problem.
   Spreads 12-14 The payoff

Or, think of it as the beginning, middle, end, payoff. Or problem, attempts to solve, failure and re-commitment to try, payoff.

Notice that in this structure, there is a pivot point—things change drastically—between spreads 8 and 9. There are two minor pivots, too, between 4-5 and 11-12. These are good places for a twist to turn the plot in a different direction.

2. The Shakespearean Sonnet
   Three quatrains (4-line stanzas) and a couplet.
   Spreads 1-4 Problem stated
   Spreads 5-8 Attempts to solve problem
   Spreads 9-12 Problem solved
   Spreads 13-14 The payoff

The main pivot point is between 12 and 13; minor pivot points occur between 4-5, 8-9. Once the story is written with this structure, do a storyboard or a book dummy to check for the illustration possibilities.

COMMON PROBLEMS

One common problem is stories that are too wordy. Because each double-page spread is a scene, you can often eliminate transitions. The page turn works like a scene-cut in film: the illustrations re-orient the reader and the words aren't needed.

Parents read picture books aloud to kids, often repeating the same book over and over. Read your story out loud. Would you mind reading it 50 times in a row? How can you adjust the language to make repetitions more satisfying?

One of the most dreaded comments from an editor is "this manuscript is too slight." Slight can mean one of several things:

1. There aren't enough illustration possibilities.
2. The theme is universal, but this telling isn't special enough. If you choose a classic theme for a story, such as a bedtime story, you must make your story stand out in the crowd. Study your competition and add twists, new conflicts, or word play to make your story unique.
3. There isn't enough story. The conflicts are too minor; the resolution is too easy. Rethink your story.
4. The series of conflicts don't add up to an overall theme. Rethink the conflicts. Consider adding an extended metaphor to connect the conflicts.
5. The story lacks universality. What is this story really about? What's happening on the surface (going to bed) may not be the real issue (sibling jealousy). When you identify the real theme, then go back and strengthen it.

SUBMITTING

Once you are satisfied, type the story in standard manuscript format without any page breaks. Don't worry about finding an illustrator and trying to provide artwork with your submission. Bui says, "Sometimes writers feel they need to submit illustrations with a story. Instead, the publisher finds the appropriate illustrator and it's our preference to take care of that." But what if you love your friend's illustrations? You take a chance if you send in a package submission: what if the editor decides to take only the text? Have you lost a friend? Adams advises, "Even if the author knows or is related to an artist, never include the illustrations." When you offer a package submission, the editor must love both, so you've cut your chances in half. Instead, wait until your text is accepted, then ask the editor if they will look at sample illustrations and a portfolio from your friend.

The creation of a picture book is a collaborative effort between a writer and illustrator; but once the editor assigns the book to an illustrator, you may have little say about the style or content of the illustrations. Adams says, "Another common error I see is a manuscript in which many of the details are specified which should be left up to the illustrator." You must trust the illustrator to be a professional and to add her unique touch to create the best story possible.

There's one last checkpoint. To bring a picture book to market, the publisher often invests $15,000-25,000. Ask yourself if this story is worth that kind of investment. Have you revised and polished it until it is perfect?

Once you've created the best text possible, consult *Children's Writer's & Illustrator's Market* for an appropriate publisher, take a deep breath and send it in.

Strong Narrative Arcs

Deborah Halverson, Assistant Editor, Harcourt, Inc., suggests studying these books as examples of strong narrative arcs.

Gleam and Glow, by Eve Bunting, illustrated by Peter Sylvada
Traditional prose story: A family is separated by war, but they reunite with a new perspective thanks to people they meet during the separation. The ending is brilliant and effective because of the emotional setup—uncertainty turns to fear, then to sadness, then to hope.

That Summer, by Tony Johnston, illustrated by Barry Moser.
Poetry: The text and illustrations use a blend of memory and present day events to carry readers through one summer with a boy whose brother is sick with a terminal illness. The younger brother starts a quilt, stitching images of his favorite things. When he can no longer finish the quilt, the older brother finishes it for him in a tangible expression of the theme of memory.

Whose Shoes?, by Anna Grossnickle Hines, illustrated by LeUyen Pham.
Simple text for young readers: A little mouse tries on the shoes of different family members, making her way through the entire family until she reaches her favorite pair of shoes: her own! The ending is a satisfying confirmation of self identity after imagining what it's like to be someone else.

The Nonfiction Proposal: Put Your Best Foot Forward

BY SUE BRADFORD EDWARDS

Mention that a nonfiction publisher only accepts proposals and the gripes and groans begin. "What goes into a proposal anyway?" "Wouldn't it just be easier to write the book?" "How can they judge my work based on a proposal?"

A nonfiction proposal is a valuable marketing tool for presenting your work to editors. Fortunately what goes into one is fairly straightforward.

POSITION YOUR MANUSCRIPT

Not only is most of the information in a book proposal straightforward, it's the type of information a professional gathers before beginning a new manuscript. The majority of proposals open with discussions of content, audience, competing titles, markets and author credentials.

The writer can format this material in two ways. An "informal proposal" can simply be a letter containing the information an editor needs about the book you are proposing. (See the One Short Page sidebar.) In a "formal proposal," the material is presented in titled sections and may total ten pages. To know which format a publisher prefers, check market listings, guidelines, and publishers' websites. For what goes into each section of a formal nonfiction book proposal, read on.

Introducing your work

Because the editor reads the cover letter and/or formal proposal before the outline and sample chapters, they want information on content up front. What is the proposed manuscript all about? How will it be presented? Author Mary Bowman-Kruhm does this succinctly in her cover letter:

> I am sending you a copy of the manuscript, Are You My Type? Temperament Typing for Teens. My co-author, Claudine Wirths, and I have simplified the concepts of temperament typing and written them at a seventh grade reading level to make the ideas accessible and understandable to the average high school-age student. I have also enclosed several activity sheets.

Three sentences detail title, purpose, audience, reading level and special sections, conveying information not entirely evident from the outline.

Who's the audience?

The writer must also show the editor that an audience for the proposed work exists. When Linda Moore Kurth proposed Keiko's Story: A Killer Whale Goes Home, interest in Keiko was so high that she included not a paragraph but a page of twelve items, two of which follow:

SUE BRADFORD EDWARDS *writes nonfiction for children and adults in St. Louis, Missouri. Her book reviews can be found in the* St. Louis Post-Dispatch. *Her articles for writers have been published in* Writer's Digest, *the* Institute of Children's Literature 2003 Yearbook, *ICL market reports,* Children's Writer *newsletter, and the SCBWI* Bulletin. *Visit her website at http://SueBradfordEdwards.8m.com.*

Four thousand people waited in the rain at Newport to witness Keiko's arrival. Included in the crowd was a family from Beaverton whose children had watched Free Willy *twenty-five times.*

Keiko has his own home page provided by the Discovery Channel. It averages 6,000 hits a day. Between 15,000 and 20,000 Free Willy Keiko Adoption kits have been sold.

In addition to demonstrating high public interest, Kurth included specific numbers which a marketing department can use to judge a project's feasibility, i.e. salability.

Discussing the audience also lets the author indicate who will purchase the book. Bowman-Kruhm did this for *Are You My Type?*:

We feel this book will be very salable to school guidance counselors, teachers, and other professionals who work with middle and high school students. Participants of workshops on typing would provide a large second audience.

She thus demonstrates that a readily defined market exists.

The competition

The author should next discuss the competition to show the market isn't saturated. Kurth begins her research into competing titles with an Amazon.com subject search and requests pertinent material through her library. For *Keiko's Story*, her search resulted in this cover letter paragraph:

The Discovery channel is limited in its number of Keiko specials. A lucky few can find him on the Web. A coloring book of Keiko is in print. Keiko souvenirs are selling well. But there are no Keiko books.

Kurth defined a ready-made market with no print competition.

Doing the Research

Many authors wonder how much research they should do before preparing a proposal. The answer depends in part on how they prefer to work.

For a bare bones outline, less research is required. "Personally, I do just enough research to get a strong feeling for what information is out there, how it can be organized, and what the main sources are that I'm going to want to use," Gary Blackwood says. "For the finished product, I do a great deal more research, from a large variety of sources, and I think it would be counterproductive to try to do all in advance; I would tend to want to rush it."

Boyd Jones does a little more research. "I read three or four books on the topic so I have a good overview and I research magazine and newspaper sources for the latest on my topic. Then I write the outline. I research in depth the topic of the first chapter, since I include it with the outline. I do much more research when I've been contracted to write the book, although I may have assembled all the materials I'll eventually need while I'm working on the outline."

This level of research can do more than simply give the author necessary data. "It also tells me if I can 'live' with the topic and sustain the momentum I need to write a book that is a good read first page to last and doesn't sound bogged down because I'm sick of the subject matter," Bowman-Kruhm says. "Interest is especially important in a long book, like the 57,000 word *Margaret Mead: A Biography*. I was tired from putting in long hours to meet my deadline, but my interest had not flagged a bit."

Three answers from three different authors. Which style is right for you?

This is also the place to show that your manuscript differs from existing work as did Bowman-Kruhm:

> *Unfortunately, although curriculum materials and books to help professionals use typing with youngsters are available, there are no books written solely for teens. We believe that* Are You My Type? *fills this void.*

Two short sentences acknowledge other books while stating how this manuscript is unique.

Marketing ideas

The author should next discuss marketing, impressing the editor with her willingness to help. Possibilities for the author include public appearances (signings, fairs, and school and library visits), a personal website, and printing post cards or bookmarks. Consulting Psychologists Press' director Lee Langhammer Law says her company considers how eager the author seems to be "in partnering in the marketing and promotion of the book." She checks to see if the author has "a clear plan for how to be involved in making the book a part of his or her platform." Enthusiasm here can make up for a short list of sales in the next section of a proposal.

Presenting credentials

Many writers get nervous when presenting their credentials if they lack top-selling books in print. The key is to demonstrate how the author is the ideal candidate for this project. In marketing *Keiko's Story* Kurth included:

> *I am a published writer and former teacher. I have contributed nature articles to the* High Desert Museum Newsletter *in Bend, Oregon and have had articles in national publications. January 1996, my "wholesome" career romance was published in hardback by Avalon. I am a member of Willamette Writers and SCBWI. Keiko and I have been eyeball to eyeball.*

Kurth demonstrates her expertise in writing nature nonfiction, knowledge of the classroom (key for educational publishers), and personal enthusiasm for Keiko—a combination only she possesses.

Writers can also "borrow" expertise. Kristin Nitz, author of *Fundamental Softball* and forthcoming titles *Fundamental Track* and *Fundamental Field Events*, explains, "In my cover letter, I noted that I had played softball in various leagues for over twenty years. In the proposal for the track and field books—where I had less first-hand knowledge—I noted that I had interviewed athletes and coaches and attended meets and practices." What expertise Nitz didn't have, she knew where to get.

As important as these sections are in positioning a proposed manuscript, not all publishers require them. Some educational publishers, such as Lucent, publish series that are planned in-house. They already know the intended audience, possible competition and how they will market it. (For information on applying for such a series, see sidebar, The Educational Side.)

Still, many educational publishers, including Marshall Cavendish, do want these sections in a proposal because they print series developed by freelance authors. "These are the things I need to present a proper proposal to my editorial group," explains Marshall Cavendish editor Joyce Stanton. To find out how to approach individual educational publishers, consult their market listings in *Children's Writer's & Illustrator's Market* and their guidelines.

THE CORE

Whether a piece will be part of an in-house series or a single trade title, the core of every proposal is the outline and sample chapters. The outline can take one of two forms, explains Lucent Books managing editor Lori Shein: "Outlines can be done in alphanumeric format, or as chapter-by-chapter summarization." Whichever form it takes, the outline is a catalog of the ideas that will be covered in each chapter. Following is the first chapter outline for Veda Boyd Jones' *Native Americans of the Northwest Pacific Coast*:

Chapter 1. The People and Their Land
I.   Description and climate of land
II. The seven language nations
    A. Tlingit
    B. Haida
    C. Tsimsyan
    D. Bella Coola
    E. Kwakiutl
    F. Nootka
    G. Coast Salish
III. Living groups
    A. Family
    B. Household
    C. Clan
    D. Villages
IV. Levels of society
    A. Nobles
    B. Commoners
    C. Slaves
    D. Nonclass = shaman

One Short Page: The Letter

An informal proposal's cover letter is vitally important. "If it isn't good, the sample chapter and outline matter little," explains freelancer Mary Bowman-Kruhm. "A writer once told me she spent the morning writing fifteen different letters. Then they all got rejected. Better to write one letter 15 different times until its perfect. Writers spend time with their groups critiquing their books; I'd suggest they critique each other's cover letters!"

In one short page, this letter must present information on content, audience, competing titles, marketing and author credentials. To keep her letters well-organized, Bowman-Kruhm "begins with a lead paragraph detailing the important points of the book." She then uses bullet points to organize the remaining information. Depending on space available and what is most applicable, she discusses:

- Photo availability
- Sources or experts for interviews
- Projected word count
- Projected date of completion
- Working title
- Why topic is timely/appropriate
- Target audience
- Why this publishing house would be interested. ("I try to be subtle in making this point," says Bowman-Kruhm.)
- Marketing information

Following the bulleted points, Bowman-Kruhm includes a "succinct bio of several sentences." Her final paragraph states that she has enclosed an outline, a brief bio that is more detailed than the one found in the preceding paragraph, and a SASE.

And, yes. She does this all in one well-tailored page.

From Outline To Final Draft

Many writers worry that their final draft will differ significantly from their outline.

How much it differs may depend on the type of manuscript. "Because I write biography," author Susanna Reich explains, "I find it fairly easy to outline a book. The person's life is already lived, so the 'plot' is a given."

Sometimes changes are necessary. For *Margaret Mead: A Biography*, the publisher's guidelines included a chapter on awards and honors. "As I wrote, I realized that the actual awards and honors did not reflect Mead's immense contributions to American society," Bowman-Kruhm says. "Her contributions were encapsulated in views she expressed in speeches and publications, especially articles for women she wrote for sixteen years for *Redbook* magazine. I downplayed her awards and honors by inserting information about them in earlier chapters." Fortunately an outline is not carved in stone and author and editor are working toward the same end—to produce the best book possible.

Boyd Jones' topical outline covers an introduction, six chapters, and the epilogue in only two pages.

A series outline is even less detailed. "For the two series I've done for Marshall Cavendish—one with six books, and one with five," says Gary Blackwood, "all the editor required was one page, with a paragraph about the focus and age level of the series overall, and a paragraph on each volume, telling what subjects would be covered."

Whatever the format, the outline should cover only the basics. "We're looking for the main idea of each chapter, what ideas or events will support and develop that main idea, and (in general) how the pieces will fit together," Shein says. "So, at this stage we don't need to see facts, quotes or examples."

An outline may seem scant, but it gives the editor all she needs to evaluate the writer's ability to logically organize her material. "Each chapter needs to have a distinct purpose (or theme) and the author must show how the ideas or events to be included in each chapter will support that theme as well as how they will fit together," Shein says. "If an outline is just a list of facts, we assume the author lacks the ability to decide on a theme and develop it logically, one idea at a time. If information repeats from chapter to chapter, we assume the author lacks the ability to organize the material. If ideas are not well developed, we assume the writer doesn't have a strong command of the material or of writing for the middle grade age level." Even then, the author may get another chance. "If it looks like she can write, but the outline or chapter is off-track or the author is having difficulty organizing the material, we usually return the outline and chapter with suggestions for reorganizing and revising," Stein says. Bare bones, the outline gives the editor something to work with, especially when paired with the author's sample chapters.

Sample chapters offer authors a chance to display their skills. When asked what she looks for when reading a proposal, Shein says, "Does the chapter have a main idea? Are ideas presented in a logical sequence so that one idea leads to the next and the next? Do the paragraphs hold together? Does the author develop important ideas and use facts, quotes or examples to support and illustrate?"

Although it's best to include the first three chapters as samples, there are exceptions. When writing about the Donner Party, for example, an author might submit the first two chapters and skip to the chapter that deals with the cannibalism to allow the editor to evaluate how to deal with something that might generate controversy. As a rule, though, stick with the chapters one through three. The chapters, in combination with the outline tell the editor if the author can pull off the proposed project.

THE EVIDENCE

A well-constructed proposal gives an editor all she needs to evaluate the planned manuscript and the author's writing. First the publisher looks at the idea. "My personal goal is to find very interesting and creative ideas," Stanton says. To develop unique ideas for an educational market, she recommends authors talk to librarians and teachers about new trends in education. "A couple of years ago," she says, "we learned that primary sources (sources that give the words of the witnesses or the first recorders of an event like manuscripts, archives, letters, diaries, and speeches) were an important trend—that teachers want children to know what those sources are and how historians work. As a result, we are publishing several interesting series involving the use of primary sources."

Editors also judge whether the idea is a good fit for their company. For an educational publisher, this means whether it matches curriculum. "Prospective authors should try to connect their topics with subjects children are studying. They might look, for example, at the California, Texas or New York curriculum," Stanton says. All publishers want potential projects to mesh with their missions.

Second to the idea itself is the author's experience and background. "Sometimes I can judge by seeing what they've published and with whom," Stanton says. "If, for example, I see some publishing houses that I respect, my eyes perk up. The list of publishing credits can include magazines, but if it's only magazines my decision depends more on the idea." An author need not be a household name but all authors need to show an interest in the long-term success of a project.

Publishers also consider a projects' overall marketability. Lee asks the following: "Do our sales projections on what we know at that point allow for a smart business proposition? Can we hit our sales and profitability targets?" This is why educational editors like Stanton want to know that a piece fits the curriculums of Texas, New York or California—the nation's three largest educational markets. Just as a manuscript idea that won't sell serves no purpose for the author, a book that won't sell serves no purpose for a publisher.

Not only does a proposal give an editor enough information to judge a project; it also benefits both author and publisher in several ways. Perhaps the most obvious benefit to submitting a proposal over a completed manuscript is the potential time saved by the author. "I have tons of ideas about which editors don't thus far share my enthusiasm," Bowman-Kruhm jokes, "and time would not be well used to write them until I have a contract or, at the least, interest

---

The Educational Side

Many educational presses such as Lucent develop series ideas in-house. "We've already created a series idea," Lucent Books managing editor Lori Shein says, "and have decided which titles we want to publish in that series. So, authors don't have to 'sell' us on a proposal."

Instead of submitting proposals to Lucent and similar companies, writers should send the acquisitions editor a résumé of published work along with nonfiction clips. Veda Boyd Jones did this and received a call from a Lucent editor who read her a list of available titles. Jones then selected the one she was most interested in and submitted an outline and sample chapters before receiving approval on the assignment.

Other educational publishers, including Marshall Cavendish, publish series proposed by freelancers. Authors can also request to write a single titles for an existing series. To do this, explains Joyce Stanton, "Send a letter, 'I've looked in your catalog and there's a series on such and such. Here are my credentials. Are you continuing the series?'" Such a contact can lead to a single book assignment.

Either approach represents an opportunity for an author to see her name in print.

expressed." Submitting proposals, the author reduces the chances of completing a host of manuscripts that won't sell.

The publisher, too, benefits in that it's easier to incorporate an editor's suggestions into a proposed piece than into a completed manuscript. "Authors may be unwilling to follow the developmental guidance of the publishing house if the manuscript is a done deal," Law says. She describes proposal development as "a true partnership between the author and editor to maximize the opportunity to the fullest." Kurth agrees, adding that with a proposal "you have the opportunity to get your foot in the door."

Authors who understand how proposals work can use them to put their best foot forward.

Need Information? Inspiration? Validation? Try a Conference

BY TERI DANIELS

The conference announcement arrives. You think, This looks good, but the trip is long; dollars come hard; and time is as tight as ever. Why bother?

Personally speaking, a writer's conference is like oxygen . . . the invisible substance that fuels one-fifth of my writing life. Other vital components are the words I read, the words I write, the mentors who shepherd them, and the readers who share them.

Could I have survived without doses of conference O_2? Of course. Would I have thrived? Maybe not. Over nine years time, at one conference or another, I met my literary agent, a children's publicist, two editors who subsequently accepted my work, critique group friends, and countless others who have vitalized my career.

Does everyone get oxygen at a writer's conference? Is there a way to breathe more deeply? Like everything else, thoughtful preparation goes a long way. Here are 12 ways to kick up the winds, and reap the most rewards from the writer's conference.

Evaluate the program. If the content and presenters are of interest, quickly reserve your spot, and, if need be, a place to stay. Canvas your writing buddies, family, and friends to enlist a travel companion. Away conferences are easier to navigate in pairs, although a lot can be gotten from going alone.

Read books by the keynote speakers. Author talks will have far more impact if you've experienced a sampling of their creative efforts in advance. At the conference, you can select favorite titles to purchase (often at a discount) and have autographed. Re-read and dissect these books by successful published authors. That exercise can make your own work better.

Review the faculty. Highlight the names of people you'd like to meet, and the sessions you're likely to attend. Then familiarize yourself with the bios and credits of these faculty members. Use a search engine (like www.google.com) to link with the info available on the web. For a refined search, bracket the name you are researching, example: "Teri Daniels" book. This will link you to websites, reviews, interviews, booksellers and articles by and about the presenter. Be sure to add those links to your favorite places to facilitate your own career.

Pack smart. Choose a compact piece of luggage on wheels that can accommodate your clothing and toiletries. Invest in a roomy tote or attaché case, preferably one with compartments for books, folders of your work, brochures, cards, pens, a notebook, eyeglasses and more. Pack wrapped snacks and a water bottle for each day, to stay alert and energized. (Often coffee at a conference means just that, coffee—not coffee *and*.) If a portfolio case is in order, consider taking a folding cart to bungee everything together.

Look the part. Even if you haven't a word in print, dress for your success. Wear neat, business-casual attire, comfortable shoes, and add a signature accessory to make your presence more memorable. But don't overdo it. You want to be remembered for all the right reasons.

Be friendly. Introduce yourself to others, and ask about their pursuits. Attendees could have talents that set them apart. At an SCBWI Mid-Year conference in New York, Coleen Pascatore

TERI DANIELS *is the author of* The Feet in the Gym, G-Rex, Just Enough, *and* Math Man. *For more info visit www.TeriDanielsBooks.com.*

said, "I'm just getting started." Yet, on break I discovered that this mother of three had ten years of public relations experience. Moreover, she self-published a dedication book to enable people to express their love and grief. *Remembering: an heirloom tribute to a loved one's life* is now in its third printing. Another conferee, Pat Kibbe, had visited Europe and Asia where she hand delivered student-created picture books to underprivileged children as ambassador for her non-profit organization, Kids to Kids International. Fascinating.

Stay on topic when querying faculty. The more focused your questions, the more pointed the responses will be. After an inquiry, offer a handshake or a business card, but never your projects on the spot. Remember, faculty members are also carrying cases with books, folders, and freebees. Your precious work might get lost or passed over.

Take advantage of publicity forums. Poster and book presentations are great ways to meet writers, agents, editors, and art directors. You can showcase published books, dummys or artwork. When displaying your work, be sure to attach name labels and tie on business cards or brochures. If you plan to represent yourself with a poster, make it compact but effective. Set your name in large, dark font, and post a few examples of your best work. Devise a way to pocket brochures, and art or business cards onto your board. And remember to avail yourself for questions. While positioned beside my poster, I met an author who does school visits as I do, and an editor who handed me his card without prompting. That was productive.

Maximize your conference time. Listen attentively, and take good seminar notes to employ later on. During breaks, seek out the professionals you've written to, but never met. If after-hours critique sessions are available, join in. Be kind and generous with your comments. If you're old hat at the read-and-review format, lead a circle. If not, follow along bravely. Critiques are enriching through the giving *and* the getting. If reading groups are not on the schedule, ask the conference moderator if a sign-up sheet could be posted. Also, request a time and place to be designated for informal, evening chat groups.

Give praise where praise is due, and criticize thoughtfully. The conference evaluation sheet is your chance to thank the committee for the enriching experience, and/or offer your perspective on how to make the next event more satisfying. Did the keynote speakers inspire you? Say so. Did you discover a gap in the program? Make suggestions. Was there a topic presented that was too narrow for the broad format, or vice versa. Do your part and point that out.

Prolong your conference experience. After effects can last indefinitely. You might be bursting with thoughts for articles, stories or promotions. Enter them into your file of ideas to act on. (This article was written the day after a conference!) If you're charged by the energy of meeting conferees, find ways to share information. I met regional advisors from as far off as Australia, editors and agents from New York, and aspiring writers and illustrators hailing from coast to coast. Snap a card with conference contacts into your Rolodex, and add new e-mails to your online address book with brief explanations.

Preserve your good notes. Read over and digest what you have written. Store your seminar notes, brochures and freebees in a labeled folder. Type the advice you'd like quick access to into a computer file. Save the memorable quotes, suggested reads, writing tips, and faculty's likes and dislikes for future use. Consider this. Two years after meeting a wonderful agent, I was able to revisit her words through my notes and secure her services.

Quotes are powerful tools. Some quotes make you think. Others make you act. Still others make you smile. Here are a few from my conference file. Author Sharon Creech on her characters: "I like when a kid asks the hardest questions a kid can ask." Author Marvin Terban on School visits: "You have twenty seconds to capture their attention. . . . Make them laugh!" Schuyler Hooke, a manager of Books of Wonder: "Allow six weeks minimum for scheduling a book signing."

Make the most of every conference you opt for with pre-planning and pro-active involvement. You'll readily inhale the fresh inspiration, new information and joyful validation that await you.

No More Piranhas! Editors' Thoughts on Conferences

BY MARILYN SINGER

Have you heard the one about the editor at a writer's conference? She'd been "on" for hours and was enjoying a much-needed moment of privacy in the bathroom. Then, from the adjacent stall, came an eager voice. "Hi," it said. "I'm so happy to finally meet you. Let me tell you about this picture book I've written . . ."

Truth or urban legend? Well, maybe a bit of both. But the fact is with more and more publishing houses closing transoms to unsolicited manuscripts and more and more "pre-published" writers desperate for entrée, this kind of story isn't far-fetched. Only slightly less dramatic stories *have* been verified, and they demonstrate the real frustration editors have with conferences. Because of these tales, I decided to ask a number of editors what they like and dislike about these events. It's my hope that both writers and organizers will benefit from their responses.

THE AMBUSH

All editors expect to receive queries and manuscripts after a conference. They welcome the opportunity to discover new authors and material. But there isn't an editor alive who likes to be accosted immediately after a presentation or during a lunch break. Several editors have likened this onslaught to a "feeding frenzy." They say that some writers even foist manuscripts or portfolios on them. As Melanie Donovan of HarperCollins says, the ambush "is more likely to hurt rather than help an author's chances of getting published and manuscripts stand more chance of being mislaid than if they were submitted via the usual means."

Translation: writers should make pitches and send manuscripts via traditional mail. At the conference, an editor will supply an address and any necessary instructions (writing "SCBWI attendee," for example, on the envelope) so that the query or work will arrive safely. A conference moderator may want to repeat these instructions—or, better yet, put them in a hand-out for attendees to take home.

THE NEW YORK MINUTE

Many editors will critique manuscripts during a conference. Critiquing is another good way to discover writers and to show them what immediately grabs an editor. But because these critiques are so brief, all an editor can really give is a first impression. Stephanie Lurie of Dutton says one of her pet peeves is when "people expect to have an in-depth discussion of a manuscript they brought along or submitted recently."

Atheneum's Ginee Seo once got hate mail in response to such a New York-minute critique: "Anonymously, of course, so I had no way of letting the poor person understand that what she witnessed was really *not* editing. Editing is not about negativity—it's about trying to figure out why something isn't working. But, of course, in a public forum it's hard not to take any kind of criticism personally."

MARILYN SINGER *is the author of over sixty children's books and the host of the AOL Children's Writers Chat. Visit her website, www.marilynsinger.net.*

Perhaps the critiques should be confined to smaller conferences where editors can have pre-scheduled one-on-one sessions. The danger with these—with conferences, period—is over-scheduling. Editors and other speakers have sometimes been run ragged with critiques, panels, speeches, etc. Good pacing is a must. In addition, Judy O'Malley of Cricket Books suggests giving the speaker a " 'keeper' who runs interference, plays time-keeper for critiquing sessions, makes sure I get time to eat and even a break here and there, a cup of coffee, water, etc. This can really help. Pacing the schedule and giving speakers that bit of TLC can mean that more authors/editors/agents who really do value these opportunities to interact with writers and illustrators can do it more often, and more sanely."

THE QUICK FIX

Everyone agrees that a good panel or Q&A session is invigorating. Editors enjoy thinking about and discussing a wealth of important topics related to children's books, especially with, as Greenwillow's Rebecca Davis puts it, "people who are passionate about the subject." "I love Q&A time," says editor Harold Underdown, "especially when people aren't censoring their questions. I remember being on a panel of editors in Philly and getting asked, 'What do editors really think of agents?' This prompted nervous laughter and a great discussion."

A good discussion can be made even better when the moderator is talented. As Timothy Travaglini of Walker Books suggests, "Audiences can be shy on occasion; they might not think of the right questions until days later; or they might never know exactly the right questions. A good moderator will not only broach new topics, but will ensure that the panelists cover everything of the most use to attendees."

But what is truly useful and what the attendees want to know is not always the same thing. Some writers are really interested in perfecting their craft, and their questions demonstrate it. Others, unfortunately, are too concerned with format or are interested in the quick fix, and their questions reflect that: "Will colored paper catch your attention?"; "Do you want things double-spaced, with one- or two-inch margins?"; "How many words should a novel be?"; "Do I need to use a fixed vocabulary for a picture book?"; "Do I need to hire an illustrator for a picture book?"; "What's hot these days?"; "Are you interested in rhyming picture books?"; "How about a novel about a really stupid kid who time travels back to the Gold Rush and strikes oil instead?"

The answers to many of these questions can be found in numerous books about children's writing or on the Internet (for example, check the FAQ, written by Anne LeMieux, David Lubar, and me, at: www.marilynsinger.net). As for the "Tell me what you want, what you really, really want" type of questions, editors tend to give the same response over and over: "I want something great."

Prior to going to conferences, writers need to do their homework. They need to learn about format and something about the industry, about what a publishing house actually publishes and how it works. They should also spend some time finding out what types of books different editors edit by researching the editors on the Internet (hint: search for the editor's name, in quotes, and a keyword such as "editor" or "books"). The conference hand-out should also list what types of books editors do or don't publish (example: "Betsy Blue Pencil edits picture books and middle-grade novels, but not YA or poetry. She is partial to realistic or historical fiction and dislikes fantasy."). After learning these basics, writers are free to focus on the essence of writing: craft. Stephanie Lurie has actually met folks who want to know how to get published, but haven't yet written a thing. "I think conferences should concentrate more on technique and less on the pot o' gold at the end of the rainbow," she says.

THE CENTER OF THE UNIVERSE

How can writers develop their technique? By reading good books, by writing a lot, and by learning from good teachers. Most editors feel that the best teachers are not editors, but established authors. Conferences used to feature stellar line-ups of these, but now the emphasis is increasingly upon Editor as Idol—a situation that doesn't please the Idol herself. As Scholastic's Dianne Hess put it, "I don't deny that it's important to have small doses of business people. But this is putting the cart before the horse. The real bottom line of publishing is being able to publish great writers. And you can learn much more about how to write from other great writers than from listening to endless chatter about what publishers are looking for."

Editors want to get off the pedestal! At conferences, they'd like to see more master classes, workshops, and critiques conducted by established authors and attended by serious-minded writers. "We aren't the center of the universe," says Harold Underdown.

And it's true. Editors are not gods. Sometimes, they even need to use the bathroom—preferably in private.

The Lone Writer: Five Top Editors Weigh in on the Value of Critique Groups

BY TANYA LEE STONE

You are the lone writer. You sit at a desk . . . or a kitchen table . . . or a corner of your child's playroom—and you write. Sometimes amidst noise and chaos, sometimes in blissful solitude—you write. You experience moments of exhilaration as brilliant words fill the page. These are often followed by the block—hair-pulling times of frustration when every phrase eludes you. Throughout it all, the daily art and craft of writing, rewriting, tweaking, shaping, molding, and revising, until finally . . . a manuscript evolves. And even with all the labor and love, not drastically unlike a newborn child, there is often that moment of, "Where did this come from?" And so it begins, you—the lone writer—are ready to share your baby with the rest of the world.

Or are you? Is the manuscript really as funny as you think it is? Does your rhyming meter work? Is your story line strong enough? Are your characters fully developed? If only you had a community of people who truly understood what you are trying to accomplish. A community that knew—or at least thought they had a pretty good idea of—what kids like to read. Then maybe those people could read your latest creation and see if they agree that your book is ready to pass muster with an editor.

But wait—you have your critique group! The lone writer's posse! You turn your latest work over to them, prepare to accept input without emotion, and wait with bated breath for their individual and collective reactions. In the meantime, perhaps you take a break from writing and briefly indulge in imagining which lucky editor will pluck your newest piece from a pile, unable to put it down.

A glimpse into an editor's world

Although a critique group extends a writer's community, the lone writer spends most of his or her time working in isolation. After all, reading and writing are solitary events. Editors work in a similar way, right? They need quiet time to read and edit. But how much do you think they get? Once, long ago, an editor had oodles of time to pore over a promising manuscript and imagine, "What a wonderful book this *could* be!" He or she would then pick up the phone, call that lucky author, and a nurturing and creative partnership would bloom.

Of course, editors still make those calls to those lucky authors; and the partnerships that develop are at the core of what makes this business so meaningful. But what has changed is that editors now have a lot less time to devote to this process. As a result, manuscripts have to

---

TANYA LEE STONE *was an editor for 13 years before becoming a full-time writer. She moderates an on-line critique group of seasoned authors and offers critique services for newer writers. After publishing nearly 30 nonfiction titles for kids, Stone began writing picture books last year. Her first two picture books, written in verse, will be available in Fall 2002 and Spring 2003 with Price Stern Sloan, an imprint of Penguin Putnam Books for Young Readers. Stone can be contacted at: tanyastone@tanyastone.com. Visit her website, www.tanyastone.com.*

With the input of her critique group, author Tanya Lee Stone has created successful manuscripts like *D is for Dreidel: A Hanukkah Alphabet Book*, illustrated by Dawn Apperley (Price Stern Sloan). *D is for Dreidel* features sweet, rhyming text corresponding with every letter of the alphabet, ending with the complete story of Hanukkah. Its follow-up *P is for Passover: A Holiday Alphabet Book*, a spring 2003 release illustrated by Margeaux Lucas, includes the complete story of Passover.

be as polished as possible in order to have a chance of being published. To get some insight into how busy editors' schedules have become, let's take a minute (or ten), to pay a visit to Emma Dryden, Vice President and Editorial Director of Margaret McElderry Books, an imprint of Simon & Schuster Children's Publishing. If you think her title took some effort to say, just take a look at her day!

Emma may wear more hats than the average bear, but most editors these days have multiple responsibilities in addition to the actual editing of books in progress and reading of new manuscripts. Each day, Emma the Editor (now take a deep breath): responds to more than 200 e-mails; writes letters and answers phone calls; reads a handful of submissions; prepares materials and presents books both at sales and acquisitions meetings; negotiates contracts; meets with art directors to choose illustrators for new books and review various stages of artwork for books in progress; meets with marketing and publicity to discuss and plan strategies for a variety of titles; meets with production managers to work out pricing of books; proofs and reviews books at various stages of production; and oversees the editorial work of her assistant editor. Whew! Now take another deep breath and add to this list the responsibilities of Emma the Vice President, such as maintaining budgets, scheduling books for the next 3 to 5 years, creating a balance for the book lists, brainstorming project ideas, and reporting to both the publisher and the president.

So, when exactly does this eagle-eyed talent scout get a chance to actually read and edit?

Although Dryden somehow finds time to read manuscripts during her workday, she also carts them home, "on weekends, at night, and on vacation." If you're beginning to feel that with all of these pressures, her spirit for the job might be dampened, here's the best part. She still says, "I love my job and cannot think of doing anything other than publishing children's books!"

However busy they are, editors love books every bit as much as authors. Lauren Thompson, Senior Editor at Scholastic Press and children's author of six books (including two *New York Times* Best-Sellers) says, "...all editors are hungry for strong new writers . . ."

The editors speak: how valuable are critique groups?

Now, back to your manuscript. The critiques from your group members have come in. What are your expectations? Are you hoping for unanimous praise and accolades? Are you willing to do an immediate and complete revision upon one member's suggestion? Chances are, if you're getting the most out of your group, the truth lies somewhere in the middle. Of course, a writer always wants readers to enjoy his or her work. But is empty praise helpful in the forum of a critique group? It certainly won't help a manuscript that is lacking get transformed into a published book. What should you glean from the six different perspectives you are likely to get from six different group members? Do editors feel such groups have value?

Not surprisingly, the editors I contacted all agreed that a *good* critique group can help a writer immensely. Thompson says, "Writing can be a lonely task, and it is good to have sympathetic company as you journey through the brisk winds of the highlands and the murky, morbid fogs of the lowlands. A critique group can provide an essential outsider's response to your work; we can gain an unnerving but helpful dose of objectivity about our work simply by hearing it read aloud by someone else. And a group that meets regularly can serve as a prompt to keep writing, to start new things or finish old things, so that you won't be the only one that month with nothing to show. . . . in today's hectic publishing world, where editors rarely have time to offer suggestions on a manuscript that is 'not quite right,' it is important for writers to look to fellow writers, rather than editors, for advice and encouragement."

Wendy Lamb, Vice President and Publishing Director of Random House imprint Wendy Lamb Books (see Insider Report on page 160), echoes this thought, "They're very helpful. We're not here to teach writing, so people should find a good group and refine their work there. They can also help you understand basic facts about contracts, what rejection letters really mean, how long to let an editor keep a manuscript, what contests are worth entering . . . tricky things where someone else's experience is invaluable."

Melanie Cecka, Senior Editor of Viking Children's Books, a division of Penguin Putnam Books for Young Readers, says, "Workshopping a manuscript with a critique group gives you an opportunity to get objective feedback on multiple levels, whether it's working with rhymed verse on a line-by-line basis, or getting responses to more substantive issues like the plot or characterization in a novel. In that way, a good critique group functions as an intermediary editor; they can help you to sound out issues of story and craft well before the manuscript reaches an editor's desk."

Rebecca Davis, Senior Editor of Greenwillow Books, an imprint of HarperCollins Publishers, has a similar perspective. She says, "I think small author critique groups can be invaluable," she says. "It's easy, when writing, to get too close to a piece, so that you can't see it clearly enough anymore. A critique group can give a writer new perspective. As fresh readers, the group members can point out places in which a manuscript is unclear, or a character's behavior doesn't seem believable, etc. And armed with the group's comments, a writer can fine tune a manuscript, so that the manuscript she submits to a publishing house is stronger."

And Dryden comes in strongly in favor of *good* (there's that operative word again) critique groups as well. "At their best, critique groups offer children's book writers a unique opportunity to share their work or work-in-progress with their peers in a safe, supportive, and honest environment, enabling writers to try out their words on an audience and to hear their own words and stories spoken out loud by someone else. Children's book writers who write to make a living must eventually allow their pieces of writing to venture out into the world to be scrutinized and criticized by editors, reviewers, teachers, librarians, and—toughest of all—kids. Often, the gentlest and safest way to start that process is by sharing pieces of writing with a critique group, who can and should offer a balance of support and helpful criticism, as well as pose thoughtful questions and possible solutions."

You're the best, I'm even better: critique group pitfalls

After all this talk about the qualities of a *good* critique group, the lone writer might now be wondering, "What is a *bad* critique group?" Well, there are definitely pitfalls to avoid. It is necessary for a critique group—whether it is made up of experienced or newer writers—to strive for a sense of balance. Cecka says, "It's probably important that there are enough people with knowledge or interest in the kind of writing you do to provide the right kind of commentary; someone who writes mostly YA fantasy may not get much from a critique group that's made up exclusively of picture book writers. Perhaps the most important criteria for evaluating a critique group is whether or not you feel you can trust and respect them as peers. A writer's group isn't about showing off your work or for pointing out the flaws in someone else's work."

One sign that a critique group is not functioning well is that everyone loves everybody's work all of the time. Of course, it's great to hear that your newest idea is "wonderful, lovely, and every kid will want to read it," but that won't get you far if it's the extent of the input you're receiving. It will not assist you in fine tuning a manuscript or making it competitive in a tough marketplace. Thompson agrees, "There are risks to critique groups. A group won't be of much help if the members are so gentle with each other that only praise is offered and no critique."

Even worse than the group in which everyone is a member of everyone else's fan club, is a group in which competition is the main driving force. Get out of this kind of group fast! Critique group members should be generous in nature and interested in nurturing a community of writers. "Writers should be aware that at their worst, critique groups can become overly competitive, particularly if some members are published and some are not," says Dryden. "Some critique groups are not balanced well enough—with one or two people dominating the conversation too often or feeling too free with negative criticism without providing any positive reinforcement. If a writer ever feels uncomfortable in a critique group for any reason, I would urge a writer to remove him or herself from the group immediately, as such a situation will only hurt a writer and their work."

Perhaps most importantly, a critique group should offer writers a safe haven in which trust and respect are the key elements. And each writer should always maintain the conviction of his or her own voice within that community. Only you know what rings true for your style, voice, and manuscript. Welcome the critiques, but be your own best filter. Thompson says, "Beginning writers may find themselves relying too much on the group's reaction rather than on their own gut feelings about a manuscript." Davis agrees, "When sifting through a group's comments remember that, as the saying goes, we can't please everyone all of the time. Some comments may make sense and be enormously helpful, others you may disagree with, and sometimes group members will come down passionately on opposite sides of an issue (just as reviewers sometimes do with published books). As the writer, you know your story and characters best and can best judge which pieces of advice will help make the story clearer, more focused, and more powerful and which pieces go against the grain."

How lone are you?

Now that we've covered the great, as well as the not so great, aspects of critique groups, it's important to mention that these groups are not right for everyone. Some authors work best left to their own devices. Writers always need to do what feels right for them. But for those who do enjoy this type of group dynamic, creating an extended community is an enormous benefit.

Dryden says, "Since the job and craft of writing is such a solitary endeavor, critique groups can provide authors with a community and with a kind of 'touchstone' for information, feedback, and conversation about writing and the process of writing."

Cecka adds, "Being an active part of a writer's community can also help you make sense of the ever-changing publishing landscape. After all, the more feelers out there, the better your prospects. Your peers may be able to recommend certain agents or editors, alert each other to calls for manuscripts, share industry news, or tips picked up from conferences. Remember that participating in a critique group—whether it's a group you meet with once a week in a local coffee house, or a group you know only through e-mail correspondence—is what being a member of the children's writing community is all about. I've had authors tell me that they value the comradery and the supportive shoulder that critique groups offer as much as—and sometimes more than—the critiques themselves."

Clearly, one word stands out when discussing the value of critique groups—community. On a personal note, I feel extremely lucky to have found a group of people that not only provide artistic help and support, but also expand and enhance my sense of community. This is one lone writer who is not so "lone" after all.

From Hocus Pocus to the Newbery: The Writing Life of Sid Fleischman

BY ANNA OLSWANGER

Sid Fleischman is the Newbery-Award winning author of *The Whipping Boy* and several Americana children's classics, including the McBroom series, *By the Great Horn Spoon!*, and *Jim Ugly*. Fleischman, who grew up in San Diego, once traveled in vaudeville as a magician before turning to writing. He's now written over 36 books for children, but started out writing for adults. His first break came during World War II when *Our Navy* paid him six dollars for a short story. "When you're a writer who's never been published, and you see yourself published, it has an impact on you," he says.

Fleischman didn't have a single major influence in his writing. "I remember reading stories by Jack London and J.P. Marquand and John Steinbeck. Those were wonderful stories and, without realizing it at the time, I chose them as my models." He admits that his adult novels all "went out of print in an hour and twenty minutes," but the main reason he never re-established himself in the adult book

Sid Fleischman

world was that he didn't feel the same rewards in writing for adults that he did for kids. "Books don't mean that much to adults," he explains. "To kids, they're primary in their lives."

Fleischman feels blessed in the progression of his career from writing for adults to screenwriting to writing for kids. "By the time I arrived at writing books for children, I had developed a wide range of literary skills, so I was prepared for the technical aspects," he says. He also feels blessed in his personal life. "My wife passed away eight years ago and, of course, I miss her, but otherwise life has been great. I had a good marriage, I have loving and talented kids, I live in a comfortable community in a nice part of the country, and I look younger than my age, so what have I got to complain about?"

Nothing apparently, and neither do the thousands of kids who read his books.

Was there a moment when you chose writing as your life's work?

No, I kind of backed into it without realizing what I was doing. I began writing magic books—these were thin little guides for magicians only—and I didn't even realize I was writing. I was just explaining how to do tricks. Then the books would come out, my name would be on the

ANNA OLSWANGER *lives in New Jersey where she directs the website for UJA Federation of Bergen County & North Hudson. A frequent traveler on Amtrak, she also teaches business writing workshops for the Center for Training and Education at Johns Hopkins University and "Writing for Physicians" for the Stony Brook University Medical School. Anna's "Jewish Book Publishing News" column appears regularly in the Association of Jewish Libraries Newsletter and online. She's a long-time contributor to CWIM. Visit her website, www.olswanger.com.*

cover, and there would be a little splash in the world of magic. I enjoyed this! But I wasn't going to make a living out of magic books, and I began thinking about writing O'Henry-type stories with trick endings. I read *Writer's Digest* and everything I could find in the library on the technique of fiction writing. I was still a magician during those years, and when the Second World War came along, I went in as a magician and came out—hocus pocus—a writer.

Did you start out wanting to be a humorous writer?

No, humor is a quirky thing. You're born with this odd eye or ear or whatever it is, and you see humor in things that pass other people by. I can't explain it. With the exception of the McBroom stories—those are tall tales and I knew I was writing comedy—I don't sit down to write a humorous book. It just happens at the typewriter for me. In real life, I'm only funny two or three times a year.

How did your childhood affect you as a writer?

We all bring whatever we've been through to our writing. I was not gifted with a terrible childhood, so I have very little material there. I had a stable home and great love. But I graduated from high school during the depths of the Depression, and then came the Second World War, so those were the cosmic events of those early years.

How did the Depression affect you?

You had to learn to look after yourself. My father couldn't send me to college so I had to learn to be an autodidact. When I decided I wanted to be a magician, I had to teach myself by going to the libraries and used bookshops and reading everything I could find on the subject. I still have some of those books I bought when I was eleven or twelve years old. When my ambition shifted to writing, I applied those same skills that I had learned as a child of the Depression, of teaching myself, because at that time you couldn't find anyone who could teach you to write. Later, when putting myself through college by giving magic shows, I discovered that colleges couldn't explain the mysteries of writing fiction. So growing up in the Depression molded that aspect of my character and developed those skills which I still use and, fortunately, passed on to my son Paul. I notice with great pleasure that he teaches himself everything, including the bagpipes and the banjo.

How did World War II affect you?

With just a couple of exceptions, I have not written about the war, but it was a great crossroads. I met people from all walks of life, people that I would never have met before and I got multiple views of the world that I didn't have. That helped as a writer.

Have you changed over the years as a writer?

Kids often ask me to write a sequel to earlier novels like *Mr. Mysterious and Company*, which was published 40 years ago. I'm not the same person or the same writer I was then. I could not write a sequel to that book. Now, I reject ideas and lines and scenes that I would have written 20 or 30 years ago. You become more critical. You've done things before and you're not interested in repeating them, so it gets harder to find material you want to run with. If you're going to spend a year or more writing a novel, you have to be very interested in that material or you're not going to bother.

You made a living as a screenwriter before you became a children's book writer. Was screenwriting good training for you?

I learned pacing and how to be efficient. I just read a novel—I won't mention the title but it's on the bestseller list—and it's so overgrown, so weedy with research and details that you need a machete to get through the undergrowth. The poor author can't have a character pick up a pencil without telling you what color it was, what number lead it was, how sharp the point was, how dirty the eraser was. Those are mistakes a writer for children doesn't make. You learn efficiency. You say the most with the least words because kids will not put up with your self-indulgence.

What's your writing day like?

I come downstairs and grab some orange juice, get to my desk, and I'm working in ten to fifteen minutes. I work for an hour or two and then I stop, have breakfast, shower and shave, and then get back to work. When I'm in the early stages of a novel—simultaneously plotting and finding the style and discovering the characters—I'm worn out by noon. God's gift to writers is the nap. I take one.

When I reach the midway point of a novel, I put in a second writing shift before dinner. Finally, coming down the home stretch, with a certain momentum built up, I do nothing but eat, sleep, and write.

Do you accept speaking engagements when you're writing a novel?

When you've been invited to speak, it's deadly to think, "Well, that's next November. I'll have time." It turns out that you need just one or two more days to finish a novel and it drives you crazy to get up, pack, and go to the airport and leave a novel that close to being finished. It's happened to me twice. With my show business background, I enjoy speaking—I'm ham enough that if you put a microphone in my hand, you've got trouble. But I've had to make up my mind, especially since I've gotten older, how I want to spend my life, whether as a writer or a performer. I've chosen writing.

Do you show your work-in-progress to anyone?

Nobody sees anything I write until I'm finished with it—nobody. My editor doesn't even know the subject matter. You want to get some approval when you write something, to have somebody read it and say, "You're a genius!" But if you spring that too early, it takes some of the wind out of your sails. It's better to keep it bottled up until you've finished the thing.

Also, since my working style is fluid, I won't risk having a friend—or an editor—trash an idea while it is still forming. That's a sure way to kill a good idea. If it is a bad idea, listen to that inner voice. You'll hear it.

How many drafts of a manuscript do you write?

I don't write a rough first draft. I write a rough first page and I do that page over and over until I get it as good as I can. Only then do I go on to the next page, and the next. These early pages are tough—they need to juggle in background, character, voice, style, story movement—all at once. And adroitly. By the time I reach page 50 or so, I no longer need to do so much rewriting. By then, I know the characters, I know how they talk, I know what their relationships are, I know what the tensions of the story are, and I've got a fix on where the story is going.

Is this a technique you recommend to new writers?

Yes. No. Just because it works for me not to plot a novel in advance doesn't mean it's going to work for you. I'm full of bad writing habits. Well, they're not bad for me, but they might be bad for you. And that goes for advice you get from other writers. It may fit you, and it may not. So find what fits and find what you're comfortable with. You don't want to write like every other writer. Cloning is for sheep. And don't be discouraged. There are always people out there happy to pull the props out from under you. Just do what you have to do, no matter what people say.

Does writing come easily for you?

You know, writing demands so many different skills: plotting, character, background, dialogue, style. Sometimes it goes swimmingly, and sometimes it doesn't. As I said, I don't plot my novels in advance. I improvise from day to day. Normally I'm a good idea man, but sometimes I have plot problems. Other times, I have problems with scenes or characters or dialogue. I'm suspicious if the story goes too easily. The really good stuff comes out of the problems you have. In solving those problems, you come up with ideas that you would never have had otherwise.

Do you think it's important to answer fan letters?

Terribly important for kids. The moment they drop the letter in the box, they're looking for an answer. After my first few books were published, the mail wasn't heavy and I could give each letter an individual reply. Certain letters now get what doesn't look like a form reply, but it is. It's difficult to keep up.

Which of your books are you the proudest of?

The Whipping Boy is one. *By the Great Horn Spoon!*, a novel about the California Gold Rush, is a second. *By the Great Horn Spoon!* has been continuously in print for more than 40 years and sells a huge number of copies every year. It's widely read in fourth grades in the West. That and *The Whipping Boy*, I suppose, will be my legacy. It's not to say there aren't others out there I'm happy with. I've had fun with the McBroom stories. I love *Mr. Mysterious and Company*— I can't tell you the magicians I've met who were turned on to magic by that novel. And I think *Scarebird* is the best piece of work I've done. I wish I could do it again. It's a picture book, one of those books you feel you wrote under special grace that doesn't visit you often. I had all kinds of problems with it, but the finished book is as close to perfection as I will come.

Reprinted with permission of Greenwillow Books.

A 2001 Greenwillow release, Sid Fleischman's *Bo and Mzzz Mad* adds to his legacy of books chock full of adventure and humor. And, like the author's Newbery-winning *The Whipping Boy*, features an orphan character, recently-orphaned Bo Gamage, who is sent to live with a distant cousin Madeleine (who calls herself Mzzz Mad), his enemy-at-first sight as the result of a long-standing family feud. "My novels are written in the dark," says Fleischman. "As I prefer not to know what's going to happen next, I'm eager to return to my desk each day and find out."

How did winning the Newbery affect your career?

The Newbery changes your life. You know something's hit you and you never quite recover. It's hard on you for the first year because you are asked to speak all over the place. You get so many phone calls and so much mail. It's pleasant and you just roll back and enjoy it and realize you've been anointed. Of course, it has a profound effect on your income because the books sell much better than they did before.

What are some of the intangible rewards of writing for you?

There's the satisfaction in knowing that your books have had an impact. You discover that from the letters you get. Kids tell you they have gotten pleasure from your books, or parents and teachers let you know that one of your books turned a resistant child on to reading. There's also the reward of doing a good job. When you finish a novel, and you've solved the problems, that's a tremendous satisfaction. And there's the reward of the lifestyle that writing has given me. I have complete freedom, although we writers work ourselves much harder than people who have a boss. I work seven days a week, and I don't know how many hours between doing all the things that go along with it—researching, writing, answering the mail. If I were working for a salary, I would want a raise!

What's the most exciting part of writing for you?

After you finish a novel, you don't know where it's going to go. It's like having a child that you watch grow, develop, and send out into the world. A book, too, has to make its way in the world. It may only sell 3,000 copies and vanish from sight. But it may end up as a movie and be translated into many languages. I have books I can't read, in languages ranging from Finnish to Korean and Japanese. You don't know when you write a book what its destiny will be.

If you couldn't be a writer, what would you be?

That's easy. I've kept up with magic. I write articles for magic journals and still invent magic tricks. If I could scrape together a living doing card tricks, that's what I would do.

Do you still perform as a magician?

I don't work professionally anymore, but when I speak at a school, I break the ice with a little magic. They think Shakespeare's going to walk in, and I want to disabuse them in a hurry, so I do a magic trick or two. That eases the tension and we become friends quickly.

Is there a connection for you between magic and writing?

I used to think that one reason I'm good at plotting is that as a magician, I learned to see around corners and I brought that to plotting. By "see around corners," I mean the unexpected. My novels are full of surprises that take a certain magician's cunning. If I think, "I want this card to reappear in a can of coffee," it may take nifty thinking to figure out how to do it. I approach story problems in the same way. Almost always, a solution surfaces.

Also, magic is a performing art. Those scenes I write in a book are really performances on the printed page. The arts cross-pollinate. Much of what I have learned behind the footlights has accompanied me to the typewriter—or computer, as I've finally joined the 21st century!

What's it like to have a son who is also a writer?

It was tough on Paul at the beginning. He started on a novel but abandoned it early on because he realized it was too much in my style. I said, "Paul, I don't have an exclusive option on this genre," but he couldn't go on. He quickly found his own voice—he has a powerful instinct for fiction—and it's a great satisfaction to watch his career develop. You can imagine the excitement in this house when he, too, won the Newbery. We're the only father and son ever to be struck by that happy lightning.

What's your advice to new writers?

It's okay to make mistakes early on. Those are finger exercises, those first stories that you write. But you have to keep in mind that you're competing with professionals when you sit down to write a story. You'd better be as good or even better than the professionals. People would regard it as ridiculous to pick up a violin and expect to play Carnegie Hall, and yet they sit down and write a story and expect it to be published. That's not realistic, especially when it comes to fiction which is full of traps and invisible technique.

How long does it takes to learn "invisible technique?"

It's a game of patience. It's not apt to happen overnight. You have to pace yourself and give yourself a long view. In five years, you can learn to write fiction. Eudora Welty said a marvelous thing and this goes for all writing: each novel teaches you how to write it, but not how to write the next one, and that's the rub. You have to learn to write good dialogue and good descriptions and you have to learn to develop characters who cast shadows. It takes time to learn these techniques.

But what's the hurry?

Reprinted with permission of HarperCollins

Prolific author Sid Fleischman earned the 1987 Newbery Medal for *The Whipping Boy*, the story of Jemmy, an orphan taken from the streets to take corporal punishment on behalf of Prince Brat as "it was forbidden to spank, thrash, cuff, smack or whip a prince." A *New York Times* book reviewer declares *The Whipping Boy* "full of adventure, suspense, humor and lively characters. This is indisputably a good, rollicking adventure." Fleischman counts the book as one that he's most proud of.

Richard Peck on Awards, History, Listening & Teaching

BY KELLY MILNER HALLS

Considering he's been published for three decades, it's hard to believe children's novelist Richard Peck started writing late in life. But a 20-year teaching career advanced a literary calling that, like the winged-heeled Hermes, almost immediately took flight, once it began.

Thirty-plus novels later, Peck's standing seemed to have peaked when he was given the American Library Association's Newbery Award in January of 2002 for *A Year Down Yonder* (Dial 2000), until George W. Bush upped the ante. On April 22, 2002, flanked by First Lady and former librarian Laura Bush, the President of the United States named Richard Peck a National Humanities Medal Recipient, and slipped the gleaming award around his neck.

Devoutly opposed to both vulgar language and censorship, Peck is exactly what his champions suggest he is—a true original, held in high esteem by both his peers and his readers. On a personal level, as well as in fiction, he has countless stories yet to tell, as this interview reveals.

Photo: Sonya Sones

Richard Peck

When was your first book published, and how many have you written since then?

Let's see. . . . I'm not sure how many. I know the first one was published in 1972, and I've written a book a year ever since. If I'm not writing a book, I'm thinking about writing a book, though the Newbery did cost me one.

How do you feel about winning the National Humanities Medal in April 2002?

Oh, it was like the Newbery—another bolt from out of the blue. I'm honored, or course. This is the first time a children's book has medalled. But I don't know what to think about it. Mrs. Bush has done so much for literacy and young people. Last fall, the weekend before September 11, she hosted the first National Book Conference—a high moment in my life.

There were 60-some writers featured. We read from our works in tents on the grounds of the Library of Congress and the U.S. Capital. Hundreds of people were expected to attend. I think thousands actually came. Mrs. Bush didn't just lend her name to it, she made it happen. Three

KELLY MILNER HALLS *is a full-time freelance writer living in Spokane, WA. Her work regularly appears in* Ask, Booklist, Book Links, *the* Chicago Tribune, Denver Post, FamilyFun, Guidepost for Teens, Teen People, *the* Washington Post, Writer's Digest *and dozens of other publications. She has six children's books in print including,* I Bought a Baby Chicken *(Boyds Mills Press), and four more on the way, including,* Editors and the Business of YA Lit, *for Scarecrow Press. Halls is the single mother of two daughters, three dogs and more cats than is prudent. She can be reached via her website, www.kellymilnerhalls.com.*

days later, that world came to an end. And we discovered that now, more than ever, we need to read to our children. Let yours be the last voice your child hears before they go to sleep.

You've written at least 34 books. Which one do you consider your best work, and why?

All of these awards have come to me for later books. So I am apparently not the best judge of my writing. But I believe *Remembering the Good Times* is the best work I can do. It centers on a subject I think needs to be considered by the young. It dramatizes the classic signs of suicide. I was glad teachers used that book in schools because I don't write them for me. I write them for young people. I certainly didn't see a Newbery for *A Year Down Yonder*, a sequel to *A Long Way from Chicago*. When the phone call came, it was, as I said, a real bolt from the blue. I'd received the silver medal for *A Long Way from Chicago*, two years before. Astonishing.

You are well-loved by your peers and colleagues. Does their admiration and friendship mean a lot to you?

It means everything to me. When I gave my acceptance speech for the Newbery, it was my opportunity to thank my colleagues. In children's literature, we don't feel competitive with each other. We're not at each other's throats. We see each other as floating faculty. It's a wonderful group of people.

You mentor new writers. Why are you so generous in that respect?

I always like to do that. When editors send me a first book by a new novelist, I think, "How exciting. What does this new voice have to say?" When I read Chris Crutcher's first novel, *Running Loose*, I found that as I came to the last few pages, I was standing. That was a very good sign.

As I get older, am longer in the field, I could begin to fear they'll know things I don't know and sweep me out. But if I embrace them, and learn from them, I am still one of them. That's the wonderful thing about writing.

It's not like football and ballet. It doesn't matter how old you are. Seeing these new writers, young people starting out, keeps you anxious—reminds you not to rest on your laurels.

Did anyone step up to mentor you when you started writing?

No. Nobody. Except for a pile of 30 young adult novels, I did it all on my own. Those were my only companions. And frankly, I never expected the book to be published. But some of my early books did well. *Are You in the House Alone*, won an Edgar Allen Poe Award. It was my first real recognition among my peers, and it seemed to me, invalid. I didn't see the book as a mystery.

It sounds like you have more stories to tell.

I do. I've decided I'm going to do more historical fiction. One of my most helpful resources as a writer is the school visit. I have the opportunity to talk with young people about what they're reading and doing. And I find they don't read any history. That may seem like a reason *not* to write history. But it's also a reason to undertake it. I love insinuating history into a story. That is what interests me the most, right now.

Why the jump from contemporary fiction to historic?

When I started out, it was a field of contemporary books on contemporary issues. And they were the books that excited me when I began. Chris Crutcher's *Running Loose* came just after I started. Terry Davis's *Vision Quest*, so true it almost couldn't be marketed to young people. Since I had just come from teaching, that immediacy appealed to me. Now that I'm older, I'm more concerned about history. I ask students, "What year was your parent born?" and to my

By the Newbery-winning author of A YEAR DOWN YONDER

FAIR WEATHER

A NOVEL BY
RICHARD PECK

Jacket art by Charles Graham, courtesy of the Chicago Historical Society. Reprinted with permission of Dial Books for Young Readers.

Fair Weather (Dial), Richard Peck's follow-up to the Newbery-winning *A Year Down Yonder*, combines the historical significance of the 1893 Chicago World's Fair, energy, humor and even black & white photographs to bring to life the year in which Ferris wheels, hamburgers and postcards were introduced. Peck began writing historical fiction because he believes that we must give history familial significance to "convince our young people that history is not dry." Booksellers chose *Fair Weather* as a Favorite Novel of the Year in *Publishers Weekly*'s "Off the Cuff" awards.

dismay, many do not know. Imagine having so few roots. Imagine not having heard and really listened to your own parents' stories. It's tragic.

Did you listen as a boy?

I think I did. As you may have noticed, there is an elderly person in all of my novels—not a traditional older person, but rather a feisty survivor. I realize you can't write a novel with the intent to change people. But you can hope to get their attention and make them think. I never name the town where Grandma Dowdel lives. That's purposeful. I don't want to.

I want my readers to imagine their grandparent's town. Imagine, my books are even translated into Japanese, so those young people can imagine a setting in Japan, assuming it translates well. The Japanese translator actually got my phone number and called, completely puzzled. She was out of her depth because these books were written in dialect. She said, " 'Don't let the door hit you where the dog bit you.' What means that?"

You are famous for your distinctive characterizations. Which of those characters most closely mirrors Richard Peck if any?

Well, they are all me, of course. As I write, I play all the parts. But I put them together as composites based on other people's memories. I go to my country cousins and ask, "What did your grandmother tell you about life here?" I do a lot of research in the library, too. But I want to go to living people who have had those stories handed down, as well. I don't use them as they are remembered. But I might think of parallel stories the facts inspire.

How do you keep historic characters authentic?

You have to come up with a voice that does not sound contemporary, even if it isn't a voice you can hear. When I was a kid, elderly people remembered going to the fair, but now all those voices are gone. I try to remember the rhythm of their speech in order to capture the past.

Speaking of speeches, you do a lot of public speaking engagements. Do you prepare your statements in advance?

I do prepare, because I don't like what comes out of my mouth when I'm not prepared. I think about the rhythms of speech, perfectly illustrated by poetry. In fact, I always put poetry—my own or someone else's—in my books to make the point that poetry and prose are not so different.

Are you adversely affected by any of the writers you currently read?

I am influenced by adult writing. I very often find it long and indulgent. I am in a field where I want to be. In children's literature, we could never resort to pornography to mask bad writing. Ours is a work of delicate balance between word and deed. A novel that is all action is a video game. A novel that is all talk is a chat room. Thankfully, we have something better to offer—a ticket out of town and a message—that nobody grows up in a group. You grow up in spite of the group, because you find your own way. When you discover you can find your own way, it's empowering.

You grew up in Chicago. Many of your books are set in Chicago. How did you wind up living in New York City?

My childhood dream was to live in New York. I decided early on, I wasn't going to settle down anywhere—even in Chicago—until I'd tried New York. When a teaching job in New York came along, I thought I would go for a year or so. That was in 1965, and I've been here ever since.

How soon after you came to New York did you start writing?

I discovered the publishers within the first year. But we ought not be too nostalgic. It wasn't easy, even then. When I entered the field in 1971, a very prominent author told me I could not make it in this field. "Johnson is not in the White House anymore," he said, "so the Great Society money is no longer raining down on schools. The great days are over, dried up, finished." But he was wrong. And there are opportunities now that weren't there when I got started—the Society of Children's Book Writers and Illustrators, for example.

What will it take for a would-be writer to make it today?

If you have two qualities—a love of language and a curiosity about other people—you have a hope in this business. So many young people can't manage it at 21 or 22 years old because they have not learned to listen. And writing is about listening. People are very generous with their stories.

Since you were a listener, an observer, do you use personal experience in your books?

I never write about my own memories. Everybody tends to be revisionist and stereotypical about their own memories. Everyone thinks they had to walk through the snowdrifts to get to school. I'll have an occasionally realistic breakthrough—yes, I did have to negotiate with my father in order to get the car to go on my own date. And yes, I never let anything keep me from winning a full scholarship to college. But nobody would read a novel about that. Other people's memories are the truly rich stores.

What skills did you take from teaching and apply to your work as a writer?

On a teaching day, you don't have time to think about yourself. You're aware that you're the oldest person in the room, perhaps. But you're surrounded by these voices. You're too busy to think about yourself. It's not so different as a writer. I'm not worried about me, when I write. I'm worried about the page.

You once said, "I fell easy prey to teachers. My mother had read to me and made me hungry for school and books. But my teachers betrayed no interest in my ideas." How did that affect your desire to write?

I think it's very hard to teach people to be writers. It's especially hard if the teacher is not a writer. But I did learn the concept of discipline before pleasure—a concept we no longer have the authority as educators to impose. But my teachers would never put a grade on a rough draft, so I never turned one in. And I never sent a rough draft to a publisher.

Are you concerned about today's children and their families? Do you sense a lack of that same strict discipline?

It's missing from the home and the school. My mother made a writer out of me in the first five years of my life, so I had something to take to school. I had a sense of the narrative and vocabulary. In fact, I had a ninth-grade vocabulary in the first grade. I wrote and spoke in emulation of the adults in my life. Parents today have abandoned that opportunity. So kids emulate the strongest teen leader. As a result, the peer group has replaced the parent.

You seem to have a fairly conservative mindset. You are very careful about not using "bad" language. And yet your books are banned. How can you explain that?

Well, I have written ghost stories. And *Are You in the House Alone* was about a rape. But censorship isn't really about books. It's about control. Every word a writer writes is censorable, because there are failed parents looking for a scapegoat. Book burners never have happy home lives. So you have to give yourself permission not to let it impact you—not to self-censor.

Now you've turned to historical fiction—the Civil War. How can you win young people over to fondly remembering the past?

All writing is a search for our roots. We, as a species, don't like the idea of coming out of a vacuum. So we are compelled to create an alternate set of memories, to replace those we don't have. If we want to convince our young people that history is not dry, we will need to turn it into a family story. Think of it. The Civil War wasn't just a series of battles. It was brother-fighting-brother. We must capture that on the page. Give history a human face.

You sound like a teacher again when you talk about historical fiction.

I *am* still a teacher. I'm still wondering, "How would I present this in class? What would the kid in the back row think of this? How can I gather these unruly sheep into my flock?" I am writing for young people. That's simply part of the job.

First Books

BY MICHELLE HOWRY

Saying the words, "I am a writer" is hard for many of us. Sure, we write sometimes. Maybe we scribble down an idea or two in the morning or before bed. We fit writing in among all the little duties and pleasures and aggravations that make up our daily lives. But sometimes it's hard to think of ourselves as "writers"—aren't real writers *different* from us somehow? More serious? More talented? More committed?

But if there's one thing that the following interviews demonstrate, it's just how wide-ranging, diverse, and inclusive the term "writer" really is. The authors in this article write in a wide variety of genres, formats, and age-levels—everything from picture books to cookbooks to YA novels. All of them worked on their projects for years before they were finally published. All of them faced some obstacles, but worked to overcome them. What unites all these writers— and what connects all of them to us—is their passion for writing. All of them are writers . . . just like you.

CLARE CRESPO
The Secret Life of Food (Hyperion)

Photo: Eric Staudenmaier

Clare Crespo has always been known among her friends as a "crazy food person." She's the one who always brings something unusual to a potluck dinner, and nothing in her kitchen can ever quite be taken at face value. A meatloaf is fashioned to look like a football. Her cupcakes are decorated to resemble sushi. Rather than gingerbread men, she makes gingerbread skeletons.

In her first book, *The Secret Life of Food*, Crespo brings readers inside her kitchen to create these, and other, wacky culinary creations. Impishly illustrated with bright, fanciful photographs by Eric Staudenmaier, the book is part cookbook, part art manual. And that was Crespo's goal—she's always thought of herself as just as much of a visual artist as a writer. "For me, food is an art supply," she says.

Crespo has been creating "food sculptures" for quite some time. In her hometown of L.A., she had several food-themed art shows in local galleries. Her website (www.yummyfun.com) presented some of her recipes in an animated format on the Web. The website started getting some attention, and Crespo was asked to teach a kids' cooking class. Before she knew it, word started getting out about her innovative, irreverent approach to food. "I was just doing what I love as an artist, and people started noticing," she says.

One of the people who noticed Crespo's art was an editor at Melcher Media, a West Coast book packager known for producing well-designed, art-intensive books. Acting like a cross between a literary agent and a book publisher, a book packager creates a fully fleshed-out book idea and sells it to a publishing house. Then the packager works with the publisher to actually design, create, and produce the book. Large publishing houses often work with book packagers on labor-intensive illustrated books that their own in-house staffs simply don't have time to produce. Crespo's kid's

MICHELLE HOWRY *is an editor of adult nonfiction books at Penguin Putnam, Inc., and the author of* Agents, Editors, and You *(Writer's Digest Books).*

cookbook was such a project—and with Melcher's help she created a dummy of the book to shop around to publishers.

While most of the recipes in *The Secret Life of Food* had been created several years earlier, it took a lot of work to bring the project from idea to published book. Crespo and Melcher shopped the book dummy around to various publishers, and they got some strong interest from Hyperion Books for Children. "Hyperion liked my recipes and aesthetic, but they wanted the book to be designed differently," she says. "It took a few months to figure out what the new design would be, what the recipes would be, and how the photography would look."

Once Crespo finally worked out a deal with Melcher and Hyperion, the hard part began: creating the book. One of the first tasks was finding the right photographer to capture the essence of her edible art. She met with many photographers and soon realized that she didn't want to use a traditional food photographer, with their reverential approach to shooting food. The look she wanted for the photographs in the book was playful, surprising, a little kooky but still appealing. Now she had to

Jacket photo © Eric Staudenmaier. Reprinted with permission of Hyperion Books for Young Readers.

To showcase her fun "food sculptures," Clare Crespo worked with a book packager to create a dummy for *The Secret Life of Food*, which was then published by Hyperion. A *Booklist* reviewer says of Crespo's debut, "adventurous kids will love the kitschy, chic style and the raucous humor, as well as Crespo's notion that 'food is an art supply.'"

find someone to help her execute it. "I was hoping that this was going to be a picture book as well as a cookbook," Crespo says.

She finally settled on Staudenmaier, an architectural photographer, because she wanted her food to be shot in the "real world." Better known for shooting buildings than gourmet meals, he was a surprising choice and one that Crespo had to justify to her publisher. "I had to defend my ideas about the design and photography, but the editors trusted me for the most part. It was a good give-and-take process." Together, they brainstormed appropriate settings for all of the dishes—Tarantula Cookies crawling up a wall, Monster Head Potatoes peeking out from underneath a bed, and Potato Flip-Flops sitting alongside a pool. "Eric was so good at finding interesting shots in the environments that I wanted the food to be in," she says. "It was a great collaboration."

One of the biggest surprises for Crespo was how much this book took over her life during its creation. For six months, she was intensively writing and rewriting the text and captions for the book, as well as overseeing the photography. In fact, all of the photography was shot in and around her home (and in the homes and backyards of friends), and she whipped up all the food for the photographs in her own kitchen. "Every surface of my house was covered in crazy food for the shoot," she says. "I'm still finding frosting in weird places! I was completely (literally) living with my book."

Readers of all ages have really responded to her book, but what's really gratifying for Crespo is how kids have reacted to *The Secret Life of Food*. "A kid came up to me recently and called me the "Monkey Pop Lady." The best part, she says, is hearing how her book inspires people to use their imaginations to create their own culinary creations. "I get a lot of letters and e-mails from kids (and grown-ups!) telling me what kind of stuff they have come up with in their own kitchens since getting my book. I love that! I hope the book shows people what's possible if you open your brain a little."

LISA KOPELKE
Excuse Me! (Simon & Schuster)

As difficult as it is for a first-time picture-book writer to get published, it's even *more* difficult to convince agents and editors to look at the work of a novice author/illustrator. It's considered to be one of the "cardinal rules" of children's publishing: picture book writers should never, never submit artwork with their books. Authors are told to leave the illustrations to the publisher, who will match their words with an experienced illustrator. But Lisa Kopelke dispelled that myth with her first book *Excuse Me!*, the tale of the trials and tribulations of a burping frog and his path toward discovering manners—and friendship.

Kopelke has no formal art background, but she's an "artist by birth" who has studied and made art all her life. Her illustrations are rich and textured, playful oil paintings full of layering and light. "I want my art to look like how chocolate tastes," she says. Though she was confident about her own art abilities, she admits she entered the writing and publishing process with some trepidation. She knew a bit about how picture books were traditionally published, and she was worried that it would be difficult to interest anyone in an unproved author/illustrator. But when she met her agent, Steven Malk, she was surprised to find that he was *excited* to be working with someone who could both illustrate and write. Her eventual editor, David Gale at Simon & Schuster, felt the same way.

While she'd been making art for years, Kopelke had always harbored a secret wish to write children's books. She'd been an avid journaler in her youth, but as adult she found it difficult to make the time to write—family, work, and myriad other distractions always seemed to get in the way. But when a move to Las Vegas in 2000 uprooted her life, she took the opportunity to focus her energies and get serious about writing. "I just sat down one day and said to myself, I've always talked about writing—I should just try it."

First-time author/illustrator Lisa Kopelke took a chance and sent material to an agent after "listening in" on an Internet chat with him. "I didn't really have a backup plan if that didn't work," she admits. But it paid off—Kopelke wrote and illustrated *Excuse Me!*, published by Simon & Schuster. Her funny picture book follows a food-loving, prone-to-belching frog as he learns some manners.

She began to do some serious research about children's writing, spending hours on the Internet and reading books by authors whose work she admired. One of the very first sites she came across was author Verla Kay's website (www.verlakay.com). Kay had compiled a website full of resources for writers—industry information, interviews with editors and agents, and online forums. It was here that Kopelke took in an online chat with agent Steven Malk.

"I had this inkling that I wanted an agent," she said, "and when I read his bio I *knew* he was the one I wanted to work with." She felt an instant connection—both were originally from San Diego, and several of his clients were writers who Kopelke admired. When it came time for her to start submitting her work, she sent her material to Malk right away. "I didn't really have a backup plan if that didn't work," she admits.

Luckily, Malk had an immediate positive reaction to her work, too. He called her the very next week, and together they embarked on an intensive writing and editing process that's still ongoing. Malk gave Kopelke some initial feedback, and he also matched her with three other young writers he represented to establish a critique group. At the time, only one of the group had been published, but since then all four have received book deals.

After a few months of work, Kopelke and Malk agreed that the manuscript was ready to start submitting to editors. One of the first and most interested editors was David Gale at Simon & Schuster. More revisions followed, but one thing Kopelke really liked was Gale's explicit, direct instructions. "He outlined exactly what he wanted to see changed, which was really awesome," she said. "Everyone's always trying to figure out what it is that editors want, and he pretty much laid it on the table for me." Finally, after one more round of revisions, they signed a contract for *Excuse Me!*. The picture book, geared for readers ages 4-8, is a fall 2002 release.

Though the back-and-forth of revision is exhausting, Kopelke credits much of her success to the constant feedback on her work offered by her agent, her editor, and others. "I need people to help guide me," she says. "When you write and constantly revise, you get so close to your work that you can't see it anymore. You can't see what's working." With the help of Malk, Gale, her critique group, and others, she was able to hone the story and make it even stronger.

"When you're just looking at a finished book, it's really intimidating," she says, "Everything appears so well planned out, from the jacket to the interior to the ending. And when you start submitting, you have to make it *look* as if you have it well thought out . . . but you also have to know that it's not set in stone." This was particularly true in her case, since she was working on the artwork as well as the words. "Once I started working with my editor and the art director at Simon & Schuster, I found that they all had a vision for the book as well, one that might not exactly match mine. But that inspired more creativity from me. A book takes on a whole new character when you start working with other people."

But it was the freedoms, not the limitations, of working on the artwork that surprised Kopelke the most. "I could try anything I wanted with the artwork," she says. "Because of today's technology, there are really no limits." With the help of her art director, Kopelke enlarged, shrunk, and used wacky media in her paintings. The result is a carefree, exciting book that captures the imagination of young readers. "Everything kind of made sense and fell into place," she says.

CATHRYN CLINTON
The Calling (Candlewick Press)

At first, a 12-year-old Christian faith healer might not seem to be the most likely protagonist for a mainstream children's novel. But Cathryn Clinton's *The Calling* (Candlewick Press) isn't an easily classifiable book. It's the story of Esta Lea Ridley, who surprises her congregation, her family, and herself by discovering that she has the ability to heal the sick, simply by laying her hands upon them. A complex, multilayered book, it's been praised for its non-preachy, matter-of-fact storytelling and its authentic depiction of rural Southern life. For Clinton, writing as Esta Lea came naturally. "I have always heard her voice in my mind," she says.

Clinton acknowledges that discussing religion and faith can be off-limits for many children's book writers. But she believes in the adage "write what you know." Clinton comes from a family of Southern preachers, and says

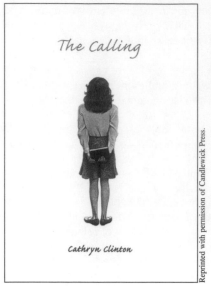

The Calling

Cathryn Clinton

Reprinted with permission of Candlewick Press.

Poet-turned-novelist Cathryn Clinton's first book *The Calling* features a 12-year-old Christian faith healer called Esta Lea. "As readers enter Esta Lea's world, Clinton provides moving insights into the nature of faith and prayer," says *Publishers Weekly* "While these are weighty underpinnings, they neither slow nor overshadow a taut story line. The audience does not need to share Esta Lea's religious beliefs in order to appreciate her conflicts and to become engrossed in her concerns."

that episodes from the novel such as Esta Lea healing a young girl's blindness and the restoration of her grandmother's hearing are drawn from real-life events. "These stories came from a variety of different sources, most of them within my family," she says. "I took all of them and put them into one gigantic story."

But while storytelling itself came easily to Clinton, writing novels for children was not her original plan. As a wife and mother of two children, she studied poetry at the University of Iowa—taking one class per semester for fourteen years to get a B.A. "I got hooked on writing," she says. Having the opportunity to study among top-notch novelists and poets at the famous Iowa Writers' Workshop was an amazing opportunity for her. Listening to some of the most talented visiting professors sharing their work, "I would just sit there mesmerized and think, *this is what I want to do*."

But while poetry was her first literary love, having kids began to awaken an interest and appreciation of children's literature. "I just read constantly to them—three books at naptime, three books at night—for years," she says. Through her children's voracious appetite for books, Clinton's attention began to turn toward books for younger readers. She enrolled in the graduate program at Vermont College to pursue an MFA in children's literature, and she started writing her first longer-form stories for her classes there. After studying poetry for so many years, working on a novel-length work was quite an adjustment. "I had spent ten years cutting, cutting, cutting my words. I was used to thinking 'small.' Now I had to learn a whole new way to write."

The MFA program was an intense experience—students were required to write 20-25 hours per week, and they were constantly studying with visiting teachers and writing in a variety of genres and formats. Just like at Iowa, she was challenged and inspired by the caliber of writers she was studying with. "The people that they brought in to do guest lectures were all the authors I'd been reading to my kids," she says.

One of the teachers she studied with at Vermont was Amy Ehrlich, an editor at Candlewick Press and a successful writer in her own right. "I was hoping to really be able to connect with Amy," Clinton says, "not only because she was an editor, but because she had written in every single genre. She's done picture books, chapter books, everything." It was with Ehrlich that Clinton developed her first novel, *A Stone in My Pocket*. Ehrlich read the book, about a young Palestinian girl living on the Gaza Strip whose father was killed during terrorist violence, and immediately saw the talent and promise in Clinton's work. It was also during this time that the two also started working on the manuscript that would eventually become *The Calling*. Clinton calls Ehrlich a "Maxwell Perkins type of editor" who believed in her as a writer and helped her craft the idea into a fully-formed story.

Over the course of the MFA program in children's writing, Clinton created a prodigious output of work—two novels and eight picture books. It was a daunting pace, she says, but "I was determined to graduate, and I didn't want it to take me another 14 years to do it." All her hard work paid off on graduation day, when she received her diploma . . . and a contract from Ehrlich to publish both her novels from Candlewick Press. *The Calling* was published in Fall 2001, and *A Stone in My Pocket* in Fall 2002.

"Both books have taken a lot longer than I thought they would to get published," she says. Between the editing, the rewriting, and the production and publication process, it's taken several years for the books to finally come to fruition. But she knows that delays and long lead times are parts of the whole publishing process, parts that a writer really doesn't have too much say over. Her control and leverage, says Clinton, is in making her manuscripts as strong as they can be while they're still in her hands. "I think that the whole process of writing is working and working and *working* until you get your words to be what you really want them to be," she says. "If you're going to be a good writer, you're going to be working at it for the rest of your life. It doesn't stop."

Neither, apparently, does Clinton, who is currently at work on a third novel, this one about a 16-year-old girl whose attempted suicide leads her to a friendship with a 60-year-old widow. "I just love fiction because you can make it into the story you always wanted it to be. Growing up you were always told not to exaggerate, and now I can exaggerate all I want."

ALEX SANCHEZ
Rainbow Boys (Simon & Schuster)

Alex Sanchez has always written. But for most of his life, he avoided writing about one major truth in his life—his homosexuality. "Being gay was hard for me to write about because of my own internalized homophobia," he says. "Even though I would write a lot, my writing wasn't very real or true to my experience—it wasn't about my feelings and my life." But in 2001, Sanchez published the YA novel *Rainbow Boys*, the story of three gay teens and the struggles they face coming to terms with their sexuality, their relationships, and themselves. "I came to the point in my life when I decided that I needed to be honest in my writing," he says. "Writing the book was part of my own coming out process."

Since its publication, *Rainbow Boys* has been hailed as groundbreaking, the book was named a Best Book for Young Adults by the American Library Association, and the School Library Journal has likened Sanchez's writing to Judy Blume's. Heady praise indeed, but Sanchez maintains that he was "just telling the story he needed to tell."

Not that it's always been easy. During one early writing workshop, Sanchez was working on a story with a gay-themed character, and his writing instructor was less than supportive. It was an incident that really set him back, but one that he ultimately credits for strengthening his resolve to continue writing. Several years later, he decided to try again. With the help of more supportive teachers at the Washington D.C.-area organization The Writer's Center, he started getting the encouragement, feedback, and support he needed.

"One very important thing for me has been surrounding myself with people who are going to give me confidence," he says. "Because writing is such a solitary process, it's important to have people who cheer me along on the way." Sanchez found another such supportive community at The Fine Arts Workshop in Provincetown, Massachusetts, during its week-long summer workshops each year. And it was an instructor at one such workshop who was so impressed by Sanchez's work that she offered a recommendation to an agent, Miriam Altshuler, who agreed to represent him.

Alex Sanchez's first novel *Rainbow Boys* follows the lives of three gay teens and the varying ways they deal with their own homosexuality and each other. Until the last few years, there have been few books published portraying gay teenagers, "or at least books in which the gay character didn't get killed at the end or commit suicide," says Sanchez. "As I got into the process of writing, it became apparent that this was the book I wished I'd had when I was young."

Reprinted with permission of Simon & Schuster.

During the next few years, Sanchez kept crafting his writing. First with Altshuler, and then with his editor at Simon & Schuster, he continued to hone his story. *Rainbow Boys* is told alternately through the different points of view of the three main characters—a device that works well to demonstrate the breadth of their experiences. "I think it added to the intensity of the story," he says.

One of the most gratifying things for Sanchez has been the overwhelming response he's received to the book. A reality of young adult publishing is that, until a few years ago, there was a real lack of books being published that portrayed gay teens, "or at least books in which the gay character didn't get killed at the end or commit suicide," Sanchez says. "As I got into the process of writing, it became apparent that this was the book I wished I'd had when I was young."

But interestingly, *Rainbow Boys* has struck a chord with others, too. "There are so many out gay and lesbian people now, it's hard to find someone who does not know someone who is openly gay," Sanchez says. "Whenever I give a reading, it's not only gay teens who come up to talk with me, it's everyone—people who share their experiences with a gay child, a gay aunt, a gay colleague. There's a lot less stigma about it, and there's also a lot more compassion and understanding and acceptance."

Right now, Sanchez is hard at work on a sequel to *Rainbow Boys* titled *Rainbow High*, which follows the three protagonists through the second half of their senior year of high school. Other books may follow, and Sanchez hopes that the success of his book also opens up doors for others who are exploring gay themes in their work. "The audience is there," he says. "My goal is to give gay and lesbian kids courage and allow them to see themselves in print. But then also to reach non-gay kids to help create empathy and understanding."

MELANIE JONES
Balls (Children's Press/Grolier)

"I think I've been a writer all my life," says Melanie Jones. "I just didn't always call myself one." She'd been writing for nearly 10 years—plugging away at stories, attending writing conferences, and even getting close to publication a few times—but she never quite felt like the real thing. That is, until she landed two book contracts within a month of each other, one for the easy reader *Balls* with Children's Press/Grolier, and one for the picture book *Pigs Rock!* with Viking. "I was in sort of a daze for a week," she says.

Her first book, *Balls*, is a rhyming "easy reader" in the Grolier Rookie Reader series. Featuring golf balls, beach balls, and everything in between, the book helps young readers learn letters and numbers using simple counting concepts and an easy to understand format. A former first grade teacher, Jones found herself naturally drawn to books written with the beginning reader in mind—books with short, simple sentences that reinforce kids' developing language skills. And with a husband and three sons who are all avid outdoors enthusiasts, writing a book about sports was a natural extension of her daily family life.

But the first incarnation of the book, focusing only on baseball and entitled *Fly Ball*, was rejected by an editor due to forces entirely outside of Jones's control—it was too similar to another title going to press in the Rookie Readers series. It wasn't a dead-end, though. "The editor gave me some positive feedback and said she'd like to see some more of my work," Jones says, and she began the hard work of refocusing and revising her story based on the suggestions. The editor at Grolier agreed to take another look, and she eventually offered Jones a contract for the book—followed just three weeks later by a call from Viking asking to publish her picture book, which she'd submitted months earlier.

While Jones's publishing spree is the sort of success that many writers dream of, her accomplishment was grounded in years of hard work. She is a longtime member of the Society of Children's Book Writers and Illustrators (SCBWI), and work on the book that was to become *Balls* started at an SCBWI writing retreat held in rural Alabama. It was an intensive, instructive workshop that Jones credits for pointing her in the right direction with her writing. "The retreat gave me just the boost I needed," she says.

Though she takes time to think about her stories everyday, Jones admits her writing routine isn't always as "consistent" as she'd like it to be. Even with the help of her critique partner and the looming deadlines that come with book contracts, Jones still finds it a struggle sometimes to keep disciplined and stay on target with her writing. She notices a difference, too, between her habits when she's writing for different age levels. With easy readers, "I don't work quite the same with picture books," she says. "Picture books take me a little longer to write, and I tend to have to revise more."

Jones sold both her books without the help of an agent, a choice that has worked out well for her. And while she says she's had great experiences working with her editors at both of the publishing houses she's sold books to, she admits she *has* thought about finding an agent for future projects. "I think getting an agent is a very personal choice, and so much of it has to do with personalities," she says. For now, she's content to work without an agent while holding out for someone she really clicks with. "The relationship has to be a good fit, or eventually there will be problems," she says.

One reason she feels comfortable working without an agent has been the strong relationships she's built with her editors. "The ending of *Balls* had to be revised to make it a little stronger," she says. "It worked out great, and the book was much better because of the changes. My editor is really good about helping me make the text as strong as it can be. It's been a collaborative effort."

Another successful collaborative relationship has been between Jones and the illustrator for *Balls*, Linda Bronson. Though her heart was "pounding" when she looked at the illustrations for the first time, Jones was thrilled with the result. She did, however, offer one suggestion after showing the illustrations to her kindergarten-age son Justin: simplify the illustrations. "He had trouble counting the balls without counting some twice—there were just too many for a beginning reader to count." In this case, her background as a teacher and a mother let her offer some valuable feedback to her editors, and the illustration was re-drawn using fewer balls. "Unless you know your audience, you may not think of things like this," she says.

Getting to know her audience is something Jones continues to strive for. She estimates she brings home about twenty books a week from her local library, and she's always encouraging other aspiring writers to "read, read, and read some more. Then when you feel like you know enough, keep reading." She must be doing something right—she's been signed for three additional easy readers with Children's Press/Grolier after the fall 2003 publication of *Balls*, and the Viking picture book *Pigs Rock!* will be published in spring 2003. "I do feel more pressure now to continue working and sell more books," she says, "And I've also learned that just because you are published, it doesn't guarantee the next book. You still have to work and polish each manuscript or it just won't be accepted."

Former first-grade teacher Melanie Jones is naturally drawn to books written with the beginning reader in mind—books with short, simple sentences that reinforce kids' developing language skills. It makes sense, then, that her first book, *Balls*, is rhyming "easy reader" in the Grolier Rookie Reader series. Featuring golf balls, beach balls, and everything in between, the book helps young readers learn letters and numbers using simple counting concepts and an easy to understand format.

Key to Symbols & Abbreviations

N Indicates a listing new in this edition.

Indicates a Canadian listing.

Indicates a publisher produces educational material.

Indicates an electronic publisher or publication.

Indicates a book packager/producer.

Indicates a change to a company's mailing address since the 2002 edition.

A Indicates a publisher accepts agented submissions only.

Indicates an award-winning publisher.

• Indicates a comment from the editors of *Children's Writer's & Illustrator's Market*.

ms or **mss** Stands for manuscript or manuscripts.

SASE Refers to a self-addressed stamped envelope.

SAE Refers to a self-addressed envelope.

IRC Stands for International Reply Coupon. These are required with SAEs sent to markets in countries other than your own.

b&w Stands for black & white.

Important Listing Information

- Listings are based on questionnaires, phone calls and updated copy. They are not advertisements nor are markets reported here necessarily endorsed by the editor of this book.
- Information in the listings comes directly from the companies and is as accurate as possible, but situations may change and needs may fluctuate between the publication of this directory and the time you use it.
- *Children's Writer's & Illustrator's Market* reserves the right to exclude any listing that does not meet its requirements.

Complaint Procedure

If you feel you have not been treated fairly by a listing in *Children's Writer's & Illustrator's Market*, we advise you to take the following steps:

- First try to contact the listing. Sometimes one phone call or a letter can quickly clear up the matter.
- Document all your correspondence with the listing. When you write to us with a complaint, provide the details of your submission, the date of your first contact with the listing and the nature of your subsequent correspondence.
- We will enter your letter into our files and attempt to contact the listing.
- The number and severity of complaints will be considered in our decision whether or not to delete the listing from the next edition.

Markets
Book Publishers

There's no magic formula for getting published. It's a matter of getting the right manuscript on the right editor's desk at the right time. Before you submit it's important to learn publishers' needs, see what kind of books they're producing and decide which publishers your work is best suited for. *Children's Writer's & Illustrator's Market* is but one tool in this process. (Those just starting out, turn to Just Getting Started? Some Quick Tips, on page 2.)

To help you narrow down the list of possible publishers for your work, we've included several indexes at the back of this book. The **Subject Index** lists book and magazine publishers according to their fiction and nonfiction needs or interests. The **Age-Level Index** indicates which age groups publishers cater to. The **Photography Index** indicates which markets buy photography for children's publications. The **Poetry Index** lists publishers accepting poetry.

If you write contemporary fiction for young adults, for example, and you're trying to place a book manuscript, go first to the Subject Index. Locate the fiction categories under Book Publishers and copy the list under Contemporary. Then go to the Age-Level Index and highlight the publishers on the Contemporary list that are included under the Young Adults heading. Read the listings for the highlighted publishers to see if your work matches their needs.

Remember, *Children's Writer's & Illustrator's Market* should not be your only source for researching publishers. Here are a few other sources of information:

- The Society of Children's Book Writers and Illustrators (SCBWI) offers members an annual market survey of children's book publishers. (Members send a SASE with $1.06 postage or get the list for free online at www.scbwi.org. SCBWI membership information can also be found at www.scbwi.org.)
- The Children's Book Council website (www.cbcbooks.org) gives information on member publishers.
- If a publisher interests you, send a SASE for submission guidelines *before* submitting. To quickly find guidelines on the Internet, visit The Colossal Directory of Children's Publishers Online at www.signaleader.com/childrens-writers/.
- Check publishers' websites. Many include their complete catalogs which you can browse. Web addresses are included in many publishers' listings.
- Spend time at your local bookstore to see who's publishing what. While you're there, browse through *Publishers Weekly*, *The Horn Book* and *Riverbank Review*.

SUBSIDY & SELF-PUBLISHING

Some determined writers who receive rejections from royalty publishers may look to subsidy and co-op publishers as an option for getting their work into print. These publishers ask writers to pay all or part of the costs of producing a book. We strongly advise writers and illustrators to work only with publishers who pay them. For this reason, we've adopted a policy not to include any subsidy or co-op publishers in *Children's Writer's & Illustrator's Market* (or any other Writer's Digest Books market books).

If you're interested in publishing your book just to share it with friends and relatives, self-publishing is a viable option, but it involves a lot of time, energy and money. You oversee all book production details. Check with a local printer for advice and information on cost.

Whatever path you choose, keep in mind that the market is flooded with submissions, so it's important for you to hone your craft and submit the best work possible. Competition from thousands of other writers and illustrators makes it more important than ever to research publishers before submitting—read their guidelines, look at their catalogs, check out a few of their titles and visit their websites.

ADVICE FROM INSIDERS

For insight and advice on getting published from a variety of perspectives, be sure to read the Insider Reports in this section. Subjects include authors **Kate DiCamillo** (page 122), **Jennifer L. Holm** (page 144), **Lemony Snicket** (page 150), and **Patricia Reilly Giff** (page 190); editors **Stephen Roxburgh** (page 136), **Wendy Lamb** (page 160) and **Megan Tingley** (page 198); illustrator **Lori McElrath-Eslick** (page 116); and children's librarian **Pat Clancy** (page 182).

Information on book publishers listed in the previous edition but not included in this edition of *Children's Writer's & Illustrator's Market* may be found in the General Index.

ABINGDON PRESS, The United Methodist Publishing House, 201 Eighth Ave. S., Nashville TN 37203. (615)749-6384. Fax: (615)749-6512. E-mail: paugustine@umpublishing.org. **Acquisitions:** Peg Augustine, children's book editor. Estab. 1789. "Abingdon Press, America's oldest theological publisher, provides an ecumenical publishing program dedicated to serving the Christian community—clergy, scholars, church leaders, musicians and general readers—with quality resources in the areas of Bible study, the practice of ministry, theology, devotion, spirituality, inspiration, prayer, music and worship, reference, Christian education and church supplies."
Fiction: All levels: multicultural, religion, special needs.
Nonfiction: All levels: religion.
How to Contact/Writers: Query; submit outline/synopsis and 1 sample chapter. Responds to queries in 3 months; mss in 6 months.
Illustration: Uses color artwork only. Reviews ms/illustration packages from artists. Query with photocopies only. Samples returned with SASE; samples not filed.
Photography: Buys stock images. Wants scenics, landscape, still life and multiracial photos. Model/property release required. Uses color prints. Submit stock photo list.
Terms: Pays authors royalty of 5-10% based on retail price. Work purchased outright from authors ($100-1,000).

ABSEY & CO., 23011 Northcrest Dr., Spring TX 77389. (281)257-2340. Fax: (281)251-4676. E-mail: abseyandco@aol.com. Website: www.absey.com. **Publisher:** Edward Wilson. "We are looking primarily for education books, especially those with teaching strategies based upon research." Publishes hardcover, trade paperback and mass market paperback originals. Publishes 5-10 titles/year. 50% of books from first-time authors; 50% from unagented writers.
Fiction: "Since we are a small, new press, we are looking for good manuscripts with a firm intended audience." Recently published *Saving the Scrolls*, by Mary Kerry.
Nonfiction: Recently published *Amazing Jones*, by Deanna Cera; and *Ancient Egyptian Jewelry*, by Carol Andrews.
How to Contact/Writers: Fiction: Query with SASE. Nonfiction: Query with outline and 1-2 sample chapters. Does not consider simultaneous submissions. Responds to queries in 3 months.
Illustration: Reviews/ms illustration packages. Send photocopies, transparencies, etc.
Photography: Reviews ms/photo packages. Send photocopies, transparencies, etc.
Terms: Pays 8-15% royalty on wholesale price. Publishes book 1 year after acceptance of ms. Manuscript guidelines for #10 SASE.
Tips: Absey publishes a few titles every year. We like the author and the illustrator working together to create something magical. Authors and illustrators have input into every phase of production.

ACTION PUBLISHING, P.O. Box 391, Glendale CA 91209. (323)478-1667. Fax: (323)478-1767. Website: www.actionpublishing.com. Book publisher. Estab. 1996. Publishes picture books and fiction. **Publisher:** Michael Metzler. **Art Acquisitions:** Art Director. Publishes 4 young readers/year; 2 middle readers/year; and 2 young adult titles/year.

Fiction: Picture book: fantasy. Young readers: adventure, fantasy. Middle readers: adventure. Recently published *The Family of Ree*, by Scott E. Sutton (ages 6-9, picture book).

How to Contact/Writers: Only interested in agented material. Current guidelines on website.

Illustration: Works with 4 illustrators/year. Reviews illustration packages from artists. Query. Contact: Publisher. Send promotional literature. Contact: Art Director. Responds only if interested. Samples returned with SASE or kept on file if interested and OK with illustrator.

Photography: Buys stock and assigns work. Contact: Art Director. "We use photos on as-needed basis. Mainly publicity, advertising and copy work." Uses 35mm or 4×5 transparencies. Submit cover letter and promo piece.

Terms: Pays authors royalty based on wholesale price. Offers advances against royalties. Pays illustrators by the project or royalty. Pays photographers by the project or per photo Sends galleys to authors. Original art returned as negotiated depending on project.

ALADDIN PAPERBACKS/SIMON PULSE PAPERBACK BOOKS, 1230 Avenue of the Americas, 4th Floor, New York NY 10020. Fax: (212) 698-7337. Website: www.simonsays.com. Paperback imprints of Simon & Schuster Children's Publishing Children's Division. Associate Vice President/Editorial Director: Ellen Krieger (middle grade/chapter books, Lisa Clancy (young adult), Julia Richardson (beginning readers, chapter books), Jennifer Klonsky (all areas). **Manuscript Acquisitions:** Attn: Submissions Editor. **Art Acquisitions:** Debra Sfetsios, Aladdin; Russel Gordon, Simon Pulse. Publishes 130 titles/year.

- Aladdin publishes primarily reprints of successful hardcovers from other Simon & Schuster imprints. They accept query letters with proposals for middle-grade series and single-title fiction, beginning readers, middle grade mysteries and commercial nonfiction. Simon Pulse primarily publishes Young Adult series and media tie-in titles, as well as reprints of successful hardcovers from other Simon & Schuster imprints. They accept query letters for young adult series and single-title fiction.

Fiction: Recently published The Unicorn's Secret chapter book series by Kathleen Duey (ages 7-10, edited by Ellen Krieger; fantasy chapter books, Aladdin Paperbacks); *Pirate Hunter*, by Brad Strickland and Tom Fuller; and *Pendragon*, by D.J. MacHale middle grade fiction, edited by Lisa Clancy.

 ALL ABOUT KIDS PUBLISHING, 6280 San Ignacio Ave., Suite C, San Jose CA 95119. (408)578-4026. Fax: (408)578-4029. E-mail: mail@aakp.com. Website: www.aakp.com. Estab. 1999. Specializes in fiction, educational material, multicultural material, nonfiction. Book publisher. **Manuscript Acquisitions:** Linda L. Guevara. **Art Acquisitions Editor:** Nadine Takvorian, art director. Publishes 10-20 picture books/year. 80% of books by first-time authors.

Fiction: Picture books, young readers: adventure, animal, concept, fantasy, folktales, history, humor, multicultural, nature/environment, poetry, religion, special needs, suspense/mystery Average word length: picture books—450 words. Recently published *The Flight of the Sunflower*, by Melissa Bourbon-Ramirez (picture book).

Nonfiction: Picture books, young readers: activity books, animal, biography, concept, history, multicultural, nature/environment, religion, special needs, textbooks. Average word length: picture books—450 words. Recently published *Fishes, Flowers & Fandangles*, by Hua Tao Zhang; *Activity Book to Teach Children Ages 5-12 Art For Teachers & Parents*.

How to Contact/Writers: Fiction: Submit complete ms. Nonfiction: Submit complete ms for picture books; outline synopsis and 2 sample chapters for young readers. Responds to mss in less than 3 months. Publishes a book 2-3 years after acceptance. Manuscript returned with SASE.

Illustration: Works with 20-30 illustrators/year. Uses both color and b&w artwork. Reviews ms/illustration packages from artists. Submit ms with dummy or ms with 2-3 pieces of final art. Contact: Linda L. Guevara, editor. Illustrations only: Arrange personal portfolio review or send résumé, portfolio and client list. Contact: Nadine Takvorian, art director. Responds in 3 months. Samples returned with SASE; samples filed.

Photography: Works on assignment only. Contact: Linda L. Guevara, editor. Model/property releases required. Uses 35mm transparencies. Submit portfolio, résumé, client list.

Terms: Pays author royalty of 5% based on retail price. Offers advances (Average amount: $1,000). Pays illustrators by the project (range: $3,000 minimum) or royalty of 3-5% based on retail price. Pays

---

● **SPECIAL COMMENTS** by the editors of *Children's Writer's & Illustrator's Market* are set off by a bullet.

photographers by the project (range: $500 minimum) or royalty of 5% based on wholesale price. Sends galleys to authors; dummies to illustrators. Originals returned to artist at job's completion. All imprints included in a single catalog. Writer's, artist's and photographer's guidelines available for SASE.

Tips: "Write from the heart and for the love of children. Submit only one manuscript per envelope. Only one per month please."

AMIRAH PUBLISHING, P.O. Box 541146. Flushing NY 11354. Phone/fax: (718)321-9004. E-mail: amirahpbco@aol.com. Website: www.ifna.net. Estab. 1992. Specializes in fiction, educational material, multicultural material. **Manuscript Acquisitions:** Yahiya Emerick. **Art Acquisitions:** Yahiya Emerick, president. Publishes 2 young readers/year; 5 middle readers; 3 young adult titles/year. 25% of books by first-time authors. "Our goal is to produce quality books for children and young adults with a spiritually uplifting application."

● Amirah accepts sumissions only through e-mail.

Fiction: Picture books, young readers, middle readers, young adults: adventure, animal, history, multicultural, religion, Islamic. Average word length: picture books—200; young readers—1,000; middle readers—5,000; young adults—5,000. Recently published *Ahmad Deen and the Curse of the Aztec Warrior*, by Yahiya Emerick (ages 8-11); *Burhaan Khan*, by Qasim Najar (ages 6-8); *The Memory of Hands*, by Reshma Baig (ages 15 to adult).

Nonfiction: Picture books, young readers, middle readers, young adults: history, religion, Islamic. Average word length: picture books—200; young readers—1,000; middle readers—5,000; young adults—5,000. Recently published *Color and Learn Salah*, by Yahiya Emerick (ages 5-7, religious); *Learning About Islam*, by Yahiya Emerick (ages 9-11, religious); *What Islam Is All About*, by Yahiya Emerick (ages 14+, religious).

How to Contact/Writers: Fiction/nonfiction: Query via e-mail only. Responds to queries in 2 weeks; mss in 3 months. Publishes a book 6-12 months after acceptance. Will consider electronic submissions via disk or modem.

Illustration: Works with 2-4 illustrators/year. Reviews ms/illustration packages from artists. Query. Contact: Qasim Najar, vice president. Illustrations only: Query with samples. Contact: Yahiya Emerick, president. Responds in 1 month. Samples returned with SASE.

Photography: Works on assignment only. Contact: Yahiya Emerick, president. Uses images of the Middle East, children, nature. Model/property releases required. Uses 4×6, matte, color prints. Submit cover letter.

Terms: Work purchased outright from authors for $1,000-3,000. Pays illustrators by the project (range: $20-40). Pays photographers by the project (range: $20-40). Sends galleys to authors; dummies to illustrators. Originals returned to artist at job's completion. Book catalog available for SASE and 2 first-class stamps. All imprints included in a single catalog. Catalog available on website.

Tips: "We specialize in materials relating to the Middle East and Muslim-oriented culture such as stories, learning materials and such. These are the only types of items we currently are publishing."

ATHENEUM BOOKS FOR YOUNG READERS, 1230 Avenue of the Americas, New York NY 10020. (212)698-2715. Website: www.simonsayskids.com. Imprint of Simon & Schuster Children's Publishing Division. Book publisher. Vice President and Editorial Director: Ginee Seo. Estab. 1960. **Manuscript Acquisitions:** Send queries with SASE to: Ginee Seo, Anne Schwartz, editorial director of Anne Schwartz Books; Richard Jackson, editorial director of Richard Jackson Books; Caitlyn Dlouhy, executive editor. "All editors consider all types of projects." **Art Acquisitions:** Ann Bobco. Publishes 15-20 picture books/year; 4-5 young readers/year; 20-25 middle readers/year; and 10-15 young adults/year. 10% of books by first-time authors; 50% from agented writers. "Atheneum publishes original hardcover trade books for children from pre-school age through young adult. Our list includes picture books, chapter books, mysteries, biography, science fiction, fantasy, middle grade and young adult fiction and nonfiction. The style and subject matter of the books we publish is almost unlimited. We do not, however, publish textbooks, coloring or activity books, greeting cards, magazines or pamphlets or religious publications. Anne Schwartz Books is a highly selective line of books within the Atheneum imprint. The lists of Charles Scribner's Sons Books for Young Readers have been folded into the Atheneum program."

● Atheneum does not accept unsolicited manuscripts. Send query letter only. Atheneum title *True Believer*, by Virginia Euwer Wolff, won a 2002 Printz Honor and the 2002 Golden Kite Award for Fiction. Anne Schwartz/Atheneum title *Goin' Someplace Special*, illustrated by Jerry Pinkney, text by Patricia McKissack, won the 2002 Coretta Scott King Illustrator Award.

How to Contact/Writers: Send query letter and 3 sample chapters. Responds to queries in 1 month; requested mss in 3 months. Publishes a book 18-24 months after acceptance. Will consider simultaneous queries from previously unpublished authors and those submitted to other publishers, "though we request that the author let us know it is a simultaneous query."

Illustration: Works with 40-50 illustrators/year. Send art samples résumé, tearsheets to Ann Bobco, Design Dept. 4th Floor, 1230 Avenue of the Americas, New York NY 10020. Samples filed. Reports on art samples only if interested.

Terms: Pays authors in royalties of 8-10% based on retail price. Pays illustrators royalty of 5-6% or by the project. Pays photographers by the project. Sends galleys and proofs to authors; proofs to illustrators. Original artwork returned at job's completion. Manuscript guidelines for #10 SAE and 1 first-class stamp.

Tips: "Atheneum has a 40-year tradition of publishing distinguished books for children. Study our titles."

A/V CONCEPTS CORP., 30 Montauk Blvd., Oakdale NY 11769. (631)567-7227. Fax: (631)567-8745. E-mail: info@edcompublishing.com. Educational book publisher. **Manuscript Acquisitions:** Laura Solimene, editorial director. **Art Acquisitions:** Phil Solimene, president. Publishes 6 young readers/year; 6 middle readers/year; 6 young adult titles/year. 20% of books by first-time authors. Primary theme of books and multimedia is classic literature, math, science, language arts, self esteem.

Fiction: Middle readers: hi-lo. Young adults: hi-lo, multicultural, special needs. "We hire writers to adapt classic literature."

Nonfiction: All levels: activity books. Young adults: hi-lo, multicultural, science, self help, textbooks. Average word length: middle readers—300-400; young adults—500-950.

How to Contact/Writers: Fiction: Submit outline/synopsis and 1 sample chapter. Responds to queries in 1 month.

Illustration: Works with 4-6 illustrators/year. Reviews ms/illustration packages from artists. Submit ms with 3-4 pieces of final art. Illustrations only: Query with samples. "No originals; send non-returnable material and samples only." Responds in 1 month. Samples returned with SASE; samples filed.

Photography: Submit samples.

Terms: Work purchased outright from authors (range $50-1,000). Pays illustrators by the project (range: $50-1,000). Pays photographers per photo (range: $25-250). Manuscript and art guidelines available for 9 × 12 SASE.

AVISSON PRESS, INC., 3007 Taliaferro Rd., Greensboro NC 27408. (336)288-6989. Fax: (336)288-6989. Estab. 1995. Specializes in multicultural material, nonfiction. **Manuscript Acquisitions:** Martin Hester, publisher. Publishes 5-7 young adult titles/year. 70% of books by first-time authors.

Nonfiction: Young adults: biography. Average word length: young adults—25,000. Recently published *Mum Bet: The Life and Times of Elizabeth Freeman*, by Mary Wilds; *Young Superstars of Tennis: The Venus and Serena Williams Story*, by Mike Fillon; *Here Comes Eleanor: A New Biography of Eleanor Roosevelt for Young People*, by Virginia Veeder Westervelt; *Eight Who Made a Difference: Pioneer Women in the Arts*, by Erica Stux.

How to Contact/Writers: Nonfiction: Submit outline/synopsis and 2 sample chapters. Responds to queries in 2 weeks; mss in 2 months. Publishes a book 9-12 months after acceptance. Will consider simultaneous submissions.

Terms: Pays author royalty of 8-10% based on wholesale price. Offers advances (Average amount: $400). Sends galleys to authors. Book catalog available for #10 SAE and 1 first-class stamp; ms guidelines available for SASE.

Tips: "We don't use illustrated books."

AVON BOOKS/BOOKS FOR YOUNG READERS, 1350 Avenue of the Americas, New York NY 10019. (212)261-6800. Fax: (212)261-6668. Website: www.harperchildrens.com. A division of Harper-Collins Children's Book Group.

• Avon is not accepting unagented submissions. See listing for HarperCollins Children's Books.

AZRO PRESS, PMB 342, 1704 Llano St. B, Santa Fe NM 87505. (505)989-3272. Fax: (505)989-3832. E-mail: books@azropress.com, Website: www.azropress.com. Estab. 1997. **Manuscript/Art Acquisitions:** Gae Eisenhardt. Imprints: Green Knees (Jaenet Guggenheim, acquisitions editor). Publishes 6 picture books/year. 90% of books by first-time authors. "We publish illustrated children's books with a southwestern flavor."

Fiction: Picture books: animal, humor, multicultural. Average word length: picture books—1,000; young readers—1,500. Recently published *Watcha Doing?*, by Agatha Featherstone (ages 2-5); *One Bullfrog*, by Sid Hausman (age 5-10, illustrated song book with CD); *Lucy's Journey to the Wild West*, by Charlotte Piepmeier; and *Grow Grow Grow*, by Barbara Riley.

Nonfiction: Picture books: activity books, animals, science.

How to Contact/Writers: Fiction/nonfiction: Submit complete ms or outline/synopsis. Responds to queries in 2 weeks; mss in 2-3 months. Publishes a book 2 years after acceptance. Will consider simultaneous submissions, electronic submissions via disk or modem.

Illustration: Works with 3-4 illustrators/year. Reviews ms/illustration packages from artists. Submit ms with 2-3 pieces of final art. Contact: Gae Eisenhardt, editor. Query with samples. Samples filed.

Terms: Pays authors royalty fo 5-10% based on wholesale price. Pays illustrators by the project (range: $3,000-4,000) or royalty of 5%. Sends galleys to authors; dummies to illustrators. Originals returned to artist at job's completion. Book catalog available for SASE. All imprints included in a single catalog. Manuscript guidelines available for SASE. Catalog available on website.

Tips: Read our submission guidelines. Go to your local bookstore and library to see what is available.

A ▼ BANTAM BOOKS FOR YOUNG READERS, (formerly Bantam Doubleday Dell), imprint of Knopf Delacorte Dell Young Readers Group (Random House Children's Books), 1540 Broadway, New York NY 10036. (212)354-6500. Website: www.randomhouse.com. Book publisher.

• Delacorte title *Lord of the Deep*, by Graham Salisbury, won the 2002 Boston Globe-Horn Book Award for Fiction and Poetry. Delacorte title *The Ropemaker*, by Peter Dickinson, won a 2002 Printz Honor.

BAREFOOT BOOKS, 3 Bow St., Cambridge MA 02138. (617)576-0660. Fax: (617)576-0049. E-mail: Alison@barefootbooks.com. Website: www.barefoot-books.com. Estab. 1993 in the UK; 1998 in the US. Specializes in fiction, trade books, multicultural material, nonfiction. **Manuscript Acquisitions:** Alison Keehn, associate editor. **Art Acquisitions:** Alison Keehn, associate editor. Publishes 35 picture books/year; 10 anthologies/year. 40% of books by first-time authors; 60% subsidy published. "The Barefoot child represents the person who is in harmony with the natural world and moves freely across boundaries of many kinds. Barefoot Books explores this image with a range of high-quality picture books for children of all ages. We work with artists, writers and storytellers from many cultures, focusing on themes that encourage independence of spirit, promote understanding and acceptance of different traditions, and foster a life-long love of learning."

Fiction: Picture books, young readers: animal, anthology, concept, fantasy, folktales, multicultural, nature/environment, poetry, spirituality. Middle readers, young adults: anthology, folktales. Average word length: picture books—500-1,000; young readers—2,000-3,000; anthologies—10,000-20,000. Recently published *There's a Cow in the Cabbage Patch*, by Clare Beaton (ages 1-7, picture book); *Daddy Island*, by Philip Wells, illustrated by Niki Daly (ages 4-7, picture book); *The Barefoot Book of Knights*, by John Matthews, illustrated by Giovanni Manna (ages 6 to adult, anthology).

Nonfiction: Picture books, young readers, middle readers, young adults: multicultural, spirituality/inspirational. Average word length: young readers—3,000-20,000. Recently published *The Genius of Leonardo*, by Guido Visconti, illustrated by Bimba Landmann; *Daughters of Eve: Strong Women of the Bible*, by Lillian Hammer Ross, illustrated by Kyra Teis.

How to Contact/Writers: Fiction: Submit complete ms for picture books; outline/synopsis and 1 sample story for collections. Nonfiction: Query. Responds to queries in 1 month; mss in 2 months. Will consider simultaneous submissions and previously published work.

Illustration: Works with 45 illustrators/year. Uses color artwork only. Reviews ms/illustration packages from artists. Query for anthology/collections or send ms with dummy for picture books. Contact: Alison Keehn, associate editor. Illustrations only: Query with samples or send promo sheet and tearsheets. Contact: Alison Keehn, associate editor. Responds only if interested. Samples returned with SASE.

Terms: Pays author royalty of 5% based on retail price. Offers advances. Sends galleys to authors. Originals returned to artist at job's completion. Book catalog available for 9×12 SAE and 5 first-class stamps; ms guidelines available for SASE. Catalog available on website.

Tips: "We are looking for books that inspire, books that are filled with a sense of magic and wonder. We also look for strong stories from all different cultures, reflecting the ways of the individual culture while also touching deeper human truths that suggest we are all one. We welcome playful submissions for the very youngest children and also anthologies of stories or poems for older readers, all focused around a universal theme. We encourage writers and artists to visit our website and read some of our books to get a sense of our editorial philosophy and what we publish before they submit to us. Always, we encourage them to stay true to their inner voice and artistic vision that reaches out for timeless stories, beyond the momentary trends that may exist in the market today."

◘ BARRONS EDUCATIONAL SERIES, 250 Wireless Blvd., Hauppauge NY 11788. (631)434-3311 or (800)645-3476, ext. 264. Fax: (631)434-3723. E-mail: wb@barronseduc.com. Website: www.barronsedu c.com. Book publisher. Estab. 1945. "Barrons tends to publish series of books, both for adults and children." **Manuscript Acquisitions:** Wayne R. Barr, acquisitions manager. **Art Acquisitions:** Bill Kuchler, art director. Publishes 20 picture books/year; 20 young readers/year; 20 middle reader titles/year; 10 young adult titles/year. 25% of books by first-time authors; 25% of books from agented writers.

Fiction: Picture books: animal, concept, multicultural, nature/environment. Young readers: Adventure, multicultural, nature/environment, fantasy, suspense/mystery. Middle readers: adventure, fantasy, horror, multicultural, nature/environment, problem novels, suspense/mystery. Young adults: horror, problem novels. Recently published *Everyday Witch*, by Sandra Forrester; *Word Wizardry* by Margaret and William Kenda.

Nonfiction: Picture books: concept, reference. Young readers: how-to, reference, self help, social issues. Middle readers: hi-lo, how-to, reference, self help, social issues. Young adults: biography, how-to, reference, self help, social issues, sports.

How to Contact/Writers: Fiction: Query. E-mail preferred: wb@barronseduc.com. Nonfiction: Submit outline/synopsis and sample chapters. "Submissions must be accompanied by SASE for response." Responds to queries in 2 months; mss in 3-4 months. Publishes a book 1 year after acceptance. Will consider simultaneous submissions.

Illustration: Works with 20 illustrators/year. Reviews ms/illustration packages from artists. Query first; 3 chapters of ms with 1 piece of final art, remainder roughs. Illustrations only: Submit tearsheets or slides plus résumé. Responds in 3-8 weeks.

Terms: Pays authors in royalties of 10-14% based on net price or buys ms outright for $2,000 minimum. Pays illustrators by the project based on retail price. Sends galleys to authors; dummies to illustrators. Book catalog, ms/artist's guidelines for 9 × 12 SAE.

Tips: Writers: "We are predominately on the lookout for preschool storybooks and concept books. No romance novels." Illustrators: "We are happy to receive a sample illustration to keep on file for future consideration. Periodic notes reminding us of your work are acceptable." Children's book themes "are becoming much more contemporary and relevant to a child's day-to-day activities. We have a great interest in children's fiction (ages 7-11 and ages 12-16) with New Age topics."

BEACH HOLME PUBLISHERS, 2040 W. 12th Ave., Suite 226, Vancouver, British Columbia V6J 2G2 Canada. (604)733-4868, (888)551-6655 (orders). Fax: (604)733-4860. E-mail: bhp@beachholme.bc. ca. Website: www.beachholme.bc.ca. Book publisher. **Manuscript Acquisitions:** Michael Carroll, publisher. **Art Acquisitions:** Michael Carroll. Publishes 5-6 young adult titles/year and 7-8 adult literary titles/ year. 40% of books by first-time authors. "We publish primarily regional historical fiction. We publish young adult novels for children aged 8-12. We are particularly interested in works that have a historical basis and are set in the Pacific Northwest, or northern Canada. Include ideas for teacher's guides or resources and appropriate topics for a classroom situation if applicable."

• Beach Holme *only* accepts work from Canadian writers.

Fiction: Young adults: contemporary, folktales, history, multicultural, nature/environment, poetry. Multicultural needs include themes reflecting cultural heritage of the Pacific Northwest, i.e., first nations, Asian, East Indian, etc. Does not want to see generic adventure or mystery with no sense of place. Average word length: middle readers—15-20,000; young adults/teens—30,000-40,000. Recently published *Tom Thomson's Last Paddle*, by Larry McCloskey (ages 9-13, young adult fiction); and *Criss Cross, Double Cross*, by Norma Charles (ages 8-13, young adult fiction).

How to Contact/Writers: Fiction: Submit outline/synopsis and 3 sample chapters. Responds to queries/ mss in 6 months. Publishes a book 6 months-1 year after acceptance. No electronic or multiple submissions.

Illustration: Works with 4-5 Canadian illustrators/year. Responds to submissions in 1-2 months if interested. Samples returned with SASE; samples filed. Originals returned at job's completion. Works mainly with Canadian illustrators.

Terms: Pays authors 10% royalty based on retail price. Offers advances (average amount: $500). Pays illustrators by the project (range: $500-1,000). Pays photographers by the project (range: $100-300). Sends galleys to authors. Book catalog available for 9 × 12 SAE and 3 first-class Canadian stamps; ms guidelines available online at website.

Tips: "Research what we have previously published and view our website to familiarize yourself with what we are looking for. Please, be informed."

BEBOP BOOKS, Imprint of Lee & Low Books Inc., 95 Madison Ave., New York NY 10016-7801. (212)779-4400. Website: www.bebopbooks.com. Estab. 2000. **Acquisitions:** Jennifer Frantz. **Executive Editor:** Louise May. Publishes 10-15 picture books/year. Many books by first-time authors. "Our goal is to publish child-centered stories that support literacy learning and provide multicultural content for children just beginning to learn to read. We make a special effort to work with writers and illustrators of diverse backgrounds. Current needs are posted on website."

Fiction: Picture books: adventure, concept, contemporary, hi-lo, multicultural, nature/environment, sports, culturally specific topics for young children.

Nonfiction: Picture books: arts/crafts, careers, concept, cooking, hi-lo, hobbies, how-to, multicultural, music/dance, nature/environment, social issues, sports.

How to Contact/Writers: Fiction/nonfiction: Submit complete ms. Responds to mss in up to 4 months; "manuscripts are acquired just once a year."

Illustration: Works with 10-15 illustrators/year. Uses color artwork only. Illustrations and photographs: Query with color samples and send client list or cover letter. Responds only if interested. Samples returned with SASE; samples filed. "We are especially interested in submissions from artists of color, and we encourage artists new to the field of children's books to send us samples of their work."

Terms: Pays authors royalty. Offers advances. Pays illustrators royalty and advance. Pays photographers royalty and advance. Book catalog available for 9×12 SAE and 89¢ postage, attn: Catalog Request. Catalog available on website.

Tips: "Bebop Books is currently specializing in emergent readers with multicultural themes. Emergent readers, often called 'little books,' are used by kindergarten and first-grade teachers to help young children develop early reading skills and strategies. Each book is a small, 12-, 16- or 24-page paperback, with full color illustrations and a story specifically written and illustrated to support beginning readers. The stories should fit within Guided Reading™ levels D-G and Reading Recovery® levels 6-12."

BEHRMAN HOUSE INC., 11 Edison Place, Springfield NJ 07081. (973)379-7200. Fax: (973)379-7280. Book publisher. Estab. 1921. Managing Editor: Bob Tinkham. **Acquisitions:** Editorial Department. Publishes 3 young reader titles/year; 3 middle reader titles/year; and 3 young adult titles/year. 12% of books by first-time authors; 2% of books from agented writers. Publishes books on all aspects of Judaism: history, cultural, textbooks, holidays. "Behrman House publishes quality books of Jewish content—history, Bible, philosophy, holidays, ethics—for children and adults."

Fiction: All levels: Judaism.

Nonfiction: All levels: Judaism, Jewish educational textbooks. Average word length: young reader—1,200; middle reader—2,000; young adult—4,000. Published *My Jewish Year*, by Adam Fisher (ages 8-9); *Partners with God*, by Gila Gevirtz (ages 8-9); and *It's a Mitzvah!*, by Bradley Artson (adult).

How to Contact/Writers: Fiction/Nonfiction: Submit outline/synopsis and sample chapters. Responds to queries in 1 month; mss in 2 months. Publishes a book 2½ years after acceptance. Will consider simultaneous submissions.

Illustration: Works with 6 children's illustrators/year. Reviews ms/illustration packages from artists. "Query first." Illustrations only: Query with samples; send unsolicited art samples by mail. Responds to queries in 1 month; mss in 2 months.

Photography: Purchases photos from freelancers. Buys stock and assigns work. Uses photos of families involved in Jewish activities. Uses color and b&w prints. Photographers should query with samples. Send unsolicited photos by mail. Submit portfolio for review.

Terms: Pays authors in royalties of 3-10% based on retail price or buys ms outright for $1,000-5,000. Offers advance. Pays illustrators by the project (range: $500-5,000). Sends galleys to authors; dummies to illustrators. Book catalog free on request.

Tips: Looking for "religious school texts" with Judaic themes or general trade Judaica.

BENCHMARK BOOKS, Imprint of Marshall Cavendish, 99 White Plains Rd., Tarrytown NY 10591. (914)332-8888. Fax: (914)332-1888. E-mail: mbisson@marshallcavendish.com. Website: www.marshallcavendish.com. **Manuscript Acquisitions:** Michelle Bisson and Joyce Stanton. Publishes 90 young reader, middle reader and young adult books/year. "We look for interesting treatments of primarily nonfiction subjects related to elementary, middle school and high school curriculum."

Nonfiction: Most nonfiction topics should be curriculum related. Average word length for books: 4,000-20,000. All books published as part of a series. Recently published *Life in the Middle Ages* (series), *The City*, *The Countryside*, *The Church*, *The Castle*, by Kathryn Hinds; *Lifeways: The Abache*, *The Cheyenne*, *The Haida*, *The Huron*, by Raymond Bial.

How to Contact/Writers: Nonfiction: submit complete ms or submit outline/synopsis and 1 or more sample chapters. Responds to queries and mss in 3 months. Publishes a book 2 years after acceptance. Will consider simultaneous submissions.

Photography: Buys stock and assigns work.

Terms: Pays authors royalty based on retail price or buys work outright. Offers advances. Sends galleys to authors. Book catalog available. All imprints included in a single catalog.

BETHANY HOUSE PUBLISHERS, 11400 Hampshire Ave. S., Minneapolis MN 55438-2852. (952)829-2500. Fax: (952)996-1304. Website: www.bethanyhouse.com. Book publisher. **Manuscript Acquisitions:** Youth Department. **Art Acquisitions:** Paul Higdon. Publishes 4 young readers/year; 18 middle-grade readers/year; and 8 young adults/year. Bethany House Publishers is a non-profit publisher seeking to publish imaginative, excellent books that reflect an evangelical worldview without being preachy. Publishes picture books under Bethany Backyard imprint.

Fiction: Children's and young adult fiction list is full.

Nonfiction: Young readers, middle readers, young adults: religion/devotional, self-help, social issues. Published *Get God*, by Kevin Johnson (young teen; discipleship); and *Hot Topics, Tough Questions*, by Bill Myers (young adult/teen, Biblically based advice).

How to Contact/Writers: Considers unsolicited 1-page queries sent by fax only. "Bethany House no longer accepts unsolicited manuscripts or book proposals." Responds in 4 months. Publishes a book 12-18 months after acceptance.

Illustration: Works with 12 illustrators/year. Reviews illustration samples from artists. Illustrations only: Query with samples. Responds in 2 months. Samples returned with SASE.

Terms: Pays authors royalty based on net sales. Pays illustrators by the project. Pays photographers by the project. Sends galleys to authors. Book catalog available for 11×14 SAE and 5 first-class stamps. Write "Catalog Request" on outside of envelope.

Tips: "Research the market, know what is already out there. Study our catalog before submitting material. We look for an evangelical message woven delicately into a strong plot and topics that seek to broaden the reader's experience and perspective."

BEYOND WORDS PUBLISHING, INC., 20827 N.W. Cornell Rd., Hillsboro OR 97124-1808. (503)531-8700. Fax: (503)531-8773. E-mail: info@beyondword.com. Website: www.beyondword.com. **Acquisitions:** Barbara Mann, managing editor children's division. Publishes 2-3 picture books/year and 7-9 nonfiction teen books/year. 50% of books by first-time authors. "Our company mission statement is 'Inspire to Integrity,' so it's crucial that your story inspires children in some way. Our books are high quality, gorgeously illustrated, meant to be enjoyed as a child and throughout life."

Fiction: Picture books: contemporary, feminist, folktales, history, multicultural, nature/environment. "We are looking for authors/illustrators; stories that will appeal and inspire." Average length: picture books— 32 pages. Recently published *Abbie Against the Storm*, by Marcia Vaughan, illustrated by Bill Farnsworth (all ages, historical fiction).

Nonfiction: Picture books, young readers: advice, biography, history, multicultural, nature/environment. *Girls Know Best* (compilation of 38 teen girls' writing—ages 7-15); *So, You Wanna Be a Writer?* (ages 9-16, advice/career).

How to Contact/Writers: Fiction: Submit complete ms. Nonfiction: Submit outline/synopsis. Responds to queries/mss in 6 months. Will consider simultaneous submissions and previously published work.

Illustration: Works with 4-6 illustrators/year. Reviews ms/illustration packages from artists. Submit ms with 2-3 pieces of final art. Illustrations only: Send résumé, promo sheet, "samples—no originals!" Responds in 6 months only if interested. Samples returned with SASE; samples filed.

Photography: Works on assignment only.

Terms: Sends galleys to authors; dummies to illustrators. Manuscript and artist's guidelines for SASE.

Tips: "Please research the books we have previously published. This will give you a good idea if your proposal fits with our company."

BLUE SKY PRESS, 555 Broadway, New York NY 10012-3999. (212)343-6100. Fax: (212)343-4831. Website: www.scholastic.com. Book publisher. Imprint of Scholastic Inc. **Acquisitions:** Bonnie Verburg. Publishes 15-20 titles/year. 1% of books by first-time authors. Publishes hardcover children's fiction and nonfiction including high-quality novels and picture books by new and established authors.

● Blue Sky is currently not accepting unsolicited submissions due to a large backlog of books.

Fiction: Picture books: adventure, animal, concept, contemporary, fantasy, folktales, history, humor, multicultural, nature/environment, poetry. Young readers: adventure, contemporary, fantasy, folktales, history, humor, multicultural, nature/environment, poetry. Young adults: adventure, anthology, contemporary, fantasy, history, humor, multicultural, poetry. Multicultural needs include "strong fictional or themes featuring non-white characters and cultures." Does not want to see mainstream religious, bibliotherapeutic, adult. Average length: picture books—varies; young adults—150 pages. Recently published *To Every Thing There Is a Season*, illustrated by Leo and Diane Dillon (all ages, picture book); *Bluish*, by Virginia Hamilton; *No, David!*, by David Shannon; *The Adventures of Captain Underpants*, by Dav Pilkey; and *How Do Dinosaurs Say Goodnight?*, by Jane Yolen, illustrated by Mark Teague.

"PICTURE BOOKS" are for preschoolers to 8-year-olds; "Young readers" are for 5- to 8-year-olds; "Middle readers" are for 9- to 11-year-olds; and "Young adults" are for ages 12 and up. Age ranges may vary slightly from publisher to publisher.

insider report

Juggling marketing and motherhood for a successful illustration career

Back when Lori McElrath-Eslick was an illustrator at Hallmark Cards, she had a conversation with a fellow artist who longed to become a children's book illustrator. McElrath-Eslick suggested her friend begin reaching for her goals by approaching kids' magazines. "It seemed to be a good place to start," she reasoned. "Not only could you learn the type of illustration that's required, but you would gain a printed portfolio of tearsheets." McElrath-Eslick ended up following her own advice. Years later when she began her own freelance career, she entered the children's market via magazine illustration.

Lori McElrath-Eslick

Ironically it was her work in magazines that led to the Michigan artist's biggest break in book publishing. Her magazine illustrations were accepted into the Bologna Book Fair competition for emerging illustrators, part of the prestigious children's publishing event held annually Italy (www.bookfair.bolognafiere.it). Her illustrations caught the eye of a publisher and McElrath-Eslick landed a book contract soon after.

What seems like a lucky break was the result of hard work and dedication. Not only is McElrath-Eslick an artist, she's also her own rep. And she's a stay-at-home mom who balances assignments with chasing after a lively three-year-old (appropriately named Chase), and spending time with her husband and teenage daughter. How does she do it? McElrath-Eslick admits she doesn't have all the answers, but she's learned a few strategies that help her enjoy the freelance life.

Boyds Mill Press contacted you for *Read for Me, Mama* after seeing your illustrations at the Bologna Book Fair. How did you get chosen for that international exhibition?

Every year the Bologna Book Fair in Italy (or, as the Italians say, *BolognaFiere*), features a competition for illustrators from around the world. I entered illustrations I did for *Ladybug*. I was amazed when I received the letter of acceptance! I decided to go to the fair—my first trip to Italy—with my husband and daughter. Not only did we have a great time, but since the editors of many U.S. publishing houses were there, I got to meet many of them. At trade shows the editors are there to do business, not interview. But I learned if I wait patiently, many have time for me. I met Jody Taylor at the Boyds Mills Press booth. The Fair publishes an annual of the winners and she took it back to Boyds Mills. Soon after I got a call from one of their editors about a manuscript, *Read for Me, Mama*, by Vashanti Rahaman.

You worked in-house at Hallmark for more than six years. How did that affect your work?

My Hallmark coworkers (among them Floyd Cooper and G. Brian Karus) and I were always very aware of the work being done in children's publishing. We held illustrators like Trina Schart Hyman, Chris Van Alsburg and Ed Young in high esteem. Hallmark invited many of those artists to talk to us about their work. Visiting artists such as Mark English, Tom Allen, Tomie dePaola and David McCally inspired us with slides of their commercial and personal work. It really influenced me to see the broad range of styles of artists who did the majority of their work for children.

How much time do you spend marketing your work?

As my own rep, I remain diligent, constantly sending out samples and following up. I'd say I spend at least 50 percent of my time marketing. I find that very frustrating, as the thing I am best at is the actual painting or illustrating. There are some parts of marketing that I like. One of the aspects I enjoy is packaging my samples and tearsheets. Within the past two years I've made a commitment to send out quarterly postcard samples of my work to a list of the "dream" folks I want to work for. I try to streamline marketing activities as much as possible. I send postcard mailers of illustrations from my children's books and sometimes samples of my personal paintings. I choose work I think is my strongest. I always enclose a SASE so I can turn around and send the same samples again.

The college I attended, Kendall College, stressed always doing a pristine presentation—and it stuck. You will be known by how you present yourself, good or bad.

You have a great website. Was it difficult to launch? Does it help you with marketing?

When I decided to launch a site, I looked at some fellow illustrators' sites and made a list of the categories and icons I liked. Then I approached a gentleman who launched a site for our church. After we settled on a sum he went to work on it. He is a gem with the technical stuff. All I do is scan and send him the updates. In return, I include his small ad on my site. And, yes, I do get many assignments through the site.

I look at the site as a portfolio. I always include my website address, www.members.aol.com/EslickArt, on my samples, so I get a lot of hits after sending mailings. Art directors don't have to wait to see more samples of my work; they can simply log on to my site.

Do you do school visits?

I became involved in school visits after I received requests from schools. I learned even more when Boyds Mills Press invited a small group of illustrators and authors to attend a workshop on how to do a school visit. After giving us speaking tips from their guru, Peter Jacobi, they videotaped us at a local school. It really helped! It's embarrassing to see yourself on tape, however necessary, and it was really telling. I do as many visits as I can. It's something I have to work in around the illustrating—but it's worth it because I always learn so much from the children's insights and reactions.

What have you learned about art directors?

I have real respect for art directors who look at my track record and trust me to come up with the best solution for the manuscript. In the beginning of any career, you work out the

A lot of children's magazine work and a trip to the Bologna Book Fair in Italy led to illustrator Lori McElrath-Eslick's work on *Read for Me, Mama*, by Vashanti Rahaman (Boyds Mills Press). McElrath-Eslick advises artists who want to break into children's book illustration to begin by approaching children's magazines: "Not only could you learn the type of illustration that's required, but you would gain a printed portfolio of tearsheets."

trust. Later, once you have some printed assignments under your belt, art directors begin to trust you. It feels good to finally not have to prove yourself. I also appreciate editors and art directors who allow me freedom, yet make good calls, letting me know when something isn't right. A good art director can pinpoint what's not working, and a very good art director can offer advice on how to make changes. We work as a team. To fight it doesn't help the work. Two heads are better than one.

Tell me about your affiliation with The Mazza Collection.

I am sometimes approached by individuals and organizations interested in buying original oil paintings I've done for publication. One of these organizations is The Mazza Collection, located in Findlay, Ohio—a museum of hundreds of children's book illustrations. (Visit to www.mazzac ollection.org to see examples.)

The director, Jerry Mallett, purchased an illustration from *Read for Me, Mama* for the museum. It portrayed a little boy sitting and reading in front of a dryer at the laundromat while clothes spin behind his head. Jerry pointed out that the colors swirling around the boy's head makes it look like while reading, ideas are forming, taking shape, and his mind is active. It meant so much to me that my idea was evident. That Jerry "got it" made me hopeful that children would also get it.

What are you working on now?

I have just been sent a manuscript for a cover and interior illustrations for a novel. I am also trying my hand at writing and have sent out a nonfiction story of a potter. So far my manuscript has received one rejection. Since it is a multiple submission, I remain hopeful. I just received the Ezra Jack Keats award and an artist-in-residence award for a week at a National Park in Michigan. I get to paint!

—*Mary Cox*

How to Contact/Writers: "Due to large numbers of submissions, we are discouraging unsolicited submissions—send query with SASE only if you feel certain we publish the type of book you have written." Fiction: Query (novels, picture books). Responds to queries in 6 months. Publishes a book 1-3 years after acceptance; depending on chosen illustrator's schedule. Will not consider simultaneous submissions.
Illustration: Works with 10 illustrators/year. Uses both b&w and color artwork. Reviews illustration packages "only if illustrator is the author." Submit ms with dummy. Illustrations only: Query with samples, tearsheets. Responds only if interested. Samples returned with SASE. Original artwork returned at job's completion.
Terms: Pays 10% royalty based on wholesale price split between author and illustrators. Advance varies.
Tips: "Read currently published children's books. Revise—never send a first draft. Find your own voice, style, and subject. With material from new people we look for a theme or style strong enough to overcome the fact that the author/illustrator is unknown in the market."

BOYDS MILLS PRESS, 815 Church St., Honesdale PA 18431. (800)490-5111 or (570)253-1164. Fax: (570)253-0179. Website: www.boydsmillspress.com. Imprint: Wordsong (poetry). Book publisher. **Manuscript Acquisitions:** Kathryn Yerkes. **Art Acquisitions:** Tim Gillner. 5% of books from agented writers. Estab. 1990. "We publish a wide range of quality children's books of literary merit, from preschool to young adult."
Fiction: All levels: adventure, contemporary, history, humor, multicultural, poetry. Picture books: animal. Young readers, middle readers, young adult: problem novels, sports. Multicultural themes include any story showing a child as an integral part of a culture and which provides children with insight into a culture they otherwise might be unfamiliar with. "Please query us on the appropriateness of suggested topics for middle grade and young adult. For all other submissions send entire manuscript." Does not want to see

talking animals, coming-of-age novels, romance and fantasy/science fiction. Recently published *Mr. Beans* by Dayton O. Hyde (novel, ages 10 and up); and *An Alligator Ate My Brother*, by Mary Olson (picture book, ages 5-8).

Nonfiction: All levels: nature/environment, science. Picture books, young readers, middle readers: animal, multicultural. Does not want to see reference/curricular text. Recently published *Uncommon Champions*, by Marty Kaminsky (ages 12 and up) and *St. Nicholas*, by Ann Tompert (ages 6 and up).

How to Contact/Writers: Fiction/Nonfiction: Submit complete ms or submit through agent. Query on middle reader, young adult and nonfiction. Responds to queries/mss in 1 month.

Illustration: Works with 25 illustrators/year. Reviews ms/illustration packages from artists. Submit complete ms with 1 or 2 pieces of art. Illustrations only: Query with samples; send résumé and slides. Responds only if interested. Samples returned with SASE. Samples filed. Originals returned at job's completion.

Photography: Assigns work.

Terms: Authors paid royalty or work purchased outright. Offers advances. Illustrators paid by the project or royalties; varies. Photographers paid by the project, per photo, or royalties; varies. Manuscript/artist's guidelines available for #10 SASE.

Tips: "Picture books—with fresh approaches, not worn themes—are our strongest need at this time. Check to see what's already on the market before submitting your story."

BROADMAN & HOLMAN PUBLISHERS, LifeWay Christian Resources, 127 Ninth Ave. N., Nashville TN 37234. Fax: (615)251-5026. Book publisher. **Senior Acquisitions & Development Editor:** Gail Rothwell. Publishes 25-30 titles/year with majority being for younger readers. Only publish a few titles/year for ages 0-3 or 9-11. 10% of books by first-time authors. "All books have Christian values/themes."

Fiction: Middle readers, young readers: adventure, concept, contemporary, religion.

Nonfiction: Picture books: religion. Young or middle readers: self-help, social issues, religion, contemporary. Recently published *Manners Made Easy: A Workbook for Student Parent and Teacher*, by June Hines Moore, illustrated by Jim Osborn (ages 7-12); *The Great Adventure* and *Thank You*, by Stephen Elkins, illustrated by Ellie Colton (children's storybook with CD based on Dove-Award winning songs, age 5 and up); *Which Came First, the Chicken or the Egg?*, by Leslie Eckard, illustrated by Judy Sakaguchi (children's songbook, ages 5-8).

How to Contact/Writers: Responds to queries in 2 weeks; mss in 2 months. Publishes a book 1 year after acceptance. Will consider simultaneous submissions.

Illustration: Works with 5-6 illustrators/year. Samples returned with SASE; samples filed.

Terms: Pays authors royalty 10-18% based on wholesale price. Offers variable advance. Original artwork returned at job's completion. Book catalog available for 9×12 SAE and 2 first-class stamps. Manuscript guidelines available for SASE.

Tips: "We're looking for picture books with good family values; Bible story re-tellings; modern-day stories for younger readers based on Bible themes and principles. Write us to ask for guidelines before submitting."

CANDLEWICK PRESS, 2067 Massachusetts Ave., Cambridge MA 02140. (617)661-3330. Fax: (617)661-0565. E-mail: bigbear@candlewick.com. Children's book publisher. Estab. 1991. **Manuscript Acquisitions:** Liz Bicknell, editorial director; Joan Powers, editorial director (novelty); Mary Lee Donovan, executive editor; Kara LaReau, senior editor; Sarah Ketchersid, editor; Cynthia Platt, editor; Deborah Wayshak, editor; Jamie Michalak, associate editor. **Art Acquisitions:** Anne Moore. Publishes 160 picture books/year; 10 middle readers/year; and 10 young adult titles/year. 10% of books by first-time authors. "Our books are truly for children, and we strive for the very highest standards in the writing, illustrating, designing and production of all of our books. And we are not averse to risk."

● Candlewick Press is not accepting queries and unsolicited mss at this time. Candlewick title *"Let's Get a Pup!" Said Kate*, written and illustrated by Bob Graham, won the 2002 Boston Globe-Horn Book Award for Picture Books. Their title *Handel, Who Knew What He Liked*, by M.T. Anderson won a 2002 Boston Globe-Horn Book Honor Award for nonfiction.

Fiction: Picture books: animal, concept, contemporary, fantasy, history, humor, multicultural, nature/environment, poetry. Middle readers, young adults: contemporary, fantasy, history, humor, multicultural, poetry, science fiction, sports, suspense/mystery. Recently published: *Stoner & Spaz* (YA fiction); *A Poke in the I* (concrete poetry collection).

Nonfiction: Picture books: concept, biography, geography, nature/environment. Young readers: biography, geography, nature/environment. Recently published *Auschwitz* (nonfiction).

Illustration: Works with 40 illustrators/year. "We prefer to see a variety of the artist's style." Reviews ms/illustration packages from artists. "General samples only please." Illustrations only: Submit résumé and portfolio to the attention of Design Dept. Responds to samples in 6 weeks. Samples returned with SASE; samples filed.

Terms: Pays authors royalty of 2½-10% based on retail price. Offers advances. Pays illustrators 2½-10% royalty based on retail price. Sends galleys to authors; dummies to illustrators. Photographers paid 2½-10% royalty. Original artwork returned at job's completion.

☑ **CAPSTONE PRESS INC.**, 7825 Telegraph Rd., Minneapolis MN 55438. Fax: (952)933-2410. Website: www.capstone-press.com. Book publisher. **Product Planning:** Helen Moore. Imprints: Capstone Press, Bridgestone Books, Pebble Books, Art Books, Blue Earth Books, Life Matters. "The mission of Capstone Press is to help people learn to read and read to learn. We publish and distribute accessible, accurate, attractive, and affordable books to serve the needs of readers, educators, and librarians."
Nonfiction: Publishes only nonfiction books for emergent, early, challenged and reluctant readers. Currently looking for experienced authors to write on vehicle, military and sport topics; also science, social studies, and pleasure reading areas. All levels: animals, arts/crafts, biography, geography, health, history, hobbies, special needs. Young adults only: Hi-lo, cooking, self help. Recently published *Christopher Columbus*, by Lola M. Schaefer (grades K-1 biography, edited by Martha Rustard); *Earth Worms: Underground Burrowers*, by Adele D. Richardson (grades 1-2 science, edited by Sarah L. Schuette); *Goldberg: Pro Wrestler Bill Goldberg*, by Michael Burgan (grades 3-4, sports biography, edited by Angie Kaelberer).
How to Contact/Writers: Does not accept submissions. Do not send mss. Instead, request an author brochure with SASE, then send query letter, résumé and samples of nonfiction writing to be considered for assignment. Responds in 3 weeks.
Photographers: Buys stock and assigns work. Contact: Photo Research Manager. Model/property release required. Uses 35mm slides, 4×5, 8×10 transparencies. Submit slides, stock photo list.
Terms: Authors paid flat fee. Photographers paid by the project or per photo. Originals returned to artist at job's completion. Book catalog available for large format SAE.
Tips: "See website prior to sending query letter."

CAROLRHODA BOOKS, INC., Division of the Lerner Publishing Group, 241 First Ave. N., Minneapolis MN 55401. (612)332-3344 or (800)328-4929. Fax: (612)332-7615. Website: www.lernerbooks.com. Imprint of Lerner. Lerner's other imprints are Runestone Press, Lerner Sports, LernerClassroom and First Avenue Editions. The acquisition editor for Lerner is Jennifer Zimian, who handles fiction and nonfiction for grades 5-12. Book publisher. Estab. 1969. **Acquisitions:** Rebecca Poole, submissions editor. Publishes 50-60 titles/year. 10% of books by first-time authors. Carolrhoda Books is a children's publisher focused on producing high-quality, socially conscious nonfiction and fiction books for young readers K through grade 12, that help them learn about and explore the world around them. List includes picture books, biographies, nature and science titles, multicultural and introductory geography books and fiction for beginning readers. Recently published *The War*, by Anais Vaugelade; *Little Wolf's Haunted Hall for Small Horrors*, by Ian Whybrow.
How to Contact/Writers: Submissions are accepted in the months of March and October only. Submissions received in any month other than March or October will be returned unopened to the sender. A SASE is required for all submissions. Please allow 6 months for a response.
Tips: Carolrhoda does not publish alphabet books, puzzle books, songbooks, textbooks, religious subject matter or plays.

CARTWHEEL BOOKS, for the Very Young, Imprint of Scholastic Inc., 557 Broadway, New York NY 10012. (212)343-6100. Website: www.scholastic.com. Estab. 1991. Book publisher. Vice President/Editorial Director: Ken Geist. **Manuscript Acquisitions:** Grace Maccarone, executive editor; Sonia Black, senior editor; Jane Gerver, executive editor. **Art Acquisitions:** Richard Deas, art director. Publishes 25-30 picture books/year; 30-35 easy readers/year; 15-20 novelty/concept books/year. "With each Cartwheel list, we strive for a pleasing balance among board books and novelty books, hardcover picture books and gift books, nonfiction, paperback storybooks and easy readers. Cartwheel seeks to acquire novelties that are books first; play objects second. Even without its gimmick, a Cartwheel book should stand alone as a valid piece of children's literature. We want all our books to be inviting and appealing, and to have inherent educational and social value. We believe that small children who develop personal relationships with books and grow up with a love of reading, become book consumers, and ultimately better human beings."
Fiction: Picture books, young readers: humor, suspense/mystery. Average work length: picture books—1-3,000; easy readers—100-3,000.
Nonfiction: Picture books, young readers: animal, history, nature/environment, science, sports. "Most of our nonfiction is either written on assignment or is within a series. We do not want to see any arts/crafts or cooking." Average word length: picture books—100-3,000; young readers—100-3,000.

insider report

Discipline, good fortune, good friends, great characters—own the world

Kate DiCamillo

Newbery Honor Award-winning author Kate DiCamillo was 29 years old when it occurred to her that if she wanted to be a writer she would actually have to write. She began a routine of rising at four a.m. to shuffle directly to her computer. "I'd get up from bed and walk straight to the desk. That was absolutely the magic hour. You're still in a kind of dream state and can get wonderful writing that way. At four o'clock, you own the world."

DiCamillo scheduled writing into her life and took it on as a job. She set a goal of writing two pages every day, five days a week. Throughout her beginning years as a writer, she read and studied the stories of authors who had "made it." Imagining that she would be there someday was an incredible thing. "I would really memorize those sections of *Writer's Digest*."

Her studying and discipline paid off big when her novel, *Because of Winn-Dixie*, was awarded the Newbery Honor in 2001. The night before the winners were announced felt like Christmas Eve. DiCamillo continuously woke to check the clock, then finally got up and began her day as usual. She was writing when the phone rang with the news. She was stunned and extremely happy after speaking with the Newbery Committee. "I spent the whole day walking into walls." As a child, she knew to look for the Newbery Medal when choosing books. "To think that my book will have that medal on it's cover, and that some kid will pick it up because of that, is just amazing."

Kids may pick up *Because of Winn-Dixie* because it's adorned with the Newbery Honor medal, but it's DiCamillo's flawless story telling ability that has made the book an incredible success. With her childhood home of Florida as the setting, the charming novel follows ten-year-old India Opal Buloni and her mangy, goofy dog, Winn-Dixie. When Opal claims the mischief-making hound as her own, she convinces her preacher father to take him in. With the help of Winn-Dixie, Opal creates friendships in her new community and comes to terms with her sadness of not knowing her mother. It's because of Winn-Dixie that Opal learns to replace emptiness with hope. The tender, humorous story has gone on to sell well over 350,000 copies.

In addition to the Newbery Honor Award, *Because of Winn-Dixie* received seven other awards and eighteen award nominations. It was placed on eight master book lists and three Best Books of the Year lists.

DiCamillo's lean style, fresh voice and knack for weaving character-driven stories with emotional undertones has brought her novels much acclaim. But even with all the awards, she doesn't buy into the fact that her talent has much to do with her success. She believes luck has played a large role. "What has happened to me isn't just the result of a good book. I've been the recipient of good fortune, starting with Kara LaReau finding my manuscript. Kara's sensibility and mine dovetailed and that's what made it work." Candlewick editor Kara LaReau inherited *Because of Winn-Dixie* when an editorial change at the publishing house occurred. LaReau championed the first novel the minute she read it. At the time LaReau made an offer on *Winn-Dixie*, DiCamillo had just finished the final draft on her second novel, *The Tiger Rising*. Candlewick purchased both books. "It all happened within a couple of months," DiCamillo says.

In *The Tiger Rising*, Rob Horton discovers a caged tiger in the woods behind his home. Rob is a pro at not-thinking and not-crying and identifies with the trapped tiger's constant pacing. Rob's so good at suppressing his grief over the death of his mother and his anger at his father that his emotions rise to the surface in the form of a rash. With the aid of his odd and feisty friend Sistene, Rob releases the tiger and is able to set his own emotions free.

Both of DiCamillo's novels are coming-of-age stories rich in emotion. Both deal with the loss of a parent and recognize the importance of friendship. The fact that her father left when she was five and that she's never been without a best friend are mirrored in her work. "My friends have been a saving grace in my life," DiCamillo says.

In 1997, weary and close to turning off her path toward success, DiCamillo confided in friend and fellow writer Jane Resh Thomas. "I told her I didn't think I could believe in myself anymore. She said, 'You don't have to believe in yourself. I'll do it for you.'" Thomas continues to be a guiding light for DiCamillo. "It's amazing how much the right words can make such a huge difference. That is a tremendous gift."

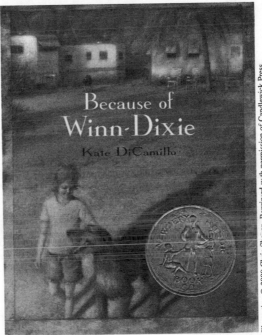

Kate DiCamillo says that having characters invade your thoughts to the point that you can hear them is one of the things an author waits for. She began writing the 2000 Newbery Honor award winner *Because of Winn-Dixie* (Candlewick Press) during a frigid winter in Minnesota. One night before she went to sleep she heard a little girl with a southern accent say to her "I have a dog named Winn-Dixie." *Because of Winn-Dixie* has recently been optioned for development as a feature film.

Illustration © 2000 Chris Sheban. Reprinted with permission of Candlewick Press

Even though DiCamillo had the support of friends, she was still in need of another kind of support—monetary. In 1998, she competed for and won the McKnight Fellowship for Writers. It was instrumental in allowing her to concentrate on writing without worrying about finances. "I was so poor when I received it, that it allowed me to sigh a huge sigh of relief."

Today, with financial worries behind her, DiCamillo continues her two-page-at-a-time writing sessions. Though she no longer rises before dawn, she still shuffles directly to her computer. DiCamillo now allows herself several sessions each day with breaks in between.

"I don't revise or edit as I go," DiCamillo says of her writing habits. "It's like I'm drawing a really rough map. I don't bother with capitalization or spelling or punctuation." The second draft is where she begins to pay attention to double spacing and other conventions of writing. "With each draft, I fine tune and revise." She rewrites several times before sending her work on to her editor. "Writing for me is nothing but rewriting. I can do ten drafts before it gets into Kara's hands because at some point, I have to let it go and realize I'll never get it perfect. There's no such thing."

Since being awarded the Newbery Honor, DiCamillo (whose third novel with Candlewick is scheduled for a fall 2003 release) tries not to think about her success while she writes. "There's a different kind of pressure now—that what I write has to live up to what I wrote before."

—*Lisa Rondinelli Albert*

Illustration © 2001 Chris Sheban. Reprinted with permission of Candlewick Press

The Tiger Rising, Kate DiCamillo's second novel, features a wild caged tiger as the animal catalyst. *Publishers Weekly* gave the novel a starred review and praised DiCamillo's demonstration of "versatility by treating themes similar to those of her first novel with a completely different approach."

How to Contact/Writers: Cartwheel Books is no longer accepting unsolicited mss or queries. All unsolicited materials will be returned unread. Fiction/nonfiction: For previously published or agented authors, submit complete ms. Responds to queries in 4 months; mss in 6 months. Publishes a book 2 years after acceptance. Will consider simultaneous submissions.

Illustration: Works with 100 illustrators/year. Reviews ms/illustration packages from artists. Send ms with dummy. Illustrations only: Query with samples; arrange personal portfolio review; send promo sheet, tearsheets to be kept on file. Contact: Art Director. Responds in 2 months. Samples returned with SASE; samples filed. Please do not send original artwork.

Photography: Buys stock and assigns work. Uses photos of kids, families, vehicles, toys, animals. Submit published samples, color promo piece.

Terms: Pays authors royalty of 2-8% based on retail price or work purchased outright for $600-5,000. Offers advances (Average amount: $3,000). Pays illustrators by the project (range: $2,000-10,000); flat fee; or advance against royalties (royalty of 1-3% based on retail price). Photographers paid by the project (range: $250-10,000); per photo (range: $250-500); or royalty of 1-3% of wholesale price. Sends galley to authors; dummy to illustrators. Originals returned to artist at job's completion. Book catalog available for 9 × 12 SAE and 2 first-class stamps; ms guidelines for SASE.

Tips: "Know what types of books we do. Check out bookstores or catalogs to see where your work would fit best."

N CAVENDISH CHILDREN'S BOOKS, Imprint of Marshal Cavendish, 99 White Plains Rd., Tarrytown NY 10591-9001. (914)332-8888. Specializes in children's trade books. **Editorial Director:** Margery Cuyler. **Art Acquisitions:** Anahid Hamparian, art director. Publishes 20-25 books/year.

Fiction/Nonfiction: All levels.

How to Contact/Writers: Do not query. Fiction/Nonfiction: Submit proposal.

Illustration: Contact: Art Director.

Terms: Pays authors royalties. Pays illustrators advance and royalty.

CHARLESBRIDGE, 85 Main St., Watertown MA 02472. (617)926-0329. Fax: (617)926-5720. E-mail: tradeeditorial@charlesbridge.com. Website: www.charlesbridge.com. Book publisher. Estab. 1980. Imprints: Talewinds and Whispering Coyote. Publishes 60% nonfiction, 40% fiction titles and picture books. Publishes nature, science, multicultural social studies and fiction picture books and board books. Charlesbridge also has an educational division. **Contact:** Trade Editorial Department, submissions editor or School Editorial Department.

Fiction: Picture books: "Strong, realistic stories with enduring themes." Considers the following categories: adventure, concept, contemporary, health, history, humor, multicultural, nature/environment, special needs, sports, suspense/mystery. Recently published: *Froggie Went A-Courtin'*, by Iza Trapani; and *Peanut's Emergency*, by Cristina Salat.

Nonfiction: Picture books: animal, biography, careers, concept, geography, health, history, multicultural, music/dance, nature/environment, religion, science, social issues, special needs, hobbies, sports. Average word length: picture books—1,500. Recently published: *The Skull Alphabet Book*, by Rozanne Lancsak Williams; and *Beaks!*, by Sneed B. Collard III.

How to Contact/Writers: Send ms and SASE. Accepts exclusive submissions only. Responds to mss in 3 months. Full ms only; no queries.

Illustration: Works with 5-10 illustrators/year. Uses color artwork only. Illustrations only: Query with samples; provide résumé, tearsheets to be kept on file. "Send no original artwork, please." Responds only if interested. Samples returned with SASE; samples filed. Originals returned at job's completion.

Terms: Pays authors and illustrators in royalties or work purchased outright. Manuscript/art guidelines available for SASE. Exclusive submissions only.

Tips: Wants "books that have humor and are factually correct. See our website for more tips."

CHICAGO REVIEW PRESS, 814 N. Franklin St., Chicago IL 60610. (312)337-0747. Fax: (312)337-5110. E-mail: publish@ipgbook.com. Website: www.ipgbook.com. Book publisher. Estab. 1973. **Manuscript Acquisitions:** Cynthia Sherry, executive editor. **Art Acquisitions:** Joan Sommers, art director. Publishes 3-4 middle readers/year and "about 4" young adult titles/year. 33% of books by first-time authors; 30% of books from agented authors. "Chicago Review Press publishes high-quality, nonfiction, educational activity books that extend the learning process through hands-on projects and accurate and interesting text. We look for activity books that are as much fun as they are constructive and informative."

Nonfiction: Picture books, young readers, middle readers and young adults: activity books, arts/crafts, multicultural, history, nature/environment, science. "We're interested in hands-on, educational books; anything else probably will be rejected." Average length: young readers and young adults—175 pages. Recently published *Oceans*, by Nancy Castaldo (ages 6-9); *The American Revolution for Kids*, by Janis Herbert (ages 9 and up); and *Monet and Impressionism for Kids*, by Carol Sabbeth (ages 9 and up).

How to Contact/Writers: Enclose cover letter and no more than table of contents and 1-2 sample chapters. Send for guidelines. Responds to queries/mss in 2 months. Publishes a book 1-2 years after acceptance. Will consider simultaneous submissions and previously published work.

Illustration: Works with 6 illustrators/year. Uses primarily b&w artwork. Reviews ms/illustration packages from artists. Submit 1-2 chapters of ms with corresponding pieces of final art. Illustrations only: Query with samples, résumé. Responds only if interested. Samples returned with SASE.

Photography: Buys photos from freelancers ("but not often"). Buys stock and assigns work. Wants "instructive photos. We consult our files when we know what we're looking for on a book-by-book basis." Uses b&w prints.

Terms: Pays authors royalty of 7½-12½% based on retail price. Offers advances of $1,000-4,000. Pays illustrators by the project (range varies considerably). Pays photographers by the project (range varies considerably). Original artwork "usually" returned at job's completion. Book catalog/ms guidelines available for $3.

Tips: "We're looking for original activity books for small children and the adults caring for them—new themes and enticing projects to occupy kids' imaginations and promote their sense of personal creativity. We like activity books that are as much fun as they are constructive. Please write for guidelines so you'll know what we're looking for."

CHILD WELFARE LEAGUE OF AMERICA, Child & Family Press, 440 First St., NW, 3rd Floor, Washington DC 20001-2085. (202)942-0263. Fax: (202)638-4004. E-mail: www.ptierney@cwla.org. Website: www.cwla.org. The Child & Family Press imprint was created in 1990. **Acquisitions:** Peggy Porter Tierney. Publishes 5 picture books/year; 1 middle reader/year. 50% books by first-time authors. "CWLA is the nation's oldest and largest membership-based child welfare organization. We are committed to engaging people everywhere in promoting the well-being of children, youth, and their families, and protecting every child from harm."

Fiction: Picture books: animal, concept, contemporary, health, multicultural, special needs. Recently published *Glenna's Seeds*, by Nancy Edward (picture book, ages 4-11); *Imagine*, by Angela Lamanno (picture book, ages 4-9); and *An American Face*, by Jan Czech (picture book, ages 4-11).

Nonfiction: Picture books, young readers, middle readers, young adults: concept, multicultural, self-help, social issues, special needs (anything relating to child welfare). Recently published *Being Adopted*, by Stephanie Herbert (picture book, ages 4-8); *I Miss My Foster Parents*, by Stefan Herbert (picture book, 4-8); and *The Visit*, by Latisha Herbert (picture book, ages 4-8).

How to Contact/Writers: Fiction/nonfiction: Submit complete ms or submit outline/synopsis and 3-4 sample chapters. Responds in 3 months. Publishes a book 1 year after acceptance. Will consider simultaneous submissions.

Illustration: Works with 5 illustrators/year. Reviews ms/illustration packages from artists. Send ms with dummy or submit ms with 3-4 pieces of final art. Contact: Jennifer Geanakos, lead designer. Illustrations only: Query with samples. Contact: Peggy Porter Tierney, acquisitions. Responds in 3 months. "We prefer to keep samples on file in case suitable for future job." Samples returned with SASE.

Photography: Buys stock. Contact: Peggy Porter Tierney, acquisitions. Uses photos of children and families. Uses color or b&w prints and 35mm, 2¼×2¼, 4×5 transparencies. Submit slides, client list, promo piece, published samples, stock photo list.

Terms: Pays authors royalty of 9-12% based on retail price. Pays illustrators royalties of 3-5% or by the project. Pays photographers by the project or per photo. Sends galleys to authors; dummies to illustrators. Writer's guidlines for SASE. Catalog available on website.

Tips: "We are looking for upbeat, imaginative children's stories, particularly with some kind of message, but without being didactic. Authors do not need to worry about illustrations or formatting. In fact, a plain text to me is preferable to a manuscript set out in pages with very amateurish drawings. Do not call to propose an idea."

CHILDREN'S BOOK PRESS, 2211 Mission St., San Francisco CA 94110. (415)821-3080. Fax: (415)821-3081. E-mail: info@cbookpress.org. Website: www.cbookpress.org. **Acquisitions:** Submissions Editor. "Children's Book Press is a nonprofit publisher of multicultural and bilingual children's literature. We publish folktales and contemporary stories reflecting the traditions and culture of minorities and new immigrants in the United States. Our goal is to help broaden the base of children's literature in this country to include more stories from the African-American, Asian-American, Hispanic and Native American communities as well as the diverse Spanish-speaking communities throughout the Americas."

Fiction: Picture books, young readers: contemporary, folktales, history, multicultural, poetry. Average word length: picture books—800-1,600.

Nonfiction: Picture books, young readers: multicultural.

How to Contact/Writers: Submit complete ms to Submissions Editor. Responds to mss in roughly 4 months. Publishes a book 1-2 years after acceptance. Will consider simultaneous submissions.

Illustration: Works with 4-5 illustrators/year. Uses color artwork only. Reviews ms/illustration packages from artists. Send ms with 3 or 4 color photocopies. Illustrations only: color copies preferable, slides if you must, no original artwork. Responds only of interested. Samples returned with SASE.

Terms: Original artwork returned at job's completion. Book catalog available; ms guidelines available via website or with SASE.

Tips: "Vocabulary level should be approximately third grade (eight years old) or below. Keep in mind, however, that many of the young people who read our books may be nine, ten, or eleven years old or older. Their life experiences are often more advanced than their reading level, so try to write a story that will appeal to a fairly wide age range. We are especially interested in humorous stories and original stories about contemporary life from the multicultural communities mentioned above by writers *from* those communities."

CHINA BOOKS & PERIODICALS, 2929 24th St., San Francisco CA 94110. (415)282-2994. Fax: (415)282-0994. E-mail: info@chinabooks.com. Website: www.chinabooks.com. Book publisher, distributor, wholesaler. Estab. 1960. **Acquisitions:** Greg Jones, editor. Publishes 1 picture book/year; 1 middle readers/year; and 1 young adult title/year. 50% of books by first-time authors. Publishes only books about China and Chinese culture. "China Books is the main importer and distributor of books and magazines from China, providing an ever-changing variety of useful tools for travelers, scholars and others interested in China and Chinese culture."

Fiction: All levels: animal, anthology, folktales, history, multicultural, nature/environment.

Nonfiction: All levels: activity books, animal, arts/crafts, cooking, how-to, multicultural, music/dance, reference, textbooks. Recently published *Sing Chinese! Popular Children's Songs & Lullabies*, by Ma Baolin and Cindy Ma (children/adult song book); and *The Moon Maiden and Other Asian Folktales*, by Hua Long (children to age 12, folktales); *West to East: A Young Girl's Journey to China*, by Qian Gao (young adult nonfiction travel journal).

How to Contact/Writers: Fiction/Nonfiction: Query. Responds to queries and mss in 2 months. Publishes a book 1 year after acceptance. Will consider simultaneous submissions, electronic submissions via disk or modem, previously published work.

Illustration: Works with 4-5 illustrators/year. Reviews ms/illustration packages from artists. Query. Illustrations only: Query with samples. Send résumé, promo sheet, tearsheets. Responds in 1 month only if interested. Samples returned with SASE; samples filed.

Terms: Pays authors 4-10% royalty based on wholesale price or work purchased outright. Pays illustrators and photographers by the project (range $400-1,500) or royalty based on wholesale price. Sends galleys to authors; dummies to illustrators. Originals returned to artist at job's completion. See website for guidelines.

N **☐** **CHRISTIAN ED. PUBLISHERS**, P.O. Box 26639, San Diego CA 92196. (858)578-4700. E-mail: slowe@cepub.com (writing); ckruger@cepub.com (illustration). Website: www.ChristianEdWarchouse.com. **Senior Editor:** Dr. Lon Ackelson. **Managing Editor:** Carol Rogers. Book publisher. Publishes 80 Bible curriculum titles/year. "We publish curriculum for children and youth, including program and student books (for youth) and take-home papers (for children)—all handled by our assigned freelance writers only."

Fiction: Young readers: contemporary. Middle readers: adventure, contemporary, suspense/mystery. "We publish fiction for Bible club take-home papers. All fiction is on assignment only."

Nonfiction: Publishes Bible curriculum and take home papers for all ages. Recently published *All-Stars for Jesus*, by Treena Herrington and Letitia Zook, illustrated by Beverly Warren (Bible club curriculum for grades 4-6); and *Honeybees Classroom Activity Sheets*, by Janet Miller and Wanda Pelfrey, illustrated by Aiko Gilson and Terry Walderhaug (Bible club curriculum for ages 2-3).

How to Contact/Writers: Fiction/Nonfiction: Query. Responds to queries in 5 weeks. Publishes a book 1 year after acceptance. Send SASE for guidelines or contact Christian Ed. at slowe@cepub.com.

Illustration: Works with 6-7 illustrators/year. Uses primarily b&w artwork. Query; include a SASE; we'll send an application form. Contact: Clint Kruger, design coordinator (ckruger@cepub.com). Responds in 1 month. Samples returned with SASE.

Terms: Work purchased outright from authors for 3¢/word. Pays illustrators by the project (range: $300-400/book). Book catalog available for 9 × 12 SAE and 4 first-class stamps; ms and art guidelines available for SASE.

Tips: "Read our guidelines carefully before sending us a manuscript or illustrations. All writing and illustrating is done on assignment only and must be age-appropriate (preschool-6th grade)."

CHRONICLE BOOKS, 85 Second St., 6th Floor, San Francisco CA 94105. (415)537-4422. Fax: (415)537-4420. Website: www.chroniclekids.com. Book publisher. **Acquisitions:** Victoria Rock, associate publisher, children's books. Publishes 35-60 (both fiction and nonfiction) books/year, 5-10% middle readers, young adult nonfiction titles. 10-25% of books by first-time authors; 20-40% of books from agented writers.

Fiction: Picture books: animal, folktales, history, multicultural, nature/environment. Young readers: animal, folktales, history, multicultural, nature/environment, poetry. Middle readers: animal, history, multicultural, nature/environment, poetry, problem novels. Young adults: multicultural needs include "projects that feature diverse children in everyday situations." Recently published *Red is a Dragon*, by Roseanne Thong, illustrated by Grace Lin; *Bintou's Braids*, by Sylviane A. Dionf, illustrated by Shane W. Evans; *Twinkle Twinkle Little Star*, by Sylvia Long.

Nonfiction: Picture books: animal, history, multicultural, nature/environment, science. Young readers: animal, arts/crafts, cooking, geography, history, multicultural and science. Middle readers: animal, arts/crafts, biography, cooking, geography, history, multicultural and nature/environment. Young adults: biography and multicultural. Recently published *Story Painter: The Life of Jacob Lawrence*, by John Duggleby; *Seven Weeks on an Iceberg*, by Keith Potter (Doodlezoo series).

How to Contact/Writers: Fiction/Nonfiction: Submit complete ms (picture books); submit outline/synopsis and 3 sample chapters (for older readers). Responds to queries/mss in 4 months. Publishes a book 1-3 years after acceptance. Will consider simultaneous submissions, as long as they are marked "multiple submission." Will not consider submissions by fax or e-mail. Must include SASE or projects will not be returned.

Illustration: Works with 15-20 illustrators/year. Wants "unusual art, graphically strong, something that will stand out on the shelves. Either bright and modern or very traditional. Fine art, not mass market." Reviews ms/illustration packages from artists. "Indicate if project *must* be considered jointly, or if editor may consider text and art separately." Illustrations only: Submit samples of artist's work (not necessarily from book, but in the envisioned style). Slides, tearsheets and color photocopies OK. (No original art.) Dummies helpful. Résumé helpful. "If samples sent for files, generally no response—unless samples are not suited to list, in which case samples are returned. Queries and project proposals responded to in same time frame as author query/proposals."

Photography: Purchases photos from freelancers. Works on assignment only. Wants nature/natural history photos.

Terms: Generally pays authors in royalties based on retail price "though we do occasionally work on a flat fee basis." Advance varies. Illustrators paid royalty based on retail price or flat fee. Sends proofs to authors and illustrators. Book catalog for 9×12 SAE and 8 first-class stamps; ms guidelines for #10 SASE.

Tips: "Chronicle Books publishes an eclectic mixture of traditional and innovative children's books. We are interested in taking on projects that have a unique bent to them—be it in subject matter, writing style, or illustrative technique. As a small list, we are looking for books that will lend our list a distinctive flavor. Primarily we are interested in fiction and nonfiction picture books for children ages infant-8 years, and nonfiction books for children ages 8-12 years. We are also interested in developing a middle grade/YA fiction program, and are looking for literary fiction that deals with relevant issues. Our sales reps are witnessing a resistance to alphabet books. And the market has become increasingly competitive. The '80s boom in children's publishing has passed, and the market is demanding high-quality books that work on many different levels."

CLARION BOOKS, 215 Park Ave. S., New York NY 10003. (212)420-5889. Website: www.houghtonmifflinbooks.com/trade/. Imprint of Houghton Mifflin Company. Book publisher. Estab. 1965. **Manuscript Acquisitions:** Dinah Stevenson, associate publisher; Michele Coppola, editor; Virginia Buckley, contributing editor; Jennifer Green, editor. **Art Acquisitions:** Joann Hill, art director.

• Clarion title *A Single Shard*, by Linda Sue Park, won the 2002 Newbery Medal. Their title *The Three Pigs*, by David Wiesner, won the 2002 Caldecott Medal. Clarion is reading manuscripts but signing books for 2004 and beyond.

How to Contact/Writers: Fiction and picture books: Send complete mss. Nonfiction: Send query with up to 3 sample chapters. Must include SASE. Will accept simultaneous submission if informed.

Illustration: Send samples (no originals).

Terms: Pays illustrators royalty; flat fee for jacket illustration. Pays royalties and advance to writers; both vary.

CLEAR LIGHT PUBLISHERS, 823 Don Diego, Santa Fe NM 87505. (505)989-9590. Fax: (505)989-9519. Website: www.clearlightbooks.com. Book publisher. **Acquisitions:** Harmon Houghton, publisher. Publishes 4 middle readers/year; and 4 young adult titles/year.
Nonfiction: Middle readers and young adults: multicultural, American Indian and Hispanic only.
How to Contact/Writers: Fiction/Nonfiction: Submit complete ms with SASE. "No e-mail submissions. Authors supply art. Manuscripts not considered without art or artists renderings." Will consider simultaneous submissions. Responds in 3 months. Only send *copies*.
Illustration: Reviews ms/illustration packages from artists. "No originals please." Submit ms with dummy and SASE.
Terms: Pays authors royalty of 10% based on wholesale price. Offers advances (average amount: up to 50% of expected net sales within the first year). Sends galleys to authors.
Tips: "We're looking for authentic American Indian art and folklore."

CONCORDIA PUBLISHING HOUSE, 3558 S. Jefferson Ave., St. Louis MO 63118. (314)268-1187. Fax: (314)268-1329. Website: cphmall.com. Book publisher. **Contact:** Peggy Kuethe. "Concordia Publishing House produces quality resources which communicate and nurture the Christian faith and ministry of people of all ages, lay and professional. These resources include curriculum, worship aids, books, multimedia products and religious supplies. We publish approximately 30 quality children's books each year. All are nonfiction based on a religious subject. We boldly provide Gospel resources that are Christ-centered, Bible-based and faithful to our Lutheran heritage."
Nonfiction: Picture books: activity books, arts/crafts, concept, poetry, contemporary, religion. Young readers, middle readers, young adults: activity books, arts/crafts, concept, contemporary, religion. Young adults: religion. "All books must contain explicit Christian content." Recently published *The Very First Christmas*, by Paul L. Maier (picture book for ages 6-10); and *Running the Race of Faith*, by Pam Ausenhus (ages over 12, youth nonfiction).
How to Contact/Writers: Submit complete ms (picture books); submit outline/synopsis and sample chapters for longer mss. May also query. Responds to queries in 1 month; mss in 3 months. Publishes a book 2 years after acceptance. Will consider simultaneous submissions. "No phone queries."
Illustration: Works with 50 illustrators/year. Illustrations only: Query with samples. Contact: Ed Luhmann, art director. Responds only if interested. Samples returned with SASE; samples filed. Originals not returned at job's completion.
Terms: Pays authors in royalties based on retail price or work purchased outright ($750-2,000). Sends galleys to author. Manuscript guidelines for 1 first-class stamp and a #10 envelope. Pays illustrators by the project ($1,000).
Tips: "Do not send finished artwork with the manuscript. If sketches will help in the presentation of the manuscript, they may be sent. If stories are taken from the Bible, they should follow the Biblical account closely. Liberties should not be taken in fantasizing Biblical stories."

COOK COMMUNICATIONS MINISTRIES, (formerly Cook Communications), 4050 Lee Vance View, Colorado Springs CO 80918. (719)536-0100. Fax: (719)536-3296. Website: www.cookministries.org. Book publisher. **Acquisitions:** Mary McNeil, acquisitions editor. Publishes 15-20 picture books/year; 6-8 young readers/year; and 6-12 middle readers/year. Less than 5% of books by first-time authors; 15% of books from agented authors. "All books have overt Christian values, but there is no primary theme."
   ● Cook accepts unsolicited mss, but prefers agented submissions.
Illustration: Works with 15 illustrators/year. "Send color material I can keep." Query with samples; send résumé, promo sheet, portfolio, tearsheets. Responds in 6 months only if interested. Samples returned with SASE; samples filed.
Terms: Pays illustrators by the project, royalty or work purchased outright. Sends dummies to illustrators. Original artwork returned at job's completion. Manuscript guidelines available for SASE. Call ms hotline at (719)536-0100, ext. 3930.

COTEAU BOOKS LTD., 401-2206 Dewdney Ave., Regina, Sasketchewan S4R 1H3 Canada. (306)777-0170. E-mail: coteau@coteaubooks.com. Website: www.coteaubooks.com. Thunder Creek Publishing Co-op Ltd. Book publisher. Estab. 1975. **Acquisitions:** Geoffrey Ursell, publisher. Publishes 3-4

A SELF-ADDRESSED, STAMPED ENVELOPE (SASE) should always be included with submissions within your own country. When sending material to other countries, include a self-addressed envelope (SAE) and International Reply Coupons (IRCs).

juvenile and/or young adult books/year, 12-14 books/year. 10% of books by first-time authors. "Coteau Books publishes the finest Canadian fiction, poetry, drama and children's literature, with an emphasis on western writers."

• Coteau Books publishes Canadian writers and illustrators only; manuscripts from the U.S. are returned unopened.

Fiction: Young readers, middle readers, young adults: adventure, contemporary, fantasy, history, humor, multicultural, nature/environment, science fiction, suspense/mystery. "No didactic, message pieces, nothing religious. No picture books. Material should reflect the diversity of culture, race, religion, creed of human-kind—we're looking for fairness and balance." Recently published *Angels in the Snow*, by Wenda Young (ages 11-14); *Bay Girl*, by Betty Dorion (ages 8-11); and *The Innocent Polly McDoodle*, by Mary Woodbury (ages 8-12).

Nonfiction: Young readers, middle readers, young adult: biography, history, multicultural, nature/environment, social issues.

How to Contact/Writers: Fiction: Submit complete ms to acquisitions editor. Include SASE or send up to 20-page sample by e-mail, as an attached file, in the Mime protocol. Responds to queries in 3-4 months; mss in 3-4 months. Publishes a book 1-2 years after acceptance. Send for guidelines.

Illustration: Works with 1-4 illustrators/year. Illustrations only: Submit nonreturnable samples. Responds only if interested. Samples returned with SASE; samples filed.

Photography: "Very occasionally buys photos from freelancers." Buys stock and assigns work.

Terms: Pays authors in royalties based on retail price. Pays illustrators and photographers by the project. Sends galleys to authors; dummies to illustrators. Original artwork returned at job's completion. Book catalog free on request with 9 × 12 SASE.

Tips: "Truthfully, the work speaks for itself! Be bold. Be creative. Be persistent! There is room, at least in the Canadian market, for quality novels for children, and at Coteau, this is a direction we will continue to take."

CRICKET BOOKS, Imprint of the Cricket Magazine Group, 332 S. Michigan Ave., Suite 1100, Chicago IL 60604. (312)939-1500. E-mail: cricketBooks@caruspub.com. Website: www.cricketbooks.net. Imprint estab. 1999; Company estab. 1973. **Manuscript Acquisitions:** Carol Saller. **Art Acquisitions:** Tony Jacobson. Publishes 24 titles/year. "For 25 years we've published the best children's literary magazines in America, and we're looking for the same high-quality material for our book imprint."

• Publisher Marc Aronson is publishing fiction and nonfiction for teenagers under his Harcato imprint. Look for news on the new imprint in industry publications.

Fiction: Young readers, middle readers, young adult/teen: adventure, animal, contemporary, fantasy, history, multicultural, humor, sports, suspense/mystery, science fiction, problem novels. Recently published *John Riley's Daughter*, by Kezi Matthews; *Two Suns in the Sky*, by Miriam Bat-Ami.

How to Contact: Fiction: submit complete ms. Nonfiction: Query. Responds to queries in 3 months; mss in 3 months. Publishes a book 18 months after acceptance. Will consider simultaneous submissions if informed.

Illustration: Works with 4 illustrators/year. Use color and b&w. Illustration only: submit samples, tear-sheets. Contact: Tony Jacobson. Responds only if interested. Samples returned with SASE; sample filed.

Terms: Authors paid royalty of 7-10% based on retail price. Offers advances. Illustrators paid royalty of 3% based on retail price. Sends galleys to authors; dummies to illustrators. Originals returned to artist at job's completion. Writer's guidelines available for SASE. Catalog available at website.

Tips: "Primarily interested in chapter books, middle-grade fiction, and young adult novels, but will also consider picture books. Study *Cricket* and *Spider* magazines to get an idea of our approach and to learn more of what we're looking for."

CROSSWAY BOOKS, Good News Publishers, 1300 Crescent, Wheaton IL 60187-5800. (630)682-4300. Fax: (630)682-4785. E-mail: editorial@gnpcb.org. Website: www.crosswaybooks.org. Book Publisher. Estab. 1938. Editorial Director: Marvin Padgett. **Acquisitions:** Jill Carter. Publishes 3-4 picture books/year; and 1-2 young adult titles/year. "Crossway Books is committed to publishing books that bring Biblical reality to readers and that examine crucial issues through a Christian world view."

Fiction: Picture books: religion. Middle readers: adventure, contemporary, history, humor, religion, Christian realism. Young adults: contemporary, history, humor, religion, Christian realism. Does not want to see horror novels, romance or prophecy novels. Not looking for picture book submissions at present time. Recently published *If I Only Had a Green Nose*, by Max Lucado, illustrated by Sergio Martinez; *Yes or No, Who Will Go?*, by Melody Carlson, illustrated by Steve Björkman.

How to Contact/Writers: Fiction: Query with outline/synopsis and up to 2 sample chapters. Responds to queries/mss in 2 months. Publishes a book 12-18 months after acceptance. Will consider simultaneous submissions.

Illustration: Works with 3-4 illustrators/year. Reviews ms/illustration packages from artists. Query. Illustrations only: Query with samples; provide résumé, promo sheet and client list. Responds to artists' queries/submissions in 2 months. Samples returned with SASE; samples filed. Originals returned at job's completion.

Terms: Pays authors royalty based on wholesale price. Pays illustrators by the project. Sends galleys to authors; dummies to illustrators. Book catalog available; ms guidelines available for SASE.

CROWN BOOKS FOR YOUNG READERS, 1540 Broadway, New York NY 10036. (212)782-9000. Website: www.randomhouse.com/kids. See Random House listing. Book publisher.
- Crown Books for Young Readers is an imprint of Random House Children's Books.

MAY DAVENPORT, PUBLISHERS, 26313 Purissima Rd., Los Altos Hills CA 94022-4539. (650)947-1275. Fax: (650)947-1373. E-mail: mdbooks@earthlink.net. Website: www.maydavenportpublishers.com. Independent book producer/packager. Estab. 1976. **Acquisitions:** May Davenport, editor/publisher. Publishes 1-2 picture books/year; and 2-3 young adult titles/year. 99% of books by first-time authors. Seeks books with literary merit. "We like to think that we are selecting talented writers who have something humorous to write about today's unglued generation in 30,000-50,000 words for teens and young adults in junior/senior high school before they become tomorrow's 'functional illiterates.' We are interested in publishing literature that teachers in middle and high schools can use in their Language Arts, English and Creative Writing courses. There's more to literary fare than the chit-chat Internet dialog and fantasy trips on television with cartoons or humanoids." This publisher is overstocked with picture book/elementary reading material.

Fiction: Young adults (15-18): contemporary, humorous fictional literature for use in English courses in junior-senior high schools in US. Average word length: 40,000-60,000. Recently published *The Lesson Plan*, by Irvin Gay (about an illiterate black boy who grows up to become a teacher, ages 15-18); *A Life on the Line*, by Michael Horton (about a juvenile delinquent boy who becomes a hero, ages 15-18); *Making My Escape*, by David Lee Finkle (about a young boy who day dreams movie-making in outer space to escape unhappy family life, ages 12-18).

Nonfiction: Teens: humorous. Recently published *The Runaway Game*, by Kevin Casey (a literary board game of street life in Hollywood, ages 15-18).

How to Contact/Writers: Fiction: Query. Responds to queries/mss in 3 weeks. "We do not answer queries or manuscripts which do not have SASE attached." Publishes a book 6-12 months after acceptance.

Illustration: Works with 1-2 illustrators/year. "Have enough on file for future reference." Responds only if interested. Samples returned with SASE; samples filed. Originals returned at job's completion.

Terms: Pays authors royalties of 15% based on retail price; negotiable. Pays "by mutual agreement, no advances." Pays illustrators by the project (range: $75-350). Book catalog, ms guidelines free on request with SASE.

Tips: "Create stories to enrich the non-reading high school readers. They might not appreciate your similies and metaphors and may find fault with your alliterations, but show them how you do it with memorable characters in today's society. Just project your humorous talent and entertain with more than two sentences in a paragraph."

DAWN PUBLICATIONS, P.O. Box 2010, Nevada City CA 95959. (530)478-0111. Fax: (530)478-0112. E-mail: glenn@dawnpub.com. Website: www.dawnpub.com. Book publisher. Publisher: Muffy Weaver. **Acquisitions:** Glenn J. Hovemann, editor. Publishes works with holistic themes dealing with nature. "Dawn Publications is dedicated to inspiring in children a deeper appreciation and understanding of nature."

Nonfiction: Picture books: animal, nature/environment. Biographies of naturalists recently published *John Muir: My Life With Nature*, by Joseph Cornell (80-page biography); and *Do Animals Have Feelings Too?*, by David L. Rice (32-page picture book).

How to Contact/Writers: Nonfiction: Query or submit complete ms. Responds to queries/mss in 3 months maximum. Publishes a book 1 year after acceptance. Will consider simultaneous submissions.

Illustration: Works with 5 illustrators/year. Will review ms/illustration packages from artists. Query; send ms with dummy. Illustrations only: Query with samples, résumé.

Terms: Pays authors royalty based on wholesale price. Offers advance. Pays illustrators by the project or royalties based on wholesale price. Book catalog available online; ms guidelines available online.

Tips: Looking for "picture books expressing nature awareness with inspirational quality leading to enhanced self-awareness. Usually no animal dialogue."

DIAL BOOKS FOR YOUNG READERS, Penguin Putnam Inc., 345 Hudson St., New York NY 10014. Website: www.penguinputnam.com. Associate Publisher/Editorial Director: Lauri Hornik. **Acquisitions:** Nancy Mercado, editor; Cecile Goyette, editor; Karen Riskin, editor. Art Director: Lily Malcom. Publishes 35 picture books/year; 3 young reader titles/year; 6 middle reader titles/year; and 9 young adult titles/year.

Fiction: Picture books, young readers: adventure, animal, contemporary, fantasy, folktales, history, humor, multicultural, nature/environment, poetry, science fiction, sports. Middle readers, young adults: adventure, contemporary, fantasy, folktales, history, humor, multicultural, poetry, problem novels, science fiction, sports, mystery/adventure. Published *A Year Down Yonder*, by Richard Peck (ages 10 and up); *The Magic Nesting Doll*, by Jacqueline K. Ogburn and illustrated by Laurel Long (all ages, picture book); *A Penguin Pup for Pinkerton*, by Steven Kellogg (ages 3-7, picture book).

Nonfiction: Will consider query letters for submissions of outstanding literary merit. Picture books, young readers: animals, biography, history, sports. Middle readers: biography, history. Young adults: biography, history, contemporary. Recently published *Thanks to My Mother*, by Schoschana Rabinovici (ages 12 and up, YA) and *Dirt on their Skirts*, by Doreen Rappaport and Lyndall Callan (ages 4-8, picture book).

How to Contact/Writers: Accepts picture book ms and queries for longer works. Do not send more than 10 pages. Responds to queries/mss. in 3 months. "We do not supply specific guidelines, but we will send you a recent catalog if you send us a 9×12 SASE with four 34¢ stamps attached. Questions and queries should only be made in writing. We will not reply to anything without a SASE." No e-mail queries.

Illustration: Works with 25 illustrators/year. To arrange a personal interview to show portfolio, send samples and a letter requesting an interview. Art samples should be sent to Dial Design and will not be returned without a SASE. "No phone calls please. Only artists with portfolios that suit the house's needs will be interviewed."

Terms: Pays authors and illustrators in royalties based on retail price. Average advance payment "varies."

✓ Ⓐ **DK PUBLISHING, INC.**, DK Ink, 375 Hudson St., New York NY 10014. Website: www.dk.com.

Acquisitions: submissions editor. Publishes 30 picture books/year; 30 young readers/year; 10 middle readers/year; and 5 young adult titles/year.

• DK Publishing does not accept unagented manuscripts.

DOG-EARED PUBLICATIONS, P.O. Box 620863, Middletown WI 53562-0863. (608)831-1410. (608)831-1410. Fax: (608)831-1410. E-mail: field@dog-eared.com. Website: www.dog-eared.com. Book publisher. Estab. 1977. Art Acquisitions: Nancy Field, publisher. Publishes 2-3 middle readers/year. 1% of books by first-time authors. "Dog-Eared Publications creates action-packed nature books for children. We aim to turn young readers into environmentally aware citizens and to foster a love for science and nature in the new generation.

Nonfiction: Middle readers: activity books, animal, nature/environment, science. Average word length varies. Recently published *Leapfrogging Through Wetlands*, by Margaret Anderson, Nancy Field and Karen Stephenson, illustrated by Michael Maydak (middle readers, activity book); *Ancient Forests*, by Margaret Anderson, Nancy Field and Karen Stephenson, illustrated by Sharon Torvik (middle readers, activity book); *Discovering Wolves*, by Nancy Field, Corliss Karassov, illustrated by Cary Hunkel (activity book).

How to Contact/Writers: Nonfiction: Currently not accepting unsolicited submissions.

Illustration: Works with 2-3 illustrators/year. Reviews mss/illustration packages from artists. Submit query and a few art samples. Contact: Nancy Field, publisher. Illustrations only: Query with samples. Contact: Nancy Field, publisher. Responds only if interested. Samples not returned; samples filed. "Interested in realistic, mature art!"

Photography: Works on assignment only.

Terms: Pays authors royalty based on wholesale price. Offers advances(amount varies). Pays illustrators royalty based on wholesale price. Sends galleys to authors. Originals returned to artist at job's completion. Brochure available for SASE and 1 first-class stamp. Brochure available on website.

DUTTON CHILDREN'S BOOKS, Penguin Putnam Inc., 345 Hudson St., New York NY 10014. (212)366-3700. Website: www.penguinputnam.com. Book publisher. President and Publisher: Stephanie Owens Lurie. **Acquisitions:** Submissions Editor. **Art Acquisitions:** Sara Reynolds, art director. Publishes approximately 60 picture books/year; 6 young reader titles/year; 16 middle reader titles/year; and 12 young adult titles/year. 10% of books by first-time authors.

• Dutton is open to query letters only.

Fiction: Picture books: adventure, animal, history, humor, multicultural, nature/environment, poetry, contemporary. Young readers: adventure, animal, contemporary, fantasy, suspense/mystery. Middle readers: adventure, animal, contemporary, fantasy, history, multicultural, nature/environment, suspense/mystery. Young adults: adventure, animal, contemporary, fantasy, history, multicultural, nature/environment, poetry, suspense/mystery. Recently published *The Tale of Wagmore Gently*, by Linda Ashman, illustrated by John Bendell-Brunello (picture book).

Nonfiction: Picture books, young readers: animal, history, multicultural, nature/environment. Middle readers: animal, biography, history, multicultural, nature/environment. Young adults: animal, biography, history, multicultural, nature/environment, social issues. Recently published *Dr. Jenner and the Speckled Monster*, by Albert Marrin; *Cop on the Beat*, by Arlene Schulman.

How to Contact/Writers: Query only. Does not accept unsolicited mss. Responds to queries in 3 months. Publishes a book 12-18 months after acceptance. Will consider simultaneous submissions.

Illustration: Works with 40-60 illustrators/year. Reviews ms/illustration packages from artists. Query first. Illustrations only: Query with samples; send résumé, portfolio, slides—no original art please. Responds to art samples in 2 months. Original artwork returned at job's completion.

Photography: Will look at photography samples and photo-essay proposals.

Terms: Pays authors royalties of 4-10% based on retail price. Book catalog, ms guidelines for SASE with 8 first-class stamps. Pays illustrators royalties of 2-10% based on retail price unless jacket illustration—then pays by flat fee.

Tips: "Avoid topics that appear frequently. In nonfiction, we are looking for history, general biography, science and photo essays for all age groups." Illustrators: "We would like to see samples and portfolios from potential illustrators of picture books (full color), young novels (b&w) and jacket artists (full color)." Foresee "even more multicultural publishing, plus more books published in both Spanish and English."

EERDMAN'S BOOKS FOR YOUNG READERS, an imprint of Eerdmans Publishing Company, 255 Jefferson Ave. SE, Grand Rapids MI 49503. (616)459-4591 or (800)253-7521. Website: www.eerdmans. com/youngreaders. Book publisher. **Manuscript Acquisitions:** Judy Zylstra, editor-in-chief. **Art Acquisitions:** Jesse Josten. Publishes 12-15 books/year.

Fiction: Picture books, middle readers: parables, religion, retold Bible stories, child or family issues, historical fiction, art/artists, poetry. No science fiction.

Nonfiction: All levels: biography, religion.

How to Contact/Writers: Fiction/Nonfiction: Query with sample chapters (novels) or submit complete ms (picture books or middle readers under 200 pages). Always include cover letter. Responds to queries in 6 weeks; mss in 3 months.

Illustration: Works with 14-16 illustrators/year. Responds to ms/art samples in 3 months. Illustrations only: Submit résumé, slides or color photocopies. Samples returned with SASE; samples filed.

Terms: Pays authors and illustrators royalties of 5-7% based on retail price. Sends galleys to authors; dummies to illustrators. Original artwork returned at job's completion. Book catalog free on request with SASE (4 first class stamps, 9 × 12 envelope); ms and/or artist's guidelines free on request, with SASE.

Tips: "We are looking for material that will help children build their faith in God and explore God's world. We accept all genres. We will not accept or respond to manuscripts, proposals or queries sent by e-mail or fax."

ENSLOW PUBLISHERS INC., Box 398, 40 Industrial Rd., Berkeley Heights NJ 07922-0398. Website: www.enslow.com. Estab. 1978. **Acquisitions:** Brian D. Enslow, vice president. Imprint: MyReportLinks. com Books. Publishes 100 middle reader titles/year; and 100 young adult titles/year. 30% of books by first-time authors.

• Enslow Imprint MyReportLinks.com Books produces books on animals, states, presidents, continents, oceans and ancient civilizations for middle readers and young adults, and offers links to online sources of information on topics covered in books.

Nonfiction: Young readers, middle readers, young adults: animal, biography, careers, health, history, hobbies, nature/environment, social issues, sports. "Enslow is moving into the elementary (Grades 3-4) level and is looking for authors who can write biography and suggest other nonfiction themes at this level." Average word length: middle readers—5,000; young adult—18,000. Published *Louis Armstrong*, by Patricia and Fredrick McKissack (grades 2-3, biography); and *Lotteries: Who Wins, Who Loses?*, by Ann E. Weiss (grades 6-12, issues book).

How to Contact/Writers: Nonfiction. Send for guidelines. Query. Responds to queries/mss in 2 weeks. Publishes a book 18 months after acceptance. Will not consider simultaneous submissions.

Illustration: Submit résumé, business card or tearsheets to be kept on file.

Terms: Pays authors royalties or work purchased outright. Sends galleys to authors. Book catalog/ms guidelines available for $2, along with an 8½ × 11 SAE and $1.67 postage or via website.

EVAN-MOOR EDUCATIONAL PUBLISHERS, 18 Lower Ragsdale Dr., Monterey CA 93940-5746. (831)649-5901. Fax: (831)649-6256. E-mail: main@evan-moor.com. Website: www.evan-moor.com. Book publisher. **Manuscript Acquisitions:** Marilyn Evans, editor. **Art Acquisitions:** Joy Evans, production director. Publishes 30-50 books/year. Less than 10% of books by first-time authors. " 'Helping Children Learn' is our motto. Evan-Moor is known for high-quality educational materials written by teachers for use in the classroom and at home. We publish teacher resource and reproducible materials in most all curriculum areas and activity books (language arts, math, science, social studies). No fiction or nonfiction literature books."

Nonfiction: Recently published *Read and Understand Science* (4 books of science stories with comprehension activities); *Literature Pockets* (5 books of projects for various genre); *Daily Word Problem* (6 books for grades 1-6).

How to Contact/Writers: Query or submit outline, table of contents, and sample pages. Responds to queries in 2 months; mss in 4 months. Publishes a book 12-18 months after acceptance. Will consider simultaneous submissions if so noted. Submission guidelines available on our website. E-mail queries are responded to quickly. View our materials on our website to determine if your project fits in our product line.

Illustration: Works with 8 illustrators/year. Uses b&w artwork primarily. Illustrations only: Query with samples; send résumé, tearsheets. Contact: Joy Evans, production director. Responds only if interested. Samples returned with SASE; samples filed.

Terms: Work purchased outright from authors, "dependent solely on size of project and 'track record' of author." Pays illustrators by the project (range: varies). Sends galleys to authors. Artwork is not returned. Book catalog available for 9 × 12 SAE; ms guidelines available for SASE.

Tips: "Writers—know the supplemental education or parent market. (These materials are *not* children's literature.) Tell us how your project is unique and what consumer needs it meets. Illustrators—you need to be able to produce quickly and be able to render realistic and charming children and animals."

FARRAR, STRAUS & GIROUX INC., 19 Union Square W., New York NY 10003. (212)741-6900. Fax: (212)633-2427. Book publisher. Imprints: Frances Foster Books, Melanie Kroupa Books. Children's Books Editorial Director: Margaret Ferguson. **Manuscript Acquisitions:** Frances Foster, publisher, Frances Foster Books; Beverly Reingold, executive editor; Wesley Adams, senior editor; Robbie Mayes, editor; Janine O'Malley, assistant editor. **Art Acquisitions:** Robin Gourley, art director, books for young readers. Estab. 1946. Publishes 40 picture books/year; 15 middle reader titles/year; and 15 young adult titles/year. 5% of books by first-time authors; 20% of books from agented writers.

• Farrar title *Everything on a Waffle*, by Polly Horrath, won a 2002 Newbery Honor.

Fiction: All levels: all categories. "Original and well-written material for all ages." Recently published *Joey Pigza Loses Control*, by Jack Gantos (ages 10 up).

Nonfiction: All levels: all categories. "We publish only literary nonfiction."

How to Contact/Writers: Fiction/Nonfiction: Query with outline/synopsis and sample chapters. Do not fax submissions or queries. Responds to queries/mss in 3 months. Publishes a book 18 months after acceptance. Will consider simultaneous submissions.

Illustration: Works with 30-60 illustrators/year. Reviews ms/illustration packages from artists. Submit ms with 1 example of final art, remainder roughs. Do not send originals. Illustrations only: Query with tearsheets. Responds if interested in 2 months. Samples returned with SASE; samples sometimes filed.

Terms: "We offer an advance against royalties for both authors and illustrators." Sends galleys to authors; dummies to illustrators. Original artwork returned at job's completion. Book catalog available for 9 × 12 SAE and $1.87 postage; ms guidelines for 1 first-class stamp.

Tips: "Study our catalog before submitting. We will see illustrator's portfolios by appointment. Don't ask for criticism and/or advice—it's just not possible. Never send originals. Always enclose SASE."

FIESTA CITY PUBLISHERS, Box 5861, Santa Barbara CA 93150-5861. (805)681-9199. E-mail: fcooke 3924@aol.com. Book publisher. **Acquisitions:** Frank Cooke, president. **Art Director:** Ann H. Cooke. Publishes 1 middle reader/year; 1 young adult/year. 25% of books by first-time authors. Publishes books about cooking and music or a combination of the two. "We are best known for children's and young teens' cookbooks and musical plays."

Fiction: Young adults: history, humor, musical plays.

Nonfiction: Young adult: cooking, how-to, music/dance, self-help. Average word length: 30,000. Does not want to see "cookbooks about healthy diets or books on rap music." Published *Kids Can Write Songs, Too!* (revised second printing), by Eddie Franck; *Bent-Twig*, by Frank E. Cooke, with some musical arrangements by Johnny Harris (a 3-act musical for young adolescents); *The Little Grammar Book*, by F. Cooke.

How to Contact/Writers: Query. Responds to queries in 4 days; on mss in 1 month. Publishes a book 1 year after acceptance. Will consider simultaneous submissions.

Illustration: Works with 1 illustrator/year. Will review ms/illustrations packages (query first). Illustrations only: Send résumé. Samples returned with SASE; samples filed.

Terms: Pays authors 5-10% royalty based on retail price.

Tips: "Write clearly and simply. Do not write 'down' to young adults (or children). Looking for self-help books on current subjects, original and unusual cookbooks, and books about music, or a combination of cooking and music." Always include SASE.

☐ ☐ FIVE STAR PUBLICATIONS, INC., P.O. Box 6698, Chandler AZ 85246-6698. (480)940-8182. Fax: (480)940-8787. E-mail: info@fivestarpublications.com. Website: www.fivestarpublications.c om. Estab. 1985. Specializes in educational material, nonfiction. Independent book packager/producer. Publishes 7 middle readers/year.

Nonfiction: Recently published *Shakespeare for Children: The Story of Romeo & Juliet*, by Cass Foster; *The Sixty-Minute Shakespeare: Hamlet*, by Cass Foster; *The Sixty-Minute Shakespeare: Twelfth Night*, by Cass Foster.

How to Contact/Writers: Nonfiction: Query.

Illustration: Works with 3 illustrators/year. Reviews ms/illustration packages from artists. Query. Contact: Sue DeFabis, project manager. Illustrations only: Query with samples. Responds only if interested. Samples filed.

Photography: Buys stock and assigns work. Works on assignment only. Contact: Sue De Fabis, project manager. Submit letter.

Terms: Pays illustrators by the project. Pays photographers by the project. Sends galleys to authors; dummies to illustrators.

FORWARD MOVEMENT PUBLICATIONS, 412 Sycamore St., Cincinnati OH 45202. (513)721-6659. Fax: (513)721-0729. E-mail: orders@forwarddaybyday.com. Website: www.forwardmovement.org.

Acquisitions: Edward S. Gleason, editor.

Fiction: Middle readers and young adults: religion and religious problem novels, fantasy and science fiction.

Nonfiction: Religion.

How to Contact/Writers: Fiction/Nonfiction: Query. Responds in 1 month. Does not accept mss via e-mail.

Illustration: Query with samples. Samples returned with SASE.

Terms: Pays authors honorarium. Pays illustrators by the project.

Tips: "Forward Movement is now exploring publishing books for children and does not know its niche. We are an agency of the Episcopal Church and most of our market is to mainstream Protestants."

FREE SPIRIT PUBLISHING, 217 Fifth Ave. N., Suite 200, Minneapolis MN 55401-1299. (612)338-2068. Fax: (612)337-5050. E-mail: help4kids@freespirit.com. Website: www.freespirit.com. Book publisher. **Acquisitions:** Editor. Publishes 16-22 titles/year for children and teens, teachers and parents. "Free Spirit Publishing is the home of SELF-HELP FOR KIDS® and SELF-HELP FOR TEENS® nonfiction, issue-driven, solution-focused books and materials for children and teens, and the parents and teachers who care for them."

● Free Spirit no longer accepts fiction or story book submissions.

Nonfiction: Areas of interest include emotional health, bullying and conflict resolution, tolerance and character development, social and study skills, creative learning and teaching, special needs learning, teaching, and parenting (gifted & talented and LD), family issues, healthy youth development, challenges specific to boys (including the parenting and teaching of boys), classroom activities, and innovative teaching techniques. We do not publish fiction or picture storybooks, books with animal or mythical characters, books with religious or New Age content, or single biographies, autobiographies, or memoirs. We prefer books written in a natural, friendly style, with little education/psychology jargon. We need books in our areas of emphasis and prefer titles written by specialists such as teachers, counselors, and other professionals who work with youth." Recently published *What Do You Really Want? How to Set A Goal and Go For It*, by Beverly Eachel; *What In the World Do You Do When Your Parents Divorce? A Survival Guide For Kids*, by Kent Winchester and Roberta Beyer.

How to Contact/Writers: "Submissions are accepted from prospective authors, including youth ages 16+, or through agents. Please review our catalog and Author Guidelines (both available online at www.fre espirit.com) before submitting proposal." Responds to queries/mss in 3-4 months. "If you'd like materials returned, enclose a SASE with sufficient postage." Write or call for catalog and submission guidelines before sending submission. Accepts queries only by e-mail. Submission guidelines available online.

Illustration: Works with 5 illustrators/year. Submit samples to production manager for consideration. If appropriate, samples will be kept on file and artist will be contacted if a suitable project comes up. Enclose SASE if you'd like materials returned.

insider report

'Books are the joy and bane of my life'

In 1994, Front Street was merely the name of Stephen Roxburgh's neighborhood block. Today, Roxburgh is president and publisher of Front Street Books, producing dozens of quality books, gaining a "tumble bumble" treasure chest full of awards, and maintaining a thriving alliance with the Cricket Magazine Group. Since its formation, Front Street has published more than 50 books, many which have inhabited top-ten lists for weeks at a time. Front Street titles such as Marilyn Nelson's *Carver: A Life in Poems* and Carolyn Coman's *What Jamie Saw*, both Newbery Honor winners, address timely issues for young adults, highlight other cultures and locations, and provide favorable resolutions. According to Roxburgh, his company's books gain widespread attention for "high literary and artistic merit, new vision, honesty,

Stephen Roxburgh

and a beautiful appearance"—Front Street's star standards for each title, whether a ghost story, magic picture book or Civil War chronicle.

When it comes to the book business, Roxburgh is a noble authority. While declaring he's read thousands of children's stories, Roxburgh has also edited and promoted a sufficient amount of them. "Books are the joy and bane of my life," says the polished scholar and lover of theatre. "The number of times I've leafed through *Middlemarch* reading favorite passages at my leisure is exceeded only by the number of times I've schlepped it up and down stairs as I moved from this place to that." Here Roxburgh defines literary success, and shares his thoughts on publishing, promotion and storytelling.

Describe your transition from academics to the business of publishing books about apple islands and cat detectives.
For several years between finishing my M.A. and Ph.D. work I did odd jobs, including working as a carpenter. Once I was refurbishing an elementary school librarian's kitchen. At the time I happened to track down a book I remember having read to me in pre-primary, Frances Hodgson Burnett's *The Secret Garden*. I would read it during my work breaks. One day the librarian came home early and found me reading it. She asked if I would like to read more good children's books and the rest is history. I loved the books she brought me and recognized that they were good by all the critical standards I knew from my studies in literature. When I went back to school to get a Ph.D. I made one of my major fields children's literature; the genre of the novel and Victorian literature were the other two. My M.A. work was primarily in English Renaissance drama. Eventually I grew tired of the university but not of children's literature. I had worked briefly with the children's librarian in her library and realized that a love of children's books doesn't mean you are meant to work with children, so I turned to publishing.

How do your daily activities at Front Street differ from your previous responsibilities at Farrar, Straus & Giroux?

At FSG, I was in charge of 15-20 people and worked with a lot of others from different departments. Too much of my days were spent in meetings, which are, for the most part, an enormous waste of time. This is a function of size and FSG was a small place. I can't imagine working at a large corporation. At Front Street we have very few meetings and my days are spent working. My responsibilities are greater because I own the company; everything is my responsibility. But the rewards are greater as well; I do get what I want.

What nourishes your fascination with children's literature?

Story. Narrative. First, last and always. In whatever form, whatever genre.

From *Bee and Jackie* to *Bruises*, Front Street has published some outstanding book covers. How do you choose illustrators, and do many freelancers approach you for assignments?

Many apply, few are chosen. I find the best artists I can—those with distinct visions—and I pretty much let them do what they do best. A little guidance goes a very long way when you are dealing with the highest caliber artists. I never choose someone based on what they have done. I choose them based on what I think they can do, and I encourage them to do it.

little chicago

adam rapp

Cover design Helen Robinson. Reprinted with permission of Front Street Books.

The startling story of young Blacky Brown, who is sexually abused by his mother's boyfriend in Adam Rapp's novel *Little Chicago*, demonstrates Stephen Roxburgh's willingness to reach out to controversial topics. Roxburgh, the president and publisher of Front Street Books, says that among his goals he wants to publish books that "deal honestly with whatever subject they address."

Considering Front Street only has a staff of four, how much promotion can an author expect from you once their book is published?

We publish about ten books a year. All four people work on every book at every phase of its lifetime. Anyone who picks up the phone or has a conversation about our list is intimately familiar with every book we publish. Our resources are carefully apportioned. We push where we feel pushing will help, and apply the amount of pressure that is necessary. Promotion is about getting attention, and to do that someone needs to be paying attention. Promotion is also about work—effort over time. That is the promotion an author can expect once his or her book is published by Front Street.

Is there a book you edited that really surprised you with the success and attention it received?

I believe that publishing a book successfully isn't about wide appeal or large numbers. For instance, a first literary novel in translation in the U.S. is most publishers' idea of failure. The market is just too small. The numbers don't work. Well, our numbers don't need to be as high as theirs because we aren't supporting a massive infrastructure. So, if I can print and sell a couple thousand copies of that literary translation, and control my costs, and the book is well reviewed, then it's a success. Based on this approach to publishing (which I hasten to add, is probably not a viable economic model) most of the surprises I've experienced have been on the upside. A book has done better, economically, than I expected. As far as critically, I'm usually not surprised. No one knows better than I the strengths and weaknesses of a book I've published.

Design Helen Robinson. Illustration Jennifer Lynn Sorenson. Reprinted with permission of Front Street.

Front Street Books title *The Shakeress*, by Kimberly Heuston, follows 12-year-old Naomi as she and her siblings lose their parents in a fire and are forced to take refuge in a Shaker village. President and publisher of Front Street Books, Stephen Roxburgh, incorporates publishing new writers into his vision for the company.

How has your vision for the company evolved since 1994?

Now that we've published 50 or so books, the name Front Street begins to have meaning. The meaning of Front Street will evolve as we publish more books. My vision is to publish books of high literary and artistic merit, new voices (almost half of every list has been first books), beautiful books that are a pleasure to hold and look at, and books that deal honestly with whatever subject they address.

Reflecting on books such as *Asphalt Angels*, based on the plight of homeless children, Front Street continues to be a cultural pioneer, making books about raw issues available to young adults. What is your response to censorship?

Censorship is blindness and the censor is the blind man. You can close your own eyes as long as you want, but you can't close anyone else's for very long. In my experience, if a book is good enough it will find an audience no matter how controversial it is. The audience may be small—not everybody wants to see everything. But I never worry about topics or issues; my only concern is their treatment, the integrity of the vision, the quality of the art, and the strength of the voice. This simplifies things. The fact is, I have published very few books that somebody hasn't found something to be upset about. It comes with the territory. My publishing strategy is to find the people who want to see what a book reveals, not avoid the disapproval of people who don't want to see things.

—*Candi Lace*

Photography: Submit samples to production manager for consideration. If appropriate, samples will be kept on file and photographer will be contacted if a suitable project comes up. Enclose SASE if you'd like materials returned.

Terms: Pays authors in royalties based on wholesale price. Offers advance. Pays illustrators by the project. Pays photographers by the project or per photo.

Tips: "Free Spirit is a niche publisher known for high-quality books featuring a positive and practical focus and jargon free approach. Study our catalog, read our author guidelines, and be sure your proposal is the right 'fit' before submitting. Our preference is for books that help parents and teachers help kids [and that help kids themselves] gain personal strengths, succeed in school, stand up for themselves and others, and otherwise make a positive difference in today's world."

FREESTONE/PEACHTREE, JR., Peachtree Publishers, 1700 Chattahooche Ave., Atlanta GA 30318-2112. (404)876-8761. Fax: (404)875-2578. Website: www.peachtree-online.com. Estab. 1997. **Manuscript Acquisitions.** Lyn Deardorff (children's, young adult). Art Acquisitions: Loraine Balsuk (all). Publishes 3-4 young adult titles/year.
• Freestone and Peachtree, Jr. are imprints of Peachtree Publishers. See the listing for Peachtree for submission information. No e-mail or fax queries, please.

FRONT STREET BOOKS, 20 Battery Park Ave., #403, Ashville NC 28801. (828)236-3097. Fax: (828)236-3098. Fax: (828)236-3098. E-mail: contactus@frontstreetbooks.com Website: www.frontstreethooks.com. Book publisher Estab 1995. **Acquisitions.** Stephen Roxburgh, publisher; Joy Neaves, editor; Nancy Zimmerman, associate publisher. Publishes 10-15 titles/year. We are a small independent publisher of books for children and young adults. We do not publish pablum: we try to publish books that will attract, if not addict, children to literature and art books that are a pleasure to look at and a pleasure to hold, books that will be revelations to young minds."
• See Front Street's website for submission guidelines and their complete catalog. Front Street focuses on fiction, but will publish poetry, anthologies, nonfiction and high-end picture books. They are not currently accepting unsolicited picture book manuscripts. Front Street title *A Step from Heaven*, by An Na, won the 2002 Printz Award. Their title *Carver: A Life in Poems*, by Marilyn Nelson won a 2002 Newbery Honor and a 2002 Coretta Scott King Honor.

Fiction: Recently published: *Many Stones*, by Carolyn Coman; *Cut*, by Patricia McCormic; *A Step from Heaven*, by An Na; *Carver: A Life in Poems*, by Marilyn Nelson; *The Comic Book Kid*, by Adam Osterweil.

How to Contact/Writers: Fiction: Submit cover letter and complete ms if under 30 pages; submit cover letter, one or two sample chapters and plot summary if over 30 pages. Nonfiction: Submit detailed proposal and sample chapters. Poetry: Submit no more than 25 poems. Include SASE with submissions if you want them returned. "It is our policy to consider submissions in the order in which they are received. This is a time-consuming practice, and we ask you to be patient in awaiting our response."
Illustration "If you are the artist or are working with an artist, we will be happy to consider your project." Submit ms, dummy and a sample piece of art "rendered in the manner and style representative of the final artwork."
Terms: Pays royalties.

☑ **GIBBS SMITH, PUBLISHER**, P.O. Box 667, Layton UT 84040. (801)544-9800. Fax: (801)544-5582. Website: gibbs-smith.com. Imprint: Gibbs Smith. Book publisher; co-publisher of Sierra Club Books for Children. Editorial Director: Suzanne Taylor. Publishes 2-3 books/year. 50% of books by first-time authors. 50% of books from agented authors.
Fiction: Picture books: adventure, contemporary, humor, multicultural, nature/environment, suspense/mystery, western. Average word length: picture books—1,000. Recently published *Bullfrog Pops!*, by Rick Walton, illustrated by Chris McAllister (ages 4-8); and *The Magic Boots*, by Scott Emerson, illustrated by Howard Post (ages 4-8).
Nonfiction: Middle readers: activity, arts/crafts, cooking, how-to, nature/environment, science. Average word length: up to 10,000. Recently published *Hiding in a Fort*, by G. Lawson Drinkard, illustrated by Fran Lee Kirby (ages 7-12); and *Sleeping in a Sack: Camping Activities for Kids*, by Linda White, illustrated by Fran Lee (ages 7-12).
How to Contact/Writers: Fiction/Nonfiction: Submit several chapters or complete ms. Responds to queries and mss in 2 months. Publishes a book 1-2 years after acceptance. Will consider simultaneous submissions. Manuscript returned with SASE.
Illustration: Works with 2 illustrators/year. Reviews ms/illustration packages from artists. Query. Submit ms with 3-5 pieces of final art. Illustrations only: Query with samples; provide résumé, promo sheet, slides (duplicate slides, not originals). Responds only if interested. Samples returned with SASE; samples filed.
Terms: Pays authors royalty of 2% based on retail price or work purchased outright ($500 minimum). Offers advances (average amount: $2,000). Pays illustrators by the project or royalty of 2% based on retail price. Sends galleys to authors; color proofs to illustrators. Original artwork returned at job's completion. Book catalog available for 9×12 SAE and postage. Manuscript guidelines available.
Tips: "We target ages 5-11."

DAVID R. GODINE, PUBLISHER, 9 Hamilton Place, Boston MA 02108. (617)451-9600. Fax: (617)350-0250. Website: www.godine.com. Book publisher. Estab. 1970. Publishes 1 picture book/year; 1 young reader title/year; 1 middle reader title/year. 10% of books by first-time authors; 90% of books from agented writers. "We publish books that matter for people who care."
• This publisher is no longer considering unsolicited mss of any type.
Fiction: Picture books: adventure, animal, contemporary, folktales, nature/environment. Young readers: adventure, animal, contemporary, folk or fairy tales, history, nature/environment, poetry. Middle readers: adventure, animal, contemporary, folk or fairy tales, history, mystery, nature/environment, poetry. Young adults/teens: adventure, animal, contemporary, history, mystery, nature/environment, poetry. Recently published *Roma and Sita*, by David Weitzman (picture book); *Ultimate Game*, by Christian Lehmann (received the Batchelder Honor Book for the American Library Association).
Nonfiction: Picture books: alphabet, animal, nature/environment. Young readers: activity books, animal, history, music/dance, nature/environment. Middle readers: activity books, animal, biography, history, music/dance, nature/environment. Young adults: biography, history, music/dance, nature/environment.
How to Contact/Writers: Query. Publishes a book 3 years after acceptance. Include SASE for return of material.
Illustration: Only interested in agented material. Works with 4-6 illustrators/year. Reviews ms/illustration packages from artists. "Submit roughs and one piece of finished art plus either sample chapters for very long works or whole ms for short works." Illustrations only: "After query, submit slides, with one full-size blow-up of art." Please do not send original artwork unless solicited. "Almost all of the children's books we accept for publication come to us with the author and illustrator already paired up. Therefore, we rarely use freelance illustrators." Samples returned with SASE; samples filed (if interested).
Tips: "Always enclose a SASE. Keep in mind that we do not accept unsolicited manuscripts and that we rarely use freelance illustrators."

☑ Ⓐ **GOLDEN BOOKS**, 1540 Broadway, New York NY 10036. (212)782-9000. Imprint of Random House Children's Books. **Editorial Directors:** Courtney Silk, color and activity; Chris Angelilli, storybooks. **Art Acquisitions:** Tracy Tyler, art director.

• See listing for Random House/Golden Books for Young Readers Group.
How to Contact/Writers: Not accepting unsolicited mss. Does not accept queries. No multiple submissions.
Fiction: They publish board books, novelty books, picture books, workbooks, series (mass market and trade).

GREENE BARK PRESS, P.O. Box 1108, Bridgeport CT 06601-1108. (203)372-4861. Fax: (203)371-5856. E-mail: greenebark@aol.com. Website: www.greenebarkpress.com. Book publisher. **Acquisitions:** Michele Hofbauer; associate publisher. Thomas J. Greene, publisher. Publishes 4-6 picture books/year. 40% of books by first-time authors. "We publish quality hardcover picture books for children. Our books and stories are selected for originality, imagery and colorfulness. Our intention is to capture a child's attention; to fire-up his or her imagination and desire to read and explore the world through books."
Fiction: Picture books, young readers: adventure, fantasy, humor. Average word length: picture books—650; young readers—1,400. Recently published *The Magical Trunk*, by Gigi Tegge; *Couldn't We Make A Difference*, by Michele Hofbauer; *Empty Pockets*, by Faye Van Wert; *To Know the Sea*, by Frances Gilbert.
How to Contact/Writers: Responds to queries in 2 months; ms in 6 months. Publishes a book 18 months after acceptance. Will consider simultaneous submissions. Prefer to review complete mss with illustrations.
Illustrations: Works with 1-2 illustrators/year. Uses color artwork only. Reviews ms/illustration packages from artists. Submit ms with 3 pieces of final art (copies only). Illustrations only: Query with samples. Responds in 2 months only if interested. Samples returned with SASE; samples filed. Originals returned at job's completion.
Terms: Pays authors royalty of 10-12% based on wholesale price. Pays illustrators by the project (range: $1,500-3,000) or 5-7½% royalty based on wholesale price. No advances. Send galleys to authors; dummies to illustrators. Book catalog available for $2.00 fee which includes mailing. All imprints included in a single catalog. Manuscript and art guidelines available for SASE or per e-mail request.
Tips: "As a guide for future publications do not look to our older backlist. Please no telephone, e-mail or fax queries."

☑ **GREENHAVEN PRESS**, Lucent Books, Imprint of the Gale Group, 10911 Technology Place, San Diego CA 92127. (858)485-7424. Website: www.gale.com. Book publisher. Estab. 1970. **Acquisitions:** Chandra Howard, acquisitions editor. Publishes 300 young adult titles/year. 35% of books by first-time authors. "Greenhaven continues to print quality nonfiction for libraries and classrooms. Our well known opposing viewpoints series is highly respected by students and librarians in need of material on controversial social issues. In recent years, Greenhaven has also branched out with a new series covering historical and literary topics."
• Greenhaven accepts no unsolicited mss. All writing is done on a work-for-hire basis.
Nonfiction: Middle readers: biography, controversial topics, history, issues. Young adults: biography, history, nature/environment. Other titles "to fit our specific series." Average word length: young adults—18,000-25,000.
How to Contact/Writers: Send query, résumé and list of published works.
Terms: Buys ms outright for $1,500-3,000. Offers advances. Sends galleys to authors.
Tips: "Please no phone calls. Also, short writing samples are appropriate, but long unsolicited manuscripts will not be read."

☑ **GREENWILLOW BOOKS**, 1350 Avenue of the Americas, New York NY 10019. (212)261-6500. Website: www.harperchildrens.com. Imprint of HarperCollins. Book publisher. Vice President/Publisher: Virginia Duncan. **Manuscript Acquisitions:** Submit to Editorial Department. **Art Acquisitions:** Paul Zakris, art director. Publishes 50 picture books/year; 5 middle readers books/year; and 5 young adult books/year. "Greenwillow Books publishes picture books, fiction for young readers of all ages, and nonfiction primarily for children under seven years of age."
• Greenwillow Books is currently accepting neither unsolicited mss nor queries. Unsolicited mail will not be opened and will not be returned. Call (212)261-6627 for an update. Greenwillow title

---

MARKET CONDITIONS are constantly changing! If you're still using this book and it is 2004 or later, buy the newest edition of *Children's Writer's & Illustrator's Market* at your favorite bookstore or order directly from Writer's Digest Books (800)448-0915.

Amber Was Brave, Essie Was Smart, by Vera B. Williams, won a 2002 Boston Globe-Horn Book Honor Award for Fiction and Poetry. Their title *Bluebird Summer*, by Deborah Hopkinson, won a 2002 Golden Kite Honor Award for Picture Book Text.

Illustration: Art samples (postcards only) should be sent in duplicate to Paul Zakris and Virginia Duncan.

Terms: Pays authors royalty. Offers advances. Pays illustrators royalty or by the project. Sends galleys to authors. Book catalog available for 9×12 SASE with $2.20 postage (no cash or checks); ms guidelines available for SASE.

Tips: "You need not have a literary agent to submit to us. We accept—and encourage—simultaneous submissions to other publishers and ask only that you so inform us. Because we receive thousands of submissions, we do not keep a record of the manuscripts we receive and cannot check the status of your manuscript. We do try to respond within ten weeks' time."

GRYPHON HOUSE, P.O. Box 207, Beltsville MD 20704-0207. (301)595-9500. Fax: (301)595-0051. E-mail: kathyc@ghbooks.com. Website: www.gryphonhouse.com. Book publisher. **Acquisitions:** Kathy Charner, editor-in-chief.

Nonfiction: Parent and teacher resource books—activity books, textbooks. Recently published *First Art: Art Experiences for Toddlers and Twos*, by MaryAnn F. Kohl; *Games to Play with Babies Third Edition*, by Jackie Silberg; *Creating Readers*, by Pam Schiller.

How to Contact/Writers: Query. Submit outline/synopsis and 2 sample chapters. Responds to queries/mss in 6 months. Publishes a book 18 months after acceptance. Will consider simultaneous submissions, electronic submissions via disk or modem.

Illustration: Works with 4-5 illustrators/year. Uses b&w artwork only. Illustrations only: Query with samples, promo sheet. Responds in 2 months. Samples returned with SASE; samples filed.

Photography: Buys photos from freelancers. Buys stock and assigns work. Submit cover letter, published samples, stock photo list.

Terms: Pays authors royalty based on wholesale price. Offers advances. Pays illustrators by the project. Pays photographers by the project or per photo. Sends edited ms copy to authors. Original artwork returned at job's completion. Book catalog and ms guidelines available via website or with SASE.

Tips: "Send a SASE for our catalog and manuscript guidelines. Look at our books, then submit proposals that complement the books we already publish or supplement our existing books. We are looking for books of creative, participatory learning experiences that have a common conceptual theme to tie them together. The books should be on subjects that parents or teachers want to do on a daily basis."

GULLIVER BOOKS, 15 E. 26th St., New York NY 10010. (212)592-1000. Imprint of Harcourt, Inc. **Acquisitions:** Elizabeth Van Doren, editorial director; Kate Harrison, associate editor; Scott Piehl, art director. Publishes 25 titles/year.

● Gulliver only accepts mss submitted by agents, previously published authors, or SCBWI members.

Fiction: Emphasis on picture books: animal, contemporary, history, humor, multicultural, nature/environment, poetry, sports, suspense/mystery. Also publishes middle grade and young adult.

Nonfiction: Publishes nonfiction. Picture books: animal, biography, history, multicultural. Also publishes some middle grade and young adult.

How to Contact/Writers: Only interested in agented material. Also accepts material from SCBWI members and previously published authors. Fiction/Nonfiction: Query or send ms for picture book. Resonds to queries/mss in 2 months.

Illustrations: Responds only if interested. Samples returned with SASE only; samples filed.

Terms: Authors and illustrators paid royalty.

HACHAI PUBLISHING, 156 Chester Ave., Brooklyn NY 11218-3020. (718)633-0100. Fax: (718)633-0103. E-mail: info@hachai.com. Website: www.hachai.com. Book publisher. **Manuscript Acquisitions:** Devorah Leah Rosenfeld, submissions editor. Publishes 3 picture books/year; 3 young readers/year; 1 middle reader/year. 75% of books published by first-time authors. "All books have spiritual/religious themes, specifically traditional Jewish content. We're seeking books about morals and values; the Jewish experience in current and Biblical times; and Jewish observance, Sabbath and holidays."

Fiction: Picture books and young readers: contemporary, historical fiction, religion. Middle readers: adventure, contemporary, problem novels, religion. Does not want to see fantasy, animal stories, romance, problem novels depicting drug use or violence. Recently published *Let's Go to Shul*, written and illustrated by Rikki Benenfeld (ages 2-5, picture book); *Get Well Soon*, by Dina Rosenfeld, illustrated by Rina Lyampe (ages 2-5, picture book); *Big Like Me! A New Baby Story*, by Ruth Finkelstein, illustrated by Esther Touson (ages 2-5, picture book); *Once Upon a Time*, by Draizy Zelcer, illustrated by Vitaliy Romanenko (ages 3-6, picture book); *The Great Potato Plan*, written and illustrated by Joy Nelkin Wieder (ages 7-10, short chapter book).

Nonfiction: Published *My Jewish ABC's*, by Draizy Zelcer, illustrated by Patti Nemeroff (ages 3-6, picture book); *Nine Spoons* by Marci Stillerman, illustrated by Pesach Gerber (ages 5-8).

How to Contact/Wrtiers: Fiction/Nonfiction: Submit complete ms. Responds to queries/mss in 6 weeks.

Illustration: Works with 4 illustrators/year. Uses primary color artwork, some b&w illustration. Reviews ms/illustration packages from authors. Submit ms with 1 piece of final art. Contact: Devorah Leah Rosenfeld, submissions editor. Illustrations only: Query with samples; arrange personal portfolio review. Responds in 6 weeks. Samples returned with SASE; samples filed.

Terms: Work purchased outright from authors for $800-1,000. Pays illustrators by the project (range: $2,000-3,500). Book catalog, ms/artist's guidelines available for SASE.

Tips: "Write a story that incorporates a moral—not a preachy morality tale. Originality is the key. We feel Hachai publications will appeal to a wider readership as parents become more interested in positive values for their children."

HAMPTON ROADS PUBLISHING COMPANY, INC., 1125 Stoney Ridge Road, Charlottesville VA 22902. (434)296-2772. Fax: (434)296-5096. E-mail: hrpc@hrpub.com. Website: www.hrpub.com. Estab. 1989. **Manuscript Acquisitions:** Pat Adler, Grace Pedalino. **Art Acquisitions:** Jane Hagaman. Publishes 3 picture books/year. 50% of books by first-time authors. Mission Statement: "to work as a team to seek, create, refine and produce the best books we are capable of producing, which will impact, uplift and contribute to positive change in the world; to promote the physical, mental, emotional and financial well-being of all its staff and associates; to build the company into a powerful, respected and prosperous force in publishing in the region, the nation and the world in which we live."

Fiction: Picture books, young readers, middle readers, young adult titles: metaphysical and spiritual. Average word length: picture books—100-200; young readers—1,000-5,000; middle readers—500-4,000. Recently published *The Wonderful Life of a Fly Who Couldn't Fly*, by Bo Lozoff; *The Legend of Wings*, by Timothy Green (ages 5-9).

Nonfiction: Young adult titles: metaphysical and spiritual.

How to Contact/Writers: Fiction: Submit complete ms for picture books. Otherwise query first. Nonfiction: Query. Responds to queries in 1 month; mss in 6 months. Publishes a book 6-12 months after acceptance. Will consider simultaneous submissions.

Illustration: Works with 2-3 illustrators/year. Reviews ms/illustration packages from artists. Submit ms with 2-3 pieces of final art (copies). Contact: Grace Pedalino, chief children's editor. Illustration only: query with samples. Contact: Jane Hagaman, art director. Responds in 1 month. Samples returned only with SASE; samples not filed.

Terms: Pays authors variable royalty. Offers advances (average amount: $1,000). Pays illustrators by the project. Occasionally pays by royalty based on retail price. Sends galleys to authors. Original returned to artist at job's completion. Book catalog available on request. Writer's guidelines available for SASE.

Tips: "Please do not send us any project books, journals or mainstream material of any kind. Please familiarize yourself with our mission statement and/or the books we publish. We encourage writers NOT to spend time and money finding their own illustrators. Preferably send manuscripts that can be recycled rather than returned. If there is no SASE, they will be recycled."

A **HARCOURT, INC.**, 525 B St., Suite 1900, San Diego CA 92101-4495. (619)699-6810. Fax: (619)699-6777. Children's Books Division includes: Harcourt Children's Books (Ms. Allyn Johnston, editorial director), Gulliver Books (Elizabeth Van Doren, editorial director), Silver Whistle Books (Paula Wiseman, editorial director), Voyager Paperbacks, Odyssey Paperbacks, and Red Wagon Books. Book publisher. **Art Acquisitions:** Art Director. Publishes 50-75 picture books/year; 5-10 middle reader titles/year; 10 young adult titles/year. 20% of books by first-time authors; 50% of books from agented writers. "Harcourt, Inc. owns some of the world's most prestigious publishing imprints—which distinguish quality products for the juvenile, educational and trade markets worldwide."

- The staff of Harcourt's children's book department is no longer accepting unsolicited manuscripts, queries or illustrations. Harcourt title *Little Rat Sets Sail*, by Monika Bang-Campbell, illustrated by Molly Bang, won a 2002 Boston Globe-Horn Book Honor Award for Picture Books. Their title *Castles, Caves and Honeycombs*, illustrated by Lauren Stringer, won a 2002 Golden Kite Honor.

Fiction: All levels: Considers all categories. Average word length: picture books—"varies greatly"; middle readers—20,000-50,000; young adults—35,000-65,000. Recently published *Home Run*, by Robert Burleigh, illustrated by Mike Wimmer (ages 6-10, picture book/biography); *Cast Two Shadows*, by Ann Rinaldi (ages 12 and up; young adult historical fiction); *Tell Me Something Happy Before I Go to Sleep*, by Joyce Dunbar, illustrated by Debi Gliori (ages 4-8, picture book).

insider report

Family history inspires award-winning historical fiction

Writers interested in historical fiction can take a lesson from author Jennifer L. Holm. Drawing on her Finnish roots, oral family histories, her great aunt's diary, and her own life as the lone sister of four brothers, Holm created a Newbery Honor-winning first novel, *Our Only May Amelia*, and it's strong follow-up *Boston Jane: An Adventure*. Both books feature spirited girls as main characters—tomboy May Amelia Jackson, who finds adventure along with hardship on the banks of Washington's Naselle River in 1899; and aspiring young lady Jane Peck, who embarks on an eventful journey from Philadelphia to the Washington territory in the 1850s.

Jennifer L. Holm

Photo: Reven Wurman

"Even as a kid, I had been intrigued by my father's stories of the family farm in Naselle, Washington, and I wondered what it must have been like to grow up in what was essentially a wilderness settled by Finnish pioneers," Holm says. "I also wanted to tell the story of a lesser-known part of the American immigrant experience, the story of the Scandinavian immigrants who came to this country late in the century and the hardships they endured in a part of the country that was still considered frontier."

Holm will follow up her two historical novels with *The Creek*, a contemporary young adult literary thriller "about terror in suburbia. So get ready to be scared!" she says. She'll also follow up with two more books in the Boston Jane trilogy.

Your great aunt Alice Amelia Holm's diary was the spark for *Our Only May Amelia*. I imagine you didn't simply read through the diary and head to your computer. What made you sit down and start writing about May Amelia?
I was a huge reader when I was young. One of our neighbors said recently his clearest memory of me as a kid was raking the lawn one-handed while I read a book with the other! In elementary school, I wrote fan letters to Lloyd Alexander and even sent a manuscript to Scholastic, which was very politely rejected.

Much later, I went to Dickinson College in Carlisle, Pennsylvania, where I majored in International Relations and planned to have a career in the foreign service. For fun, I audited a creative writing course and was intimidated beyond belief. But one of my professors who I really consider my mentor, a religion professor named Ralph Slotten, encouraged me to write poetry. For years I kept up a poetry correspondence with him, and a lot of the poems I wrote were about childhood, and that kind of kept the flame going.

There had always been a rich cache of family stories, and my aunts made a point of mailing oral histories to all of the kids—me and my brothers and cousins. I just sort of stuck them in a drawer, even the diary I've talked about. Then during a sad time in my twenties after a very close cousin died and my dad was ill, and it seemed that my whole life was falling apart, I started writing what became *Our Only May Amelia*. I was having a hard time dealing with my dad being sick, I think, and I wrote as a distraction. I started pulling out those oral histories, which were from his family, and the book became this love letter to him and his family's experience. Now, when I look back, I think I was pretty depressed then, and a lot of that grief and loss poured out onto the page. Poor May Amelia has a lot of bad stuff happen to her!

The many details you convey of the history and the area in which your novels take place really adds a richness to them. What tips can you offer on doing historical research?

Having a large family from the area who lived through the history and has passed down stories is obviously very helpful. I'm not saying "write what you know," but if you're interested in history, you shouldn't ignore the oral history of your own family.

Beyond that, my favorite resources are archives. I worked in an archive in college and I used to spend hours poring over boxes of stuff. Crazy, amazing stuff—whatever alumni had donated to the college over the years. Some guy donated his entire JFK memorabilia collection complete with plaster busts! But some of it was incredible. Like letters between students in the 1700s talking about a big "to-do" going on in Philadelphia! And the archivist/librarian I worked for was incredibly knowledgeable, and so encouraging.

I would recommend, if you're interested in doing historical fiction, that you buddy up with any archivist from a library or historical society who specializes in what you're writing about. Historians in general love to be asked questions, so don't be shy. You may wind up with a whole new set of fascinating friends.

While Jennifer L. Holm's enthusiastic young fans are begging for a movie version of Newbery Honor novel *Our Only May Amelia* (HarperCollins), "Steven Spielberg hasn't come calling yet," she says. However, Seattle Children's Theater opens its 2002-2003 season with the novel's first-ever staging. In addition to the Newbery Honor, *Our Only May Amelia* boasts 2000 Notable Children's Book (ALA), 1999 Parents' Choice Silver Award, and 1999 Publishers Weekly Best Book. Check out May Amelia's website at www.jenniferholm.com/books/may/.

Reprinted with permission of HarperCollins.

You've said you don't read other people's books while you're writing. Why is that? When you're not writing, what do like to read? Had you read many books for young readers (as an adult) when you began writing *May Amelia*?

Reading is my favorite thing in life. Literally. And writing requires so much discipline, more than anything I've ever done. You are your own boss. So I don't read anything (except newspapers and maybe a few trashy fashion magazines) when I'm writing. That way reading a book is this big treat dangled at the end of a draft. And the other reason is because if I'm reading someone I really love, I get intimidated that nothing I will ever write will be as good as what they wrote, and it just gets me down.

When I'm not writing, I read voraciously across all genres—literature, mystery, horror, romance, some nonfiction. I'm kind of in a chick-lit phase right now. I love Joanna Trollope and Elinor Lipman and Alice Hoffman is an old favorite.

I hadn't read any children's literature since I was a kid when I began writing Our *Only May Amelia*. Now, between drafts, I read books I get from conferences or from my publisher. Which is a good thing, because the children's publishing scene these days is completely different from what I was reading growing up.

How did winning a Newbery Honor on your first book change your writing life? Did you feel added pressure as you worked on your follow-up?

Well, first of all, it was a complete surprise. This is my Newbery story. See, there's this whole protocol where the Newbery committee calls the winners in the morning before the press

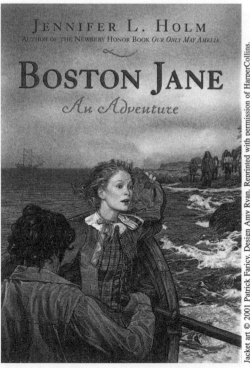

Jacket art © 2001 Patrick Faricy. Design Amy Ryan. Reprinted with permission of HarperCollins.

Boston Jane: An Adventure (HarperCollins), the first installment to Jennifer L. Holm's planned trilogy, follows 16-year-old Jane Peck from Philadelphia to Oregon during the mid-19th century. Reviewers praise Holm for her attention to historic details in this novel with regard to both the settlers and the Native Americans of the region. Holm recommends visiting your local library or historical society if you are interested in writing historical fiction. Librarians and historians will be eager to help and "you may wind up with a whole new set of fascinating friends." Look for the sequel, *Boston Jane: Wilderness Days*, a September 2002 release, and *Boston Jane: The Claim* due out in September 2003.

conference to tell them that they've won. On the morning of the call, the Newbery Committee couldn't find me! I missed the famous call. They called all over looking for me to give me the good news, but my dad had gotten ill over the weekend and so I was holed up in a hospital in Pennsylvania. Needless to say, when I finally got around to checking my messages later that afternoon, it was great!

When the Newbery happened, I was still working at an ad agency, and writing in my spare time, even though I had already sold more manuscripts to HarperCollins. But afterward, my dad said to me, "Maybe you should think about quitting your job and make a go of this full-time." It was kind of a scary concept to me—you know, not getting a steady paycheck—but I took his advice and finally did it last spring. So I guess you could say that winning the Newbery Honor changed my life because I now introduce myself at parties as a writer, rather than a producer who writes.

You accepted an invitation to visit a mother-daughter book club in New Jersey. How did that come about? Have you gotten a lot of this kind of enthusiasm from your readers?
That was so hilarious. I got an e-mail from this girl in New Jersey telling me that her mother-daughter book club had read *Our Only May Amelia* and could I please come out and visit them? As an added enticement, she said that her mom would pick me up at the train station and cook me dinner. I said I couldn't but ended up calling and chatting with the gang of them on speakerphone.

Then some time later, she e-mailed me again and said they'd read *Boston Jane* and would I please please please come out and that her mom would cook the *greatest dinner ever!* How could I refuse? And I admit, dinner was fabulous. (They even had cherry pie in honor of Jane.)

Girls are an enthusiastic bunch. On one school visit they all dressed up as May Amelia and another girl just sent me a videotape of her acting out May Amelia in her family's barn. It really seems to strike a cord with so many of them. They keep begging for a movie to be made but Steven Spielberg hasn't come calling yet, so if anyone knows him . . .

What's your best advice for unpublished writers of novels for young readers?
Keep your day job. Being a penniless writer living in a garret is a recipe for disaster, I think. It's really hard to be creative when you can't pay the rent. I sold several books over several years before I became a full-time writer, and even now it still scares me.

And also, finish what you start. A lot of people who come up to me at signings are looking for encouragement on projects they've just started. They've written a chapter or two and want someone to buy it before they write more. But I would encourage you to have a finished manuscript. It shows editors that you're capable of crafting a complete book. And if you enjoy writing, that should be no problem.

Remember, rejection is part of the game, so hang in there. I got tons of rejections, and still do. Every time you send out that manuscript, just remember that it's postage—it's not life or death. If you're not having success with one manuscript, put it away for a while and work on something new. You can always go back to it.

And if you're having writers' block, have a bowl of chocolate ice cream. It usually does the trick for me.

—Alice Pope

Nonfiction: All levels: animal, biography, concept, history, multicultural, music/dance, nature/environment, science, sports. Average word length: picture books—"varies greatly"; middle readers—20,000-50,000; young adults—35,000-65,000. Recently published *Lives of the Presidents*, by Kathleen Krull; illustrated by Kathryn Hewitt (ages 8-12, illustrated nonfiction).
How to Contact/Writers: Only interested in agented material.
Illustration: Only interested in agented material.
Photography: Works on assignment only.
Terms: Pays authors and illustrators in royalty based on retail price. Pays photographers by the project. Sends galleys to authors; dummies to illustrators. Original artwork returned at job's completion. Book catalog available for 8×10 SAE and 4 first-class stamps; ms/artist's guidelines for business-size SASE. All imprints included in a single catalog.

[A] [♥] **HARPERCOLLINS CHILDREN'S BOOKS,** 1350 Avenue of the Americas, New York NY 10019. (212)261-6500. Website: www.harpercollins.com. Book publisher. Editor-in-Chief: Kate Morgan Jackson. **Art Acquisitions:** Harriett Barton, Barbara Fitzsimmon, directors. Imprints: Laura Geringer Books, Joanna Cotler Books, Greenwillow Books, Amistad, Rayo. Paperback Imprints: Harper Trophy, Harper Tempest, Avon. Merchandise Imprint: Harper Festival.
  • HarperCollins is not accepting unsolicited and/or unagented mss not addressed to a specific editor. Harper/Joanna Cotler Books title *I Stink*, by Kate McMullan, illustrated by Jim McMullan, won a 2002 Boston Globe-Horn Book Honor Award for Picture Books. Their title *The Stray Dog*, by Marc Simont, won a 2002 Caldecott Honor. Their title *Freewill*, by Chris Lynch, won a 2002 Printz Honor.
Fiction: Picture books: adventure, animal, anthology, concept, contemporary, fantasy, folktales, hi-lo, history, multicultural, nature/environment, poetry, religion. Middle readers: adventure, hi-lo, history, poetry, suspense/mystery. Young adults/teens: fantasy, science fiction, suspense/mystery. All levels: multicultural. "Artists with diverse backgrounds and settings shown in their work."
Nonfiction: Picture books: animal, arts/crafts, biography, geography, multicultural, nature/environment. Middle readers: how-to.
Illustration: Responds only if interested.
How to Contact/Illustrators: Send samples. Do not send original art.
Terms: Pays authors and illustrators royalty. Pays flat fee for jacket art.

[✓] **HARVEST HOUSE PUBLISHERS,** 990 Owen Loop North, Eugene OR 97402. (541)343-0123. Fax: (541)342-6410. Book publisher. Publishes 1-2 picture books/year and 2 young reader titles/year. Books follow a Christian theme.
  • Harvest House no longer accepts unsolicited manuscripts.

[🍎] **HAYES SCHOOL PUBLISHING CO. INC.,** 321 Pennwood Ave., Wilkinsburg PA 15221-3398. (412)371-2373. Fax: (800)543-8771. E-mail: chayes@hayespub.com. Website: www.hayespub.com. **Acquisitions:** Mr. Clair N. Hayes. Estab. 1940. Produces folders, workbooks, stickers, certificates. Wants to see supplementary teaching aids for grades K-12. Interested in all subject areas. Will consider simultaneous and electronic submissions.
How to Contact/Writers: Query with description or complete ms. Responds in 6 weeks. SASE for return of submissions.
Illustration: Works with 3-4 illustrators/year. Responds in 6 weeks. Samples returned with SASE; samples filed. Originals not returned at job's completion.
Terms: Work purchased outright. Purchases all rights.

[✓] **HEALTH PRESS,** P.O. Box 37470, Albuquerque NM 87176. (505)888-1394 or (877)411-0707. Fax: (505)888-1521. E-mail: goodbooks@healthpress.com. Website: www.healthpress.com. Book publisher. **Acquisitions:** Contact Editor. Publishes 4 young readers/year; 4 middle readers/year. 100% of books by first-time authors.
Fiction: Young readers, middle readers: health, special needs. Average word length: young readers—1,000-1,500; middle readers—1,000-1,500. Recently published *Pennies, Nickels and Dimes*, by Elizabeth Murphy.
Nonfiction: Young readers, middle readers: health, special needs.
How to Contact/Writers: Submit complete ms. Responds in 1 month. Publishes a book 9 months after acceptance. Will consider simultaneous submissions.
Terms: Pays authors royalty. Sends galleys to authors. Book catalog available.

[N] **HENDRICK-LONG PUBLISHING COMPANY,** P.O. 1247, Friendswood TX 77549. Fax: (281)482-6169. E-mail: hendrick-long@worldnet.att.net. Book publisher. Estab. 1969. **Acquisitions:**

Vilma Long, vice president. Publishes 4 young reader titles/year; 4 middle reader titles/year. 20% of books by first-time authors. Publishes fiction/nonfiction about Texas of interest to young readers through young adults/teens.

Fiction: Middle readers: history books on Texas and the Southwest. No fantasy or poetry. Recently published *Young Pioneers in Texas*, written and illustrated by Betsy Warren (grades 4-6); *Maggie Houston, My Father's Honor*, by Jane Cook, illustrated by Janie Falcon (grades 4-6).

Nonfiction: Middle, young adults: history books on Texas and the Southwest, biography, multicultural. Recently published *Texas Brain Twisters*, by Jodie Weddle.

How to Contact/Writers: Fiction/Nonfiction: Query with outline/synopsis and sample chapter. Responds to queries in 1 month; mss in 2 months. Publishes a book 18 months after acceptance. No simultaneous submissions. Include SASE.

Illustration: Works with 2-3 illustrators/year. Uses primarily b&w interior artwork; color covers only. Illustrations only: Query first. Submit résumé or promotional literature or photocopies or tearsheets—no original work sent unsolicited. Responds only if interested.

Terms: Pays authors in royalty based on selling price. Advances vary. Pays illustrators by the project or royalty. Sends galleys to authors; dummies to illustrators. Manuscript guidelines for 1 first-class stamp and #10 SAE.

Tips "Material **must** pertain to Texas or the Southwest. Check all facts about historical figures and events in both fiction and nonfiction. Be accurate."

HOLIDAY HOUSE INC., 425 Madison Ave., New York NY 10017. (212)688-0085. Fax: (212)421-6134. Book publisher. Estab. 1935. Vice President/Editor-in-Chief: Regina Griffin. **Acquisitions:** Suzanne Reinochl, editor. Publishes 35 picture books/year; 3 young reader titles/year; 10 middle reader titles/year; and 3 young adult titles/year. 20% of books by first-time authors; 10% from agented writers.

- Holiday House title *John & Abigail Adams: An American Love Story*, by Judith St. George, won a 2002 Golden Kite Honor.

Fiction: All levels: adventure, contemporary, ghost, historical, humor, school. Recently published *A Child's Calendar*, by John Updike, illustrated by Trina Schart Hyman; *I Was a Third Grade Science Project*, by M.J. Auch; and *Darkness Over Denmark*, by Ellen Levine.

Nonfiction: All levels: animal, biography, concept, contemporary, geography, historical, math, nature/environment, science, social studies.

How to Contact/Writers: Send queries only to Editor. Responds to queries in 2 months. If we find your book idea suited to our present needs, we will notify you by mail. Once a ms has been requested, the writers should send in the exclusive submission, with a SASE, otherwise the ms will not be returned.

Illustration: Works with 35 illustrators/year. Reviews ms illustration packages from artists. Send ms with dummy. Do not submit original artwork or slides. Color photocopies or printed samples are preferred. Responds only if interested. Samples returned with SASE or filed.

Terms: Pays authors and illustrators an advance against royalties. Originals returned at job's completion. Book catalog, ms/artist's guidelines available for a SASE.

Tips: "Fewer books are being published. It will get even harder for first timers to break in."

HENRY HOLT & CO., LLC, 115 W. 18th St., New York NY 10011. (212)886-9200. Website: www.henryholt.com. Book publisher. **Manuscript Acquisitions:** Laura Godwin, editor-in-chief/associate publisher of Books for Young Readers dept.; Nina Ignatowicz, executive editor; Christy Ottaviano, executive editor, Reka Simonsen, editor. Adriane Frye, associate editor; Kate Farrell, associate editor. **Art Acquisitions:** Martha Rago, creative director. Publishes 20-40 picture books/year; 4-6 chapter books/year; 10-15 middle grade titles/year; 8-10 young adult titles/year. 15% of books by first-time authors; 40% of books from agented writers. "Henry Holt and Company Books for Young Readers is known for publishing quality books that feature imaginative authors and illustrators. We tend to publish many new authors and illustrators each year in our effort to develop and foster new talent."

Fiction: Picture books: animal, anthology, concept, folktales, history, humor, multicultural, nature/environment, poetry, special needs, sports. Middle readers: adventure, contemporary, history, humor, multicultural, special needs, sports, suspense/mystery. Young adults: contemporary, multicultural, problem novel, sports.

Nonfiction: Picture books: animal, arts/crafts, biography, concept, geography, history, hobbies, multicultural, music, dance, nature/environment, sports. Middle readers, young readers, young adult: biography, history, multicultural, sports.

How to Contact/Writers: Fiction/Nonfiction: Submit complete ms with SASE. Responds in 3 months. Will not consider simultaneous or multiple submissions.

insider report

Creating a following with something fresh: tales of unfortunate orphans and unhappy endings

"If you are interested in stories with happy endings, you would be better off reading some other book," warns author Lemony Snicket in *The Bad Beginning*, the first book in his A Series of Unfortunate Events. "In this book, not only is there no happy ending, there is no happy beginning and very few happy things in the middle." But Lemony Snicket's own story as an author is full of happy things. So if you are interested in articles full of woe and misery, you would be better off reading some other article.

Lemony Snicket

A *New York Times* book reviewer said: "Had the gloom-haunted Edward Gorey found a way to have a love child with Dorothy Parker, their issue might well have been Lemony Snicket." "Lemony Snicket" is actually the alter ego of author Daniel Handler, who penned a few adult novels prior to delving into writing for a middle grade audience. Handler stumbled into writing A Series of Unfortunate Events after HarperCollins editor Susan Rich suggested he give it a shot. Rich had seen Handler's novel *The Basic Eight*, which centers on a group of high schoolers, and thought Handler had good voice for fiction for a young readers. He unearthed a mock-gothic adult novel he had been working on, and with Rich's help, transformed it into the beginnings of *The Bad Beginning* and the other books in A Series of Unfortunate Events.

The darkly hilarious series with alliterative titles like *The Reptile Room*, *The Ersatz Elevator*, and *The Vile Village* follows the lives of the three Baudelaire children, who, in the first book in the series, become orphans on page 8 when their rich and loving parents die in a fire that burns down their mansion and destroys all their possessions. The kids will inherit a fortune when the oldest Baudelaire, 14-year-old Violet, comes of age. The children, Violet along with younger siblings Klaus and Sunny, are shipped from unfortunate family member to unfortunate family member (their guardians don't generally bode well), all the while pursued by master of disguise and could-be relative Count Olaf, who is out to steal the Baudelaire family fortune.

Each of Baudelaire children has distinct qualities that inform their characters. Violet is an inventor. One can tell the wheels in her head are turning through her habit of tying her long hair back in a ribbon whenever she's thinking of an invention, as "she never wanted to be distracted by something as trivial as her hair." Twelve-year-old Klaus is the middle child and only Baudelaire brother. He was very smart and has read a number of the books in the extensive Baudelaire library—before it burned down, of course. The youngest of the siblings, Sunny, is a baby with a few exceptionally sharp teeth. Her mode of operation is biting people and things, and emitting nonsense sounds like "Gack" and "Odo yow" which are understood only by her older brother and sister.

Since their release in 1999, Lemony Snicket's books have sold more than a million copies, and have shown up regularly on *The New York Times* Best-Seller List, alongside everyone's favorite British boy wizard. "I really thought these books would be noble failures," confesses Handler. "I thought they'd attract a small, cultist following among children who liked dark stories and who had parents who were amenable to providing them with such books, and it's been a surprise and a delight, but more a surprise, that they've taken off the way they have."

Handler as Snicket is really onto something. He's come up with a new concept in what can often be a formulaic industry, yet his writing is, as one reviewer describes it, "self-consciously, generously, joyously" formulaic. The narrator of the doom-and-gloom tales is very present, often interjecting with a definition of a word he's chosen. And readers have really responded— "responded" in this case means bought tons and tons of books. One young reader declared in a review on Amazon.com: "Lemony Snicket is the best writer the world has ever seen."

And Handler and his publishers have gone whole-hog with the gimmick of warning readers away from the books. The opening letter to readers, the book jackets, the website www.lemo nysnicket.com, bookstore displays, and even Lemony Snicket book signings (with Handler "filling in" for Mr. Snicket, who, for various bizarre reasons never seems to make it to his appearances) offer a clear message: *Don't read these books.* This message, Handler says, is a comment on the "overanxious, condescending voice that children hear wherever they go in

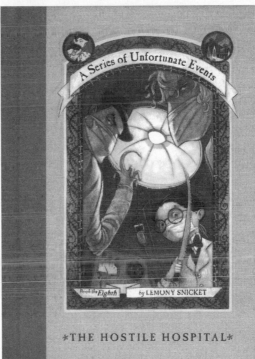

In spite of repeated warnings from Lemony Snicket (a.k.a. Daniel Handler) to shut this book immediately, young readers by the millions continue to brave the sad story of the Baudelaire orphans. A recent episode in Snicket's A Series of Unfortunate Events, *The Hostile Hospital*, (HarperCollins) finds the orphans having as terrible a time as ever. Snicket's alter-ego, Daniel Handler, began writing the middle-grade novels on the suggestion of HarperCollins editor, Susan Rich.

Reprinted with permission of HarperCollins.

Reprinted with permission of HarperCollins.

Described by *Publishers Weekly* as "a devious romp masquerading as an autobiography," *Lemony Snicket: The Unauthorized Autobiography* gives readers the inside scoop on everything they want to know about the mysterious Lemony Snicket—sort-of . "The 13 (naturally) chapters burst with red herrings, non sequiturs, mysterious letters, diary entries and so on not to mention fading black-and-white photographs with captions such as Total strangers and W?H?O?" says *Publishers Weekly*. "The narrative makes for a most satisfying tease, larded with such Snicketisms as For various reasons, portions of this chapter have been changed or made up entirely, including this sentence."

their culture, in books, on TV, and in the library. When Mr. Snicket says to the readers *I don't think you want to read this book*, children find it appealing that that sort of voice is being made fun of."

Readers overwhelmingly seem anxious to participate in the whole world of the books. "I never get a letter to Daniel Handler, even though my real name is certainly widely available," says the author. "They always come to Mr. Snicket, they're often reporting sightings of Count Olaf or evidence they have to offer, or they're just concerned for the children. I don't think they are actually 100 percent believing the stories. I think they're just eager to participate in the world the book offers, which is flattering. You never love a book the way you love a book when you're ten. It's an overwhelming privilege to be in that space in people's heads."

Handler himself enjoys telling stories as Snicket. "I'm really excited about the books I'm writing, and if I weren't I'd do something else." He'll end A Series of Unfortunate Events with volume 13. "I'd like to have the series be one nice, neat arc, and not continue indefinitely." Book 9, *The Carnivorous Carnival* was a June 2002 release, on the heels of *Lemony Snicket: The Unauthorized Autobiography* (May 2002).

So what will happen in Book 13? "I know more or less," Handler says. "I like to leave myself plenty of room to improvise. People always ask me if there's going to be a happy ending, and I remind them that happy is a comparative term. The ending will be happy compared to some endings they can think of, and unhappy compared to others." Handler's career as a children's author, however, seems destined for happiness by anyone's account.

—*Alice Pope*

Illustration: Works with 50-60 illustrators/year. Reviews ms/illustration packages from artists. Random samples OK. Illustrations only: Submit tearsheets, slides. Do *not* send originals. Responds to art samples in 1 month. Samples returned with SASE; samples filed. If accepted, original artwork returned at job's completion.

Terms: Pays authors/illustrators royalty based on retail price. Sends galleys to authors; proofs to illustrators.

HOUGHTON MIFFLIN CO., Children's Trade Books, 222 Berkeley St., Boston MA 02116-3764. (617)351-5000. Fax: (617)351-1111. E-mail: childrens_books@hmco.com. Website: www.houghtonmifflin books.com. Book publisher. **Manuscript Aquisitions:** Hannah Rodgers, submissions coordinator. Kim Keller, managing editor; Ann Rider, Margaret Raymo, senior editors; Amy Flynn, editor; Eden Edwards, Sandpiper Paperback editor; Walter Lorraine, Walter Lorraine Books editor; Kate O'Sullivan, assistant editor. **Art Acquisitions:** Bob Kosturko, art director. Averages 60 titles/year. Publishes hardcover originals and trade paperback reprints and originals. Imprints include Clarion Books. "Houghton Mifflin gives shape to ideas that educate, inform, and above all, delight."

- Houghton Mifflin title *Black Potatoes: the Story of the Great Irish Famine*, by Susan Campbell Bartoletti, won the 2002 Golden Kite Award for Nonfiction. Their title *The Lamp, the Ice, and the Boat Called Fish*, illustrated by Beth Krommes, won the 2002 Golden Kite Award for Illustration.

Fiction: All levels: all categories except religion. "We do not rule out any theme, though we do not publish specifically religious material." *The Strange Egg*, by Mary Newell DePalma (ages 4-8, picture book); *Gathering Blue*, by Lois Lowry (ages 10-14, novel); and *The Circuit*, by Francisco Jimenez (ages 10 and up).

Nonfiction: All levels: all categories except religion. Recently published *Slap, Squeak, and Scatter*, by Steve Jenkins (ages 6-10; picture book); *The Man-Eating Tigers of Sundarbans*, by Sy Montgomery (ages 4-8, photo); *Girls Think of Everything*, by Catherine Thimmesh, illustrated by Melissa Sweet (ages 8-12).

How to Contact/Writers: Fiction: Submit complete ms. Nonfiction: Submit outline/synopsis and sample chapters. Always include SASE. Response within 4 months.

Illustration: Works with 60 illustrators/year. Reviews ms/illustration packages from artists. Manuscript/illustration packages or illustrations only: Query with samples (colored photocopies are fine); provide tearsheets. Responds in 4 months. Samples returned with SASE; samples filed if interested.

Terms: Pays standard royalty based on retail price; offers advance. Illustrators paid by the project and royalty. Manuscript and artist's guidelines available for SASE.

HUNTER HOUSE PUBLISHERS, P.O.Box 2914, Alameda CA 94501-0914. Fax: (510)865-4295. E-mail: acquisitions@hunterhouse.com. Website: www.hunterhouse.com. Book publisher. **Manuscript Acquisitions:** Jeanne Brondino. Publishes 0-1 titles for teenage women/year. 50% of books by first-time authors; 5% of books from agented writers.

Nonfiction: Young adults: health, multicultural, self-help (self esteem), social issues, violence prevention. "We emphasize that all our books try to take multicultural experiences and concerns into account. We would be interested in a social issues or self-help book on multicultural issues." Books are therapy/personal growth-oriented. Does *not* want to see books for young children; fiction; illustrated picture books; autobiography. Published *Turning Yourself Around: Self-Help Strategies for Troubled Teens*, by Kendall Johnson, Ph.D.; *Safe Dieting for Teens*, by Linda Ojeda, Ph.D.

How to Contact/Writers: Query; submit overview and chapter-by-chapter synopsis, sample chapters and statistics on your subject area, support organizations or networks and marketing ideas. "Testimonials from professionals or well-known authors are crucial." Responds to queries in 3 months; mss in 6 months. Publishes a book 18 months after acceptance. Will consider simultaneous submissions.

Photography: Purchases photos from freelancers. Buys stock images.

Terms: Payment varies. Sends galleys to authors. Book catalog available for 9×12 SAE and $1.25 postage; ms guidelines for standard SAE and 1 first-class stamp.

Tips: Wants therapy/personal growth workbooks; teen books with solid, informative material. "We do few children's books. The ones we do are for a select, therapeutic audience. No fiction! Please, no fiction."

HYPERION BOOKS FOR CHILDREN, 114 Fifth Ave., New York NY 10011-5690. (212)633-4400. Fax: (212)633-4833. Website: www.hyperionchildrensbooks.com. Trade imprint of Disney Publishing Worldwide. Book publisher. **Manuscript Acquisitions:** Editorial Director. **Art Acquisitions:** Anne Diebel, art director. 10% of books by first-time authors. Publishes various categories.

- Hyperion/Jump at the Sun title *Martin's Big Words*, illustrated by Bryan Collier, text by Doreen Rappaport, won a 2002 Caldecott Honor and Coretta Scott King Illustrator Honor. Their title *Money-Hungry*, by Sharon G. Flake, won a 2002 Coretta Scott King Honor.

Fiction: Picture books, young readers, middle readers, young adults: adventure, animal, anthology (short stories), contemporary, fantasy, folktales, history, humor, multicultural, poetry, science fiction, sports, suspense/mystery. Middle readers, young adults: commercial fiction. Recently published *Emily's First 100 Days of School*, by Rosemary Wells (ages 3-6, *New York Times* bestseller); *Artemis Fowl*, by Eoin Colfer (YA novel, *New York Times* bestseller); *Dumpy The Dump Truck*, series by Julie Andrews Edwards and Emma Walton Hamilton (ages 3-7).

Nonfiction: All trade subjects for all levels.

How to Contact/Writers: Only interested in agented material.

Illustration: Works with 100 illustrators/year. "Picture books are fully illustrated throughout. All others depend on individual project." Reviews ms/illustration packages from artists. Submit complete package. Illustrations only: Submit résumé, business card, promotional literature or tearsheets to be kept on file. Responds only if interested. Original artwork returned at job's completion.

Photography: Works on assignment only. Publishes photo essays and photo concept books. Provide résumé, business card, promotional literature or tearsheets to be kept on file.

Terms: Pays authors royalty based on retail price. Offers advances. Pays illustrators and photographers royalty based on retail price or a flat fee. Sends galleys to authors; dummies to illustrators. Book catalog available for 9×12 SAE and 3 first-class stamps.

HYPERION PRESS LIMITED, 300 Wales Ave., Winnipeg, Manitoba R2M 2S9 Canada. (204)256-9204. Fax: (204)255-7845. E-mail: tamos@escape.ca. Website: www.escape.ca/~tamos. Book Publisher. **Acquisitions:** Dr. M. Tutiah, editor. Publishes authentic-based, retold folktales/legends for ages 4-9. "We are interested in a good story or well researched how-to material."

Fiction: Young readers, middle readers: folktales/legends. Recently published *The Wise Washerman*, by Deborah Froese, illustrated by Wang Kui; *The Cricket's Cage*, written and illustrated by Stefan Czernecki; and *The Peacock's Pride*, by Melissa Kajpust, illustrated by Jo'Anne Kelly.

How to Contact/Writers: Fiction: Query. Responds in 3 months.

Illustration: Reviews ms/illustration packages from artists. Manuscript/illustration packages and illustration only: Query. Samples returned with SASE.

Terms: Pays authors royalty. Pays illustrators by the project. Sends galleys to authors; dummies to illustrators. Book catalog available for 8½×11 SAE and $2.00 postage (Canadian).

ILLUMINATION ARTS, P.O. Box 1865, Bellevue WA 98009. (425)644-7185. Fax: (425)644-9274. E-mail: liteinfo@illumin.com. Website: www.illumin.com. Book publisher. Estab. 1987. "All of our books are inspirational/spiritual (nonreligious) picture books. We specialize in children's books, but they are designed to appeal to all readers, including adults. We are so selective and painstaking in every detail that our company has established a reputation for producing award-winning books." **Acquisitions:** Ruth Thompson, editorial director.

Fiction: Average word length: up to 1,500 words. Recently published *The Tree*, by Dana Lyons, illustrated by David Danioth; *The Whoosh of Gadoosh*, by Pat Skene, illustrated by Doug Keith.

How to Contact/Writers: Fiction: Submit complete ms. Responds to queries in 1-2 months, with SASE only. No electronic or CD submissions for text or art. Publishes a book 2 years after acceptance. Will consider simultaneous submissions.

Illustration: Works with 3 illustrators/year. Uses color artwork only. Reviews ms/illustration packages from artists. Query or send ms with dummy. Illustrations only: Query with samples; send résumé and promotional literature to be kept on file. Contact: Terri Cohlene, creative director. Responds in 1 week. Samples returned with SASE or filed.

Terms: Pays authors and illustrators royalty based on wholesale price. Originals returned to artist at job's completion. Book fliers available for SASE.

Tips: "Follow our guidelines. Be patient. The market is competitive. We receive 1,500 submissions annually and publish 4-5 books a year."

IMAJINN BOOKS, P.O. Box 162, Hickory Corners MI 49060-0162. (269)671-4633. Fax: (269)671-4535. E-mail: editors@imajinnbooks.com. Website: www.imajinnbooks.com. Estab. 1998. Specializes in fiction, trade books. **Manuscript Acquisitions:** Linda Kichline, senior editor. Publishes 2-4 middle readers/year; and 2-4 young adult titles/year. 100% of books by first-time authors. "We provide full-length middle grade and young adult science fiction and fantasy novels with fast-paced action. We want underlying moral lessons in the stories without preaching. We want children to have respect for adults. We want to see children interact with each other over their problems and help each other find solutions for them. We want books that will appeal to both boys and girls."

Fiction: Middle readers, young adults: fantasy, science ficiton. Average word length: middle readers—50,000-70,000; young adults—50,000-70,000. Recently published *Penelope Quagmire and the Lizard Men from Outer Space*; and *Penelope Quagmire and the Planet of the Zombies*, by Hall W. Lanse (ages 8-12).
How to Contact/Writers: Query or submit outline/synopsis. Responds to queries in 2 months; mss in 8 months. Publishes book 24-30 months after acceptance. Will consider electronic submissions via disk or modem.
Terms: Pays authors royalty of 6-10% based on retail price. Offers advances (Average amount: $25-100). Book catalog available for #10 SAE and 2 first-class stamps; ms guidelines available for SASE. Catalog available on website.

IMPACT PUBLISHERS, INC., P.O. Box 6016, Atascadero CA 93423-6016. (805)466-5917. Fax: (805)466-5919. E-mail: info@impactpublishers.com. Website: www.impactpublishers.com. Estab. 1970. Nonfiction publisher. **Manuscript Acquisitions:** Melissa Froehner, children's editor. **Art Acquisitions:** Sharon Skinner, art director. Imprints: Little Imp Books, Rebuilding Books, The Practical Therapist Series. Publishes 1 young reader/year; 1 middle reader/year; and 1 young adult title/year. 20% of books by first-time authors. "Our purpose is to make the best human services expertise available to the widest possible audience."
Nonfiction: Young readers, middle readers, young adults: self-help. Recently published *The Divorce Helpbook for Kids*, by Cynthia MacGregor (ages 8-12, children's/divorce/emotions).
How to Contact/Writers: Nonfiction: Query or submit complete ms, cover letter, résumé. Responds to queries in 8-10 weeks; mss in 10-12 weeks. Will consider simultaneous submissions or previously published work.
Illustration: Works with 1 or less illustrator/year. Uses b&w artwork only. Reviews ms/illustration packages from artists. Query. Contact: Children's Editor. Illustrations only: query with samples. Contact: Sharon Skinner, production manager. Responds only if interested. Samples returned with SASE; samples filed. Originals returned to artist at job's completion.
Terms: Pays authors royalty of 10-12%. Offers advances. Pays illustrators by the project. Sends galleys to authors. Book catalog available for #10 SAE with 2 first-class stamps; ms guidelines available for SASE. All imprints included in a single catalog.

INCENTIVE PUBLICATIONS, INC., 3835 Cleghorn Ave., Nashville TN 37215-2532. (615)385-2934. Fax: (615)385-2967. E-mail: info@incentivepublications.com. Website: www.incentivepublications. com. Estab. 1969. "Incentive publishes developmentally appropriate instructional aids for tots to teens."
Acquisitions: Jennifer Streams. Approximately 20% of books by first-time authors. "We publish only educational resource materials (for teachers and parents of children from pre-school age through high school). We publish *no fiction*. Incentive endeavors to produce developmentally appropriate research-based educational materials to meet the changing needs of students, teachers and parents. Books are written by teachers for teachers for the most part."
Nonfiction: Black & white line illustrated books, young reader, middle reader: activity books, arts/craft, multicultural, science, health, how-to, reference, animal, history, nature/environment, special needs, social issues, supplemental educational materials. "Any manuscripts related to child development or with content-based activities and innovative strategies will be reviewed for possible publication." Recently published *Romeo & Juliet Curriculum Guide*, by Laura Maravilla; ESL Games, Puzzles and Inventive Exercises Series, by Imogene Forte and Mary Ann Pangle.
How to Contact/Writers: Nonfiction: Submit outline/synopsis, sample chapters and SASE. Usually responds to queries/mss in 1 month. Responds to queries in 6 weeks; mss in 2 months. Typically publishes a book 18 months after acceptance. Will consider simultaneous submissions.
Illustration: Works with 2-6 illustrators/year. Responds in 1 month if reply requested (send SASE). Samples returned with SASE; samples filed. Need 4-color cover art; b&w line illustration for content.
Terms: Pays authors in royalties (5-10% based on wholesale price) or work purchased outright (range: $500-1,000). Pays illustrators by the project (range: $200-1,300). Pays photographers by the project. Original artwork not returned. Book catalog and ms and artist guidelines for SAE and $1.78 postage.
Tips: Writers: "We buy only educational teacher resource material that can be used by teachers and parents (home schoolers). Please do not submit fiction! Incentive Publications looks for a whimsical, warm style of illustration that respects the integrity and age of the child. We work primarily with local artists, but not exclusively."

ipicturebooks, Website: www.ipicturebooks.com. Online book publisher. "ipicturebooks is the #1 brand for children's e-books on the Internet. It is designed to appeal to parents, children, teachers and librarians seeking in-print, out-of print and original enhanced e-books for use on home computers, school and library networked computers, proprietary and open hand-helds and dedicated e-book readers. It will sell e-books by individual downloaded copy, site licenses and subscription models. ipicturebooks will also introduce a variety of 'enhanced' e-books, ranging from original ebooks illustrated digitally, to 'custom' e-books in which a child's name appears to 'e-pop up books' to e-books with spoken text to e-books with music and animation." See website for submission information for writers and illustrators, as well as sample e-books.

JAYJO BOOKS, L.L.C., A Guidance Channel Company, 135 Dupont St., P.O. Box 760, Plainview NY 11803-0760. (516)349-5520. Fax: (516)349-5521. E-mail: jayjobooks@guidancechannel.com. Website: www.jayjo.com. Estab. 1993. Specializes in educational material. Independent book packager/producer. **Manuscript Acquisitions:** Sally Germain. Publishes 3-5 picture books/year; 3-5 young readers/year. 25% of books by first-time authors. "Our goal is to provide quality children's health education through entertainment and teaching, while raising important funds for medical research and education."
Fiction: Picture books, young readers, middle readers, young adults: health, special needs, chronic conditions. Average word length: picture books—1,800; young readers—1,800; middle readers—1,800. Recently published *Taking Dyslexia to School*, by Lauren E. Moynihan (ages 5-10); *Taking Down Syndrome to School*, by Jenna Glatzer (ages 5-10).
Nonfiction: Picture books, young readers, middle readers: health, special needs, chronic conditions. Average word length: picture books—1,500; young readers—1,500; middle readers—1,500.
How to Contact/Writers: Fiction/Nonfiction: Send query. Responds in 3 months. Publishes a book 2 years after acceptance. Will consider simultaneous submissions.
Illustration: Works with 2 illustrators/year. Uses color artwork only. Illustrations only: Query with samples. Responds in 3 months. Samples returned with SASE; samples filed.
Terms: Work purchased outright from authors. Pays illustrators by the project. Book catalog and guidelines available for #10 SAE and 1 first-class stamp. Manuscript guidelines for SASE.
Tips: "Send query letter. Since we only publish books adapted to our special format, we contact appropriate potential authors and work with them to customize manuscripts."

JEWISH LIGHTS PUBLISHING, P.O. Box 237, Rt. 4, Sunset Farm Offices, Woodstock VT 05091. (802)457-4000. Fax: (802)457-4004. E-mail: everyone@longhillpartners.com. Website: www.jewishlights.com. A division of LongHill Partners, Inc. Book publisher. Imprint: Sky Light Paths Publishing. President: Stuart M. Matlins. **Manuscript Acquisitions:** Submissions Editor. **Art Acquisitions:** Bridget Taylor. Publishes 2 picture books/year; 1 young reader/year. 50% of books by first-time authors; 1% of books from agented authors. All books have spiritual/religious themes. "Jewish Lights publishes books for people of all faiths and all backgrounds who yearn for books that attract, engage, educate and spiritually inspire. Our authors are at the forefront of spiritual thought and deal with the quest for the self and for meaning in life by drawing on the Jewish wisdom tradition. Our books cover topics including history, spirituality, life cycle, children's, self-help, recovery, theology and philosophy. We do *not* publish autobiography, biography, fiction, *haggadot*, poetry or cookbooks. At this point we plan to do only two books for children annually, and one will be for younger children (ages 4-10)."
Fiction: Picture books, young readers, middle readers: spirituality. "We are not interested in anything other than spirituality." Recently published *God Said Amen*, by Sandy Eisenberg Sasso, illustrated by Avi Katz (ages 4-9, picture book); and *Cain and Abel*, by Sandy Eisenberg Sasso, illustrated by Joan Keller Rothenberg (ages 8 and up).
Nonfiction: Picture book, young readers, middle readers: activity books, spirituality. Recently published *When a Grandparent Dies: A Kid's Own Remembering Workbook for Dealing with Shiva and the Year Beyond*, by Nechama Liss-Levinson, Ph.D. (ages 7-11); and *Sharing Blessings: Children's Stories for Exploring the Spirit of the Jewish Holidays*, written by Rabbi Michael Klayman and Rahel Musleah, illustrated by Mary O'Keefe Young (ages 6-10, picture book).
How to Contact/Writers: Fiction/Nonfiction: Query with outline/synopsis and 2 sample chapters; submit complete ms for picture books. Include SASE. Responds to queries/mss in 3-4 months. Publishes a book 6 months after acceptance. Will consider simultaneous submissions and previously published work.
Illustration: Works with 2 illustrators/year. Reviews ms/illustration packages from artists. Query. Illustrations only: Query with samples; provide résumé. Samples returned with SASE; samples filed.
Terms: Pays authors royalty of 10% of revenue received. Offers advances. Pays illustrators by the project or royalty. Pays photographers by the project. Sends galleys to authors; dummies to illustrators. Book catalog available for 6½×9½ SAE and 59¢ postage; ms guidelines available for SASE.
Tips: "Explain in your cover letter why you're submitting your project to *us* in particular. (Make sure you know what we publish.)"

JOURNEY FORTH BOB JONES UNIVERSITY PRESS, (formerly Bob Jones University Press), 1700 Wade Hampton Blvd., Greenville SC 29614. (803)242-5100, ext. 4350. E-mail: jb@bjup.com. Website:

www.bjup.com/books/FreelanceOpportunities. Book publisher. Estab. 1974. **Acquisitions:** Mrs. Nancy Lohr, editor. Publishes 4 young reader titles/year; 4 middle reader titles/year; and 4 young adult titles/year. 30% of books by first-time authors. "Our books reflect the highest Christian standards of thought, feeling, and action, are uplifting or instructive and enhance moral purity. Themes advocating secular attitudes of rebellion or materialism are not acceptable. We are looking for books that present a fully developed main character capable of dynamic changes, who experiences the central conflict of the plot, which should have plenty of action and not be didactic in tone."

Fiction: Young readers, middle readers, young adults: adventure, animal, concept, contemporary, easy-to-read, fantasy, history, multicultural, nature/environment, sports, spy/mystery. Average word length: young readers—10,000; middle readers—30,000; young adult/teens—50,000. Published *The Treasure of Pelican Cove*, by Milly Howard (grades 2-4, adventure story); and *Over the Divide*, by Catherine Farnes (young adult, contemporary).

Nonfiction: Average word length: young readers—10,000; middle readers—30,000; young adult/teens—50,000. Published *With Daring Faith*, by Becky Davis (grades 5-8, biography); and *Someday You'll Write*, by Elizabeth Yates (how-to).

How to Contact/Writers: Fiction: Send the first five chapters and synopsis. "Do not send stories with magical elements. We are not currently accepting picture books. We do not publish these genres: romance, science fiction, poetry and drama." Nonfiction: Query or submit complete ms or submit outline/synopsis and sample chapters. Responds to queries in 3 weeks; mss in 3 months. Publishes book "approximately one year" after acceptance. Will consider simultaneous submissions.

Illustration: Works with 4 illustrators/year. Responds only if interested. Samples returned with SASE; samples filed.

Terms: Pays authors royalty based on wholesale price. Or work purchased outright. Pays illustrators by the project. Originals returned to artist at job's completion. Book catalog and ms guidelines free on request. Send SASE for book catalog and mss guidelines.

Tips: "Writers—give us original, well-developed characters in a suspenseful plot that has good moral tone. Artists—we need strong color as well as black & white illustrations. Looking for quality illustrations of people in action in realistic settings. Be willing to take suggestions and follow specific directions. We are committed to producing high-quality books for children."

KAMEHAMEHA SCHOOLS PRESS, 1887 Makuakane St., Honolulu HI 96817. (808)842-8880. Fax: (808)842-8895. E-mail: kspress@ksbe.edu. Website: www.ksbc.edu/pubs/KSPress/catalog.html. Estab. 1933. Specializes in educational and multicultural material. **Manuscript Acquisitions:** Lilinoe Andrews. "Kamehameha Schools Press publishes in the areas of Hawaiian history, Hawaiian culture, Hawaiian language and Hawaiian studies."

Nonfiction: Middle readers, young adults: biography, history, multicultural, Hawaiian folklore. Recently published *From the Mountains to the Sea: Early Hawaiian Life*, by Julie Stewart Williams, illustrated by Robin Yoko Racoma (pre-contact Hawaiian life and culture).

How to Contact/Writers: Query. Responds to queries in 2 months; mss in 3 months. Publishes a book 12-18 months after acceptance.

Illustration: Uses b&w artwork only. Illustrations only: Query with samples. Responds only if interested. Samples not returned.

Terms: Work purchased outright from authors. Pays illustrators by the project. Sends galleys to authors. Book catalog available for #10 SASE and 1 first-class stamp. All imprints included in a single catalog. Catalog available on website.

Tips: "Writers and illustrators *must* be knowledgeable in Hawaiian history/culture and be able to show credentials to validate their proficiency. Greatly prefer to work with writers/illustrators available in the Honolulu area."

KAR-BEN PUBLISHING, INC. (formerly Kar-Ben Copies, Inc.), a division of Lerner Publishing Group, 6800 Tildenwood Lane, Rockville MD 20852-4371. (301)984-8733. Fax: (301)881-9195. E-mail: karben@aol.com. Website: www.karben.com. Book publisher. Estab. 1975. **Manuscript Acquisitions:** Madeline Wikler and Judy Groner, editorial directors. Publishes 5-10 picture books/year; 20% of books by first-time authors. All of Kar-Ben Copies' books are on Jewish themes for young children and families.

THE SUBJECT INDEX, located in the back of this book, lists book publishers and magazines according to the fiction and nonfiction subjects they seek.

Fiction: Picture books, young readers: adventures, concept, contemporary, fantasy, folktales, history, humor, multicultural, religion, special needs, suspense/mystery; *must be* on a Jewish theme. Average word length: picture books—2,000. Recently published *The Hardest Word*, by Jacqueline Jules; *Sammy Spiders First Trip to Israel*, by Sylvia Rouss; *The Shabbat Box*, by Lesley Simpson.

Nonfiction: Picture books, young readers: activity books, arts/crafts, biography, careers, concept, cooking, history, how-to, multicultural, religion, social issues, special needs; must be of Jewish interest. Average word length: picture books—2,000. Recently published *Bible Story Crafts for Little Hands*, by Ruth Brinn; *Mitzvah Magic*, by Danny Siegel.

How to Contact/Writers: Fiction/nonfiction: Submit complete ms. Responds to queries/ms in 6 weeks. Publishes a book 1 year after acceptance. Will consider simultaneous submissions. "Story should be short, no more than 3,000 words."

Illustration: Works with 5-6 illustrators/year. Prefers "four-color art in any medium that is scannable." Reviews ms/illustration packages from artists. Submit whole ms and sample of art (no originals). Illustrations only: Submit tearsheets, photocopies, promo sheet or anything representative that does *not* need to be returned. "Submit samples which show skill in children's book illustration." Enclose SASE for response. Responds to art samples in 2 weeks.

Terms: Pays authors in royalties of 5-6% of net purchased outright (range: $2,000-3,000). Offers advance (average amount: $1,000). Pays illustrators royalty of 8-10% based on wholesale price or by the project (range: $500-3,000). Sends galleys to authors. Original artwork returned at job's completion. Book catalog free on request. Manuscript guidelines for 9×12 SAE and 2 first-class stamps.

Tips: Looks for "books for young children with Jewish interest and content, modern, non-sexist, not didactic. Fiction or nonfiction with a *Jewish* theme—can be serious or humorous, life cycle, Bible story, or holiday-related."

KEY PORTER BOOKS, 70 The Esplanade, Toronto, Ontario M5E 1R2 Canada. (416)862-7777. Fax: (416)862-2304. Website: www.keyporter.com. Book publisher. Publishes 4 picture books/year; and 4 young readers/year. 30% of books by first-time authors.

Fiction: Young readers, middle readers, young adult: animal, anthology, concept, health, multicultural, nature/environment, science fiction, special needs, sports, suspense/mystery. Does not want to see religious material. Average word length: picture books—1,500; young readers—5,000.

Nonfiction: Picture books: animal, history, nature/environment, reference, science. Middle readers: animal, careers, history, nature/environment, reference, science and sports. Average word length: picture books—1,500; middle readers—15,000. Recently published *New Animal Discoveries*, by Ronald Orenstein (ages 8-12); *Footnotes: Dancing the World's Best Love Ballads*, by Frank Augustyn and Shelley Tanaka (ages 8-10).

How to Contact/Writers: Only interested in agented material from Canadian writers; *no unsolicited mss.*

Photography: Buys photos from freelancers. Buys stock and assigns work. Captions required. Uses 35mm transparencies. Submit cover letter, résumé, duplicate slides, stock photo list.

KIDS CAN PRESS, 29 Birch Ave., Toronto, Ontario M4V 1E2 Canada. (800)265-0884. E-mail: info@kidscan.com. Website: www.kidscanpress.com. Estab. 1973. Specializes in fiction, trade books, nonfiction. **Contact:** Acquisitions Editor. **Contact:** Art Director. Publishes 6-10 picture books/year; 10-15 young readers/year; 20-30 middle readers/year; 2-3 young adult titles/year. 10-15% of books by first-time authors.

• Kids Can Press is currently accepting unsolicited mss from Canadian authors only.

Fiction: Picture books, young readers: concept. All levels: adventure, animal, contemporary, fantasy, folktales, history, humor, multicultural, nature/environment, poetry, special needs, sports, suspense/mystery. Average word length: picture books—1,000-2,000; young readers—750-1,500; middle readers—10,000-15,000; young adults —over 15,000. Recently published *Oma's Quilt*, by Paulette Bourgeois, illustrated by Stéphane Jorlisch (picture book); *The Secret of Sagawa Lake*, by Mary Labatt (early novel-mystery); and *The Best Figure Skater in the Whole Wide World*, by Linda Bailey, illustrated by Alan and Lea Daniel (picture book).

Nonfiction: Picture books: activity books, animal, arts/crafts, biography, careers, concept, health, history, hobbies, how-to, multicultural, nature/environment, science, social issues, special needs, sports; young readers: activity books, animal, arts/crafts, biography, careers, concept, history, hobbies, how-to, multicultural; middle readers: cooking, music/dance. Average word length: picture books—500-1,250; young readers—750-2,000; middle readers—5,000-15,000. Recently published *The Kids Winter Handbook*, by Jane Drake and Ann Love, illustrated by Heather Collins (informational activity); *Animals at Work*, by Etta Kaner, illustrated by Pat Stephens (animal/nature); and *Quilting*, by Biz Storms, illustrated by June Bradford (craft book).

How to Contact/Writers: Fiction/nonfiction: Submit outline/synopsis and 2-3 sample chapters. For picture books submit complete ms. Responds in 6 months. Publishes a book 18-24 months after acceptance. **Illustration:** Works with 40 illustrators/year. Reviews ms/illustration packages from artists. Send color copies of illustration portfolio, cover letter outlining other experience. Contact: Art Director. Illustrations only: Send tearsheets, color photocopies. Contact: Art Director, Kids Can Press, 2250 Military Rd., Tonawanda NY 14150. Responds only if interested. Samples returned with SASE; samples filed.

☑ Ⓐ **KINGFISHER**, Imprint of Larousse Kingfisher Chambers, 215 Park Ave. South, New York NY 10003. (212)420-5800. Fax: (212)686-1082. Website: www.lkcpub.com. **Contact:** Phil Gray.
   ● Kingfisher is not currently accepting unsolicited mss. All solicitations must be made by a recognized literary agent. Kingfisher is an award-winning publisher of nonfiction and fiction for children of all ages. They publish high-quality books with strong editorial content and world class illustration at a competitive price, offering value to parents and educators.

[N] ▼ **KNOPF DELACORTE DELL YOUNG READERS GROUP**, (formerly Alfred A. Knopf Books for Young Readers), 1540 Broadway, New York NY 10036. (212)782-9000. Website: www.randomh ouse.com/kids. Division of Random House Children's Books. Vice-President, Editor-at-Large: Janet Schulman. 90% of books published through agents. "Knopf is known for high quality literary fiction and is willing to take risks with writing styles. It publishes for children ages 5 and up."
   ● Knopf title *Woody Guthrie Poet of the People*, written and illustrated by Bonnie Christensen, won a 2002 Boston Globe-Horn Book Honor Award for Nonfiction.
Fiction: Unsolicited mss are only being accepted as submissions to either the Marguerite de Angeli Contest for middle-grade contemporary or historical fiction or the Delacorte Press Contest for contemporary young adult fiction. Send a SASE for contest rules.
Illustration: Illustration only: Contact: Isabel Warren-Lynch, Liney Li, art directors. Responds only if interested. Samples returned with SASE; samples filed.
Terms: Pays illustrators and photographers by the project or royalties. Original artwork returned at job's completion.

[N] **WENDY LAMB BOOKS**, Imprint of Random House, 1540 Broadway, New York NY 10036. Fax: (212)782-9451. Specializes in trade books, fiction, multicultural material. **Manuscript Acquisitions:** Wendy Lamb. Publishes 3 middle readers/year; and 8 young adult titles/year. 33% of books by first-time authors. Recently published *Island Boyz*, by Graham Salisbury; *Pictures of Hollis Woods*, by Patricia Reilly Giff; *Tribes*, by Arthur Slade.
How to Contact/Writers: Fiction/nonfiction: Query. Responds to queries in 3 weeks; mss in 4 months. Publishes book 18 months after acceptance. Will consider electronic submissions via disk or modem; previously published work.
Illustration: Reviews ms/illustration packages from artists. Query.

LEE & LOW BOOKS INC., 95 Madison Ave., New York NY 10016-7801. (212)779-4400. E-mail: info@leeandlow.com. Website: www.leeandlow.com. Book publisher. Estab. 1991. **Acquisitions:** Philip Lee, publisher; Louise May, executive editor. Publishes 12-14 picture books/year. 50% of books by first-time authors. Lee & Low publishes only picture books with multicultural themes. "One of our goals is to discover new talent and produce books that reflect the multicultural society in which we live."
   ● Lee & Low Books is dedicated to publishing culturally authentic literature. The company makes a special effort to work with writers and artists of color and encourages new voices. See listing for their new imprint BeBop Books.
Fiction: Picture books: concept. Picture books, young readers: anthology, contemporary, history, multicultural, poetry. "We are not considering folktales or animal stories." Picture book, middle reader: contemporary, history, multicultural, nature/environment, poetry, sports. Average word length: picture books—1,000-1,500 words. Recently published *Love to Langston*, by Tony Medina, illustrated by R. Gregory Christie; *The Pot that Juan Built*, by Nancy Andrews-Goebel, illustrated by David Diaz; and *Love to Mamá*, edited by Pat Mora, illustrated by Pauls S. Barragán M.
Nonfiction: Picture books: concept. Picture books, middle readers: biography, history, multicultural, science and sports. Average word length: picture books—1,500. Recently published *Ray Charles*, by Sharon Bell Mathis, illustrated by George Ford; and *¡Béisbol! Latino Baseball Pioneers and Legends*, by Jonah Winter.
How to Contact/Writers: Fiction/Nonfiction: Submit complete ms. No e-mail submissions. Responds in 4 months. Publishes a book 1-2 years after acceptance. Will consider simultaneous submissions. Guidelines on website.

insider report

'Creating something of value is hard'

As a youngster, Wendy Lamb never sat around dreaming of becoming a children's book editor. She was too busy reading.

"In fourth grade," Lamb says, "I gave 250 book reports, which is actually kind of scary. Nowadays, they'd probably send me to a counselor. In those days, they gave me an A-plus."

These days, Lamb is still receiving high marks. The one-time extreme reader is now Vice President/Publishing Director of Wendy Lamb Books. Random House launched the imprint in Spring 2002.

Lamb grew up in New Canaan, Connecticut, and was very close to the wife and eldest daughter of legendary editor Maxwell Perkins. "Although my parents were cultured people, there was this passion for books in the Perkins' household that was unusual,"

Wendy Lamb

Photo: Maryanne Russell

Lamb says. "And I was just the perfect kid to wander into that world. I certainly knew what an editor was and I did get this kind of idealized sense of the meaning of books in this world."

Lamb, considered one of the most insightful editors in the field, has worked with some of the finest talent in the business, including Walter Dean Myers, Patricia Reilly Giff, Gary Paulsen and Christopher Paul Curtis. Lamb pulled Curtis' manuscript for *The Watsons Go to Birmingham—1963* from a pile of contest entries when she was an editor at Delacorte. *Watsons* went on to win a Newbery Honor. Curtis' second book, *Bud, Not Buddy*, which Lamb edited, won the 2000 Newbery Medal.

Is it true you've always wanted to write Broadway plays?
I've worked on a couple musicals as a lyricist. I wrote the book of lyrics for a show produced in New York. I really loved all that; I still like doing it. It's sort of interesting how helpful that is for my job. Thinking about how to communicate. It's connected. The theater of it is children's book-ish. I find there's a certain connection between those two zones that I like.

When did you first know that editing was going to be your thing?
I don't know if that ever happened [*laughs*]. No, after college, I took this publishing course—the Radcliffe Publishing Course—and came to New York and got a job at HarperCollins, just Harper back then. But then I ran away and did other things and wrote. So I didn't really settle into a career as a full-time editor, and actually I thought I'd kind of blown it. I started out working full-time and then I just ran out the door at 26 and went to graduate school and had adventures, and just wrote my musicals. After I came back to full-time editing, the Children's Book Council asked me to give a talk about my career and I thought well, *I'm* not the one to be giving this talk.

So during the Radcliffe course you weren't thinking, "Wendy Lamb Books by the year 2001"?

No way. There, I didn't even know what I'd do. I went around having interviews to do publicity for adult books, or to work on magazines. I had many interviews; I was open to all sorts of things. The only thing I knew I *didn't* want to do was work in textbooks. But it was really lucky because children's books was the place for me.

I was a reader at Harper. All I did was read slush all day. It was a terrible job, actually.

You didn't discover *anyone*?

No, I didn't. I did it for 10 months and then I was thrilled to get to be somebody's secretary.

When the CBC asked me to give a talk they wanted me to talk about the book that changed my career. I think they were thinking of books that have won prizes. But, actually, I said you know, the book that changed my career was the book I never found while at Harper's in my first 10 months. That changed my career because it showed me right away how hard it was. I immediately saw, *ohhh*, it's a long haul. And I sort of think of this whole thing as cheerfully slogging toward greatness. And the thing about having an imprint is, I don't have any secrets or shortcuts. I don't. I wish I did. All I know is it's a slog. But it's good, it's cheerful.

During your presentation at the 2001 SCBWI Conference, you said: "If it weren't for bad childhoods, I wouldn't have a job."

Well, it was a joke. But most people, if they had a happy time in high school, don't end up

"In fourth grade I gave 250 book reports," says Wendy Lamb, Vice President/Publishing Director of the new Random House imprint, Wendy Lamb Books. A lifelong book lover, Lamb would find plenty to write about in WLB's latest release *Daughter of Venice*, by Donna Jo Napoli, a YA novel inspired by the first woman to earn a doctorate degree.

Jacket illustration Steven Adler. Design Trish Parcell. Reprinted with permission of Random House.

writing YA too often. It's kind of interesting how *angst*, how being an outsider, is what seems to drive people to write for teenagers. For some people, high school was a wonderful time. It was a successful and happy time. Do they ever write books? Well, maybe not. Maybe they weren't driven to it. I think Christopher Paul Curtis had a happy childhood and he is now writing YA. He says his book is kind of sadder; it has a darker theme. I did hear Mary Pope Osborne say she had a happy childhood and she writes to bring that to other kids. She wants them to feel the fun she had.

You've said, "Creating something of value is hard." Do you think many beginning writers expect it to be much easier than it is?
Absolutely. You know, it seems easy. Children's books seem easy. Nobody wants to work that hard on them. Especially when you're not being paid that much. If you look at it in a practical way, suppose you get a $5,000 advance and then I make you work on it for another year? That's insane, financially. So people have to want to do it for another reason.

You have a quote on your wall from Churchill: "Success is going from failure to failure without losing your enthusiasm." That seems like a funny quote for someone who was awarded her own imprint.
Well . . . I don't know. In a way, no book is ever as good as the ideal book in my head. There's always this crazy, ideal book. "Oh God, this could be the best book on the planet!" But of course, that's just crazy. Every book could be better. But there's a time when it's done. And that time is when an author has given everything they have to that book. It is over for them emotionally. And then it's finished. Magically, mysteriously, that seems to coincide with when it's due.
—*Barbara J. Odanaka*

Illustration Joel Nakamura. Design Melissa J. Knight. Reprinted with permission of Random House.

Wendy Lamb Books' recent release *Tribes*, the first U.S. title by Canadian author Arthur Slade, is somewhat of a dark comedy. The main character, Percy, is a fatherless high school senior who finds that the only way he can handle the mysterious rites of the 12th grade is to categorize and analyze: the Jock Tribe, the Teacher Tribe, the Born-Again Tribe, and so on. Percy runs into complications as he realizes that those he studies are real people too. Slade previously won the 2001 Governor General's Award and the Saskatchewan Book Award in Canada.

Illustration: Works with 12-14 illustrators/year. Uses color artwork only. Reviews ms/illustration packages from artists. Contact: Louise May. Submit ms with dummy. Illustrations only: Query with samples, résumé, promo sheet and tearsheets. Responds only if interested. Samples returned with SASE; samples filed. Original artwork returned at job's completion.

Photography: Buys photos from freelancers. Works on assignment only. Model/property releases required. Submit cover letter, résumé, promo piece and book dummy.

Terms: Pays authors royalty. Offers advances. Pays illustrators royalty plus advance against royalty. Photographers paid royalty plus advance against royalty. Sends galleys to authors; proofs to illustrators. Book catalog available for 9 × 12 SAE and $1.43 postage; ms and art guidelines available via website or with SASE.

Tips: "We strongly urge writers to visit our website and familiarize themselves with our list before submitting. Materials will only be returned with SASE."

LEGACY PRESS, Imprint of Rainbow Publishers, P.O. Box 261129, San Diego CA 92196. (858)271-7600. Book publisher. Estab. 1997. **Manuscript/Art Acquisitions:** Christy Scannell, editorial director. Publishes 3 young readers/year; 3 middle readers/year; 3 young adult titles/year. Publishes nonfiction, Bible-teaching books. "We publish growth and development books for the evangelical Christian—from a non-denominational viewpoint—that may be marketed primarily through Christian bookstores."

Nonfiction: Young readers, middle readers, young adults: reference, religion. Recently published *God's Girls* (devotions and crafts for girls age 9-12) and *Gotta Have God* (3-book series of devotionals for boys ages 2-12) both illustrated by Aline Heiser.

How to Contact/Writers: Nonfiction: Submit outline/synopsis and 3-5 sample chapters. Responds to queries in 6 weeks; on ms in 3 months. Publishes a book 18 months after acceptance. Will consider simultaneous submissions and previously published work.

Illustration: Works with 5 illustrators/year. Reviews ms/illustration packages from artists. Submit ms with 5-10 pieces of final art. Illustrations only: Query with samples to be kept on file. Responds in 6 weeks. Samples returned with SASE.

Terms: Pays authors royalty or work purchased outright. Offers advances. Pays illustrators by the project. Sends galley to authors. Book catalog available for business size SASE; ms guidelines for SASE.

Tips: "Get to know the Christian bookstore market. We are looking for innovative ways to teach and encourage children about the Christian life. No picture books please."

LERNER PUBLICATIONS CO., 241 First Ave. N., Minneapolis MN 55401. (612)332-3344. Fax: (612)332-7615. E-mail: info@lernerbooks.com. Website: www.lernerbooks.com. Book publisher. Estab. 1959. **Manuscript Acquisitions:** Jennifer Zimian, submissions editor. Primarily nonfiction for readers of all grade levels. List includes titles encompassing nature, geography, natural and physical science, current events, ancient and modern history, world art, special interest, sports, world cultures, and numerous biography series.

How to Contact/Writers: Submissions are accepted in the months of March and October only. Lerner Publications does not publish alphabet books, puzzle books, song books, textbooks, workbooks, religious subject matter or plays. Work received in any month other than March or October will be returned unopened. A SASE is required for authors who wish to have their materials returned. Please allow 6 months for a response. No phone calls please.

LIGHTWAVE PUBLISHING, 26275 98th Ave., Maple Ridge, British Columbia V2W 1K3 Canada. (604)462-7890. Fax: (604)462-8208. E-mail: mikal@lightwavepublishing.com. Website: www.lightwavepublishing.com. **Assistant:** Mikal Marrs. Estab. 1991. Independent book packager/producer specializing in Christian material. Publishes over 30 titles/year. "Our mission is helping parents pass on their Christian faith to their children."

Fiction: Picture books: religion adventure, concept. Young readers: concept, religion. Middle readers: adventure, religion. Young adults: religion.

Nonfiction: Picture books, young readers: activity books, concept, religion. Middle readers, young adults: concept, religion. Average word length: young readers—2,000; middle readers—20,000; young adults—30,000. Recently published *Focus On The Family's Guide to Spiritual Growth of Children*, edited by Osborne, Bruner, Trent; *The Memory Verse Bible*, by K. Christie Bowler.

How to Contact/Writers: Fiction/Nonfiction: Does not accept unsolicited mss. Only interested in writers who will work for hire. Query. Responds to queries in 6 weeks; mss in 2 months. Publishes book 1 year after acceptance.

Illustration: Works with 5-10 illustrators/year. Reviews ms/illustration packages from artists. Submit ms "any way the artist wants to." Contact: Terry Van Roon, art director. Responds only if interested. Samples not returned; samples filed.

Photography: Buys stock and assigns work. Model/property releases required. Uses color prints and digital.

Terms: Work purchased outright from authors. Payment varies. Pays illustrators by the project. Payment varies. Pays photographers by the project. Payment varies. Book catalog available for SASE (Canadian postage or IRC). Writer's guidelines available for SASE (Canadian postage or IRC). Catalog available on website.

Tips: "We only do work-for-hire writing and illustrating. We have our own projects and ideas then find writers and illustrators to help create them. No royalties. Interested writers and illustrators are welcome to contact us. Please don't put U.S. stamps on SASE."

LINNET BOOKS, Imprint of The Shoe String Press Inc., 2 Linsley St., North Haven CT 06473-2517. (203)239-2702. Fax: (203)239-2568. E-mail: books@shoestringpress.com. Website: www.shoestring press.com or www.linnetbooks.com. Estab. 1952. Specializes in nonfiction, educational material, multicultural material. **Manuscript Acquisitions:** Diantha C. Thorpe. Imprints: Linnet Books, Linnet Professional Publications, Archon Books—Diantha C. Thorpe, acquisitions for all. Publishes 12-15 books/year.

Nonfiction: Young readers: activity books, animal. Middle readers: animal, biography, geography, history, multicultural, music/dance, nature/environment, reference, science. Young adults: biography, history, multicultural, nature/environment, reference. Recently published *Chaucer's England*, by Diana Childress; *Four to The Pole! The American Women's Expedition to Antarctica 1992-93*, by Nancy Loewen and Ann Bancroft; *Tragic Prelude: Bleeding Kansas*, by Karen Zeinert.

How to Contact/Writers: Manuscript guidelines on website. Nonfiction: Query or submit outline/synopsis and 3 sample chapters. Responds to queries in 6 weeks; mss in 4 months. Publishes a book 1 year after receipt of edited ms. Will consider simultaneous submissions "only if, when we indicate serious interest, the author withdraws from other publishers."

Illustration: Uses mainly b&w artwork. Illustrations only: Query with samples. "We keep on file—send only disposable ones."

Photography: Buys stock. "We keep work on file, but generally our authors are responsible for photo illustrations." Uses 5×7 glossy b&w prints. Send "anything that tells us what you specialize in."

Terms: Pays authors variable royalty. Offers advances. Sends galleys to authors. Book catalog available annually.

LION BOOKS, PUBLISHER, Suite B, 210 Nelson, Scarsdale NY 10583. (914)725-2280. Fax: (914)725-3572. Imprint of Sayre Ross Co. Book publisher. **Acquisitions:** Harriet Ross. Publishes 5 middle readers/year; 10 young adults/year. 50-70% of books by first-time authors. Publishes books "with ethnic and minority accents for young adults, including a variety of craft titles dealing with African and Asian concepts."

Nonfiction: Activity, art/crafts, biography, history, hobbies, how-to, multicultural. Average word length: young adult—30,000-50,000.

How to Contact/Writers: Query, submit complete ms. Responds to queries in 3 weeks; ms in 2 months.

Illustration: Responds in 2 weeks.

Terms: Work purchased outright (range: $500-5,000). Average advance: $1,000-2,500. Illustrators paid $500-1,500. Sends galleys to author. Book catalog free on request.

LITTLE, BROWN AND COMPANY CHILDREN'S BOOKS, An AOL Time Warner Book Group Company, Time-Life Bldg., 1271 Avenue of the Americas, New York NY 10020. (212)522-8700. Website: www.twbookmark.com. Book publisher. Estab. 1837. **Editorial Director:** Maria Modugno. Art Director: Sheila Smallwood. Editorial Director of Megan Tingley Books: Megan Tingley; Senior Editor: Cynthia Eagan. Publishes picture books, board books, pop-up and lift-the-flap editions, chapter books and general fiction and nonfiction titles for middle and young adult readers.

• Little, Brown does not accept unsolicited mss.

Fiction: Picture books: adventure, animal, contemporary, fantasy, folktales, history, humor, multicultural, nature/environment. Young adults: contemporary, health, humor, multicultural, nature/environment, suspense/mystery. Multicultural needs include "any material by, for and about minorities." Average word length: picture books—1,000; young readers—6,000; middle readers—15,000-25,000; young adults—20,000-40,000. Recently published *Cirque du Freak: The Vampire's Assistant*, by Darren Shan (ages 10 and up); *The Magical, Mystical, Marvelous Coat*, by Catherine Ann Cullen (ages 4-8; picture book); *Toot and Puddle: I'll be Home for Christmas*, by Holly Hobbie (ages 4-8; picture book).

Nonfiction: Middle readers, young adults: arts/crafts, history, multicultural, nature, social issues, sports, science. Average word length: middle readers—15,000-25,000; young adults—20,000-40,000. Recently published *Baby on the Way*, by Dr. William Sears (ages 4-8); *The Big Dig: Reshaping An American City*, by Peter Vanderwarker (ages 9 and up; photo essay).

How to Contact/Writers: Only interested in agented material. Fiction: Submit complete ms. Nonfiction: Submit cover letter, previous publications, a proposal, outline and 3 sample chapters. Do not send originals. Responds to queries in 2 weeks. Responds to mss in 2 months.

Illustration: Works with 55 illustrators/year. Illustrations only: Query art director or managing editor with b&w and color samples; provide résumé, promo sheet or tearsheets to be kept on file. Responds to art samples in 2 months. Do not send originals; copies only.

Photography: Works on assignment only. Model/property releases required; captions required. Publishes photo essays and photo concept books. Uses 35mm transparencies. Photographers should provide résumé, promo sheets or tearsheets to be kept on file.

Terms: Pays authors royalties based on retail price. Pays illustrators and photographers by the project or royalty based on retail price. Sends galleys to authors; dummies to illustrators. Artist's and writer's guidelines for SASE.

Tips: "Publishers are cutting back their lists in response to a shrinking market and relying more on big names and known commodities. In order to break into the field these days, authors and illustrators research their competition and try to come up with something outstandingly different."

[N] LLEWELLYN WORLDWIDE LTD., P.O. Box 64383, St. Paul MN 55164-0383. (651)291-1970. Fax: (651)291-1908. E-mail: childrensbooks@llewellyn.com. Website: www.llewellyn. com. Estab. 1901. Specializes in trade books, nonfiction, fiction. **Manuscript Acquisitions:** Megan C. Atwood. 50% of books by first-time authors. "Our mission is to provide quality, well-written books that develop and introduce New Age, occult and/or metaphysical topics in an entertaining and edgy way, either in a fiction or nonfiction format, to both the 8- to 12-year-old and the 12- to 18-year-old demographic."

Fiction: Middle readers, young adults: New Age/metaphysical slant. Recently published *The Fortune Teller's Club: The Lost Girl*, by Dotti Enderle (middle grade, suspense/mystery); *Witches' Chillers: Witches' Night Out*, by Silver Ravenwolf (young adult, suspense/mystery); *Seasons of Magic*, by Laurel Reinhardt (middle grade, religion).

Nonfiction: Picture books: hobbies, religion, self-help. Middle readers, young adults: how-to, religion, self-help, New Age/metaphysical slant. Recently published *SpellCraft for Teens*, by Gwinevere Rain (young adult, how-to); *Teen Witch*, by Silver Ravenwolf (young adult, religion, how-to); *Wild Girls*, by Patricia Monaghan (young adult, how-to).

How to Contact/Writers: Fiction: Query or submit complete ms. Submit outline/synopsis and 1-2 sample chapters. Nonfiction: Query or submit complete ms. Submit outline/synopsis and 1-2 sample chapters.

Responds to queries/mss in 2 months. Will consider simultaneous submissions, electronic submissions via e-mail—only for queries and proposals, previously published work.

Terms: Pays authors royalty of 10% based on wholesale price. Sends galleys to authors. Book catalog available for 9×12 SASE and 4 first-class stamps; ms guidelines available for SASE.

Tips: "Please be sure to only send in those submissions that hit the Middle Grade (ages 8-12) and Young Adult (ages 12-18) market. We do not accept any proposals for a younger audience at this time. We are interested in quality manuscripts specifically with a metaphysical or occult slant that fits our genre. Generally speaking, always request guidelines from a publishing company and follow the instructions before submitting. Also, be sure to familiarize yourself with a publishing company's repertoire of books to make sure that your proposal fits the company's genre."

[ ] LOBSTER PRESS, 1620 Sherbrooke St. W., Suite C&C, Montréal, Quebec H3H 1C9 Canada. (514)904-1100. Fax: (514)904-1101. E-mail: editorial@lobsterpress.com. Website: www.lobsterpress.com. Estab. 1997. **Editorial Coordinator:** Gabriella Mancini. Publishes 4 picture books/year; 4 young reader/ year. "Driven by a desire to produce quality books that bring families together."

● Lobster Press is not currently accepting ms or queries

Fiction: Picture books, young readers, middle readers, young adults: adventure, animal, contemporary, health, history, multicultural, nature/environment, special needs, sports, suspense/mystery. Average word length: picture books—200-1,000. Recently published *Going on a Journey to the Sea*, by Jane Barclay, illustrated by Doris Barrette (picture book); *When Pigs Fly*, by Valerie Coulman, illustrated by Rogé (picture book); *Shoes for Amélie*, by Connie Colker Steiner, illustrated by Denis Rodier (young readers).

Nonfiction: Young readers, middle readers and adults/teens: animal, biography, careers, geography, hobbies, how-to, multicultural, nature/environment, references, science, self-help, social issues, sports, travel. Average word length: middle readers—40,000. Recently published *The Lobster Kids' Guide to Exploring New Orleans*, by Barri Bronston; *7 Secrets of Highly Successful Kids*, by Peter Kuitenbrouwer; *The Sex Book*, by Jane Pavanel.

How to Contact/Writers: Fiction: submit complete ms. Nonfiction: submit complete ms or submit outline/synopsis and 2 sample chapters. Responds to queries and mss only if interested. Does not return unread ms. Publishes a book 18 months after acceptance.

Illustration: Works with 5 illustrators/year. Uses line drawings and color artwork. Reviews ms/illustration packages from artists. Query with samples. Illustrations only: query with samples. Samples not returned; samples kept on file.

Terms: Pays authors 5-10% royalty based on retail price. Offers advances (average amount: $2,000-4,000). Pays illustrators by the project (range: $1,000-2,000) or 2-7% royalty based on retail price. Sends galleys to authors; dummies to illustrators. Originals returned to artist at job's completion. Writer's and artist's guidelines available on website.

Tips: "Do not send manuscripts or samples registered mail or with fancy envelopes or bows and ribbons—everything is received and treated equally. Please do not call and ask for an appointment. We do not meet with anyone unless we are going to use their work."

N LUCENT BOOKS, Imprint of The Gale Group, 10911 Technology Place, San Diego CA 92127. Website: www.galegroup.com/lucent. **Managing Editor:** Lori Shein.
- See also listing for Greenhaven Press.

MAGINATION PRESS, 750 First Street NE, Washington DC 20002-2984. Website: www.maginationpress.com. Book publisher. **Acquisitions:** Darcie Conner Johnston, managing editor. Publishes up to 15 picture books and young reader titles/year. "We publish books dealing with the psycho/therapeutic treatment or resolution of children's problems and psychological issues, many written by mental health professionals."
- Magination Press is an imprint of the American Psychological Association.

Fiction: All levels: concept, health, multicultural, special needs. Middle readers, young adults: problem novels. Recently published *Too Nice*, by Marjorie White Pellegrino, illustrated by Bonnie Matthews (ages 8-12 edited by Darcie Johnston); *Why Are You So Sad? A Child's Book About Parental Depression*, by Beth Andrews, illustrated by Nicole Wong (ages 4-8 edited by Darcie Johnston).

Nonfiction: All levels: health, social issues, special needs, self help. Picture books, young readers, middle readers: activity.

How to Contact/Writers: Fiction/nonfiction: Submit complete ms. Responds in 6 months. Materials returned only with a SASE. Publishes a book 12-18 months after acceptance.

Illustration: Works with 10-15 illustrators/year. Reviews ms/illustration packages. Will review artwork for future assignments. Responds only if interested, or immediately if SASE or response card is included. We keep all samples on file.

How to Contact/Illustrators: Illustrations only: Query with samples. Original artwork returned at job's completion.

Terms: Pays authors 5-15% in royalties based on actual revenues (net). Pays illustrators by the project; royalties are negotiable. Book catalog and ms guidelines on request with SASE.

MAVAL PUBLISHING, INC., Imprint of Editora Maval, 567 Harrison St., Denver CO 80206. (303)320-1035. Fax: (303)320-1546. E-mail: maval@maval.com. Website: www.maval.com. Book publisher. Estab. 1991. **Acquisitions:** George Waintrub, manager; Mary Hernandez, manuscripts coordinator. Publishes 10 picture books/year. 50% of books by first-time authors.

Fiction: Picture books, young readers, middle readers: adventure, animal, anthology, contemporary, fantasy, health, history, multicultural, nature/environment. Picture books, young readers: concept. Picture books: folktales, sports.

Nonfiction Picture books, young readers, middle readers: adventure, animal, anthology, contemporary, fantasy, health, history, multicultural, nature/environment. Picture books, Young readers: concept. Picture books: folktales, sports.

How to Contact/Writers: Fiction/Nonfiction: Submit outline/synopsis and 1-2 sample chapters. Responds to queries/mss in 3 months. Publishes a book 6-12 months after acceptance. Will consider simultaneous submissions and previously published work.

Illustration: Works with 2 illustrators/year. Reviews ms/illustration packages from artists. Submit manuscript with 1-2 pieces of final art. Contact: George Waintrub, manager. Illustrations only: Query with samples. Contact: George Waintrub, manager. Responds in 2 months. Samples not returned.

Photography: Buys stock.

Terms: Pays authors royalty of 5-7% based on retail price. Pays illustrators royalty of 5-7%. Book catalog and writer's guidelines available for SASE. All imprints included in a single catalog. Catalog available on website.

MARGARET K. McELDERRY BOOKS, 1230 Avenue of the Americas, New York NY 10020. (212)698-7000. Fax: (212)698-2796. E-mail: childrens.submissions@simonandschuster.com. Website: www.simonsayskids.com. Imprint of Simon & Schuster Children's Publishing Division. Editor at Large: Margaret K. McElderry. **Manuscript Acquisitions:** Emma D. Dryden, vice president and editorial director. **Art Acquisitions:** Ann Bobco, executive art director. Publishes 10-12 picture books/year; 2-4 young reader titles/year; 8-10 middle reader titles/year; and 5-7 young adult titles/year. 10% of books by first-time authors; 33% of books from agented writers. "Margaret K. McElderry Books publishes original hardcover trade books for children from pre-school age through young adult. This list includes picture books, easy-to-read books, and fiction for eight to twelve-year-olds, poetry, fantasy and young adult fiction. The style and subject matter of the books we publish is almost unlimited. We do not publish textbooks, coloring and activity books, greeting cards, magazines and pamphlets or religious publications."

● Margaret K. McElderry Books is not currently accepting unsolicited mss. Queries are accepted via mail and e-mail. McElderry title *Saffy's Angel*, by Hilary McKay, won a 2002 Boston Globe-Horn Book Honor Award for Fiction and Poetry. Their title *The Life History of a Star*, by Kelly Easton won a 2002 Golden Kite Honor.

Fiction: Young readers: adventure, contemporary, fantasy, history. Middle readers: adventure, contemporary, fantasy, humor, mystery. Young adults: contemporary, fantasy, mystery, poetry. "Always interested in publishing humorous picture books, original beginning reader stories, and strong poetry." Average word length: picture books—500; young readers—2,000; middle readers—10,000-20,000; young adults—45,000-50,000. Recently published *Bear Snores On*, by Karma Wilson, illustrated by Jane Chapman; *If the Shoe Fits*, by Laura Whipple, illustrated by Laura Beingessner; *Green Boy*, by Susan Cooper; *Saffy's Angel*, by Hilary McKay.

Nonfiction: Young readers, young adult teens, biography, history. Average word length: picture books—500-1,000; young readers—1,500-3,000; middle readers—10,000-20,000; young adults—30,000-45,000. *Shout, Sister, Shout!*, by Roxane Orgill.

How to Contact/Writers: Fiction/nonfiction: Submit query and sample chapters with SASE; may also include brief résumé of previous publishing credits. Accepts queries through e-mail. "Please clarify in your e-mail that your query is intended for Margaret K. McElderry Books." Responds to queries in 1 month; mss in 3 months. Publishes a book 18 months after contract signing. Will consider simultaneous submissions (only if indicated as such).

Illustration: Works with 20-30 illustrators/year. Query with samples; provide promo sheet or tearsheets; arrange personal portfolio review. Contact: Ann Bobco, executive art director. Responds to art samples in 3 months. Samples returned with SASE or samples filed.

Terms: Pays authors royalty based on retail price. Pay illustrators royalty based on retail price. Pays photographers by the project. Sends galleys to authors; dummies to illustrators. Original artwork returned at job's completion. Manuscript guidelines free on request with SASE.

Tips: "We're looking for strong, original fiction. We are always interested in picture books for the youngest age reader."

MEADOWBROOK PRESS, 5451 Smetana Dr., Minnetonka MN 55343-9012. (952)930-1100. Fax: (952)930-1940. Website: www.meadowbrookpress.com. Book publisher. **Manuscript Acquisitions:** Angela Wiechmann, submissions editor. **Art Acquisitions:** Paul Woods, art director. Publishes 1-2 middle readers/year; and 2-4 young readers/year. 20% of books by first-time authors; 10% of books from agented writers. Publishes children's activity books, arts-and-crafts books and how to books.

● Meadowbrook does not accept unsolicited children's picture books, short stories or novels. They are primarily a nonfiction press. The publisher offers specific guidelines for children's poetry. Be sure to specify the type of project you have in mind when requesting guidelines.

Nonfiction: Young readers, middle readers: activity books, arts/crafts, hobbies, how-to, multicultural, self help. Average word length: varies. Recently published *Children's Busy Book* (activity book) and *Long Shot* (middle readers).

How to Contact/Writers: Nonfiction: Query or submit outline/synopsis with SASE. Responds to queries in 3 months. Publishes a book 1-2 years after acceptance. Send a business-sized SASE and 2 first-class stamps for free writer's guidelines and book catalog before submitting ideas. Will consider simultaneous submissions.

Illustration: Works with 10-12 illustrators/year. Reviews ms/illustration packages from artists. Submit ms with 2-3 pieces of nonreturnable samples. Illustrations only: Responds only if interested. Samples filed.

Photography: Buys photos from freelancers. Buys stock. Model/property releases required. Submit cover letter.

Terms: Pays authors in royalties of 5-7½% based on retail price. Offers average advance payment of $2,000-4,000. Pays illustrators per project. Pays photographers per photo. Originals returned at job's completion. Book catalog available for 5 × 11 SASE and 2 first-class stamps; ms guidelines and artists guidelines available for SASE.

Tips: "Illustrators and writers should send for our free catalog and guidelines before submitting their work to us. Also, illustrators should take a look at the books we publish to determine whether their style is consistent with ours. Writers should also note the style and content patterns of our books. Please correspond with us by mail before telephoning with questions about your submission. We work with the printed word and will respond more effectively to your questions if we have something in front of us."

MERIWETHER PUBLISHING LTD., 885 Elkton Dr., Colorado Springs CO 80907-3557. Fax: (719)594-9916. E-mail: merpeds@aol.com. Website: www.meriwetherpublishing.com. Book publisher. Estab. 1969. Executive Editor: Arthur L. Zapel. **Manuscript Acquisitions:** Ted Zapel, educational drama; Rhonda Wray, religious drama. "We do most of our artwork in-house; we do not publish for the children's elementary market." 75% of books by first-time authors; 5% of books from agented writers. "Our niche is drama. Our books cover a wide variety of theatre subjects from play anthologies to theatrecraft. We publish books of monologs, duologs, short one-act plays, scenes for students, acting textbooks, how-to speech and theatre textbooks, improvisation and theatre games. Our Christian books cover worship on such topics as clown ministry, storytelling, banner-making, drama ministry, children's worship and more. We also publish anthologies of Christian sketches. We do not publish works of fiction or devotionals."

Fiction: Middle readers, young adults: anthology, contemporary, humor, religion. "We publish plays, not prose-fiction."

Nonfiction: Middle readers: activity books, how-to, religion, textbooks. Young adults: activity books, drama/theater arts, how-to church activities, religion. Average length: 250 pages. Recently published *Grammar Wars* by Tom Ready (language arts) and *Worship Sketches 2 Perform* by Steven James.

How to Contact/Writers: Nonfiction: Query or submit outline/synopsis and sample chapters. Responds to queries in 3 weeks; mss in 2 months. Publishes a book 6-12 months after acceptance. Will consider simultaneous submissions.

Illustration: Works with 2 illustrators/year. Query first. Query with samples; send résumé, promo sheet or tearsheets. Samples returned with SASE. Samples kept on file. Originals returned at job's completion.

Terms: Pays authors in royalties of 10% based on retail price. Outright purchase $200-1,000. Royalties based on retail or wholesale price. Book catalog for SAE and $2 postage; ms guidelines for SAE and 1 first-class stamp.

Tips: "We are currently interested in finding unique treatments for theater arts subjects: scene books, how-to books, musical comedy scripts, monologs and short plays for teens."

MILKWEED EDITIONS, 1011 Washington Ave. S., Suite 300, Minneapolis MN 55415-1246. (612)332-3192. Fax: (612)215-2550. E-mail: editor@milkweed.org. Website: www.milkweed.org. Book Publisher. Estab. 1980. **Manuscript Acquisitions:** Emilie Buchwald, publisher. Publishes 3-4 middle readers/year. 25% of books by first-time authors. "Milkweed Editions publishes with the intention of making a humane impact on society, in the belief that literature is a transformative art uniquely able to convey the essential experiences of the human heart and spirit. To that end, Milkweed Editions publishes distinctive voices of literary merit in handsomely designed, visually dynamic books, exploring the ethical, cultural, and esthetic issues that free societies need continually to address."

Fiction: Middle readers: adventure, contemporary, fantasy, multicultural, nature/environment, suspense/mystery. Does not want to see anthologies, folktales, health, hi-lo, picture books, poetry, religion, romance, sports. Average length: middle readers—90-200 pages. Recently published *The $66 Summer*, by John Armistead (multicultural, mystery); *The Ocean Within*, by V.M. Caldwell (contemporary, nature); *No Place*, by Kay Haugaard (multicultural).

How to Contact/Writers: Fiction: Submit complete ms. Responds to mss in 6 months. Publishes a book 1 year after acceptance. Will consider simultaneous submissions.

Illustration: Works with 2-4 illustrators/year. Reviews ms/illustration packages from artists. Query; submit ms with dummy. Illustrations only: Query with samples; provide résumé, promo sheet, slides, tearsheets and client list. Samples filed or returned with SASE; samples filed. Originals returned at job's completion.

Terms: Pays authors royalty of 7½% based on retail price. Offers advance against royalties. Illustrators' contracts are decided on an individual basis. Sends galleys to authors. Book catalog available for $1.50 to cover postage; ms guidelines available for SASE or at www.milkweed.org. Must include SASE with ms submission for its return.

THE MILLBROOK PRESS, P.O. Box 335, 2 Old New Milford Rd., Brookfield CT 06804. (203)740-2220. Fax: (203)775-5643. Website: www.millbrookpress.com. Book publisher. Estab. 1989. **Manuscript**

Acquisitions: Editorial Assistant. **Art Acquisitions:** Associate Art Director. Publishes 20 picture books/
year; 50 young readers/year; 30 middle readers/year; and 20 young adult titles/year. 10% of books by
first-time authors; 20% of books from agented authors. Publishes nonfiction, concept-oriented/educational
books. Publishes under Twenty-First Century Books imprint also.

Nonfiction: Picture books: animal, biography, history, multicultural, nature/environment, science. Young
readers: animal, arts/crafts, biography, careers, cooking, geography, health, hi-lo, history, multicultural,
nature/environment, religion, science, sports. Middle readers: biography, careers, geography, health, hi-lo,
history, multicultural, nature/environment, religion, science, social issues, sports. Young adults: biography,
history, multicultural, nature/environment, reference, science, social issues. Average word length: young
readers—5,000; middle readers—10,000; young adult/teens—20,000. Published *Wildshots: The World of
the Wildlife Photographer*, by Nathan Aaseng (grades 5-8, nature and photography); *Meet My Grandmother:
She's A Children's Book Author*, by Lisa Tucker McElroy, photographs by Joel Benjamin (grades 2-4,
current events/history); *Little Numbers*, by Edward Packard, illustrated by Sal Murdocca (grades K-3,
math/concepts); *Crafts From Your Favorite Children's Songs*, by Kathy Ross, illustrated by Vicky Enright
(grades K-3, arts and crafts); *Adoption Today*, by Ann E. Weiss (grade 7-up, social studies). No fiction,
picture books, activity books or other novelty submissions.

How to Contact/Writers: Send for guidelines with SASE *before* submitting. We do not accept unsolicited manuscripts, guidelines give specific instructions.

Illustration: Work with approximately 30 illustrators/year. Illustrations only: Query with samples; provide
résumé, business card, promotional literature or tearsheets to be kept on file. No samples returned. Samples
filed. Responds only if interested.

Photography: Buys stock.

Terms: Pays author royalty of 5-7½% based on wholesale price or work purchased outright. Offers
advances. Pays illustrators by the project, royalty of 3-7% based on wholesale price. Sends galleys to
authors. Manuscript and artist's guidelines by SASE. Address to: Manuscript Guidelines, The Millbrook
Press . . . Book catalog for 9×11 SASE. Address to: Catalogues, The Millbrook Press . . .

MITCHELL LANE PUBLISHERS, INC., P.O. Box 619, Bear DE 19701. (302)834-9646. Fax:
(302)834-4164. E-mail: mitchelllane@mitchelllane.com. Website: www.mitchelllane.com. Book publisher.
Acquisitons: Barbara Mitchell, president. Publishes 20 young adult titles/year. "We publish multicultural
biographies of role models for children and young adults."

Nonfiction: Young readers, middle readers, young adults: biography, multicultural. Average word length:
4,000-50,000 words. Recently published *Robert Jarrick and the First Artificial Heart*, by John Bankston
(unlocking the Secrets of Science); and *Francisco Vasquez de Coronado*, by Jim Whiting (Latinos in
American History).

How to Contact/Writers: Nonfiction: Query or submit outline/synopsis and 3 sample chapters. Responds to queries only if interested. Publishes a book 18 months after acceptance. Most assignments are
work-for-hire.

Illustration: Works with 2-3 illustrators/year. Reviews ms/illustration packages from artists. Query. Illustration only: query with samples; arrange personal portfolio review; send résumé, portfolio, slides, tearsheets. Responds only if interested. Samples not returned; samples filed.

Photography: Buys stock images. Needs photos of famous and prominent minority figures. Captions
required. Uses b&w prints. Submit cover letter, résumé, published samples, stock photo list.

Terms: Pays authors 5-10% royalty based on wholesale price or work purchased outright for $250-2,000.
Pays illustrators by the project (range: $40-250). Sends galleys to authors.

Tips: "Most of our assignments are work-for-hire. Submit résumé and samples of work to be considered
for future assignments."

△ MONDO PUBLISHING, 980 Avenue of the Americas, New York NY 10018. (212)268-3560. Fax:
(212)268-3561. Website: www.mondopub.com. Book publisher. **Acquisitions:** editorial staff. Publishes 60
picture and chapter books/year. 10% of books by first-time authors. Publishes various categories. "Our
motto is 'creative minds creating ways to create lifelong readers.' We publish for both educational and
trade markets, aiming for the highest quality books for both."

● Mondo Publishing only accepts agented material.

Fiction: Picture books, young readers, middle readers: adventure, animal, contemporary, fantasy, folktales,
history, humor, multicultural, nature/environment, poetry, sports. Multicultural needs include: stories about
children in different cultures or about children of different backgrounds in a U.S. setting. Recently published
Right Outside My Window, by Mary Ann Hoberman; *Jake Greenthumb*, by Loki (ages 4-8).

Nonfiction: Picture books, young readers, middle readers: animal, biography, geography, how-to, multicultural, nature/environment, science, sports. Recently published *Seahorses*, by Sylvia James; *How to Make
a Collage*, by Sue and Will Johnson.

How to Contact/Writers: Accepting mss from agented or previously published writers only. Fiction/ Nonfiction: Query or submit complete ms. Responds to queries in 1 month; mss in 6 months. Will consider simultaneous submissions. Manuscripts returned with SASE. Queries must also have SASE.

Illustration: Works with 40 illustrators/year. Reviews ms/illustration packages from illustrators. Illustration only: Query with samples, résumé, portfolio. Responds only if interested. Samples returned with SASE; samples filed. Send attention: Art Deptartment.

Photography: Occasionally uses freelance photographers. Buys stock images. Uses mostly nature photos. Uses color prints, transparencies, slides or digital images.

Terms: Pays authors royalty of 2-5% based on wholesale/retail price for trade titles. Offers advance based on project. Pays illustrators by the project (range: 3,000-9,000), royalty of 2-4% based on retail price. Pays photographers by the project or per photo. Sends galleys to authors depending on project. Originals returned to artists at job's completion. Book catalogs available for 9×12 SASE with $3.20 postage.

Tips: "Prefer illustrators with book experience or a good deal of experience in illustration projects requiring consistency of characters and/or setting over several illustrations. Prefer manuscripts targeted to trade market plus crossover to educational market."

MORGAN REYNOLDS PUBLISHING, 620 S. Elm St., Suite 223, Greensboro NC 27406. (336)275-1311. Fax: (336)275-1152. E-mail: editorial@morganreynolds.com. Website: www.morganreynolds.com. **Acquisitions:** Laura Shoemaker, editor. Book publisher. Publishes 18 young adult titles/year. 50% of books by first-time authors. Morgan Reynolds publishes nonfiction books for juvenile and young adult readers. We prefer lively, well-written biographies of interesting figures for our biography series. Subjects may be contemporary or historical. Books for our Great Events series should depict insightful and exciting looks at critical periods.

Nonfiction: Middle readers, young adults/teens: biography, history. Average word length: 17,000-20,000. Recently published *Ms.: The Story of Gloria Steinem*, by Elizabeth Wheaton; and *I Too Sing America: The Story of Langston Hughes*, by Martha E. Rhynes.

How to Contact/Writers: Prefers to see entire ms. Query; submit outline/synopsis with 3 sample chapters. Responds to queries/mss in 6 weeks. Publishes a book 1 year after acceptance. Will consider simultaneous submissions.

Terms: Pays authors negotiated price. Offers advances and royalties. Sends galleys to authors. Manuscript guidelines available for SASE. Visit website for complete catalog.

Tips: "Familiarize yourself with our titles before sending a query or submission. Visit our website."

Ⓝ MOUNT OLIVE COLLEGE PRESS, 634 Henderson St., Mount Olive NC 28365. (919)658-2502. Book publisher. Estab. 1990. **Acquisitions:** Pepper Worthington, editor. Publishes 1 middle reader/year. 85% of books by first-time authors.

Fiction: Middle readers: animal, humor, poetry. Average word length: middle readers—3,000 words.

Nonfiction: Middle readers: nature/environment, religion, self help. Average word length: middle readers—3,000 words.

How to Contact/Writers: Submit complete ms or outline/synopsis and 3 sample chapters. Responds to queries in 2 years.

Illustration: Uses b&w artwork only. Submit ms with 50% of final art. Contact: Pepper Worthington, editor. Responds in 1 year if interested. Samples not returned.

Terms: Payment negotiated individually. Book catalog available for SAE and 1 first-class stamp.

Ⓝ TOMMY NELSON®, Imprint of Thomas Nelson, Inc., P.O. 24100, Nashville TN 37214. (615)889-9000. Fax: (615)902-3330. Website: www.tommynelson.com. Book publisher. **Acquisitions:** Laura Minchew, Senior Vice President/Publisher. Publishes 15 picture books/year; 20 young readers/year; and 25 middle readers/year. Evangelical Christian publisher.

Fiction: Picture books: concept, humor, religion. Young readers: adventure, concept, humor, religion. Middle readers: adventure, humor, religion, sports, suspense/mystery. Young adults: adventure, problem novels, religion, sports, suspense/mystery. Recently published *Prayer of Jabez* series (4 books), and *Nightmare Academy*, by Frank Reretti.

Nonfiction: Picture books, young readers: activity books, religion, self help. Middle readers, young adults: reference, religion, self help. Recently published *He Chose You*, by Max Lucado.

How to Contact/Writers: Does not accept unsolicited mss, queries or proposals.

Illustration: Query with samples. Responds only if interested. Samples filed. Contact: Patti Evans, art director.

Tips: "Know the CBA market—and avoid preachiness."

NEW CANAAN PUBLISHING COMPANY INC., P.O. Box 752, New Canaan CT 06840. Phone/Fax: (203)966-3408. E-mail: djm@newcanaanpublishing.com. Website: www.newcanaanpublishing.com. Book publisher. Vice President: Kathy Mittelstadt. Publishes 2 picture books/year; 2 young readers/year; 2 middle readers/year; and 2 young adult titles/year. 50% of books by first-time authors. "We seek books with strong educational or traditional moral content and books with Christian themes."
Fiction: All levels: adventure, history, religion (Christianity), suspense/mystery. Picture books: phonics readers. "Stories about disfunctional families are not encouraged." Average word length: picture books—1,000-3,000; young readers—8,000-30,000; middle readers—8,000-40,000; young adults—15,000-50,000. Recently published *Journey to the Edge of Nowhere*, by Janet Baird; *Rainbows and Other Promises*, by Laurie Swinwood; *Olive, The Orphan Reindeer*, by Michael Christie, illustrated by Margeaux Lucas.
Nonfiction: All levels: geography, history, how-to, reference, religion (Christian only), textbooks. Average word length: picture books—1,000-3,000; young readers—8,000-30,000; middle readers—8,000-40,000; young adults—15,000-50,000.
How to Contact/Writers: Submit outline/synopsis or complete ms with biographical information and writing credentials. Responds to queries/mss in 6 months. Publishes a book 12-18 months after acceptance. Will consider electronic submissions via disk or modem.
Illustration: Works with 3-5 illustrators/year. Reviews ms/illustration packages from artists. Query or send ms with dummy. Illustrations only: Query with samples; send résumé, promo sheet. Responds in 1-2 months. Samples returned with SASE.
Terms: Pays authors royalty of 7-12% based on wholesale price. Royalty may be shared with illustrator where relevant. Pays illustrators royalty of 4-6% as share of total royalties. Book catalog available for SAE; ms guidelines available for SASE.
Tips: "We are diligent but small, so please be patient."

N NEW VOICES PUBLISHING, Imprint of KidsTerrain, Inc., P.O. Box 560, Wilmington MA 01887. (978)658-2131. Fax: (978)988-8833. E-mail: RSCHIANO@KidsTERRAIN.com. Website: www.KidsTERRAIN.com. Estab. 2000. Specializes in fiction. **Manuscript Acquisitions:** Rita Schiano. **Art Acquisitions:** Rita Schiano, executive editor. Publishes 7 picture books/year. 95% of books by first-time authors.
Fiction: Picture books, young readers: multicultural. Average word length: picture books—500; young readers—500-1,200. Recently published *The Magic in Me*, by Maggie Moran, illustrated by Chie Sasaki; *Aunt Rosa's House*, by Maggie Moran, illustrated by Chie Sasaki (ages 4-8); and *Last Night I Left Earth for Awhile*, written and illustrated by Natalie L. Brown-Douglas (ages 4-8).
How to Contact/Writers: Fiction: Query or submit complete ms. Responds to queries in 2 weeks; mss in 2 months. Publishes book 12-18 months after acceptance. Will consider simultaneous submissions.
Illustration: Works with 2 illustrators/year. Uses color artwork only. Reviews ms/illustration packages from artists. Query. Illustrations only: Query with samples. Contact: Executive Editor. Responds in 2 weeks. Samples returned with SASE.
Terms: Pays authors royalty of 10-15% based on wholesale price. Pays illustrators by the project or royalty. Sends galleys to authors. Offers writer's guidelines for SASE.

✓ NORTH LIGHT BOOKS, Imprint of F&W Publications, 4700 E. Galbraith Rd., Cincinnati OH 45236. (513)531-2690. Fax: (513)531-7107. E-mail: Trica.Waddell@fwpubs.com. Website: www.artistsnetwork.com. Trade book publisher specializing in children's arts and crafts books. **Acquisitions Editor:** Tricia Waddell. Publishes 4-6 arts and crafts books for ages 6-12/year. 90% of books by first-time authors.
Nonfiction: All levels: Arts/Crafts. Average word length: nonfiction—7,500 words. Recently published: *Artistic Drawing*, by Kat Rakel-Ferguson (ages 6-9, fine art); *Nature Crafts*, by Joy Williams (ages 6-9, craft); *Painting on Rocks for Kids*, by Lin Welford.
How to Contact/Writers: Query with project/craft samples. Responds to queries/mss in 2 months. Will consider simultaneous submissions and electronic submissions via disk or modem. Book published 18 months after acceptance.
Terms: Authors paid flat fee or royalty; negotiable. Offers advance (average amount: $2,000). Original projects returned at job's completion. All company's imprints available in a single catalog.
Tips: "If you submit arts or crafts ideas for kids, make sure they aren't cookie cutter crafts. Also, try to find new twists on old projects. We're looking for arts and crafts today's children will want to do without focusing on new, trendy materials."

THE AGE-LEVEL INDEX, located in the back of this book, lists book publishers and magazines according to the age-groups for which they need material.

Ⓐ **NORTH-SOUTH BOOKS**, 11 E. 26th St., 17th Floor, New York NY 10010. (212)706-4545. Website: www.northsouth.com. **Acquisitions:** Andrea Spooner, editor-in-chief, Sea Star Books; Ellen Friedman, vice president and art director. U.S. office of Nord-Siid Verlag, Switzerland. Publishes 100 titles/year.

• North-South does not accept queries or unsolicited manuscripts.

Fiction: Picture books.

How to Contact/Writers: Only interested in agented material.

Illustration: Uses artists for picture book illustration.

Terms: Pays authors and illustrators advance and royalties.

🗔 ☑ **NORTHWORD BOOKS FOR YOUNG READERS**, North Word Press, 18705 Lake Dr. E., Chanhassen MN 55317. (952)936-4700. Fax: (942)932-0386. Website: www.northwordpress.com. Specializes in mass market books, fiction, trade books, educational material, nonfiction. "Our mission at NorthWord Books for Young Readers is to publish books for children that encourage a love for the natural world." **Manuscript Acquisitions:** Aimee Jackson, executive editor; Kristen McCurry, nonfiction series. **Art Acquisitions:** Aimee Jackson, executive editor. Publishes 12-15 books/year—2-4 picture picture books (ages 5-8), 4-5 nonfiction (ages 5-8, 7-11, 8-10).

Fiction: Picture books, young readers: animal, nature/environment. Average word length: picture books— 1,000; young readers—1,000-3,000. Recently published *The Family of Earth*, by Schim Schimmel (ages 4-7, picture book); *We are Wolves* and *We are Bears*, both written by Molly Grooms and illustrated by Lucia Guamotta (ages 4-7, picture books/natural history); *Penguin ABC* and *Penguin 123*, by Kevin Schafer (ages 3-5, concept books, edited by Aimee Jackson).

Nonfiction: Picture books, young readers, middle readers: activity books, animal, arts/crafts, cooking, hobbies, how-to, nature/environment. Recently published *My Cat and How to Have a Happy, Healthy Pet* and *My Dog*, by Lynn Cole (ages 6-10, nonfiction pet care books); *Rocks, Fossils, and Arrowheads*, by Laura Evert, illustrated by Linda Garrow (ages 7-10, interactive "field guide" book—nonfiction series).

How to Contact/Writers: Fiction: Submit complete ms. Query. Responds in 3 months. Publishes a book 1-2 years after acceptance. Will consider simultaneous submissions.

Illustration: Works with 5 illustrators/year. Uses color artwork only. Reviews ms/illustration packages from artists. Query. Contact: Aimee Jackson, executive editor. Illustrations only: Query with samples; send résumé and tearsheets. Responds in 3 months only if interested. Samples returned with SASE.

Photography: Buys stock images. Contact: Photo Editor. Uses photos of animals *wildlife and natural history*. "Film must be labeled with species (common and Latin names), the more information on photo the better." Uses 35mm, $2\frac{1}{4} \times 2\frac{1}{4}$, 4×5 transparencies. Submit cover letter, published samples, stock photo list.

Terms: Payment depends on project—most nonfiction series is flat fee if commissioned by us—some (fiction, usually) is advance against royalty (usually net). Sends galleys for review; dummies to illustrators. Originals returned to artist at job's completion. Book catalog available for SASE or call for catalog. Writer's, artist's and photographer's guidelines available for SASE.

Tips: "Always research the publisher you are applying to. Make sure your work is appropriate for that house. Send to acquiring editor for manuscript, illustration and photography. And always allow *plenty* of time for review. *Do not* call editor to see if they 'got your submissions.' Include a return postcard to acknowledge receipt of work."

🗔 **THE OLIVER PRESS, INC.**, Charlotte Square, 5707 W. 36th St., Minneapolis MN 55416-2510. (952)926-8981. Fax: (952)926-8965. E-mail: queries@oliverpress.com. Website: www.oliverpress.com. Book publisher. **Acquisitions:** Denise Sterling, Jenna Anderson. Publishes 8 young adult titles/year. 10% of books by first-time authors. "We publish collective biographies of people who made an impact in one area of history, including science, government, archaeology, business and crime. Titles from The Oliver Press can connect young adult readers with their history to give them the confidence that only knowledge can provide. Such confidence will prepare them for the lifelong responsibilities of citizenship. Our books will introduce students to people who made important discoveries and great decisions."

Nonfiction: Middle reader, young adults: biography, history, multicultural, social issues, history of science and technology. "Authors should only suggest ideas that fit into one of our existing series. We would like to add to our Innovators series on the history of technology and our Business Builders series on leaders of industry." Average word length: young adult—20,000 words. Recently published *Business Builders in Real Estate*, by Nathan Aaseng (ages 10 and up, collective biography); *Women with Wings*, by Jacqueline McLean (ages 10 and up, collective biography); *Space Flight: Crossing the Last Frontier*, by Jason Richie (ages 10 and up, collective biography); and *Ranchers, Homesteaders, and Traders: Frontiersmen of the South-Central States*, by Kieran Doherty (ages 10 and up, collective biography).

How to Contact/Writers: Nonfiction: Query with outline/synopsis. Responds in 6 months. Publishes a book approximately 1 year after acceptance.

Photography: Rarely buys photos from freelancers. Buys stock images. Looks primarily for photos of people in the news. Captions required. Uses 8×10 b&w prints. Submit cover letter, résumé and stock photo list.

Terms: Pays authors negotiable royalty. Work purchased outright from authors (fee negotiable). Pays photographers per photo (negotiable). Sends galleys to authors upon request. Book catalog and ms guidelines available online or for SASE.

Tips: "Authors should read some of the books we have already published before sending a query to The Oliver Press."

N. ☐ ONSTAGE PUBLISHING, 214 E. Moulton St. NE, Decatur AL 35601. (256)308-2300, (888)420-8879. Website: www.onstagebooks.com. Estab. 1999. Specializes in mass market books, nonfiction, fiction, educational material. **Manuscript Acquisitions:** Dianne Hamilton. Publishes 1 picture book; 1 young readers; 2 middle readers; 1 young adult title/year. 80% of books by first-time authors.

Fiction: Picture books: adventure, contemporary, history, nature/environment, suspense/mystery. Young readers, middle readers: adventure, contemporary, fantasy, history, nature/environment, science fiction, suspense/mystery. Young adults: adventure, contemporary, fantasy, history, humor, science fiction, suspense/mystery. Average word length: picture books—50-100; young readers—100-300; middle readers—5,000 and up; young adults—25,000 and up. Recently published *The Secret of Crybaby Hollow*, by Darren Butler (a middle grade mystery book, ages 8-12, the Abbie Girl Spy adventures).

Nonfiction: All levels: animal, biography, history, music/dance, nature/environment, science, sports. Average word length: picture books—100-2,500; young readers—500-2,500; middle readers—1,000-3,000; young adults—5,000 and up. Recently published *Write Away*, by Margaret Green and Laurel Griffith (educational instruction book designed by elementary teacher that lays out a series of creative writing exercises for grades 1-6); *The Miracle at the Pump*, by Darren Butler, illustrated by Linda Lee (activity book for ages 5-8 based on the early life of Helen Keller).

How to Contact/Writers: Fiction/nonfiction: submit complete ms. Responds to queries/mss in 1 month. Publishes a book 2 years after acceptance. Will consider simultaneous submissions.

Illustration: Reviews ms/illustration packages from artists. Submit ms with 3 pieces of final art. Contact: Dianne Hamilton, senior editor. Illustrations only: arrange personal portfolio review. Responds in 6 weeks. Samples returned with SASE.

Photography: Works on assignment only. Contact: Art Department. Model/property releases required; captions required. Uses color, 5×7, semi gloss prints. Submit cover letter, published samples, stock photo list.

Terms: Pays authors/illustrators/photographers advance plus royalties. Sends galleys to authors; dummies to illustrators. Book catalog available for 9×12 SAE and 3 first-class stamps; ms guidelines available for SASE. Return of original artwork is negotiable. All imprints included in a single catalog. Catalog available on website.

Tips: "Study our catalog and get a sense of the kind of books we publish, so that you know whether your project is likely to be right for us. Electronic publishing will have an impact in the next five years, as choices, more information and more books will be accessible for the consumer. This is a market we are watching."

☒ ORCA BOOK PUBLISHERS, P.O. Box 5626 Station B, Victoria, British Columbia V8R 6S4 Canada. (604)380-1229. Fax: (604)380-1892. Book publisher. Estab. 1984. Publisher: R. Tyrrell. **Acquisitions:** Maggie deVries, children's book editor. Publishes 10 picture books/year; 4 middle readers/year; and 4 young adult titles/year. 25% of books by first-time authors. "We only consider authors who are Canadian or who live in Canada."

Fiction: Picture books: animals, contemporary, history, nature/environment. Middle readers: contemporary, history, nature/environment, problem novels. Young adults: adventure, contemporary, history, multicultural, nature/environment, problem novels, suspense/mystery. Average word length: picture books—500-2,000; middle readers—20,000-35,000; young adult—25,000-45,000. Published *Tall in the Saddle*, by Anne Carter, illustrated by David McPhail (ages 4-8, picture book); *Me and Mr. Mah*, by Andrea Spalding, illustrated by Janet Wilson (ages 5 and up, picture book); and *Alone at Ninety Foot*, by Katherine Holubitsky (young adult).

How to Contact/Writers: Fiction: Submit complete ms if picture book; submit outline/synopsis and 3 sample chapters. Nonfiction: Query with SASE. "All queries or unsolicited submissions should be accompanied by a SASE." Responds to queries in 2 months; mss in 3 months. Publishes a book 18-24 months after acceptance.

Illustration: Works with 8-10 illustrators/year. Reviews ms/illustration packages from artists. Submit ms with 3-4 pieces of final art. "Reproductions only, no original art please." Illustrations only: Query with samples; provide résumé, slides. Responds in 2 months. Samples returned with SASE; samples filed.

Terms: Pays authors royalty of 5% for picture books, 10% for novels, based on retail price. Offers advances (average amount: $2,000). Pays illustrators royalty of 5% minimum based on retail price and advance on royalty. Sends galleys to authors. Original artwork returned at job's completion if picture books. Book catalog available for legal or 8½×11 manila SAE and $2 first-class postage. Manuscript guidelines available for SASE. Art guidelines not available.

Tips: "American authors and illustrators should remember that the U.S. stamps on their reply envelopes cannot be posted in any country outside of the U.S."

☑ **ORCHARD BOOKS**, 557 Broadway, New York NY 10012. (212)343-6782. Fax: (212)343-4890. Website: www.scholastic.com. Imprint of Scholastic, Inc. Book publisher. Editorial Director: Ken Geist. **Manuscript Acquisitions:** Amy Griffin, senior editor. **Art Acquisitions:** David Saylor, art director. "We publish approximately 25 books yearly including fiction, poetry, picture books, and young adult novels." 10% of books by first-time authors.

• Orchard is not accepting unsolicited manuscripts; query letters only.

Fiction: All levels: animal, contemporary, history, humor, multicultural, nature/environment, poetry. Recently published *Flora's Blanket*, by Deb Gliori; *Giraffes Can't Dance*, by Giles Andreae, illustrated by Guy Parker-Rees; *Forbidden Forest: The Story of Little John and Robin Hood*, by Michael Cadnum.

Nonfiction: "We rarely publish nonfiction." Recently published *A Dragon in the Sky*, by Pringle Marshall.

How to Contact/Writers: Query only with SASE. Responds in 3 months.

Illustration: Works with 15 illustrators/year. Art director reviews ms/illustration portfolios. Submit "tearsheets or photocopies or photostats of the work." Responds to art samples in 1 month. Samples returned with SASE. No disks or slides, please.

Terms: Most commonly an advance against list royalties. Sends galleys to authors; dummies to illustrators. Original artwork returned at job's completion.

Tips: "Read some of our books to determine first whether your manuscript is suited to our list."

☐ **OUR SUNDAY VISITOR, INC.**, 200 Noll Plaza, Huntington IN 46750. (260)356-8400. Fax: (260)359-9117. E-mail: booksed@osv.com; jlindsey@osv.com; mdubruiel@osv.com; bmcnamara@osv.com. Website: www.osv.com. Book publisher. **Acquisitions:** Jacquelyn M. Lindsey, Michael Dubruiel, Beth McNamara. Art Director: Eric Schoenig. Publishes primarily religious, educational, parenting, reference and biographies. OSV is dedicated to providing books, periodicals and other products that serve the Catholic Church.

• Our Sunday Visitor, Inc., is publishing only those children's books that tie in to sacramental preparation. Contact the acquisitions editor for manuscript guidelines and a book catalog.

Nonfiction: Picture books, middle readers, young readers, young adults. Recently published *I Am Special*, by Joan and Paul Plum, illustrated by Andee Most (kindergarten program).

How to Contact/Writers: Query, submit complete ms, or submit outline/synopsis, and 2-3 sample chapters. Responds to queries in 2 months; mss in 2 months. Publishes a book 18-24 months after acceptance. Will consider simultaneous submissions, electronic submissions via disk or modem, previously published work.

Illustration: Reviews ms/illustration packages from artists. Illustration only: Query with samples. Contact: Aquisitions Editor. Responds only if interested. Samples returned with SASE; samples filed. Original artwork returned at job's completion.

Photography: Buys photos from freelancers. Contact: Acquisitions Editor.

Terms: Pays authors royalty of 10-12% net. Pays illustrators by the project (range: $200-1,500). Sends galleys to authors; dummies to illustrators. Book catalog available for SASE; ms guidelines available for SASE.

Tips: "Stay in accordance with our guidelines."

THE OVERMOUNTAIN PRESS, P.O. Box 1261, Johnson City TN 37605. (423)926-2691. Fax: (423)929-2464. E-mail: bethw@overmtn.com. Website: www.overmtn.com. Also www.silverdaggermysteries.com. Estab. 1970. Specializes in regional history trade books. **Manuscript Acquisitions:** Elizabeth L. Wright, senior editor. Publishes 3 picture books/year; 2 young readers/year; 2 middle readers/year. 50% of books by first-time authors. "We are primarily a publisher of southeastern regional history, and we have recently published several titles for children. We consider children's books about Southern Appalachia only!"

Fiction: Picture books: folktales, history. Young readers, middle readers: folktales, history, suspense/mystery. Average word length: picture books—800-1,000; young readers—5,000-10,000; middle readers—20-30,000. Recently published *Bloody Mary: The Mystery of Amanda's Magic Mirror*, by Patrick Bone (young, middle reader); *Zebordee's Miracle*, by Ann G. Cooper, illustrated by Adam Hickam (pre-elementary, picture book); and *Appalachian ABCs*, by Francie Hall, illustrated by Kent Oehm (pre-elementary, picture book).

Nonfiction: Picture books, young readers, middle readers: biography (regional), history (regional). Average word length: picture books—800-1,000; young readers—5,000-10,000; middle readers—20-30,000. Recently published *Ten Friends: A Child's Story About the Ten Commandments*, written and illustrated by Gayla Dowdy Seale (preschool-elementary, picture book).

How to Contact/Writers: Fiction/Nonfiction: Submit outline/synopsis and 2 sample chapters. Responds to queries in 2 months; mss in 6 months. Publishes book 1 year after acceptance. Will consider simultaneous submissions and previously published work.

Illustration: Works with 4 illustrators/year. Uses color artwork only. Reviews ms/illustration packages from artists. Send ms with dummy with at least 3 color copies of sample illustrations. Illustrations only: Send résumé. Responds only if interested. Samples not returned; samples filed.

Terms: Pays authors royalty of 5-15% based on wholesale price. Pays illustrators royalty of 5-10% based on wholesale price or by author/illustrator negotiations (author pays). Sends galleys to authors; dummies to illustrators. Originals sometimes returned to artist at job's completion. Book catalog available for 8½ × 11 SAE and 4 first-class stamps; ms guidelines available for SASE. All imprints included in a single catalog. Catalog available on website.

Tips: "Because we are fairly new in the children's market, we will not accept a manuscript without complete illustrations. We are compiling a database of freelance illustrators which is available to interested authors. Please call if you have questions regarding the submission process or to see if your product is of interest. The children's market is huge! If the author can find a good local publisher, he or she is more likely to get published. We are currently looking for authors to represent our list in the new millennium. At this point, we are accepting regional (Southern Appalachian) manuscripts only. *Please* call if you have a question regarding this policy."

RICHARD C. OWEN PUBLISHERS, INC., P.O. Box 585, Katonah NY 10536. (800)262-0783. Fax: (914)232-3977. Website: www.rcowen.com. Book publisher. **Acquisitions:** Janice Boland, children's books editor/art director. Publishes 20 picture story books/year. 90% of books by first-time authors. We publish "child-focused books, with inherent instructional value, about characters and situations with which five-, six-, and seven-year-old children can identify—books that can be read for meaning, entertainment, enjoyment and information. We include multicultural stories that present minorities in a positive and natural way. Our stories show the diversity in America." Is not interested in lesson plans, or books of activities for literature studies or other content areas.

Fiction: Picture books, young readers: adventure, animal, contemporary, folktales, hi-lo, humor, multicultural, nature/environment, poetry, science fiction, suspense/mystery. Does not want to see holiday, religious themes, moral teaching stories. "No talking animals with personified human characteristics, jingles and rhymes, alphabet books, stories without plots, stories with nostalgic views of childhood, soft or sugar-coated tales. No stereotyping." Average word length: under 500 words. Recently published *Digging to China*, by Katherine Goldsby, illustrated by Viki Woodworth; *The Red-Tailed Hawk*, by Lola Schaefer, illustrated by Stephen Taylor; and *Dogs at School*, by Suzanne Hardin, illustrated by Jo-Ann Friar.

Nonfiction: Picture books, young readers: animals, careers, hi-lo, history, how-to, music/dance, geography, multicultural, nature/environment, science, sports. Multicultural needs include: "Good stories respectful of all heritages, races, cultural—African-American, Hispanic, American Indian." Wants lively stories. No "encyclopedic" type of information stories. Average word length: under 500 words. Recently published *New York City Buildings*, by Ann Mace, photos by Tim Holmstron.

How to Contact/Writers: Fiction/nonfiction: Submit complete ms and cover letter. Responds to mss in 1 year. Publishes a book 2-3 years after acceptance. See website for guidelines.

Illustration: Works with 20 illustrators/year. Uses color artwork only. Illustration only: Send color copies/reproductions or photos of art or provide tearsheets; do not send slides or originals. Include SASE and cover letter. Responds only if interested; samples filed.

Photography: Buys photos from freelancers. Contact: Janice Boland, art director. Include SASE and cover letter. Wants photos that are child-oriented; candid shots; not interested in portraits. "Natural, bright, crisp and colorful—of children and of interesting subjects and compositions attractive to children. If photos are assigned, we buy outright—retain ownership and all rights to photos taken in the project." Sometimes interested in stock photos for special projects. Uses 35mm, 2¼ × 2¼, color transparencies.

Terms: Pays authors royalties of 5% based on wholesale price or outright purchase (range: $25-500). Offers no advances. Pays illustrators by the project (range: $100-2,500). Pays photographers by the project (range: $100-2,000) or per photo ($100-150). Original artwork returned 12-18 months after job's completion. Book brochure, ms/artists guidelines available for SASE.

Tips: Seeking "stories (both fiction and nonfiction) that have charm, magic, impact and appeal; that children living in today's society will want to read and reread; books with strong storylines, child-appealing language, action and interesting, vivid characters. Write for the ears and eyes and hearts of your readers—use an economy of words. Visit the children's room at the public library and immerse yourself in the best children's literature."

PACIFIC PRESS, P.O. Box 5353. Nampa ID 83653-5353. (208)465-2500. Fax: (208)465-2531. E-mail: booksubmissions@pacificpress.com. Website: www.pacificpress.com/writers/books.htm. Estab. 1874. Specializes in Christian material. **Manuscript Acquisitions:** Tim Lale. **Art Acquisitions:** Randy Maxwell, creative director. Publishes 1 picture book/year; 2 young readers/year; 2 middle readers/year. 5% of books by first-time authors. Pacific Press brings the Bible and Christian lifestyle to children.
Fiction: Picture books, young readers, middle readers, young adults: religion. Average word length: picture books—100; young readers—1,000; middle readers—15,000; young adults—40,000. Recently published *Don't Let Your Heart Feel Funny*, by Jerry Thomas; *Petunia the Ugly Pig*, by Heather Grovet; *The Palamino*, by Katy Pistole.
Nonfiction: Picture books, young readers, middle readers, young adults: religion. Average word length: picture books—100; young readers—1,000; middle readers—15,000; young adults—40,000. Recently published *Before I Was a Kid*, by Rita Spears-Stewart; *God Spoke to a Girl*, by Dorothy Nelson; *His Messenger*, by Ruth Wheeler.
How to Contact/Writers: Fiction/Nonfiction: Query or submit outline/synopsis and 3 sample chapters. Responds to queries in 2 months; mss in 3 months. Publishes a book 6-9 months after acceptance. Will consider electronic submissions via disk or modem.
Illustration: Works with 2 illustrators/year. Uses color artwork only. Query. Responds only if interested. Samples returned with SASE.
Photography: Buys stock and assigns work. Model/property releases required.
Terms: Pays author royalty of 6-15% based on wholesale price. Offers advances (Average amount: $1,500). Pays illustrators royalty of 6-15% based on wholesale price. Pays photographers royalty of 6-15% based on wholesale price. Sends galleys to authors. Originals returned to artist at job's completion. Book catalog available for 10×12 SAE and 5 first-class stamps; ms guidelines for SASE. All imprints included in a single catalog. Catalog available on website www.adventistbookcenter.com.
Tips: Pacific Press is owned by the Seventh-day Adventist Church. The Press rejects all material that is not Bible-based.

PACIFIC VIEW PRESS, P.O. Box 2657, Berkeley CA 94702. (510)849-4213. Fax: (510)843-5835. E-mail: PVP@sirius.com. Book publisher. **Acquisitions:** Pam Zumwalt, president. Publishes 1-2 picture books/year. 50% of books by first-time authors. "We publish unique, high-quality introductions to Asian cultures and history for children 8-12, for schools, libraries and families. Our children's books focus on hardcover illustrated nonfiction. We look for titles on aspects of the history and culture of the countries and peoples of the Pacific Rim, especially China, presented in an engaging, informative and respectful manner. We are interested in books that all children will enjoy reading and using, and that parents and teachers will want to buy."
Nonfiction: Young readers, middle readers: Asia-related multicultural only. Recently published *Kneeling Carabao and Dancing Giants: Celebrating Filipino Festivals*, by Rena Krasno, illustrated by Ileana C. Lee (ages 8-12, nonfiction on festivals and history of Philippines); and *Made in China: Ideas and Inventions from Ancient China*, by Suzanne Williams, illustrated by Andrea Fong (ages 10-12, nonfiction on history of China and Chinese inventions).
How to Contact/Writers: Query with outline and sample chapter. Responds in 3 months.
Illustration: Works with 2 illustrators/year. Responds only if interested. Samples returned with SASE.
Terms: Pays authors royalty of 8-12% based on wholesale price. Pays illustrators by the project (range: $2,000-5,000).
Tips: "We welcome proposals from persons with expertise, either academic or personal, in their area of interest. While we do accept proposals from previously unpublished authors, we would expect submitters to have considerable experience presenting their interests to children in classroom or other public settings and to have skill in writing for children."

PARENTING PRESS, INC., P.O. Box 75267, Seattle WA 98125. (206)364-2900. Fax: (206)364-0702. E-mail: office@parentingpress.com. Website: www.parentingpress.com. Book publisher. Estab. 1979. Publisher: Carolyn Threadgill. **Acquisitions:** Elizabeth Crary, (parenting) and Carolyn Threadgill (children and parenting). Publishes 4-5 books/year for parents or/and children and those who work with them. 40% of books by first-time authors. "Parenting Press publishes educational books for children in story format—no straight fiction. Our company publishes books that help build competence in parents and children. We are known for practical books that teach parents and can be used successfully by parent educators, teachers, and educators who work with parents. We are interested in books that help people feel good about themselves because they gain skills needed in dealing with others. We are particularly interested in material that provides 'options' rather than 'shoulds.' "

● Parenting Press's guidelines are available on their website.

Fiction: Picture books: concept. Publishes social skills books, problem-solving books, safety books, dealing-with-feelings books that use a "fictional" vehicle for the information. "We rarely publish straight fiction." Recently published *Heidi's Irresistible Hat, Willy's Noisy Sister, Amy's Disappearing Pickle*, by Elizabeth Crary, illustrated by Susan Avishai (ages 4-10); and *The Way I Feel*, written and illustrated by Janan Cain, a book that promotes emotional literacy.

Nonfiction: Picture books: health, social skills building. Young readers: health, social skills building books. Middle readers: health, social skills building. No books on "new baby; coping with a new sibling; cookbooks; manners; books about disabilities (which we don't publish at present); animal characters in anything; books that tell children what they should do, instead of giving options." Average word length: picture books—500-800; young readers—1,000-2,000; middle readers—up to 10,000. Published *Kids to the Rescue*, by Maribeth and Darwin Boelts (ages 4-12); *Bully on the Bus*, by Carl Bosch (ages 7-11).

How to Contact/Writers: Query. Responds to queries/mss in 3 months, "after requested." Publishes a book 18 months after acceptance. Will consider simultaneous submissions.

Illustrations: Works with 3-5 illustrators/year. Reviews ms/illustration packages from artists. "We do reserve the right to find our own illustrator, however." Query. Illustrations only: Submit "résumé, samples of art/drawings (no original art); photocopies or color photocopies okay." Responds only if interested. Samples returned with SASE; samples filed, if suitable.

Terms: Pays authors royalties of 3-8% based on wholesale price. Pays illustrators (for text) by the project; 3-5% royalty based on wholesale price. Pays illustrators by the project ($250-3,000). Sends galleys to authors; dummies to illustrators. Book catalog/ms/artist's guidelines for #10 SAE and 1 first-class stamp.

Tips: "Make sure you are familiar with the unique nature of our books. All are aimed at building certain 'people' skills in adults or children. Our publishing for children follows no trend that we find appropriate. Children need nonfiction social skill-building books that help them think through problems and make their own informed decisions." The traditional illustrated story book does not *usually* fit our requirements because it does all the thinking for the child.

☒ PAULINE BOOKS & MEDIA, 50 St. Paul's Ave., Jamaica Plain MA 02130-3491. (617)522-8911. Website: www.pauline.org. Estab. 1932. Specializes in Christian material. **Manuscript Acquisitions:** Sr. Patricia Edward Jablonski, F.S.P. **Art Acquisitions:** Art Director, Design Dept. Publishes 2 picture books/year; 5 young readers/year; 3-5 middle readers/year; and 1-2 young adult titles/year. 20% of books by first-time authors. "We communicate the Gospel message through all available forms of media, responding to the needs and hopes of all people in the spirit of St. Paul."

Nonfiction: Picture books, young readers, middle readers, young adults: religion. Average word length: picture books—150-500; young readers—15,000-25,000; middle readers—8,000-10,000. Recently published *Saint Juan Diego and Our Lady of Guadalupe*, by Josephine Nobisso (ages 10-12, biography); *Pope John Paul II*, by Toni Ragot (ages 12-14, comic book); *Kids Explore America's Catholic Heritage*, by the Young Writers Workshop (ages 9-12, history of the Catholic Church in the U.S. with stories of persons who exemplify contemporary Catholic life in America).

How to Contact/Writers: Nonfiction: Submit outline/synopsis and 3 sample chapters. Responds to queries in 2 months; mss in 3 months. Publishes book 2-3 years after acceptance. Will consider simultaneous submissions, electronic submissions via disk or modem.

Illustration: Works with 20-30 illustrators/year. Uses color artwork only. Illustrations only: Send résumé, promotional literature, client list, tearsheets. Contact: Art Director, Design Department. Responds only if interested. Samples returned with SASE.

Photography: Buys stock and assigns work. Contact: Art Director, Design Department. Looking for children, animals and nature (not New England) photos. Model/property releases required; captions required. Uses color or b&w, 4×6, either matte or semigloss prints. Submit cover letter, résumé, client list, promo piece, published samples, stock photo list.

Terms: Pays authors royalty of 5-10% based on wholesale price. Offers advances (Average amount: $200). Pays illustrators by the project (range: $600-5,000) or royalty of 5% based on wholesale price. Pays photographers by the project. Sends galleys to authors. Book catalog available for 10½×13½ SAE and 7 first-class stamps; ms and art guidelines available for SASE. Catalog available on website.

Tips: "Please be sure that all material submitted is consonant with Christian teaching and values. We generally do not accept anthropomorphic stories, fantasy or poetry.

PEACHTREE PUBLISHERS, LTD., 1700 Chattahoochee Ave., Atlanta GA 30318-2112. (404)876-8761. Fax: (404)875-2578. E-mail: hello@peachtree-online.com. Website: www.peachtree-online.com. Book publisher. Imprints: Peachtree Jr. and Freestone. Estab. 1977. **Acquisitions:** Helen Harriss. **Art Director:** Loraine Joyner. Production Manager: Melanie McMahon. Publishes 20-24 titles/year.

Fiction: Picture books, young readers: adventure, animal, concept, history, nature/environment. Middle readers: adventure, animal, history, nature/environment, sports. Young adults: fiction, mystery, adventure. Does not want to see science fiction, romance.

Nonfiction: Picture books: animal, history, nature/environment. Young readers, middle readers, young adults: animal, biography, nature/environment. Does not want to see religion.

How to Contact/Writers: Fiction/Nonfiction: Submit complete ms. Responds to queries/mss in 4 months. Publishes a book 1-1½ years after acceptance. Will consider simultaneous submissions.

Illustration: Works with 8-10 illustrators/year. Illustrations only: Query production manager or art director with samples, résumé, slides, color copies to keep on file. Responds only if interested. Samples returned with SASE; samples filed.

Terms: Manuscript guidelines for SASE, or call for a recorded message.

PEEL PRODUCTIONS, P.O. Box 546, Columbus NC 28722. (828)894-8838. Fax: (801)365-9898. E-mail: editor@peelbooks.com. Book publisher. **Acquisitions:** Susan Dubosque, editor. Publishes 1 picture book/year; and 5 how-to-draw books/year.

Nonfiction: Young readers, middle readers: activity books (how to draw).

How to Contact/Writers: Fiction/Nonfiction: Submit outline/synopsis and 2 sample chapters. Responds to queries in 1 month; mss in 6 weeks. Publishes a book 1 year after acceptance. Will consider simultaneous submissions.

Terms: Pays authors royalty. Offers advances. Sends galleys to authors. Book catalog available for SAE and 2 first-class stamps. Manuscript guidelines available for SASE.

PELICAN PUBLISHING CO. INC., P.O. Box 3110, Gretna LA 70054-3110. (504)368-1175. Website: www.pelicanpub.com. Book publisher. Estab. 1926. **Manuscript Acquisitions:** Nina Kooij, editor-in-chief. **Art Acquisitions:** Tracey Clements, production manager. Publishes 18 young readers/year and 3 middle reader titles/year. 15% of books from agented writers. "Pelican publishes hardcover and trade paperback originals and reprints. Our children's books (illustrated and otherwise) include history, holiday, and regional. Pelican's mission is to publish books of quality and permanence that enrich the lives of those who read them."

Fiction: Young readers: history, holiday and regional. Middle readers: Louisiana history. Multicultural needs include stories about African-Americans, Irish-Americans, Jews, Asian-Americans, Cajuns and Hispanics. Does not want animal stories, general Christmas stories, "day at school" or "accept yourself" stories. Maximum word length: 1,100 young readers; middle readers—40,000. Recently published *The Warlord's Puzzle*, by Virginia Walton Pilegard (ages 5-8, folktale).

Nonfiction: Young readers: biography, history. Middle readers: Louisiana history. Recently published *The Governors of Louisiana*, by Miriam G. Reeves (ages 8-12, biography).

How to Contact/Writers: Fiction/Nonfiction: Query. Responds to queries in 1 month; mss in 3 months. Publishes a book 9-18 months after acceptance.

Illustration: Works with 15 illustrators/year. Reviews ms/illustration packages from artists. Query first. Illustrations only: Query with samples (no originals). Responds only if interested. Samples returned with SASE; samples kept on file.

Terms: Pays authors in royalties; buys ms outright "rarely." Sends galleys to authors. Illustrators paid by "various arrangements." Book catalog and ms guidelines available on website or for SASE.

Tips: "No anthropomorphic stories, pet stories (fiction or nonfiction), fantasy, poetry, science fiction or romance. Writers: Be as original as possible. Develop characters that lend themselves to series and always be thinking of new and interesting situations for those series. Give your story a strong hook—something that will appeal to a well-defined audience. There is a lot of competition out there for general themes. We look for stories with specific 'hooks' and audiences, and writers who actively promote their work."

PERFECTION LEARNING CORPORATION, Cover to Cover, 10520 New York, Des Moines IA 50322. (515)278-0133. Fax: (515)278-2980. E-mail: acquisitions@plconline.com. Website: www.perfectionlearning.com. Book publisher, independent book producer/packager. **Manuscript Acquisitions:** S. Thies (3-12 books), Rebecca Christian (curriculum). **Art Acquisitions:** Randy Messer, art director. Publishes 20 early chapter books/year; 40-50 middle readers/year; 25 young adult titles/year.

• Perfection Learning Corp. publishes *all* hi-lo children's books on a variety of subjects.

Fiction: Grades 3-12, ages 8-18: adventure, animal, contemporary, fantasy, folktales, history, humor, multicultural, nature/environment, poetry, science fiction, special needs, sports, suspense/mystery. Average word length: early chapter books—4,000; middle readers—10,000-14,000; young adults: 10,000-30,000. Recently published *Soccer Battles*; *The Club*, by Michael Strickland and Lisa Bahlinger.

Nonfiction: All levels: animal, biography, careers, geography, health, history, hobbies, multicultural, nature/environment, science, social issues, special needs, sports. Multicultural needs include contemporary fiction by authors who are of the culture. Does not want to see ABC or picture books. Average word length: early chapter books—4,000; middle readers—10,000-14,000; young adults—10,000-14,000.

How to Contact/Writers: Fiction/Nonfiction: Submit a few sample chapters and synopsis. Responds to queries/mss in 3 months. Publishes a book 18 months after acceptance.

Illustration: Works with 15-20 illustrators/year. Illustration only: Query with samples; send résumé, promo sheet, client list, tearsheets. Contact: Randy Messer, art director. Responds only if interested. Samples returned with SASE; samples filed.

Photography: Buys photos from freelancers. Contact: Randy Messer, art director. Buys stock and assigns work. Uses children. Uses color or up to 8×10 b&w glossy prints; $2\frac{1}{4} \times 2\frac{1}{4}$, 4×5 transparencies. Submit cover letter, client list, stock photo list, promo piece (color or b&w).

Terms: Pays authors "depending on going rate for industry." Offers advances. Pays illustrators by the project. Pays photographers by the project. Original artwork returned on a "case by case basis."

Tips: "Our materials are sold through schools for use in the classroom. Talk to a teacher about his/her needs."

PHILOMEL BOOKS, Penguin Putnam Inc., 345 Hudson St., New York NY 10014. (212)414-3610. Website: www.penguinputnam.com. Putnam Books. Book publisher. Estab. 1980. **Manuscript Acquisitions:** Patricia Gauch, editorial director; Emily Earle, assistant editor; Michael Green, senior editor. **Art Acquisitions:** Gina DiMassi, design assistant. Publishes 18 picture books/year; 2 middle-grade/year; 2 young readers/year; 4 young adult/year. 5% of books by first-time authors; 80% of books from agented writers. "We look for beautifully written, engaging manuscripts for children and young adults."

• Philomel Books is not accepting unsolicited manuscripts.

Fiction: All levels: adventure, animal, anthology, contemporary, fantasy, folktales, hi-lo, history, humor, poetry, sports, multicultural. Middle readers, young adults: problem novels, science fiction, suspense/mystery. No concept picture books, mass-market "character" books, or series. Average word length: 1,000 for picture books; 1,500 young readers; 14,000 middle readers; 20,000 young adult.

Nonfiction: Picture books, young readers, middle readers: hi-lo. "Creative nonfiction on any subject." Average word length: 2,000 for picture books; 3,000 young readers; 10,000 middle readers.

How to Contact/Writers: Not accepting unsolicited mss. Fiction: Submit outline/synopsis and first two chapters. Nonfiction: Query. Responds to queries in 3 months; mss in 4 months.

Illustration: Works with 20-25 illustrators/year. Reviews ms/illustration packages from artists. Query with art sample first. Illustrations only: Query with samples. Send résumé and tearsheets. Responds to art samples in 1 month. Original artwork returned at job's completion. Samples returned with SASE or kept on file.

Terms: Pays authors in royalties. Average advance payment "varies." Illustrators paid by advance and in royalties. Sends galleys to authors; dummies to illustrators. Book catalog, ms guidelines free on request with SASE (9×12 envelope for catalog).

Tips: Wants "unique fiction or nonfiction with a strong voice and lasting quality. Discover your own voice and own story—and persevere." Looks for "something unusual, original, well-written. Fine art. The genre (fantasy, contemporary, or historical fiction) is not so important as the story itself and the spirited life the story allows its main character. We are also interested in receiving adolescent novels, particularly novels that contain regional spirit, such as a story about a young boy or girl written from a Southern, Southwestern or Northwestern perspective."

**FOR EXPLANATIONS OF THESE SYMBOLS,
SEE THE INSIDE FRONT AND BACK COVERS OF THIS BOOK**

PHOENIX LEARNING RESOURCES, 12 W. 31st St., New York NY 10001-4415. (212)629-3887. (212)629-5648. E-mail: john@phoenixlr.com. Website: www.phoenixlr.com. Book publisher. Executive Vice President: John A. Rothermich. Publishes 20 textbooks/year. Publisher's goal is to provide proven skill building materials in reading, language, math and study skills for today's student, grades K-adult.

Nonfiction: Middle readers, young readers, young adults: hi-lo, textbooks. Recently published *Reading for Concepts*, Third Edition.

How to Contact/Writers: Nonfiction: Submit outline/synopsis. Responds to queries in 2 weeks; mss in 1 month. Will consider simultaneous submissions and previously published work.

Photography: Buys stock. Contact: John A. Rothermich, executive vice president. Uses color prints and 35mm, 2¼×2¼, 4×5 transparencies. Submit cover letter.

Terms: Pays authors royalty based on wholesale price or work purchased outright. Pays illustrators and photographers by the project. Sends galleys to authors. Book catalog available for SASE.

Tips: "We look for classroom-tested and proven materials."

PIANO PRESS, P.O. Box 85, Del Mar CA 92014-0085. (858)481-5651. Fax: (858)755-1104. E-mail: PianoPress@aol.com. Website: www.pianopress.com. Estab. 1998. Specializes in music-related fiction, educational material, multicultural material, nonfiction. **Manuscript Acquisitions:** Elizabeth C. Axford, M.A., editor. "We publish music-related books, either fiction or nonfiction, coloring books, songbooks and poetry."

Fiction: Picture books, young readers, middle readers, young adults: folktales, multicultural, poetry, music. Average word length: picture books—1,500-2,000. Recently published *Strum a Song of Angels*, by Linda Oatman High and Elizabeth C. Axford; *Music and Me*, by Kimberly White and Elizabeth C. Axford.

Nonfiction: Picture books, young readers, middle readers, young adults: multicultural, music/dance. Average word length: picture books—1,500-2,000. Recently published *The Musical ABC*, by Dr. Phyllis J. Perry and Elizabeth C. Axford; Merry Christmas Happy Hanukkah—A Multilingual Songbook & CD, by Elizabeth C. Axford.

How to Contact/Writers: Fiction/Nonfiction: Query. Responds to queries in 3 months; mss in 6 months. Publishes a book 1 year after acceptance. Will consider simultaneous submissions, electronic submissions via disk or modem.

Illustration: Works with 1 or 2 illustrators/year. Reviews ms/illustration packages from artists. Query. Contact: Editor. Illustrations only: Query with samples. Contact: Editor. Responds in 3 months. Samples returned with SASE; samples filed.

Photography: Buys stock and assigns work. Contact: Editor. Looking for music-related, multicultural. Model/property releases required. Uses glossy or flat, color or b&w prints. Submit cover letter, résumé, client list, published samples, stock photo list.

Terms: Pays author royalty of 5-10% based on retail price. Pays illustrators royalty of 5-10% based on retail price. Pays photographers royalty of 5-10% based on retail price. Sends galleys to authors; dummies to illustrators. Originals returned to artist at job's completion. Book catalog available for #10 SAE and 2 first-class stamps. All imprints included in a single catalog. Catalog available on website.

Tips: "We are looking for music-related material only for any juvenile market. Please do not send nonmusic-related materials. Query first before submitting anything."

THE PLACE IN THE WOODS, "Different" Books, 3900 Glenwood Ave., Golden Valley MN 55422-5307. (763)374-2120. Fax: (952)593-5593. E-mail: placewoods@aol.com. Book publisher. **Acquisitions:** Roger Hammer, publisher/editor. Publishes 2 elementary-age titles/year and 1 middle readers/year; 1 young adult titles/year. 100% of books by first-time authors. Books feature primarily diversity/multicultural/disability themes, many by first-time authors and illustrators.

Fiction: All levels: adventure, animal, contemporary, fantasy, folktales, hi-lo, history, humor, poetry, multicultural, special needs. Recently published *Little Horse*, by Frank Minogue, illustrated by Beth Crire (young adult fiction); *Simon the Daredevil Centipede*, by Phil Segal, illustrated by Alisa Caiarelli (early elementary fiction).

Nonfiction: All levels: hi-lo, history, multicultural, special needs. Multicultural themes must avoid negative stereotypes. "Generally, we don't publish nonfiction, but we would look at these."

How to Contact/Writers: Fiction/Nonfiction: Submit complete ms. Responds to queries/mss in 1 month with SASE. "No multiple or simultaneous submissions. Please indicate a time frame for response."

Illustration: Works with 4 illustrators/year. Uses primarily b&w artwork only. Reviews ms/illustration packages from authors. Query; submit ms. Contact: Editor. Illustration only: Query with samples. Responds in 1 month. Include SASE. "We buy all rights."

Photography: Buys photos from freelancers. Works on assignment only. Uses photos that appeal to children. Model/property releases required; captions required. Uses any b&w prints. Submit cover letter and samples with SASE.

Terms: Work purchased outright from authors ($50-250). Pays illustrators by the project (range: $10-500). Pays photographers per photo. For all contracts, "initial payment repeated with each printing." Original artwork not returned at job's completion. Guidelines available for SASE.

PLAYERS PRESS, INC., P.O. Box 1132, Studio City CA 91614-0132. (818)789-4980. Book publisher. Imprints: Showcase Publishing; Gaslight Productions; Health Watch Books. Estab. 1965. **Manuscript Acquisitions:** Robert W. Gordon, vice president/editorial director. **Art Acquisitions:** Attention: Art Director. Publishes 7-25 young readers dramatic plays and musicals/year; 2-10 middle readers dramatic plays and musicals/year; and 4-20 young adults dramatic plays and musicals/year. 35% of books by first-time authors; 1% of books from agented writers. Players Press philosophy is "to create is to live life's purpose."
Fiction: All levels: plays. Recently published *Play From African Folktales*, by Carol Rorty (collection of short plays); *Punch and Judy*, a play by William-Alan Landes; and *Silly Soup!*, by Carol Kerty (a collection of short plays with music and dance).
Nonfiction: Picture books, middle readers, young readers, young adults. "Any children's nonfiction pertaining to the entertainment industry, performing arts and how-to for the theatrical arts only." Needs include activity, arts/crafts, careers, history, how-to, music/dance, reference and textbook. Recently published *Scenery*, by J. Stell (How to Build Stage Scenery); *Monologues for Teens*, by Vernon Howard (ideal for teen performers); *Humorous Monologues*, by Vernon Howard (ideal for young performers); *Actor's Résumés*, by Richard Devin (how to prepare an acting résumé).
How to Contact/Writers: Fiction/nonfiction: Submit plays or outline/synopsis and sample chapters of entertainment books. Responds to queries in 1 month; mss in 1 year. Publishes a book 10 months after acceptance. No simultaneous submissions.
Illustration: Works with 2-6 illustrators/year. Use primarily b&w artwork. Illustrations only: Submit résumé, tearsheets. Responds to art samples in 1 week only if interested. Samples returned with SASE; samples filed.
Terms: Pays authors royalties based on wholesale price. Pay illustrators by the project (range: $5-5,000). Pays photographers by the project (up to 1,000); royalty varies. Sends galleys to authors; dummies to illustrators. Book catalog and ms guidelines available for 9×12 SASE.
Tips: Looks for "plays/musicals and books pertaining to the performing arts only. Illustrators: send samples that can be kept for our files."

PLAYHOUSE PUBLISHING, 1566 Akron-Peninsula Rd., Akron OH 44313. (330)926-1313. Fax: (330)926-1315. E-mail: info@playhousepublishing.com. Website: www.playhousepublishing.com. Specializes in mass market Christian and educational material. **Acquisitions:** Deborah D'Andrea, creative director. Imprints: Picture Me Books, Nibble Me Books. Publishes 10-15 picture books/year, 2-5 young readers/year. 50% of books by first-time authors. "Playhouse Publishing is dedicated to finding imaginative new ways to inspire young minds to read, learn and grow—one book at a time."
Fiction: Picture books: adventure, animal, concept, fantasy, folktales, humor, nature/environment, sports. Average word length: board books—75; picture books—500. Recently published: *Picture Me Sparkle Princess*, by Cathy Hapka, illustrated by Heather Hill; *My Family*, by Merry North, illustrated by Lynne Schwaner; *Campbell's® Alphabet Soup Book*, by Jackie Wolf, illustrated by Campbell's®.
How to Contact/Writers: Fiction: Query or submit outline/synopsis. Responds to queries/mss in 2-4 months. Publishes a book 18 months after acceptance. Will consider simultaneous submissions and electronic submissions via disk or modem.
Illustration: Works with 7 illustrators/year. Uses color artwork only. Reviews ms/illustration packages. Query or submit ms with 1-2 pieces of final art. Illustrations only: Query with samples. Send résumé, promosheet and tearsheets. Contact: Deborah D'Andrea, creative director. Responds in 1 month. Samples returned with SASE.
Photography: Works on assignment only. Model/property release required. Uses color prints.
Terms: Work purchased outright from authors. Illustrators and photographers paid by the project. Book catalog available for 9×12 SASE. All imprints included in single catalog. Catalog available online.

PLEASANT COMPANY PUBLICATIONS, 8400 Fairway Place, Middleton WI 53562-2554. Phone/fax: (608)836-4768. Website: www.americangirl.com. Book publisher. Editorial Director: Judy Woodburn. **Manuscript Acquisitions:** Submissions Editor, Jodi Evert, editorial director fiction/picture books; Michelle Watkins, editorial director, American Girl Library; Peg Ross, History mysteries. **Art Acquisitions:** Jane Varda, art director. Imprints: The American Girls Collection, American Girl Library, History Mysteries, AG Fiction. Publishes 30 middle readers/year. 10% of books by first-time authors. Publishes fiction and nonfiction for girls 7 and up. "Pleasant Company's mission is to educate and entertain girls with high-quality products and experiences that build self-esteem and reinforce positive social and moral values."

A look at children's books through the eyes of a librarian

While some authors forget regular sleeping hours, wearily considering their next grand dose of dialogue, how many are fueled by the possibility of their books achieving "entrance display presence" at county libraries? Realistically, only a handful of children's writers may contemplate weekly "hot sheets" and public libraries as soaring rewards for their efforts. However, libraries are just as important as bookstores and book clubs when it comes to a book's public debut, and in turn, its potential success and longevity.

Pat Clancy

Does subject matter influence purchasing decisions in libraries? Will children's media specialists recommend award-winning, *Booklist* favorites over lesser-known titles? Are image-heavy magazines really popular among young readers? Here, Children's Library Associate Pat Clancy offers insight from Northwest Library in Columbus, Ohio, a branch that boasted a circulation of almost a million at the end of 2001. An enthusiast of medieval historical fiction, boxed sets of Tolkien and rooms full of enchanting fantasy tales, Clancy has been involved in children's education for nearly twenty years.

In your ventures from theatrical avenues to theories in religion, how did you become a children's library associate?
After 15 years of working in a Catholic Youth Ministry, I decided I needed a change. I already had a job teaching American Sign Language at a local college lined up, but that was only two courses. I needed something to pay the bills that would give me a somewhat flexible schedule. I saw this job advertised and thought, "I grew up in a household of books and reading, I have planned programs for young people—even used stories when giving retreats—and perhaps my signing skills would come in handy." I have been fortunate to do a "Stories and Sign" story time, and my love of fantasy literature has enabled me to lead a fantasy book club for school-age young people. I do not think being a children's library associate is my last stop in the journey. Like many people I would love to have both the time and the inspiration to write.

In your activity groups, how often do you incorporate the Internet or television?
I don't really. I try to point out relevant websites. There are some good author and book sites for some of the fantasy literature like Redwall and the author T.A. Barron. In the activities I lead I really want the young people to use their own creative imaginations so the story can become their story, as well as their interpretation, not someone else's.

When a parent asks for suggestions, how do you determine what material may be appropriate for a child who resists reading as a leisure activity?
I like to ask the parent what interests their young person—sports, animals, etc. Then I try to

find a book or reading material that will match those interests. It is always ideal when a young person is there so you can have the conversation directly with her or him. In my experience it seems to be mostly boys who are reluctant readers. So I try to recommend shorter funny books to capture their interest as well as nonfiction. Sometimes you have to convince the parents that nonfiction is also legitimate reading. Whatever will get the young people reading, whether it is a magazine or nonfiction, for instance, can be a jumping point for suggesting other reading materials.

With so many vivid and sophisticated picture books and educational workbooks available, are magazines such as *Spider*, *Appleseeds* and *Children's Digest* popular among readers?
We have found that most patrons will check out topic-specific magazines such as *American Girl*, *Boys' Life* and *National Geographic*. The other more literary magazines do not tend to circulate as often. Perhaps because there are so many children's books nowadays.

As an education specialist, how do you feel about children's books such as *Are You There God, It's Me Margaret?*, *Little Red Riding Hood* and the Goosebumps series being banned from public libraries?
I personally feel that books should not be banned from a public library. Every individual has a right to choose what they want to read. What an individual chooses to have on their shelves at home is up to them. We are a nation founded on freedom and diversity. I believe a public library should be a gathering place for materials that reflect this. I understand the argument that books are purchased with taxpayer dollars, but not just a few taxpayers are contributing. I would not want someone to tell me what religion I should be practicing nor do I want someone dictating what books I can and can't read. The issue of censorship seems so broad. From what I have been reading, some group could challenge almost any book as being objectionable.

How do you handle complaints regarding books you've recommended or a title on the shelf a concerned parent finds distasteful?
This will seem really immodest but I haven't had any complaints about titles that I've recommended. I really try to listen to the patrons and understand the kinds of literature they are looking for, and not force a book on anyone just because I loved it. If someone really objects to fantasy that involves magic I will not lead her there. If a patron complains about a title they find, I try to talk about equal access of books, but offer that they may share their concerns with our director and give them the form to do so. I then pass that on to the appropriate person.

Within an environment where kids have access to every topic imaginable, do they often ask you for guidance about books related to sexual identity or acculturation, for example, or do they discover the books in solitude?
The library I work at has a separate young adult section with a young adult librarian so I have not had to deal with questions concerning literature about sexual identity. I do try to familiarize myself with materials out there so I can handle the question sensitively if it arises. I also try to be aware of books on different cultures, both fiction and nonfiction, so I can point those out to patrons should they ask. This information has become especially important since September 11.

Are you compelled to suggest award-winning books and titles on *Booklist* first? If not, how often do you refer to current lists and reviews?

I don't feel compelled to suggest award-winning books first. It depends on what a patron is looking for. I do try to keep up with current lists and reviews. Most times I prefer to recommend titles I've read myself or I know others have read and enjoyed. I also try to recommend books that are age appropriate. I admit I am a snob when it comes to things like picture books based on original classics, such as the Little House books or Narnia. I also have the reputation of being a stickler about series. With very few expectations they should be read in order. And seeing the movie version of the first of the series does not, in my opinion, qualify for reading the first book. However, I am a customer service professional, so while I will state my opinion regarding series order, I will get the patron whichever book they are requesting.

While *Booklist* elaborates on about 2,500 children's titles a year, do any particular genres tend to get slighted when the library's budget is configured? Do you have any input during this process?

As a children's library associate I really don't have any input into the process of what is priority ordering or the budget. If I come across a book or series that I really like or feel we should have, I pass suggestions on to the person who does that ordering. We are very fortunate in the library where I work to presently have a very healthy budget when it comes to ordering. It doesn't appear to me that one area is slighted over another.

Do you have much reading time "on the job," and how do you select titles to survey during this time allocated—again, new arrivals and reviewed books first?

With planning story time and other tasks, I am not really given time on the job for reading. I do try to read new arrivals and admit I gravitate to the new fantasy and science fiction. Truly there is not enough time in the day, and every now and then, I want a grown-up book to read, not just juvenile literature. While nothing beats a book in the hands, books on tape have helped me keep up with my reading.

Lastly, what is your favorite children's book? . . . Okay, up to three if you can't choose one.

My all-time favorite picture book is *Harold and the Purple Crayon*, by Crockett Johnson. It is the first book I can remember reading that showed me what one could do with one object and your imagination. My most recent favorite is *Sammy and the Dinosaurs*, by Ian Whybrow, because it shows the power of connection and belonging. My favorite juvenile fiction is a toss up so I will name two and thus give you four favorites. The first is *A Wrinkle in Time*, by Madeleine L'Engle. And lastly, *Little Women*, by Louisa May Alcott, because I think I always felt like Jo March— never quite sure of where I fit in. I have yet to find that dream of becoming a writer like she did but the dream is there, so maybe one day!

—*Candi Lace*

● Pleasant Company does not accept ideas or manuscripts for The American Girls Collection, but does accept manuscripts for stand-alone historical fiction, and is seeking manuscripts for AG fiction, its contemporary middle-grade fiction imprint for girls 10 and up. Request writers' guidelines for more information. Pleasant Company publishes *American Girl* magazine. See the listing for *American Girl* in the Magazines section.

Fiction: Middle readers: adventure, animal, contemporary, fantasy, suspense/mystery. Recently published *Meet Kit*, by Valerie Tripp, illustrated by Walter Rane (ages 7-12, historical fiction); *Smoke Screen*, by Amy Goldman Koss (ages 10 and up, contemporary fiction); *Trouble at Fort La Pointe*, by Kathleen Ernst (ages 10 an up, historical fiction/mystery).

Nonfiction: Middle readers: activity books, arts/crafts, cooking, history, hobbies, how-to, self help, sports. Recently published *Help! A Girl's Guide to Divorce and Stepfamilies*, by Nancy Holyoke, illustrated by Scott Nash (ages 8 and up; self-help); *Paper Punch Art*, by Laura Torres (ages 8 and up; craft); and *Quiz Book 2*, by Sarah Jane Brian, illustrated by Debbie Tilley (ages 8 and up; activity).

How to Contact/Writers: Fiction/nonfiction: Query or submit entire ms. Responds to queries/mss in 3 months. Will consider simultaneous submissions.

Illustration: Works with 10 illustrators/year. Reviews ms/illustration packages from artists. Illustrations only: Query with samples. Contact: Jane Varda, senior art director. Responds only if interested. Samples returned with SASE; copies of samples filed.

Photography: Buys stock and assigns work. Submit cover letter, published samples, promo piece.

Terms: Pays authors royalty or work purchased outright. Pays illustrators by the project. Pays photographers by the project. Sends galleys to authors; dummies to illustrators. Originals returned to artist at job's completion. Book catalog available for 8½ × 11 SAE and 4 first-class stamps. All imprints included in a single catalog.

PROMETHEUS BOOKS, 59 John Glenn Dr., Amherst NY 14228-2197. Fax: (716)564-2711. E-mail: slmitchell@prometheusbooks.com. Website: www.PrometheusBooks.com. Book publisher. Estab. 1969. **Acquisitions:** Steven L. Mitchell, editor-in-chief. Publishes 1-2 titles/year. 50% of books by first-time authors; 30% of books from agented writers. "We hope more books will be published that focus on real issues children face and real questions they raise. Our primary focus is to publish children's books with alternative viewpoints: humanism, free thought, skepticism toward the paranormal, moral values, critical reasoning, human sexuality, and independent thinking based upon science and reasoning. Our niche is the parent who seeks informative books based on these principles. We are dedicated to offering customers the highest-quality books. We are also committed to the development of new markets both in North America and throughout the world."

Nonfiction: All levels: sex education, moral education, critical thinking, nature/environment, science, self help, skepticism, social issues. Average word length: picture books—2,000; young readers—10,000; middle readers—20,000; young adult/teens—60,000. Recently published *A Solstice Tree For Jenny*, by Karen Shrugg (ages 4 and up); *All Families Are Different*, by Sid Gordon (ages 7 and up); and *Flat Earth? Round Earth?*, by Theresa Martin (ages 7 and up).

How to Contact/Writers: Submit complete ms with sample illustrations (b&w). Responds to queries in 1-3 weeks; mss in 1-2 months. Publishes a book 12-18 months after acceptance. SASE required for return of ms/proposal.

Illustration: Works with 1-2 illustrators/year. "We will keep samples in a freelance file, but freelancers are rarely used." Reviews ms/illustration packages from artists. "Prefer to have full work (manuscript and illustrations); will consider any proposal." Include résumé, photocopies.

Terms: Pays authors royalty of 5-15% based on wholesale price and binding. "Author hires illustrator; we do not contract with illustrators." Pays photographers per photo (range: $50-100). Sends galleys to author. Book catalog is free on request.

Tips: We do not accept projects with anthropomorphic characters. We stress realistic children in realistic situations. "Books should reflect secular humanist values, stressing nonreligious moral education, critical thinking, logic, and skepticism. Authors should examine our book catalog and website to learn what sort of manuscripts we're looking for."

PUFFIN BOOKS, Penguin Putnam Inc., 345 Hudson St., New York NY 10014-3657. (212)366-3600. Website: www.penguinputnam.com/childrens. Imprint of Penguin Putnam Inc. **Acquisitions:** Sharyn November, senior editor. Publishes trade paperback originals (very few) and reprints. Publishes 175-200 titles/year. Receives 600 queries and mss/year. 1% of books by first-time authors; 5% from unagented writers. "Puffin Books publishes high-end trade paperbacks and paperback originals and reprints for preschool children, beginning and middle readers, and young adults."

Fiction: Picture books, young adult novels, middle grade and easy-to-read grades 1-3. "We publish mostly paperback reprints. We publish few original titles." Recently published *Go and Come Back*, by Joan Ablelove; *Speak*, by Laurie Halse Anderson.

Nonfiction: Biography, children's/juvenile, illustrated book, young children's concept books (counting, shapes, colors). Subjects include education (for teaching concepts and colors, not academic), women in history. " 'Women in history' books interest us." Reviews artwork/photos. Send color photocopies. Recently published *Rachel Carson: Pioneer of Ecology*, by "Fadlinski" (history); *Grandma Moses*, by O'Neill Ruff (history). Publishes the Alloy Books series.

How to Contact/Writers: Fiction: Submit complete picture book ms or 3 sample chapters with SASE. Nonfiction: Submit 5 pages of ms with SASE. "It could take up to 5 months to get response." Publishes book 1 year after acceptance. Will consider simultaneous submissions, if so noted.

Terms: Pays royalty. Offers advance (varies). Book catalog for 9 × 12 SASE with 7 first-class stamps; send request to Marketing Department.

G.P. PUTNAM'S SONS, Penguin Putnam Inc., 345 Hudson St., New York NY 10014. (212)414-3610. Website: www.penguinputnam.com. Book publisher. **Manuscript Acquisitions:** Kathy Dawson, executive editor; Susan Kochan, senior editor, John Rudolph. **Art Acquisitions:** Cecilia Yung, art director, Putnam and Philomel. Publishes 20 picture books/year; 10 middle readers/year; and 2 young adult titles/year. 5% of books by first-time authors; 50% of books from agented authors.

• Putnam title *Hope Was Here*, by Joan Bauer, won a 2001 Newbery Honor Medal. Their *Miracle's Boys*, by Jacqueline Woodson, won the 2001 Coretta Scott King Author Award.

Fiction: Picture books: animal, concept, contemporary, humor, multicultural, special needs. Young readers: adventure, contemporary, history, humor, multicultural, special needs, suspense/mystery. Middle readers: adventure, contemporary, history, humor, multicultural, problem novels, special needs, sports, suspense/mystery. Young adults: contemporary, history, problem novels, special needs. "Multicultural books should reflect different cultures accurately but unobtrusively." Regarding special needs, "stories about physically or mentally challenged children should portray them accurately and without condescension." Does not want to see series, romances. Average word length: picture books—200-1,500; middle readers—10,000-30,000; young adults—40,000-50,000. Recently published *Gumbrella*, by Barry Root (ages 4-8); and *Stand Tall*, by Joan Bauer (ages 10-14).

Nonfiction: Picture books: animal, concept, nature/environment. Subject must have broad appeal but inventive approach. Average word length: picture books—200-1,500. Recently published *Atlantic*, by G. Brian Karas (ages 4-8, 32 pages).

How to Contact/Writers: Fiction/nonfiction: Query with outline/synopsis and 3 sample chapters. Unsolicited picture book mss only. Responds to queries in 3 weeks; mss in 2 months. Publishes a book 2 years after acceptance. Will consider simultaneous submissions on queries only.

Illustration: Works with 40 illustrators/year. Reviews ms/illustration packages from artists. Manuscript/illustration packages and illustration only: Query. Responds only if interested. Samples returned with SASE; samples filed.

Terms: Pays authors royalty based on retail price. Pays illustrators by the project or royalty based on retail price. Sends galleys to authors. Original artwork returned at job's completion. Book catalog and ms and artist's guidelines available for SASE.

Tips: "Study our catalogs and get a sense of the kind of books we publish, so that you know whether your project is likely to be right for us."

RAINBOW PUBLISHERS, (formerly Rainbow Books), P.O. Box 261129, San Diego CA 92196. (858)271-7600. Book publisher. Estab. 1979. **Acquisitions:** Christy Scannell, editorial director. Publishes 5 young readers/year; 5 middle readers/year; and 5 young adult titles/year. 50% of books by first-time authors. "Our mission is to publish Bible-based, teacher resource materials that contribute to and inspire spiritual growth and development in kids ages 2-12."

Nonfiction: Young readers, middle readers, young adult/teens: activity books, arts/crafts, how-to, reference, religion. Does not want to see traditional puzzles. Recently published *Worship Bulletins for Kids*, by Mary Rose Pearson and Jeanne Grieser (series of 2 books for ages 3-12).

How to Contact/Writers: Nonfiction: Submit outline/synopsis and 3-5 sample chapters. Responds to queries in 6 weeks; mss in 3 months. Publishes a book 18 months after acceptance. Will consider simultaneous submissions, submissions via disk and previously published work.

Illustration: Works with 2-5 illustrators/year. Reviews ms/illustration packages from artists. Submit ms with 2-5 pieces of final art. Illustrations only: Query with samples. Responds in 6 weeks. Samples returned with SASE; samples filed.

Terms: For authors work purchased outright (range: $500 and up). Pays illustrators by the project (range: $300 and up). Sends galleys to authors. Book catalog available for 10×13 SAE and 2 first-class stamps; ms guidelines available for SASE.

Tips: "Our Rainbow imprint carries reproducible books for teachers of children in Christian ministries, including crafts, activities, games and puzzles. Our Legacy imprint (new in '97) handles nonfiction titles for children in the Christian realm, such as Bible story books, devotional books, and so on. Please write for guidelines and study the market before submitting material."

RANDOM HOUSE/GOLDEN BOOKS FOR YOUNG READERS GROUP, (formerly Random House Books for Young Readers), 1540 Broadway, New York NY 10036. (212)782-9000. Random House, Inc. Book publisher. Estab. 1935. "Random House Books aims to create books that nurture the hearts and minds of children, providing and promoting quality books and a rich variety of media that entertain and educate readers from 6 months to 12 years." Vice President/Publishing Director: Kate Klimo. Vice President/Associate Publishing Director/Art Director: Cathy Goldsmith. **Acquisitions:** Easy-to-Read Books (step-into-reading and picture books): Heidi Kilgras, executive editor. Stepping Stones and middle grade fiction: Jennifer Dussling, senior editor. **Art Acquisitions:** Jan Gerardi. 100% of books published through agents; 2% of books by first-time authors.

• Random House accepts only agented material. Random House title *Only Passing Through: The Story of Sojourner Truth*, illustrated by R. Gregory Christie (text by Anne Rockwell), won a 2001 Coretta Scott King Illustrator Honor Award.

How to Contact/Writers: Not accepting unsolicited mss and reserves the right not to return any work.

Illustration: Reviews ms/illustration packages from artists through agent only.

Terms: Pays authors in royalties; sometimes buys mss outright. Sends galleys to authors. Book catalog free on request.

RED DEER PRESS, Rm 813, Mackimmie Library Tower, 2500 University Dr. NW, Calgary, Alberta T2N 1N4 Canada. (403)220-4334. Fax: (403)210-8191. E-mail: rdp@ucalgary.ca. Website: www.reddeerpress.com. Imprints: Northern Lights Books for Children, Northern Lights Young Novels. Book publisher. Estab. 1975. **Manuscript/Art Acquisitions:** Peter Carver, children's editor. Publishes 3 picture books/year; 4 young adult titles/year. 20% of books by first-time authors. Red Deer Press is known for their "high-quality international children's program that tackles risky and/or serious issues for kids."

Fiction: Picture books, young readers: adventure, contemporary, fantasy, folktales, history, humor, multicultural, nature/environment, poetry; middle readers, young adult/teens: adventure, contemporary, fantasy, folktales, hi-lo, history, humor, multicultural, nature/environment, problem novels, suspense/mystery. Recently published *Courage to Fly*, by Troon Harrison, illustrated by Zhong-Yang Huung (ages 4-7, picture book); *Amber Waiting*, by Nan Gregory, illustrated by Macdonald Denton (ages 4-7, picture book); *Tom Finder*, by Martine Leavitt (14 and up).

How to Contact/Writers: Fiction/Nonfiction: Query or submit outline/synopsis. Responds to queries in 6 months; ms in 8 months. Publishes a book 18 months after acceptance. Will consider simultaneous submissions.

Illustration: Works with 4-6 illustrators/year. Illustrations only: Query with samples. Responds only if interested. Samples not returned; samples filed for six months. Canadian illustrators only.

Photography: Buys stock and assigns work. Model/property releases required. Submit cover letter, résumé and color promo piece.

Terms: Pays authors royalty (negotiated). Occasionally offers advances (negotiated). Pays illustrators and photographers by the project or royalty (depends on the project). Sends galleys to authors. Originals returned to artist at job's completion. Guidelines not available.

Tips: "Red Deer Press is currently not accepting children's manuscripts unless the writer is an established Canadian children's writer with an original project that fits its publishing program. Writers, illustrators and photographers should familiarize themselves with RD Press's children's publishing program."

RED WHEELBARROW PRESS, INC., E-mail: publisher@rwpress.com. Website: www.rwpress.com. Estab. 1997. Trade book publisher specializing in fiction (with slant) and educational material. **Manuscript Acquisitions:** L.C. Sajbel, publisher.

• Red Wheelbarrow is currently not accepting submissions until further notice.

RENAISSANCE HOUSE, Imprint of Laredo Publishing, 9400 Lloydcrest Dr., Beverly Hills CA 90210. (800)547-5113. Fax: (310)358-5282. E-mail: laredopub@cs.com. Website: www.renaissancehouse.net. Estab. 1991. Specializes in trade books, educational material, multicultural material. Independent book packager/producer. **Manuscript Acquisitions:** Raquel Benatar. **Art Acquisitions:** Sam Laredo. Publishes 5 picture books/year; 10 young readers/year; 10 middle readers/year; 5 young adult titles/year. 25% of books by first-time authors.

Fiction: Picture books: animal, folktales, multicultural. Young readers: animal, anthology, folktales, multicultural. Middle readers, young adult/teens: anthology, folktales, multicultural, nature/environment. Recently published *Isabel Allende, Memories for a Story* (English-Spanish, age 9-12, biography); *Stories of the Americas*, a series of legends by several authors (ages 9-12, legend).

How to Contact/Writers: Submit outline/synopsis. Responds to queries/mss in 3 weeks. Publishes a book 1 year after acceptance. Will consider simultaneous submissions, electronic submissions via disk or modem.

Illustration: Works with 25 illustrators/year. Uses color artwork only. Reviews ms/illustration packages from artists. Send ms with dummy. Contact: Sam Laredo. Illustrations only: Send tearsheets. Contact: Raquel Benatar. Responds in 3 weeks. Samples not returned; samples filed.

Terms: Pays authors royalty of 5-10% based on retail price. Pays illustrators by the project. Sends galleys to authors; dummies to illustrators. Originals returned to artist at job's completion. Book catalog available for 9×12 SASE and $3 postage. All imprints included in a single catalog. Catalog available on website.

RISING MOON, P.O. Box 1389, Flagstaff AZ 86002-1389. (928)774-5251. Fax: (928)774-0592. E-mail: editorial@northlandpub.com. Website: www.northlandpub.com. Book publisher. **Manuscript Acquisitions:** Theresa Howell, editor. **Art Acquisitions:** Address to Art Director. Publishes 10-12 picture books/year; 10% of books by first-time authors. "Rising Moon is looking for stories with broad subjects, wide appeal, universal themes, and exceptional bilingual (Spanish/English) stories. Southwest Kids is looking for original stories with a Southwest flavor, fractured fairy tales and board books."

How to Contact/Writers: Rising Moon is accepting picture book mss from agented authors and previously published authors only; Southwest Kids is now accepting unsolicited picture book mss. We are no longer publishing middle-grade children's fiction. Please submit the entire ms for children's picture books, include a cover letter with information regarding any previously published work, and provide a self-addressed, stamped envelope (SASE) of adequate size and postage with your submission. No e-mail submissions.

Illustration: Works with 8-10 illustrators/year. Uses color artwork only. Reviews illustration packages from artists. Submit color samples (printed/color lasers) to art director with résumé, samples, promo sheet, slides, tearsheets. Samples returned with SASE only.

Terms: Pays authors royalty based on retail or wholesale price. Pays illustrators by the project or royalty based on retail or wholesale price. Sends galleys to authors; dummies to illustrators. Originals returned at job's completion. Visit our website at www.northlandpub.com for writer's and artist's guidelines and complete catalog.

ROARING BROOK PRESS, Imprint of The Millbrook Press, 2 Old New Milford Rd., Brookfield CT 06804. (203)740-2220. Fax: (203)775-5643. Estab. 2000. Specializes in fiction, trade books. **Manuscript Acquisitions:** Simon Boughton. Query only with SASE. **Art Acquisitions:** Simon Boughton. Publishes approximately 40 titles/year. 1% of books by first-time authors. This publisher's goal is "to publish distinctive high-quality children's literature for all ages. To be a great place for authors to be published. To provide personal attention and a focused and thoughtful publishing effort for every book and every author on the list."

Fiction: Picture books, young readers, middle readers, young adults: adventure, animal, contemporary, fantasy, history, humor, multicultural, nature/environment, poetry, religion, science fiction, sports, suspense/mystery. Recently published *Get to Work, Trucks*, by Don Carter (preschool, picture book); *Across a Dark, Wild Sea*, by Don Brown (grades 1-4, picture book); and *Objects in Mirror*, by Ronder Thomas Young (grades 6-9, young adult novel).

How to Contact/Writer: Primarily interested in agented material. Not accepting unsolicited mss or queries. Will consider simultaneous submissions.

Illustration: Primarily interested in agented material. Works with 25 illustrators/year. Contact: Simon Boughton, publisher. Illustrations only: Query with samples. Do not send original art; copies only through the mail. Contact: Simon Boughton, publisher. Responds to agented queries/submissions in 1 month; unsolicited in 3 months. Samples returned with SASE.

Photography: Works on assignment only.

Terms: Pays authors royalty based on retail price. Pays illustrators royalty or flat fee depending on project. Sends galleys to authors; dummies to illustrators, if requested.

Tips: "You should find a reputable agent and have him/her submit your work."

RONSDALE PRESS, 3350 W. 21st Ave., Vancouver, British Columbia V6S 1G7 Canada. (604)738-4688. Fax: (604)731-4548. E-mail: ronhatch@pinc.com. Website: ronsdalepress.com. Book publisher. Estab. 1988. **Manuscript/Art Acquisitions:** Veronica Hatch, children's editor. Publishes 2 children's books/year. 80% of titles by first-time authors. "Ronsdale Press is a Canadian literary publishing house that publishes 8 to 10 books each year, two of which are children's titles. Of particular interest are books involving children exploring and discovering new aspects of Canadian history."
Fiction: Middle readers, young adults: Canadian historical novels. Average word length: for middle readers and young adults—40,000. Recently published *The Tenth Pupil*, by Constance Horne (ages 9-14); *Beginnings*, edited by Ann Walsh (anthology of short stories, ages 9 and up); *Eyewitness*, by Margaret Thompson (ages 8-14); and *Hurricanes over London*, by Charles Reid (ages 8-14).
Nonfiction: Middle readers, young adults: animal, biography, history, multicultural, social issues. Average word length: young readers—90; middle readers—90.
How to Contact/Writers: Fiction/Nonfiction: Submit complete ms. Responds to queries in 2 weeks; ms in 2 months. Publishes a book 1 year after acceptance. Will consider simultaneous submissions.
Illustrations: Works with 2 illustrators/year. Reviews ms/illustration packages from artists. Requires only cover art. Responds in 2 weeks. Samples returned with SASE. Originals returned to artist at job's completion.
Terms: Pays authors royalty of 10% based on retail price. Pays illustrators by the project $800-1,200. Sends galleys to authors. Book catalog available for 8½×11 SAE and $1 postage; ms and art guidelines available for SASE.
Tips: "Ronsdale Press publishes well-written books that have a new slant on things or books that can take an age-old story and give it a new spin. We are particularly interested in novels for middle readers and young adults with a historical component that offers new insights into a part of Canada's history. We publish only Canadian authors."

THE ROSEN PUBLISHING GROUP INC., 29 E. 21st St., New York NY 10010. (212)777-3017. Fax: (212)777-0277. E-mail: rosened@erols.com. Website: www.rosenpub.com. **Art Acquisitions:** Cindy Reiman, photo director. Imprints: Rosen (Young Adult) (Iris Rosoff, editorial director); Rosen Central (Iris Rosoff, editorial director); PowerKids Press (Kristin Eck, editorial director).
Nonfiction: Picture books: biography, health, hi-lo, nature/environment, science, self-help, social issues, special needs. Young readers: biography, health, hi-lo, multicultural, nature/environment, science, self-help, social issues, special needs. Middle readers: biography, careers, health, multicultural, nature/environment, science, self-help, social issues, special needs. Young adult: careers, health, multicultural, science, self-help. Average word length: young readers—800-950; middle readers—5,000-7,500; young adults—between 8,000 and 30,000. Recently published *Body Talk: A Girl's Guide to What's Happening to Your Body*.
How to Contact/Writers: Nonfiction: Query with outline/synopsis and sample chapter as well as SASE. No unsolicited mss, no phone calls.
Photography: Buys stock and assigns work. Contact: Cindy Reiman, photo manager.
Terms: Pays flat fee or royalty, depending on book.
Tips: "Our list is specialized, and we publish only in series. Authors should familiarize themselves with our publishing program and policies before submitting."

ST. ANTHONY MESSENGER PRESS, 1615 Republic St., Cincinnati OH 45210-1298. (513)241-5615. Fax: (513)241-0399. E-mail: books@americancatholic.org. Website: www.AmericanCatholic.org. Book publisher. Managing Editor: Lisa Biedenbach. **Manuscript Acquisitions:** Katie Carroll. 25% of books by first-time authors. Imprints include Franciscan Communications (print and video) and Ikonographics (video). "Through print and electronic media marketed in North America and worldwide, we endeavor to evangelize, inspire and inform those who search for God and seek a richer Catholic, Christian, human life. We also look for books for parents and religious educators."
Fiction: "We are not currently accepting queries."
Nonfiction: Picture books, young readers, middle readers, young adults: religion. "We like all our resources to include anecdotes, examples, etc., that appeal to a wide audience. All of our products try to reflect cultural and racial diversity. All our books must be explicitly Catholic." Recently published *Friend Jesus: Prayers for Children*, by Gaynell Bordes Cronin; *Growing Up a Friend of Jesus: A Guide for Discipleship for Children*, by Francoise Darcy-Berube and John Paul Berube (middle readers); *Can You Find Jesus? Introducing Your Child to the Gospel*, by Philip Gallery and Janet Harlow (ages 5-10); *People of the Bible: Their Life and Customs*, by Claire Musatti (ages 5-10).
How to Contact/Writers: Query or submit outline/synopsis and sample chapters. Responds to queries in 6 weeks; mss in 2 months. Publishes a book 12-18 months after acceptance.

insider report

Orange juice, ideas & discipline: a bestselling author's power breakfast

"Dress your imaginary person everyday, grab her by the hair and drop her into a conflict," says award-winning children's writer Patricia Reilly Giff. "As long as you allow flexibility in her voice, she will inevitably figure out the rest." While Giff has published more than 90 books, she sustains a school bus full of ideas for future picture books, historical fiction novels and another riveting detective series. Giff insists the befitting key to her success has been nothing other than productivity.

From the Newbery Honor-winning book, *Lily's Crossing*, to the engaging Polk Street School vignettes, Giff has dazzled young audiences all over the world since she began "talking on paper obsessively" years ago in a makeshift closet-office. While she no longer writes propped up against clothing shelves, Giff is a

Patricia Reilly Giff

dedicated morning writer and matron of cherished characters. The imaginary individuals she's tugged by the hair and toppled into a conflict have incorporated pirate queens and Poopsie Pomerantz, candy corn contest winners and cool-itch kids, man-eating rodents and monster rabbits—all who ultimately come together to prove that ordinary people are special. "After shifting my hours of writing in a cramped (but nurturing) cubbyhole with one window to the spacious family room or outdoor veranda, the process is no different today than years ago," says Giff. "As long as I continue to write each morning, a story unfolds that someone will relate to."

Whether the action takes place at a pet parade or in a bowl of alphabet soup, each of Giff's books is based on personal experiences or tales students relayed during her 20 years as an elementary school teacher. Before embarking on a fulltime writing career, Giff earned an M.A. from St. John's University, a Professional Diploma in Reading and a Doctorate of Humane Letters from Hofstra University, which were achieved alongside teaching and family responsibilities. Once she decided to immerse herself in writing children's literature instead of only reading and interpreting it, Giff retired from teaching. Now, as an education consultant for Dell Yearling and Young Yearling Books, as well as an adviser and instructor to aspiring children's writers, Giff is satisfied with her modified roles involving children's literacy and cultural enrichment.

Also a guest speaker at multiple conferences, schools and libraries, another tag on this writer's industrious schedule includes the co-partnership of The Dinosaur's Paw, a children's bookstore named after one of her Kids of the Polk Street School novels. At the store, Giff facilitates a writing course for adults and oversees the Grandparent's Club, a group of subscribers who receive monthly book selections.

When asked if the Grandparents Club, her young readers, parents, or other writers may influence the stories she creates, Giff says, "Well, it's no secret that the essence of childhood influences me. The pictures I depict are all based on the joys and sorrows of growing up.

"If I have a hard time conjuring up an idea, I concentrate hard and mentally plant myself in second or third grade like I had during my first exciting hours of 'dressing characters.' Those days I bought that core time for myself," explains Giff. "Back then I made sure the kids had their milk money and lunches packed the night before." And today, Giff hides "*The New York Times*, Amazon book reviews or the 20th version of *Little Women*," until the allocated time has been spent on writing. Once she is satisfied with the result—"satisfied, not necessarily ecstatic each round"—she takes care of returning business calls, examining reviews and preparing for speaking engagements.

Along the way of militantly regimenting a writing schedule, Giff says the four editors she's collaborated with over the years have also spurred her dedication. Whether teaming up on a quick-phrased, whimsical picture book or well-researched, emotional historical novel, each editor has enriched Giff's professional and personal life. Proudly, she cites no complaints or misfortunes concerning her author-editor alliances—"even during a cranky morning or two."

While Giff has attained a world of success through creating early reader and young adult books, she claims that hard work is precisely why she is published, not an aggressive editor, staggering talent or a gamut of writing courses she mastered in college. After all, 90 books indicate a lot of revisions, among other related obligations. Thus, as you are formulating sentences in your own closet-office, cubicle or country cottage, remember Poopsie Pomerantz's creator's advice: "Write now! You do have the time each day, as little or lots—shortcuts, such as dreadful procrastination, are not optional."

—*Candi Lace*

Author of over 90 books, Patricia Reilly Giff dropped her latest character into a big conflict. In *Pictures of Hollis Woods* (Wendy Lamb Books), Hollis Woods is an abandoned 12-year-old girl torn between her desire to run away with her elderly, forgetful guardian and her longing for the Regans, the one family that offered her a home. Giff says that while she no longer writes inside a closet-office, her actual writing process has not changed throughout the years.

pictures of hollis woods

PATRICIA REILLY GIFF
Author of the Newbery Honor Book *Lily's Crossing*

Photo: Clarissa Leahy. Design Kenny Holcomb. Reprinted with permission of Random House.

Illustration: Works with 2 illustrators/year. "We design all covers and do most illustrations in-house, unless illustrations are submitted with text." Reviews ms/illustration packages from artists. Query with samples, résumé. Contact: Jeanne Kortekamp, art director. Responds to queries in 1 month. Samples returned with SASE; samples filed. Originals returned at job's completion.

Photography: Purchases photos from freelancers. Contact: Jeanne Kortekamp, art director. Buys stock and assigns work.

Terms: Pays authors royalties of 10-12% based on net receipts. Offers average advance payment of $1,000. Pays illustrators by the project. Pays photographers by the project. Sends galleys to authors. Book catalog and ms guidelines free on request.

Tips: "Know our audience—Catholic. We seek popularly written manuscripts that include the best of current Catholic scholarship. Parents, especially baby boomers, want resources for teaching children about the Catholic faith for passing on values. We try to publish items that reflect strong Catholic Christian values."

SCHOLASTIC CANADA LTD., 175 Hillmount Rd., Markham, Ontario L6C 1Z7 Canada. (905)887-READ. Fax: (905)887-1131. Website: www.scholastic.ca; for ms/artist guidelines: www.scholastic.ca/guideline.html. Imprints: North Winds Press; Les Éditions Scholastic. **Acquisitions:** Editor, children's books. Publishes hardcover and trade paperback originals. Publishes 30 titles/year; imprint publishes 4 titles/year. 3% of books from first-time authors; 50% from unagented writers. Canadian authors, theme or setting required.

Fiction: Children's/juvenile, young adult. Recently published *Dear Canada, with Nothing but Our Courage*, by Karleen Bradford (ages 8 and up, edited by Sandy Bogart Johnston); *After the War*, by Carol Matas (novel).

Nonfiction: Animals, history, hobbies, nature, recreation, science, sports. Reviews artwork/photos as part of ms package. Send photocopies. Recently published *Whose Bright Idea Was It?*, by Larry Verstraete (about amazing inventions).

How to Contact/Writers: Query with synopsis, 3 sample chapters and SASE. Nonfiction: Query with outline, 1-2 sample chapters and SASE (IRC or Canadian stamps only). Responds in 3 months. Publishes book 1 year after acceptance.

Terms: Pays 5-10% royalty on retail price. Offers advance: $1,000-5,000 (Canadian). Book catalog for 8½×11 SAE with 2 first-class stamps (IRC or Canadian stamps only).

SCHOLASTIC INC., 555 Broadway, New York NY 10012. (212)343-6100. Website: www.scholastic.com.

• Scholastic does not accept unsolicited manuscripts. Their title *The Dinosaurs of Waterhouse Hawkins*, illustrated by Brian Selznick, text by Barbara Kerley, won a 2002 Caldecott Honor.

Illustration: Works with 50 illustrators/year. Does not review ms/illustration packages. Illustrations only: send promo sheet and tearsheets. Responds only if interested. Samples not returned. Original artwork returned at job's completion.

Terms: All contracts negotiated individually; pays royalty. Sends galleys to author; dummies to illustrators.

SCHOLASTIC PRESS, 557 Broadway, New York NY 10012. (212)343-6100. Website: www.scholastic.com. Book publisher. Imprint of Scholastic Inc. **Manuscript Acquisitions:** Dianne Hess, executive editor (picture book fiction/nonfiction); Lauren Thompson, senior editor (picture book fiction/nonfiction); Tracy Mack, executive editor (picture book, middle grade, YA). **Art Acquisitions:** David Saylor, Scholastic Press, Reference, Paperback. Publishes 60 titles/year. 1% of books by first-time authors.

Fiction: Looking for strong picture books, middle grade novels (ages 8-11) and interesting and well written young adult novels. Not looking for any more fiction series.

Nonfiction: Interested "unusual approaches to commonly dry subjects, such as biography, math, history or science."

How to Contact/Writers: Fiction/nonfiction: "Send query with 1 sample chapter and synopsis. Don't call!" Picture books: submit complete ms.

Illustrations: Works with 30 illustrators/year. Uses both b&w and color artwork. Contact: Art Director. Illustration only: Query with samples; send tearsheets. Responds only if interested. Samples returned with SASE. Original artwork returned at job's completion.

Terms: Pays authors by varying royalty (usually standard trade roles) or outright purchase (rarely). Offers variable advance. Pays illustrators by the project (range: varies) or standard royalty based on retail price.

Tips: "Read *currently* published children's books. Revise, rewrite, rework and find your own voice, style and subject. We are looking for authors with a strong and unique voice who can tell a great story and have the ability to evoke genuine emotion. Children's publishers are becoming more selective, looking for irresistable talent and fairly broad appeal, yet still very willing to take risks, just to keep the game interesting."

SEEDLING PUBLICATIONS, INC., 4522 Indianola Ave., Columbus OH 43214-2246. (614)267-7333. Fax: (614)267-4205.Website: www.SeedlingPub.com. **Acquisitions:** Josie Stewart. 20% of books by first-time authors. Publishes books for the beginning reader in English. "Natural language and predictable text are requisite to our publications. Patterned text is acceptable, but must have a unique storyline. Poetry, books in rhyme, full-length picture books or chapter books are not being accepted at this time. Illustrations are not necessary."

Fiction: Beginning reader books: adventure, animal, fantasy, hi-lo, humor, multicultural, nature/environment, special needs. Multicultural needs include stories which include children from many cultures and Hispanic-centered storylines. Does not accept texts longer than 16 pages or over 150-200 words or stories in rhyme. Average word length: young readers—100. Recently published *Yoshiko's Surprise*, by Clare Mishica; *In Search of Something Delicious*, by Betty Erickson.

Nonfiction: Beginning reader books: animal, concept, hi-lo, multicultural, music/dance, nature/environment, science, special needs, sports. Does not accept texts longer than 16 pages or over 150-200 words. Average word length: young readers—100. Recently published *Gerbils Measure Up*, by Josie Stewart and Lynn Salem (ages 3-7, early reader).

How to Contact/Writers: Fiction/Nonfiction: Submit complete ms. Responds in 6 months. Publishes a book 1-2 years after acceptance. Will consider simultaneous submissions.

Illustration: Works with 4-5 illustrators/year. Uses color artwork only. Reviews ms/illustration packages from artists. Submit ms with dummy. Illustrations only: Send color copies. Responds only if interested. Samples returned with SASE only; samples filed if interested.

Photography: Buys photos from freelancers. Works on assignment only. Model/property releases required. Uses color prints and 35mm transparencies. Submit cover letter and color promo piece.

Terms: Pays authors royalty of 5% based on retail price or work purchased outright. Pays illustrators and photographers by the project. Original artwork is not returned at job's completion. Book catalog available with postage for 3 ounces.

Tips: "Follow our guidelines carefully and test your story with children and educators."

SILVER MOON PRESS, 160 Fifth Ave., New York NY 10010. (212)242-6499. Fax: (212)242-6799. E-mail: mail@silvermoonpress.com. Website: www.silvermoonpress.com. Publisher: David Katz. Managing Editor: Hope Killcoyne. **Marketing Coordinator:** Karin Lillebo. Book publisher. Publishes 2 books for grades 4-6. 25% of books by first-time authors; 10% books from agented authors. "We publish books of entertainment and educational value and develop books which fit neatly into curriculum for grades 4-6. Silver Moon Press publishes mainly American historical fiction with a strong focus on the Revolutionary War and Colonial times. History comes alive when children can read about other children who lived when history was being made!"

Fiction: Middle readers: historical, multicultural and mystery. Average word length: 14,000. Recently published *A Message for General Washington*, by Vivian Schurfranz; and *A Secret Party in Boston Harbor*, by Kris Hemphill (both historical fiction, ages 8-12); *Treason Stops at Oyster Bay*, by Anna Leah Sweetzer.

How to Contact/Writers: Fiction: Query. Send synopsis and/or a few chapters, along with a SASE. Responds to queries in 1 month; mss in 2 months. Publishes a book 1-2 years after acceptance. Will consider simultaneous submissions, or previously published work.

Illustration: Works with 2-3 illustrators/year. Reviews ms/illustration packages from artists. Query. Illustrations only: Query with samples, résumé, client list. Responds only if interested. Samples returned with SASE; samples filed. Original artwork returned at job's completion.

Photography: Buys photos from freelancers. Buys stock and assigns work. Uses archival, historical, sports photos. Captions required. Uses color, b&w prints; 35mm, 2¼×2¼, 4×5, 8×10 transparencies. Submit cover letter, résumé, published samples, client list, promo piece.

Terms: Pays authors royalty or work purchased outright. Pays illustrators by the project, no royalty. Pays photographers by the project, per photo, no royalty. Sends galleys to authors; dummies to illustrators. Book catalog available for 8½×11 SAE and 77¢ postage.

SIMON & SCHUSTER BOOKS FOR YOUNG READERS, 1230 Avenue of the Americas, New York NY 10020. (212)698-7000. Fax: (212)698-2796. E-mail: childrens.submissions@simonandschuster.c om. Website: www.simonsayskids.com. Imprint of Simon & Schuster Children's Publishing Division. **Manuscript Acquisitions:** David Gale, editorial director, Kevin Lewis, senior editor; Jessica Schulte, editor. **Art Acquisitions:** Dan Petash, art director. Publishes 75 books/year. "We publish high-quality fiction and nonfiction for a variety of age groups and a variety of markets. Above all we strive to publish books that will offer kids a fresh perspective on their world."

● Simon & Schuster Books for Young Readers does not accept unsolicited manuscripts. Queries are accepted via mail and e-mail.

Fiction: Picture books: animal, concept. Middle readers, young adult: adventure, suspense/mystery. All levels: anthology, contemporary, history, humor, poetry, nature/environment. Recently published *Giggle, Giggle, Quack*, by Doreen Cronin, illustration by Betsy Lewin (picture book, ages 3-7); *Gingerbread*, by Rachel Cohn (young adult fiction, ages 13 and up).

Nonfiction: All levels: biography, history, nature/environment. Picture books: concept. "We're looking for picture book or middle grade nonfiction that has a retail potential. No photo essays." Recently published *America: A Patriotic Primer*, by Lynne Cheney, illustrated by Robin Preiss Glasser (picture book nonfiction, all ages).

How to Contact/Writers: Accepting query letters only, preferably by e-mail. Please note the appropriate imprint in the subject line. Responds to queries/mss in 2 months. Publishes a book 2-4 years after acceptance. Will consider simultaneous submissions.

Illustration: Works with 70 illustrators/year. Do not submit original artwork. Editorial reviews ms/illustration packages from artists. Submit query letter to Submissions Editor. Illustrations only: Query with samples; samples filed. Provide promo sheet, tearsheets. Responds only if interested. Originals returned at job's completion.

Terms: Pays authors royalty (varies) based on retail price. Pays illustrators or photographers by the project or royalty (varies) based on retail price. Original artwork returned at job's completion. Manuscript/artist's guidelines available via website or free on request (call (212)698-2707).

Tips: "We're looking for picture books centered on a strong, fully-developed protagonist who grows or changes during the course of the story; YA novels that are challenging and psychologically complex; also imaginative and humorous middle-grade fiction. And we want nonfiction that is as engaging as fiction. Our imprint's slogan is 'Reading You'll Remember.' We aim to publish books that are fresh, accessible and family-oriented; we want them to have an impact on the reader."

SOMERVILLE HOUSE INC., 24 Dinnick Crescent, Toronto, Ontario M4N 1L5 Canada. (416)489-7769. Fax: (416)486-4458. E-mail: somer@sympatico.ca. Website: www.somervillehouse.com. Somerville publishes books and develops products and is an expert in merging media for the Youth and Family markets—the web, wireless phones, pagers, electronic games, handheld personal computers, books and toys. **Acquisitions and Business Development:** Jane Somerville, publisher/president. Produces 5-10 titles/year in nonfiction and novelty formats.

● Somerville is currently accepting unsolicited mss in the areas of natural science, activities, sports and novelty formats.

Nonfiction: Recently published *The Hummingbird Book and Feeder*, by Neil Dawe; and *The Titantic Book and Submersible Model*, by Steve Santini.

How to Contact/Writers: Only interested in agented material. Responds to queries/mss in 3 months.

Illustration: Works with 20-30 illustrators/year. Responds only if interested. Samples not returned; samples filed.

SOUNDPRINTS, 353 Main Ave., Norwalk CT 06851-1552. (203)846-2274. Fax: (203)846-1776. E-mail: soundprints@soundprints.com. Website: www.soundprints.com. Estab. 1987. Specializes in trade books, educational material, multicultural material, fact-based fiction. **Manuscript Acquisitions:** Chelsea Shriver, assistant editor. **Art Acquisitions:** Marcin Pilchowski. Publishes 4 picture books/year; 8 young readers/year. Soundprints publishes children's books accompanied by plush toys and read-along cassettes that deal with wildlife, history and nature. All content must be accurate and realistic and is curated by experts for veracity. Soundprints will begin publishing early reader chapter books in the spring of 2002.

Fiction: Picture books: animal. Young readers: animal, multicultural, nature/environment. Middle readers: history, multicultural.

Nonfiction: Picture books: animals. Young readers: animal, multicultural, nature/environment. Middle readers: history, multicultural. *Koala Country: Story of an Australian Eucalyptus Forest*, by Deborah Dennard, illustrated by James McKinnon (grades 1-4); *Box Turtle at Silver Pond*, by Susan Korman, illustrated by Stephen Marchesi (grades ps-2); *Bear on His Own*, by Laura Gales Gatvin (ages 18 months to 3 years).

How to Contact/Writers: Fiction/Nonfiction: Submit published writing samples. Responds in 3 months. Publishes book 2 years after acceptance.

Illustration: Works with 12 illustrators/year. Uses color artwork only. Query. Contact: Chelsea Shriver, assistant editor. Query with samples. Samples not returned.

Terms: Work purchased outright from authors for $1,000-2,500. Pays illustrators by the project. Book catalog available for 8½×11 SASE; ms and art guidelines available for SASE. Catalog available on website.

Tips: "As a small publisher with very specific guidelines for our well-defined series, we are not able to accept unsolicited manuscripts for publication. All of our authors are contracted on a 'work for hire basis,' meaning that they create manuscripts to our specifications, depending on our need. While we generally work with an established group of authors who know our needs as a publisher, we are always interested in reviewing the work of new potential authors. If you would like to submit some published writing samples, we would be happy to review them and keep them on file for future reference. Please send all writing smaples to Chelsea Shriver, assistant editor."

SOURCEBOOKS, INC., 1935 Brookdale Rd., Suite 139, Naperville IL 60563-9245. (630)961-3900. Fax: (630)961-2168. Website: www.sourcebooks.com. Book publisher. **Manuscript Acquisitions:** Todd Stocke, editorial director; Hillel Black, agented manuscripts; Deborah Werksman, gift, humor, relationships. **Art Acquisitions:** Norma Underwood, director of production.
How to Contact/Writers: Fiction/Nonfiction: Query or submit outline/synopsis. Responds to queries/ mss in 3 months. Publishes a book 1 year after acceptance. Will consider simultaneous submissions, electronic submissions via disk or modem and previously published work.
Illustration: Works with 10 illustrators/year. Reviews ms/illustration packages from artists. Query. Illustrations only: Query with samples. Samples returned with SASE; samples filed.
Photography: Buys stock.
Terms: Send galleys to authors. Originals returned to artist at job's completion. Book catalog for 9×12 SASE. All imprints included in a single catalog. Manuscript guidelines available for SASE or via website.

THE SPEECH BIN, INC., 1965 25th Ave., Vero Beach FL 32960. (561)770-0007. Fax: (561)770-0006. Book publisher. Estab. 1984. **Acquisitions:** Jan J. Binney, senior editor. Publishes 10-12 books/year. 50% of books by first-time authors; less than 15% of books from agented writers. "Nearly all our books deal with treatment of children (as well as adults) who have communication disorders of speech or hearing or children who deal with family members who have such disorders (e.g., a grandparent with Alzheimer's disease or stroke)."
   • The Speech Bin is currently overstocked with fiction.
Fiction: Picture books: animal, easy-to-read, health, special needs. Young readers, middle readers, young adult: health, special needs, communication disorders.
Nonfiction: Picture books, young readers, middle readers, young adults: activity books, health, textbooks, special needs, communication disorders.
How to Contact/Writers: Fiction/Nonfiction: Query. Responds to queries in 6 weeks; mss in 3 months. Publishes a book 10-12 months after acceptance. "Will consider simultaneous submissions *only* if notified; too many authors fail to let us know if manuscript is simultaneously submitted to other publishers! We *strongly* prefer sole submissions. No electronic or faxed submissions."
Illustration: Works with 4-5 illustrators/year ("usually in-house"). Reviews ms/illustration packages from artists. Manuscript/illustration packages and illustration only: "Query first!" Submit tearsheets (no original art). SASE required for reply or return of material. No electronic or faxed submissions without prior authorization.
Photography: Buys stock and assigns work. Looking for scenic shots. Model/property releases required. Uses glossy b&w prints, 35mm or 2¼×2¼ transparencies. Submit résumé, business card, promotional literature or tearsheets to be kept on file.
Terms: Pays authors in royalties based on selling price. Pay illustrators by the project. Photographers paid by the project or per photo. Sends galleys to authors. Original artwork returned at job's completion. Book catalog for $1.43 postage and 9×12 SAE; ms guidelines for #10 SASE.
Tips: "No calls, please. All submissions and inquiries must be in writing."

STANDARD PUBLISHING, 8121 Hamilton Ave., Cincinnati OH 45231. (513)931-4050. Fax: (513)931-0950. E-mail: customerservice@standardpub.com. Website: www.standardpub.com. Book publisher. Estab. 1866. Managing Director Consumer Product: Diane Stortz. **Manuscript Acquisitions:** Ruth Frederick, children's ministry director. **Art Acquisitions:** Coleen Davis, art director; Rob Glover, consumer product senior designer. Many projects are written in-house. No juvenile or young adult novels. 25-40% of books by first-time authors; 1% of books from agented writers. Publishes picture books, board book, nonfiction, devotions and resources for teachers.
Fiction: Recently published: *Jesus Must Be Really Special*, by Jennie Bishop, illustrated by Amy Wumman.
Nonfiction: Recently published *Playtime Devotions*, by Christine Tangvald, illustrated by Tamara Schmitz.

How to Contact/Writers: Responds in 6 weeks to queries, mss in 3 months.
Illustration: Works with 20 new illustrators/year. Illustrations only: Submit cover letter and photocopies. Responds to art samples only if interested. Samples returned with SASE; samples filed.
Terms: Pays authors royalties based on net price or work purchased outright (range varies by project). Pays illustrators (mostly) by project. Pays photographers by the photo. Sends galleys to authors on most projects. Book catalog available for $2 and 8½×11 SAE; ms guidelines for letter-size SASE.
Tips: "We look for manuscripts that help draw children into a relationship with Jesus Christ; help children develop insights about what the Bible teaches; make reading an appealing and pleasurable activity."

STEMMER HOUSE PUBLISHERS, INC., 2627 Caves Rd., Owings Mills MD 21117-9919. (410)363-3690. Fax: (410)363-8459. E-mail: stemmerhouse@home.com. Website: www.stemmer.com. Book publisher. Estab. 1975. **Acquisitions:** Barbara Holdridge, president. Publishes 1-3 picture books/year. "Sporadic" numbers of young reader, middle reader titles/year. 60% of books by first-time authors. "Stemmer House is best known for its commitment to fine illustrated books, excellently produced."
  • Stemmer House is not currently accepting fiction.
Nonfiction: Picture books: animal, multicultural, nature. All level: animals, nature/environment. Multicultural needs include Native American, African. Recently published *Will You Sting Me? Will You Bite?*, by Sarah Swan Miller.
How to Contact/Writers: Fiction/Nonfiction: Query or submit outline/synopsis and sample chapters. Responds only with SASE. Responds to queries/mss in 1 week. Publishes a book 18 months after acceptance. Will consider simultaneous submissions. No submissions via e-mail.
Illustration: Works with 2-3 illustrators/year. Uses color artwork only. Reviews ms/illustration packages from artists. Query first with several photocopied illustrations. Illustrations only: Submit tearsheets and/or slides (with SASE for return). Responds in 2 weeks. Samples returned with SASE; samples filed "if noteworthy."
Terms: Pays authors royalties of 4-10% based on net sales price. Offers average advance payment of $300. Pays illustrators royalty of 4-10% based on net sales price. Pays photographers 4-10% royalty based on net sales price. Sends galleys to authors. Original artwork returned at job's completion. Book catalog and ms guidelines for 9×12 SASE or via website.
Tips: Writers: "Simplicity, literary quality and originality are the keys." Illustrators: "We want to see ms/illustration packages—don't forget the SASE!"

SUPER MANAGEMENT, Smarty Pants A/V, 15104 Detroit, Suite 2, Lakewood OH 44107-3916. (216)221-5300. Fax: (216)221-5348. Estab. 1988. Specializes in mass market books, fiction, educational material, Christian material, audio with each book. **Acquisitions:** S. Tirk, CEO/President. Publishes 12 young readers/year. 5% of books by first-time authors. "We do mostly the classics or well known names such as Paddington Bear."
Fiction: Picture books: adventure, animal, folktales, multicultural, nature/environment, poetry. Average word length: young readers—24 pages. Recently published *The Best of Mother Goose*, from the "Real M.G."; *Beatrix Potter*, *Paddington Bear*.
Nonfiction: Picture books, young readers: activity books, animal, music/dance, nature/environment. Average word length: picture books—24 pages; middle readers—24 pages.
How to Contact/Writers: Fiction: Submit complete ms. Responds in 3 weeks. Publishes a book 6-12 months after acceptance. Will consider simultaneous submissions and previously published work.
Illustration: Only interested in agented material. Works with several illustrators/year. Uses color artwork only. Reviews ms/illustration packages from artists. Submit ms with dummy with return prepaid envelope. Contact: S. Tirk, CEO/President. Illustrations only: send promo sheet. Responds in 3 weeks to queries. Samples returned with SASE.
Photography: Works on assignment only. Model/property releases required. Uses color prints. Submit color promo piece.
Terms: Pays author negotiable royalty. Buys artwork and photos outright. Manuscript and art guidelines available for SASE.
Tips: "We deal with mostly children's classics and well-known characters."

TEACHER IDEAS PRESS, Libraries Unlimited, P.O. Box 6633, Englewood CO 80155-6633. (303)770-1220. Fax: (303)220-8843. E-mail: lu-books@lu.com. Website: www.lu.com/tip. Estab. 1965. Specializes in educational material, multicultural material. Independent book packager/producer.
Nonfiction: Young readers, middle readers, young adult: activity books, multicultural, reference, teacher resource books. Recently published *Science Through Children's Literature, 2002*, by Butzow (grades K-

6, lit-based activity book); *More Novels & Plays: 30 Creative Teaching Guides for Grades 6-12*, by Worthington; and *Native American Today: Resources & Activities for Educators*, by Hirschfelder (grades 4-8).

How to Contact/Writers: Nonfiction: Query or submit outline/synopsis. Responds to queries in 6 weeks. Publishes a book 6-9 months after acceptance. Will consider simultaneous submissions or electronic submissions via disk or modem.

Terms: Pays authors royalty of 10-15%. Send galleys to authors. Book catalog available for 9×12 SASE and 3 first-class stamps. Writer's guidelines available for SASE. Catalog and ms guidelines available online at www.lu.com.

Tips: "We encourage queries from writers with classroom experience as teachers, although we will consider others. Activity Books, annotated bios, story collections with supplemental materials, and books with many reproducibles are welcome for consideration."

N ⚜ THISTLEDOWN PRESS LTD., 633 Main St., Saskatoon, Saskatchewan S7H 0J8 Canada. (306)244-1722. Fax: (306)244-1762. E-mail: tdpress@thistledown.sk.ca. Website: www.thistledown.sk.ca. Book publisher. **Manuscript Acquisitions:** Patrick O'Rourke, editor-in-chief; Jesse Stothers. **Art Acquisitions:** A.M. Forrie, art director. Publishes numerous middle reader and young adult titles/year. "Thistledown originates books by Canadian authors only, although we have co-published titles by authors outside Canada. We do not publish children's picture books."

Fiction: Middle readers, young adults: adventure, anthology, contemporary, fantasy, humor, poetry, romance, science fiction, suspense/mystery. Average word length: middle readers—35,000; young adults—40,000. Recently published *Up All Night*, edited by R.P. MacIntyre (YA anthology); *Alice, I Think*, by Susan Juby (YA novel); *Offside*, by Cathy Bereridge (YA novel).

How to Contact/Writers: Submit outline/synopsis and sample chapters. Responds to queries in 1 month, mss in 6 months. Publishes a book about one year after acceptance. No simultaneous submissions.

Illustration: Prefers agented illustrators but "not mandatory." Works with few illustrators. Illustrations only: Query with samples, promo sheet, slides, tearsheets. Responds only if interested. Samples returned with SASE; samples filed.

Terms: Pays authors royalty of 10-12% based on retail price. Pays illustrators and photographers by the project (range: $250-750). Sends galleys to authors. Original artwork returned at job's completion. Book catalog free on request. Manuscript guidelines for #10 envelope and IRC.

Tips: "Send cover letter including publishing history and SASE."

TILBURY HOUSE, PUBLISHERS, 2 Mechanic St., #3, Gardiner ME 04345. (207)582-1899. Fax: (207)582-8227. E-mail: tilbury@tilburyhouse.com. Website: www.tilburyhouse.com. Book publisher. Publisher: Jennifer Elliott. Publishes 1-3 young readers/year.

Fiction: Picture books, young readers, middle readers: multicultural, nature/environment. Special needs include books that teach children about tolerance and honoring diversity. Recently published *Shy Mama's Halloween*, by Anne Broyles, illustrated by Leane Morin; and *Lucy's Family Tree*, by Karen Halversen Shreck, illustrated by Stephen Gassler.

Nonfiction: Picture books, young readers, middle readers: multicultural, nature/environment. Recently published *Sea Soup: Zooplankton*, by Mary Cerullo, with photography by Bill Curtsinger; and *Shelterwood*, by Susan Hand Shetterly, illustrated by Rebecca Haley McCall.

How to Contact/Writers: Fiction/Nonfiction: Submit outline/synopsis. Responds to queries/mss in 1 month. Publishes a book 1-2 years after acceptance. Will consider simultaneous submissions "with notification."

Illustration: Works with 2 illustrators/year. Illustrations only: Query with samples. Contact: J. Elliott, associate publisher. Responds in 1 month. Samples returned with SASE. Original artwork returned at job's completion.

Photography: Buys photos from freelancers. Contact: J. Elliott, publisher. Works on assignment only.

Terms: Pays authors royalty based on wholesale price. Pays illustrators/photographers by the project; royalty based on wholesale price. Sends galleys to authors. Book catalog available for 6×9 SAE and 55¢ postage.

Tips: "We are primarily interested in children's books that teach children about tolerance in a multicultural society and honoring diversity. We are also interested in books that teach children about environmental issues."

✓ Ⓐ MEGAN TINGLEY BOOKS, Imprint of Little, Brown and Company, Time and Life Building, 1271 Avenue of the Americas, New York NY 10020. (212)572-8700. Website: www.twbookmark.com.

insider report

Working with talented people in a creative environment

If you happen to be in the greater Boston area on a Saturday morning, do yourself a favor and tune into 91.5 FM. There, on station WMFO, you just might catch the voice of children's book editor Megan Tingley.

Megan Tingley . . . on the radio? That's right. The Vice President/Editorial Director of Megan Tingley Books spends Saturday mornings co-hosting a show called Brand New Day from the Medford campus of Tufts University.

Spinning an eclectic mix of tunes might seem a radical departure from Tingley's day job. Actually, it's not such a stretch.

"Almost everything I like to do has to do with the process of editing—taking different elements and assembling them in a pleasing, compelling way," Tingley says. "I've recently taken up

Megan Tingley

gardening, which involves the same skills—pruning, nurturing, planting, replanting, finding that spot with just the right mixture of sun and rain."

Tingley, whose imprint was launched at Little, Brown in Spring 2000, is praised by industry insiders for her willingness to take chances on fresh ideas. Her Fall 2002 list includes a picture book with an actual purple feather inside (*The Perfect Purple Feather*, by Hanoch Piven) along with a memoir of a boy in a Sudanese refugee camp who goes on to graduate from Harvard (*Of Beetles & Angels*, by Mawi Asgedom).

Tingley is "willing to look at things from every angle," says bestselling artist/author Todd Parr, who has worked exclusively with Tingley since she "discovered" Parr at a New York licensing show. Tingley "sees what's underneath your work," Parr says. "If she believes in something, she gets behind it 200 percent. Maybe 300 percent."

Says Tingley: "I always love the process of working with talented people in a creative environment toward a final goal, whether it be opening night, a perfectly produced radio interview, or a book."

How did you first become interested in editing children's books?
From age 12 to 21, I worked with kids in various capacities—as a babysitter, camp counselor, teacher and reading tutor at a family homeless shelter. I had also always been an avid reader my whole life. I took some creative writing courses in college and quickly discovered I liked editing more than writing. I loved the workshop approach and seeing a story grow through the revision process.

When I graduated from Macalester College in 1986 with a degree in Comparative Literature, I felt I had two career options: teaching or editing. The first publishing job that came my way was as entry-level editorial assistant to Melanie Kroupa at Joy Street Books/Little, Brown.

Photo: Ben Willman

When I walked into her office stuffed with books, plants and toys and talked to her about publishing children's books, I realized I had found the perfect fit for me: kids + reading + editing!

What were some of your favorite books as a child?

My family lived in Paris while I was growing up (age 5 to 9) and during that time I had access mainly to European, especially British, children's books. The books that left the strongest impressions on me were probably from that period: *Winnie the Pooh*, *Babar*, and *Madeline*, of course, and then, as I got older, all the fairytale collections edited by Andrew Lang (*The Green Fairy Book*, *The Pink Fairy Book*, etc.), *The Chronicles of Narnia*, My Naughty Little Sister series (because I was a naughty little sister!), *Little Princess*, *Ballet Shoes* and all the boarding school novels by Enid Blyton. A real favorite was *James and the Giant Peach*. I must have read it 10

Illustration © 2002 Todd Parr. Reprinted with permission of Little, Brown.

Author/illustrator Todd Parr's latest Megan Tingley Books' title, *It's Okay to Be Different*, offers young readers insights like, "It's okay to eat macaroni and cheese in the bathtub." Parr, who works exclusively with Tingley, says she's "willing to look at things from every angle. If she believes in something, she gets behind it 200 percent. Maybe 300 percent."

times and I pored over every detail in Nancy Elkholm Burkert's exquisite black and white drawings. It's surprising to me that I loved fairytales, fantasies, and series fiction so much as a young reader and yet I'm not drawn to publishing these genres as an editor now.

There are a few picture books which stand out clearly from my childhood: *Harvey's Hideout*, by Russell Hoban; the Frances books, by Lillian Hoban; *Big Sister, Little Sister*, by Charlotte Zolotow; and *A Snowy Day*, by Ezra Jack Keats.

Who or what has been the greatest influence on your career?

I would say without a doubt it is my family. I could not have the career I have today without the rich cultural experiences I had in my childhood. My parents were huge readers and we always had lots of books around the house. For the years we lived in France, we only had an old black and white TV set and there were only one or two channels with mostly news, old movies, or the occasional variety show. There also wasn't nearly the emphasis on extra-curricular sports as there is in the States. So, we spent all our free time reading books or putting on plays, puppet shows, playing with dolls, etc.

In school in Paris, the writing assignments always had to be accompanied by an illustration and we were actually graded on the creativity and style of the pages. I recently rediscovered some of my old notebooks from third and fourth grade, and each page had a detailed hand-drawn map, a collage of photos from magazines, a picture to illustrate a poem, or a colorful border around the text. So, early on, I was introduced to the idea of putting pictures and words together.

Reprinted with permission of Little, Brown.

Working as an assistant editor in 1990, Megan Tingley first discovered Julie Ann Peters' work in the midst of the slush pile. Twelve years later, as Vice President/Editorial Director of Megan Tingley Books, Tingley and Peters have published six books together. Peters' latest is a YA love story about two girls, *Keeping You a Secret*, due out Spring 2003.

When we moved back to the States, we lived in a very small New Hampshire town of about 3,000 people. There wasn't much to do and my mother encouraged me to join a local theater company. That experience clearly inspired my sense of characters, drama, colors, style, pacing, tension, humor—all the things that make good children's books—as well as taught me how to work with creative people. Early exposure to museums, ballet, puppet shows, musicals, etc. all helped me develop my own personal taste and critical skills that inform my work as an editor.

What is the most rewarding aspect of your job?
Seeing writers and artists grow and develop their talent. I save everything—old letters, manuscripts, sketches—and it's just amazing to see where some people start out and where they end up.

What has been your most exciting slush pile discovery?
I found a first novel, a chapter book called *The Stinky Sneakers Contest*, by Julie Anne Peters, around 1990. I was an assistant editor at the time, and it was the first novel I ever discovered and edited. Of course, the funny title caught my attention right away as I thought kids would get a kick out of that concept and then the author's cover letter had a distinctive style, which is very unusual.

Julie has a very natural, humorous voice and it's the same in her letters and e-mails as it is in her fiction. Julie and I worked so hard on that book. Happily, we are still working together ten years later and have gone on to publish six more books. Her newest novel (*Keeping You A Secret*, due out in Spring 2003) is a YA love story between two girls. It's very satisfying to see her grow into this deeper genre—and she still always comes up with great titles!

How do you see the field evolving over the next ten years? Will children's books look the same as they do now?
I'd say children's books will still look the same over the next ten years, but the business of publishing will continue to evolve into an "adult book" publishing model. By that I mean acquiring books with the expectation that they must be financially successful in the first year. I wonder if books like *Harvey's Hideout* would be deemed "commercial" by publishing houses today?

Which part of your job would you most like to eliminate, if you could?
This one's easy: having to say "no" to so many writers and artists!
—*Barbara J. Odanaka*

Estab. 2000. Specializes in trade books, nonfiction, fiction, multicultural material. **Manuscript Acquisitions:** Alvina Ling, Mary Gruetzke. **Art Acquisitions:** Roslyn Lee, managing editor. Publishes 10 picture books/year; 1 middle readers/year; 1 young adult title/year. 2% of books by first-time authors.
● Megan Tingley Books accepts agented material only.
Fiction: Average word length: picture books—under 1,000 words. Recently published *You Read to Me, I'll Read to You: Very Short Stories to Read Together*, by Mary Ann Hoberman, illustrated by Michael Emberley (ages 4 and up, picture book); *It's Okay to be Different*, by Todd Parr (all ages, picture book); *Define Normal*, by Julie Peters.
Nonfiction: All levels: activity books, animal, arts/crafts, biography, concept, cooking, history, multicultural, music/dance, nature/environment, science, self help, social issues, special needs. Recently published *Twin Tales: The Magic & Mystery of Multiple Births*, by Donna Jackson (ages 10 and up, picture book); *Imaginative Inventions*, by Charise Harper (ages 4-8, picture book); *The Girls' Book of Friendship*, by Catherine Dee (ages 10 and up, middle reader).

How to Contact/Writers: Accepts agented material only. Query. Responds to mss in 3 months. Publishes a book 2 years after acceptance. Will consider simultaneous submissions, previously published work.

Illustration: Works with 15 illustrators/year. Reviews ms/illustration packages from artists. Query. Contact: Alvina Ling, assistant editor. Illustrations only: Query with samples. Contact: Alvina Ling, assistant editor. Responds only if interested. Samples not returned; samples kept on file.

Photography: Buys stock images. Contact: Alvina Ling, assistant editor. Submit cover letter, samples.

Terms: Pays authors royalty of 5% based on retail price or work purchased outright. Pays illustrators by the project, 5% royalty based on retail price. Pays photographers by the project, royalty 5% based on retail price. Sends galleys to authors. Originals returned to artist at job's completion. All imprints included in a single catalog. Book catalog and art guidelines available for SASE.

TRADEWIND BOOKS, 1809 Maritime Mews, Granville Island, Vancouver, British Columbia V6H 3W7 Canada.(604)662-4405. Fax: (604)730-0154. E-mail: tradewindbooks@eudoramail.com. Website: tradewindbooks.com. Estab. 1994. Trade book publisher. **Manuscript Acquisitions:** Michael Katz, publisher. **Art Acquisitions:** Carol Frank, art director. Publishes 3 picture books and 2 young adult titles/year. 25% of books by first-time authors.

Fiction: Picture books: adventure, animal, multicultural, folktales. Average word length: 900 words. Recently published *Huevos Rancheros*, written and illustrated by Stefan Czernecki; *Pigmalion*, by Glenda Leznoff, illustrated by Rachel Berman; *The Jade Necklace*, by Paul Lee, illustrated by Grace Lin.

Nonfiction: Picture books: animal and nature/environment.

How to Contact/Writers: Fiction: Submit complete ms. Will consider simultaneous submissions. Do not send query letter. Responds to mss in 6 weeks. Unsolicited submissions accepted only if authors have read a selection of books published by Tradewind Books. Submissions must include a reference to these books.

Illustration: Works with 3-4 illustrators/year. Uses color artwork only. Reviews ms/illustration packages from artists. Send ms with dummy. Illustrations only: Query with samples. Responds only if interested. Samples returned with SASE; samples filed.

Photography: Works on assignment only. Uses color prints.

Terms: Royalties negotiable. Offers advances against royalties. Originals returned to artist at job's completion. Book catalog available for 3×5 SAE and 3 first-class stamps. Catalog available on website.

TRICYCLE PRESS, Imprint of Ten Speed Press, P.O. Box 7123, Berkeley CA 94707. (510)559-1600. Fax: (510)559-1637. Website: www.tenspeed.com. Estab. 1993. **Acquisitions:** Nicole Geiger, publisher. Publishes 12-14 picture books/year; 3 activity books/year; 2 middle readers/year; 1 'tween fiction/year; 4 board books/year. 25% of books by first-time authors. "Tricycle Press looks for something outside the mainstream; books that encourage children to look at the world from a different angle. Tricycle Press, like its parent company, Ten Speed Press, is known for its quirky, offbeat books. We publish high quality trade books."

Fiction: Board books, picture books, middle reader: adventure, animal, contemporary, fantasy, history, multicultural, nature, poetry, suspense/mystery. Picture books, young readers: concept. Middle readers: anthology, novels. Average word length: picture books—800. Recently published *Hey, Little Ant*, by Phil and Hannah Hoose (ages 5-8 picture book); *King and King*, by Linda de Haan and Stern Nijland.

Nonfiction: Picture books, middle readers: activity books, animal, arts/crafts, biography, careers, concept, cooking, history, how-to, multicultural, music/dance, nature/environment, science. Recently published *Q is for Quark Science: An Alphabet Book*, by David M. Schwartz (ages 9 and up, picture book); *Honest Pretzels and 64 Other Amazing Recipes for Cooks Ages 8 & Up*, by Mollie Katzen (activity book); and *The Young Adventurer's Guide to Everest*, by Jonathan Chester (ages 8 and up, nonfiction picture book).

How to Contact/Writers: Fiction: Submit complete ms for picture books. Submit outline/synopsis and 2-3 sample chapters for chapter book. "No queries!" Nonfiction: Submit complete ms. Responds to mss in 6 months. Publishes a book 1-2 years after acceptance. Welcomes simultaneous submissions and previously published work. Do not send original artwork; copies only, please. No electronic or faxed submissions.

Illustration: Works with 12 illustrators/year. Uses color and b&w. Reviews ms/illustration package from artists. Submit ms with dummy and/or 2-3 pieces of final art. Illustrations only: Query with samples, promo sheet, tearsheets. Contact: Nicole Geiger. Responds only if interested. Samples returned with SASE; samples filed. Original artwork returned at job's completion unless work for hire.

Photography: Works on assignment only. Contact: Nicole Geiger. Uses 35mm transparencies. Submit samples.

Terms: Pays authors royalty of 7½-8½% based on net receipts. Offers advances. Pays illustrators and photographers royalty of 7½-8½% based on net receipts. Sends galleys of novels to authors. Book catalog for 9×12 SASE (3 first-class stamps). Manuscript guidelines for SASE (1 first-class stamp). Guidelines available at www.tenspeed.com.

Tips: "We are looking for something a bit outside the mainstream and with lasting appeal (no one-shot-wonders)."

UAHC PRESS, 633 Third Ave., New York NY 10017. (212)650-4120. Fax: (212)650-4119. E-mail: press@uahc.org. Website: www.uahc.press.com. Book publisher. Estab. 1876. **Manuscript/Art Acquisitions:** Rabbi Hara Person, managing editor. Publishes 4 picture books/year; 2 young readers/year; 2 middle readers/year; 2 young adult titles and 4 textbooks/year. "The Union of American Hebrew Congregations Press publishes textbooks for the religious classroom, children's tradebooks and scholarly work of Jewish education import—no adult fiction and no YA fiction."

Fiction: Picture books, young readers, middle readers: religion. Average word length: picture books— 150; young readers—500; middle readers—3,000. Recently published *A Tree Trunk Seder*, written and illustrated by Camille Kress (toddler's board book); *Solomon and the Trees*, by Matt Biers-Ariel, illustrated by Esti Silverberg-Kiss (ages 4-8, picture book); *Sophie and the Shofar*, written by Fran Manuskin and illustrated by Rosalind Charney Kaye (ages 3-7, Jewish fiction).

Nonfiction: Picture books, young readers, middle readers, young adult/teens: religion. Average word length: picture books—150; young readers—500; middle readers—3,000; young adult/teens—20,000. Recently published *My Jewish Holiday Fun Book*, written and illustrated by Ann Koffsky (ages 5-9, activity book); *Until the Messiah Comes*, by Kenneth Roseman (ages 10-13, do-it-yourself Jewish adventure); and *The Chocolate Chip Challah Activity Books*, written and illustrated by Lisa Rauchwerger (ages 5-10, activity book).

How to Contact/Writers: Fiction: Submit outline/synopsis and 2 sample chapters. Nonfiction: Submit complete ms. Responds to queries/ms in 4 months. Publishes a book 18 months-2 years after acceptance. Will consider simultaneous submissions.

Illustration: Works with 5 illustrators/year. Reviews ms/illustration packages from artists. Send ms with dummy. Illustrations only: Send portfolio to be kept on file. Responds in 2 months. Samples returned with SASE. Looking specifically for Jewish themes.

Photography: Buys stock and assigns work. Uses photos with Jewish content. Prefer modern settings. Submit cover letter and promo piece.

Terms: Offers advances. Pays photographers by the project (range: $200-3,000) or per photo (range:$20-100). Book catalog free; ms guidelines for SASE.

Tips: "Look at some of our books. Have an understanding of the Reform Jewish community. We sell mostly to Jewish congregations and day schools.' "

VIKING CHILDREN'S BOOKS, Penguin Putnam Inc., 345 Hudson St., New York NY 10014-3657. (212)414-3600. Website: www.penguinputnam.com. **Acquisitions:** Catherine Frank, assistant editor, picture books, middle grade and young adult fiction; Tracy Gates, executive editor, picture books, middle grade, and young adult fiction; Melanie Cecka, senior editor, easy-to-read and fiction. **Art Acquisitions:** Denise Cronin, Viking Children's Books. Publishes hardcover originals. Publishes 80 books/year. Receives 7500 queries/year. 25% of books from first-time authors; 33% from unagented writers. "Viking Children's Books is known for humorous, quirky picture books, in addition to more traditional fiction and publishes the highest quality trade books for children including fiction, nonfiction, and novelty books for pre-schoolers through young adults." Publishes book 1-2 years after acceptance of artwork. Hesitantly accepts simultaneous submissions.

- Viking Children's Books is not accepting unsolicited submissions. Viking title *This Land Was Made for You and Me. The Life and Songs of Woody Guthrie*, by Elizabeth Partridge, won the 2002 Boston Globe-Horn Book Award for Nonfiction.

Fiction: All levels: adventure, animal, anthology, contemporary, hi-lo, humor, multicultural, suspense/mystery, easy-to-read, history, poetry, religion, sports. Middle readers, young adults/teens: problem novels, fantasy, romance, science fiction. Recently published *Pinocchio the Boy*, by Lane Smith (ages 4-8, picture book); *Catalyst*, by Laurie Halse Anderson (ages 12 and up, novel).

Nonfiction: Picture books: activity books, biography, concept. Young readers, middle readers, young adult: biography, history, reference, religion, science, sports. Middle readers: animal, biography, geography, hi-lo, history, hobbies, multicultural, music/dance, nature/environment, religion, science, social issues, sports. Young adult/teens: animal, biography, cooking, geography, hi-lo, history, multicultural, music/dance, nature/environment, reference, religion, science, social issues, sports. Recently published *Understanding September 11th*, by Mitch Frank (ages 12 and up, nonfiction).

Illustration: Works with 40 illustrators/year. Responds to artist's queries/submissions only if interested. Samples returned with SASE or samples filed. Originals returned at job's completion.

How to Contact/Writers: Picture books: submit entire ms and SASE. Novels: submit outline with 3 sample chapters and SASE. Nonfiction: query with outline, one sample chapter and SASE. Responds to queries/mss in 8 months.

Terms: Pays 2-10% royalty on retail price or flat fee. Advance negotiable.

Tips: Mistake often made is that "authors disguise nonfiction in a fictional format."

WALKER AND COMPANY, Books for Young Readers, 435 Hudson St., New York NY 10014-3941. (212)727-8300. Fax: (212)727-0984. Website: www.walkerbooks.com. Division of Walker Publishing Co. Inc. Book publisher. Estab. 1959. **Manuscript Acquisitions:** Emily Easton, publisher; Timothy Travaglini, editor. **Art Acquisitions:** Marlene Fungseth, design director. Publishes 16 picture books/year; 4-6 middle readers/year; 2-4 young adult titles/year. 5% of books by first-time authors; 65% of books from agented writers.

Fiction: Picture books: adventure, history, humor, poetry. Middle readers: adventure, contemporary, history, humor, multicultural, poetry. Young adults: adventure, contemporary, humor, historical fiction, suspense/mystery. Recently published *Welcome to Kindergarten*, by Anne Rockwell, (ages 3-5, edited by E. Easton, picture book); *Playing the Field*, by Janette Rallison (ages 10-14, edited by T. Travaglini, editor, middle grade novel); *Walk Away Home*, by Paul Many (12 and up, edited by E. Easton, teen/young adult novel).

Nonfiction: Picture book, middle readers: biography, history. Recently published *Champion: The Story of Muhammad Ali*, by Jim Haskins, illustrated by Eric Velasquez (ages 6-10, edited by T. Travaglini, picture book, biography); *The Great Ships*, by Patrick O'Brien (ages 3-7, edited by T. Travaglini, picture book history); *The Signers*, by Dennis Fradin, illustrated by Michael McCurdy (10 and up, edited by E. Easton, illustrated nonfiction). Multicultural needs include "contemporary, literary fiction and historical fiction written in an authentic voice. Also high interest nonfiction with trade appeal."

How to Contact/Writers: Fiction/nonfiction: Submit outline/synopsis and sample chapters; query for novels. Responds to queries/mss in 3 months. Send SASE for writer's guidelines.

Illustration: Works with 10-12 illustrators/year. Uses color artwork only. Editorial department reviews ms/illustration packages from artists. Query or submit ms with 4-8 samples. Illustrations only: Tearsheets. "Please do not send original artwork." Responds to art samples only if interested. Samples returned with SASE.

Terms: Pays authors royalties of 5-10%; pays illustrators royalty or flat fee. Offers advance payment against royalties. Original artwork returned at job's completion. Sends galleys to authors. Book catalog available for 9×12 SASE; ms guidelines for SASE.

Tips: Writers: "Make sure you study our catalog before submitting. We are a small house with a tightly focused list." Illustrators: "Have a well-rounded portfolio with different styles." Does not want to see folktales, ABC books, paperback series, genre fiction. "Walker and Company is committed to introducing talented new authors and illustrators to the children's book field."

WHAT'S INSIDE PRESS, P.O. Box 16965, Beverly Hills CA 90209. (800)269-7757. Fax: (800)856-2160. E-mail: whatsin@aol.com. Website: whatsinsidepress.com. Estab. 1998. Specializes in fiction. **Manuscript Acquisitions:** Shalen Williams. Publishes 5-10 picture books; 5-10 picture books. 50% of books by first-time authors. "The goal of What's Inside Press is to publish books that embrace the simple joys and journeys of childhood."

Fiction: Picture books: adventure, concept, contemporary, fantasy, humor. Young adults: contemporary, humor, problem novels. Recently published *The Tree in the Field of Mathingamy Theme*, by Walter Caldwell (picture book); and *Slam*, by Kinsley Foster (young adult novel, ages 11-17).

Illustration: Works with 4 illustrators/year. Uses color artwork only. Reviews ms/illustration packages from artists. Send postcard sample. Responds in 2 months only if interested. Samples not returned; samples filed.

Terms: Pays authors royalty 8-14% based on wholesale price. Offers advances (Average amount: $500). Pays illustrators by the project (range: $1,000-5,000). Book catalog available for catalog size SASE and 4 first-class stamps. Manuscript guidelines available for SASE. Catalog available on website.

Tips: "Be patient in receiving your reply. Send queries via regular mail or e-mail only–no certified or express mail. Write to tell a story, not just to get published! Keep believing in your writing and don't give up! E-publishing will change children's publishing little if at all. The magic of books is here to stay!"

WHITECAP BOOKS, 351 Lynn Ave., North Vancouver, British Columbia V7J 2C4 Canada. (604)980-9852. E-mail: whitecap@whitecap.ca. Book publisher. **Acquisitions:** Leanne McDonald, rights and acquisitions. Publishes 4 young readers and 2 middle readers/year.

Fiction: Picture books for children 3-7. Recently published *The Chinese Violin*, by Madeleine Thien and Joe Chang (ages 4-7).

Nonfiction: Young readers, middle readers: animal, nature/environment. Does not want to see text that writes down to children. Recently published *Welcome to the World of Wild Horses*, by Diane Swanson (ages 5-7); *Dot to Dot in the Sky: Stories in the Stars*, by Joan Hinz (ages 8-11); *Whose Teeth Are These*, by Wayne Lynch (ages 5-7).

How to Contact/Writers: Nonfiction: Query. Responds to queries in 1 month; ms in 3 months. Publishes a book 6 months after acceptance. Will consider simultaneous submissions. Please send international postal voucher if submission is from US.

Illustration: Works with 1-2 illustrators/year. Reviews ms/illustration packages from artists. Query. Illustrations only: Query with samples—"never send original art." Contact: Robin Rivers. Samples returned with SASE with international postal voucher for Canada if requested.

Photography: Buys stock. "We are always looking for outstanding wildlife photographs." Uses 35mm transparencies. Submit cover letter, client list, stock photo list.

Terms: Pays authors a negotiated royalty or purchases work outright. Offers advances. Pays illustrators by the project or royalty (depends on project). Pays photographers per photo (depends on project). Originals returned to artist at job's completion unless discussed in advance. Manuscript guidelines available for SASE with international postal voucher for Canada.

Tips: "Writers and illustrators should spend time researching what's already available on the market. Whitecap specializes in nonfiction for children and adults. Whitecap Fiction focuses on humorous events or extraordinary animals. Please review previous publications before submitting."

ALBERT WHITMAN & COMPANY, 6340 Oakton St., Morton Grove IL 60053-2723. (847)581-0033. Fax: (847)581-0039. Website: www.albertwhitman.com. Book publisher. Estab. 1919. **Manuscript Acquisitions:** Kathleen Tucker, editor-in-chief. **Art Acquisitions:** Carol Gildar, art director. Publishes 30 books/year. 20% of books by first-time authors; 15% of books from agented authors.

Fiction: Picture books, young readers, middle readers: adventure, concept (to help children deal with problems), fantasy, history, humor, multicultural, suspense. Middle readers: problem novels, suspense/mystery. "We are interested in contemporary multicultural stories—stories with holiday themes and exciting distinctive novels. We publish a wide variety of topics and are interested in stories that help children deal with their problems and concerns. Does not want to see "religion-oriented, ABCs, pop-up, romance, counting." Published *Pumpkin Jack*, by Will Hubbell; *Mabela the Clever*, by Margaret Read MacDonald, illustrated by Tim Coffey; *Girl, You're Amazing!*, by Virginina Kroll, illustrated by Melisande Potter.

Nonfiction: Picture books, young readers, middle readers: animal, arts/crafts, health, history, hobbies, multicultural, music/dance, nature/environment, science, sports, special needs. Does not want to see "religion, any books that have to be written in or fictionalized biographies." Published *Shelter Dogs*, by Peg Kehret; *I Have a Weird Brother Who Digested a Fly*, by Joan Hulub, illustrated by Patrick Girouard; and *The Riches of Oseola McCarty*, by Evelyn Coleman, illustrated by Daniel Minter.

How to Contact/Writers: Fiction/Nonfiction: Submit query, outline and sample chapter. For picture books send entire ms. Include cover letter. Responds to queries in 6 weeks; mss in 4 months. Publishes a book 18 months after acceptance. Will consider simultaneous submissions "but let us know if it is one."

Illustration: Do not send originals. Reviews ms/illustration packages from artists. Illustrations only: Query with samples. Send slides or tearsheets. Samples returned with SASE; samples filed. Originals returned at job's completion. Responds in 2 months.

Photography: Publishes books illustrated with photos but not stock photos—desires photos all taken for project. "Our books are for children and cover many topics; photos must be taken to match text. Books often show a child in a particular situation (e.g., kids being home-schooled, a sister whose brother is born prematurely)." Photographers should query with samples; send unsolicited photos by mail.

Terms: Pays authors royalty. Pays illustrators and photographers royalty. Book catalog for 8×10 SAE and 3 first-class stamps.

Tips: "In both picture books and nonfiction, we are seeking stories showing life in other cultures and the variety of multicultural life in the U.S. We also want fiction and nonfiction about mentally or physically challenged children—some recent topics have been autism, stuttering, diabetes. Look up some of our books first, to be sure your submission is appropriate for Albert Whitman & Co."

JOHN WILEY & SONS, INC., 111 River St., Hoboken NJ 07030. (201)748-6000. Website: www.wiley.com. Book publisher. **Acquisitions:** Kate Bradford, senior editor. Publishes 18 middle readers/year; 2 young adult titles/year. 10% of books by first-time authors. Publishes educational nonfiction: primarily history, science, and other activities.

Nonfiction: Middle readers: activity books, animal, arts/crafts, biography, cooking, geography, health, history, hobbies, how-to, nature/environment, reference, science, self help. Young adults: activity books, arts/crafts, health, hobbies, how-to, nature/environment, reference, science, self help. Average word length middle readers—20,000-40,000. Recently published: *Sports Science*, by Jim Wiese (ages 8-12, science/ activity); *Outrageous Women of the American Frontier*, by Mary Forbee (ages 10-14, US history).

How to Contact/Writers: Query. Submit outline/synopsis, 2 sample chapters and an author bio. Responds to queries in 1 month; mss in 3 months. Publishes a book 1 year after acceptance. Will consider simultaneous and previously published submissions.

Illustration: Works with 6 illustrators/year. Uses primarily black & white artwork. Reviews ms/illustration packages from artists. Query. Illustrations only: Query with samples, résumé, client list. Responds only if interested. Samples filed. Original artwork returned at job's completion. No portfolio reviews.

Photography: Buys photos from freelancers.

Terms: Pays authors royalty of 10-12% based on wholesale price, or by outright purchase. Offers advances. Pays illustrators by the project. Photographers' pay negotiable. Sends galleys to authors. Book catalog available for SASE.

Tips: "We're looking for topics and writers that can really engage kids' interest—plus we're always interested in a new twist on time-tested subjects."

WILLIAMSON PUBLISHING CO., Box 185, Charlotte VT 05445. (802)425-2102. Fax: (802)425-2199. E-mail: susan@williamsonbooks.com. Website: www.williamsonbooks.com. Book publisher. Estab. 1983. **Manuscript Acquisitions:** Susan Williamson, editorial director. **Art Acquisitions:** Jack Williamson, publisher. Publishes 12-15 young readers titles/year. 50% of books by first-time authors; 10% of books from agented authors. Publishes "very successful nonfiction series (Kids Can!® Series—3,000,000 sold) on subjects such as history, science, arts/crafts, geography. Successfully launched *Little Hands*® series for ages 2-6, *Kaleidoscope Kids*® series (age 7 and up) and *Quick Startsfor Kids!*® series (ages 7 +). Our mission is to help every child fulfill his/her potential and experience personal growth.

Nonfiction: Hands-on active learning books, animals, African-American, arts/crafts, Asian, biography, careers, geography, health, history, hobbies, how-to, math, multicultural, music/dance, nature/environment, Native American, science, writing and journaling. Does not want to see textbooks, picture books, poetry, fiction. "We are looking for books in which learning and doing are inseparable." Published *Awesome Ocean Science*, by Cindy Littlefield, illustrated by Sarah Rakitin (ages 7-14, exploring science); *All Around Town*, by Judy Press, illustrated by Karen Weiss (ages 2-6, early learning skills); *And Who Really Discovered America?*, by Avery Hart, illustrated by Michael Kline (ages 7 and up, learning to be discerning historians).

How to Contact/Writers: Query with annotated TOC/synopsis and 1 sample chapter. Responds to queries in 4 months; mss in 4 months. Publishes book, "about 1 year" after acceptance. Writers may send a SASE for guidelines. Please do not query via e-mail.

Illustration: Works with at least 6 illustrator and 6 designers/year. "We're interested in expanding our illustrator and design freelancers." Uses primarily b&w artwork; some 2-color and 4-color. Responds only if interested. Samples returned with SASE; samples filed. Please do not send samples via e-mail.

Photography: Buys photos from freelancers; uses archival art and photos.

Terms: Pays authors royalty based on wholesale price or purchases outright. Pays illustrators by the project. Pays photographers per photo. Sends galleys to authors. Book catalog available for 8½ × 11 SAE and 6 first-class stamps; ms guidelines available for SASE.

Tips: "Please do not send any fiction or stories of any kind. We're interested in interactive learning books with a creative approach packed with interesting information, written for young readers ages 2-6 and 4-10. In nonfiction children's publishing, we are looking for authors with a depth of knowledge shared with children through a warm, embracing style. Our publishing philosophy is based on the idea that all children can succeed and have positive learning experiences. Children's lasting learning experiences involve participation."

WINDSTORM CREATIVE LTD., 7419 Ebbert Dr. SE, Port Orchard WA 98367. Website: www.arabyfai r.com. **Acquisitions:** Ms. Cris Newport, senior editor. Publishes trade paperback originals and reprints. Publishes 10 titles/year. 50% of books from first-time authors; 50% from unagented writers. WSC consists of the following imprints: Little Blue Works—Children's titles and young adult novels released in paper and on multimedia CD-ROM; Lightning Rod Ltd—Internet & Episode Guides; WSC—Cutting-edge fiction. Publishes genre fiction and poetry primarily in paper and on multimedia CD-ROM; RAMPANT Gaming—Role-playing and other games for ages 14 and up—Paper Frog—theater and film. "WSC publishes work that is revolutionary in content. In order to understand what we mean by this, please read several of our books from the different imprints. We do not publish work that is racist, homophobic, sexist or graphically violent in content. All of our authors and artists should expect to be proactive in marketing their work. If you do not wish to read from and/or sign your books and/or artwork, you should not submit work to us."

Fiction: All levels and categories. Published *Surprise for Ray*, by Ann Marie Stephens, illustrated by Michael Bolan; *Miss Panda Series*, by Ambika Mather Kamat/K. Michael Crawford (Multimedia CD-ROM); and *Tonight I Heard the Ghost Cat*, by Jennifer Anna, illustrated by Patrick Dengate.

Nonfiction: All levels and categories.

How to Contact/Writers: You must visit the website for guidelines and information before submitting to us.

Illustration: Works with 10 illustrators/year. Visit website for guidelines.

Photography: Buys photos from freelancers. See website.

Terms: Pays 10-15% royalty based on wholesale price. Will consider simultaneous submissions. Artists and photographers are paid flat fee for covers only. All other work is paid on royalty basis. Royalty payment is 10% of gross monies received."

Tips: "We reserve the right to destroy any submissions that deviate from our format."

WINDWARD PUBLISHING, Imprint of Finney Company, 3943 Meadowbrook Rd., Minneapolis MN 55426. (952)938-9330. Fax: (952)938-7353. E-mail: feedback@finney-hobar.com. Website: www. finney-hobar.com. Estab. 1947. Specializes in mass market books, trade books, nonfiction, educational material. **Manuscript/Art Acquisitions:** Alan E. Krysan. Publishes 1 picture book/year; 2-4 young readers, middle readers, young adult titles/year. 25% of books by first-time authors.

Fiction: Young readers, middle readers, young adults: adventure, animal, nature/environment. Recently published *Billy's Search for Florida Undersea Treasure*, illustrated by Russ Smiley (ages 5-10, story picture book).

Nonfiction: Young readers, middle readers, young adults: activity books, animal, careers, nature/environment, science. Young adults: textbooks. Recently published *Sea Turtles Hatching*, by Katherine Orr (ages 5-8, nature); *Occupational Guidance for Agriculture* (ages 12 and up, careers); *Reading a Ruler* (ages 12 and up, how-to).

How to Contact/Writers: Fiction: Query. Nonfiction: Submit outline/synopsis and 3 sample chapters. Responds to queries in 1 month; mss in 2 months. Publishes book 6-8 months after acceptance. Will consider simultaneous submissions and previously published work.

Illustration: Reviews ms/illustration packages from artists. Send ms with dummy. Contact: Alan E. Krysan, president. Query with samples. Contact: President. Responds in 2 months. Samples returned with SASE; samples filed.

Photography: Buys stock and assigns work. Contact: President. Photography needs depend on project—mostly ocean and beach subject matter. Uses color, 4×6, glossy prints. Submit cover letter, résumé, stock photo list.

Terms: Author's payment negotiable by project. Offers advances (Average amount: $500). Illustrators and photographers payment negotiable by project. Sends galleys to authors; dummies to illustrators. Originals returned to artist at job's completion. Book catalog available for 6×9 SAE and 3 first-class stamps; ms guidelines available for SASE. Catalog mostly available on website.

WM KIDS, Imprint of White Mane Publishing Co., Inc., P.O. Box, 708, 63 W. Burd St., Shippensburg PA 17257. (717)532-2237. Fax: (717)532-6110. E-mail: marketing@whitemane.com. Book publisher. Estab. 1987. **Acquisitions:** Harold Collier. White Mane Books, Burd Street Press, White Mane Kids, Ragged Edge Press (Harold Collier, acquisitions editor). Publishes 10 middle readers/year. 50% of books are by first-time authors.

Fiction: Middle readers, young adults: history. Average word length: middle readers—30,000. Recently published *Freedom Calls: Journey of a Slave Girl*, by Ken Knapp Sawyer (historical fiction, grades 5 and up); *Young Heroes of History*, by Alan Kay (grades 5 and up).

Nonfiction: Middle readers, young adults: history. Average word length: middle readers—30,000. Recently published *Slaves Who Dared: The Story of Ten African American Heroes*, by Mary Garrison (young adult).

How to Contact/Writers: Fiction: Query. Nonfiction: Submit outline/synopsis and 2-3 sample chapters. Responds to queries in 1 month; mss in 3 months. Publishes a book 12-15 months after acceptance. Will consider simultaneous submissions.

VISIT OUR WEBSITES at www.writersmarket.com and www.writersdigest.com, for helpful articles, hot new markets, daily market updates, writers' guidelines and much more.

Illustration: Works with 3 illustrators/year. Reviews ms/illustration packages from artists. Submit ms with 3 pieces of final art. Contact: Harold Collier, acquisitions editor. Responds in 1 month. Samples returned with SASE.

Photography: Buys stock and assigns work. Submit cover letter and portfolio.

Terms: Pays authors royalty of 7-10%. Pays illustrators by the project. Pays photographers by the project. Sends galleys for review. Originals returned to artist at job's completion. Book catalog and writer's guidelines available for SASE. All imprints included in a single catalog.

Magazines

Children's magazines are a great place for unpublished writers and illustrators to break into the market. Illustrators, photographers and writers alike may find it easier to get book assignments if they have tearsheets from magazines. Having magazine work under your belt shows you're professional and have experience working with editors and art directors and meeting deadlines.

But magazines aren't merely a breaking-in point. Writing, illustration and photo assignments for magazines let you see your work in print quickly, and the magazine market can offer steady work and regular paychecks (a number of them pay on acceptance). Book authors and illustrators may have to wait a year or two before receiving royalties from a project. The magazine market is also a good place to use research material that didn't make it into a book project you're working on. You may even work on a magazine idea that blossoms into a book project.

TARGETING YOUR SUBMISSIONS

It's important to know the topics typically covered by different children's magazines. To help you match your work with the right publications, we've included several indexes in the back of this book. The **Subject Index** lists both book and magazine publishers by the fiction and nonfiction subjects they're seeking.

If you're a writer, use the Subject Index in conjunction with the **Age-Level Index** to narrow your list of markets. Targeting the correct age group with your submission is an important consideration. Most rejection slips are sent because a writer has not targeted a manuscript to the correct age. Few magazines are aimed at children of all ages, so you must be certain your manuscript is written for the audience level of the particular magazine you're submitting to. Magazines for children (just as magazines for adults) may also target a specific gender.

If you're a poet, refer to the **Poetry Index** to find which magazines publish poems.

Each magazine has a different editorial philosophy. Language usage also varies between periodicals, as does the length of feature articles and the use of artwork and photographs. Reading magazines *before* submitting is the best way to determine if your material is appropriate. Also, because magazines targeted to specific age groups have a natural turnover in readership every few years, old topics (with a new slant) can be recycled.

If you're a photographer, the **Photography Index** lists children's magazines that use photos from freelancers. Using it in combination with the subject index can narrow your search. For instance, if you photograph sports, compare the Magazine list in the Photography Index with the list under Sports in the Subject Index. Highlight the markets that appear on both lists, then read those listings to decide which magazines might be best for your work.

Since many kids' magazines sell subscriptions through direct mail or schools, you may not be able to find a particular publication at bookstores or newsstands. Check your local library, or send for copies of the magazines you're interested in. Most magazines in this section have sample copies available and will send them for a SASE or small fee.

Also, many magazines have submission guidelines and theme lists available for a SASE. Check magazines' websites, too. Many offer excerpts of articles, submission guidelines and theme lists and will give you a feel for the editorial focus of the publication.

For insights into children's magazines from experienced editors, turn to the Insider Reports with *Cricket*'s **Deborah Vetter** (page 220), *Discovery Trail*'s **Sinda Zinn** (page 228) and *High-*

lights for Children's **Marileta Robinson** (page 236).

Information on magazines listed in the previous edition but not included in this edition of *Children's Writer's & Illustrator's Market* **may be found in the General Index.**

ADVENTURES, WordAction Publications, (formerly *Wonder Time*), 6401 The Paseo, Kansas City MO 64131. (816)333-7000. Fax: (816)333-4439. E-mail: psmits@nazarene.org. **Editor:** Pamela Smits. Weekly magazine. Circ. 45,000. "*Wonder Time* is a full-color story paper for first and second graders. It is designed to connect Sunday School learning with daily living experiences of the primary child. *Wonder Time*'s target audience is children ages six to eight. The readability goal should be at beginning readers level. The intent of *Wonder Time* is to: Provide a life-related paper enabling Christian values, encourage good choices and provide reinforcement for biblical concepts taught in WordAction Sunday School curriculum."
Fiction: Contemporary, inspirational, religious. "We need ethnic balance—stories and illustrations from a variety of experiences." Buys 52 mss/year. Average word length: 100-150. Byline given.
How to Contact/Writers: Fiction: Send complete ms. Responds to queries/mss in 6 weeks. Send SASE for themes and guidelines.
Terms: Pays on acceptance. Pays $25 per story for all rights.
Tips: "Basic themes reappear regularly. Please write for a theme list. Ask for guidelines, sample copies, theme list *before* submitting. Send SASE."

ADVOCATE, PKA'S PUBLICATION, PKA Publication, 301A Rolling Hills Park, Prattsville NY 12468. (518)299-3103. **Publisher**: Patricia Keller. Bimonthly tabloid. Estab. 1987. Circ. 12,000. "*Advocate* advocates good writers and quality writings. We publish art, fiction, photos and poetry. *Advocate*'s submitters are talented people of all ages who do not earn their livings as writers. We wish to promote the arts and to give those we publish the opportunity to be published through a for-profit means rather than in a not-for-profit way. We do this by selling advertising and offering reading entertainment."
   • Gaited Horse Association newsletter is now included in our publication. Horse-oriented stories, poetry, art and photos are currently needed.
Fiction: Middle readers and young adults/teens: adventure, animal, contemporary, fantasy, folktales, health, humorous, nature/environment, problem-solving, romance, science fiction, sports, suspense/mystery. Looks for "well written, entertaining work, whether fiction or nonfiction." Buys approximately 42 mss/year. Average word length: 1,500. Byline given. Wants to see more humorous material, nature/environment and romantic comedy.
Nonfiction: Middle readers and young adults/teens: animal, arts/crafts, biography, careers, concept, cooking, fashion, games/puzzles, geography, history, hobbies, how-to, humorous, interview/profile, nature/environment, problem-solving, science, social issues, sports, travel. Buys 10 mss/year. Average word length: 1,500. Byline given.
Poetry: Reviews poetry any length.
How to Contact/Writers: Fiction/nonfiction: send complete ms. Responds to queries in 6 weeks/mss in 2 months. Publishes ms 2-18 months after acceptance.
Illustration: Uses b&w artwork only. Uses cartoons. Reviews ms/illustration packages from artists. Submit a photo print (b&w or color), an excellent copy of work (no larger than 8×10) or original. Illustrations only: "Send previous unpublished art with SASE, please." Responds in 2 months. Samples returned with SASE; samples not filed. Credit line given.
Photography: Buys photos from freelancers. Model/property releases required. Uses color and b&w prints. Send unsolicited photos by mail with SASE. Responds in 2 months. Wants nature, artistic and humorous photos.
Terms: Pays on publication with contributor's copies. Acquires first rights for mss, artwork and photographs. Pays in copies. Original work returned upon job's completion. Sample copies for $4. Writer's/illustrator/photo guidelines for SASE.
Tips: "Artists and photographers should keep in mind that we are a b&w paper. Please do not send postcards. Use envelope with SASE."

AIM MAGAZINE, America's Intercultural Magazine, P.O. Box 1174, Maywood IL 60153-8174. Website: www.aimmagazine.org. **Contact:** Ruth Apilado (nonfiction), Mark Boone (fiction). **Photo Editor:** Betty Lewis. Quarterly magazine. Circ. 8,000. Readers are high school and college students, teachers, adults interested in helping to purge racism from the human blood stream by the way of the written word—that is our goal! 15% of material aimed at juvenile audience.

Fiction: Young adults/teens: adventure, folktales, humorous, history, multicultural, "stories with social significance." Wants stories that teach children that people are more alike than they are different. Does not want to see religious fiction. Buys 20 mss/year. Average word length: 1,000-4,000. Byline given.

Nonfiction: Young adults/teens: biography, interview/profile, multicultural, "stuff with social significance." Does not want to see religious nonfiction. Buys 20 mss/year. Average word length: 500-2,000. Byline given.

How to Contact/Writers: Fiction: Send complete ms. Nonfiction: Query with published clips. Responds to queries/mss in 1 month. Will consider simultaneous submissions.

Illustration: Buys 6 illustrations/issue. Preferred theme: Overcoming social injustices through nonviolent means. Reviews ms/illustration packages from artists. Query first. Illustrations only: Query with tearsheets. Responds to art samples in 1 month. Samples filed. Original artwork returned at job's completion "if desired." Credit line given.

Photography: Wants "photos of activists who are trying to contribute to social improvement."

Terms: Pays on acceptance. Buys first North American serial rights. Pays $15-25 for stories/articles. Pays in contributor copies if copies are requested. Pays $25 for b&w cover illustration. Photographers paid by the project. Sample copies for $5.

Tips: "Write about what you know."

AMERICAN CAREERS, Career Communications, Inc., 6701 W. 64th St., Overland Park KS 66202. (913)362-7788. Fax: (913)362-4864. **Articles Editor:** Mary Pitchford. **Art Director:** Jerry Kanabel. Published 3 times/year. Estab. 1990. Circ. 400,000. Publishes career and education information for middle and high school students.

Nonfiction: Buys 20 mss/year. Average word length: 300-800. Byline given.

How to Contact/Writers: Nonfiction: Query with published clips. Responds to queries in 2 months. Publishes ms 6-24 months after acceptance. Will consider simultaneous submissions, electronic submissions.

Tips: Send a query in writing with résumé and clips.

AMERICAN CHEERLEADER, Lifestyle Ventures LLC, 250 W. 57th St., Suite 420, New York NY 10107. (212)265-8890. Fax: (212)265-8908. E-mail: editors@americancheerleader.com. Website: www.americancheerleader.com. **Editorial Director:** Julie Davis. **Managing Editor:** Alyssa Roenigk. **Editor:** Sheila Noone. Bimonthly magazine. Estab. 1995. Circ. 200,000. Special interest teen magazine for kids who cheer.

Nonfiction: Young adults: biography, interview/profile (sports personalities), careers, fashion, beauty, health, how-to (cheering techniques, routines, pep songs, etc.), problem-solving, sports, cheerleading specific material. "We're looking for authors who know cheerleading." Buys 20 mss/year. Average word length: 750-2,000. Byline given.

How to Contact/Writers: Query with published clips. Responds to queries/mss in 3 months. Publishes ms 3 months after acceptance. Will consider electronic submission via disk or modem.

Illustration: Buys 6 illustrations/issue; 30-50 illustrations/year. Works on assignment only. Reviews ms/illustration packages from artists. Illustrations only: Query with samples; arrange portfolio review. Responds only if interested. Samples filed. Originals not returned at job's completion. Credit line given.

Photography: Buys photos from freelancers. Looking for cheerleading at different sports games, events, etc. Uses 35mm, 2¼×2¼ transparencies and 5x7 prints. Query with samples; provide résumé, business card, tearsheets to be kept on file. "After sending query, we'll set up an interview." Responds only if interested.

Terms: Pays on publication. Buy all rights for mss, artwork and photographs. Pays $100-1,000 for stories. Pays illustrators $50-200 for b&w inside, $100-300 for color inside. Pays photographers by the project $300-750; per photo (range. $25-100). Sample copies for $4.

Tips: "Authors: We invite proposals from freelance writers who are involved in or have been involved in cheerleading—i.e. coaches, sponsors or cheerleaders. Our writing style is upbeat, and 'sporty' to catch and hold the attention of our teen readers. Articles should be broken down into lots of sidebars, bulleted lists, etc. Photographers and illustrators must have teen magazine experience or high profile experience."

AMERICAN CHEERLEADER JUNIOR, Lifestyle Ventures, 250 W. 57th St., #420, New York NY 10107. (212)265-8890. Fax: (212)265-8908. Website: www.americancheerleaderjunior.com. **Articles Editor:** Sheila Noone. **Art Director:** Kristin Fennell. Quarterly magazine. Estab. 2001. "We celebrate the young cheerleaders across the country and provide ways to improve their abilities, friendships and community service." 95% of publication aimed at juvenile market.

Fiction: Middle readers: sports. Byline given.

Nonfiction: Picture-oriented, young readers, middle readers: arts/crafts, games/puzzles, health, how-to, humorous, sports. Average word length: 400. Byline given.

Poetry: Reviews poetry.

How to Contact/Writers: Fiction/nonfiction: Query with published clips. Responds in 1-2 months. Will consider electronic submission via disk or modem.

Illustration: Buys 2-4 illustrations/issue; 8-10 illustrations/year. Uses color artwork only. Works on assignment only. Reviews ms/illustration packages from artists. Contact: Kristin Fennell, art director. Illustrations only: query with samples, arrange portfolio review. Contact: Kristin Fennell. Responds only if interested. Samples not returned; samples filed. Credit line given.

Photography: Looking for photos depicting action, cheer, friendship. Model/property release required. Uses color prints and 35mm transparencies. Query with samples; arrange a personal interview to show portfolio. Responds only if interested.

Terms: Pays on publication. Buys exclusive magazine rights or negotiates for rights. Buys first rights for artwork; all rights for photos. Additional payment for ms/illustration packages and for photos accompanying articles. Payment for illustrators varies. Payment for photographers varies. Samples copies free for SAE. Writer's guidelines free for SASE.

Tips: "We look for fun, wholesome illustrations aimed at athletic and energetic kids."

AMERICAN GIRL, Pleasant Company, 8400 Fairway Place, P.O. Box 620986, Middleton WI 53562-0984. (608)836-4848. E-mail: im_agmag_editor@pleasantco.com. Website: www.americangirl.com. **Executive Editor:** Kristi Thom. **Managing Editor:** Barbara Stretchberry. **Contact:** Editorial Dept. Assistant. Bimonthly magazine. Estab. 1992. Circ. 750,000. "For girls ages 8-12. We run fiction and nonfiction, historical and contemporary."

Fiction: Middle readers: contemporary, historical, multicultural, suspense/mystery, good fiction about anything. No romance, science fiction or fantasy. No preachy, moralistic tales or stories with animals as protagonists. Only a girl or girls as characters—no boys. Buys approximately 6 mss/year. Average word length: 1,000-2,300. Byline given.

Nonfiction: How-to, interview/profile, history. Any articles aimed at girls ages 8-12. Buys 3-10 mss/year. Average word length: 600. Byline sometimes given. No historical profiles about obvious female heroines—Annie Oakley, Amelia Earhart; no romance or dating.

How to Contact/Writers: Fiction: Query with published clips. Nonfiction: Query. Responds to queries/mss in 3 months. Will consider simultaneous submissions.

Illustration: Works on assignment only.

Terms: Pays on acceptance. Buys first North American serial rights. Pays $500 minimum for stories; $300 minimum for articles. Sample copies for $3.95 and 9×12 SAE with $1.93 in postage (send to Magazine Department Assistant). Writer's guidelines free for SASE.

Tips: "Keep (stories and articles) simple but interesting. Kids are discriminating readers, too. They won't read a boring or pretentious story. We're looking for short (maximum 175 words) how-to stories and short profiles of girls for 'Girls Express' section, as well as word games, puzzles and mazes."

ANALOG SCIENCE FICTION AND FACT, Dell Magazines, 475 Park Ave., New York NY 10016. (212)686-7188. Fax: (212)686-7414. E-mail: analog@dellmagazines.com. Website: www.analogsf.com. **Articles Editor:** Stanley Schmidt. **Fiction Editor:** Stanley Schmidt. **Art Director:** Victoria Green. Magazine published 11 times/year (one double issue). Estab. 1930. Circ. 60,000. "We publish science fiction and science fact articles aimed at intelligent scientifically literate adults. Some bright teenagers read us, but we are *not* a children's magazine."

Fiction: Young adults: science fiction. Buys 70 mss/year. Average word length: 80,000 maximum. "We use very few stories between 20,000 and 40,000 words; longer ones are occassionally serialized." Byline given.

Nonfiction: Young adults: nature/environment, science. Buys 11 mss/year. Average word length: 3,000-5,000.

How to Contact/Writers: Fiction: Query for serials (over 20,000 words) only. Send complete ms if under 20,000 words. Responds to /mss in 1 month. Publishes ms 1 year after acceptance.

Illustration: Buys 4 illustrations/issue; 45 illustrations/year. Works on assignment only. Illustrations only: Query with samples. Send portfolio, slides. Contact: Victoria Green, art director. Responds only if interested. Samples returned with SASE.

Terms: Pays on acceptance. Buys first North American serial rights, nonexclusive foreign serial rights. Pays $20-4,000 for stories. Sample copies for $5. Writer's/illustrators guidelines for SASE; also available on website.

Tips: "Read the magazine to get a feel for what our readers like."

☑ **APPLESEEDS, The Magazine for Young Readers**, Cobblestone Publishing, A Division of Carus Publishing, 140 E. 83rd St., New York NY 10028. E-mail: swbuc@aol.com. Website: www.cobblestonepub. com/pages/writersAPPguides.html. **Editor:** Susan Buckley. Magazine published monthly except June, July and August. *AppleSeeds* is a theme-based social studies magazine from Cobblestone Publishing for ages 7-10. Published 9 times/year.

• *AppleSeeds* is aimed toward readers ages 7-10. See website for current theme list.

How to Contact/Writers: Nonfiction: Query only. See website for submission guidelines and theme list.

Tips: "Submit queries specifically focused on the theme of an upcoming issue. We generally work 6 months ahead on themes. We look for unusual perspectives, original ideas, and excellent scholarship. We accept no unsolicited manuscripts. Writers should check our website for current guidelines, topics, and query deadlines. We use very little fiction. Illustrators should not submit unsolicited art."

ASK, Arts and Sciences for Kids, 332 S. Michigan Ave., Suite 1100, Chicago IL 60604. (312)939-1500. Fax: (312)939-8150. E-mail: ask@caruspub.com. Website: www.caruspub.com. **AA Director:** Karen Kohn. Bimonthly magazine. Estab. 2002. "*ASK* encourages children between the ages of 7 and 10 to inquire about the world around them. Nonfiction articles, poetry, activities, and reprints from trade books will be considered for publication."

Fiction: Middle readers: adventure, animal, contemporary.

Nonfiction: Young readers, middle readers: animal, arts/crafts, biography, careers, games/puzzles, geography, health, history, humorous, interview/profile, math, multicultural, nature/environment, problem-solving, science, social issues, sports. Buys 30-40 mss/year. Average word length: 250-900. Byline given.

Poetry: Reviews poetry.

How to Contact/Writers: Nonfiction: Query. Responds to queries in 6 weeks; mss in 3 months. Will consider electronic submission via disk or modem, previously published work.

Illustration: Buys 10 illustrations/issue; 60 illustrations/year. Works on assignment only. Reviews ms/illustration packages from artists. Contact: Karen Kohn, art director. Illustrations only: Query with samples. Contact: Karen Kohn, art director.

BABYBUG, Carus Publishing Company, P.O. Box 300, Peru IL 61354. (815)224-6656. **Editor:** Paula Morrow. **Art Director:** Suzanne Beck. Published 10 times/year (monthly except for combined May/June and July/August issues). Estab. 1994. "A listening and looking magazine for infants and toddlers ages 6 to 24 months, *Babybug* is 6 ¼ × 7, 24 pages long, printed in large type (26-point) on high-quality cardboard stock with rounded corners and no staples."

Fiction: Looking for very simple and concrete stories, 4-6 short sentences maximum.

Nonfiction: Must use very basic words and concepts, 10 words maximum.

Poetry: Maximum length 8 lines. Looking for rhythmic, rhyming poems.

How to Contact/Writers: "Please do not query first." Send complete ms with SASE. "Submissions without SASE will be discarded." Responds in 3 months.

Illustration: Uses color artwork only. Works on assignment only. Reviews ms/illustration packages from artists. "The manuscripts will be evaluated for quality of concept and text before the art is considered." Contact: Suzanne Beck. Illustrations only: Send tearsheets or photo prints/photocopies with SASE. "Submissions without SASE will be discarded." Responds in 3 months. Samples filed.

Terms: Pays on publication for mss; after delivery of completed assignment for illustrators. Buys first rights with reprint option or (in some cases) all rights. Original artwork returned at job's completion. Rates vary ($25 minimum for mss; $250 minimum for art). Sample copy for $5. Guidelines free for SASE.

Tips: "*Babybug* would like to reach as many children's authors and artists as possible for original contributions, but our standards are very high, and we will accept only top-quality material. Before attempting to write for *Babybug*, be sure to familiarize yourself with this age child." (See listings for *Cricket*, *Cicada*, *Ladybug*, *Muse* and *Spider*.)

☑ **BOYS' LIFE**, Boy Scouts of America, 1325 W. Walnut Hill Lane, Irving TX 75038. (972)580-2366. Website: www.boyslife.org. **Editor-in-Chief:** J.D. Owen. **Managing Editor:** W.E. Butterworth, IV. **Senior Editor:** Michael Goldman. **Fiction Editor:** Rich Haddaway. **Director of Design:** Joseph P. Connolly. **Art**

"PICTURE-ORIENTED MATERIAL" is for preschoolers to 8-year-olds; "Young readers" are for 5- to 8-year-olds; "Middle readers" are for 9- to 11-year-olds; and "Young adults/teens" are for ages 12 and up. Age ranges may vary slightly from magazine to magazine.

Director: Scott Feaster. Monthly magazine. Estab. 1911. Circ. 1,300,000. *Boys' Life* is "a 4-color general interest magazine for boys 8 to 18 who are members of the Cub Scouts, Boy Scouts or Venturers; a 4-color general interest magazine for all boys."

Fiction: Middle readers: adventure, humor, science fiction, spy/mystery. Does not want to see "talking animals and adult reminiscence." Buys only 12-16 mss/year. Average word length: 1,000-1,500. Byline given.

Nonfiction: "Subject matter is broad. We cover everything from professional sports to American history to how to pack a canoe. A look at a current list of the BSA's more than 100 merit badge pamphlets gives an idea of the wide range of subjects possible. Even better, look at a year's worth of recent issues. Column headings are science, nature, earth, health, sports, space and aviation, cars, computers, entertainment, pets, history, music and others." Average word length: 500-1,500. Columns 300-750 words. Byline given.

How to Contact/Writers: Fiction: Send query or complete ms with cover letter and SASE to fiction editor. Nonfiction: Major articles query articles editor. Columns query associate editor with SASE for response. Responds to queries/mss in 2 months.

Illustration: Buys 10-12 illustrations/issue; 100-125 illustrations/year. Works on assignment only. Reviews ms/illustration packages from artists. "Query first." Illustrations only: Send tearsheets. Responds to art samples only if interested. Samples returned with SASE. Original artwork returned at job's completion. Credit line given.

Terms: Pays on acceptance. Buys first rights. Pays $750 and up for fiction; $400-1,500 for major articles; $150-400 for columns; $250-300 for how-to features. Pays illustrators $1,500-3,000 for color cover; $100-1,500 color inside. Sample copies for $3 plus 9×12 SASE. Writer's/illustrator's/photo guidelines available for SASE.

Tips: "We strongly urge you to study at least a year's issues to better understand the type of material published. Articles for *Boys' Life* must interest and entertain boys ages 8 to 18. Write for a boy you know who is 12. Our readers demand crisp, punchy writing in relatively short, straightforward sentences. The editors demand well-reported articles that demonstrate high standards of journalism. We follow *The New York Times* manual of style and usage. All submissions must be accompanied by SASE with adequate postage."

☑ **BOYS' QUEST**, P.O. Box 227, Bluffton OH 45817-0227. (419)358-4610. Fax: (419)358-5027. **Articles Editor:** Marilyn Edwards. **Art Submissions:** Anne Hohenbrink. Bimonthly magazine. Estab. 1995. "*Boys' Quest* is a magazine created for boys from 6 to 13 years, with youngsters 8, 9 and 10 the specific target age. Our point of view is that every young boy deserves the right to be a young boy for a number of years before he becomes a young adult. As a result, *Boys' Quest* looks for articles, fiction, nonfiction, and poetry that deal with timeless topics, such as pets, nature, hobbies, science, games, sports, careers, simple cooking, and anything else likely to interest a young boy."

Fiction: Young readers, middle readers: adventure, animal, history, humorous, nature/environment, problem-solving, sports, jokes, building, cooking, cartoons, riddles. Does not want to see violence, teenage themes. Buys 30 mss/year. Average word length: 200-500. Byline given.

Nonfiction: Young readers, middle readers: animal, arts/crafts, biography, cooking, games/puzzles, history, how-to, humorous, math, problem-solving, science. Prefer photo support with nonfiction. Buys 30 mss/year. Average word length: 200-500. Byline given.

Poetry: Reviews poetry. Maximum length: 21 lines. Limit submissions to 6 poems.

How to Contact/Writers: All writers should consult the theme list before sending in articles. To receive current theme list, send a SASE. Fiction/Nonfiction: Query or send complete ms (preferred). Send SASE with correct postage. No faxed material. Responds to queries in 2 weeks; mss in 1 month (if rejected); 4 months (if scheduled). Publishes ms 3 months-3 years after acceptance. Will consider simultaneous submissions and previously published work.

Illustration: Buys 6 illustrations/issue; 36-45 illustrations/year. Uses b&w artwork only. Works on assignment only. Reviews ms/illustration packages from artists. Send ms with dummy. Illustrations only: Query with samples, arrange portfolio review. Send portfolio, tearsheets. Responds in 1 month. Samples returned with SASE; samples filed. Credit line given.

Photography: Photos used for support of nonfiction. "Excellent photographs included with a nonfiction story is considered very seriously." Model/property releases required. Uses b&w, 5×7 or 3×5 prints. Query with samples; send unsolicited photos by mail. Responds in 3 weeks.

Terms: Pays on publication. Buys first North American serial rights for mss. Buys first rights for artwork. Pays 5¢/word for stories and articles. Additional payment for ms/illustration packages and for photos accompanying articles. Pays $150-200 for color cover. Pays photographers per photo (range: $5-10). "*Boys' Quest*, as a new publication, is aware that its rates of payment are modest at this time. But we pledge to increase those rewards in direct proportion to our success. Meanwhile, we will strive to treat our contributors and their work with respect and fairness. That treatment, incidentally, will include quick decision on all submissions." Originals returned to artist at job's completion. Sample copies for $4. Writer's/illustrator's/photo guidelines free for SASE.

Tips: "We are looking for lively writing, most of it from a young boy's point of view—with the boy or boys directly involved in an activity that is both wholesome and unusual. We need nonfiction with photos and fiction stories—around 500 words—puzzles, poems, cooking, carpentry projects, jokes and riddles. Nonfiction pieces that are accompanied by black and white photos are far more likely to be accepted than those that need illustrations. We will entertain simultaneous submissions as long as that fact is noted on the manuscript." (See listing for *Hopscotch*.)

BREAD FOR GOD'S CHILDREN, Bread Ministries, Inc., P.O. Box 1017, Arcadia FL 34265-1017. (863)494-6214. Fax: (863)993-0154. E-mail: bread@sunline.net. Website: www.breadministries.org. **Editor:** Judith M. Gibbs. Bimonthly magazine. Estab. 1972. Circ. 10,000 (US and Canada). "*Bread* is designed as a teaching tool for Christian families." 85% of publication aimed at juvenile market.

Fiction: Young readers, middle readers, young adult/teen: adventure, religious, problem-solving, sports. Looks for "teaching stories that portray Christian lifestyles without preaching." Buys approximately 20 mss/year. Average word length: 900-1,500 (for teens); 600-900 (for young children). Byline given.

Nonfiction: Young readers, middle readers: animal. All levels: how-to. "We do not want anything detrimental to solid family values. Most topics will fit if they are slanted to our basic needs." Buys 3-4 mss/year. Average word length: 500-800. Byline given.

Illustration: "The only illustrations we purchase are those occasional good ones coming with a story we accept."

How to Contact/Writers: Fiction/nonfiction: Send complete ms. Responds to mss in 6 months "if considered for use." Will consider simultaneous submissions and previously published work.

Terms: Pays on publication. Pays $10-50 for stories; $25 for articles. Sample copies free for 9 × 12 SAE and 5 first-class stamps (for 2 copies).

Tips: "We want stories or articles that illustrate overcoming by faith and living solid, Christian lives. Know our publication and what we have used in the past . . . know the readership . . . know the publisher's guidelines. Stories should teach the value of morality and honesty without preaching. Edit carefully for content and grammar."

CALLIOPE, Exploring World History, Cobblestone Publishing Company, 30 Grove St., Suite C, Peterborough NH 03458. (603)924-7209. Fax: (603)924-7380. Website: www.cobblestonepub.com. **Managing Editor:** Lou Waryncia. **Co-editors:** Rosalie Baker and Charles Baker. **Art Director:** Ann Dillon. Magazine published 9 times/year. "*Calliope* covers world history (East/West), and lively, original approaches to the subject are the primary concerns of the editors in choosing material."

● *Calliope* themes for 2003 include Tang Dynasty, The Qu'ran, Olmec and Tolmec, and Galileo and the Scientific Revolution. For additional themes and time frames, visit the website.

Fiction: Middle readers and young adults: adventure, folktales, plays, history, biographical fiction. Material must relate to forthcoming themes. Word length: up to 800.

Nonfiction: Middle readers and young adults: arts/crafts, biography, cooking, games/puzzles, history. Material must relate to forthcoming themes. Word length: 300-800.

Poetry: Maximum line length: 100. Wants "clear, objective imagery. Serious and light verse considered."

How to Contact/Writers: "A query must consist of the following to be considered (please use nonerasable paper): a brief cover letter stating subject and word length of the proposed article; a detailed one-page outline explaining the information to be presented in the article; an extensive bibliography of materials the author intends to use in preparing the article; a self-addressed stamped envelope. Writers new to *Calliope* should send a writing sample with query. If you would like to know if your query has been received, please also include a stamped postcard that requests acknowledgment of receipt. In all correspondence, please include your complete address as well as a telephone number where you can be reached. A writer may send as many queries for one issue as he or she wishes, but each query must have a separate cover letter, outline, bibliography and SASE. Telephone queries are not accepted. Handwritten queries will not be considered. Queries may be submitted at any time, but queries sent well in advance of deadline *may not be answered for several months*. Go-aheads requesting material proposed in queries are usually sent five months prior to publication date. Unused queries will be returned approximately three to four months prior to publication date."

Illustration: Illustrations only: Send tearsheets, photocopies. Original work returned upon job's completion (upon written request).

Photography: Buys photos from freelancers. Wants photos pertaining to any forthcoming themes. Uses b&w/color prints, 35mm transparencies. Send unsolicited photos by mail (on speculation).

Terms: Buys all rights for mss and artwork. Pays 20-25¢/word for stories/articles. Pays on an individual basis for poetry, activities, games/puzzles. "Covers are assigned and paid on an individual basis." Pays photographers per photo ($15-100 for b&w; $25-100 for color). Sample copy for $4.95 and SAE with $2 postage. Writer's/illustrator's/photo guidelines for SASE. (See listings for *AppleSeeds, Cobblestone, Faces, Footsteps* and *Odyssey*.)

CAMPUS LIFE, Christianity Today, International, 465 Gundersen Dr., Carol Stream IL 60188. (630)260-6200. Fax: (630)260-0114. E-mail: clmag@campuslife.net. Website: www.campuslife.net. **Articles and Fiction Editor:** Chris Lutes. Bimonthly magazine. Estab. 1944. Circ. 100,000. "Our purpose is to help Christian high school students navigate adolescence with their faith intact."
Fiction: Young adults: humorous, problem-solving. Buys 5-6 mss/year. Byline given.
Poetry: Reviews poetry.
How to Contact/Writers: Fiction/nonfiction: Query.
Illustration: Works on assignment only. Reviews illustration packages from artists. Contact: Doug Fleenor, senior designer. Illustrations only: Query; send promo sheet. Responds only if interested. Credit line given.
Terms: Pays on acceptance. Original artwork returned at job's completion. Writer's/illustrator's/photo guidelines for SASE.

CAREER WORLD, General Learning Communications, 900 Skokie Blvd., Suite 200, Northbrook IL 60062-4028. (847)205-3000. Fax: (847)564-8197. **Articles Editor:** Carole Rubenstein. Monthly (school year) magazine. Estab. 1972. A guide to careers, for students grades 6-12.
Nonfiction: Young adults/teens: education, how-to, interview/profile, career awareness and development. Byline given.
How to Contact/Writers: Nonfiction: Query with published clips and résumé. "We do not want any unsolicited manuscripts." Responds to queries in 2 weeks.
Illustration: Buys 5-10 illustrations/year. Works on assignment only. Reviews ms/illustration packages from artists. Manuscript/illustration packages and illustration only: Query; send promo sheet and tearsheets. Credit line given.
Photography: Purchases photos from freelancers.
Terms: Pays on publication. Buys all rights for ms. Pays $150 and up for articles. Pays illustrators by the project. Writer's guidelines free, but only on assignment.

CAT FANCY, The Magazine for Responsible Cat Owners, Fancy Publications, P.O. Box 6050, Mission Viejo CA 92690. (949)855-8822. Fax: (949)855-3045. Website: www.catfancy.com. Monthly magazine. Estab. 1965. Circ. 300,000. "Our magazine is for cat owners who want to know more about how to care for their pets in a responsible manner. We want to see 500-750-word articles showing children relating to or learning about cats in a positive, responsible way. We'd love to see more craft projects for children." 3% of material aimed at juvenile audience.
Fiction: Middle readers, young adults/teens: animal (all cat-related). Does not want to see stories in which cats talk. Buys 2 mss/year. Average word length: 750-1,000. Byline given. Never wants to see work showing cats being treated abusively or irresponsibly or work that puts cats in a negative light. Never use mss written from cats' point of view. Query first.
Nonfiction: Middle readers, young adults/teens: careers, arts/crafts, puzzles, profiles of children who help cats (all cat-related). Buys 3-9 mss/year. Average word length: 450-1,000. Byline given. Would like to see more crafts and how-to pieces for children.
Poetry: Reviews short poems only. "No more than five poems per submission please."
How To Contact/Writers: Fiction/nonfiction: Send query only. Responds to queries in 2 months. Publishes ms (juvenile) 4-12 months after acceptance. Send SASE for writer's guidelines.
Illustration: Buys 2-10 illustrations/year. "Most of our illustrations are assigned or submitted with a story. We look for realistic images of cats done with pen and ink (no pencil)." Illustration only: "Submit photocopies of work; samples of spot art possibilities." Samples returned with SASE. Responds in 2 months. Credit line given.
Photography: "Cats only, in excellent focus and properly lit. Send SASE for photo needs and submit according to them."
Terms: Pays on publication. Buys first North American serial rights. Buys one-time rights for artwork and photos. Originals returned to artist at job's completion. Pays $50-200 for stories; $75-400 for articles; $35-50 for crafts or puzzles; $20 for poems. Pays illustrators $50-200 for color inside. Photographers paid per photo (range: $35-200). Writer's/artist's/photo guidelines free for #10 SAE and 1 first-class stamp.
Tips: "Perhaps the most important tip we can give is: consider what 9- to 14-year-olds want to know about cats and what they enjoy most about cats, and address that topic in a style appropriate for them.

Writers, keep your writing concise, and don't be afraid to try again after a rejection. Illustrators, we use illustrations mainly as spot art; occasionally we make assignments to illustrators whose spot art we've used before."

CATHOLIC FORESTER, Catholic Order of Foresters, P.O. Box 3012, 355 Shuman Blvd., Naperville IL 60566-7012. (630)983-4900. Fax: (630)983-3384. E-mail: cofpr@aol.com. **Articles Editor:** Patricia Baron. **Art Director:** Keith Halla. Bimonthly magazine. Estab. 1883. Circ. 100,000. Targets members of the Catholic Order of Foresters. In addition to the organization's news, it offers general interest pieces on health, finance, travel, family life. Also use inspirational and humorous fiction.
Fiction: Young readers, middle readers, young adults: humorous, nature/environment, religious. Buys 10-20 mss/year. Average word length: 500-1,500.
How to Contact/Writers: Fiction: Submit complete ms. Responds in 4 months. Will consider previously published work.
Illustration: Buys 8-12 illustrations/issue. Uses color artwork only. Works on assignment only.
Photography: Buys photos with accompanying ms only.
Terms: Pays on acceptance. Buys first North American serial rights, reprint rights, one-time rights. Sample copies for 9×12 SAE and 3 first-class stamps. Writer's guidelines free for SASE.

CELEBRATE, Word Action Publishing Co., Church of the Nazarene, 6401 The Paseo, Kansas City MO 64131. (816)333-7000, ext. 2358. Fax: (816)333-4439. E-mail: mhammer@nazarene.org. Website: www.wordaction.com. **Editor:** Melissa Hammer. **Editorial Assistant**: Andrea Simms. Weekly publication. Estab. 2001. Circ. 30,000. "This weekly take-home paper connects Sunday School learning to life for preschoolers (age 3 and 4), kindergartners (age 5 and 6) and their families." 75% of publication aimed at juvenile market; 25% parents.
Nonfiction: Picture-oriented material: arts/crafts, cooking, poems, action rhymes, piggyback songs (theme based). 50% of mss nonfiction. Byline given.
Poetry: Reviews poetry. Maximum length: 4-8 lines. Unlimited submissions.
How to Contact/Writers: Nonfiction: query. Responds to queries in 1 month. Responds to mss in 6 weeks. Publishes ms 1 year after acceptance. Will accept electronic submission via e-mail.
Terms: Pays on acceptance. Buys all rights, multi-use rights. Pays a minimum of $2 for songs and rhymes; 25¢/line for poetry; $15 for activities, crafts, recipes. Compensation includes 4 contributor copies. Sample copy for SASE.
Tips: "Limited acceptance at this time."

N ▣ CHICKADEE, The Owl Group, 49 Front St. E., 2nd Floor, Toronto, Ontario M5E 1B3 Canada. (416)340-2700. Fax: (416)340-9769. E-mail: owl@owl.on.ca. Website: www.owlkids.com. **Contact:** Angela Keenlyside, managing editor. Magazine published 10 times/year. Estab. 1979. Circ. 110,000. "*Chickadee* is a hands-on publication designed to interest 6- to 9-year-olds in science, nature and the world around them. It features games, stories, crafts, experiments. Every effort is made to provide *Chickadee* readers with fresh ideas that are offered in an innovative and surprising way. Lively writing and a strong visual component are necessary strengths in any piece written for *Chickadee*."
Fiction: Picture-oriented material, new readers: animal, humorous, nature/environment. Does not want to see religious, anthropomorphic animal, romance material, material that talks down to kids. Buys 6 mss/year. Average word length: 800-900. Byline given.
Nonfiction: Picture-oriented material, new readers: animal (facts/characteristics), arts/crafts, games/puzzles, humorous, nature/environment, science. Does not want to see religious material. Buys 2-5 mss/year. Average word length: 300-800. Byline given.
Poetry: Limit submissions to 5 poems at a time.
How to Contact/Writers: Fiction/nonfiction: Send complete ms. SAE and international postage coupon for answer and return of ms. Responds to mss in 3 months unless return postage is missing. Will consider simultaneous submissions. "We prefer to read complete manuscript on speculation."
Illustration: Buys 3-5 illustrations/issue; 40 illustrations/year. Preferred theme or style: realism/humor (but not cartoons). Works on assignment only. Illustration only: Send promo sheet. Reports on art samples only if interested. Samples returned with SASE. Credit line given.
Photography: Looking for animal (mammal, insect, reptile, fish, etc.) and nature photos, kids, sports, science, bizarre, edgy. Uses 35mm and 2¼×2¼ transparencies. Write to request photo package for $1 money order, attention Kim Gillingham, researcher.
Terms: Pays on publication. Buys all rights for mss. Buys one-time rights for photos. Original artwork returned at job's completion. Pays $10-250 for stories. Pays illustrators $100-650 for color inside, pays photographers per photo (range: $100-350). Sample copies for $4. Writer's guidelines free. All requests must include SAE and international postage coupon.

Tips: "The magazine publishes fiction and nonfiction that encourages kids to read and learn more about the world around them. The majority of *Chickadee*'s content is stories, puzzles, activities and observation games for young kids to enjoy on their own. Each issue also includes a longer story or poem that can be enjoyed by older kids." (See listings for *Chirp* and *OWL*.)

CHILD, G&N USA Pulishing, 375 Lexington Ave., New York NY 10017. (212)499-2000. Fax: (212)499-2038. Website: www.child.com. **Executive Editor:** Andrea Barbalich. **Photo Editor:** Topaz LeTourneau. Monthly magazine. Estab. 1984. Circ. 1 million. "Child provides parents of children from birth to age 12 with the newest thinking, information, and advice they need to raise their families in a constantly changing, time-pressed world."

Nonfiction: Freelance writers are invited to submit query letters and published clips only. The topics are children's health, parenting and marital relationship issues, child behavior and development, and personal essays pertaining to family life. Buys 5 mss/year.

How to Contact/Writers: Responds to queries in 10 weeks.

Illustration: Only interested in agented material.

Terms: Pays on acceptance. Buys first rights. Sample copies for $3.95. Writer's guidelines for SASE.

CHILD LIFE, Children's Better Health Institute, P.O. Box 567, Indianapolis IN 46206. Parcels and packages: please send to 1100 Waterway Blvd., 46202. (317)636-8881. Fax: (317)684-8094. Website: www.chil dlifemag.org. **Editor:** Jack Gramling. **Art Director:** Phyllis Lybarger. Magazine published 8 times/year. Estab. 1921. Circ. 80,000. Targeted toward kids ages 9-11. Focuses on health, sports, fitness, nutrition, safety, academic excellence, general interests, and the nostalgia of *Child Life's* early days. "We publish jokes, riddles and poems by children." Kids should include name, address, phone number (for office use) and school photo. "No mass duplicated, multiple submissions."

● *Child Life* is no longer accepting manuscripts for publication. See listings for *Children's Playmate*, *Humpty Dumpty's Magazine*, *Jack And Jill*, *Turtle Magazine* and *U*S*Kids*.

Tips: "We use kids' submissions from our age range—9 to 11. Those older or younger should try one of our sister publications: *Children's Digest*, *Children's Playmate*, *Humpty Dumpty's Magazine*, *Jack And Jill*, *Turtle Magazine*, *U*S*Kids*."

CHILDREN'S DIGEST, Children's Better Health Institute, 1100 Waterway Blvd., P.O. Box 567, Indianapolis IN 46206. (317)634-1100. Fax: (317)684-8094. Website: www.childrensdigestmag.org.

CHILDREN'S PLAYMATE, Children's Better Health Institute, 1100 Waterway Blvd., Box 567, Indianapolis IN 46206. (317)636-8881. Website: www.childrensplaymatemag.org. **Editor:** Terry Harshman. **Art Director:** Chuck Horsman. Magazine published 8 times/year. Estab. 1929. Circ. 135,000. For children ages 6-8 years; approximately 50% of content is health-related.

Fiction: Average word length: 100-300. Byline given.

Nonfiction: Young readers: arts/crafts, easy recipes, games/puzzles, health, medicine, safety, science, sports. Buys 16-20 mss/year. Average word length: 300-500. Byline given.

Poetry: Maximum length: 20-25 lines.

How to Contact/Writers: Fiction/nonfiction: Send complete ms. Responds to mss in 3 months. Do not send queries.

Illustration: Works on assignment only. Reviews ms/illustration packages from artists. Query first.

Terms: Pays on publication for illustrators and writers. Buys all rights for mss and artwork. Pays 17¢/word for stories. Pays minimum $25 for poems. Pays $275 for color cover illustration; $90 for b&w inside; $70-155 for color inside. Sample copy $1.75. Writer's/illustrator's guidelines for SASE. (See listings for *Child Life*, *Children's Digest*, *Humpty Dumpty's Magazine*, *Jack and Jill*, *Turtle Magazine* and *U*S* Kids*.)

CHIRP, The Owl Group, 49 Front St. E., 2nd Floor, Toronto, Ontario M5E 1B3 Canada. Fax: (416)340-9769. E-mail: owl@owl.on.ca. Website: www.owlkids.com. **Editor:** Mary Vincent or Jackie Farquhar. Published monthly during school year. *Discovery* magazine for children ages 3-6. "*Chirp* aims to introduce preschool non-readers to reading for pleasure about the world around them."

Fiction: Picture-oriented material: nature/environment, adventure, animal, multicultural, problem-solving, sports. Word length: 250 maximum.

Nonfiction: Picture-oriented material: fun, easy craft ideas, animal, games/puzzles, how-to, multicultural, nature/environment, problem-solving.

Poetry: Wants rhymes and poetry. Maximum length: 8 lines.

How to Contact/Writers: Query. Responds to queries/mss in 3 months.

Illustration: Uses approximately 15 illustrations/issue; 135 illustrations/year. Samples returned with SASE. Originals returned at job's completion. Credit line given.

Terms: Pays on acceptance. Buys all rights. Pays on publication. Pays writers $250 (Canadian); illustrators $150-650 (Canadian); photographers paid per photo ($150-375 Canadian). Sample copies available for $4 (Canadian).

Tips: "Chirp editors prefer to read completed manuscripts of stories and articles, accompanied by photographs or suggestions of visual references where they are appropriate. All craft ideas should be based on materials that are found around the average household." (See listings for *Chickadee* and *OWL*.)

CICADA, Carus Publishing Company, P.O. Box 300, 315 Fifth St., Peru IL 61354. (815)224-6656. Fax: (815)224-6615. E-mail: CICADA@caruspub.com. Website: www.cicadamag.com. **Editor-in-Chief:** Mari-anne Carus. **Executive Editor:** Deborah Vetter. **Associate Editor:** Tracy C. Schoenle. **Senior Art Director:** Ron McCutchan. Bimonthly magazine. Estab. 1998. *Cicada* publishes fiction and poetry with a genuine teen sensibility, aimed at the high school and college-age market. The editors are looking for stories and poems that are thought-provoking but entertaining.

Fiction: Young adults: adventure, animal, contemporary, fantasy, history, humorous, multicultural, nature/environment, romance, science fiction, sports, suspense/mystery, stories that will adapt themselves to a sophisticated cartoon, or graphic novel format. Buys up to 60 mss/year. Average word length: about 5,000 words for short stories; up to 15,000 for novellas only—we run one novella per issue.

Nonfiction: Young adults: first-person, coming-of-age experiences that are relevant to teens and young adults (example-life in the Peace Corps). Buys 6 mss/year. Average word length: about 5,000 words. Byline given.

Poetry: Reviews serious, humorous, free verse, rhyming (if done well) poetry. Maximum length: up to 25 lines. Limit submissions to 5 poems.

How to Contact/Writers: Fiction/nonfiction: send complete ms. Responds to mss in 3 months. Publishes ms 1-2 years after acceptance. Will consider simultaneous submissions if author lets us know.

Illustration: Buys 20 illustrations/issue; 120 illustrations/year. Uses color artwork for cover; b&w for interior. Works on assignment only. Reviews ms/illustration packages from artists. Send ms with 1-2 sketches and samples of other finished art. Contact: Ron McCutchan, senior art director. Illustrations only: Query with samples. Contact: Ron McCutchan, senior art director. Responds in 6 weeks. Samples returned with SASE; samples filed. Credit line given.

Photography: Wants documentary photos (clear shots that illustrate specific artifacts, persons, locations, phenomena, etc., cited in the text) and "art" shots of teens in photo montage/lighting effects etc. Uses b&w 4×5 glossy prints. Submit portfolio for review. Responds in 6 weeks.

Terms: Pays on publication. Buys all rights for mss. Buys all rights for artwork and photographs. Pays up to 25¢/word for mss; up to $3/line for poetry. Pays illustrators $750 for color cover; $50-150 for b&w inside. Pays photographers per photo (range: $50-150). Sample copies for $8.50. Writer's/illustrator's/photo guidelines for SASE.

Tips: "Please don't write for a junior high audience. We're looking for complex character development, strong plots, and thought-provoking themes for young people in high school and college. Don't forget humor!" (See listings for *Babybug, Cricket, Ladybug, Muse* and *Spider*.)

CLASS ACT, Class Act, Inc., P.O. Box 802, Henderson KY 42419-0802. E-mail: classact@henderson.net. Website: www.henderson.net/~classact. **Editor:** Mary Anderson. **Articles Editor:** Susan Thurman. Monthly, September-May. Newsletter. Estab. 1993. Circ. 300. "We are looking for practical, ready-to-use ideas for the English/language arts classroom (grades 6-12)."

Nonfiction: Young adults/teens: games/puzzles, how-to. Does not want to see esoteric material; no master's thesis; no poetry (except articles about how to write poetry). Buys 20 mss/year. Average word length: 200-2,000. Byline given.

How to Contact/Writers: Send complete ms. E-mail submissions (no attachments) and submissions on disk using Word encouraged. Responds to queries/mss in 1 month. Usually publishes ms 3-12 months after acceptance. Will consider simultaneous submissions. Must send SASE.

Terms: Pays on acceptance. Pays $10-40 per article. Buys all rights. Sample copy for $3 and SASE.

Tips: "We're interested only in language arts-related articles for teachers and students. Writers should realize teens often need humor in classroom assignments. In addition, we are looking for teacher-tested ideas that have already worked in the classroom. We currently have more puzzles than we need and are looking for prose rather than puzzles. Be clever. We've already seen a zillion articles on homonyms and haikus. If a SASE isn't sent, we'll assume you don't want a response."

COBBLESTONE: Discover American History, Cobblestone Publishing Co., 30 Grove St., Suite C, Peterborough NH 03458. (603)924-7209. Fax: (603)924-7380. Website: www.cobblestonepub.com. **Editor:** Meg Chorlian. **Art Director:** Ann Dillon. **Managing Editor:** Lou Waryncia. Magazine published 9

insider report

'Only the rarest kind of best can be good enough for the young'

There's no argument, Carus Publishing has a reputation. A reputation for high quality literature that challenges young readers to grow.

Deborah Vetter

In 1973, *Cricket* began publication as the first magazine under the now vast Carus umbrella. "*Cricket* began as a perfect-bound magazine with black-and-white illustrations," says *Cricket* executive editor Deborah Vetter, "and it was geared for children ages 6 to12. Every issue had an 'easy story' for beginning readers." Then along came *Ladybug* and *Spider* for preschoolers and beginning readers. "We dropped the easy story and changed *Cricket*'s age range to 9 through 14," says Vetter. "Along the way we also went to a saddle-bound format and full-color illustrations." Add to the bug list *Babybug* and *Cicada* and the age range expands to include toddlers and high school students.

It's no secret that magazine publishers today face many challenges. Greatest among these, according to Vetter, is competition. "There are so many magazines out there. The Cricket Magazine Group is addressing this challenge by diversifying and publishing to many markets. In addition to our five 'bug' magazines (*Babybug, Ladybug, Spider, Cricket* and *Cicada*) we have our Chicago-based nonfiction magazines—*Muse, Ask,* and *Click.* The Cobblestone group is also a division of the Cricket Magazine Group now. They publish *Cobblestone, Calliope, Odyssey, Dig, AppleSeeds, Footsteps,* and *Faces.*"

All of this equals greater opportunities for writers who are prepared to meet the Carus challenge. To help them do that, Deborah Vetter takes writers behind the scenes.

The Carus magazines have the reputation for being very sophisticated in their treatment of readers. How does this sophistication shape your magazine?
Our mission from the very beginning has been to respect children's intelligence and never talk down to them. We also want to create in young people a love of reading and an appreciation for good writing and illustration.

What advice do you have for writers who are still trying to break in?
Marianne Carus, *Cricket*'s founder and editor-in-chief, likes to quote Walter de la Mare, who once said, "Only the rarest kind of best in anything can be good enough for the young." That philosophy has driven the Cricket Magazine Group over the past 30 years. For writers who are still trying to break in, I would say read widely in children's literature, keep writing (practice makes perfect!), and above all, be persistent.

Carus Publications began with *Cricket*, a publication for children ages 6-12. To stay competitive in the modern market, Carus has diversified into a virtual plethora of bugs including *Babybug*, *Ladybug*, *Spider*, *Cricket* and *Cicada* as well as nonfiction magazines *Muse*, *Ask*, and *Click*, and the recently added Cobblestone Publishing Group magazines, including *Cobblestone*, *Calliope*, *Odyssey*, *Dig*, *AppleSeeds*, *Footsteps*, and *Faces*. (See *Children's Writer's & Illustrator's Market* Magazine Listings.)

Of the wide range of manuscripts *Cricket* **buys, from fantasy and contemporary fiction to how-to and science pieces, what do these manuscripts have in common?**
Clear, engaging writing; authenticity; good internal structure and development of plot, characters, setting, ideas, concepts, etc.

Which type of manuscript is the most difficult to sell to *Cricket***? Why?**
We're always looking for science articles. However, we want more than purely descriptive, fact-filled pieces; we want clear, engaging writing and a premise. That last element shows us how science works and is often lacking from science writing. What concept or theory are you presenting and/or supporting? A sense of wonder is always good, too. It inspires an appreciation of the incredible world in which we live!

When you read over a bibliography for a nonfiction project, what do you look for?
I'm looking for depth of research. In other words, don't just rely on other books written for children. Use adult sources as well. Track down primary sources rather than relying on other authors' interpretations. You also want to make sure your research is up to date. Interview someone active in the field. Don't rely solely on the Internet for your research.

Cricket **uses a system of first readers. How does this system work?**
We receive about 2,000 magazine manuscripts per month in our offices in Peru, Illinois. Authors we publish often are "set up" and read in-house, and they receive personal replies. All other submissions are sent to our first readers, who read everything and return promising submissions to the office so the editors can take a second look. Out of every 100 submissions, about 5 are returned, and out of those 5, about 1 is accepted for publication.

What kinds of things might you ask a writer to change for a rewrite?
Sometimes a story is a "cusp" story; that is, it falls between two of our magazines. This happens a lot with *Cricket* and *Cicada*. The subject matter may be sophisticated, but the writing style is too young. We may offer suggestions on how an author might tailor the story for one magazine's age group or the other. Another problem is rushed endings in which the author races through the climax and ties everything up too neatly. "Pie-in-the-sky endings," we call them.

What's your advice for a writer who's been asked to resubmit a manuscript?
Don't rush it! A rushed revision is almost always a failed revision. Drop the editor a note letting her know you plan to revise and estimate when the manuscript might be ready. Then do an in-depth, organic revision, rather than a surface, cosmetic revision. When you're done, set the manuscript aside for a week or two. At the end of that time, go back and see if you missed something or if something doesn't "feel" right. Revise as many times as you need to before resubmitting. Remember that changing any one element, such as a character's motivation in a scene, may have a ripple effect throughout the entire story.

Which types of manuscripts offer the best opportunity for writers to break into *Cricket***?**
Whatever an author does best is what we want to see. The writing speaks for itself!
—*Sue Bradford Edwards*

times/year. Circ. 33,000. "*Cobblestone* is theme-related. Writers should request editorial guidelines which explain procedure and list upcoming themes. Queries must relate to an upcoming theme. It is recommended that writers become familiar with the magazine (sample copies available)."

● *Cobblestone* themes through 2003 are available on website.

Nonfiction: Middle readers (school ages 8-14): activities, biography, games/puzzles (no word finds), history (world and American), interview/profile, science, travel. All articles must relate to the issue's theme. Buys 120 mss/year. Average word length: 600-800. Byline given.

Poetry: Up to 100 lines. "Clear, objective imagery. Serious and light verse considered." Pays on an individual basis. Must relate to theme.

How to Contact/Writers: Fiction/nonfiction: Query. "A query must consist of all of the following to be considered: a brief cover letter stating the subject and word length of the proposed article, a detailed one-page outline explaining the information to be presented in the article, an extensive bibliography of materials the author intends to use in preparing the article, a self-addressed stamped envelope. Writers new to *Cobblestone* should send a writing sample with query. If you would like to know if your query has been received, please also include a stamped postcard that requests acknowledgment of receipt. In all correspondence, please include your complete address as well as a telephone number where you can be reached. A writer may send as many queries for one issue as he or she wishes, but each query must have a separate cover letter, outline, bibliography and SASE. Telephone queries are not accepted. Handwritten queries will not be considered. Queries may be submitted at any time, but queries sent well in advance of deadline *may not be answered for several months*. Go-aheads requesting material proposed in queries are usually sent five months prior to publication date. Unused queries will be returned approximately three to four months prior to publication date."

Illustration: Buys 4 color illustrations/issue; 36 illustrations/year. Preferred theme or style: Material that is simple, clear and accurate but not too juvenile. Sophisticated sources are a must. Works on assignment only. Reviews ms/illustration packages from artists. Query. Illustrations only: Send photocopies, tearsheets, or other nonreturnable samples. "Illustrators should consult issues of *Cobblestone* to familiarize themselves with our needs." Responds to art samples in 2 weeks. Samples returned with SASE; samples not filed. Original artwork returned at job's completion (upon written request). Credit line given.

Photography: Photos must relate to upcoming themes. Send transparencies and/or color prints. Submit on speculation.

Terms: Pays on publication. Buys all rights to articles and artwork. Pays 20-25¢/word for articles/stories. Pays on an individual basis for poetry, activities, games/puzzles. Pays photographers per photo ($15-100 for b&w; $25-100 for color). Sample copy $4.95 with 7½×10½ SAE and 5 first-class stamps; writer's/illustrator's/photo guidelines free with SAE and 1 first-class stamp.

Tips: Writers. "Submit detailed queries which show attention to historical accuracy and which offer interesting and entertaining information. Study past issues to know what we look for. All feature articles, recipes, activities, fiction and supplemental nonfiction are freelance contributions." Illustrators: "Submit color samples, not too juvenile. Study past issues to know what we look for. The illustration we use is generally for stories, recipes and activities." (See listings for *AppleSeeds, Calliope, Dig, Faces, Footsteps* and *Odyssey*.)

☑ **COLLEGE BOUND MAGAZINE**, Ramholtz Publishing, Inc., 1200 South Ave., Suite 202, Staten Island NY 10314. (718)761-4800. 5700. Fax: (718)761-3300. E-mail: editorial@collegebound.net. Website: www.collegebound.net. **Articles Editor:** Gina LaGuardia. **Art Director:** Suzanne Vidal. Monthly magazine and website. Estab. 1987. Circ. 75,000 (regionals), 725,000 (nationals). *College Bound Magazine* is written by college students for high school juniors and seniors. It is designed to provide an inside view of college life, with college students from around the country serving as correspondents. The magazine's editorial content offers its teen readership personal accounts on all aspects of college, from living with a roommate, choosing a major, and joining a fraternity or sorority, to college dating, interesting courses, beating the financial aid fuss, and other college-bound concerns. *College Bound Magazine* is published six times regionally throughout the tri-state area. Special issues include the National Editions (published each September and February) and Spring California, Chicago, Texas, Florida and New England issues. The magazine offers award-winning World Wide Web affiliates starting at *CollegeBound.NET*, at www.collegebound.net.

Nonfiction: Young adults: careers, college prep, fashion, health, how-to, interview/profile, problem-solving, social issues, college life. Buys 70 mss/year. Average word length: 400-1,100 words. Byline given.

How to Contact/Writers: Nonfiction: Query with published clips. Responds to queries in 5 weeks; mss in 6 weeks. Publishes ms 2-3 months after acceptance. Will consider electronic submission via disk or modem, previously published work (as long as not a competitor title).

Illustration: Buys 2-3 illustrations/issue. Uses color artwork only. Works on assignment only. Reviews ms/illustration packages from artists. Query. Contact: Suzanne Vidal, art director. Illustrations only: Query with samples. Responds in 2 months. Samples kept on file. Credit line given.

Terms: Pays on publication. Buys first North American serial rights, all rights or reprint rights for mss. Buys first rights for artwork. Originals returned if requested, with SASE. Pays $25-100 for articles 30 days upon publication. All contributors receive 2 issues with payment. Pays illustrators $25-125 for color inside. Sample copies free for #10 SASE and $3 postage. Writer's guidelines for SASE.

Tips: "Review the sample issue and get a good feel for the types of articles we accept and our tone and purpose."

CRICKET, Carus Publishing Company, (formerly *Cricket Magazine*), P.O. Box 300, Peru IL 61354. (815)224-6656. Website: www.cricket.com. **Articles/Fiction Editor-in-Chief:** Marianne Carus. **Executive Editor:** Deborah Vetter. **Associate Editor:** Tracy Schoenle. **Associate Editor:** Julia M. Messina. **Senior Art Director:** Ron McCutchan. Monthly magazine. Estab. 1973. Circ. 72,000. Children's literary magazine for ages 9-14.

Fiction: Middle readers, young adults/teens: contemporary, fantasy, folk and fairy tales, history, humorous, science fiction, suspense/mystery. Buys 140 mss/year. Maximum word length: 2,000. Byline given.

Nonfiction: Middle readers, young adults/teens: adventure, architecture, archaeology, biography, foreign culture, games/puzzles, geography, natural history, science and technology, social science, sports, travel. Multicultural needs include articles on customs and cultures. Requests bibliography with submissions. Buys 40 mss/year. Average word length: 200-1,500. Byline given.

Poetry: Reviews poems, 1-page maximum length. Limit submissions to 5 poems or less.

How to Contact/Writers: Send complete ms. Do not query first. Responds to mss in 3 months. Does not like but will consider simultaneous submissions. SASE required for response.

Illustration: Buys 35 illustrations (14 separate commissions)/issue; 425 illustrations/year. Uses b&w and full-color work. Preferred theme or style: "strong realism; strong people, especially kids; good action illustration; no cartoons. All media, but prefer other than pencil." Reviews ms/illustration packages from artists "but reserves option to re-illustrate." Send complete ms with sample and query. Illustrations only: Provide tearsheets or good quality photocopies to be kept on file. SASE required for response/return of samples. Responds to art samples in 2 months.

Photography: Purchases photos with accompanying ms only. Model/property releases required. Uses color transparencies, b&w glossy prints.

Terms: Pays on publication. Buys all rights. Do not send original artwork. Pays up to 25¢/word for unsolicited articles; up to $3/line for poetry. Pays $750 for color cover; $75-150 for b&w, $150-250 for color inside. Pays $750 for color cover; $75-150 for b&w, $150-250 for color inside. Writer's/illustrator's guidelines for SASE.

Tips: Writers: "Read copies of back issues and current issues. Adhere to specified word limits. *Please* do not query." Illustrators: "Edit your samples. Send only your best work and be able to reproduce that quality in assignments. Put name and address on *all* samples. Know a publication before you submit—is your style appropriate?" (See listings for *Babybug, Cicada, Ladybug, Muse* and *Spider*.)

CRUSADER, Calvinist Cadet Corps, P.O. Box 7259, Grand Rapids MI 49510. (616)241-5616. Website: www.calvinistcadets.org. **Editor:** G. Richard Broene. **Art Director:** Robert deJonge. Magazine published 7 times/year. Circ. 12,000. "Our magazine is for members of the Calvinist Cadet Corps—boys aged 9-14. Our purpose is to show how God is at work in their lives and in the world around them. Our magazine offers nonfiction articles and fast-moving fiction—everything to appeal to interests and concerns of boys, teaching Christian values subtly."

Fiction: Middle readers, boys/early teens: adventure, humorous, multicultural, problem-solving, religious, sports. Buys 12 mss/year. Average word length: 900-1,500.

Nonfiction: Middle readers, boys/early teens: arts/crafts, games/puzzles, hobbies, how-to, humorous, interview/profile, problem-solving, science, sports. Buys 6 mss/year. Average word length: 400-900.

How to Contact/Writers: Fiction/nonfiction: Send complete ms. Responds to queries in 1 month; on mss in 2 months. Will consider simultaneous submissions.

Illustration: Buys 1 illustration/issue; buys 6 illustrations/year. Works on assignment only. Reviews ms/ illustration packages from artists. Responds in 5 weeks. Samples returned with SASE. Originals returned to artist at job's completion. Credit line given.

Photography: Buys photos from freelancers. Wants nature photos and photos of boys.

Terms: Pays on acceptance. Buys first North American serial rights; reprint rights. Pays 4-5¢/word for stories/articles. Pays illustrators $50-200 for b&w/color cover or b&w inside. Sample copy free with 9 × 12 SAE and 4 first-class stamps.

Tips: "Our publication is mostly open to fiction; send SASE for a list of themes (available yearly in January). We use mostly fast-moving fiction that appeals to a boy's sense of adventure or sense of humor. Avoid preachiness; avoid simplistic answers to complicated problems; avoid long dialogue with little action. Articles on sports, outdoor activities, bike riding, science, crafts, etc. should emphasize a Christian perspective but avoid simplistic moralisms."

THE CRYSTAL BALL, The Starwind Press, P.O. Box 98, Ripley OH 45167. (937)392-4549. E-mail: susannah@techgallery.com. Articles/Fiction Editor: Marlene Powell. **Assistant Editor:** Susannah C. West. Quarterly magazine. Estab. 1997. Circ. 1,000. Publishes science fiction and fantasy for young adults.
Fiction: Young adults: fantasy, folktale, science fiction. Buys 8-12 mss/year. Average word length: 1,500-5,000. Byline given.
Nonfiction: Young adults: biography, how-to, interview/profile, science. Buys 8-12 mss/year. Average word length: 1,000-3,000.
Poetry: Only publishes poetry by kids.
How to Contact/Writers: Fiction: send complete ms. Nonfiction: query. Responds to queries and mss in 4 months. Publishes ms 6-12 months after acceptance. Will consider previously published work if published in noncompeting market.
Illustration: Buys 6-8 illustrations/issue; 24-32 illustrations/year. Uses b&w camera ready artwork only. Works on assignment only. Reviews ms/illustration packages from artists. Send ms with dummy. Contact: Marlene Powell, editor. Illustrations only: query with samples. Contact: Marlene Powell, editor. Responds in 4 months if SASE enclosed. Samples kept on file. Credit line given.
Photography: Looking for photos to illustrate nonfiction pieces. Uses b&w, line shots or already screened. Responds in 3 months.
Terms: Pays on acceptance. Buys first North American serial rights for mss, artwork and photos. Original artwork returned at job's completion if requested. Pays $5-20 for stories and articles. Additional payment for photos accompanying article. Pays illustrators $5-20 for b&w inside and cover. Pays photographers per photo (range: $5-20). Sample copies for $3. Writer's/illustrator's guidelines for SASE.
Tips: Be familiar with the science fiction/fantasy genre.

DANCE MAGAZINE, 111 Myrtle St., Suite 203, Oakland CA 94607. (510)839-6060. Fax: (510)839-6066. Website: www.dancemagazine.com. **Editor-in-Chief:** KC Patrick. **Art Director:** James Lambertus. Monthly magazine. Estab. 1927. Circ. 50,000. Covers "all things dance—features, news, reviews, calendar. We have a Young Dancer section." Byline given.
How to Contact: Fiction: Query with published clips.
Photography: Uses dance photos.
Terms: Pays on publication. Buys first rights. Additional payment for ms/illustration packages and for photos accompanying articles. Pays photographers per photo. Sample copies for $4.95.
Tips: "Study the magazine for style."

DIG, (formerly *Archaeology's Dig*), Cobblestone Publishing, 30 Grove St., Suite C, Peterburough NH 03450. (603)924-7209. Fax: (603)924-7380. E-mail: cfbakeriii@meganet.net. Website: www.digonsite.c om. **Editor:** Rosalie Baker. **Editorial Director:** Lou Waryncia. **Art Director:** Ann Rillon. Bimonthly magazine. Estab. 1999. Circ. 60,000. An archaeology magazine for kids ages 8-14. Publishes entertaining and educational stories about discoveries, dinosaurs, etc.
• *Dig* was purchased by Cobblestone Publishing.
Nonfiction: Middle readers, young adults: biography, games/puzzles, history, science, archaeology. Buys 50 mss/year. Average word length: 400-800. Byline given.
How to Contact/Writers: Fiction/nonfiction: Query. "A query must consist of all of the following to be considered: a brief cover letter stating the subject and word length of the proposed article, a detailed one-page outline explaining the information to be presented in the article, an extensive bibliography of materials the author intends to use in preparing the article, and a SASE. Writers new to *Dig* should send a writing sample with query. If you would like to know if query has been received, include a stamped postcard that requests acknowledgement of receipt." Multiple queries accepted (include separate cover letter, outline, bibliography, SASE)—may not be answered for many months. Go-aheads requesting material proposed in queries are usually sent 5 months prior to publication date. Unused queries will be returned approximately 3-4 months prior to publication date.

THE AGE-LEVEL INDEX, located in the back of this book, lists book publishers and magazines according to the age-groups for which they need material.

Illustration: Buys 10-15 illustrations/issue; 60-75 illustrations/year. Uses color artwork only. Works on assignment only. Reviews ms/illustration packages from artists. Query. Contact: Ken Feisel, art director. Illustrations only: Query with samples. Arrange portfolio review. Send tearsheets. Contact: Ken Feisel, art director. Responds in 2 months only if interested. Samples not returned; samples filed. Credit line given.

Photography: Uses anything related to archaeology, history, artifacts, dinosaurs and current archaeological events that relate to kids. Uses color prints and 35mm transparencies. Provide résumé, business card, promotional literature or tearsheets to be kept on file. Responds only if interested.

Terms: Pays on publication. Buys all rights for mss. Buys first North American rights for artwork and photos. Original artwork returned at job's completion. Pays 50¢/word. Additional payment for ms/illustration packages and for photos accompanying articles. Pays illustrators $1,000 and up for color cover; $150-2,000 for color inside. Pays photographers by the project (range: $500-1,000). Pays per photo (range: $100-500).

Tips: "We are looking for writers who can communicate archaeological and paleontological concepts in a conversational style for kids. Writers should have some idea where photography can be located to support their work."

DISCOVERIES, Children's Ministries, 6401 The Paseo, Kansas City MO 64131. (816)333-7000. Fax: (816)333-4439. E-mail: vfolsom@nazarene.org. **Editor**: Virginia Folsom. **Executive Editor**: Larry Morris. **Editorial Assistant:** Kathy Hendrixson. Weekly tabloid. "*Discoveries* is a leisure-reading piece for third and fourth graders. It is published weekly by WordAction Publishing. The major purpose of the magazine is to provide a leisure-reading piece which will build Christian behavior and values and provide reinforcement for Biblical concepts taught in the Sunday School curriculum. The focus of the reinforcement will be life-related, with some historical appreciation. *Discoveries'* target audience is children ages eight to ten in grades three and four. The readability goal is third to fourth grade."

Fiction: Middle readers: adventure, contemporary, humorous, religious. "Fiction—stories should vividly portray definite Christian emphasis or character-building values, without being preachy. The setting, plot and action should be realistic." 500-word maximum. Byline given.

Nonfiction: Puzzles that fit the theme list and trivia about any miscellaneous area of interest to 8- to 10-year-olds (hobbies, fun activities, to do in your spare time, interesting facts). Please document sources.

How to Contact/Writers: Fiction: Send complete ms. Responds to queries/mss in 1 month.

Terms: Pays "approximately one year before the date of issue." Buys multi-use rights. Pays 5¢/word. Contributor receives 3 complimentary copies of publication. Sample copy free for #10 SASE with 1 first-class stamp. Writer's/artist's guidelines free with #10 SAE.

Tips: "*Discoveries* is committed to reinforcement of the Biblical concepts taught in the Sunday School curriculum. Because of this, the themes needed are mainly as follows: faith in God, obedience to God, putting God first, choosing to please God, accepting Jesus as Savior, finding God's will, choosing to do right, trusting God in hard times, prayer, trusting God to answer, importance of Bible memorization, appreciation of Bible as God's Word to man, Christians working together, showing kindness to others, witnessing. Because of this stories must follow our theme list. Please request one before attempting to submit copy."

DISCOVERY, John Milton Society for the Blind, 475 Riverside Dr., Room 455, New York NY 10115. (212)870-3335. Fax: (212)870-3226. E-mail: jglover@jmsblind.org. Website: www.jmsblind.org. **Assistant Editor**: Jennifer Glover. **Executive Director & Editor**: Darcy Quigley. Quarterly braille magazine. Estab. 1935. Circ. 2,000. "*Discovery* is a free Christian braille magazine for blind and visually impaired youth ages 8-18. 95% of material is stories, poems, quizzes and educational articles, reprinted from 20 Christian and other magazines for youth. Original pieces from individual authors must be ready to print with little or no editing involved. We cannot offer reprint fees. Christian focus."

Fiction: Young readers, middle readers, young adults/teens: all categories and issues pertaining to blind; adventure, animal, contemporary, fantasy, folktales, health, history, humorous, multicultural, nature/environment, problem solving, religious. Does not want stories in which blindness is described as a novelty. It should be part of a story with a larger focus. Buys less than 10 mss/year. Average word length: 1,500 words (maximum). Byline given.

Nonfiction: Young readers, middle readers, young adults/teens: animal, biography, careers, concept, cooking, games/puzzles, geography, health, history, hobbies, how-to, humorous, interview/profile, multicultural, nature/environment, problem solving, religion, science, social issues. Also want inspirational stories involving visually impaired. Buys less than 10 mss/year. Average word length: 1,500 words (maximum). Byline given.

Poetry: Reviews poetry. Maximum length: 500 words.

How to Contact/Writers: Fiction/nonfiction: Send complete ms. Responds to queries/mss in 2 months. Publishes ms 3-12 months after acceptance. Will consider simultaneous submissions, previously published work.

Terms: Acquires reprint rights. Authors do not receive payment, only sample copy. Sample copies free with SASE.

Tips: "95% of the material in *Discovery* is reprinted from Christian and other periodicals for youth. Previously unpublished material must therefore be ready to print with little or no editing involved. Please send complete manuscripts or request our 'Writers' Guidelines' which includes a list of periodicals we reprint from."

DISCOVERY TRAILS, Gospel Publishing House, 1445 N. Boonville Ave., Springfield MO 65802-1894. (417)862-2781. E-mail: rl-discoverytrails@gph.org. Website: www.radiantlife.org. **Articles Editor:** Sinda S. Zinn. **Art Director:** Diane Lamb. Quarterly take-home paper. Circ. 20,000. "*Discovery Trails* provides fiction stories that promote Christian living through application of biblical principles. Puzzles and activities are fun ways to learn more about God's Word and "bytes" of information are provided to inspire readers to be in awe of God's wonderful creation."

Fiction: Middle readers: adventure, animal, contemporary, humorous, nature/environment, problem-solving, religious, suspense/mystery. Buys 100 or less mss/year.

Nonfiction: Middle readers: animal, arts/crafts, how-to, humorous, nature/environment, problem-solving, religion. Buys 50-100 mss/year. Average word length: 200-500. Byline given.

Poetry: Reviews poetry. Limit submissions, at one time, to 2 poems.

How to Contact/Writers: Fiction/nonfiction: Send complete ms. Responds in 1 month. Publishes ms 15-24 months after acceptance. Will consider simultaneous submissions or previously published work. Please indicate such.

Illustration: Buys 1 illlustration issue; 50-60 illustrations/year from assigned freelancers. Uses color artwork only. Works on assignment only. Send promo sheet, portfolio. Contact: Diane Lamb, art coordinator. Responds only if interested. Samples returned with SASE; samples filed. Credit line given.

Terms: Pays on acceptance. Pays authors 7-10¢ per word. Buys first rights or reprint rights for mss. Buys reprint rights for artwork. Original artwork returned at job's completion. Sample copies for 6 × 9 SAE and 2 first-class stamps. Writer's guidelines for SASE.

✅ **DOLPHIN LOG**, The Cousteau Society, P.O. Box 112, 61 E. Eighth St., New York NY 10003. (800)441-4395. Website: www.dolphin.org. **Editor:** Lisa Rao. Bimonthly magazine for children ages 7-13. Circ. 80,000. Entirely nonfiction subject matter encompasses all areas of science, natural history, marine biology, ecology and the environment as they relate to our global water system. The philosophy of the magazine is to delight, instruct and instill an environmental ethic and understanding of the interconnectedness of living organisms, including people. Of special interest are articles on ocean- or water-related themes which develop reading and comprehension skills.

Nonfiction: Middle readers, young adult: animal, games/puzzles, geography, interview/profile, nature/environment, science, ocean. Multicultural needs include indigenous peoples, lifestyles of ancient people, etc. Does not want to see talking animals. No dark or religious themes. Buys 10 mss/year. Average word length: 500-700. Byline given.

How to Contact/Writers: Nonfiction: Query first. Unsolicited mss returned unopened. Responds to queries in 3 months; mss in 6 months.

Illustration: Buys 1 illustration/issue; buys 6 illustrations/year. Preferred theme: Biological illustration. Reviews ms/illustration packages from artists. Illustrations only: Query; send résumé, promo sheet, slides. Reports on art samples in 8 weeks only if interested. Credit line given to illustrators.

Photography: Wants "sharp, colorful pictures of sea creatures. The more unusual the creature, the better." Submit duplicate slides only. Query for submissions/rates.

Terms: Pays on publication. Buys first North American serial rights; reprint rights. Pays $75-250 for articles. Pays $100-400 for illustrations. Pays $75-200/color photos. Sample copy $2.50 with 9 × 12 SAE and 3 first-class stamps. Writer's/illustrator's guidelines free with #10 SASE.

Tips: Writers: "Write simply and clearly and don't anthropomorphize." Illustrators: "Be scientifically accurate and don't anthropomorphize. Some background in biology is helpful, as our needs range from simple line drawings to scientific illustrations which must be researched for biological and technical accuracy."

DRAMATICS, Educational Theatre Association, 2343 Auburn Ave., Cincinnati OH 45219. (513)421-3900. E-mail: dcorathers@edta.org. Website: www.edta.org. **Articles Editor:** Don Corathers. **Art Director:** William Johnston. Published monthly September-May. Estab. 1929. Circ. 35,000. "Dramatics is for students (mainly high school age) and teachers of theater. Mix includes how-to (tech theater, acting, direct-

insider report

Seeking quality material with concrete spiritual themes

Every writer and illustrator knows exactly what they hope to discover when they see their SASE in their mailbox: an acceptance letter.

And editors like *Discovery Trails*' Sinda Zinn know what they hope to find inside that manilla envelope lying on top of the slush pile: a successful manuscript.

For a religious publication such as *Discovery Trails*, a manuscript must work on multiple levels. First of all, it needs to be well-written. This poses a problem far too often. Judging by much of what she receives, Zinn says, "Many writers assume that Christian publications will buy poor-quality manuscripts with pat endings, worn story plots, and poor writing." Nothing could be further from the truth.

Sinda Zinn

Discovery Trails editors want to find the same quality that those at secular magazines, such as *Dig*, *Girl's Quest* and *Turtle* seek: a writer's very best work and nothing else. "The first thing I notice," Zinn says, "is the condition of the manuscript. That often tells us that it is a 'first' submission and not the 'fifth' one. Crisp, clean, well-done are the first things we notice—which does not apply to electronic submissions, of course." Add to this list typo-free pages, careful word choices that reflect quality writing, and stories that are "age-level appropriate" for *Discovery Trails*' 10- to 12- year-old audience and you have the basics of what Zinn hopes to discover in the slush pile.

But because *Discovery Trails* is a Christian publication, there is one more thing essential to a high-quality submission. Whether it is a fictional mystery, humor or adventure story or nonfiction history, science, or nature article, Zinn describes this necessary quality as "a spiritual emphasis, a child acting according to Christian principles. Each in some way touches on our relationship to God and how He wants us to live or how He provides for all of nature in a variety of ways." This emphasis is missing or present only superficially in many of the submissions Zinn receives.

To go beyond a superficial treatment, the spiritual theme has to be more than a catchy motto. " 'God is there for you' is jargon," Zinn explains. "Instead, make it practical and concrete. Get beyond the abstract to what it means to kids. Why do they want to read your piece? What does it mean to them? Be specific." Get to the details to bring your work alive.

This spiritual focus is missing more often in fiction (which usually has a moral, but not a specific spiritual/God-related emphasis) than in nonfiction. "Usually if it's a nonfiction piece," Zinn says, "it will have had a spiritual focus in the first place for them to send it to us."

Although nonfiction authors are better at including this spiritual focus, Zinn still has a nonfiction wish list. First on this list is quality puzzles. "Fiction and a puzzle are always included

DISCOVERY trails

FOR KIDS IN SEARCH OF THE TRUTH!

APRIL 28, 2002

STOP, LOOK, AND LISTEN

By Judy Stoner

"**S**top!" shouted five-year-old Rosalia, pausing at the edge of the sidewalk.

Daniel ignored her and started across the street. "Come on!" he yelled over his shoulder.

"No!" she shouted back. "Mrs. Martin said you're supposed to stop, look, and listen before you cross the street."

Daniel sighed and rolled his eyes. His sister had been so much easier to take care of before she was old enough to be in Mrs. Martin's Sunday School class. Now every annoying thing she did was because, "Mrs. Martin said this" or "Mrs. Martin said that."

Daniel watched as Rosalia looked to her left, then to her right. Then she just stood there.

"What are you doing now?" he shouted. "Come on!"

"I'm listening."

"Well, if you don't hurry up, I'm going on without you." Daniel was about to turn and leave when Rosalia finally skipped across the street. She smiled and took hold of his hand. Daniel shook his hand free. He didn't want anyone from school to see him holding hands with his sister.

At the grocery store, Rosalia ran straight to the candy rack. "Can I have some candy? Please? Please?"

"No," Daniel answered. "Mom gave me just enough money for bread and milk."

"Well, if it isn't Danny-boy, the baby-sitter," a voice behind them said.

Daniel whirled to see Bruce and Kevin, two of the boys from his class, standing behind him. They still wore their soccer uniforms. Daniel's heart gave a little lurch. He had wanted to try out for the soccer team, but he had to watch Rosalia after school.

"And he's got the baby with him too," Kevin teased.

"Let the baby have some candy," Bruce ordered.

"I don't have enough money for candy," Daniel said.

Bruce looked over his shoulder. "Just take some candy," he whispered to Rosalia, "No one will see you."

"Mrs. Martin said you shouldn't take things that aren't yours," Rosalia said in a loud voice.

Daniel suppressed a smile. For once he was glad his sister listened to her Sunday School teacher.

Kevin grabbed a candy bar and stuffed it into his pocket. "See how easy it is. I do it all the time and never get caught. Go ahead; no one is watching."

"But Mrs. Martin said God is always watching," Rosalia said.

Both boys doubled up with laughter. "The baby thinks God can see her," Bruce mocked Rosalia's voice.

Rosalia gave Daniel a hurt look. Tears sprang to her eyes. "Isn't that right, Daniel? That's what Mrs. Martin said."

Daniel put his arm around his little sister. "Mrs. Martin is right," he whispered to Rosalia. "God is watching you all of the time. Now stay here while I get the milk and bread."

Daniel hurried to the back of the grocery store. The two boys met him at the end of the aisle. Bruce stuck out his foot and tripped Daniel, sending him sprawling.

Daniel jumped to his feet. He knew he shouldn't fight, but sometimes a guy could only take so much. He swung his arm back, ready to punch Bruce.

Daniel could hear the words Rosalia had been saying

(Continued on back)

Illustration by Doug Jones

Bruce looked over his shoulder. "Just take some candy," he whispered to Rosalia. "No one will see you."

Illustration © 2002 Doug Jones. Reprinted with permission of *Discovery Trails*.

Discovery Trails is a Sunday school take-home paper for children ages 10-12 published by Radiant Life curriculum guides, a part of the Assemblies of God company, Gospel House Publishing. *Trails* editor Sinda Zinn says she is constantly on the lookout for "high-quality" mysteries, adventures and humor with spiritual emphasis.

in each issue, but we often have only the article and the fiction and choose to create the lesson-related puzzles ourselves," explains Zinn. She is on the lookout for "unique puzzles and activities that are more visually stimulating and mentally challenging. Puzzles need more variety—anyone can buy a computer puzzle program to make word finds, etc."

Second on her nonfiction wish list are articles based on the "funny, weird questions that kids really ask and the answers of course. They should be about something that would get readers' attention and that they would be interested in reading."

Last but not least on the nonfiction list are "real-life stories with kids as heroes, submitted with pictures." When asked how she defines a hero, Zinn pauses and then answeres, "Someone who does something extraordinary such as calling 911 to save a life. Or something to help solve a problem in their community—true life stories."

Zinn's wish list also includes fiction. Because she receives very few mysteries, which she feels are among the hardest pieces of fiction to write, she hopes to receive "exciting, imaginative mysteries with spiritual emphasis."

The final item on her wish list is adventure stories. Although she does receive adventures, they are seldom fresh. She encourages authors to go beyond overdone themes including "raccoons stealing," "bears in woods," "knights in armor," "talking animals," or "angels talking to kids." She also reminds writers that no fictional story should contain actions that could, if copied, put a child in danger.

To be ideal for *Discovery Trails*, even the best work must fit their theme list. "We try to correlate *Discovery Trails* to the curriculum," Zinn explains. Interested writers can download the theme list from www.radiantlife.org/pdfs/dt_themes.pdf. Topics are listed seasonally (fall, spring, winter and summer) for three years at a time and range from things such as God the Son/Prophecies of Jesus Birth (12/1/2002) to Obey God's Laws/Value Others (6/19/2005). "Manuscripts should be submitted at least 18 months ahead of the print date," says Zinn who reminds writers that "fiction fills up first because we receive more of those manuscripts."

When the name for Zinn's publication was chosen, careful consideration was given to its audience. "We wanted to change from *Junior Trails* but keep some part of the title for recognition," Zinn explains, "and we felt that 'discovery' was a big part of the life of kids this age." Writers who keep this sense of discovery in mind as they put together their very best work may make a discovery of their own when they open the SASE they enclosed with their manuscript.

—Sue Bradford Edwards

ing, etc.), informational, interview, photo feature, humorous, profile, technical. "We want our student readers to grow as theater artists and become a more discerning and appreciative audience. Material is directed to both theater students and their teachers, with strong student slant."

Fiction: Young adults: drama (one-act and full-length plays.) Does not want to see plays that show no understanding of the conventions of the theater. No plays for children, no Christmas or didactic "message" plays. "We prefer unpublished scripts that have been produced at least once." Buys 5-9 plays/year. Emerging playwrights have better chances with résumé of credits.

Nonfiction: Young adults: arts/crafts, careers, how-to, interview/profile, multicultural (all theater-related). "We try to portray the theater community in all its diversity." Does not want to see academic treatises. Buys 50 mss/year. Average word length: 750-3,000. Byline given.

How to Contact/Writers: Send complete ms. Responds in 3 months (longer for plays). Published ms 3 months after acceptance. Will consider simultaneous submissions and previously published work occasionally.

Illustration: Buys 0-2 illustrations/year. Works on assignment only. Arrange portfolio review; send résumé, promo sheets and tearsheets. Responds only if interested. Samples returned with SASE; sample not filed. Credit line given.

Photography: Buys photos with accompanying ms only. Looking for "good-quality production or candid photography to accompany article. We very occasionally publish photo essays." Model/property release and captions required. Uses 5×7 or 8×10 b&w glossy prints and 35mm transparencies. Query with résumé of credits. Responds only if interested.

Terms: Pays on acceptance. Buys one-time rights, occasionally reprint rights. Buys one-time rights for artwork and photos. Original artwork returned at job's completion. Pays $100-400 for plays; $50-400 for articles; up to $100 for illustrations. Pays photographers by the project or per photo. Sometimes offers additional payment for ms/illustration packages and photos accompanying a ms. Sample copy available for $2.50 and 9×12 SAE. Writer's and photo guidelines available for SASE or via website.

Tips: "Obtain our writer's guidelines and look at recent back issues. The best way to break in is to know our audience—drama students, teachers and others interested in theater—and write for them. Writers who have some practical experience in theater, especially in technical areas, have an advantage, but we'll work with anybody who has a good idea. Some freelancers have become regular contributors."

☑ DYNAMATH, Scholastic Inc., 555 Broadway, Room 367, New York NY 10012-3999. (212)343-6458. Fax: (212)343-6333. E-mail: dynamath@scholastic.com. Website: www.scholastic.com/dynamath. **Editor:** Matt Friedman. **Art Director:** James Sarfati. Monthly magazine. Estab. 1981. Circ. 225,000. Purpose is "to make learning math fun, challenging and uncomplicated for young minds in a very complex world."

Nonfiction: Middle readers: animal, arts/crafts, cooking, fashion, games/puzzles, health, history, hobbies, how-to, humorous, math, multicultural, nature/environment, problem-solving, science, social issues, sports—all must relate to math and science topics.

How to Contact/Writers: Nonfiction: Query with published clips, send ms. Responds to queries in 1 month; mss in 6 weeks. Publishes ms 4 months after acceptance. Will consider simultaneous submissions.

Illustration: Buys 4 illustrations/issue. Illustration only: Query first; send résumé and tearsheets. Responds on submissions only if interested. Credit line given.

Terms: Pays on acceptance. Buys all rights for mss, artwork, photographs. Originals returned to artist at job's completion. Pays $50-450 for stories.

FACES, People, Places & Cultures, Cobblestone Publishing Company, 30 Grove St., Peterborough NH 03458. (603)924-7209. Fax: (603)924-7380. E-mail: facesmag@yahoo.com. Website: www.cobbleston epub.com. **Editor**: Elizabeth Crooker Carpentiere. **Editorial Director**: Lou Warnycia. **Art Director**: Ann Dillon. Magazine published 9 times/year (September-May). Circ. 15,000. *Faces* is a theme-related magazine; writers should send for theme list before submitting ideas/queries. Each month a different world culture is featured through the use of feature articles, activities and photographs and illustrations.

• See website for 2003 theme list.

Fiction: Middle readers, young adults/teens: adventure, folktales, history, multicultural, plays, religious, travel. Does not want to see material that does not relate to a specific upcoming theme. Buys 9 mss/year. Maximum word length: 800. Byline given.

Nonfiction: Middle readers and young adults/teens: animal, anthropology, arts/crafts, biography, cooking, fashion, games/puzzles, geography, history, how-to, humorous, interview/profile, nature/environment, religious, social issues, sports, travel. Does not want to see material not related to a specific upcoming theme. Buys 63 mss/year. Average word length: 300-800. Byline given.

Poetry: Clear, objective imagery; up to 100 lines. Must relate to theme.

How to Contact/Writers: Fiction/nonfiction: Query with published clips and 2-3 line biographical sketch. "Ideas should be submitted six to nine months prior to the publication date. Responses to ideas are usually sent approximately four months before the publication date."

Illustration: Buys 3 illustrations/issue; buys 27 illustrations/year. Preferred theme or style: Material that is meticulously researched (most articles are written by professional anthropologists); simple, direct style preferred, but not too juvenile. Works on assignment only. Roughs required. Reviews ms/illustration packages from artists. Illustrations only: Send samples of b&w work. "Illustrators should consult issues of *Faces* to familiarize themselves with our needs." Reports on art samples only if interested. Samples returned with SASE. Original artwork returned at job's completion (upon written request). Credit line given.

Photography: Wants photos relating to forthcoming themes.

Terms: Pays on publication. Buys all rights for mss and artwork. Pays 20-25¢/word for articles/stories. Pays on an individual basis for poetry. Covers are assigned and paid on an individual basis. Pays illustrators $50-300 for color inside. Pays photographers per photo ($25-100 for color). Sample copy $4.95 with $7\frac{1}{2} \times 10\frac{1}{2}$ SAE and 5 first-class stamps. Writer's/illustrator's/photo guidelines via website or free with SAE and 1 first-class stamp.

Tips: "Writers are encouraged to study past issues of the magazine to become familiar with our style and content. Writers with anthropological and/or travel experience are particularly encouraged; *Faces* is about world cultures. All feature articles, recipes and activities are freelance contributions." Illustrators: "Submit b&w samples, not too juvenile. Study past issues to know what we look for. The illustration we use is generally for retold legends, recipes and activities." (See listing for *AppleSeeds, Calliope, Cobblestone, Footsteps* and *Odyssey*.)

Focus on the Family CLUBHOUSE; Focus on the Family CLUBHOUSE JR., Focus on the Family, 8605 Explorer Dr., Colorado Springs CO 80920. (719)531-3400. Fax: (719)531-3499. Website: www.clubh ousemagazine.org. **Editor:** Jesse Florea *Clubhouse*; Annette Bourland, editor *Clubhouse Jr.* **Art Director:** Timothy Jones. Monthly magazine. Estab. 1987. Combined circulation is 210,000. "*Focus on the Family Clubhouse* is a 24-page Christian magazine, published monthly, for children ages 8-12. Similarly, *Focus on the Family Clubhouse Jr.* is published for children ages 4-8. We want fresh, exciting literature that promotes biblical thinking, values and behavior in every area of life."

Fiction: Young readers, middle readers: adventure, contemporary, multicultural, nature/environment, religious. Middle readers: history, sports, science fiction. Multicultural needs include: "interesting, informative, accurate information about other cultures to teach children appreciation for the world around them." Buys approximately 6-10 mss/year. Average word length: *Clubhouse*, 500-1,400; *Clubhouse Jr.*, 250-1,100. Byline given on all fiction and puzzles.

Nonfiction: Young readers, middle readers: arts/crafts, cooking, games/puzzles, how-to, multicultural, nature/environment, religion, science. Young readers: animal. Middle readers, young adult/teen: interview/profile. Middle readers: sports. Buys 3-5 mss/year. Average word length: 200-1,000. Byline given.

Poetry: Wants to see "humorous or biblical" poetry for 4-8 year olds. Maximum length: 250 words.

How to Contact/Writers: Fiction/nonfiction: send complete ms. Responds to queries/mss in 6 weeks.

Illustration: Buys 8 illustrations/issue. Uses color artwork only. Works on assignment only. Reviews ms/illustration packages from artists. Submit ms with rough sketches. Contact: Tim Jones, art director. Illustrations only: Query with samples, arrange portfolio review or send tearsheets. Contact: Tim Jones, art director. Responds in 3 months. Samples returned with SASE; samples kept on file. Credit line given.

Photography: Buys photos from freelancers. Uses 35mm transparencies. Photographers should query with samples; provide résumé and promotional literature or tearsheets. Responds in 2 months.

Terms: Pays on acceptance. Buys first North American serial rights for mss. Buys first rights or reprint rights for artwork and photographs. Original artwork returned at job's completion. Additional payment for ms/illustration packages. Pays writers $150-300 for stories; $50-150 for articles. Pays illustrators $300-700 for color cover; $200-700 for color inside. Pays photographers by the project or per photo. Sample copies for 9×12 SAE and 3 first-class stamps. Writer's/illustrators/photo guidelines for SASE.

Tips: "Test your writing on children. The best stories avoid moralizing or preachiness and are not written *down* to children. They are the products of writers who share in the adventure with their readers, exploring the characters they have created without knowing for certain where the story will lead. And they are not always explicitly Christian, but are built upon a Christian foundation (and, at the very least, do not contradict biblical views or values)."

FOOTSTEPS, The Magazine of African American History, Cobblestone Publishing Co., 30 Grove St., Suite C, Peterborough NH 03458. (603)924-7204 or (800)821-0115. Fax: (608)924-7380. Website: www.cobblestonepub.com. **Editor:** Charles F. Baker. Magazine on African American history for readers ages 8-14.

 ● *Footsteps'* themes for 2003 include Paul Robeson, Black Churches, Langston Hughes and the Harlem Renaissance, and Black Scientists. For additional themes and time frames, visit the website.

Fiction: Middle readers: adventure, history, multicultural. Word length: up to 700 words.

Nonfiction: Middle readers: history, interviews/profile. Word length: 300-750 words.

How to Contact/Writers: Query with cover letter, outline, bibliography and SASE. "All material must relate to the theme of a specific upcoming issue in order to be considered."

Terms: Writer's guidelines available on website.

Tips: "We are looking for articles that are lively, age-appropriate, and exhibit an original approach to the theme of the issue. Cultural sensitivity and historical accuracy are extremely important."

THE FRIEND MAGAZINE, The Church of Jesus Christ of Latter-day Saints, 50 E. North Temple, Salt Lake City UT 84150-3226. (801)240-2210. **Editor:** Vivian Paulsen. **Art Director:** Mark Robison. Monthly magazine for 3-11 year olds. Estab. 1971. Circ. 275,000.

Needs: Children's/true stories—adventure, ethnic, some historical, humor, mainstream, religious/inspirational, nature. Length: 1,000 words maximum. Publishes short stories length 250 words.

Poetry: Reviews poetry. Maximum length: 20 lines.

How to Contact/Writers: Send complete ms. Responds to mss in 2 months.

Illustration: Illustrations only: Query with samples; arrange personal interview to show portfolio; provide résumé and tearsheets for files.

Terms: Pays on acceptance. Buys all rights for mss. Pays 12¢/word for unsolicited fiction articles; $25 and up for poems; $12 for recipes, activities and games. Contributors are encouraged to send for sample copy for $1.50, 9 × 11 envelope and four 34¢ stamps. Free writer's guidelines.

Tips: "*The Friend* is published by The Church of Jesus Christ of Latter-day Saints for boys and girls up to twelve years of age. All submissions are carefully read by *The Friend* staff, and those not accepted are returned within two months when a self-addressed, stamped envelope is enclosed. Submit seasonal material at least eight months in advance. Query letters and simultaneous submissions are not encouraged. Authors may request rights to have their work reprinted after their manuscript is published."

☑ **FUN FOR KIDZ**, P.O. Box 227, Bluffton OH 45817-0227. (419)358-4610. **Articles Editor:** Marilyn Edwards. Bimonthly magazine. Estab. 2002. "*Fun for Kidz* is a magazine created for boys and girls ages 6-13, with youngsters 8, 9, and 10 the specific target age. The magazine is designed as an activity publication to be enjoyed by both boys and girls on the alternative months of *Hopscotch* and *Boys' Quest* magazine."

• *Fun for Kidz* is theme-oriented. Upcoming themes include: Pets, Gardening, Camping, Winter Wonder and Indoor Fun, among others. Send SASE for theme list.

Fiction: Picture-oriented material, young readers, middle readers: adventure, animal, humorous, nature/environment, sports. Average word length: 300-700.

Nonfiction: Picture-oriented material, young readers, middle readers: animal, arts/crafts, cooking, games/puzzles, nature/environment, sports, carpentry projects. Average word length: 300-700. Byline given.

Poetry: Reviews poetry.

How to Contact/Writers: Fiction/nonfiction: Send complete ms. Will consider simultaneous submissions.

Illustration: Works on assignment mostly. "We are anxious to find artists capable of illustrating stories and features. Our inside art is pen & ink." Query with samples. Samples kept on file.

Photography: "We use a number of back & white photos inside the magazine; most support the articles used."

Terms: Pays on publication. Buys first American serial rights. Buys first American serial rights and photos for artwork. Pays 5¢/word; $10/poem or puzzle; $35 for art (full page); $25 for art (partial page). Pays illustrators $5-10 for b&w photos.

Tips: "Our point of view is that every child deserves the right to be a child for a number of years before he or she becomes a young adult. As a result, *Fun for Kidz* looks for activities that deal with timeless topics, such as pets, nature, hobbies, science, games, sports, careers, simple cooking, and anything else likely to interest a child."

GIRLS' LIFE, Monarch, 4517 Harford Rd., Baltimore MD 21214. (410)426-9600. Fax: (410)254-0991. Website: www.girlslife.com. **Senior Editor**: Sarah Cordi. **Creative Director**: Chun Kim. Bimonthly magazine. Estab. 1994. General interest magazine for girls, ages 10-15.

Fiction: Romance.

Nonfiction: Arts/crafts, fashion, interview/profile, social issues, sports, travel, hobbies. Buys appoximately 25 mss/year. Word length varies. Byline given. "No fiction!"

How to Contact/Writers: Nonfiction: Query with descriptive story ideas, résumé and published writing samples. Responds in 6 weeks. Publishes ms 3 months after acceptance. Will consider simultaneous submissions. No phone calls.

Illustration: Buys 4 illustrations/issue. Uses color artwork only. Works on assignment only. Reviews ms/illustration packages from artists. Send ms with dummy. Illustration only: Query with samples; send tearsheets. Contact: Chun Kim, creative director. Responds only if interested. Samples returned with SASE; samples filed. Credit line given.

Photography: Buys photos from freelancers. Uses 35mm transparencies. Provide samples. Responds only if interested.

Terms: Pays on publication. Original artwork returned at job's completion. Pays $500-800 for features; $150-350 for departments. Sample copies available for $5. Writer's guidelines for SASE or via website.

Tips: "Don't call with queries. Make query short and punchy."

■ ☑ **GO-GIRL.COM**, The Collegebound Network, 1200 South Ave., Suite 202, Stanten Island NY 10314. (718)761-4800. Fax: (718)761-3300. E-mail: editorial@collegebound.net. Website: www.go-girl.com. **Articles Editor:** Gina LaGuardia. Weekly online magazine. Estab. 1997. "Go-Girl.com is one of The CollegeBound Network's affiliate of websites, and is devoted to empowering teen girls to become 'academic divas.' Student surfers have access to real people who guide them through their college and career choices. Our content is highly interactive—students can enter challenging contests, win scholarships and prizes, meet other students, and discover valuable information on academic and lifestyle issues of interest to them."

Nonfiction: Young adults: biography, careers, fashion, health, how-to, interview/profile, social issues, travel, celebrity education. Buys 50 mss/year. Average word length: 100-900. Byline given.

How to Contact/Writer: Nonfiction: Query. Responds to queries in 6 weeks; mss in 7 weeks. Publishes ms 2-3 months after acceptance. Will consider simultaneous submissions, electronic submission via disk or modem (upon acceptance).

Terms: Pays on publication. Buys first rights. Pays $50-100 for articles. Writer's guidelines for SASE.

GUIDE MAGAZINE, Review and Herald Publishing Association, 55 W. Oak Ridge Dr., Hagerstown MD 21740. (301)393-4038. Fax: (301)393-4055. E-mail: guide@rhpa.org. Website: www.guidemagazine.org. **Editor**: Randy Fishell. **Designer**: Brandon Reese. Weekly magazine. Estab. 1953. Circ. 32,000. "Ours is a weekly Christian journal written for middle readers and young adults (ages 10-14), presenting true stories relevant to the needs of today's young person, emphasizing positive aspects of Christian living."

Nonfiction: Middle readers, young adults/teens: adventure, animal, character-building, contemporary, games/puzzles, humorous, multicultural, problem-solving, religious. "We need true, or based on true, happenings, not merely true-to-life. Our stories and puzzles must have a spiritual emphasis." No violence. No articles. "We always need humor and adventure stories." Buys 150 mss/year. Average word length: 500-600 minimum, 1,000-1,200 maximum. Byline given.

How to Contact/Writers: Nonfiction: Send complete ms. Responds in 1 month. Will consider simultaneous submissions. "We can only pay half of the regular amount for simultaneous submissions." Responds to queries/mss in 6 weeks. Credit line given.

Terms: Pays on acceptance. Buys first North American serial rights; first rights; one-time rights; second serial (reprint rights); simultaneous rights. Pays 6-12¢/word for stories and articles. "Writer receives several complimentary copies of issue in which work appears." Sample copy free with 6×9 SAE and 2 first-class stamps. Writer's guidelines for SASE.

Tips: "Children's magazines want mystery, action, discovery, suspense and humor—no matter what the topic. For us, truth is stronger than fiction."

■ **GUIDEPOSTS FOR KIDS**, 1050 Broadway, Suite 6, Chesterton IN 46304. Fax: (219)926-3839. E-mail: gp4k@guideposts.org. Website: www.gp4k.com. **Editor-in-Chief**: Mary Lou Carney. **Managing Editor:** Rosanne Tolin. **Art Director**: Mike Lyons. **Art Coordinator**: Rose Pomeroy. Electronic magazine. Estab. 1998. 62,000 plus unique visitors/month. "*Guideposts for Kids* online by Guideposts for kids 6-13 years old (emphasis on upper end of that age bracket). It is a value-centered, electronic magazine that is *fun* to visit. The site hosts a long list of interactive and editorial features including games, puzzles, how-tos, stories, poems, and facts and trivia.

• *Guideposts for Kids* is online only.

Fiction: Middle readers: adventure, animal, contemporary, fantasy, folktales, historical, humorous, multi-cultural, nature/environment, problem-solving, science fiction, sports, suspense/mystery. Multicultural needs include: Kids in other cultures—school, sports, families. Does not want to see preachy fiction. "We want real stories about real kids doing real things—conflicts our readers will respect; resolutions our readers will accept. Problematic. Tight. Filled with realistic dialogue and sharp imagery. No stories about 'good' children always making the right decision. If present at all, adults are minor characters and *do not* solve kids' problems for them." Buys approximately 25 mss/year. Average word length: 200-900. Byline given.

Nonfiction: Middle readers: animal, current events, games/puzzles, history, how-to, humorous, interview/ profile, multicultural, nature/environment, problem-solving, profiles of kids, science, seasonal, social issues, sports. "Make nonfiction issue-oriented, controversial, thought-provoking. Something kids not only *need* to know but *want* to know as well." Buys 20 mss/year. Average word length: 200-1,300. Byline usually given.

How to Contact/Writers: Fiction: Send complete ms. Nonfiction: Query or send ms. Responds to queries/mss in 6 weeks.

Photography: Looks for "spontaneous, *real* kids in action shots."

Terms: Pays on acceptance. Buys electronic and nonexclusive print rights. "Features range in payment from $50-200; fiction from $75-250. We pay higher rates for stories exceptionally well-written or well-researched. Regular contributors get bigger bucks, too." Writer's guidelines free for SASE.

Tips: "Make your manuscript good, relevant and playful. No preachy stories about Bible-toting children. *Guideposts for Kids* is not a beginner's market. Study our e-zine magazine. (Sure, you've heard that before—but it's *necessary*!) Neatness *does* count. So do creativity and professionalism. SASE essential if sending a query by snail mail." (See listing for *Guideposts for Teens*.)

GUIDEPOSTS FOR TEENS, 1050 Broadway, Suite 6, Chesterton IN 46304. (219)929-4429. Fax: (219)926-3839. E-mail: gp4t@guideposts.org. Website: www.gp4teens.com. **Editor-in-Chief:** Mary Lou Carney. **Art Director:** Michael Lyons. **Art Coordinator:** Rose Pomeroy. Bimonthly magazine. Estab. 1998. "We are an inspirational magazine that offers teens advice, humor and true stories—lots of true stories. These first-person (ghostwritten) stories feature teen protagonists and are filled with action, adventure, overcoming adversity and growth—set against the backdrop of God at work in everyday life."
Nonfiction: Young adults: how-to, quizzes, celebrity interviews, true stories. Average word length: 300-2,000. Byline sometimes given.
How to Contact/Writers: Nonfiction: Query. Responds to queries/mss in 6 weeks. Will consider simultaneous submissions or electronic submission via disk or modem. Send SASE for writer's guidelines.
Illustration: Uses color artwork only. Works on assignment only. Reviews ms/illustration packages from artists. Query. Contact: Michael Lyons, art director. Illustrations only: Query with samples. Responds only if interested. Samples kept on file. Credit line given.
Photography: Buys photos separately. Wants location photography and stock; digital OK. Uses color prints and 35mm, 2¼×2¼, 4×5 or 8×10 transparencies. Query with samples; provide web address. Responds only if interested.
Terms: Pays on acceptance. Buys all rights for mss. Buys one-time rights for artwork. Original artwork returned at job's completion. Pays $300-500 for true stories; $100-300 for articles. Additional payment for photos accompanying articles. Pays illustrators $125-1,500 for color inside (depends on size). Pays photographers by the project (range: $100-1,000). Sample copies for $4.50 from: Guideposts, 39 Seminary Hill Rd., Carmel NY 10512. Attn: Special Handling.
Tips: "Study our magazine! Language and subject matter should be current and teen-friendly. No preaching, please! (Your 'takeaway' should be inherent.) We are most in need of inspirational action/adventure, sports, and relationship stories. We also need short (250-word) true stories with a miracle/'aha' ending for our 'Soul Food' department. For illustrators: We get illustrators from two basic sources: submissions by mail and submissions by Internet. We also consult major illustrator reference books. We prefer color illustrations, 'on-the-edge' style. We accept art in almost any digital or reflective format."

☑ **HIGH ADVENTURE**, Assemblies of God, 1445 N. Boonville Ave., Springfield MO 65802. (417)862-2781, Ext. 4177. Fax: (417)831-8230. E-mail: rangers@ag.org. Website: royalranger.ag.org. **Editor:** Jerry Parks. Quarterly magazine. Circ. 86,000. Estab. 1971. Magazine is designed to provide boys ages 5-17 with worthwhile, enjoyable, leisure reading; to challenge them in narrative form to higher ideals and greater spiritual dedication; and to perpetuate the spirit of Royal Rangers through stories, ideas and illustrations. 75% of material aimed at juvenile audience.
Fiction: Buys 100 mss/year; adventure, humorous, problem solving, religious, sports, travel. Maximum word length: 1,000. Byline given.
Nonfiction: Articles: Christian living, devotional, Holy Spirit, salvation, self-help, biography, missionary stories, news items, testimonies, inspirational stories based on true-life experiences, arts/crafts, games/puzzles, geography, health, hobbies, how-to, humorous, nature/environment, problem solving, sports, travel.
How to Contact/Writers: Fiction/nonfiction: Send complete ms. Responds to queries in 6-8 weeks. Will consider simultaneous submissions. Samples returned with SASE by request. Prefer hardcopy and media (3.5, Zip or Jaz).
Terms: Pays on publication. Buys first or all rights. Pays 6¢/word for articles ($30-35 for one page; 60-65 for two pages); $25-30 for cartoons; $15 for puzzles, $5 for jokes. Sample copy free with 9×12 SASE. Free writer's/illustrator's guidelines with SASE.
Tips: Obtain writer's guidelines. Articles are not subject to a theme-associated listing, but can be seasonal in nature or as described above.

HIGHLIGHTS FOR CHILDREN, 803 Church St., Honesdale PA 18431. (570)253-1080. E-mail: eds@highlights-corp.com. Website: www.highlights.com. **Contact:** Manuscript Coordinator. **Editor:** Christine French Clark. **Art Director:** Janet Moir McCaffrey. Monthly magazine. Estab. 1946. Circ. 2.5 million. "Our motto is 'Fun With a Purpose.' We are looking for quality fiction and nonfiction that appeals to children, encourages them to read, and reinforces positive values. All art is done on assignment."

THE SUBJECT INDEX, located in the back of this book, lists book publishers and magazines according to the fiction and nonfiction subjects they seek.

insider report

Bringing children's magazines into the 21st century

Highlights.

Marileta Robinson

Say it and many writers and illustrators flash back to their childhoods. Poring over the Hidden Pictures to find a toothbrush or apple hidden somewhere in the line drawing of a barnyard scene. Flipping forward to read Goofus and Gallant or the Timbertoes before tackling the longer stories and articles. Given these kinds of connections, it's no wonder *Highlights for Children* received ten thousand submissions in 2001 alone.

Like many other freelancers, Marileta Robinson submitted her work to this old favorite. She sold them her very first story, "Mr. Goat's Bad Good Idea," in 1976. Sales to *Highlights* continued, and when she decided to seek full time work in 1988, she got another lucky break. Not only was *Highlights* the first stop on her list, they were hiring. She started there as an assistant editor, editing rebuses and fiction for beginning readers.

In her current position as a senior editor, Robinson edits fiction for younger readers, writes "The Timbertoes," and coordinates the International Edition. Through her varied experience, she has discovered the many challenges of putting together a magazine for an audience that includes both pre-readers and middle readers. "We make the appeal as broad as possible by not including anything that is too babyish or too adult," says Robinson. "Young children enjoy having older stories read to them, and older children who are not strong readers or who simply want an easier read enjoy the younger features. We offer a great deal of variety, knowing that every child is bound to find something of interest at his or her reading level."

Robinson offered the following advice to freelancers wishing to break into magazine writing and *Highlights for Children* in particular.

What advice do you have for writers wanting to break into the children's magazine market in general?

Figure out your niche. What special talent, background, focus, or style do you have to offer that's unique and valuable? Do you travel and write well about your travels? Do you collect authentic folk tales? Do you have a silly sense of humor that kids love? Do you have a special understanding about a particular culture or period of history? Are you a skilled interviewer? These are qualities that will make your name stick in an editor's mind.

What do you have to say to writers who may be tempted to write for the *Highlights* they remember from their childhood without looking at the current magazine? How has it changed?

Marileta Robinson, senior editor of *Highlights for Children* emphasizes that while the magazine has changed to fit the needs of today's children, the idea of the publication has stayed the same. "Goofus and Gallant now ride skateboards and play video games, but they still deal with issues of thoughtfulness, honesty, and respect."

That is a timely question. Many of the fiction stories we get do seem to be set in the era of the author's childhood. To encourage more up-to-date stories, we chose "stories about today's kids" as the theme of our fiction contest for 2002. Writers need to absorb the culture of today's children in order to create convincing contemporary characters. What do kids do for fun? What kinds of family situations are common? What are schools and classrooms like now? What media and advertising are kids exposed to? Even though many of the problems kids deal with are timeless, the settings should not feel old fashioned if the story is set in the present day.

It helps to be very familiar with our magazine before you write for us. In general, for realistic stories we prefer protagonists no older than twelve or younger than five or six, but of course there are exceptions. For nonfiction, the author needs to be able to relate complex ideas in such a way that a nine- or ten-year-old child would find them understandable and interesting. We also like to see shorter, simpler articles for our younger readers.

Which type of manuscript is most difficult to sell to *Highlights*?
We would love to see more realistic stories about contemporary children, but they are not easy to write for us. The characters must be realistic without being too trendy. The problems in the stories must be appropriate for young ears as well as of interest to older children. And our standards for the quality of writing are high.

What about nonfiction?
Our standards for nonfiction are also high. The subject must be well-researched, which means the author must go beyond consulting one or two encyclopedias. We prefer primary sources and interviews when possible. The writing must be engaging and appropriate for our readers.

Writers of nonfiction should also be aware of our need for articles about recent developments in science and technology and contemporary role models in all fields.

Does *Highlights* feel that they are competing with television and computers for the attention of young minds?
Yes, we know children have many more demands on their time and attention today.

Without compromising quality, we are moving toward making our stories and articles shorter and as easily accessible as possible.

In spite of the many changes, is there anything about *Highlights* that has remained the same?
Values have always been the backbone of our editorial philosophy. Goofus and Gallant now ride skateboards and play video games, but they still deal with issues of thoughtfulness, honesty, and respect. Our mission has remained the same: to help children grow into responsible, creative members of society by providing inspiring and fun-to-read stories, articles, and activities.

What one word best describes *Highlights* today?
Fun. If kids don't have fun when they open our pages, they won't come back.

And obviously with a publishing run that began in 1946 and continues today, both readers and freelancers have found something in *Highlights* that keeps them coming back for more.
—*Sue Bradford Edwards*

Fiction: Picture-oriented material, young readers, middle readers: adventure, animal, contemporary, fantasy, folktales, history, humorous, multicultural, problem-solving, sports. Multicultural needs include first person accounts of children from other cultures and first-person accounts of children from other countries. Does not want to see war, crime, violence. "We see too many stories with overt morals." Would like to see more contemporary, multicultural and world culture fiction, sports pieces, mystery stories, action/adventure stories, humorous stories, and fiction for younger readers. Buys 150 mss/year. Average word length: 400-800. Byline given.

Nonfiction: Picture-oriented material, young readers, middle readers: animal, arts/crafts, biography, careers, games/puzzles, geography, health, history, hobbies, how-to, interview/profile, multicultural, nature/environment, problem solving, science, sports. Multicultural needs include articles set in a country *about* the people of the country. Does not want to see trendy topics, fads, personalities who would not be good role models for children, guns, war, crime, violence. "We'd like to see more nonfiction for younger readers—maximum of 500 words. We still need older-reader material, too—500-800 words." Buys 200 mss/year. Maximum word length: 800. Byline given.

How to Contact/Writers: Send complete ms. Responds to queries in 1 month; mss in 6 weeks.

Illustration: Buys 25-30 illustrations/issue. Preferred theme or style: Realistic, some stylization. Works on assignment only. Reviews ms/illustration packages from artists. Illustrations only: photocopies, promo sheet, tearsheets, or slides. Résumé optional. Portfolio only if requested. Contact: Janet Moir McCaffrey, art director. Responds to art samples in 2 months. Samples returned with SASE; samples filed. Credit line given.

Terms: Pays on acceptance. Buys all rights for mss. Pays $50 and up for unsolicited articles. Pays illustrators $1,000 for color cover; $25-200 for b&w inside, $100-500 for color inside. Sample copies $3.95 and 9×11 SASE with 4 first-class stamps. Writer's/illustrator's guidelines free with SASE.

Tips: "Know the magazine's style before submitting. Send for guidelines and sample issue if necessary." Writers: "At *Highlights* we're paying closer attention to acquiring more nonfiction for young readers than we have in the past." Illustrators: "Fresh, imaginative work encouraged. Flexibility in working relationships a plus. Illustrators presenting their work need not confine themselves to just children's illustrations as long as work can translate to our needs. We also use animal illustrations, real and imaginary. We need crafts, puzzles and any activity that will stimulate children mentally and creatively. We are always looking for imaginative cover subjects. Know our publication's standards and content by reading sample issues, not just the guidelines. Avoid tired themes, or put a fresh twist on an old theme so that its style is fun and lively. We'd like to see stories with subtle messages, but the fun of the story should come first. Write what inspires you, not what you think the market needs."

☑ **HOPSCOTCH, The Magazine for Girls**, The Bluffton News Publishing and Printing Company, P.O. Box 164, Bluffton OH 45817-0164. (419)358-4610. **Editor**: Marilyn Edwards. **Contact:** Diane Winebar, editorial assistant. Bimonthly magazine. Estab. 1989. Circ. 14,000. For girls from ages 6-12, featuring traditional subjects—pets, games, hobbies, nature, science, sports, etc.—with an emphasis on articles that show girls actively involved in unusual and/or worthwhile activities."

Fiction: Picture-oriented material, young readers, middle readers: adventure, animal, history, humorous, nature/environment, sports, suspense/mystery. Does not want to see stories dealing with dating, sex, fashion, hard rock music. Buys 30 mss/year. Average word length: 300-700. Byline given.

Nonfiction: Picture-oriented material, young readers, middle readers: animal, arts/crafts, biography, cooking, games/puzzles, geography, hobbies, how-to, humorous, math, nature/environment, science. Does not want to see pieces dealing with dating, sex, fashion, hard rock music. "Need more nonfiction with quality photos about a *Hopscotch*-age girl involved in a worthwhile activity." Buys 46 mss/year. Average word length: 400-700. Byline given.

Poetry: Reviews traditional, wholesome, humorous poems. Maximum word length: 300; maximum line length: 20. Will accept 6 submissions/author.

How to Contact/Writers: All writers should consult the theme list before sending in articles. To receive a current theme list, send a SASE. Fiction: Send complete ms. Nonfiction: Query, send complete ms. Responds to queries in 2 weeks; on mss in 2 months. Will consider simultaneous submissions.

Illustration: Buys illustrations for 6-8 articles/issue; buys 50-60 articles/year. "Generally, the illustrations are assigned after we have purchased a piece (usually fiction). Occasionally, we will use a painting—in any given medium—for the cover, and these are usually seasonal." Uses b&w artwork only for inside; color for cover. Review ms/illustration packages from artists. Query first or send complete ms with final art. Illustrations only: Send résumé, portfolio, client list and tearsheets. Responds to art samples with SASE in 1 month. Credit line given.

Photography: Purchases photos separately (cover only) and with accompanying ms only. Looking for photos to accompany article. Model/property releases required. Uses 5×7, b&w prints; 35mm transparencies. Black & white photos should go with ms. Should show girl or girls ages 6-12.

Terms: For mss: pays a few months ahead of publication. For mss, artwork and photos, buys first North American serial rights; second serial (reprint rights). Original artwork returned at job's completion. Pays 5¢/word and $5-10/photo. "We always send a copy of the issue to the writer or illustrator." Text and art are treated separately. Pays $150-200 for color cover. Photographers paid per photo (range: $5-15). Sample copy for $4 and 8 × 12 SASE. Writer's/illustrator's/photo guidelines free for #10 SASE.

Tips: "Remember we publish only six issues a year, which means our editorial needs are extremely limited. Please look at our guidelines and our magazine . . . and remember, we use far more nonfiction than fiction. If decent photos accompany the piece, it stands an even better chance of being accepted. We believe it is the responsibility of the contributor to come up with photos. Please remember, our readers are 6-12 years— most are 7-10—and your text should reflect that. Many magazines try to entertain first and educate second. We try to do the reverse of that. Our magazine is more simplistic, like a book to be read from cover to cover. We are looking for wholesome, non-dated material." (See listing for *Boys' Quest*.)

N **HORSEPOWER, Magazine for Young Horse Lovers**, Corinthian Publishing Co. Ltd., P.O. Box 670, Aurora, Ontario L4G 4J9 Canada. (800)505-7428. Fax: (905)841-1530. E-mail: info@horse-canada.c om. Website: www.horse-canada.com. **Editor:** Susan Stafford. Bimonthly magazine. Estab. 1988. Circ. 10,000. "*Horsepower* offers how-to articles and stories relating to horse care for kids ages 8-16, with a focus on safety."

Fiction: Middle readers, young adults: adventure, health, history, humorous, problem-solving sports. Buys 6-10 mss/year. Average word length: 500-1,000.

Nonfiction: Middle readers, young adults: arts/crafts, biography, careers, fashion, games/puzzles, health, history, hobbies, how-to, humorous, interview/profile, problem-solving, travel. Buys 6-10 mss/year. Average word length: 500-1,200. Byline given.

How to Contact/Writers: Fiction: query. Nonfiction: send complete ms. Responds to queries in 6 months; mss in 3 months. Publishes ms 6 months after acceptance. Will consider simultaneous submissions, electronic submission via disk or modem, previously published work.

Illustration: Buys 3 illustrations/year. Reviews ms/illustration packages from artists. Send ms with dummy. Contact: Editor. Query with samples. Responds only if interested. Samples returned with SASE; samples kept on file. Credit line given.

Photography: Look for photos of kids and horses, instructional/educational, relating to riding or horse care. Uses b&w and color 4×6, 5×7, matte or glossy prints. Query with samples. Responds only if interested.

Terms: Pays on publication. Buys one-time rights for mss. Original artwork returned at job's completion if SASE provided. Pays $50-75 for stories. Additional payment for ms/illustration packages and for photos accompanying articles. Pays illustrators $25-50 for color inside. Pays photographers per photo (range: $10-15). Sample copies for $1. Writer's/illustrator's/photo guidelines for SASE.

Tips: "Articles must be easy to understand, yet detailed and accurate. How-to or other educational features must be written by, or in conjunction with, a riding/teaching professional. Fiction is not encouraged, unless it is outstanding and teaches a moral or practical lesson."

N **HULLABALOO**, 954 Gayley Ave., Los Angeles CA 90024. (310)709-1040. E-mail: editor@hullabal oomagazine.com. Website: www.hullabaloomagazine.com. **Articles Editor:** Deidre Cutter. Bimonthly magazine. Estab. 2002. "*Hullabaloo* is a new children's magazine featuring a different country with each issue. Through storytelling, fun facts, children's interviews and more, the reader explores the country from a child's perspective." 100% of publication aimed at juvenile market.

● See *Hullabaloo*'s website for a list of upcoming countries to be covered in the magazine. These
      include Guatemala (March 2003), Finland (May 2003) and India (July 2003).

Fiction: Young readers: folktale. Middle readers: adventure, animal, contemporary, folktale, history, humorous, multicultural. Buys 18-24 mss/year. Average word length: 800-1,500. Byline given.

Nonfiction: Young readers: animal, arts/crafts, games/puzzles, math, travel. Middle readers: arts/crafts, biography, games/puzzles, geography, humorous, interview/profile, math, multicultural, science, travel. Buys up to 60 mss/year. Average word length: 400-750 or 50-200. Byline given.

Poetry: Accepts country-specific poems in style of country (ex: haiku) or regarding specific country. Maximum length: 16 lines.

How to Contact/Writers: Fiction: send complete ms. Nonfiction: query with published clips or send complete ms. Responds to queries in 3 weeks; mss in 6 weeks. Publishes ms 6 months after acceptance. Will consider simultaneous submissions, electronic submission via disk or previously published work.

Illustration: Buys 20 illustrations/issue; 120 illustrations/year. Works on assignment only. Reviews ms/ illustration packages from artists. Send ms with dummy. Contact: Deidre Cutter, editor. Illustrations only: Query with samples; send tearsheets. Contact: Editor. Responds only if interested. Samples returned with SASE; samples kept on file. Credit line given.

Photography: Looking for country-specific photos of people, important places and landmarks, celebrations and festivals, daily life. Model/property release required. Uses color or b&w prints; 300 dpi digital photos; slides. Query with samples; send unsolicited photos by mail; provide résumé, promotional literature or tearsheets. Responds in 1 month if interested.

Terms: Pays on publication. Buys first North American serial rights. Buys first rights or reprint rights and promotional rights (for both). Original artwork returned at job's completion. Pays 20¢/word minimum for stories; 15¢/word minimum for articles. Additional payment for ms/illustration packages and for photos accompanying articles. Pays illustrators $500 and up for color cover; $25 and up for b&w, $75 and up for for color inside. Pays photographers per photo (range: $5 and up). Sample copies for $5.50. Writer's/illustrator's/photo guidelines for SASE.

Tips: "Know the magazine's style before submitting. All submissions should be specific to an upcoming country (see website or submission guidelines for list). We include many styles in the magazine—shorter nonfiction articles (50-200 words) are conversational 'sound-bytes' of interesting information for kids."

A HUMPTY DUMPTY'S MAGAZINE, Children's Better Health Institute, 1100 Waterway Blvd., P.O. Box 567, Indianapolis IN 46206. (317)636-8881. Fax: (317)684-8094. Website: www.humptydumpty mag.org. **Editor:** Nancy S. Axelrad. **Art Director:** Rob Falco. Magazine published 8 times/year—Jan/Feb; Mar; April/May; June; July/Aug; Sept; Oct/Nov; Dec. *HDM* is edited for children ages 4-6. It includes fiction (easy-to-reads; read alouds; rhyming stories; rebus stories), nonfiction articles (some with photo illustrations), poems, crafts, recipes, and puzzles. Content encourages development of better health habits.

> • *Humpty Dumpty's Magazine* is not currently accepting unsolicited manuscripts. *Humpty Dumpty's* publishes material promoting health and fitness with emphasis on simple activities, poems and fiction.

Fiction: Picture-oriented stories: adventure, animal, contemporary, fantasy, folktales, health, humorous, multicultural, nature/environment, problem-solving, science fiction, sports. Does not want to see "bunny-rabbits-with-carrot-pies stories! Also, talking inanimate objects are very difficult to do well. Beginners (and maybe everyone) should avoid these." Buys 8-10 mss/year. Maximum word length: 300. Byline given.

Nonfiction: Picture oriented articles: animal, arts/crafts, concept, games/puzzles, health, how-to, humorous, nature/environment, no-cook recipes, science, social issues, sports. Buys 6-10 mss/year. Prefers very short nonfiction pieces—200 words maximum. Byline given.

How to Contact/Writers: Send complete ms. Nonfiction: Send complete ms with bibliography if applicable. "No queries, please!" Responds to mss in 3 months. Send seasonal material at least 8 months in advance.

Illustration: Buys 13-16 illustrations/issue; 90-120 illustrations/year. Preferred theme or style: Realistic or cartoon. Works on assignment only. Illustrations only. Query with slides, printed pieces or photocopies. Contact: Brad Turner, art director. Samples are not returned; samples filed. Responds to art samples only if interested. Credit line given.

Terms: Writers: Pays on publication. Artists: Pays within 1-2 months. Buys all rights. "One-time book rights may be returned if author can provide name of interested book publisher and tentative date of publication." Pays up to 22¢/word for stories/articles; payment varies for poems and activities. 10 complimentary issues are provided to author with check. Pays $275 for color cover illustration; $35-90 per page b&w inside; $70-155 for color inside. Sample copies for $1.75. Writer's/illustrator's guidelines free with SASE.

I.D., Cook Communications Ministries, 4050 Lee Vance View, Colorado Springs CO 80918. (719)536-0100. Fax: (719)536-3296. Website: www.cookministries.org. **Editor:** Gail Rohlfing. **Design Manager:** Paul Segsworth. **Designer:** Joe Matisek. Weekly magazine. Estab 1991. Circ. 100,000. "*I.D.* is a class-and-home paper for senior high Sunday school students. Stories relate to Bible study."

Nonfiction: Young adults/teens: animal, arts/crafts, biography, careers, concept, geography, health, history, how-to, humorous, interview/profile, multicultural, nature/environment, problem solving, religion, science, social issues, sports. "Sometimes material sent to us is too 'preachy.'" By assignment only. Average word length: 600-1,000. Byline sometimes given if written in the first person.

How to Contact/Writers: Send complete ms. Responds in 6 months. Publishes ms 15 months after acceptance. Will consider simultaneous submissions.

Illustrations: Buys 5 illustrations/year. Uses b&w and color artwork. Reviews ms/illustration packages from artists. Submit ms with rough sketches. Illustrations only: Query. Works on assignment only. Responds only if interested.

Terms: Pays on acceptance. Pays $50-300 for stories and articles.

INSIGHT, Teens Meeting Christ, 55 W. Oak Ridge Dr., Hagerstown MD 21740. (301)393-4038. Fax: (301)393-4055. E-mail: insight@rhpa.org. Website: www.insightmagazine.org. **Articles Editor:** Michelle Sturm. **Art Director:** Sebastian Bruce. **Photo Editor:** Sebastian Bruce. Weekly magazine. Estab. 1970. Circ. 20,000. "Our readers crave true stories written by teens or written about teens that convey a strong spiritual or portray a spiritual truth." 100% of publication aimed at teen and college-age market.

Nonfiction: Young adults: animal, biography, fashion, health, humorous, interview/profile, multicultural, nature/environment, problem-solving, social issues, sports, travel: first-person accounts preferred. Buys 200 mss/year. Average word length: 500-1,500. Byline given.

Poetry: Reviews poetry. Publishes poems written by teens. Maximum length: 250-500 words.

How to Contact/Writers: Nonfiction: Send complete ms. Responds to queries in 2 months. Publishes ms 6-12 months after acceptance. Will consider simultaneous submissions, electronic submission via disk or modem, previously published work.

Illustration: Works on assignment only. Reviews ms/illustration packages from artists. Query. Contact: Sebastian Bruce, design. Illustrations only: Query with samples. Contact: Sebastian Bruce, designer. Samples kept on file. Credit line given.

Photography: Looking for photos that will catch a young person's eye with unique elements such as juxtaposition. Model/property release required; captions not required but helpful. Uses color prints and 35mm, 2¼×2¼, 4×5, 8×10 transparencies. Query with samples; provide business card, promotional literature or tearsheets to be kept on file. Responds only if interested.

Terms: Pays on publication. Buys first North American serial rights for mss. Buys one-time rights for artwork and photos. Original artwork returned at job's completion. Pays $10-100 for stories; $10-100 for articles. Pays illustrators $100-300 for b&w (cover); $100-300 for color cover; $100-300 for b&w (inside), $100-300 for color inside. Pays photographers by the project. Sample copies for 9×14 SAE and 4 first-class stamps.

Tips: "Do your best to make your work look 'hip,' 'cool' appealing to young people."

INTEEN, Urban Ministries, Inc., 1551 Regency Ct., Calumet City IL 60409. (708)868-7100, ext. 239. Fax: (708)868-7105. E-mail: umil551@aol.com. **Editor:** Katara A. Washington. **Art Acquisitions:** Larry Taylor. Quarterly magazine. Estab. 1970. "We publish Sunday school lessons for urban teens and features for the same group."

● Contact *Inteen* for guidelines. They work on assignment only—do not submit work.

Nonfiction: Young adults/teens: careers, games/puzzles, how-to, interview/profile, religion. "We make 40 assignments/year."

Terms: Pays $75-150 for stories.

JACK AND JILL, Children's Better Health Institute, 1100 Waterway Blvd., P.O. Box 567, Indianapolis IN 46206. (317)636-8881. Website: www.jackandjillmag.org. **Editor:** Daniel Lee. **Art Director:** Emilie Frazier. Magazine published 8 times/year. Estab. 1938. Circ. 360,000. "Write entertaining and imaginative stories *for* kids, not just *about* them. Writers should understand what is funny to kids, what's important to them, what excites them. Don't write from an adult 'kids are so cute' perspective. We're also looking for health and healthful lifestyle stories and articles, but don't be preachy."

Fiction: Young readers and middle readers: adventure, contemporary, folktales, health, history, humorous, nature, sports. Buys 30-35 mss/year. Average word length: 700. Byline given.

Nonfiction: Young readers, middle readers: animal, arts/crafts, cooking, games/puzzles, history, hobbies, how-to, humorous, interview/profile, nature, science, sports. Buys 8-10 mss/year. Average word length: 500. Byline given.

Poetry: Reviews poetry.

How to Contact/Writers: Fiction/nonfiction: Send complete ms. Responds to mss in 3 months. Guidelines by request with a #10 SASE.

Illustration: Buys 15 illustrations/issue; 120 illustrations/year. Responds only if interested. Samples not returned; samples filed. Credit line given.

Terms: Pays on publication; minimum 17¢/word. Pays illustrators $275 for color cover; $35-90 for b&w, $70-155 for color inside. Pays photographers negotiated rate. Sample copies $1.25. Buys all rights.

Tips: See listings for *Child Life*, *Children's Digest*, *Children's Playmate*, *Humpty Dumpty's Magazine*, *Turtle Magazine* and *U*S* Kids*. Publishes writing/art/photos by children.

THE KIDS HALL OF FAME NEWS, The Kids Hall of Fame, 3 Ibsen Court, Dix Hills NY 11746. (631)242-9105. Fax: (631)242-8101. E-mail: VictoriaNesnick@TheKidsHallofFame.com. Website: www. TheKidsHallofFame.com. **Publisher:** Victoria Nesnick. **Art/Photo Editor:** Amy Gilvary. Quarterly magazine. Estab. 1998. "We spotlight and archive extraordinary positive achievements of contemporary and historical kids internationally under age 20. Their inspirational stories are meant to provide positive peer role models and empower kids to say, 'If that kid can do it, so can I,' or 'I can do better.' Our magazine is the prelude to The Kids Hall of Fame set of books (one volume per year) and museum."

How to Contact/Writers: Query with published clips or send complete manuscripts with SASE for response. Go to website for nomination form for The Kids Hall of Fame.

Tips: "Nomination stories must be positive and inspirational. See sample stories and nomination form on our website. Request writers' guidelines and list of suggested nominees. Evening telephone queries acceptable."

LADYBUG, The Magazine for Young Children, Carus Publishing Company, P.O. Box 300, Peru IL 61354. (815)224-6656. **Editor:** Paula Morrow. **Art Director:** Suzanne Beck. Monthly magazine. Estab. 1990. Circ. 130,000. Literary magazine for children 2-6, with stories, poems, activities, songs and picture stories.

Fiction: Picture-oriented material: adventure, animal, fantasy, folktales, humorous, multicultural, nature/environment, problem-solving, science fiction, sports, suspense/mystery. "Open to any easy fiction stories." Buys 50 mss/year. Average word length 300-850 words. Byline given.

Nonfiction: Picture-oriented material: activities, animal, arts/crafts, concept, cooking, humorous, math, nature/environment, problem-solving, science. Buys 35 mss/year.

Poetry: Reviews poems, 20-line maximum length; limit submissions to 5 poems. Uses lyrical, humorous, simple language.

How to Contact/Writers: Fiction/nonfiction: Send complete ms. Queries not accepted. Responds to mss in 3 months. Publishes ms up to 2 years after acceptance. Will consider simultaneous submissions if informed. Submissions without SASE will be discarded.

Illustration: Buys 12 illustrations/issue; 145 illustrations/year. Prefers "bright colors; all media, but use watercolor and acrylics most often; same size as magazine is preferred but not required." To be considered for future assignments: Submit promo sheet, slides, tearsheets, color and b&w photocopies. Responds to art samples in 3 months. Submissions without SASE will be discarded.

Terms: Pays on publication for mss; after delivery of completed assignment for illustrators. For mss, buys first publication rights; second serial (reprint). Buys first publication rights plus promotional rights for artwork. Original artwork returned at job's completion. Pays 25¢/word for prose; $3/line for poetry. Pays $750 for color (cover) illustration, $50-100 for b&w (inside) illustration, $250/page for color (inside). Sample copy for $5. Writer's/illustrator's guidelines free for SASE.

Tips: Writers: "Get to know several young children on an individual basis. Respect your audience. We want less cute, condescending or 'preachy-teachy' material. Less gratuitous anthropomorphism. More rich, evocative language, sense of joy or wonder. Keep in mind that people come in all colors, sizes, physical conditions. Be inclusive in creating characters. Set your manuscript aside for at least a month, then reread critically." Illustrators: "Include examples, where possible, of children, animals, and—most important—action and narrative (i.e., several scenes from a story, showing continuity and an ability to maintain interest)." (See listings for *Babybug, Cicada, Cricket, Muse* and *Spider*.)

LISTEN, Drug-Free Possibilities for Teens, The Health Connection, 55 West Oak Ridge Dr., Hagerstown MD 21740. (301)393-4019. Fax: (301)393-4055. E-mail: listen@healthconnection.org. **Editor:** Anita Jacobs. Monthly magazine, 9 issues. Estab. 1948. Circ. 50,000. "*Listen* offers positive alternatives to drug use for its teenage readers. Helps them have a happy and productive life by making the right choices."

Fiction: Young adults: health, humorous, problem-solving peer pressure. Buys 50 mss/year. Average word length: 1,000-1,200. Byline given.

Nonfiction: Young adults: biography, games/puzzles, hobbies, how-to, health, humorous, problem solving, social issues, drug-free living. Wants to see more factual articles on drug abuse. Buys 50 mss/year. Average word length: 1,000-1,200. Byline given.

How to Contact/Writers: Fiction/nonfiction: Query. Responds to queries in 6 weeks; mss in 2 months. Will consider simultaneous submissions, electronic submission via disk or e-mail and previously published work.

Illustration: Buys 8-10 illustrations/issue; 72 illustrators/year. Reviews ms/illustration packages from artists. Manuscript/illustration packages and illustration only: Query. Contact: Doug Bendall, designer. Responds only if interested. Originals returned at job's completion. Samples returned with SASE. Credit line given.

Photography: Purchases photos from freelancers. Photos purchased with accompanying ms only. Uses color and b&w photos; 35mm, 2¼×2¼. Query with samples. Looks for "youth oriented—action (sports, outdoors), personality photos."

Terms: Pays on acceptance. Buys exclusive magazine rights for ms. Buys one-time rights for artwork and photographs. Pays $50-200 for stories/articles. Pays illustrators $500 for color cover; $75-225 for b&w

inside; $135-450 for color inside. Pays photographers by the project (range: $125-500); pays per photo (range: $125-500). Additional payment for ms/illustration packages and photos accompanying articles. Sample copy for $1 and 9 × 12 SASE and 2 first class stamps. Writer's guidelines free with SASE.

Tips: "*Listen* is a magazine for teenagers. It encourages development of good habits and high ideals of physical, social and mental health. It bases its editorial philosophy of primary drug prevention on total abstinence from tobacco, alcohol, and other drugs. Because it is used extensively in public high school classes, it does not accept articles and stories with overt religious emphasis. Four specific purposes guide the editors in selecting materials for *Listen*: (1) To portray a positive lifestyle and to foster skills and values that will help teenagers deal with contemporary problems, including smoking, drinking, and using drugs. This is *Listen*'s primary purpose. (2) To offer positive alternatives to a lifestyle of drug use of any kind. (3) To present scientifically accurate information about the nature and effects of tobacco, alcohol, and other drugs. (4) To report medical research, community programs, and educational efforts which are solving problems connected with smoking, alcohol, and other drugs. Articles should offer their readers activities that increase one's sense of self-worth through achievement and/or involvement in helping others. They are often categorized by three kinds of focus: (1) Hobbies. (2) Recreation. (3) Community Service.

THE MAGAZINE OF FANTASY & SCIENCE FICTION, Spilogale, Inc., P.O. Box 3447, Hoboken NJ 07030. Phone/fax: (201)876-2551. E-mail: FandSF@aol.com. Website: www.fsfmag.com. **Articles Editor:** Gordon Van Gelder. **Fiction Editor:** Gordon Van Gelder. Estab. 1949. Circ. 50,000. "We are one of the longest-running magazines devoted to fantasy and science fiction."

Fiction: Young adults: fantasy, science fiction. "We have no formula for fiction. We are looking for stories that will appeal to science fiction and fantasy readers. The SF element may be slight, but it should be present. We prefer character-oriented stories. We receive a lot of fantasy fiction, but never enough science fiction or humor." Buys 80-120 mss/year. Average word length: 25,000 maximum. Byline given.

Nonfiction: Buys 0-1 ms/year. Byline given.

How to Contact/Writers: Fiction: Send complete ms. Responds to mss in up to 2 months. Publishes ms 9 months after acceptance. Will consider previously published work.

Illustration: Buys 1 illustration/issue; 11 illustrations/year. Uses color artwork only. Works on assignment only. Responds only if interested.

Terms: Pays on acceptance. Buys first North American serial rights. Original artwork returned at job's completion. Pays 5-8¢/word. Sample copies for $5. Writer's guidelines for SASE.

Tips: "We are not aimed primarily at young readers, but we value our young readers and we have published many works that have become classics for youngsters (such as Daniel Keyes's 'Flowers for Algernon' and 'The Brave Little Toaster', by Thomas M. Disch). Read a sample issue before submitting."

MUSE, Carus Publishing, 332 S. Michagan Ave, Suite 1100, Chicago IL 60604. (312)939-1500. Fax: (312)939-8150. E-mail: muse@caruspub.com. Website: www.musemag.com **Editor:** Diana Lutz. **Art Director:** Karen Kohn. **Photo Editor:** Carol Parden. Estab. 1996. Circ. 60,000. "The goal of *Muse* is to give as many children as possible access to the most important ideas and concepts underlying the principal areas of human knowledge. It will take children seriously as developing intellects by assuming that, if explained clearly, the ideas and concepts of an article will be of interest to them. Articles should meet the highest possible standards of clarity and transparency aided, wherever possible, by a tone of skepticism, humor, and irreverence."

   • *Muse* is not accepting unsolicited manuscripts or queries.

Nonfiction: Middle readers, young adult: animal, biography, history, interview/profile, math, multicultural, nature/environment, problem-solving, science, social issues.

Illustration: Buys 6 illustrations/issue; 40 illustrations/year. Uses color artwork only. Works on assignment only. Reviews ms/illustration packages. Send ms with dummy. Illustrations only: Query with samples. Send résumé, promo sheet and tearsheets. Responds only if interested. Samples returned with SASE. Credit line given.

Photography: Needs vary. Query with samples. Responds only if interested.

Terms: Pays within 60 days of acceptance. Buys first publications rights; all rights for feature articles. Pays 50¢/word for assigned articles; 25¢/word for unsolicited manuscripts. Writer's guidelines and sample copy available for $5.

Tips: "*Muse* may on occasion publish unsolicited manuscripts, but the easiest way to be printed in *Muse* is to send a query. However, manuscripts may be submitted to the Cricket Magazine Group for review, and any that are considered suitable for *Muse* will be forwarded. Such manuscripts will also be considered for publication in *Cricket*, *Spider* or *Ladybug*." (See listing for *Ask*, *Babybug*, *Cricket*, *Ladybug* and *Spider*.)

MY FRIEND, The Catholic Magazine for Kids, Pauline Books & Media, 50 St. Pauls Ave., Jamaica Plain, Boston MA 02130-3491. (617)522-8911. Fax: (617)541-9805. E-mail: myfriend@pauline.org. Website: www.myfriendmagazine.com. **Editor:** Sr. Maria Grace Dateno, FSP. **Art Director:** Sister Helen Lane, FSP. Monthly magazine. Estab. 1979. Circ. 12,000. "*My Friend* is a 32-page monthly Catholic magazine for boys and girls. Its' goal is to celebrate the Catholic Faith—as it is lived by today's children and as it has been lived for centuries. Its pages are packed with fun, learning, new experiences, information, crafts, global awareness, friendships and inspiration. Together with it's web-page, *My Friend* provides kids and their families a wealth of information and contacts on every aspect of the Faith."

Fiction: Young readers, middle readers: adventure, Christmas, contemporary, humorous, multicultural, nature/environment, problem-solving, religious, sports. Buys 30 mss/year. Average word length: 750-1,100. Byline given.

Nonfiction: Young readers, middle readers: humorous, interview/profile, media literacy, problem-solving, religious, multicultural, social issues. Does not want to see material that is not compatible with Catholic values; no "New Age" material. Staff writes doctrinal articles and prepares puzzles. Buys 10 mss/year. Average word length: 450-750. Byline given.

How to Contact/Writers: Fiction/nonfiction: Send complete ms. Responds to queries/mss in 2 months.

Terms: Pays on acceptance for mss. Buys first rights for mss; variable for artwork. Original artwork returned at job's completion. Pays $80-150 for stories/articles. Sample copy $2 with 9 × 12 SAE and 4 first-class stamps. Writer's guidelines and theme list free with SASE.

Tips: Writers: "We are looking for fresh perspectives into a child's world that are imaginative, unique, challenging, informative, current and fun. We prefer articles that are visual, not necessarily text-based—articles written in 'windows' style with multiple points entry. Illustrators: Please contact us! Preferred style: realistic or slightly cartoon-style depictions of children. For the most part, we need illustrations for fiction stories."

NATIONAL GEOGRAPHIC KIDS, (formerly *National Geographic World*) National Geographic Society, 1145 17th St. NW, Washington DC 20036-4688. (202)857-7000. Fax: (202)775-6112. Website: www.nationalgeographic.com/world. **Editor:** Melina Bellows. **Art Director**: Ursula Vosseler. **Photo Director**: Leah P. Roberts. Monthly magazine. Estab. 1975. Circ. 870,000.

NATURE FRIEND MAGAZINE, 2673 Twp. Rd., Sugarcreek OH 44681. (330)852-1900. Fax: (330)852-3285. **Articles Editor:** Marvin Wengerd. Monthly magazine. Estab. 1983. Circ. 10,000.

Fiction: Picture-oriented material, conversational, no talking animal stories.

Nonfiction: Picture-oriented material, animal, how-to, nature. No talking animal stories. No evolutionary material. Buys 50 mss/year. Average word length: 500. Byline given.

How to Contact/Writers: Nonfiction: Send complete ms. Responds to mss in 4 months. Will consider but must note simultaneous submissions.

Illustration: Buys approximately 8 illustrations/issue from freelancers; 96 illustrations/year. Responds to artist's submissions in 1 month. Works on assignment only. Credit line given.

Photography: Pays $75 for front cover, $50 for back cover, $75 for centerfold, $30 for text photos. Submit slides or transparencies on CD with color printout.

Terms: Pays on publication. Buys one-time rights. Pays $15 minimum. Payment for illustrations: $15-80/b&w, $50-100/color inside. Two sample copies and writer's guidelines for $5 with 9 × 12 SAE and $2 postage. Writer's guidelines for $2.50.

Tips: Looks for "main articles, puzzles and simple nature and science projects. Needs conversationally-written stories about unique animals or nature phenomena. Please examine samples and writer's guide before submitting." Current needs: science and nature experiments for ages 8-12.

NEW MOON: The Magazine For Girls & Their Dreams, New Moon Publishing, Inc., P.O. Box 3620, Duluth MN 55803-3620. (218)728-5507. Fax: (218)728-0314. E-mail: girl@newmoon.org. Website: www.newmoon.org. **Managing Editors:** Deb Mylin. Bimonthly magazine. Estab. 1992. Circ. 25,000. *New Moon* is for every girl who wants her voice heard and her dreams taken seriously. *New Moon* portrays strong female role models of all ages, backgrounds and cultures now and in the past. 100% of publication aimed at juvenile market.

Fiction: Middle readers, young adults: adventure, animal, contemporary, fantasy, folktales, history, humorous, multicultural, nature/environment, problem-solving, religious, science fiction, sports, suspense/mystery, travel. Buys 3 mss/year from adults and 3 mss/year from girls. Average word length: 900-1,200. Byline given.

Nonfiction: Middle readers, young adults: animal, arts/crafts, biography, careers, cooking, games/puzzles, health, history, hobbies, humorous, interview/profile, math, multicultural, nature/environment, problem-solving, science, social issues, sports, travel, stories about real girls. Does not want to see how-to stories. Wants more stories about real girls doing real things written by girls. Buys 6-12 adult-written mss/year. 30 girl-written mss/year. Average word length: 600. Byline given.

How to Contact/Writers: Fiction/Nonfiction: Does not return or acknowledge unsolicited mss. Send only copies. Responds only if interested. Will consider simultaneous submissions and electronic submission e-mail.

Illustration: Buys 6-12 illustrations/year from freelancers. *New Moon* seeks 4-color cover illustrations as well as b&w illustrations for inside. Reviews ms/illustrations packages from artists. Query. Submit ms with rough sketches. Illustration only: Query; send portfolio and tearsheets. Samples not returned; samples filed. Responds in 6 months only if interested. Credit line given.

Terms: Pays on publication. Buys all rights for mss. Buys one-time rights, reprint rights, for artwork. Original artwork returned at job's completion. Pays 6-12¢/word for stories; 6-12¢/word for articles. Pays in contributor's copies. Pays illustrators $400 for color cover; $50-300 for b&w inside. Sample copies for $6.50. Writer's/cover art guidelines for SASE or available on website.

Tips: "Please refer to a copy of *New Moon* to understand the style and philosophy of the magazine. Writers and artists who understand our goals have the best chance of publication. We're looking for stories about real girls; women's careers, and historical profiles. We publish girl's and women's writing only." Publishes writing/art/photos by girls.

A **NICK JR. MAGAZINE**, Nickelodeon Magazines, Inc., 1633 Broadway, 7th Floor, New York NY 10019. (212)654-6389. Fax: (212)654-4840. Website: www.nickjr.com. **Articles Editor:** Wendy Smolen, deputy editor. **Art Director:** Josh Klenert. **Director:** Don Morris. Bimonthly magazine. Estab. 1999. Circ. 500,000. A magazine where kids play to learn and parents learn to play. 50% of publication aimed at juvenile market.

Fiction: Picture-oriented material: adventure, animal, contemporary, humorous, multicultural, nature/environment, problem-solving, sports. Byline sometimes given.

Nonfiction: Picture-oriented material: animal, arts/crafts, concept, cooking, games/puzzles, hobbies, how-to, humorous, math, multicultural, nature/environment, problem-solving, science, social issues, sports. Byline sometimes given.

How to Contact/Writers: Only interested in agented material. Fiction/nonfiction: Query or submit complete ms. Responds to queries/mss in 3-12 weeks. Will consider simultaneous submissions.

Illustration: Only interested in agented material. Works on assignment only. Reviews ms/illustration packages from artists. Query or send ms with dummy. Contact: Wendy Smolen, deputy editor. Illustrations only: arrange portfolio review; send résumé, promo sheet and portfolio. Contact: Josh Klenert, art director. Responds only if interested. Samples not returned; samples kept on file. Credit line sometimes given.

Photography: Looking for photos of children. Model/property release required.
Query with résumé of credits; provide résumé, business card, promotional literature or tearsheets. Responds only if interested.

Terms: Writer's guidelines for SASE.

ODYSSEY, Adventures in Science, Cobblestone Publishing Company, 30 Grove St., Suite C, Peterborough NH 03458. (603)924-7209. Fax: (603)924-7380. E-mail: odyssey@cobblestonepub.com. Website: www.odysseymagazine.com. (Also see www.cobblestonepub.com.) **Editor:** Elizabeth E. Lindstrom. **Managing Editor:** Lou Waryncia. **Art Director**: Ann Dillon. Magazine published 9 times/year. Estab. 1979. Circ. 22,000. Magazine covers earth, general science and technology, astronomy and space exploration for children ages 10-16. All material must relate to the theme of a specific upcoming issue in order to be considered.

 • *Odyssey* themes for 2003 include The Technology of Spying, Invisible Highways: The Science of Migrations, Under Pressure, and Stats: Talking Numbers. See website for more information.

Fiction: Middle readers and young adults/teens: science fiction, science, astronomy. Does not want to see anything not theme-related. Average word length: 900-1,200 words.

Nonfiction: Middle readers and young adults/teens: interiors, activities. Don't send anything not theme-related. Average word length: 200-750, depending on section article is used in.

How to Contact/Writers: "A query must consist of all of the following to be considered (please use nonerasable paper): a brief cover letter stating the subject and word length of the proposed article; a detailed one-page outline explaining the information to be presented in the article; an extensive bibliography of materials the author intends to use in preparing the article; a SASE. Writers new to *Odyssey* should send a writing sample with query. If you would like to know if your query has been received, please also include a stamped postcard that requests acknowledgment of receipt. In all correspondence, please include your complete address as well as a telephone number and e-mail address where you can be reached. A writer may send as many queries for one issue as he or she wishes, but each query must have a separate cover letter, outline, bibliography, and SASE. Telephone queries are not accepted. Handwritten queries will not be considered. Queries may be submitted at any time, but queries sent well in advance of deadline *may* *not be answered for several months.* Go-aheads requesting material proposed in queries are usually sent four months prior to publication date. Unused queries will be returned approximately three to four months prior to publication date."

Illustration: Buys 3 illustrations/issue; 27 illustrations/year. Works on assignment only. Reviews ms/illustration packages from artists. Query. Contact: Beth Lindstrom, editor. Illustration only: Query with samples. Send tearsheets, photocopies. Responds in 2 weeks. Samples returned with SASE; samples not filed. Original artwork returned upon job's completion (upon written request).

Photography: Wants photos pertaining to any of our forthcoming themes. Uses b&w and color prints; 35mm transparencies. Photographers should send unsolicited photos by mail on speculation.

Terms: Pays on publication. Buys all rights for mss and artwork. Pays 20-25¢/word for stories/articles. Covers are assigned and paid on an individual basis. Pays photographers per photo ($15-100 for b&w; $25-100 for color). Sample copy for $4.95 and SASE with $2 postage. Writer's/illustrator's/photo guidelines for SASE. (See listings for *AppleSeeds, Calliope, Cobblestone, Dig, Faces* and *Footsteps*.)

ON THE LINE, Mennonite Publishing House, 616 Walnut Ave., Scottdale PA 15683. (724)887-8500. Fax: (724)887-3111. E-mail: otl@mph.org. **Editor:** Mary Clemens Meyer. Magazine published monthly. Estab. 1970. Circ. 5,500. "*On The Line* is a children's magazine for ages 9-14, emphasizing self-esteem and Christian values. Also emphasizes multicultural awareness, care of the earth and accepting others with differences."

Fiction: Middle readers, young adults: contemporary, history, humorous, nature/environment, problem-solving, religious, science fiction, sports. "No fantasy or fiction with animal characters." Buys 45 mss/year. Average word length: 1,000-1,800. Byline given.

Nonfiction: Middle readers, young adults: arts/crafts, biography, cooking, games/puzzles, health, history, hobbies, how-to, humorous, sports. Does not want to see articles written from an adult perspective. Average word length: 200-600. Byline given.

Poetry: Wants to see light verse, humorous poetry.

How to Contact/Writers: Fiction/nonfiction: Send complete ms. "No queries, please." Responds to mss in 1 month. Will consider simultaneous submissions. Prefers no e-mail submissions.

Illustration: Buys 5-6 illustrations/issue; buys 60 illustrations/year. "Inside illustrations are done on assignment only to accompany our stories and articles—our need for new artists is limited." Looking for new artists for cover illustrations—full-color work. Illustrations only: "Prefer samples they do not want returned; these stay in our files." Responds to art samples only if interested.

Terms: Pays on acceptance. For mss buys one-time rights; second serial (reprint rights). Buys one-time rights for artwork and photos. Pays 3-5¢/word for assigned/unsolicited articles. Pays $50 for full-color inside illustration; $150 for full-color cover illustration. Photographers are paid per photo, $25-50. Original artwork returned at job's completion. Sample copy free with 7×10 SAE. Free writer's guidelines.

Tips: "We focus on the age 12-13 group of our age 9-14 audience."

OWL, The Discovery Magazine for Children, Bayard Press, 49 Front St. E, Toronto, Ontario M5E 1B3 Canada. (416)340-2700. Fax: (416)340-9769. E-mail: owl@owl.on.ca. Website: www.owlkids.com. **Editor:** Marybeth Leatherdale. Monthly magazine. Circ. 75,000. "*OWL* helps children over eight discover and enjoy the world of science, nature and technology. We look for articles that are fun to read, that inform from a child's perspective, and that motivate hands-on interaction. *OWL* explores the reader's many interests in the natural world in a scientific, but always entertaining, way."

Nonfiction: Middle readers: animal, biology, games/puzzles, high-tech, humor, nature/environment, science, social issues, sports, travel. Especially interested in puzzles and game ideas: logic, math, visual puzzles. Does not want to see religious topics, anthropomorphizing. Buys 6 mss/year. Average word length: 500-1,500. Byline given.

How to Contact/Writers: Nonfiction: Query with outline and published clips. Responds to queries/mss in 4 months.

Photography: Looking for shots of animals and nature. "Label the photos." Uses 2¼×2¼ and 35mm transparencies. Photographers should query with samples. Send for photo package before submission. State availability of photos with submission.

MARKET CONDITIONS are constantly changing! If you're still using this book and it is 2004 or later, buy the newest edition of *Children's Writer's & Illustrator's Market* at your favorite bookstore or order directly from Writer's Digest Books (800)448-0915.

Terms: Pays on publication. Buys first North American and world rights for mss, artwork and photos. Pays $200-500 (Canadian) for assigned/unsolicited articles. Pays up to $650 (Canadian) for illustrations. Photographers are paid per photo. Sample copies for $4.28. Writer's guidelines for SAE (large envelope if requesting sample copy) and money order for $1 postage (no stamps please).

Tips: Writers: "*OWL* is dedicated to entertaining kids with contemporary and accurate information about the world around them. *OWL* is intellectually challenging but is never preachy. Ideas should be original and convey a spirit of humor and liveliness." (See listings for *Chickadee* and *Chirp*.)

PARENTS AND CHILDREN TOGETHER ONLINE, A magazine for parents and children on the World Wide Web, EDINFO Press/Family Literary Centers, 2805 East 10th St., Suite 140, Bloomington IN 47408. (800)759-4723. E-mail: erics@indiana.edu. Website: http://eric.indiana.edu\pcto.html. **Editor-in-Chief:** Mei-yu Lu. Quarterly online magazine. Estab. 1990 (in print format). Circ. 9,000 via worldwide web. "Our magazine seeks to promote family literacy by providing original articles and stories for parents and children via the worldwide web." 50% of publication aimed at juvenile market.

Fiction: We accept all categories except the overtly religious. Would like to see more humorous stories. We welcome stories from all cultural backgrounds. Buys 32 mss/year. Byline given.

Nonfiction: All categories are looked at and considered. We especially look for articles with photographs and/or illustrations included. We welcome articles about children and subjects that children will find interesting, that reflect diverse cultural backgrounds. We like articles about animals, but we do get quite a few of them. Buys 24 mss/year. Byline given.

Poetry: Reviews poetry. Limit submissions to 3 poems. "We accept poems written for children that children will enjoy—not poems about childhood by an adult looking back nostalgically. Humorous, but not just silly, poems especially appreciated."

How to Contact/Writers: Fiction/nonfiction: Send complete ms. Responds to queries in 1 week; mss in 3 months. Publishes ms 3-6 months after acceptance. Will consider simultaneous submissions, electronic submissions via disk or modem and previously published work.

Illustration: Buys 12 illustrations/issue; 48 illustrations/year. Uses color artwork only. Reviews ms/illustration packages from artists. Query with ms dummy. Contact: Editor. Illustrations only: Query with samples. Contact: Editor. Reports on art samples in 1 month. Samples returned with SASE. Credit line given.

Photography: Looking for children and parents together, either reading together or involved in other interesting activities. Also, children with grandparents. Uses color prints and 35mm transparencies. Query with samples. Send unsolicited photos by mail. Responds in 1 month.

Terms: Buys first North American serial rights for mss. Art/photos use on web with copyright retained by artist/photographer. "We are a free online publication, and cannot afford to pay our contributors at present." Sample copies for $9. Writer's guidelines free for SASE.

Tips: "We are a good market for writers, artists and photographers who want their material to reach a wide audience. Since we are a free publication, available without charge to anyone with a web browser, we cannot offer our contributors anything more than a large, enthusiastic audience for their work. Our stories and articles are read by thousands of children and parents every month via their families' internet-connected computer."

✔ POCKETS, Devotional Magazine for Children, The Upper Room, 1908 Grand, P.O. Box 340004, Nashville TN 37203-0004. (615)340-7333. Fax: (615)340-7267. E-mail: pockets@upperroom.org. Website: www.upperroom.org/pockets. **Articles/Fiction Editor:** Lynn W. Gilliam. **Art Director:** Chris Schechner, 408 Inglewood Dr., Richardson TX 75080. Magazine published 11 times/year. Estab. 1981. Circ. 99,000. "*Pockets* is a Christian devotional magazine for children ages 6-12. Stories should help children experience a Christian lifestyle that is not always a neatly wrapped moral package but is open to the continuing revelation of God's will."

Fiction: Picture-oriented, young readers, middle readers: adventure, contemporary, occasional folktales, multicultural, nature/environment, problem-solving, religious. Does not accept violence or talking animal stories. Buys 40-45 mss/year. Average word length: 600-1,400. Byline given.

Nonfiction: Picture-oriented, young readers, middle readers: cooking, games/puzzles, interview/profile, religion. Does not accept how-to articles. "Our nonfiction reads like a story." Multicultural needs include: stories that feature children of various racial/ethnic groups and do so in a way that is true to those depicted. Buys 10 mss/year. Average word length: 400-1,000. Byline given.

How to Contact/Writers: Fiction/nonfiction: Send complete ms. "Do not accept queries." Responds to mss in 6 weeks. Will consider simultaneous submissions.

Illustration: Buys 40-50 illustrations/issue. Preferred theme or style: varied; both 4-color and 2-color. Works on assignment only. Illustrations only: Send promo sheet, tearsheets.

RANGER RICK, National Wildlife Federation, 11100 Wildlife Center Dr., Reston VA 20190. (703)438-6000. Website: www.nwf.org.
- Ranger Rick is no longer accepting unsolicited queries or mss.

READ, Weekly Reader Corporation, 200 First Stamford Place, P.O. Box 120023, Stamford CT 06912-0023. Fax: (203)705-1661. E-mail: sbarchers@weeklyreader.com. Website: www.weeklyreader.com. **Managing Editor:** Suzanne Barchers. Magazine published 18 times during the school year. Language arts periodical for use in classrooms for students ages 12-16; motivates students to read and teaches skills in listening, comprehension, speaking, writing and critical thinking.
Fiction: Wants short stories, narratives and plays to be used for classroom reading and discussions. Middle readers, young adult/teens: adventure, animal, contemporary, fantasy, folktales, history, humorous, multicultural, nature/environment, sports. Average word length: 1,000-2,500.
Nonfiction: Middle readers, young adult/teen: animal, games/puzzles, history, humorous, problem solving, social issues.
How to Contact: Responds to queries/mss in 6 weeks.
Illustration: Buys 2-3 illustrations/issue; 20-25 illustration jobs/year. Responds only if interested. Samples returned with SASE. Credit line given.
Terms: Pays on publication. Rights purchased varies. Pays writers $100-800 for stories/articles. Pays illustrators $650-850 for color cover; $125-750 for b&w and color inside. Pays photographers by the project (range: $450-650); per photo (range: $125-650). Samples copies free for digest-sized SAE and 3 first-class stamps.
Tips: "We especially like plot twists and surprise endings. Stories should be relevant to teens and contain realistic conflicts and dialogue. Plays should have at least 12 speaking parts for classroom reading. Avoid formula plots, trite themes, underage material, stilted or profane language, and sexual suggestion. Get to know the style of our magazine as well as our teen audience. They are very demanding and require an engaging and engrossing read. Grab their attention, keep the pace and action lively, build to a great climax, and make the ending satisfying and/or surprising. Make sure characters and dialogue are realistic. Do not use cliché, but make the writing fresh—simple, yet original. Obtain guidelines and planned editorial calendar first. Be sure submissions are relevant."

SCHOOL MATES, USCF's Magazine for Beginning Chess Players, United States Chess Federation, 3054 Rt. 9W, New Windsor NY 12553. (845)562-8350. Fax: (845)561-CHES. E-mail: magazines@uschess.org. Website: www.uschess.org. **Editor:** Peter Kurzdorfer. **Graphic Designer:** Jami Anson. Quarterly magazine. Estab. 1987. Circ. 37,000. Magazine for beginning and scholastic chess players. Offers instructional articles, features on famous players, scholastic chess coverage, games, puzzles, occasional fiction, listing of chess tournaments.
Nonfiction: Young readers, middle readers, young adults: games/puzzles, chess. Middle readers, young adults: interview/profile (chess-related). "No *Mad Magazine* type humor. No sex, no drugs, no alcohol, no tobacco. No stereotypes. We want to see chess presented as a wholesome, non-nerdy activity that's fun for all. Good sportsmanship, fair play, and 'thinking ahead' are extremely desirable in chess articles. Also, celebrities who play chess."
Poetry: Infrequently published. Must be chess related.
How to Contact/Writers: Send complete ms. Responds to queries/mss in 5 weeks.
Illustration: Buys 10-25 illustrations/year. Prefers b&w and ink; cartoons OK. Illustration only: Query first. Responds only if interested. Credit line sometimes given. "Typically, a cover is credited while an illustration inside gets only the artist's signature in the work itself."
Photography: Purchases photos from freelancers. Wants "action shots of chess games (at tournament competitions), well-done portraits of popular chess players."
Terms: Pays on publication. Buys one-time rights for mss, artwork and photos. For stories/articles, pays $20-100. Pays illustrators $50-75 for b&w cover; $20-50 for b&w inside. Pays photographers per photo (range: $25-75). Sample copies free for 9×12 SAE and 2 first-class stamps. Writer's guidelines free on request.
Tips: Writers: "Lively prose that grabs and sustains kids' attention is desirable. Don't talk down to kids or over their heads. Don't be overly 'cute.'" Illustration/photography: "Whimsical shots are often desirable."

SCIENCE WEEKLY, Science Weekly Inc., P.O. Box 70638, Chevy Chase MD 20813. (301)680-8804. Fax: (301)680-9240. E-mail: sciencew@erols.com. Website: www.scienceweekly.com. **Editor:** Deborah Lazar. Magazine published 16 times/year. Estab. 1984. Circ. 200,000.
- *Science Weekly* uses freelance writers to develop and write an entire issue on a single science topic. Send résumé only, not submissions. Authors must be within the greater DC, Virginia, Maryland area. *Science Weekly* works on assignment only.

Nonfiction: Young readers, middle readers, (K-8th grade): science/math education, education, problem-solving.
Terms: Pays on publication. Prefers people with education, science and children's writing background. *Send résumé* only. Samples copies free with SAE and 2 first-class stamps.

SCIENCE WORLD, Scholastic Inc., 555 Broadway, New York NY 10012-3999. (212)343-6299. Fax: (212)343-6333. E-mail: scienceworld@scholastic.com. **Editor:** Mark Bregman. **Art Director:** Susan Kass. Magazine published biweekly during the school year. Estab. 1959. Circ. 400,000. Publishes articles in Life Science/Health, Physical Science/Technology, Earth Science/Environment/Astronomy for students in grades 7-10. The goal is to make science relevant for teens.
  • *Science World* publishes a separate teacher's edition with lesson plans and skills pages to accompany feature articles.
Nonfiction: Young adults/teens: animal, concept, geography, health, nature/environment, science. Multicultural needs include: minority scientists as role models. Does not want to see stories without a clear news hook. Buys 20 mss/year. Average word length: 500-750. Byline given. Currently does not accept unsolicited mss.
How to Contact/Writers: Nonfiction: Query with published clips and/or brief summaries of article ideas. Responds to queries in 3 months.
Illustration: Buys 2 illustrations/issue; 28 illustrations/year. Works on assignment only. Illustration only: Query with samples, tearsheets. Contact: Susan Kass, art director. Responds only if interested. Samples returned with SASE; samples filed "if we use them." Credit line given.
Photography: Model/property releases required; captions required including background information. Provide résumé, business card, promotional literature or tearsheets to be kept on file. Responds only if interested.
Terms: Pays on acceptance. Buys all right for mss/artwork. Originals returned to artist at job's completion. For stories/articles, pays $200. Pays photographers per photo.

SEVENTEEN MAGAZINE, Primedia, 850 Third Ave., 9th Floor, New York NY 10022. (212)407-9700. Fax: (212)407-9899. Website: www.seventeen.com. **Editor-in-Chief:** Annemarie Iverson. **Deputy Editor:** Tamara Glenny. **Art Director:** Carol Pagliuco. Monthly magazine. Estab. 1944. Circ. 2.5 million. "*Seventeen* is a young woman's first fashion and beauty magazine."
Fiction: "We consider all good literary short fiction." Buys 6-12 mss/year. Average word length: 800-4,000. Byline given.
Nonfiction: Young adults: animal, beauty, entertainment, fashion, careers, health, hobbies, how-to, humorous, interview/profile, multicultural, relationships, religion, social issues, sports. Buys 150 mss/year. Word length: Varies from 800-1,000 words for short features and monthly columns to 800-2,500 words for major articles. Byline given.
How to Contact/Writers: Fiction: Send complete ms. Nonfiction: Query with published clips or send complete ms. "Do not call." Responds to queries/mss in 3 months. Will consider simultaneous submissions.
Terms: Pays on acceptance. Strongly recommends requesting writers guidelines with SASE and reading recent issues of the magazine.
Tips: Send for guidelines before submitting.

SHARING THE VICTORY, Fellowship of Christian Athletes, 8701 Leeds, Kansas City MO 64129. (816)921-0909. Fax: (816)921-8755. Website: www.fca.org. **Articles/Photo Editor:** David Smale. **Art Director:** Frank Grey. Magazine published 9 times a year. Estab. 1982. Circ. 85,000. "Purpose is to present to coaches and athletes, and all whom they influence, the challenge and adventure of receiving Jesus Christ as Savior and Lord."
Nonfiction: Young adults/teens: religion, sports. Buys 30 mss/year. Average word length: 700-1,200. Byline given.
How to Contact/Writers: Nonfiction: Query with published clips. Responds in 6 weeks. Publishes ms 3 months after acceptance. Will consider simultaneous submissions, electronic submissions via disk or modem and previously published work. Writer's guidelines available on website.
Photography: Purchases photos separately. Looking for photos of sports action. Uses color prints and 35mm transparencies.
Terms: Pays on publication. Buys first rights and second serial (reprint) rights. Pays $150-400 for assigned and unsolicited articles. Photographers paid per photo. Sample copies for 9×12 SASE and $1. Writer's/photo guidelines for SASE.
Tips: "Be specific—write short. Take quality, sharp photos." Wants interviews and features, articles on athletes with a solid Christian base; be sure to include their faith and testimony. Interested in colorful sports photos.

SHINE brightly, GEMS Girls' Clubs, Box 7259, Grand Rapids MI 49510. (616)241-5616. Fax: (616)241-5558. E-mail: sara@gemsgc.org. Website: www.gospelcom.net/gems. **Editor:** Jan Boone. **Managing Editor:** Sara Lynne Hilton. Monthly (with combined May/June/July/August summer issue) magazine. Circ. 16,000. "*Shine brightly* is designed to help girls ages 9-14 see how God is at work in their lives and in the world around them."

Fiction: Middle readers: adventure, animal, contemporary, health, history, humorous, multicultural, nature/environment, problem-solving, religious, sports. Does not want to see unrealistic stories and those with trite, easy endings. Buys 30 mss/year. Average word length: 400-1,000. Byline given.

Nonfiction: Middle readers: animal, arts/crafts, careers, cooking, fashion, games/puzzles, health, hobbies, how-to, humorous, nature/environment, multicultural, problem-solving, religious, social issues, sports, travel. Buys 9 mss/year. Average word length: 200-800. Byline given.

How to Contact/Writers: Send for annual update for publication themes. Fiction/nonfiction: Send complete ms. Responds to mss in 1 month. Will consider simultaneous submissions.

Illustration: Buys 3 illustrations/year. Prefers ms/illustration packages. Works on assignment only. Responds to submissions in 1 month. Samples returned with SASE. Credit line given.

Terms: Pays on publication. Buys first North American serial rights, first rights, second serial (reprint rights) or simultaneous rights. Original artwork not returned at job's completion. Pays $5-30 for stories; $5-30 for assigned articles; $5-30 for unsolicited articles. "We send complimentary copies in addition to pay." Pays $25-75 for color cover illustration; $25-50 for color inside illustration. Pays photographers by the project ($25-75 per photo). Writer's guidelines for SASE.

Tips: Writers: "The stories should be current, deal with adolescent problems and joys, and help girls see God at work in their lives through humor as well as problem-solving."

SKATING, U.S. Figure Skating Association, 20 First St., Colorado Springs CO 80906. (719)635-5200. Fax: (719)635-9548. E-mail: skatingmagazine@usfsa.org. **Articles Editor:** Laura Fawcett. Magazine published 10 times/year. Estab. 1923. Circ. 45,000. "The mission of *SKATING* is to communicate information about the sport (figure skating) to the USFSA membership and figure skating fans, promoting USFSA programs, personalities, events and trends that affect the sport."

Nonfiction: Young readers, middle readers, young adults. biography, health, sports. Buys 30 mss/year. Average word length: 750-2,000. Byline given.

How to Contact/Writers: Nonfiction: Query with published clips. Responds to queries/mss in 1 month. Publishes ms 2 months after acceptance. Prefers electronic submissions via disk or e-mail.

Illustration: Buys 1 illustration/year. Works on assignment only. Reviews ms/illustration packages from artists. Query. Contact: Laura Fawcett, editor. Illustrations only: Query with samples. Contact: Laura Fawcett, editor. Responds only if interested. Samples returned with SASE; or filed. Credit line given.

Photography: Uses photos of kids learning to skate on ice. Model/property release required; captions required. Uses color most sizes matte or glossy prints, 35mm transparencies. Contact by e-mail if interested in submitting. Responds only if interested.

Terms: Pays on publication. Buys first rights for mss, artwork and photos. Original artwork returned at job's completion. Pays $75-150 for stories and articles. Additional payment if photos are used. Pays photographers per photo (range: $15-35). Sample copies for SAE. Writer's/photo guidelines for SASE.

Tips: "*SKATING* covers Olympic-eligible skating, primarily focusing on the U.S. We do *not* cover professional skating. We are looking for fun, vibrant articles on USFSA members of all age levels and skills, especially synchronized skaters and adult skaters."

SKIPPING STONES, A Multicultural Children's Magazine, P.O. Box 3939, Eugene OR 97403. (541)342-4956. E-mail: skipping@efn.org. Website: www.efn.org/~skipping. **Articles/Photo/Fiction Editor:** Arun N. Toké. Bimonthly magazine. Estab. 1988. Circ. 2,500. "*Skipping Stones* is a multicultural, nonprofit children's magazine designed to encourage cooperation, creativity and celebration of cultural and ecological richness. We encourage submissions by minorities and under represented populations."

● *Skipping Stones* themes for November/December 2002 include Cultural Celebrations, Holidays and features Bolivia and Brazil. Check website for 2003 themes, ideas, and submission guidelines.

Fiction: Middle readers, young adult/teens: contemporary, meaningful, humorous. All levels: folktales, multicultural, nature/environment. Multicultural needs include: bilingual or multilingual pieces; use of words from other languages; settings in other countries, cultures or multi-ethnic communities.

Nonfiction: All levels: animal, biography, cooking, games/puzzles, history, humorous, interview/profile, multicultural, nature/environment, creative problem-solving, religion and cultural celebrations, sports, travel, social and international awareness. Does not want to see preaching or abusive language; no poems by authors over 18 years old; no suspense or romance stories for the sake of the same. Average word length: 500-750. Byline given.

How to Contact/Writers: Fiction: Query. Nonfiction: Send complete ms. Responds to queries in 1 month; mss in 4 months. Will consider simultaneous submissions; reviews artwork for future assignments. Please include your name on each page. Manuscripts should not exceed 750 words.

Illustration: Prefers color and/or b&w drawings, especially by teenagers and young adults. Will consider all illustration packages. Manuscript/illustration packages: Query; submit complete ms with final art; submit tearsheets. Responds in 4 months. Credit line given.

Photography: Black & white photos preferred, but color photos with good contrast are welcome. Needs: youth 7-17, international, nature, celebration.

Terms: Acquires first and reprint rights for mss and photographs. Pays in copies for authors, photographers and illustrators. Sample copies for $5 with SAE and 4 first-class stamps. Writer's/illustrator's guidelines for 4×9 SASE.

Tips: "We want material meant for children and young adults/teenagers with multicultural or ecological awareness themes. Think, live and write as if you were a child—naturally, uninhibited." Wants "material that gives insight on cultural celebrations, lifestyle, custom and tradition, glimpse of daily life in other countries and cultures. Photos, songs, artwork are most welcome if they illustrate/highlight the points. Translations are invited if your submission is in a language other than English. Upcoming themes will include cultural celebrations, living abroad, disability, hospitality customs of various cultures, cross-cultural communications, African, Asian and Latin American cultures, humor, international, and turning points in life, caring for the earth, the Internet's Impact on Multicutural Awareness."

SOCCER JR., The Soccer Magazine for Kids, Scholastic Inc., 27 Unquowa Rd., Fairfield CT 06430-5015. (203)259-5766. Fax: (203)256-1119. E-mail: soccerjr@soccerjr.com. Website: www.soccerjr.com. **Editor:** Joseph Provey. **Art Director:** Jon Walker. Bimonthly magazine. Estab. 1992. Circ. 100,000. *Soccer Jr.* is for soccer players 8-14 years old. "The editorial focus of *Soccer Jr.* is on the fun and challenge of the sport. Every issue contains star interviews, how-to tips, lively graphics, action photos, comics, games, puzzles and contests. Fair play and teamwork are emphasized in a format that provides an off-the-field way for kids to enjoy the sport."

Nonfiction: Young readers, middle readers, young adults/teens: sports (soccer). Buys 10-12 mss/year.

How to Contact/Writers: Nonfiction: Send query letter. Publishes ms 3-12 months after acceptance. Will consider simultaneous submissions.

Terms: Payment varies.

Tips: "We ask all potential writers to understand *Soccer Jr.*'s voice. We write to kids, not to adults. We request a query for any feature ideas, but any fiction pieces can be sent complete. All submissions, unless specifically requested, are on a speculative basis. Please indicate if a manuscript has been submitted elsewhere or previously published. Please give us a brief personal bio, including your involvement in soccer, if any, and a listing of any work you've had published. We prefer manuscripts in Microsoft Word, along with an attached hard copy." The magazine also accepts stories written by children.

☑ **SPELLBOUND MAGAZINE**, Eggplant Productions, 135 Shady Lane, Bolingbroke IL 60440. (630)460-7959. Fax: (801)720-0706. E-mail: spellbound@eggplant-productions.com. Website: www.eggplantproductions.com/spellbound. **Articles Editor:** Raechel Henderson Moon. Quarterly magazine. Estab. 1999. Circ. 300. "*Spellbound Magazine*'s goal is to introduce new readers to the fantasy genre in all its wonderful forms. We publish intelligent fiction, nonfiction and poetry to excite kids. We like artwork that is fun."

• *Spellbound* only accepts e-mail submissions. All postal submissions are returned unread.

Fiction: Middle readers, young adults: fantasy, folktale, multicultural. Buys 20 mss/year. Average word length: 500-2,500. Byline given.

Nonfiction: Middle readers, young adults: myths/legends. Buys 1-2 mss/year. Average word length: 500-1,000. Byline given.

Poetry: Reviews free verse, traditional, rhyming poetry. Maximum length: 36 lines. Limit submissions to 5 poems.

How to Contact/Writers: Fiction: Send complete ms. Nonfiction: Query. Responds to queries in 2 weeks; mss in 1 month. Publishes ms 6 months after acceptance. Will consider simultaneous submissions; only considers electronic submission via modem.

Illustration: Buys 3-4 illustrations/issue; 12-16 illustrations/year. Uses b&w artwork only. Reviews ms/illustration packages from artists. Submit through e-mail to spellbound@eggplant-productions.com. Contact: Raechel Henderson Moon, editor. Illustrations only: Query with samples. Contact: Raechel Henderson Moon, editor. Responds in 2 weeks. Samples kept on file. Credit line given.

Terms: Pays on publication. Buys first world English-language rights for mss. Buys one-time rights for art. Pays $5 stories; $5 for articles and poetry. Artists are paid 2 contributor copies and $1.50 per interior art; 3 contributor copies and $5 for cover art. Sample copies for $5.

Tips: "Keep in mind that this is a market for children, but don't let that limit your work. We see too much that preaches or talks down to readers or that relies on old plot lines. Write the kind of story or poem that you would like to have read when you were 11. Then send it our way."

SPIDER, The Magazine for Children, Carus Publishing Company, P.O. Box 300, Peru IL 61354. (815)224-6656. Website: www.cricketmag.com. **Editor-in-Chief:** Marianne Carus. **Editor:** Heather Delabre. **Art Director**: Tony Jacobson. Monthly magazine. Estab. 1994. Circ. 73,000. *Spider* publishes high-quality literature for beginning readers, primarily ages 6-9.
Fiction: Young readers: adventure, contemporary, fantasy, folktales, science fiction. "Authentic, well-researched stories from all cultures are welcome. No didactic, religious, or violent stories, or anything that talks down to children." Average word length: 300-1,000. Byline given.
Nonfiction: Young readers: animal, arts/crafts, cooking, games/puzzles, geography, history, math, multicultural, nature/environment, problem-solving, science. "Well-researched articles on all cultures are welcome. Would like to see more games, puzzles and activities, especially ones adaptable to *Spider*'s takeout pages. No encyclopedic or overtly educational articles." Average word length: 300-800. Byline given.
Poetry: Serious, humorous, nonsense rhymes. Maximum length: 20 lines.
How to Contact/Writers: Fiction/nonfiction: Send complete ms with SASE. Do not query. Responds to mss in 3 months. Publishes ms 2-3 years after acceptance. Will consider simultaneous submissions and previously published work.
Illustration: Buys 20 illustrations/issue; 240 illustrations/year. Uses color artwork only. "Any medium—preferably one that can wrap on a laser scanner—no larger than 20×24. We use more realism than cartoon-style art." Works on assignment only. Reviews ms/illustration packages from artists. Submit ms with rough sketches. Illustrations only: Send promo sheet and tearsheets. Responds in 6 weeks. Samples returned with SASE; samples filed. Credit line given.
Photography: Buys photos from freelancers. Buys photos with accompanying ms only. Model/property releases required; captions required. Uses 35mm or $2\frac{1}{4} \times 2\frac{1}{4}$ transparencies. Send unsolicited photos by mail; provide résumé and tearsheets. Responds in 6 weeks.
Terms: Pays on publication for text; within 45 days from acceptance for art. Buys first, one-time or reprint rights for mss. Buys first and promotional rights for artwork; one-time rights for photographs. Original artwork returned at job's completion. Pays up to 25¢/word for previously unpublished stories/articles. Authors also receive 2 complimentary copies of the issue in which work appears. Additional payment for ms/illustration packages and for photos accompanying articles. Pays illustrators $750 for color cover; $200-300 for color inside. Pays photographers per photo (range: $25-75). Sample copies for $5. Writer's/illustrator's guidelines for SASE.
Tips: Writers: "Read back issues before submitting." (See listings for *Babybug, Cicada, Cricket, Muse* and *Ladybug*.)

SPORTS ILLUSTRATED FOR KIDS, 135 W. 50th St., New York NY 10020-1393. (212)522-4876. Fax: (212)522-0120. Website: www.sikids.com. **Managing Editor:** Neil Cohen. **Art Director:** Beth Bugler. **Photo Editor:** Andrew McCloskey. Monthly magazine. Estab. 1989. Circ. 950,000. Each month *SI Kids* brings the excitement, joy, and challenge of sports to life for boys and girls ages 8-14 via: action photos, dynamic designs, interactive stories; a spectrum of sports: professional, extreme, amateur, women's and kids; profiles, puzzles, playing tips, sports cards; posters, plus drawings and writing by kids. 100% of publication aimed at juvenile market.
Nonfiction: Middle readers, young adults: biography, games/puzzles, interview/profile, sports. Buys less than 20 mss/year. Average word length: 500-700. Byline given.
How to Contact/Writers: Nonfiction: Query. Responds in 6 weeks. Will consider simultaneous submissions.
Illustration: Only interested in agented material. Buys 50 illustrations/year. Works on assignment only. Reviews ms/illustration packages from artists. Submit ms/illustration package with SASE. Contact: Beth Bugler, art director. Illustrations only: Send promo sheet and samples. Contact: Beth Bugler, art director. Responds in 1 month. Samples kept on file. Credit line given.
Photography: Looking for action sports photography. Uses color prints and 35mm transparencies. Submit portfolio for review. Responds in 1 month.
Terms: Pays 25% on acceptance 75% on publication. Buys all rights for mss. Buys all rights for artwork. Buys all rights for photos. Original artwork returned at job's completion. Pays $500 for 500-600 word articles. by the project—$400; $500/day; per photo (range: $75-1,000). Sample copies free for 9×12 SASE. Writer's guidelines for SASE or via website.

STORY FRIENDS, Mennonite Publishing House, 616 Walnut Ave., Scottdale PA 15683. (724)887-8500. Fax: (724)887-3111. E-mail: RSTUTZ@mph.org. **Editor:** Rose Mary Stutzman. **Art Director:** Jim Butti. Estab. 1905. Circ. 6,000. Monthly magazine that reinforces Christian values for children ages 4-9.

Fiction: Picture-oriented material: contemporary, humorous, multicultural, nature/environment, problem-solving, religious, relationships. Multicultural needs include fiction or nonfiction pieces which help children be aware of cultural diversity and celebrate differences while recognizing similarities. Buys 45 mss/year. Average word length: 300-800. Byline given.

Nonfiction: Picture-oriented: animal, humorous, interview/profile, multicultural, nature/environment. Buys 10 mss/year. Average word length: 300-800. Byline given.

Poetry: Average length: 4-12 lines.

How to Contact/Writers: Fiction/nonfiction: Send complete ms. Responds to mss in 10 weeks. Will consider simultaneous submissions.

Illustration: Works on assignment only. Send tearsheets with SASE. Responds in 2 months. Samples returned with SASE; samples filed. Credit line given.

Photography: Occasionally buys photos from freelancers. Wants photos of children ages 4-8.

Terms: Pays on acceptance. Buys one-time rights or reprint rights for mss and artwork. Original artwork returned at job's completion. Pays 3-5¢/word for stories and articles. Pays photographers $15-30 per photo. Writer's guidelines free with SAE and 2 first-class stamps.

Tips: "Become immersed in high quality children's literature."

TURTLE MAGAZINE, For Preschool Kids, Children's Better Health Institute, 1100 Waterway Blvd., P.O. Box 567, Indianapolis IN 46206-0567. (317)636-8881. Fax: (317)684-8094. Website: www.turtlemag. org. **Editor:** Terry Harshman. **Art Director:** Bart Rivers. Monthly/bimonthly magazine published 8 times/year. Circ. 300,000. *Turtle* uses read-aloud stories, especially suitable for bedtime or naptime reading, for children ages 2-5. Also uses poems, simple science experiments, easy recipes and health-related articles.

Fiction: Picture-oriented material: adventure, contemporary, fantasy, health-related, history, holiday themes, humorous, multicultural, nature/environment, problem-solving, sports, suspense/mystery. Avoid stories in which the characters indulge in unhealthy activities. Buys 20 mss/year. Average word length: 150-300. Byline given. Currently accepting submissions for Rebus stories only.

Nonfiction: Picture-oriented material: animal, arts/crafts, cooking, games/puzzles, geography, health, multicultural, nature/environment, science, sports. "We use very simple experiments illustrating basic science concepts. These should be pretested. We also publish simple, healthful recipes." Buys 24 mss/year. Average word length: 100-300. Byline given.

Poetry: "We're especially looking for short poems (4-8 lines) and slightly longer action rhymes to foster creative movement in preschoolers. We also use short verse on our inside front cover and back cover."

How to Contact/Writers: Fiction/nonfiction: "Prefer complete manuscript to queries." Responds to mss in 3 months.

Photography: Buys photos from freelancers with accompanying ms only.

Terms: Pays on publication. Buys all rights for mss/artwork; one-time rights for photographs. Pays up to 22¢/word for stories and articles (depending upon length and quality) and 10 complimentary copies. Pays $25 minimum for poems. Pays $30-70 for b&w inside. Sample copy $1.75. Writer's guidelines free with SASE.

Tips: "Our need for health-related material, especially features that encourage fitness, is ongoing. Health subjects must be age-appropriate. When writing about them, think creatively and lighten up! Always keep in mind that in order for a story or article to educate preschoolers, it first must be entertaining—warm and engaging, exciting, or genuinely funny. Here the trend is toward leaner, lighter writing. There will be a growing need for interactive activities. Writers might want to consider developing an activity to accompany their concise manuscripts." (See listings for *Child Life, Children's Digest, Children's Playmate, Humpty Dumpty's Magazine, Jack and Jill* and *U*S* Kids*.)

U*S* KIDS, Children's Better Health Institute, 1100 Waterway Blvd., P.O. Box 567, Indianapolis IN 46206. (317)636-8881. Website: www.uskidsmag.org. **Editor:** Daniel Lee. **Art Director:** Tim LaBelle. Magazine published 8 times a year. Estab. 1987. Circ. 230,000.

Fiction: Young readers: adventure, animal, contemporary, health, history, humorous, multicultural, nature/environment, problem-solving, sports, suspense/mystery. Buys limited number of stories/year. Query first. Average word length: 500-800. Byline given.

Nonfiction: Young readers: animal, arts/crafts, cooking, games/puzzles, health, history, hobbies, how-to, humorous, interview/profile, multicultural, nature/environment, science, social issues, sports, travel. Wants to see interviews with kids ages 5-10, who have done something unusual or different. Buys 30-40 mss/year. Average word length: 400. Byline given.

Poetry: Maximum length: 8-24 lines.

How to Contact/Writers: Fiction: Send complete ms. Responds to queries and mss in 3 months.

Illustration: Buys 8 illustrations/issue; 70 illustrations/year. Color artwork only. Works on assignment only. Reviews ms/illustration packages from artists. Query. Illustrations only: Send résumé and tearsheets. Responds only if interested. Samples returned with SASE; samples kept on file. Does not return originals. Credit line given.

Photography: Purchases photography from freelancers. Looking for photos that pertain to children ages 5-10. Model/property release required. Uses color and b&w prints; 35mm, 2¼×2¼, 4×5 and 8×10 transparencies. Photographers should provide résumé, business card, promotional literature or tearsheets to be kept on file. Responds only if interested.

Terms: Pays on publication. Buys all rights for mss. Purchases all rights for artwork. Purchases one-time rights for photographs. Pays 25¢/word minimum. Additional payment for ms/illustration packages. Pays illustrators $155/page for color inside. Photographers paid by the project or per photo (negotiable). Sample copies for $2.95. Writer's/illustrator/photo guidelines for #10 SASE.

Tips: "Write clearly and concisely without preaching or being obvious." (See listings for *Child Life*, *Children's Digest*, *Children's Playmate*, *Humpty Dumpty's Magazine*, *Jack and Jill* and *Turtle Magazine*.)

W.O.W. (Wild Outdoor World®), 44 N. Last Chance Gulch, Suites 17-20, Helena MT 59601-4120. (406)449-1335. Fax: (406)449-9197. E-mail: wowgirl@quest.net. **Editorial Director:** Carolyn Zieg Cunningham. **Executive Editor:** Kay Morton Ellerhoff. **Design Editor:** Bryan Knaff. Publishes 5 issues/year. Estab. 1993. Circ. 200,000. "A magazine for young conservationists (age 8-12)." W.O.W. is distributed in fourth grade classrooms throughout the US and Canada.

Nonfiction: Middle readers: adventure (outdoor), animal, nature/environment, sports (outdoor recreation), travel (to parks, wildlife refuges, etc.). Average word length: 800 maximum. Byline given.

How to Contact/Writers: Nonfiction: Query. Responds in 6 months.

Illustration: Buys 2 illustrations/issue; 12-15 illustrations/year. Prefers work on assignment. Reviews ms/illustration packages from artists. Illustrations only: Query; send slides, tearsheets. Responds in 2 months. Samples returned with SASE; samples sometimes filed. Credit line given.

Photography: *Must* be submitted in 20-slide sheets and individual protectors, such as KYMAC. Looks for "children outdoors—camping, fishing, doing 'nature' projects." Model/property releases required. Photo captions required. Uses 35mm transparencies. Does not accept unsolicited photography. Contact: Theresa Morrow Rush, production director. Responds in 2 months.

Terms: Sample copies for $3.95 and 8½×11 SAE. Writer's/illustrator's/photo guidelines for SASE.

Tips: "We are seriously overloaded with manuscripts and do not plan to buy very much new material in the next year."

WEE ONES E-MAGAZINE, 1321 Ridge Rd., Baltimore MD 21228. E-mail: info@weeonesmag.com. Website: www.weeonesmag.com. **Editor:** Jennifer Reed. Monthly online magazine. Estab. 2001. "We are an online children's magazine for children ages 3-10. Our mission is to use the Internet to encourage kids to read. We promote literacy and family unity." 50% of publication aimed at juvenile market.

Fiction: Picture-oriented material: adventure, contemporary, health, history, humorous, multicultural, nature/environment, problem solving, sports, rebus with illustrations. Buys 60 mss/year. Average word length: up to 500. Byline given.

Nonfiction: Picture-oriented material: animal, arts/crafts, biography, concept, cooking, games/puzzles, geography, health, history, hobbies, how-to, humorous, multicultural, nature/environment, problem-solving, science, sports, travel. Buys 30 mss/year. Average word length: up to 500. Byline given.

Poetry: Uses rhyming poetry. Limit submissions to 3 poems.

How to Contact/Writers: Fiction/nonfiction: Send complete ms via e-mail. Responds to mss in 1 month. Publishes ms 6-12 months after acceptance. Will consider simultaneous submissions, electronic submissions via modem.

Illustration: Buys 6 illustrations/issue. Works on assignment only. Reviews ms/illustration packages from artists. Query. Contact: Jeff Reed, art editor. Illustrations only: Query with samples. Contact: Jeff Reed, art editor. Responds only if interested. Samples returned with SASE or kept on file. Credit line given.

Photography: Uses photos of children in various activities. Uses color b&w 4×6 prints. Responds only if interested.

Terms: Pays on publication. Buys one time electronic rights for mss, artwork and photos. Pays 3¢/word for stories and articles. Additional payment for ms/illustration packages and for photos accompanying articles. Pays $5-20 for b&w and color inside. Pays photographers per photo (range: $3). Writer's/illustrator's/photo guidelines for SASE.

Tips: "*Wee Ones* is the first online children's magazine. We are not in print! We reach over 80 countries and receive 35,000 hits per month. Study our magazine before submitting. Our guidelines are located on our site. Your chances on getting accepted depend widely only how well you follow our guidelines and submit *only* through e-mail."

WEEKLY READER, Weekly Reader Corporation, 200 First Stamford Place, Stamford CT 06912-0023. (203)705-3500. Website: www.weeklyreader.com. **Managing Editors:** Sue LaBella (grade 2), Fran Downey (grades 3-4). Weekly magazine. Estab. 1902. Circ. 8 million. Classroom periodicals bring news to kids from pre-K to high school in 17 grade-specific periodicals. Publication aimed at juvenile market.

WHAT MAGAZINE, What! Publishers Inc. 108-93 Lombard Ave., Winnipeg, Manitoba R3B 3B1 Canada. (204)985-8160. Fax: (204)957-5638. E-mail: l.malkin@m2ci.mb.ca. **Articles Editor:** Barb Chabai. **Art Director:** Brian Kauste. Magazine published 6 times/year. Estab. 1987. Circ. 250,000. "Informative and entertaining teen magazine for both genders. Articles deal with issues and ideas of relevance to Canadian teens. The magazine is distributed through schools so we aim to be cool and responsible at the same time."
Nonfiction: Young adults (13 and up): biography, careers, concept, health, how-to, humorous, interview/profile, nature/environment, science, social issues, sports. "No cliché teen stuff. Also, we're getting too many heavy pitches lately on teen pregnancy, AIDS, etc." Buys 8 mss/year. Average word length: 675-2,100. Byline given.
How to Contact/Writers: Nonfiction: Query with published clips. Responds to queries/mss in 2 months. Publishes ms 2 months after acceptance.
Terms: Pays on publication plus 30 days. Buys first rights for mss. Pays $100-500 (Canadian) for articles. Sample copies when available for 9×12 and $1.45 (Canadian). Writer's guidelines free for SASE.
Tips: "Teens are smarter today than ever before. Respect that intelligence in queries and articles. Aim for the older end of our age-range (14-19) and avoid cliché. Humor works for us almost all the time."

WINNER, The Health Connection, 55 W. OakRidge Dr., Hagerstown MD 21740. (301)393-4010. Fax: (301)393-4055. E-mail: Winner@healthconnection.org. **Articles Editor:** Anita Jacobs. **Art Director:** Tina Ivaney. Monthly magazine (September-May). Estab. 1958. Publishes articles that will promote choosing a positive lifestyle for children in grades 4-6.
Fiction: Young readers, middle readers: contemporary, health, nature/environment, problem-solving, antitobacco, alcohol, and drugs. Byline sometimes given.
Nonfiction: Young readers, middle readers: biography, games/puzzles, health, hobbies, how-to, problem-solving, social issues. Buys 20 mss/year. Average word length: 600-700. Byline sometimes given.
How to Contact/Writers: Fiction/nonfiction: Query. Responds in 6 weeks. Publishes ms 6-12 months after acceptance. Will consider simultaneous submissions, electronic submission via disk or e-mail.
Illustration: Buys 3 illustrations/issue; 30 illustrations/year. Uses color artwork only. Works on assignment only. Reviews ms/illustration packages from artists. Send ms with dummy. Contact: Tina Ivaney, art director. Responds only if interested. Samples returned with SASE.
Terms: Pays on acceptance. Buys first rights for mss. Original artwork returned at job's completion. Additional payment for ms/illustration packages. Sometimes additional payment when photos accompany articles. Pays $200-400 for color inside. Writer's and illustrator's guidelines free for SASE. Sample magazine $1.00; include 9x12 envelope with 2 first-class stamps.
Tips: Keep material upbeat and positive for elementary age children.

WITH, The Magazine for Radical Christian Youth, Faith & Life Resources, 722 Main, P.O. Box 347, Newton KS 67114. (316)283-5100. Fax: (316)283-0454. E-mail: deliag@gcmc.org. **Editor:** Carol Duerksen. Published 6 times a year. Circ. 5,800. Magazine published for Christian teenagers, ages 15-18. "We deal with issues affecting teens and try to help them make choices reflecting a radical Christian faith."
Fiction: Young adults/teens: contemporary, fantasy, humorous, multicultural, problem-solving, religious, romance. Multicultural needs include race relations, first-person stories featuring teens of ethnic minorities. Buys 15 mss/year. Average word length: 1,000-2,000. Byline given.
Nonfiction: Young adults/teens: first-person teen personal experience (as-told-to), how-to, humorous, multicultural, problem-solving, religion, social issues. Buys 15-20 mss/year. Average word length: 1,000-2,000. Byline given.
Poetry: Wants to see religious, humorous, nature. "Buys 1-2 poems/year." Maximum length: 50 lines.
How to Contact/Writers: Send complete ms. Query on first-person teen personal experience stories and how-to articles. (Detailed guidelines for first-person stories, how-tos, and fiction available for SASE.) Responds to queries in 3 weeks; mss in 6 weeks. Will consider simultaneous submissions.
Illustration: Buys 6-8 assigned illustrations/issue; buys 64 assigned illustrations/year. Uses b&w and 2-color artwork only. Preferred theme or style: candids/interracial. Reviews ms/illustration packages from artists. Query first. Illustrations only: Query with portfolio (photocopies only) or tearsheets. Responds only if interested. Credit line given.
Photography: Buys photos from freelancers. Looking for candid photos of teens (ages 15-18), especially ethnic minorities. Uses 8×10 b&w glossy prints. Photographers should send unsolicited photos by mail.

Terms: Pays on acceptance. For mss buys first rights, one-time rights; second serial (reprint rights). Buys one-time rights for artwork and photos. Original artwork returned at job's completion upon request. Pays 6¢/word for unpublished mss; 4¢/word for reprints. Will pay more for assigned as-told-to stories. Pays $10-25 for poetry. Pays $50-60 for b&w cover illustration and b&w inside illustration. Pays photographers per project (range: $120-180). Sample copy for 9 × 12 SAE and 4 first-class stamps. Writer's/illustrator's guidelines for SASE.

Tips: "We want stories, fiction or nonfiction, in which high-school-age youth of various cultures/ethnic groups are the protaganists. Stories may or may not focus on cross-cultural relationships. We're hungry for stuff that makes teens laugh—fiction, nonfiction and cartoons. It doesn't have to be religious, but must be wholesome. Most of our stories would not be accepted by other Christian youth magazines. They would be considered too gritty, too controversial, or too painful. Our regular writers are on the *With* wavelength. Most writers for Christian youth magazines aren't." For writers: "Fiction and humor are the best places to break in. Send SASE and request guidelines." For photographers: "If you're willing to line up models and shoot to illustrate specific story scenes, send us a letter of introduction and some samples of your work."

WRITER'S INTL. FORUM, "For Those Who Write to Sell," Bristol Services Intl., P.O. Box 2109, Sequim WA 98382. E-mail: services@bristolservicesintl.com. Website: www.bristolservicesintl.com. **Editor:** Sandra E. Haven. Estab. 1990. "Periodic writing competitions held exclusively at our website." Up to 25% aimed at writers of juvenile literature. "We have published past winning short stories and essays along with a professional critique. Website includes writing lessons and information."

Fiction: Middle readers, young readers, young adults/teens: adventure, contemporary, fantasy, humorous, nature/environment, problem-solving, religious, romance, science fiction, suspense/mystery. "No experimental formats; no poetry." Byline and bio information printed.

How to Contact/Writers: Send SASE or see website to determine if a contest is currently open. Only send mss if a contest is open.

Terms: See details at website.

◆◆ **YES MAG, Canada's Science Magazine for Kids,** Peter Piper Publishing Inc., 3968 Long Gun Place, Victoria, British Columbia V8N 3A9 Canada. Fax: (250)477-5390. E-mail: editor@yesmag.ca. Website: www.yesmag.ca. **Editor:** Shannon Hunt. **Art/Photo Director:** David Garrison. Managing Editor: Jude Isabella. Bimonthly magazine. Estab. 1996. Circ. 15,000. "*YES Mag* is designed to make science accessible, interesting, exciting, and FUN. Written for children ages 8 to 14, *YES Mag* covers a range of topics including science and technology news, environmental updates, do-at-home projects and articles about Canadian students and scientists."

Nonfiction: Middle readers: animal, health, math, nature/environment, science. Buys 70 mss/year. Average word length: 250-1,250. Byline given.

How to Contact/Writers: Nonfiction: Query with published clips or send complete ms (on spec only). Responds to queries/mss in 3 weeks. Generally publishes ms 3 months after acceptance. Will consider simultaneous submissions, previously published work.

Illustration: Buys 2 illustrations/issue; 10 illustrations/year. Uses color artwork only. Works on assignment only. Reviews ms/illustration packages from artists. Query. Contact: David Garrison, art director. Illustration only: Query with samples. Contact: David Garrison, art director. Responds in 3 weeks. Samples filed. Credit line given.

Photography: "Looking for science, technology, nature/environment photos based on current editorial needs." Photo captions required. Uses color prints. Provide résumé, business card, promotional literature, tearsheets if possible. Responds in 3 weeks.

Terms: Pays on publication. Buys one-time rights for mss. Buys one-time rights for artwork/photos. Original artwork returned at job's completion. Pays $25-125 for stories and articles. Sample copies for $4. Writer's guidelines for SASE.

Tips: "We do not publish fiction or science fiction. Visit our website for more information, sample articles and writers guidelines. We accept queries via e-mail. Articles relating to the physical sciences and mathematics are encouraged."

YOUNG & ALIVE, Christian Record Services, P.O. Box 6097, Lincoln NE 68506. (402)488-0981. Fax: (402)488-7582. E-mail: editorial@christianrecord.org. Website: www.christianrecord.org. **Articles Editor:** Ms. Gaylena Gibson. Quarterly magazine. Estab. 1976. Circ. 28,000. "We seek to provide wholesome, entertaining material for teens and others through age 25."

Nonfiction: Young adult/teen: animal, biography, careers, games/puzzles, health, history, humorous, interview/profile, multicultural, nature/environment, problem-solving, religion ("practical Christianity"), sports, travel. Buys 40-50 mss/year from freelancers. Word length: 700-1,400. Byline given.

How to Contact/Writers: Send complete ms. Responds to queries in 2 months; mss in 18 months. Publishes a ms "at least 2 years" after acceptance. Considers simultaneous submissions and previously published work. "Please don't send the work as a previously published piece; send a clean copy."
Illustration: Works on assignment only. Reviews ms/illustration packages from artists. Send ms with dummy. Contact Gaylena Gibson, editor.
Photography: Buys photos with accompanying ms only. Model/property release required; captions required. Uses color or b&w 3×5 or 8×10 prints.
Terms: Pays on acceptance. Buys one-time rights for ms and photos. Original artwork returned at job's completion. Pays 4-5¢/word for stories/article. Pays $25-40 for b&w inside illustration. Pays photographers by the project ($25-75). Sample copies available for 8×10 SASE and 5 first-class stamps. Writers guidelines available for SASE.

YOUNG RIDER, The Magazine for Horse and Pony Lovers, Fancy Publications, P.O. Box 8237, Lexington KY 40533. (859)260-9800. Fax: (859)260-9812. Website: www.youngrider.com. **Editor:** Lesley Ward. Bimonthly magazine. Estab. 1994. "*Young Rider* magazine teaches young people, in an easy-to-read and entertaining way, how to look after their horses properly, and how to improve their riding skills safely."
Fiction: Young adults: adventure, animal, horses, horse celebrities, famous equestrians. Buys 10 mss/year. Average word length: 1,500 maximum. Byline given.
Nonfiction: Young adults: animal, careers, health (horse), sports, riding. Buys 8-10 mss/year. Average word length: 1,000 maximum. Byline given.
How to Contact/Writers: Fiction/nonfiction: Query with published clips. Responds to queries in 2 weeks. Publishes ms 6-12 months after acceptance. Will consider simultaneous submissions, electronic submissions via disk or modem, previously published work.
Illustration: Buys 2 illustrations/issue; 10 illustrations/year. Works on assignment only. Reviews ms/illustration packages from artists. Query. Contact: Lesley Ward, editor. Illustrations only: Query with samples. Contact: Lesley Ward, editor. Responds in 2 weeks. Samples returned with SASE. Credit line given.
Photography: Buys photos with accompanying ms only. Uses color, slides, photos—in focus, good light. Model/property release required; captions required. Uses color 4×6 prints, 35mm transparencies. Query with samples. Responds in 2 weeks.
Terms: Pays on publication. Buys first North American serial rights for mss, artwork, photos. Original artwork returned at job's completion. Pays $150 maximum for stories; $250 maximum for articles. Additional payment for ms/illustration packages and for photos accompanying articles. Pays $70-140 for color inside. Pays photographers per photo (range: $65-155). Sample copies for $3.50. Writer's/illustrator's/photo guidelines for SASE.
Tips: "Fiction must be in third person. Read magazine before sending in a query. No 'true story from when I was a youngster.' No moralistic stories. Fiction must be up-to-date and humorous, teen-oriented. Need horsey interest or celebrity rider features. No practical or how-to articles—all done in-house."

☑ **YOUTH UPDATE**, St. Anthony Messenger Press, 28 W. Liberty St., Cincinnati OH 45202. (513)241-5615. E-mail: carolann@americancatholic.org. Website: www.AmericanCatholic.org. **Articles Editor:** Carol Ann Morrow. **Art Director:** June Pfaff Daley. Monthly newsletter. Estab. 1982. Circ. 23,000. "Each issue focuses on one topic only. *Youth Update* addresses the faith and Christian life questions of young people and is designed to attract, instruct, guide and challenge its audience by applying the gospel to modern problems and situations. The students who read *Youth Update* vary in their religious education and reading ability. Write for average high school students. These students are 15-year-olds with a C+ average. Assume that they have paid attention to religious instruction and remember a little of what 'sister' said. Aim more toward 'table talk' than 'teacher talk.' "
Nonfiction: Young adults/teens: religion. Buys 12 mss/year. Average word length: 2,200-2,300. Byline given.
How to Contact/Writers: Nonfiction: Query. Responds to queries/mss in 3 months. Will consider computer printout and electronic submissions via disk, after query approval.
Photography: Buys photos from freelancers. Uses photos of teens (high-school age) with attention to racial diversity and with emotion.
Terms: Pays on acceptance. Buys first North American serial rights for mss. Buys one-time rights for photographs. Pays $400-550 for articles. Pays photographers per photo ($50-75 minimum). Sample copy free with #10 SASE. Writer's guidelines free on request.
Tips: "Read the newsletter yourself—3 issues at least. In the past, our publication has dealt with a variety of topics including: dating, Lent, teenage pregnancy, baptism, loneliness, violence, confirmation and the Bible. When writing, use the *New American Bible* as translation. Interested in church-related topics."

YOUTH WEEKLY.COM, Because You Need to Know, 8359 Elk Grove Florin Rd., Suite 103, #188, Sacramento CA 95829. E-mail: admin@youthweekly.net. Website: www.youthweekly.com. **Articles Editor:** Michelle Gonzalez. Online magazine updated weekly. Estab. 2002. 80% of publication aimed at juvenile market.

Fiction: Middle readers, young adults: adventure, animal, contemporary, fantasy, folktale, health, history, humorous, multicultural, nature/environment, problem solving, science fiction, sports. Buys over 100 mss/year. Average word length: 600-3,000.

Nonfiction: Young adults: animal, arts/crafts, biography, concept, games/puzzles, geography, health, history, hobbies, humorous, interview/profile, multicultural, nature/environment, problemsolving, science, social issues, sports. Buys over 50 mss/year. Average word length: 1,000-2,000. Byline given.

Poetry: Reviews poetry. Maximum length: 30 lines. Limit submissions to 2 poems.

How to Contact/Writers: Fiction/nonfiction: send complete ms. Responds to mss in 1 month. Publishes ms 1-3 months after acceptance. Will consider electronic submission via disk or modem, previously published work.

Illustration: Buys 0-5 illustrations/issue. Uses both b&w and color artwork. Works on assignment only. "Check online submission page for current needs."Responds only if interested. Samples returned with SASE. Credit line given.

Terms: Pays on publication. Buys electronic rights for 1 year. Buys electronic rights for artwork; electronic rights for photos. Original artwork returned at job's completion. Pays $2 minimum for stories; $2 minimum for articles. "Payment will increase pending sponsorship." Writer's/illustrator's guidelines available online.

Tips: "Please read our website and archives prior to submitting. As our website is read by all ages. We do not accept any stories which include profanity, glorified or graphic violence, or extreme sexual content. We want intelligent material that will educate youth about the world around them.

**FOR EXPLANATIONS OF THESE SYMBOLS,
SEE THE INSIDE FRONT AND BACK COVERS OF THIS BOOK**

Greeting Cards, Puzzles & Games

In this section you'll find companies that produce puzzles, games, greeting cards and other items (like coloring books, stickers and giftwrap) especially for kids. These are items you'll find in children's sections of bookstores, toy stores, department stores and card shops.

Because these markets create an array of products, their needs vary greatly. Some may need the service of freelance writers for greeting card copy or slogans for buttons and stickers. Others are in need of illustrators for coloring books or photographers for puzzles. Artists should send copies of their work that art directors can keep on file—never originals. Carefully read through the listings to find companies' needs, and send for guidelines and catalogs if they're available, just as you would for book or magazine publishers.

If you'd like to find out more about the greeting card industry beyond the market for children, there are a number of resources to help you. The Greeting Card Association is a national trade organization for the industry. For membership information, contact the GCA at 1156 15th St. NW, Suite 900, Washington DC 20005, (202)393-1778, www.greetingcard.org. *Greetings Etc.* (Edgel Communications), a quarterly trade magazine covering the greeting card industry, is the official publication of the Greeting Card Association. For information call (973)252-0100. Illustrators should check out *Greeting Card Designs*, by Joanne Fink. For a complete list of companies, consult the latest edition of *Artist's & Graphic Designer's Market* (Writer's Digest Books). Writers should see *You Can Write Greeting Cards*, by Karen Ann Moore (Writer's Digest Books).

Information on greeting card, puzzle and game companies listed in the previous edition but not included in this edition of *Children's Writer's & Illustrator's Market* may be found in the General Index.

⬛ ABBY LOU ENTERTAINMENT, 1411 Edgehill Place, Pasadena CA 91103. (612)795-7334. Fax:(626)795-4013. E-mail: ale@full-moon.com. President: George LeFave. Estab. 1985. Animation production company and book publisher. "We are looking for top creative children's illustrators with classic artwork. We are a children's book publisher moving into greeting cards—nature illustrations with characters." Publishes greeting cards (Whispering Gardens), coloring books, puzzles, games, posters, calendars, books (Adventures in Whispering Gardens). 100% of products are made for kids or have kid's themes.
Writing: Needs freelance writing for children's greeting cards and other children's products. Makes 6 writing assignments/year. For greeting cards, accepts both rhymed and unrhymed verse ideas. Other needs for freelance writing include the theme of "Listen to your heart and you will hear the whispers." To contact, send cover letter, résumé, client list, writing samples. Responds in 2 weeks. Materials not returned; materials filed. For greeting cards, pays flat fee of $500, royalty of 3-10%; negotiable or negotiable advance against royalty. For other writing, pays is negotiated. Pays on acceptance. Buys one-time rights; negotiable. Credit line given.
Illustration: Need freelance illustration for children's greeting cards, posters and TV related property. Makes 12 illustration assignments/year. Prefers a "classical look—property that needs illustration is **Adventures in Whispering Gardens** and multidimentional entertainment property." Uses color artwork only. To contact send cover letter, published samples, slides, color photocopies and color promo pieces. Materials not returned; materials filed. For greeting cards and other artwork, payment is negotiable. Pays on acceptance or publication. Rights purchased are negotiable. Credit line given
Tips: "Give clear vision of what you want to do in the business and produce top quality, creative work.

✅ AMCAL, INC., 2500 Bisso Lane, Suite 200, Concord CA 94520. (925)689-9930. Fax: (925)689-0108. Website: www.amcalart.com. Vice President/Creative Development: Judy Robertson. Estab. 1975. Cards, calendars, desk diaries, boxed Christmas cards, journals, mugs, and other high quality gift and stationery products.

Illustration: Receives over 150 submissions/year. "AMCAL publishes high quality full color, narrative and decorative art for a wide market from traditional to contemporary. "Currently we are seeking updated interpretations of classic subjects such as florals and animals, strong decorative icons that are popular in the market place as well as in country folk art and decorative styles. Know the trends and the market. Juvenile illustration should have some adult appeal. We don't publish cartoon, humorous or gag art, or bold graphics. We sell to small, exclusive gift retailers and large chains. Submissions are always accepted for future lines." To contact, send samples, photocopies, slides and SASE for return of submission. Responds in approximately 1 month. Pays on publication. Payment negotable/usually advance on royalty. Rights purchased negotable. Guideline sheets for #10 SASE and 1 first-class stamp.
Tips: To learn more about AMCAL and our products, please visit our website at: www.amcalart.com.

ARISTOPLAY, LTD., 8122 Main St., Dexter MI 48130. (734)424-0123. Fax: (734)424-0124. Website: www.aristoplay.com. Art Director: Doreen Consiglio. Estab. 1979. Produces educational board games and card decks, activity kits—all educational subjects. 100% of products are made for kids or have kids' themes.
Illustration: Needs freelance illustration and graphic designers (including art directors) for games, card decks and activity kits. Makes 2-4 illustration assignments/year. To contact, send cover letter, résumé, published samples or color photocopies. Responds back in 1 month if interested. For artwork, pays by the project, $500-5,000. Pays on acceptance (½-sketch, ½-final). Buys all rights. Credit line given.
Photography: Buys photography from freelancers. Wants realistic, factual photos.
Tips: "Creating board games requires a lot of back and forth in terms of design, illustration, editorial and child testing; the more flexible you are, the better. Also, factual accuracy is important." Target age group 4-14. "We are an educational game company. Writers and illustrators working for us must be willing to research the subject and period of focus."

AVANTI PRESS, INC., 155 W. Congress, Suite 200, Detroit MI 48226. (313)961-0022. Submit nonoriginal images to this address: Avanti, 6 W. 18th St., 12th Floor, New York NY 10011. (212)414-1025. Fax: (212)414-1055. Website: www.avantipress.com. **Photo Editors:** Bridget Hoyle and Judith Rosenbaum. Estab. 1979. Greeting card company. Publishes photographic greeting cards—nonseasonal and seasonal.
Photography: Purchases photography from freelancers. Buys stock and assigns work. Buys approximately 150 stock images/year. Makes approximately 150 assignments/year. Wants "narrative, storytelling images, graphically strong and colorful!" Accepts only photographs. Uses b&w/color prints; any size or format. Pays either a flat fee or a royalty which is discussed at time of purchase." Pays on acceptance. Buys exclusive product rights (world-wide card rights). Credit line given. Photographer's guidelines for SASE or via website.
Tips: At least 75% of products have kids' and pets themes. Submit seasonal material 9 months-1 year in advance. "All images submitted should express some kind of sentiment which either fits an occasion or can be versed and sent to the recipient to convey some feeling."

THE BEISTLE COMPANY, P.O. Box 10, Shippensburg PA 17257. (717)532-2131. Fax: (717)532-7789. E-mail: beistle@mail.cvn.net. Website: www.beistle.com. **Product Manager:** C. Michelle Luhrs-Wiest. Estab. 1900. Paper products company. Produces decorations and party goods, posters—baby, baptism, birthday, holidays, educational, wedding/anniversary, graduation, ethnic themes, and New Year parties. 50% of products are made for kids or have kids' themes.
Illustration: Needs freelance illustration for decorations, party goods, school supplies, point-of-purchase display materials and gift wrap. Makes 100 illustration assignments/year. Prefers fanciful style, cute 4- to 5-color illustration in gouache and/or computer illustration. To contact, send cover letter, résumé, client list, promo piece. To query with specific ideas, phone, write or fax. Responds only if interested. Materials returned with SASE; materials filed. Pays by the project or by contractual agreement; price varies according to type of project. Pays on acceptance. Buys all rights. Artist's guidelines available for SASE.
Tips: Submit seasonal material 6 months in advance.

CARDMAKERS, P.O. Box 236, 66 High Bridge Rd., Lyme NH 03768-0236. (603)795-4422. Fax: (603)795-4222. E-mail: info@cardmakers.com. Website: cardmakers.com. Owner: Peter Diebold. Estab. 1978. "We publish whimsical greeting cards with an emphasis on Christmas and business-to-business."

A SELF-ADDRESSED, STAMPED ENVELOPE (SASE) should always be included with submissions within your own country. When sending material to other countries, include a self-addressed envelope (SAE) and International Reply Coupons (IRCs).

Writing: To contact, send cover letter and writing samples with SASE. Responds in 3 months. Returns materials if accompanied by SASE. Pays on acceptance. Buys all rights. Credit line given. Writer's guidelines available for SASE.

Illustration: Needs freelance illustration for greeting cards. Makes 30-50 illustration assignments/year. Looking for happy holidays, "activity" themes—nothing with an "edge." To contact, send cover letter, published samples, color photocopies, promo pieces and SASE. Query with specific ideas, keep it simple. Responds in 3 months. Materials returned with SASE. For greeting cards, pays flat fee of $100-400. Pays on acceptance. Credit line given. Artist's guidelines available for SASE.

Photography: Buys stock images. Wants humor. To contact, send cover letter, published samples, SASE. Responds in 3 months. Returns material with SASE. Pays per photo (range: $100-400 for b&w, $100-400 for color). Pays on acceptance. Buys exclusive product rights. Credit line given. Guidelines available for SASE.

Tips: Submit seasonal material 9 months in advance. "Be brief. Be polite. We look at all our mail. No calls, no fax, no e-mails. E-mails, requests for catalogs will get no response. Contact us through the U.S. Postal Service only. Worst times to submit—September-December. The best submissions we see are simple, right to the point, color samples with a 'check-off' stamped, return postcard eliciting comments/expression of interest."

COURAGE CARDS AND GIFTS, (formerly Courage Cards), 3915 Golden Valley Rd., Golden Valley MN 55422. (763)520-0211. Fax: (763)520-0299. E-mail: artsearch@courage.org. Website: www.courage.cards.org. **Art and Production:** Laura Brooks. Estab. 1959. Nonprofit greeting card company. Courage Cards helps support Courage Center, a nonprofit provider of rehabilitation services for children and adults with disabilities. Publishes holiday/seasonal greeting cards. 10% of cards are made using kid art.

Illustration: Needs freelance illustration for children's greeting cards. Makes 40 illustration assignments/year. Prefers colorful holiday, peace, ethnic, diversity art. Uses color artwork only. To contact, request guidelines and application—send art with submission. Responds in 3 months. Returns materials if accompanied by SASE. For greeting cards, pays flat fee of $350. Pays on publication. Buys reprint rights. Artist photo and profile on the back of every card; credit line given. Guidelines and application for art search available on website.

Tips: "Please contact us for specific guidelines for the annual art search."

A CREATE-A-CRAFT, P.O. Box 941293, Plano TX 75094-1293. **Contact:** Editor. Estab. 1967. Greeting card company. Produces greeting cards (create-a-card), giftwrap, games (create-a-puzzle), coloring books, calendars (create-a-calendar), posters, stationery and paper tableware products for all ages.

Writing: Needs freelance writing for children's greeting cards and other children's products. Makes 5 writing assignments/year. For greeting cards, accepts both rhymed and unrhymed verse ideas. Other needs for freelance writing include rhymed and unrhymed verse ideas on all products. To contact, send via recognized agent only. Responds only if interested. Material not returned. For greeting cards, payment depends on complexity of project. Pays on publication. Buys all rights. Writer's guidelines available for SASE and $2.50—includes sample cards.

Illustration: Works with 3 freelance artists/year. Buys 3-5 designs/illustrations/year. Primary age concentration is 4-8 year old market. Prefers artists with experience in cartooning. Works on assignment only. Buys freelance designs/illustrations mainly for greetings cards and T-shirts. Also uses freelance artists for calligraphy, P-O-P displays, paste-up and mechanicals. Considers pen & ink, watercolor, acrylics and colored pencil. Prefers humorous and "cartoons that will appeal to families. Must be cute, appealing, etc. No religious, sexual implications or off-beat humor." Produces material for all holidays and seasons. Contact only through artist's agent. Some samples are filed; samples not filed are not returned. Responds only if interested. Write for appointment to show portfolio of original/final art, final reproduction/product, slides, tearsheets, color and b&w. Original artwork is not returned. "Payment depends upon the assignment, amount of work involved, production costs, etc. involved in the project." Pays after all sales are tallied. Buys all rights. For guidelines and sample cards, send $2.50 and #10 SASE.

Tips: Submit 6 months in advance. "Demonstrate an ability to follow directions exactly. Too many submit artwork that has no relationship to what we produce. No phone calls accepted. Follow directions given. Do not ignore them. We do not work with anyone who does not follow them."

DESIGN DESIGN INC., P.O. Box 2266, Grand Rapids MI 49501. (616)774-2448. Fax: (616)774-4020. President: Don Kallil. Creative Director: Tom Vituj. Estab. 1986. Greeting card company. 5% of products are made for kids or have kids themes.

Writing: Needs freelance writing for children's greeting cards. Prefers both rhymed and unrhymed verse ideas. To contact, send cover letter and writing samples. Materials returned with SASE; materials not filed. For greeting cards, pays flat fee. Buys all rights or exclusive product rights; negotiable. No credit line given. Writer's guidelines for SASE.

Illustration: Needs freelance illustration for children's greeting cards and related products. To contact, send cover letter, published samples, color or b&w photocopies, color or b&w promo pieces or portfolio. Returns materials with SASE. Pays by royalty. Buys all rights or exclusive product rights; negotiable. Artist's guidelines available for SASE. Do not send original art.

Photography: Buys stock and assigns work. Looking for the following subject matter: babies, animals, dog, cats, humorous situations. Uses 4×5 transparencies or high quality 35mm slides. To contact, send cover letter with slides, stock photo list, color copies, published samples and promo piece. Materials returned with SASE; materials not filed. Pays royalties. Buys all rights or exclusive product rights; negotiable. Photographer's guidelines for SASE. Do not send original photography.

Tips: Seasonal material must be submitted 1 year in advance.

FAX-PAX USA, INC., 37 Jerome Ave., Bloomfield CT 06002. (860)242-3333. Fax: (860)242-7102. **Editor:** Stacey L. Savin. Estab. 1990. Buys 1 freelance project/year. Publishes art and history flash cards. Needs include US history, natural history.

Writing/Illustration: Buys all rights. Pays on publication. Cannot return material.

Tips: "We need concise, interesting, well-written 'mini-lessons' on various subjects including U.S. and natural history."

GREAT AMERICAN PUZZLE FACTORY, INC., 16 S. Main St., Norwalk CT 06854. (203)838-4240. Fax: (203)866-9601. E-mail: Frankd@greatamericanpuzzle.com. Website: www.greatamericanpuzzle.com. **Art Director:** Frank DeStefano. Estab. 1976. Produces puzzles. 70% of products are made for kids or have kids' themes.

Illustration: Needs freelance illustration for puzzles. Makes over 20 freelance assignments/year. To contact, send cover letter, color photocopies and color promo pieces (no slides or original art) with SASE. Responds in 1 month. Artists guidelines available for SASE. Rights purchased vary. Buys all rights to puzzles. Pays on publication. Payment varies.

Photography: Needs local cityscapes for regional puzzles. "Photos that we have used have been of wildlife. We do occasionally use city skylines. These are only for custom jobs, though, and must be 4×5 or larger format."

Tips: Targets ages 4-12 and adult. "Go to a toy store and look at puzzles. See what is appropriate. No slides. Send color copies (3-4) for style. Looking for whimsical, fantasy and animal themes with a bright, contemporary style. Not too washy or cute. No people, babies, abstracts, landscapes or still life. We often buy reprint rights to existing work. Graphic, children's-book style work is ideal for puzzles." Submit seasonal material 1 year in advance.

INTERNATIONAL PLAYTHINGS, INC., 75D Lackawanna Ave., Parsippany NJ 07054-1712. (973)316-2500. Fax: (973)316-5883. E-mail: irene.breznak@intplay.com. Website: www.intplay.com. Product Manager: Irene Breznak. Estab. 1968. Toy/game company. Distributes and markets children's toys, games and puzzles in specialty toy markets. 100% of products are made for kids or have kids' themes.

Illustration: Needs freelance illustration for children's puzzles and games. Makes 10-20 illustration assignments/year. Prefers fine-quality, original illustration for children's puzzles. Uses color artwork only. To contact, send published samples, slides, portfolio, or color photocopies or promo pieces. Responds in 1 month only if interested. Materials filed. For artwork, pays by the project (range: $500-2,000). Pays on publication. Buys one-time rights, negotiable.

Tips: "Mail correspondence only, please. No phone calls. Send child-themed art, not cartoon-y. Use up-to-date themes and colors."

NOVO CARD PUBLISHERS, INC., 3630 W. Pratt Ave., Lincolnwood IL 60712. (847)763-0077. Fax: (847)763-0020. E-mail: art@novocard.net. Website: www.novocard.net. **Contact:** Art Department. Estab.

MARKET CONDITIONS are constantly changing! If you're still using this book and it is 2004 or later, buy the newest edition of *Children's Writer's & Illustrator's Market* at your favorite bookstore or order directly from Writer's Digest Books (800)448-0915.

1926. Greeting card company. Company publishes greeting cards, note/invitation packs and gift envelopes for middle market. Publishes greeting cards (Novo Card/Cloud-9). 40% of products are made for kids or have kids' themes.

Writing: Needs freelance writing for children's greeting cards. Makes 400 writing assignments/year. Other needs for freelance writing include invitation notes. To contact send writing samples. Responds in approximately 1 month only if interested. Materials returned only with SASE. For greeting cards, pays flat fee of $2/line. Pays on acceptance. Buys all rights. No royalties. Credit line sometimes given. Writer's guidelines available for SASE.

Illustration: Needs freelance illustration for children's greeting cards. Makes 500 illustration assignments/year. Prefers just about all types: traditional, humor, contemporary, etc. To contact, send published samples, slides and color photocopies. Responds in approximately 2 months if interested. Materials returned with SASE. For greeting cards, payment negotiable. Pays on acceptance. Buys all greeting card and stationary rights. Credit line sometimes given. Artist's guidelines available for SASE.

Photography: Buys stock and assigns work. Buys more than 100 stock images/year. Wants all types. Uses color and b&w prints; 35mm transparencies. To contact, send slides, stock photo list, published samples, paper copies acceptable. Responds in approximately 2 months. Materials returned with SASE. Pays negotiable rate. Pays on acceptance. Buys all greeting card and stationary rights. Credit line sometimes given. Guidelines for SASE.

Tips: Submit seasonal material 10-12 months in advance. "Novo has extensive lines of greeting cards: everyday, seasonal (all) and alternative lives (over 24 separate lines of note card packs and gift enclosures). Our lines encompass all types of styles and images."

P.S. GREETINGS/FANTUS PAPER PRODUCTS, 5730 North Tripp Ave., Chicago IL 60646. (773)267-6069. Fax: (773)267-6055. Website: www.psgreetings.com. Send samples: Attn: Art Director. Estab. 1950. Greeting card company. Publishes boxed and individual counter greeting cards. Seasons include: Christmas, every major holiday and everyday. 30% of products are made for kids or have kid's themes. No phone calls please.

Writing: Needs freelance writing for children's greeting cards. Makes 10-20 writing assignments/year. To contact, send writing samples. Responds in 1 month. Material returned only if accompanied with SASE. For greeting cards, pays flat fee/line. Pays on acceptance. Buys greeting card rights. Credit line given. Writer's guidelines free with SASE.

Illustration: Needs freelance illustration for children's greeting cards. Makes about 30-50 illustration assignments/year. Open to all mediums, all themes. To contact, send published samples, color promo pieces and color photocopies only. Responds in 1 month. Material returned only if accompanied with SASE. Pays flat fee upon acceptance. Buys greeting card rights. Credit line given. Artist's guidelines free with SASE (speculative and on assignment).

Photography: Buys photography from freelancers. Speculative and on assignment. Wants florals, animals, seasonal (Christmas, Easter, valentines, etc.). Uses 35mm transparencies. To contact, send slides. Responds in 1 month. Materials returned with SASE; materials filed. Pays flat fee upon acceptance. Buys greeting card rights. Credit line given. Photographer's guidelines free with SASE.

Tips: Seasonal material should be submitted 8 months in advance.

SHULSINGER JUDAICA, LTD., 799 Hinsdale St., Brooklyn NY 11207. (718)345-3300. Fax: (718)345-1540. **Merchandiser:** Raizy Lasker. Estab. 1979. Greeting card, novelties and paper products company. "We are a Judaica company, distributing products such as greeting cards, books, paperware, puzzles, games, novelty items—all with a Jewish theme." Publishes greeting cards, novelties, coloring books, children's books, giftwrap, tableware and puzzles. 60% of products are made for kids or have kids' themes to party stories, temples, bookstores, supermarkets and chain stores.

Writing: Looks for greeting card writing which can be sent by children to adults and sent by adults to children (of all ages). Makes 10-20 freelance writing assignments/year. To contact, send cover letter. To query with specific ideas, write to request disclosure form first. Responds in 2 weeks. Materials returned with SASE; materials filed. For greeting cards, pays flat fee (this includes artwork). Pays on acceptance. Buys exclusive product rights.

Illustration: Needs freelance illustration for children's greeting cards, books, novelties, games. Makes 10-20 illustration assignments/year. "The only requirement is a Jewish theme." To contact, send cover letter and photocopies, color if possible. To query with specific ideas, write to request disclosure form first. Responds in 2 weeks. Returns materials with SASE; materials filed. For children's greeting cards, pays flat fee (this includes writing). For other artwork, pays by the project. Pays on acceptance. Buys exclusive product rights. Credit line sometimes given. Artist's guidelines not available.

Tips: Seasonal material should be submitted 6 months in advance. "An artist may submit an idea for any item that is related to our product line. Generally, there is an initial submission of a portfolio of the artist's work, which will be returned at the artist's expense. If the art is appropriate to our specialized subject matter, then further discussion will ensue regarding particular subject matter. We request a sampling of at least 10 pieces of work, in the form of tearsheets, or printed samples, or high quality color copies that can be reviewed and then kept on file if accepted. If art is accepted and published, then original art will be returned to artist. Shulsinger Judaica, Ltd. maintains the right to re-publish a product for a mutually agreed upon time period. We pay an agreed upon fee per project."

TALICOR, INC., 14175 Telephone Ave., Suite A, Chino CA 91710. (909)517-1962. Fax: (909)517-1962. E-mail: webmaster@talicor.com. Website: www.talicor.com. **President:** Lew Herndon. Estab. 1971. Game and puzzle manufacturer. Publishes games and puzzles (adults' and children's). 70% of products are made for kids or have kids' themes.
Writing: Makes 1 writing assignment/month.
Illustration: Needs freelance illustration for games and puzzles. Makes 12 illustration assignments/year. To contact, send promo piece. Responds in 6 months. Materials returned with SASE; materials filed. For artwork, pays by the hour, by the project or negotiable royalty. Pays on acceptance. Buys negotiable rights.
Photography: Buys stock and assigns work. Buys 6 stock images/year. Wants photos with wholesome family subjects. Makes 6 assignments/year. Uses 4×5 transparencies. To contact, send color promo piece. Responds only if interested. Materials returned with SASE; materials filed. Pays per photo, by the hour, by the day or by the project (negotiable rates). Pays on acceptance. Buys negotiable rights.
Tips: Submit seasonal material 6 months in advance.

Play Publishers & Producers

Writing plays for children and family audiences is a special challenge. Whether creating an original work or adapting a classic, plays for children must hold the attention of audiences that often include children and adults. Using rhythm, repetition and dramatic action are effective ways of holding the attention of kids. Pick subjects children can relate to, and never talk down to them.

Theater companies often have limited budgets so plays with elaborate staging and costumes often can't be produced. Touring companies want simple sets that can be moved easily. Keep in mind that they may have as few as three actors, so roles may have to be doubled up.

Many of the companies listed here produce plays with roles for adults and children, so check the percentage of plays written for adult and children's roles. Most importantly, study the types of plays a theater wants and doesn't want. Many name plays they've recently published or produced, and some have additional guidelines or information available. For more listings of theaters open to submissions of children's and adult material and information on contests and organizations for playwrights, consult *Dramatists Sourcebook* (Theatre Communications Group, Inc.).

Information on play publishers listed in the previous edition but not included in this edition of *Children's Writer's & Illustrator's Market* may be found in the General Index.

A.D. PLAYERS, 2710 W. Alabama, Houston TX 77098. (713)526-2721. Fax: (713)522-5475. E-mail: adplayer@hearn.org. Website: www.adplayers.org. Estab. 1967. Produces 4-5 children's plays/year in new Children's Theatre Series; 5 musicals/year. Produces children's plays for professional productions.
Needs: 99-100% of plays/musicals written for adult roles; 0-1% for juvenile roles. "Cast must utilize no more than five actors. Need minimal, portable sets for proscenium or arena stage with no fly space and no wing space." Does not want to see large cast or set requirements or New Age themes. Recently produced plays: *Samson: The Hair Off His Head*, by William Shryoch (courage and obedience for preK-grade 6); *The Wizard of Oz*, by Danny Siebert (new adaptation for preK-grade 6).
How to Contact: Send script with SASE. No tapes or pictures. Will consider simultaneous submissions and previously performed work. Responds in 9 months.
Terms: Buys some residual rights. Payment negotiated. Submissions returned with SASE.
Tips: "Children's musicals tend to be large in casting requirements. For those theaters with smaller production capabilities, this can be a liability for a script. Try to keep it small and simple, especially if writing for theaters where adults are performing for children. We are interested in material that reflects family values, emphasizes the importance of responsibility in making choices, encourages faith in God and projects the joy and fun of telling a story."

ALABAMA SHAKESPEARE FESTIVAL, #1 Festival Dr., Montgomery AL 36117. (334)271-5300. Fax: (334)271-5348. E-mail: asf@asf.net. Website: www.asf.net. **Literary Manager:** Gwen Orel. Estab. 1972. Produces 1 children's play/year.
Needs: Produces children's plays for professional LORT (League of Regional Theaters) theatre. 90% of plays/musicals written for adult roles; 10% for juvenile roles. Must have moderate sized casts (2-10 characters); have two stages (750 seat house/250 seat house). Interested in works for the Southern Writers' Project (contact ASF for information). Does not want to see plays exclusively for child actors. Recently produced plays: *Cinderella*, by Lynn Stevens (fairytale for elementary ages); *Wiley and the Hairy Man*, by Susan Zeder (southern folk tale for elementary ages).
How to Contact: Send full mss which meet/address the focus of the Southern Writers' Project. Musicals: Query with synopsis, character breakdown and set description; scripts which meet/address the focus of the Southern Writers' Project. Will consider simultaneous submissions and previously performed work. Responds in 1 year. Send submissions to Literary Manager.
Terms: Submissions returned with SASE.

Tips: "Created in 1991 by Artistic Director Kent Thompson, the Alabama Shakespeare Festival's Southern Writers' Project is an exploration and celebration of its rich Southern cultural heritage. In an attempt to reach this goal the project seeks: to provide for the growth of a 'new' voice for Southern writers and artists; to encourage new works dealing with Southern issues and topics including those that emphasize African American experiences; to create theatre that speaks in a special way to ASF's unique and racially diverse audiences. In this way the Southern Writers' Project strives to become a window to the complexities and beauty found in this celebrated region of our country, the South."

☑ **ANCHORAGE PRESS PLAYS, INC.**, (formerly Anchorage Press, Inc.), P.O. Box 2901, Louisville KY 40201-2901. (502)583-2288. Fax: (502)583-2281. E-mail: applays@bellsouth.net. Website: www.appl ays.com. **Publisher:** Marilee Miller. Estab. 1935. Publishes 6-8 children's plays/year; 2-3 children's musicals/year.
Needs: "There is no genre, subject of preferred interest. We want plays of high literary/theatrical quality. Like music, such material—by nature of the stage—will appeal to any age capable of following a story. Obviously some appeal more to primary ages, some secondary." Does not want send-ups or pedantic/subject matter. "Plays—like ice cream—work only if they are superb. Teaching is not the purpose of theatre—entertainment is, and that may include serious subjects fascinatingly explored." Recently produced plays: *Ezigbo the Spirit Child*, by Max Bush; *Paper Lanterns Paper Cranes*, by Brian Kral; *Amy Crocket: M.V.P.*, by Frumi Cohen.
How to Contact: Query for guidelines first. Will consider simultaneous submissions and previously performed work "essential to be proven." Responds in 2 months.
Terms: Buys all stage rights. Pays royalty (varies extensively from 50% minimum to 80%). Submissions returned with SASE.
Tips: "Get copy of play submissions guidelines from website. SASE essential."

APPLE TREE THEATRE, 595 Elm Place, Suite 210, Highland Park IL 60035. (847)432-8223. Fax: (847)432-5214. E-mail: appletreetheatre@yahoo.com. Website: www.appletreetheatre.com. Contact: Literary Manager. Produces 3 children's plays/year.
Needs: Produces professional, daytime and educational outreach programs for grades 4-9. 98% of plays written for adult roles; 2% for juvenile roles. Uses a unit set and limited to 9 actors. No musicals. Straight plays only. Does not want to see: "children's theater," i.e. . . . Peter Rabbit, Snow White. Material *must* be based in social issues. Recently produced plays: *Diary of Anne Frank*, by Frances Goodrich and Albert Hackett (about the Holocaust, ages 10-up); *Roll of Thunder, Hear My Cry*, adapted from the novel by Mildred Taylor (about Civil rights, racial discrimination in Mississippi in 1930s, ages 10-up).
How to Contact: Query first. Query with synopsis, character breakdown and set description. Will consider simultaneous submissions and previously performed work. Responds in 2 months.
Terms: Payment negotiated per contract. Submissions returned with SASE.
Tips: "Never send an unsolicited manuscript. Include reply postcard for queries."

BILINGUAL FOUNDATION OF THE ARTS, 421 N. Avenue 19th, Los Angeles CA 90031. (323)225-4044. Fax: (323)225-1250. E-mail: bfa99@earthlink.net. Website: www.bfatheatre.org. Artistic Director: Margarita Galban. **Contact:** Estela Saarlata. Estab. 1973. Produces 4 children's plays/year; 2 children's musicals/year.
Needs: Produces children's plays for professional productions. 60% of plays/musicals written for adult roles; 40% for juvenile roles. No larger than 8 member cast. Recently produced plays: *Second Chance*, by A. Cardona and A. Weinstein (play about hopes and fears in every teenager for teenagers); *Choices*, by Gannon Daniels (violence prevention, teens); *Fool 4 Kool*, Leane Schirmer and Guillermo Reyes.
How to Contact: Plays: Query with synopsis, character breakdown and set description and submit complete ms. Musicals: Query with synopsis, character breakdown and set description and submit complete ms with score. Will consider simultaneous submissions and previously performed work. Responds in 6 months.
Terms: Pays royalty; per performance; buys material outright; "different with each play."
Tips: "The plays should reflect the Hispanic experience in the U.S."

BIRMINGHAM CHILDREN'S THEATRE, P.O. Box 1362, Birmingham AL 35201-1362. (205)458-8181. Fax: (205)458-8895. E-mail: bertb@bct123.org. Website: www.bct123.org. **Managing Director:** Bert Brosowsky. Estab. 1947. Produces 8-10 children's plays/year; some children's musicals/year.
Needs: "BCT is an adult professional theater performing for youth and family audiences September-May." 99% of plays/musicals written for adult roles; 1% for juvenile roles. "Our 'Wee Folks' Series is limited to 4-5 cast members and should be written with preschool-grade 1 in mind. We prefer interactive plays for this age group. We commission plays for our 'Wee Folks' Series (preschool-grade 1), our Chil-

dren's Series (K-6) and our Young Adult Series (6-12)." Recently produced plays: *To Kill a Mockingbird*, dramatized by Christopher Sergel (YA series); *Young King Arthur*, by Michael Price Nelson (children's series); *Three Billy Goats Gruff*, by Jean Pierce (Wee Folks' Series). No adult language. Will consider musicals, interactive theater for Wee Folks Series. Prefer children's series and young adult series limited to 4-7 cast members.

How to Contact: Query first, query with synopsis, character breakdown and set description. Responds in 4 months.

Terms: Buys negotiable rights. Submissions returned with SASE.

Tips: "We would like our commissioned scripts to teach as well as entertain. Keep in mind the age groups (defined by each series) that our audience is composed of. Send submissions to the attention of Bert Brosowsky, managing director."

N BOARSHEAD THEATER, 425 S. Grand Ave., Lansing MI 48933. (517)484-7800. Fax: (517)484-2564. **Artistic Director:** John Peakes. **Director of P.R., Marketing and Outreach:** Carey McConkey. Estab. 1966. Produces 3 children's plays/year.

Needs: Produces children's plays for professional production. Majority of plays written for young adult roles. Prefers 5 characters or less for touring productions, 5 plus characters for mainstage productions; one unit set, simple costumes. Recently produced plays: *The Lion, the Witch & the Wardrobe*, by Joseph Robinette (fantasy for ages 6-12); *1,000 Cranes*, by Katharine Schultz Miller. The Planet of the Perfectly Awful People; and *Patchwork*. Does not want to see musicals.

How to Contact: Query with synopsis, character breakdown and set description. Send to Education Director. Include 10 pages of representative dialogue. Will consider previously performed work. Responds in 2 weeks on queries; 4 months "if we ask for submissions."

Terms: Submissions returned with SASE. If no SASE, send self-addressed stamped post card for reply.

CALIFORNIA THEATRE CENTER, P.O. Box 2007, Sunnyvale CA 94087. (408)245-2979. Fax: (408)245-0235. E-mail: ctc@ctcinc.org. Website: www.ctcinc.org. **General Director:** Gayle Cornelison. Estab. 1975. Produces 15 children's plays and 1 musical for professional productions.

Needs: 75% of plays/musicals written for adult roles; 20% for juvenile roles. Prefers material suitable for professional tours and repertory performance; one-hour time limit, limited technical facilities. Recently produced *Most Valuable Player*, by Mary Hall Surface (U.S. history for grades 3 and up); *Sleeping Beauty*, by Gayle Cornelison (fairy tale for ages K-5).

How to Contact: Query with synopsis, character breakdown and set description. Send to: Will Huddleston. Will consider previously performed work. Responds in 6 months.

Terms: Rights negotiable. Pays writers royalties; pays $35-50/performance. Submissions returned with SASE.

Tips: "We sell to schools, so the title and material must appeal to teachers who look for things familiar to them. We look for good themes, universality. Avoid the cute. We also do a summer conservatory that requires large cast plays."

CHILDREN'S STORY SCRIPTS, Baymax Productions, PMB 130, 2219 W. Olive Ave., Burbank CA 91506-2648. (818)787-5584. E-mail: baymax@earthlink.net. **Editor:** Deedra Bebout. Estab. 1990. Produces 1-10 children's scripts/year.

Needs: "Except for small movements and occasionally standing up, children remain seated in Readers Theatre fashion." Publishes scripts sold primarily to schools or wherever there's a program to teach or entertain children. "All roles read by children except K-2 scripts, where kids have easy lines, leader helps read the narration. Prefer multiple cast members, no props or sets." Subject matter: scripts on all subjects that dovetail with classroom subjects. Targeted age range—K-8th grade, 5-13 years old. Recently published plays: *A Clever Fox*, by Mary Ellen Holmes (about using one's wits, grades 2-4); *Memories of the Pony Express*, by Sharon Gill Askelson (grades 5-8). No stories that preach a point, no stories about catastrophic disease or other terribly heavy topics, no theatrical scripts without narrative prose to move the story along, no monologues or 1-character stories.

How to Contact: Submit complete ms. Will consider simultaneous submissions and previously performed work (if rights are available). Responds in 2 weeks.

Terms: Purchases all rights; authors retain copyrights. "We add support material and copyright the whole package." Pays writers in royalties (10-15% on sliding scale, based on number of copies sold). SASE for reply and return of submission.

Tips: "We're only looking for stories related to classroom studies—educational topics with a freshness to them. Our scripts mix prose narration with character dialogue—we do not publish traditional, all-dialogue plays." Writer's guidelines packet available for business-sized SASE with 2 first-class stamps. Guidelines explain what Children's Story Scripts are, give 4-page examples from 2 different scripts, give list of suggested topics for scripts.

CIRCA '21 DINNER THEATRE, P.O. Box 3784, Rock Island IL 61204-3784. (309)786-2667. Fax: (309)786-4119. Website: circa21.com. **Producer:** Dennis Hitchcock. Estab. 1977. Produces 3 children's musicals/year.
Needs: Produces children's plays for professional productions. 95% of musicals written for adult roles; 5% written for juvenile roles. "Prefer a cast of four to eight—no larger than ten. Plays are produced on mainstage sets." Recently produced plays: *Jungle Book*, by Ty Stover and Michael Hoagland (ages 8-adult); *Jack & The Beanstalk*, by Prince Street Players (ages 4-adult).
How to Contact: Send complete script with audiotape of music. Responds in 3 months.
Terms: Payment negotiable.

I.E. CLARK PUBLICATIONS, P.O. Box 246, Schulenburg TX 78956-0246. (979)743-3232. Fax: (979)743-4765. E-mail: ieclark@cvtv.net. **General Manager:** Donna Cozzaglio. Estab. 1956. Publishes 3 or more children's plays/year; 1 or 2 children's musicals/year.
Needs: Publishes plays for all ages. Published plays: *Little Women*, by Thomas Hischak (dramatization of the Alcott novel for family audiences); *Heidi*, by Ann Pugh, music by Betty Utter (revision of our popular musical dramatization of the Johanna Spyri novel). Does not want to see plays that have not been produced.
How to Contact: Submit complete ms and audio or video tape. Will consider simultaneous submissions and previously performed work. Responds in 4 months.
Terms: Pays writers in negotiable royalties. SASE for return of submission.
Tips: "We publish only high-quality literary works. Request a copy of our writer's guidelines before submitting. Please send only one manuscript at a time and be sure to include videos and audiotapes."

COLUMBIA ENTERTAINMENT COMPANY, % Betsy Phillips, 309 Parkade, Columbia MO 65202-1447. (573)874-5628. **Contest Director:** Betsy Phillips. Estab. 1988. Produces 0-2 children's plays/year; 0-1 children's musicals/year.
Needs: "We produce children's theatre plays. Our theatre school students act all the roles. We cast adult and children roles with children from theatre school. Each season we have 5 plays done by adults (kid parts possible)—3 theatre school productions. We need large cast plays-20+, as plays are produced by theater school classes (ages 12-14). Any set changes are completed by students in the play." Musical needs: Musicals must have songs written in ranges children can sing. Recently produced: *Musical! The Bard is Back*, by Stephen Murray; *The Haunting of Shakespeare*, by Claudia Haas.
How to Contact: Plays: Submit complete ms; use SASE to get form. Musicals: Submit complete ms and score; tape of music must be included, use SASE to get entry form. Will consider simultaneous submissions and previously performed work. Responds in 6 months. All scripts are read by a minimum of 3 readers. The authors will receive a written evaluation of the strengths and weaknesses of the play.
Terms: "We have production rights sans royalties for one production. Production rights remain with author." Pays $250 1st prize. Submissions returned with SASE.
Tips: "Please write a play/musical that appeals to all ages. We always need lots of parts, especially for girls."

CONTEMPORARY DRAMA SERVICE, Division of Meriwether Publishing Ltd., 885 Elkton Dr., Colorado Springs CO 80907-3557. (719)594-4422. Fax: (719)594-9916. E-mail: merpcds@aol.com. Website: www.meriwetherpublishing.com. **Executive Editor:** Arthur L. Zapel. Estab. 1979. Publishes 60 children's plays/year; 15 children's musicals/year.
Needs: Prefer shows with a large cast. 50% of plays/musicals written for adult roles; 50% for juvenile roles. Recently published plays: *Jitterbug Juliet*, by Mark Dissette and Bill Francoeur (a musical); *Cinderella*, by Kirk Buis (a comedy spoof); *Encounters Before Dawn*, by Keith Madsen (a Lenten play). "We publish church plays for elementary level for Christmas and Easter. Most of our secular plays are for teens or college level." Does not want to see "full-length, three-act plays unless they are adaptations of classic works or have unique comedy appeal."
How to Contact: Query with synopsis, character breakdown and set description; "query first if a musical." Will consider simultaneous submissions or previously performed work. Responds in 1 month.
Terms: Purchases first rights. Pays writers royalty (10%) or buys material outright for $200-1,000. SASE for return of submission.

Tips: "If the writer is submitting a musical play, an audiocassette of the music should be sent. We prefer plays with humorous action. We like comedies, spoofs, satires and parodies of known works. A writer should provide credentials of plays published and produced. Writers should not submit items for the elementary age level."

DALLAS CHILDREN'S THEATER, 2215 Cedar Springs, Dallas TX 75201. Website: www.dct.org. **Artistic Director:** Robyn Flatt. Estab. 1984. Produces 10 children's plays/year.
Needs: Produces children's plays for professional theater. 80% of plays/musicals written for adult roles; 20% for juvenile roles. Prefer cast size between 8-12. Musical needs: "We do produce musical works, but prefer non-musical. Availability of music tracks is a plus." Does not want to see: anything not appropriate for a youth/family audience. Recently produced plays: *And Then They Came For Me*, by James Still (story of Holocaust survivor Eva Schloss, ages 8 and up); *Deadly Weapons*, by Laurie Brooks (violence and responsibility for actions among teens, ages 13 and up).
How to Contact: Plays: Query with synopsis, character breakdown and set description. Musicals: Query with synopsis, character breakdown and set description. Will consider previously performed work. Responds in up to 1 year. Please, no phone calls.
Terms: Rights are negotiable. Payment is negotiable. Submissions returned with SASE. All scripts should be sent to the attention of Artie Olaisen.
Tips: "We are only interested in full-length substantive works. Please no classroom pieces. Our mainstage season serves a multi-generational family audience."

DRAMATIC PUBLISHING, INC., 311 Washington St., Woodstock IL 60098. (815)338-7170. Fax: (815)338-8981. E-mail: plays@dramaticpublishing.com. Website: www.dramaticpublishing.com. **Acquisitions Editor:** Linda Habjan. Estab. 1885. Publishes 10-15 children's plays/year; 4-6 children's musicals.
Needs: Recently published: *Anastasia Krupnik*, by Meryl Friedman, based on the book by Lois Lowry; *A Village Fable*, by James Still, adapted from *In the Suicide Mountain*, by John Gardner; *The Little Prince*, adapted by Rick Cummins and John Scoullar.
How to Contact: Submit complete ms/score and CD/videotape (if a musical); include SASE if materials are to be returned. Responds in 3 months. Pays writers in royalties.
Tips: "Scripts should be from ½ to 1½ hours long and not didactic or condescending. Original plays dealing with hopes, joys and fears of today's children are preferred to adaptations of old classics. No more adapted fairytales."

DRAMATICS MAGAZINE, 2343 Auburn Ave., Cincinnati OH 45219-2815. (513)421-3900. Fax: (513)421-7077. Website: www.edta.org. **Editor:** Don Corathers. Estab. 1929. Publishes 6 young adult plays/year.
Needs: Most of plays written for high school actors. 14-18 years old (grades 9-12) appropriate for high school production and study. We prefer not to receive plays geared for young children. Recently produced plays: *Nine Ten*, by Warren Leight (life in NYC before September 11, as seen at jury duty, ages 15 and up); *Reese and Babe* (a woman apologizes to a clown for killing has monkey, after the woman's husband buries her car, ages 15 and up).
How to Contact: Plays: Submit complete ms. Musicals: Not accepted. Will consider simultaneous submissions, electronic submissions via disk/modem, previously performed work. Responds in 6 months.
Terms: Buys one-time publication rights. Payment varies. Submissions returned with SASE.
Tips: Our readers are savvy theater makers. Give them more than stereotypes and fairy tales to work with.

EARLY STAGES CHILDREN'S THEATRE @ STAGES REPERTORY THEATRE, 3201 Allen Parkway, Suite 101, Houston TX 77019. (713)527-0220. Fax: (713)527-8669. E-mail: chesleyk@stagesthea tre.com. Website: www.stagestheatre.com. **Artistic Director:** Rob Bundy. Early Stages Director: Chesley Krohn. Estab. 1978. Produces 5 children's plays/year; 1-2 children's musicals/year.
Needs: In-house professional children's theatre. 100% of plays/musicals written for adult roles. Cast size must be 8 or less. Performances are in 2 theaters—Arena has 230 seats; Thrust has 180 seats. Musical needs: Shows that can be recorded for performance; no live musicians. Touring Needs: Small cast (no more than 5) addressing relevant issues for middle and high school students and teachers—2003 tour of *In Between*, by R.N. Sandberg. Recently produced plays: *Cinderella*, by Sidney Berger, music by Rob Laudes, *The Courage of Mandy Kate Brown*, by Kate Pogue (a tale of the Underground Railroad).
How to Contact: Plays/musicals: Query with synopsis, character breakdown and set description. Will consider simultaneous submissions and previously performed work. Responds only if interested.
Terms: Manuscripts optioned exclusively. Pays 3-8% royalties. Submissions returned with SASE.

Tips: "Select pieces that are intelligent, as well as entertaining, and that speak to a child's potential for understanding. We are interested in plays/musicals that are imaginative and open to full theatrical production."

EL CENTRO SU TEATRO, 4725 High, Denver CO 80216. (303)296-0219. Fax: (303)296-4614. E-mail: elcentro@suteatro.org. Website: www.suteatro.org. **Artistic Director:** Anthony J. Garcia. Estab. 1971. Produces 2 children's plays/year.
Needs: "We are interested in plays by Chicanos or Latinos that speak to that experience. We do not produce standard musicals. We are a culturally specific company." Recently produced *Joaquim's Christmas*, by Anthony J. Garcia (children's Christmas play for ages 7-15); and *The Dragonslayer*, by Silviana Woods (young boy's relationship with grandfather for ages 7-15); *And Now Miguel*, by Jim Krungold. Does not want to see "cutesy stuff."
How to Contact: Query with synopsis, character breakdown and set description. Will consider simultaneous submissions and previously performed work. Responds in 6 months. Buys regional rights.
Terms: Pays writers per performance: $35 1st night, $25 subsequent. Submissions returned with SASE.
Tips: "People should write within their realm of experience but yet push their own boundaries. Writers should approach social issues within the human experience of their character."

 **ELDRIDGE PUBLISHING CO. INC.**, P.O. Box 14367, Tallahassee FL 32317. (800)447-8243. Fax: (800)453-5179. E-mail: info@histage.com. Website: www.histage.com or www.95church.com. **Editor:** Nancy Vorhis. Estab. 1906. Publishes approximately 25 children's plays/year; 4-5 children's musicals/year.
Needs: Prefers simple staging; flexible cast size. "We publish for junior and high school, community theater and children's theater (adults performing for children), all genres, also religious plays." Recently published plays: *Oliver T*, by Craig Sodaro ("Oliver Twist" reset behind 1950s TV for ages 12-14); *teensomething*, book, music, lyrics by Michael Mish (a revue of teen life for ages 12-19). Prefers work which has been performed or at least had a staged reading.
How to Contact: Submit complete ms, score and tape of songs (if a musical). Will consider simultaneous submissions if noted. Responds in 3 months.
Terms: Purchases all dramatic rights. Pays writers royalties of 50%; 10% copy sales; buys material outright for religious market.
Tips: "Try to have your work performed, if at all possible, before submitting. We're always on the lookout for comedies which provide a lot of fun for our customers. But other more serious topics that concern teens, as well as intriguing mysteries and children's theater programs are of interest to us as well. We know there are many new talented playwrights out there, and we look forward to reading their fresh scripts."

ENCORE PERFORMANCE PUBLISHING, P.O. Box 692, Orem UT 84059. (801)376-6199. Fax: (807)795-3965. E-mail: encoreplay@aol.com. Website: www.Encoreplay.com. **Contact:** Mike Perry. Estab. 1978. Publishes 20-30 children's plays/year; 10-20 children's musicals/year.
Needs: Prefers close to equal male/female ratio if possible. Adaptations for K-12 and older. 60% of plays written for adult roles; 40% for juvenile roles. Recently published plays: *Boy Who Knew No Fear*, by G. Riley Mills/Mark Levenson (adaptation of fairy tale, ages 8-16); *Two Chains*, by Paul Burton (about drug abuse, ages 11-18).
How to Contact: Query first with synopsis, character breakdown, set description, production history, and song list if musical. Will only consider previously performed work. Responds in 2 months.
Terms: Purchases all publication and production rights. Author retains copyright. Pays writers in royalties (50%). SASE for return of submission.
Tips: "Give us issue and substance, be controversial without offense. Use a laser printer! Don't send an old manuscript. Make yours look the most professional."

N THE ENSEMBLE THEATRE, 3535 Main, Houston TX 7002. (713)520-0055, ext. 317. Fax: (713)520-1269. **Artistic Director:** Jackson Randolph. Estab. 1976. Produces 6 children's plays/year; 1 children's musical/year.
Needs: Produces children's plays for professional productions (in-house and touring). 70% of plays/musicals written for adult roles; 30% for juvenile roles. Limited to cast of 6 or less, with limited staging, costuming and props. Musical needs: appropriate for limited or recorded accompaniment. Recently published *Tales of the Mouse*, by Anita Gustafson (you're not too small to be smart for ages 4-11); *Once on this Island*, by Lynn Ahrens (love and belief for ages 6-96).
How to Contact: Plays: Query with synopsis, character breakdown and set description; submit complete ms. Musicals: Query with synopsis, character breakdown and set description. Will consider simultaneous submissions and previously performed work. Responds only if interested.
Terms: Pays $20-75/performance.
Tips: "Entertain, educate and enlighten."

FLORIDA STUDIO THEATRE, 1241 N. Palm Ave., Sarasota FL 34236. (941)366-9017. Fax: (941)955-4137. E-mail: james@fst2000.org. Website: www.fst2000.org. **Artistic Director:** Richard Hopkins. **Coordinator:** James Ashford. Estab. 1973. Produces 3 children's plays/year; 1-3 children's musicals/year.
Needs: Produces children's plays for professional productions. "Prefer small cast plays (5-8 characters) that use imagination more than heavy scenery." Will consider new plays and previously performed work.
How to Contact: Query with synopsis, character breakdown, 5 pages of sample dialogue. Responds in 3 months. Rights negotiable. Payment negotiable. Submissions returned with SASE.
Tips: "Children are a tremendously sophisticated audience. The material should respect this."

THE FOOTHILL THEATRE COMPANY, P.O. Box 1812, Nevada City CA 95959-1812. (530)265-9320. Fax: (530)265-9325. E-mail: info@foothilltheatre.org. Website: www.foothilltheatre.org. **Literary Manager:** Gary Wright. Estab. 1977. Produces 0-2 children's plays/year; 0-1 children's musicals/year. Professional nonprofit theater.
Needs: 95% of plays/musicals written for adult roles; 5% for juvenile roles. "Small is better, but will consider anything." Produced *Peter Pan*, by J.M. Barrie (kids vs. grownups, for all ages); *Six Impossible Things Before Breakfast*, by Lee Potts & Marilyn Hetzel (adapted from works of Lewis Carroll, for all ages). Does not want to see traditional fairy tales.
How to Contact: Query with synopsis, character breakdown and set description. Will consider simultaneous submissions and previously performed work. Responds in 6 months.
Terms: Buys negotiable rights. Payment method varies. Submissions returned with SASE.
Tips: "Trends in children's theater include cultural diversity, real life issues (drug use, AIDS, etc.), mythological themes with contemporary resonance. Don't talk down to or underestimate children. Don't be preachy or didactic—humor is an excellent teaching tool."

SAMUEL FRENCH, INC., 45 W. 25th St., New York NY 10010. (212)206-8990. Fax: (212)206-1429. **Senior Editor:** Lawrence Harbison. Estab. 1830. Publishes 2 or 3 children's plays/year; "variable number of musicals."
Needs: Subject matter: "all genres, all ages. No puppet plays. No adaptations of any of those old 'fairy tales.' No 'Once upon a time, long ago and far away.' No kings, princesses, fairies, trolls, etc."
How to Contact: Submit complete ms and demo tape (if a musical). Responds in 8 months.
Terms: Purchases "publication rights, amateur and professional production rights, option to publish next 3 plays." Pays writers "book royalty of 10%; variable royalty for professional and amateur productions. SASE for return of submissions.
Tips: "Children's theater is a very tiny market, as most groups perform plays they have created themselves or have commissioned."

☑ HAYES SCHOOL PUBLISHING CO. INC., 321 Pennwood Ave., Pittsburgh PA 15221. (412)371-2373. Fax: (412)371-6408. Website: www.hayespub.com. Contact: Mr. Clair N. Hayes III. Estab. 1940.
Needs: Wants to see supplementary teaching aids for grades K-12. Interested in all subject areas, especially music, foreign language (French, Spanish, Latin), early childhood education.
How to Contact: Query first with table of contents or outline and 3-4 sample pages. Will consider simultaneous and electronic submissions. Responds in 6 weeks.
Terms: Purchases all rights. Work purchased outright. SASE for return of submissions.

HEUER PUBLISHING COMPANY, P.O. Box 248, Cedar Rapids IA 52406. (319)364-6311. Fax: (319)364-1771. E-mail: editor@hitplays.com. Website: www.hitplays.com. **Associate Editor:** Geri Albrecht. Estab. 1928. Publishes 10-15 plays/year for young audiences and community theaters; 5 musicals/year.

Needs: "We publish plays and musicals for schools and community theatres (amateur)." 100% for juvenile roles. Single sets preferred. Props should be easy to find and costumes, other than modern dress, should be simple and easy to improvise. Stage effects requiring complex lighting and/or mechanical features should be avoided. Musical needs: "We need musicals with large, predominantly female casts. We publish plays and musicals for middle, junior and senior high schools." Recently published plays: *Pirate Island*, by Martin Follose (popular for all producing groups); *Virgil's Wedding*, by Eddie McPherson (delightful characters and non-stop laughter).
How to Contact: Plays/musicals: Query with synopsis. Will consider simultaneous submissions and previously performed work. Responds in 2 months.
Terms: Buys amateur rights. Pays royalty or purchases work outright. Submissions returned with SASE.
Tips: "We sell almost exclusively to junior and smaller senior high schools so the subject matter and language should be appropriate for schools and young audiences."

LAGUNA PLAYHOUSE YOUTH THEATRE, P.O. Box 1747, Laguna Beach CA 92652. (949)497-2787. Fax: (949)497-7109. E-mail: jlauderdale@lagunaplayhouse.com. Website: www.lagunaplayhouse.c om. **Artistic Director:** Joe Lauderdale. Estab. 1986. Produces 4 mainstage (including musical) and 3 touring shows/year.
Needs: The Laguna Playhouse is a LORTC theater company with TYA contract for touring shows and nonprofessionals in mainstage shows. 40% of plays/musicals written for adult roles; 60% for juvenile roles. Musical needs: Small combos of 4-7 people with some doubling of instruments possible. Recently produced plays: *Alexander and the Terrible, Horrible, No Good, Very Bad Day*, by Judith Viorst and Shelley Markham; and *The Good Times Are Killing Me*, by Lynda Barry.
How to Contact: Submit letter of intent and synopsis. Musicals should also submit recording. Responds in 8 months.
Terms: Pays 4-6% royalties.
Tips: "The majority of our mainstage works are literary based. Our touring shows have small casts (4-6 people) and are on California Reading Curriculum lists. One show per season is targeted for junior high and high school and may deal with intense or controversial ideas."

MERRY-GO-ROUND YOUTH THEATRE, P.O. Box 506, Auburn NY 13021. (315)255-1305. Fax: (315)252-3815. E-mail: youthmgr@dreamscape.com. Website: www.merry-go-round.com. **Producing Director:** Ed Sayles. Estab. 1958. Produces 10 children's plays/year; 3 children's musicals/year.
Needs: 100% of plays/musicals written for adult roles. Cast maximum, 4-5 and staging must be tourable. Recently produced plays: *Seagirl*, by Francis Elitzig (Chinese folktale); *There Once Was a Longhouse, Where Now There is Your House*, (Native Americans of New York state).
How to Contact: Plays/musicals: query with synopsis, character breakdown and set description; submit complete ms and score. Will consider simultaneous submissions, electronic submissions via disk/modem and previously performed work. Responds in 2 months.
Terms: "Realize that our program is grade/curriculum specific. And understanding of the NYS Learning Standards may help a writer to focus on a point of curriculum that we would like to cover."

NEBRASKA THEATRE CARAVAN, 6915 Cass St., Omaha Ne 68132. (402)553-4890, ext. 154. Fax: (402)553-6288. E-mail: caravan@omahaplayhouse.com. Website: www.omahaplayhouse.com. **Director:** Richard L. Scott. Estab. 1976. Produces 2 children's plays/year; 1-2 children's musicals/year.
Needs: Produces children's plays for professional productions with a company of 5-6 actors touring. 100% of plays/musicals written for adult roles; setting must be adaptable for easy touring. 75 minute show for grades 7-12; 60 minutes for elementary. Musical need: 1 piano or keyboard accompaniment. Recently produced plays: *A Thousand Cranes*, by Kathryn Schultz Miller (Sadako Susaki, for ages K-8).
How to Contact: Plays: query with synopsis, character breakdown and set description. Musicals: query first. Will consider simultaneous submissions and previously performed work. Responds in 3 months.
Terms: Pays $35-40/performance; pays commission—option 1—own outright, option 2—have right to produce at any later date—playwright has right to publish and produce. Submissions returned with SASE.
Tips: "Be sure to follow guidelines."

THE NEW CONSERVATORY THEATRE CENTER, 25 Van Ness Ave., San Francisco CA 94102-6033. (415)861-4914. Fax: (415)861-6988. E-mail: email@nctcsf.org. Website: www.nctcsf.org. **Executive Director:** Ed Decker. Estab. 1981. Produces 11 children's plays/year; 1 children's musical/year.
Needs: Limited budget and small casts only. Produces children's plays as part of "a professional theater arts training program for youths ages 4-19 during the school year and 2 summer sessions. The New Conservatory also produces educational plays for its touring company. We do not want to see any preachy

or didactic material." Recently produced plays: *Aesop's Funky Fables*, adapted by Dyan McBride (fables, for ages 4-9); *A Little Princess*, by Frances Hodgson Burnett, adapted by June Walker Rogers (classic story of a young girl, for ages 5-10).

How to Contact: Query with synopsis, character breakdown and set description, or submit complete ms and score. Responds in 3 months.

Terms: Rights purchased negotiable. Pays writers in royalties. SASE for return of submission.

Tips: "Wants plays with name recognition, i.e., *The Lion, the Witch and the Wardrobe* as well as socially relevant issues. Plays should be under 50 minutes in length."

NEW PLAYS INCORPORATED, P.O. Box 5074, Charlottesville VA 22905-0074. (434)979-2777. Fax: (434)984-2230. E-mail: patwhitton@aol.com. Website: www.newplaysforchildren.com. **Publisher:** Patricia Whitton Forrest. Estab. 1964. Publishes 3-4 plays/year; 1 or 2 children's musicals/year.

Needs: Publishes "generally material for kindergarten through junior high." Recently published: *On The Line*, audience participation play, by Carol Koty (woolen mill strikes in Lawrence, MA); *Dye Frye* and *Wicked John and the Devil*, Appalachian Folk Plays, by Loren Crawford.

How to Contact: Submit complete ms and score. Will consider simultaneous submissions and previously performed work. Responds in 2 months (usually).

Terms: Purchases exclusive rights to sell acting scripts. Pays writers in royalties (50% of production royalties; 10% of script sales). SASE for return of submission.

Tips: "Write the play you really want to write (not what you think will be saleable) and find a director to put it on."

NEW YORK STATE THEATRE INSTITUTE, 37 First St., Troy NY 12180. (518)274-3200. Fax: (518)274-3815. E-mail: nysti@capital.net. Website: www.nysti.org. **Artistic Director:** Patricia B. Snyder. **Associate Artistic Director:** Ed Lange. Estab. 1976. Produces 5 children's plays/year; 1-2 children's musicals/year.

Needs: Produces family plays for professional theater. 90% of plays/musicals are written for adult roles; 10% for juvenile roles. Does not want to see plays for children only. Produced plays: *A Tale of Cinderella*, by Will Severin, W.A. Frankonis and George David Weiss (all ages); *Miracle On 34th Street*, by Valentine Davies.

How to Contact: Query with synopsis, character breakdown and set description; submit tape of songs (if a musical). Will consider simultaneous submissions and previously performed work. Responds in 1 month for queries. SASE for return of submission.

Tips: Writers should be mindful of "audience *sophistication*. We do not wish to see material that is childish. Writers should submit work that is respectful of young people's intelligence and perception—work that is appropriate for families, but that is also challenging and provocative."

PHOENIX THEATRE'S COOKIE COMPANY, 100E. McDowell, Phoenix AZ 85004. (602)258-1974. Fax: (602)253-3626. E-mail: phoenixtheatre@yahoo.com. Website: phoenixtheatre.net. **Artistic Director:** Alan J. Prewitt. Estab. 1980. Produces 4 children's plays/year.

Needs: Produces theater with professional adult actors performing for family audiences. 95% of plays/ musicals written for adult roles; 5% for juvenile roles. Requires small casts (4-7), small stage, mostly 1 set, flexible set or ingenious sets for a small space. "We're just starting to do plays with music—no musicals per se." Does not want to see larger casts, multiple sets, 2 hour epics. Recently produced *Holidays on the Prairie*, by Alan J. Prewitt (a single mother with children faces the Santa Fe Trail, for ages 4-12); *The Sleeping Beauty*, by Alan J. Prewitt (classic tale gets "truthful parent" twist, for ages 4-12)).

How to Contact: Plays/musicals: Query with synopsis, character breakdown and set description. Will consider simultaneous submissions. Responds only if interested within 1 month.

Terms: Submissions returned with SASE.

Tips: "Only submit innovative, imaginative work that stimulates imagination and empowers the child. We specialize in producing original scripts based on classic children's literature."

PIONEER DRAMA SERVICE, P.O. Box 4267, Englewood CO 80155-4267. (303)779-4035. Fax: (303)779-4315. E-mail: editors@pioneerdrama.com. Website: www.pioneerdrama.com. **Submissions Editor:** Beth Somers. Publisher: Steven Fendrich. Estab. 1960. Publishes more than 10 new plays and musicals/ year.

Needs: "We are looking for plays up to 90 minutes long, large casts and simple sets." Publishes plays for ages middle school-12th grade and community theatre. Recently published plays/musicals: *Wonderland*, by James De Vita, music and lyrics by Bill Francoeur; *Folktales for Fun*, by Carlos Perez. Wants to see "script, scores, tapes, pics and reviews."

How to Contact: Query with synopsis, character breakdown, running time and set description. Submit complete ms and score (if a musical) with SASE. Will consider simultaneous submissions, e-mail submissions with prior approval only, previously performed work. Contact: Beth Somers, submissions editor. Responds in 4 months. Send for writer's guidelines.

Terms: Purchases all rights. Pays writers in royalties (10% on sales, 50% royalties on productions). Research Pioneer through catalog and website.

Tips: "Research the company. Include a cover letter and a SASE."

N SEATTLE CHILDREN'S THEATRE, 201 Thomas St., Seattle WA 98109. Fax: (206)443-0442. Website: www.sct.org. **Literary Manager:** Madeleine Oldham. Estab. 1975. Produces 5 full-length children's plays/year; 1 full-length children's musical/year. Produces children's plays for professional productions (September-June).

Needs: "We generally use adult actors even for juvenile roles." Produced plays: *The King of Ireland's Son*, by Paula Wing (mythology and Hero Quest for ages 8 and older); *Pink and Say*, by Oyamo (adaptation from Patricia Polacco); *Holes*, by Louis Sacher. Does not want to see anything that condescends to young people—anything overly broad in style.

How to Contact: Accepts agented scripts or those accompanied by a professional letter of recommendation (director or dramaturg). Responds in 1 year.

Terms: Rights vary. Payment method varies. Submissions returned with SASE.

Tips: "Please *do not* send unsolicited manuscripts. We prefer sophisticated material (our weekend performances have an audience that is half adults)."

✓ TADA!, 15 W. 28th St., 3rd Floor, New York NY 10001. (212)252-1619. Fax: (212)252-8763. E-mail: tada@tadatheater.com. Website: www.tadatheater.com. **Artistic Director:** Janine Nina Trevens. Estab. 1984. Produces 5 staged readings of children's plays and musicals/year; 0-5 children's plays/year; 2-3 children's musicals/year.

Needs: "All actors are children, ages 8-17." Produces children's plays for professional, year-round theater. 100% of plays/musicals written for juvenile roles. Recently produced musicals: *Sleepover*, by Phillip Freedman and James Belloff (peer acceptance, for ages 3 and up); *The Little House of Cookies*, by Janine Nina Trevens and Joel Gelpe (international communication and friendship). Does not want to see fairy tales or material that talks down to children.

How to Contact: Query with synopsis, character breakdown and set description; submit complete ms, score and tape of songs (if a musical). Responds in 1 year "or in October following the August deadline for our Annual Playwriting Competition. (Send two copies of manuscript if for competition)."

Terms: Rights purchased "depend on the piece." Pays writers in royalties of 1-6% and/or pays commissioning fee. SASE a must for return of submissions.

Tips: "For plays for our Annual Playwriting Competition, submit between January and August 15. We're looking for plays with current topics that specific age ranges can identify with, with a small cast of children and one or two adults. Our company is multi-racial and city-oriented. We are not interested in fairy tales. We like to produce material that kids relate to and that touches their lives today."

THEATREWORKS/USA, 151 W. 26th, 7th Floor, New York NY 10001. (212)647-1100. Fax: (212)924-5377. E-mail: info@theatreworksusa.org. Website: www.theatreworks.org. **Artistic Director:** Barbara Pasternack. **Assistant Artistic Director:** Michael Alltop. Estab. 1960. Produces 3-4 children's plays and musicals/year.

Needs: Cast of 5 or 6 actors. Play should be 1 hour long, tourable. Professional children's theatre comprised of adult equity actors. 100% of shows are written for adult roles. Produced plays: *The Mystery of King Tut*, by Mindi Dickstein and Daniel Messé (Ancient Egypt); *Sarah, Plain and Tall*, by Larry O'Keefe, Nell Benjamin and Julia Jordan (adaptation).

How to Contact: Query first with synopsis, character breakdown and sample songs. Will consider previously performed work. Responds in 3 months.

Terms: Pays writers royalties of 6%. SASE for return of submission.

Tips: "Plays should be not only entertaining, but 'about something.' They should touch the heart and the mind. They should not condescend to children."

MARKET CONDITIONS are constantly changing! If you're still using this book and it is 2004 or later, buy the newest edition of *Children's Writer's & Illustrator's Market* at your favorite bookstore or order directly from Writer's Digest Books (800)448-0915.

Young Writer's & Illustrator's Markets

The listings in this section are special because they publish work of young writers and artists (under age 18). Some of the magazines listed exclusively feature the work of young people. Others are adult magazines with special sections for the work of young writers. There are also a few book publishers listed that exclusively publish the work of young writers and artists. Many of the magazines and publishers listed here pay only in copies, meaning authors and illustrators receive one or more free copies of the magazine or book to which they contributed.

As with adult markets, markets for children expect writers to be familiar with their editorial needs before submitting. Many of the markets listed will send guidelines to writers stating exactly what they need and how to submit it. You can often get these by sending a request with a self-addressed, stamped envelope (SASE) to the magazine or publisher, or by checking a publication's website (a number of listings include web addresses). In addition to obtaining guidelines, read through a few copies of any magazines you'd like to submit to—this is the best way to determine if your work is right for them.

A number of kids' magazines are available on newsstands or in libraries. Others are distributed only through schools, churches or home subscriptions. If you can't find a magazine you'd like to see, most editors will send sample copies for a small fee.

Before you submit your material to editors, take a few minutes to read Before Your First Sale on page 8 for more information on proper submission procedures. You may also want to check out two other sections—Contests & Awards and Conferences & Workshops. Some listings in these sections are open to students (some exclusively)—look for the phrase **open to students** in bold. Additional opportunities for writers can be found in *The Young Writers Guide to Getting Published* (Writer's Digest Books) and *A Teen's Guide to Getting Published: the only writer's guide written by teens for teens*, by Danielle and Jessica Dunn (Prufrock Press). More information on these books are given in the Helpful Resources section in the back of this book.

Information on companies listed in the previous edition but not included in this edition of *Children's Writer's & Illustrator's Market* **may be found in the General Index**.

THE ACORN, 1530 Seventh St., Rock Island IL 61201. (309)788-3980. Newsletter. Estab. 1989. **Editor:** Betty Mowery. Audience consists of "kindergarten-12th grade students, parents, teachers and other adults. Purpose in publishing works for children: "to expose children's manuscripts to others and provide a format for those who might not have one. We want to showcase young authors who may not have their work published elsewhere and present wholesome writing material that will entertain and educate—audience grades K-12." Children must be K-12 (put name, address, grade on manuscripts). Guidelines available for SASE.

Magazines: 100% of magazine written by children. Uses 6 fiction pieces (500 words); 20 pieces of poetry (32 lines). No payment; purchase of a copy isn't necessary to be printed. Sample copy $3. Subscription $10 for 4 issues. Submit mss to Betty Mowery, editor. Send complete ms. Will accept typewritten, legibly handwritten and/or computer printout. Include SASE. Responds in 1 week. Will not respond without SASE.

Artwork: Publishes artwork by children. Looks for "all types; size 4 × 5. Use black ink in artwork." No payment. Submit artwork either with ms or separately to Betty Mowery. Include SASE. Responds in 1 week.

Tips: "My biggest problem is not having names on the manuscripts. If the manuscript gets separated from the cover letter, there is no way to know whom to respond to. Always put name, age or grade and address on manuscripts, and if you want your material returned, enclose a SASE. Don't send material with killing of humans or animals, or lost love poems or stories. Write about what you know and do not overwrite."

AMERICAN GIRL, 8400 Fairway Place, Middleton WI 53562. (608)836-4848. Fax: (608)831-7089. Website: www.americangirl. **Contact:** Magazine Department Assistant. Bimonthly magazine. Audience consists of girls ages 8-12 who are joyful about being girls. Purpose in publishing works by young people: "self-esteem boost and entertainment for readers. *American Girl* values girls' opinions and ideas. By publishing their work in the magazine, girls can share their thoughts with other girls! Young writers should be 8-12 years old. We don't have writer's guidelines for children's submissions. Instruction for specific solicitations appears in the magazine."
Magazines: 20% of magazine written by young people. "A few pages of each issue feature articles that include children's answers to questions or requests that have appeared in a previous issue of *American Girl*." Pays in copies. Submit to address listed in magazine. Will accept legibly handwritten ms. Include SASE. Responds in 3 months.
Tips: "Please, no stories, poems, etc. about American Girls Collection Characters (Felicity, Samantha, Molly, Kirsten, Addy, Josefina or Kit). Inside *American Girl*, there are several departments that call for submissions. Read the magazine carefully and submit your ideas based on what we ask for."

BEYOND WORDS PUBLISHING, INC., 20827 NW Cornell Rd., Suite 500, Hillsboro OR 97124-9808. (503)531-8700. Fax: (503)531-8773. E-mail: barbara@beyondword.com. Website:www.beyondword .com. Book publisher. **Managing Editor of Children's Division:** Barbara Mann. Publishes 2-3 picture books/year; 4-6 YA nonfiction books. Looks for "books that inspire integrity in children ages 5-15 and encourage creativity and an appreciation of nature." Wants to "encourage children to write, create, dream and believe that it is possible to be published. The books must be unique, be of national interest, and the author must be personable and promotable." Writer's guidelines available with SASE.
Books: Holds yearly writing contests for activity/advice books written by and for children/teens. Publishes historical fiction and multicultural picture books. Also publishes nonfiction advice books for children, such as guides for kids about pertinent concerns. Submit mss to Barbara Mann, managing editor of children's division. Responds in 6 months.
Artwork/Photography: Publishes artwork by children. Submit artwork to Managing Editor.
Tips: "Write about issues that affect your life. Trust your own instincts. You know best!"

BLUE JEAN ONLINE, (formerly *Blue Jean Magazine: For Teen Girls Who Dare*), 1115 E. Main St., Box 60, Rochester NY 14609. (716)288-6980. E-mail: editors@bluejeanonline.com. Website: www.blu ejeanonline.com. Bimonthly online magazine. "*Blue Jean Magazine, Blue Jean Online* and Blue Jean Press showcase the writing, artwork and creativity of young women around the world. Our cover stories profile interesting and exciting teen girls and young women in action. You will find no supermodels, tips on dieting or fashion spreads on our pages. We publish teen-produced poetry, artwork, photography, fiction and much more!" Audience is girls ages 12-19. Purpose in showcasing work by young women: "to stay true to what really matters, which is publishing what young women are thinking, saying and doing." Writer's guidelines available on request for SASE.
Magazine: 90% of magazine written by young people. Uses 1 fiction story; 8-14 nonfiction stories (250-3,000 words), 1-3 poems. Pays adult freelancers $75 per Body and Mind article, After High School article. Payment will be sent with 2 complimentary issues within 30 days of publication. Submit complete mss per submission guidelines. Will accept typewritten mss. Include SASE. Responds in 4 months at most. "Many times within two months."
Artwork: Publishes artwork and photography by teens. Will consider a variety of styles! Artwork must be submitted by a teen artist (ages 12-19). Submit art between 2 pieces of paperboard or cardboard. Include SASE with enough postage for return. Responds in 3-4 months.
Tips: "Submissions may be sent via mail or e-mail. Do not inquire about your work by calling. Replies guaranteed when material sent through mail with SASE."

CHILDREN WRITING FOR CHILDREN NONPROFIT (CWC), 7142 Dustin Rd., Galena OH 43021-7959. (800)759-7171. Website: www.cwcbooks.org. **Executive Director:** Susan Schmidt. Purpose of organization: A non-profit corporation established to educate the public at large about children's issues through literary works created by children and to celebrate and share the talents of children as authors. Books must be written and/or illustrated by children and young adults. "We look for kids to write about personal experiences that educate and reveal solutions to problems." Open submissions are accepted.

Books published to date include those dealing with cancer, child abuse, cerebral palsy, Tourette's syndrome, avoiding teen violence, children grieving over the loss of a parent or sibling and living with parents addicted to drugs and alcohol.
Books: Publishing focus is on nonfiction writings about children's issues such as peer pressure, illness, and special challenges or opportunities. Stories with educational value are preferred. Writer's guidelines available with SASE. Pays royalties, but no advances. Will accept typewritten, legibly handwritten and computer-printed ms. Include SASE for ms return and/or comments. Responds in 3 months.
Artwork/Photography: Publishes books with artwork and/or photography accompanying nonfiction stories written and illustrated by children. Please submit photocopies of art—no originals please.
Tips: Write about personal experiences in challenging situations, painting a word picture of the people involved, the story, how you resolved or responded to the situation and what you learned or gained from the experience.

CICADA, Carus Publishing Company, P.O. Box 300, Peru IL 61354. (815)224-6656. Fax: (815)224-6615. E-mail: cicada@caruspub.com. Website: www.cicadamag.com. **Editor-in-Chief:** Marianne Carus. Editor: Deborah Vetter. Senior Art Director: Ron McCutchan. Bimonthly magazine.
 • *Cicada* publishes work of writers and artists of high-school age (must be at least 14 years old). See the *Cicada* listing in the magazines section for more information, or check their website or copies of the magazine.

THE CLAREMONT REVIEW, 4980 Wesley Rd., Victoria, British Columbia Canada V8Y 1Y9. (604)658-5221. Fax: (250)658-5387. E-mail: aurora@home.com. Website: www.theClaremontReview.com. Magazine. Publishes 2 books/year by young adults. Publishes poetry and fiction with literary value by students aged 13-19 anywhere in English-speaking world. Purpose in publishing work by young people: to provide a literary venue. Sponsors annual poetry contest.
Magazines: Uses 10-12 fiction stories (200-2,500 words); 30-40 poems. Pays in copies. Submit mss to editors. Submit complete ms. Will accept typewritten mss. SASE. Responds in 6 weeks (except during the summer).
Artwork: Publishes artwork by young adults. Looks for b&w copies of imaginative art. Pays in copies. Send picture for review. Negative may be requested. Submit art and photographs to editors. SASE. Responds in 6 weeks.
Tips: "Read us first—it saves disappointment. Know who we are and what we publish. We're closed July and August. SASE a must. American students send I.R.C.'s as American stamps *do not* work in Canada."

CREATIVE WITH WORDS, Thematic anthologies, Creative with Words Publications, P.O. Box 223226, Carmel CA 93922. Fax: (831)655-8627. E-mail: cwwpub@usa.net. Website: members.tripod.com/CreativeWithWords. **Editor:** Brigitta Geltrich. Nature Editor: Bert Hower. Publishes 14 anthologies/year. Estab. 1975. "We publish the creative writing of children (4 anthologies written by children; 4 anthologies written by adults; 4-6 anthologies written by all ages)." Audience consists of children, families, schools, libraries, adults, reading programs. Purpose in publishing works by children: to offer them an opportunity to get started in publishing. "Work must be of quality, typed, original, unedited, and not published before; age must be given (up to 19 years old) and home address." SASE must be enclosed with all correspondence and mss. Writer's guidelines and theme list available on request with SASE, via e-mail or on website.
Books: Considers all categories except those dealing with sensationalism, death, violence, pornography and overly religious. Uses fairy tales, folklore items (up to 1,500 words) and poetry (not to exceed 20 lines, 46 characters across). Published *Nature Series: Seasons, Nature, School, Love* and *Relationships* (all children and adults). Pays 20% discount on each copy of publication in which fiction or poetry by children appears. Best of the month is published on website, and author receives one free copy of issue. Submit mss to Brigitta Geltrich, editor. Query; child, teacher or parent can submit; teacher and/or parents must verify originality of writing. Will accept typewritten and/or legibly handwritten mss. SASE. "Will not go through agents or overly protective 'stage mothers'." Responds in 1 month after deadline of any theme.
Artwork/Photography: Publishes b&w artwork, b&w photos and computer artwork created by children (language art work). Pays 20% discount on every copy of publication in which work by children appears. Submit artwork to Brigitta Geltrich, editor, and request info on payment.
Tips: "Enjoy the English language, life and the world around you. Look at everything from a different perspective. Look at the greatness inside all of us. Be less descriptive and use words wisely. Let the reader experience a story through a viewpoint character, don't be overly dramatic. Match illustrations to the meaning of the story or poem."

FREE SPIRIT PUBLISHING INC., 217 Fifth Ave. N, Suite 200, Minneapolis MN 55401-1730. (612)338-2068. Fax: (612)337-5050. E-mail: help4kids@freespirit.com. Website: www.freespirit.com.

Publishes 15-20 books/year. "We specialize in SELF-HELP FOR KIDS® and SELF-HELP FOR TEENS®. Our main audience is children and teens, but we also publish for parents, teachers, therapists, youth workers and others involved in caring for kids. Our main interests include the development of self-esteem, school skills, creative thinking and problem-solving abilities, assertiveness and making a difference in the world. We do not publish fiction or poetry. Request catalog, author guidelines before submitting work. Send SASE.

Books: Publishes self-help for kids, how-to, classroom activities. Pays advance and royalties. Submit mss to acquisitions editor. Send query and sample table of contents. Will accept typewritten mss. SASE required. Responds in 4 months.

Artwork/Photography: Submit samples to acquisitions editor.

Tips: "Free Spirit publishes very specific material, and it helps when writers request and study our catalog before submitting work to us, and refer to our author guidelines (our catalog and guidelines are available by mail or via our website.) We do not accept general self-help books, autobiographies or children's books that feature made-up stories. Our preference is books that help kids to gain self-esteem, succeed in school, stand up for themselves, resolve conflicts and make a difference in the world. We do not publish books that have animals as the main characters."

GREEN KNEES, Imprint of Azro Press, PMB 342, 1704 Llano St. B, Santa Fe NM 87505. (505)989-3272. Fax: (505)989-3832. E-mail: books@azropress.com. Website: www.greenknees.com. Book. Publishes 1 book/year by children. "Green Knees is primarily interested in picture books and easy readers written and illustrated by children who are 13 years old or younger." The book must have been written by a child under 13 and illustrations done by the author or children in the same grade or school. Writer's guidelines available on request.

Books: Publishes picture books and young readers; interested in animal stories and humor. Length: 1,000 words for fiction. Submit mss to Jaenet Guggenheim. Query or submit complete ms or synopsis and sample illustration (if longer than 40 pages). Send a copy of the ms, do not send original material. Will accept typewritten or electronically (disk or e-mail). Include SASE. Responds in 2 months.

Artwork/Photography: Publishes artwork by children.

HIGH SCHOOL WRITER, P.O. Box 718, Grand Rapids MN 55744-0718. (218)326-8025. Fax: (218)326-8025. E-mail: writer@mx3.com. Editor: Barbara Eiesland. Magazine published 6 times during the school year. "The *High School Writer* is a magazine written *by* students *for* students. All submissions must exceed contemporary standards of decency." Purpose in publishing works by young people: to provide a real audience for student writers—and text for study. Submissions by junior high and middle school students accepted for our junior edition. Senior high students' works are accepted for our senior high edition. Students attending schools that subscribe to our publication are eligible to submit their work." Writer's guidelines available on request.

Magazines: Uses fiction, nonfiction (2,000 words maximum) and poetry. Submit mss to editor. Submit complete ms (teacher must submit). Will accept typewritten, computer-generated (good quality) mss.

Tips: "Submissions should not be sent without first obtaining a copy of our guidelines (see page 2 of every issue). Also, submissions will not be considered unless student's school subscribes."

N HIGHLIGHTS FOR CHILDREN, 803 Church St., Honesdale PA 18431. (570)253-1080. Magazine. Published monthly. "We strive to provide wholesome, stimulating, entertaining material that will encourage children to read. Our audience is children ages 2-12." Purpose in publishing works by young people: to encourage children's creative expression.

Magazines: 15-20% of magazine written by children. Uses stories and poems. Also uses jokes, riddles, tongue twisters. Features that occur occasionally: "What Are Your Favorite Books?" (8-10/year), Recipes (8-10/year), "Science Letters" (15-20/year). Special features that invite children's submissions on a specific topic occur several times per year. Recent examples include "Pet Stories," "Favorite Songs," "Kids at Work," and "Help the Cartoonists." Pays in copies. Submit complete ms to the editor. Will accept typewritten, legibly handwritten and computer printout mss. Responds in 6 weeks.

A SELF-ADDRESSED, STAMPED ENVELOPE (SASE) should always be included with submissions within your own country. When sending material to other countries, include a self-addressed envelope (SAE) and International Reply Coupons (IRCs).

Artwork: Publishes artwork by children. Pays in copies. No cartoon or comic book characters. No commercial products. Submit b&w or color artwork for "Our Own Pages." Features include "Creatures Nobody Has Ever Seen" (5-8/year) and "Illustration Job" (18-20/year). Responds in 6 weeks.

■ KWIL KIDS PUBLISHING, The Little Publishing Company That Kwil Built, Kwilville, P.O. Box 29556, Maple Ridge, British Columbia V2X 2V0 Canada. Phone/fax: (604)465-9101. E-mail: kwil@telus.net. Website: www.members.home.com/kwilkids/. Publishes greeting cards, newspaper column, newsletter and web page. Publishes weekly column in local paper, four quarterly newsletters. "*Kwil Kids* come in all ages, shapes and sizes—from 4-64 and a whole lot more! Kwil does not pay for the creative work of children but provides opportunity/encouragement. We promote literacy, creativity and written 'connections'. through written and artistic expression and publish autobiographical, inspirational, fantastical, humorous stories of gentleness, compassion, truth and beauty. Our purpose is to foster a sense of pride and enthusiasm in young writers and artists, to celebrate the voice of youth and encourage growth through joy-filled practice and cheerleading, not criticism." Must include name, age, school, address and parent signature (if a minor). Will send guideline upon request and an application to join "The Kwil Club."
Books: Publishes autobiographical, inspirational, creative stories (alliterative, rhyming refrains, juicy words) fiction; short rhyming and non-rhyming poems (creative, fun, original, expressive, poetry). Length: 1,000 words for fiction; 8-16 lines for poetry. No payment—self-published and sold "at cost" only (1 free copy). Submit mss to Kwil publisher. Submit complete ms; send copy only—expect a reply but will not return ms. Will accept typewritten and legibly handwritten mss and e-mail. Include SASE. Publishes greeting cards with poems, short stories and original artwork. Pays 5¢ royalty on each card sold (rounded to the nearest dollar and paid once per year) as a fundraiser. Responds in April, August and December.
Newsletter: 95% of newsletter written by young people. Uses 15 short stories, poems, jokes (20-100 words). No payment—free newsletters only. Submit complete ms. Will accept typewritten and legibly handwritten mss and e-mail. Kwil answers every letter in verse. Responds in April, August and December.
Artwork: Publishes artwork and photography by children with writing. Looks for black ink sketches to go with writing and photos to go with writing. Submit by postal mail only; white background for sketches. Submit artwork/photos to Kwil publisher. Include SASE. Responds in 3 months.
Tips: "We love stories that teach a lesson or encourage peace, love and a fresh, new understanding. Just be who you are and do what you do. Then all of life's treasures will come to you."

☑ POTLUCK CHILDREN'S LITERARY MAGAZINE, (847)948-1139. Fax: (847)317-9492. E-mail: submissions@potluckmagazine.org or susan@potluckmagazine.org. Website: www.potluckmagazine .org. Quarterly magazine. "We look for works with imagery and human truths. Editors are available to assist in editing and to answer any questions or comments the writer may have concerning their work. The purpose of *Potluck* is to educate today's young writers, to encourage creative expression and to provide a professional forum in which their voices can be heard. Educational articles are written by guest authors, teachers and writing instructors, to help them enrich their writing skills, become better writers and to prepare them for the adult markets of their future. Recent articles dealt with work presentation, tracking submissions and rights, writing strong narratives, and how to prevent abrupt or neverending endings." Writer's guidelines available on request with a SASE or online.
Magazines: 99% of magazine written by young people. Uses fiction (500 words); nonfiction (500 words); poetry (30 lines); book reviews (250 words). Pays with copy of issue published. Submit mss to Susan Napoli Picchietti, editor. Submit complete ms; teacher may send group submissions, which have different guidelines. Will accept typewritten and e-mailed mss (no attachments work within body of e-mail). Include SASE. Responds 6 weeks after deadline.
Artwork/Photography: Publishes artwork by young artists. Looks for all types of artwork—no textured works. Must be 8½×11 only. Pays in copies. Do not fold submissions. Include proper postage and envelope. Color photocopy accepted. Submit artwork to Susan Napoli Picchietti, editor. Include SASE. Responds in 6 weeks.
Tips: "Relax—observe and acknowledge all that is around you. Life gives us a lot to draw on. Don't get carried away with style—let your words speak for themselves. If you want to be taken seriously as a writer, you must take yourself seriously. The rest will follow. Enjoy yourself and take pride in every piece, even the bad—they keep you humble."

SKIPPING STONES, Multicultural Children's Magazine, P.O. Box 3939, Eugene OR 97403. (541)342-4956. E-mail: skipping@efn.org. Website: www.efn.org/~skipping. **Articles/Poems/Fiction Editor:** Arun N. Toké. 5 issues a year. Estab. 1988. Circulation 2,500. "*Skipping Stones* is a multicultural, nonprofit, children's magazine to encourage cooperation, creativity and celebration of cultural and environmental richness. It offers itself as a creative forum for communication among children from different lands and backgrounds. We prefer work by children under 18 years old. International, minorities and under-represented populations receive priority, multilingual submissions are encouraged."

● *Skipping Stones'* theme for the 2002 Youth Honor Awards is the Internet's impact on multicultural issues. Send SASE for guidelines and more information on the awards.

Magazines: 50% written by children and teenagers. Uses 5-10 fiction short stories and plays (500-750 words); 5-10 nonfiction articles, interviews, letters, history, descriptions of celebrations (500-750 words); 15-20 poems, jokes, riddles, proverbs (250 words or less) per issue. Pays in contributor's copies. Submit mss to editor. Submit complete ms for fiction or nonfiction work; teachers and parents can also submit their contributions. Submissions should include "cover letter with name, age, address, school, cultural background, inspiration piece, dreams for future." Will accept typewritten, legibly handwritten and computer/word processor mss. Include SASE. Responds in 4 months. Accepts simultaneous submissions.

Artwork/Photography: Publishes artwork and photography for children. Will review all varieties of ms/illustration packages. Wants comics, cartoons, b&w photos, paintings, drawings (preferably ink & pen or pencil), 8×10, color photos OK. Subjects include children, people, celebrations, nature, ecology, multicultural. Pays in contributor's copies.

Terms: "*Skipping Stones* is a labor of love. You'll receive complimentary contributor's (up to four) copies depending on the length of your contribution and illustrations. We may allow others to reprint articles and art or photographs." Responds to artists in 4 months. Sample copy for $5 and 4 first-class stamps.

Tips: "Let the 'inner child' within you speak out—naturally, uninhibited." Wants "material that gives insight on cultural celebrations, lifestyle, custom and tradition, glimpse of daily life in other countries and cultures. Please, no mystery for the sake of mystery! Photos, songs, artwork are most welcome if they illustrate/highlight the points. Upcoming features: Living abroad, turning points, inspirations and outstanding moments in life, cultural celebrations around the world, consciousness, caring for the earth, current events, and the Internet's impact."

STONE SOUP, The Magazine by Young Writers and Artists, Children's Art Foundation, P.O. Box 83, Santa Cruz CA 95063. (831)426-5557. Fax: (831)426-1161. E-mail: editor@stonesoup.com. Website: www.stonesoup.com. **Articles/Fiction Editor, Art Director:** Ms. Gerry Mandel. Magazine published 6 times/year. Circ. 20,000. "We publish fiction, poetry and artwork by children through age 13. Our preference is for work based on personal experiences and close observation of the world. Our audience is young people through age 13, as well as parents, teachers, librarians." Purpose in publishing works by young people: to encourage children to read and to express themselves through writing and art. Writer's guidelines available upon request with a SASE.

Magazines: Uses animal, contemporary, fantasy, history, problem-solving, science fiction, sports, spy/mystery/adventure fiction stories. Uses 5-10 fiction stories (100-2,500 words); 5-10 nonfiction stories (100-2,500 words); 2-4 poems per issue. Does not want to see classroom assignments and formula writing. Buys 65 mss/year. Byline given. Pays on publication. Buys all rights. Pays $35 each for stories and poems, $35 for book reviews. Contributors also receive 2 copies. Sample copy $4. Free writer's guidelines. "We don't publish straight nonfiction, but we do publish stories based on real events and experiences." Send complete ms to editor. Will accept typewritten and legibly handwritten mss. Include SASE. Responds in 1 month.

Artwork/Photography: Publishes any type, size or color artwork/photos by children. Pays $20 for b&w or color illustrations. Contributors receive 2 copies. Sample copy $4. Free illustrator's guidelines. Send originals if possible. Send submissions to editor. Include SASE. Responds in 1 month. Original artwork returned at job's completion. All artwork must be by children through age 13.

Tips: "Be sure to enclose a SASE. Only work by young people through age 13 is considered. Whether your work is about imaginary situations or real ones, use your own experiences and observations to give your work depth and a sense of reality. Read a few issues of our magazine to get an idea of what we like."

WHOLE NOTES, P.O. Box 1374, Las Cruces NM 88004-1374. (505)541-5744. E-mail: rnhastings@zianet.com. **Editor:** Nancy Peters Hastings. Magazine published twice yearly. "We encourage interest in contemporary poetry by showcasing outstanding creative writing. We look for original, fresh perceptions in poems that demonstrate skill in using language effectively, with carefully chosen images and clear ideas. Our audience (general) loves poetry. We try to recognize excellence in creative writing by children as a way to encourage and promote imaginative thinking." Writer's guidelines available for SASE.

 SPECIAL COMMENTS by the editors of *Children's Writer's & Illustrator's Market* are set off by a bullet.

Magazines: Every fourth issue is 100% by children. Writers should be 21 years old or younger. Uses 30 poems/issue (length open). Pays complimentary copy. Submit mss to editor. Submit complete ms. "No multiple submissions, please." Will accept typewritten and legibly handwritten mss. SASE. Responds in 2 months.

Artwork/Photography: Publishes artwork and photographs by children. Looks for b&w line drawings which can easily be reproduced; b&w photos. Pays complimentary copy. Send clear photocopies. Submit artwork to editor. SASE. Responds in 2 months.

Tips: Sample issue is $3. "We welcome translations. Send your best work. Don't send your only copy of your poem. Keep a photocopy."

WORD DANCE, Playful Productions, Inc., P.O. Box 10804, Wilmington DE 19850-0804. (302)894-1950. Fax: (302)894-1957. E-mail: playful@worddance.com. Website: www.worddance.com. **Director:** Stuart Unger. Magazine. Published quarterly. "We're a magazine of creative writing and art that is for *and* by children in kindergarten through grade eight. We give children a voice."

Magazines: Uses adventure, fantasy, humorous, etc. (fiction); travel stories, poems and stories based on real life experiences (nonfiction). Publishes 250 total pieces of writing/year; maximum length: 3 pages. Submit mss to Stuart Ungar, articles editor. Sample copy $3. Free writer's guidelines and submissions form. SASE. Responds in 9 months.

Artwork: Illustrations accepted from young people in kindergarten through grade 8. Accepts illustrations of specific stories or poems and other general artwork. Must be high contrast. Query. Submit complete package with final art to art director. SASE. Responds in 8 months.

Tips: "Submit writing that falls into one of our specific on-going departments. General creative writing submissions are much more competitive."

☑ **THE WRITERS' SLATE**, (The Writing Conference, Inc.), P.O. Box 664, Ottawa KS 66067. Phone/fax: (785)242-1995. E-mail: jbushman@writingconference.com. Website: www.writingconference.com. Magazine. Publishes 3 issues/year. *The Writers' Slate* accepts original poetry and prose from students enrolled in kindergarten-12th grade. The audience is students, teachers and librarians. Purpose in publishing works by young people: to give students the opportunity to publish and to give students the opportunity *to read* quality literature written by other students. Writer's guidelines available on request.

Magazines: 90% of magazine written by young people. Uses 10-15 fiction, 1-2 nonfiction, 10-15 other mss per issue. Submit mss to Dr. F. Todd Goodson, editor, Kansas State University, 364 Bluemont Hall, Manhattan KS 66506-5300. Submit complete ms. Will accept typewritten mss. Responds in 1 month. Include SASE with ms if reply is desired.

Artwork: Publishes artwork by young people. Bold, b&w, student artwork may accompany a piece of writing. Submit to Dr. F. Todd Goodson, editor. Responds in 1 month.

Tips: "Always accompany submission with a letter indicating name, home address, school, grade level and teacher's name. If you want a reply, submit a SASE."

Resources
Agents & Art Reps

This section features listings of literary agents and art reps who either specialize in or represent a good percentage of children's writers or illustrators. While there are a number of children's publishers who are open to nonagented material, using the services of an agent or rep can be beneficial to a writer or artist. Agents and reps can get your work seen by editors and art directors more quickly. They are familiar with the market and have insights into which editors and art directors would be most interested in your work. Also, they negotiate contracts and will likely be able to get you a better deal than you could get on your own.

Agents and reps make their income by taking a percentage of what writers and illustrators receive from publishers. The standard percentage for agents is 10-15 percent; art reps generally take 25-30 percent. We have not included any agencies in this section that charge reading fees.

WHAT TO SEND

When putting together a package for an agent or rep, follow the guidelines given in their listings. Most agents open to submissions prefer initially to receive a query letter describing your work. For novels and longer works, some agents ask for an outline and a number of sample chapters, but you should send these only if you're asked to do so. Never fax or e-mail a query letter or sample chapters to agents without their permission. Just as with publishers, agents receive a large volume of submissions. It may take them a long time to reply, so you may want to query several agents at one time. It's best, however, to have a complete manuscript considered by only one agent at a time. Always include a self-addressed, stamped envelope (SASE).

For initial contact with art reps, send a brief query letter and self-promo pieces. Again, follow the guidelines given in the listings. If you don't have a flier or brochure, send photocopies. Always include a SASE.

For those who both write and illustrate, some agents listed will consider the work of author/illustrators. Read through the listings for details.

An Organization for Agents

In some listings of agents you'll see references to AAR (The Association of Authors' Representatives). This organization requires its members to meet an established list of professional standards and code of ethics.

The objectives of AAR include keeping agents informed about conditions in publishing and related fields; encouraging cooperation among literary organizations; and assisting agents in representing their author-clients' interests. Officially, members are prohibited from directly or indirectly charging reading fees. They offer writers a list of member agents on their website. They also offer a list of recommended questions an author should ask an agent. They can be contacted at AAR, P.O. Box 237201, Ansonia Station NY 10003. Website: www.aar-online.org.

As you consider approaching agents and reps with your work, keep in mind that they are very choosy about who they take on to represent. Your work must be high quality and presented professionally to make an impression on them. For insights from an agent, see the Insider Report with **Erin Murphy** on page 288. For more listings of agents and more information and tips see *Guide to Literary Agents*; for additional listing of art reps see *Artist's & Graphic Designer's Market* (both Writer's Digest Books).

Information on agents and art reps listed in the previous edition but not included in this edition of *Children's Writer's & Illustrator's Market* may be found in the General Index.

AGENTS

☑ **BOOKS & SUCH**, 4788 Carissa Ave., Santa Rosa CA 95405. (707)538-4184. Fax: (626)398-0246. E-mail: jkgbooks@aol.com. **Contact:** Janet Kobobel Grant. Estab. 1996. Associate member of CBA. Represents 35 clients. 12% of clients are new/unpublished writers. Specializes in "the Christian booksellers market but is expanding into the ABA market with children's and young adult projects."
- Before becoming an agent, Janet Grant was an editor for Zondervan and managing editor for *Focus on the Family*.
Represents: 15% juvenile books. Considers: nonfiction, fiction, picture books, young adult.
How to Contact: Query with SASE. Considers simultaneous queries. Responds in 1 month on queries; 6 weeks on mss. Returns material only with SASE.
Recent Sales: *The Roadrunner Reader* series (Cook Communications).
Needs: Actively seeking "material appropriate to the Christian market or that would crossover to the ABA market as well." Obtains new clients through recommendations and conferences.
Terms: Agent receives 15% commission on domestic and foreign sales. Offers written contract. 2 months notice must be given to terminate contract. Charges for postage, photocopying, fax and express mail.
Tips: "The heart of my motivation is to develop relationships with the authors I serve, to do what I can to shine the light of success on them, and to help be a caretaker of their gifts and time."

RUTH COHEN, INC. LITERARY AGENCY, P.O. Box 2244, LaJolla CA 92038-2244. (858)456-5805. **Contact:** Ruth Cohen. Currently accepting new clients. Estab. 1982. Member of AAR, Authors Guild, Sisters in Crime, Romance Writers of America, SCBWI. Represents 45 clients. 15% of clients are new/previously unpublished writers. Specializes in "quality writing in contemporary fiction; women's fiction; mysteries; thrillers and juvenile fiction."
- Prior to opening her agency, Ruth Cohen served as directing editor at Scott Foresman & Company (now HarperCollins).
Represents: 40% juvenile. Considers: fiction, picture books, middle grade, young adult.
How to Contact: *No unsolicited mss.* Accepts queries by mail only. Send outline plus 2 sample chapters. "Please indicate your phone number or e-mail address." *Must include SASE.* Responds in 3 weeks on queries.
Needs: Obtains new clients through recommendations from others and through submissions.
Terms: Agent receives 15% commission on domestic sales; 20% on foreign sales, "if a foreign agent is involved." Offers written contract, binding for 1 year "continuing to next." Charges for foreign postage, phone calls, photocopying submissions and overnight delivery of mss when appropriate.
Tips: "As the publishing world merges and charges, there seem to be fewer opportunities for new writers to succeed in the work that they love. We urge you to develop the patience, persistence and perseverance that have made this agency so successful. Prepare a well-written and well-crafted manuscript, and our combined best efforts can help advance both our careers."

THE CONTENT COMPANY INC., 5111 JFK Blvd. E, West New York NJ 07093. (201)558-0323. Fax: (201)558-0307. E-mail: info@theliteraryagency.com. Website: www.theliteraryagency.com, therightsagency.com. **Contact:** Lauren Mactas. Estab. 1979. Represents 20 clients. 5% of clients are new writers. 30% of material handled is books for young readers. Staff includes Peter Elek (illustration/picture books).
- Prior to starting an agency, Peter Elek worked as an art director/ production director for book and magazine publishing.
Represents: Considers nonfiction/picture books. "Your strength is based on proven success combining text and imagery—interpreting author's vision." Actively seeking fresh, original, nonderivative ideas— proving the author/illustrator identifies with a child's psyche. Not looking for "issues" and "causes"

books, nor single stories featuring a character that can be made into a series, nor ideas that envision licensed product to make them palatable! Books that "would make a great animated TV series" are discouraged as well.

How to Contact: Query with SASE or send outline and 2 sample chapters for longer works. Accepts queries by e-mail. Prefers to read material exclusively. Responds in 3 weeks to queries; 2 months to mss. Returns material only with SASE. Obtains clients through recommendations from others.

Recent Sales: Sold 6 books for young readers in the last year. *Ghosts of the Abyss* (Simon & Schuster); *I'm Gonna Like Me*, by Laura Cornell (Jamie Lee Curtis) (Joanna Cotler Books/HarperCollins); *A Day in History Series* (Hyperion).

Terms: Agent receives 15% commission on domestic sales; 20% on foreign sales. Offers written contract. 1-month notice must be given to terminate contract (with surviving terms).

Writing Conferences: Will attend LIBF in London March 2003; Bologna in Bologna Italy April 2003; Book Expo in Los Angeles May 2003.

Tips: "We are not editorially driven, but after 25 years we recognize good writing. We are a market driven company that provides emotional and professional support to our clients. We enhance and mediate the author/illustrator-publisher/editor relationship but don't feel the need to interpose our will on that relationship."

N: DUNHAM LITERARY, INC., 156 Fifth Ave., Suite 625, New York NY 10010-7002. Website: www.dunhamlit.com. **Contact:** Jennie Dunham. Seeking both new and established writers but prefers to work with established writers. Estab. 2000. Member of AAR and SCBWI. Represents 50 clients. 15% of clients are new/previously unpublished writers. 50% of material handled is books of young readers. Staff includes Jennie Dunham (all ages of children's books from novelty through young adult.)

Represents: Considers fiction, picture books, middle grade, young adult. "Most agents represent children's books or adult books, and my agency represents both." Actively seeking mss with great story and voice. Not looking for activity books, workbooks, educational books.

How to Contact: Query with SASE. Consider simultaneous queries and submissions. Responds in 1 week to queries; 2 months to mss. Returns material only with SASE. Obtains clients through recommendations from others.

Recent Sales: Sold 30 books for young readers in the last year. *The Wonderful Wizard of Oz*, by Robert Sabuda (Little Simon); *Clever Beatrice*, illustrated by Heather Solomon (Atheneum); *Gauchada*, by C. Drew Lamm (Knopf); *Molly and the Magic Wishbone*, by Barbara McClintock (Farrar, Straus & Giroux); *Blister*, by Susan Shreve (Arthur A. Levine Books); *Who Will Tell My Brother?*, by Marlene Carvell (Hyperion).

Terms: Agent receives 15% commission on domestic sales; 20-25% on foreign sales. Offers written contract. 60 days notice must be given to terminate contract.

Fees: The agency takes expenses from the clients' earnings for specific expenses documented during the marketing of a client's work in accordance with the AAR (Association of Authors' Representatives) Canon of Ethics. For example, photocopying, messenger, express mail, UPS, etc. The client is not asked to pay for these fees up front.

DWYER & O'GRADY, INC., P.O. Box 239, Lempster NH 03605-0239. (603)863-9347. Fax: (603)863-9346. **Contact:** Elizabeth O'Grady. Estab. 1990. Member of SCBWI. Represents 20 clients. Represents only writers and illustrators of children's books.
  • Dwyer & O'Grady is currently not accepting new clients.

Member Agents: Elizabeth O'Grady (children's books), Jeff Dwyer (children's books).

Represents: 100% juvenile books. Considers: nonfiction, fiction, picture books, young adult.

Needs: Obtains new clients through referrals or direct approach from agent to writer whose work they've read. Does not accept unsolicited mss.

Terms: Agent receives 15% commission on domestic sales; 20% on foreign sales. Offers written contract. Thirty days notice must be given to terminate contract. Charges for "photocopying of longer manuscripts or mutually agreed upon marketing expenses."

Tips: Agents from Dwyer & O'Grady attend Book Expo; American Library Association; Society of Children's Book Writers & Illustrators conferences. Clients include: Kim Ablon, Tom Bodett, Odds Bodkin, Donna Clair, Leonard Jenkins, Rebecca Rule, Steve Schuch, Virginia Stroud, Natasha Tarpley, Zong-Zhou Wang, Rashida Watson, Peter Sylvada, Mary Azarian, and E.B. Lewis.

ETHAN ELLENBERG LITERARY AGENCY, 548 Broadway, #5-E, New York NY 10012. (212)431-4554. Fax: (212)941-4652. E-mail: eellenberg@aol.com. Website: http://EthanEllenberg.com. **Contact:** Ethan Ellenberg. Estab. 1983. Represents 70 clients. 10% of clients are new/previously unpublished writers. Children's books are an important area for us.

● Prior to opening his agency, Ethan Ellenberg was contracts manager of Berkley/Jove and associate contracts manager for Bantam.

Represents: "We do a lot of children's books." Considers: nonfiction, fiction, picture books, young adult.

How to Contact: Children's submissions—send full ms. Young adults—send outline plus 3 sample chapters. Accepts queries by e-mail; does not accept attachments to e-mail queries or fax queries. Considers simultaneous queries and submissions. Responds in 10 days to queries; 1 month to mss. Returns materials only with SASE.

Terms: Agent receives 15% on domestic sales; 10% on foreign sales. Offers written contract, "flexible." Charges for "direct expenses only: photocopying, postage."

Tips: "We do consider new material from unsolicited authors. Write a good clear letter with a succinct description of your book. We prefer the first three chapters when we consider fiction, but for children's book submissions, we prefer the full manuscript. For all submissions you must include SASE for return or the material is discarded. It's always hard to break in, but talent will find a home. We continue to seek natural storytellers and nonfiction writers with important books." This agency sold over 100 titles in the last year, including *The Invisible Enemy*, by Martha Jocelyn.

☑ **BARRY GOLDBLATT LITERARY AGENCY INC.**, 320 Seventh Ave., #266, Brooklyn NY 11215. (718)832-8787. Fax: (718)832-5558. E-mail: bgliterary@earthlink.net. **Contact:** Barry Goldblatt. Estab. 2000. Member of SCBWI. Represents 25 clients. 40% of clients are new/previously unpublished writers. 100% of material handled is books for young readers. Staff includes Barry Goldblatt (picture books, middle grade and young adult novels).

Represents: Considers picture books, fiction, middle grade, young adult.

How to Contact: Send entire ms for picture books; outline and 3 sample chapters for fiction. Prefers to read material exclusively. Responds in 3 weeks to queries; 2 months to mss. Returns material only with SASE. Obtains clients through recommendations from others.

Recent Sales: Sold 10 books for young readers in the last year.

Terms: Agent receives 15% commission on domestic sales; 20% on foreign and dramatic sales.

Tips: "I structure my relationship with each client differently, according to their wants and needs. I'm mostly hands-on, but some want more editorial input, others less. I'm pretty aggressive selling work, but I'm fairly laid back in how I deal with clients. I'd say I'm quite friendly with most of my clients, and I like it that way. To me this is more than just a simple busines relationship."

🅽 **KIRCHOFF/WOHLBERG, INC., AUTHORS' REPRESENTATION DIVISION**, 866 United Nations Plaza, #525, New York NY 10017. (212)644-2020. Fax: (212)223-4387. Director of Operations: John R. Whitman. Estab. 1930s. Member of AAR. Represents 50 authors. 10% of clients are new/previously unpublished writers. Specializes in juvenile through young adult trade books and textbooks.

Member Agents: Liza Pulitzer-Voges (juvenile and young adult authors).

Represents: 80% juvenile books, 20% young adult. "We are interested in any original projects of quality that are appropriate to the juvenile and young adult trade book markets. But we take on very few new clients as our roster is full."

How to Contact: "Send a query that includes an outline and a sample; SASE required." Responds in 1 month to queries; 2 months to mss. Please send queries to the attention of Liza Pulitzer-Voges.

Needs: "Usually obtains new clients through recommendations from authors, illustrators and editors."

Terms: Agent receives standard commission "depending upon whether it is an author only, illustrator only, or an author/illustrator book." Offers written contract, binding for not less than 1 year.

Tips: "Kirchoff/Wohlberg has been in business since 1930 and sold over 50 titles in the last year."

BARBARA S. KOUTS, LITERARY AGENT, P.O. Box 560, Bellport NY 11713. (631)286-1278. **Contact:** Barbara Kouts. Currently accepting new clients. Estab. 1980. Member of AAR. Represent 50 clients. 10% of clients are new/previously unpublished writers. Specializes in adult fiction and nonfiction and children's books.

Represents: 60% juvenile books. Considers: nonfiction, fiction, picture books, ms/illustration packages, middle grade, young adult.

How to Contact: Accepts queries by mail only. Responds in 1 week to queries; 6 weeks to mss.

Needs: Obtains new clients through recommendations from others, solicitation, at conferences, etc.

VISIT OUR WEBSITES at www.writersmarket.com and www.writersdigest.com, for helpful articles, hot new markets, daily market updates, writers' guidelines and much more.

Recent Sales: *Sacajawea*, by Joseph Bruchac (Harcourt); *Born Blue*, by Han Nolan (Harcourt); *Froggy Plays in the Band*, by Jonathan London (Viking).

Terms: Agent receives 15% commission on domestic sales; 20% on foreign sales. Charges for photocopying.

Tips: "Write, do not call. Be professional in your writing."

RAY LINCOLN LITERARY AGENCY, Elkins Park House, Suite 107-B, 7900 Old York Rd., Elkins Park PA 19027. (215)635-0827. Fax: (215)782-8882. **Contact:** Mrs. Ray Lincoln. Estab. 1974. Represents 30 clients. 35% of clients are new/previously unpublished writers. Specializes in biography, nature, the sciences, fiction in both adult and children's categories.

Member Agents: Jerome A. Lincoln.

Represents: 20% juvenile books. Considers nonfiction, fiction, young adult, chapter and picture books.

How to Contact: Query first, then on request send outline, 2 sample chapters and SASE. "I send for balance of manuscript if it is a likely project." Responds in 2 weeks on queries; 1 month on mss.

Needs: Obtains new clients usually from recommendations.

Terms: Agent receives 15% commission on domestic sales; 20% on foreign sales. Offers written contract, binding "but with notice, may be cancelled." Charges only for overseas telephone calls. "I request authors to do manuscript photocopying themselves. Postage or shipping charge on manuscripts accepted for representation by agency."

Tips: "I always look for polished writing style, fresh points of view and professional attitudes." Recent sales of this agency include *The Best Halloween Ever*, by Barbara Robinson; *The Loser*, by Jerry Spinelli; *Moe McTooth*, by Eileen Spinelli (Houghton Mifflin); and *Towanda and Me*, by Susan Katz (Orchard Books).

GINA MACCOBY LITERARY AGENCY, P.O. Box 60, Chappaqua NY 10514. (914)238-5630. **Contact:** Gina Maccoby. Estab. 1986. Represents 35 clients. Represents writers and illustrators of children's books.

Represents: 50% juvenile books. Considers nonfiction, fiction, young adult.

How to Contact: Query with SASE. "Please, no unsolicited mss." Considers simultaneous queries and submissions. Responds to queries in 2 months. Returns materials only with SASE.

Needs: Usually obtains new clients through recommendations from own clients.

Terms: Agent receives 15% commission on domestic sales; 25% on foreign sales. Charges for photocopying. May recover certain costs such as airmail postage to Europe or Japan or legal fees.

Tips: This agency sold 18 titles last year including *The Crying Rocks*, by Janet Taylor Lisle.

☑ BARBARA MARKOWITZ LITERARY AGENCY, P.O. Box 41709, Los Angeles CA 90041. **Contact:** Barbara Markowitz. Seeking both new and established writers. Estab. 1980. Member of SCBWI. Represents 12 clients. 80% of clients are new/previously unpublished writers. 50% of material handled is books for 8-11 year old, mid-level readers. Staff includes Judith Rosenthal (young adult, historical fiction); Barbara Markowitz (mid-level and young adult, contemporary fiction).

● Prior to opening her agency, Barbara Markowitz owned Barbara Bookstores in Chicago.

Represents: Considers fiction, middle grade, young adult (11-15 year olds) historical fiction. Actively seeking contemporary and historical fiction no more than 35,000 words for 8-11 year olds and 11-15 year olds. Not looking for fable, fantasy, fairytales; no illustrated; no science fiction; no books about dogs, cats, pigs.

How to Contact: Query with SASE or send outline and 3 sample chapters. Considers simultaneous queries and submissions. Responds in 1 week to queries; 6 weeks to mss. Returns material only with SASE. "If no SASE provided, I discard." Obtains new clients through recommendations from others, queries/solicitations.

Recent Sales: *Letting Go of Bobby James*, by Valerie Hobbs (Frances Foster/FSG); *My Father Was a Corporate Werewolf*, by Henry Garfield (Richard Jackson/Atheneum).

Terms: Agent receives 15% commission on domestic sales; 15% on foreign sales. Offers written contract, binding for 1 year. 1-month notice must be given to terminate contract. Charges clients for postage only.

Tips: Markowitz agenting style is "very hands on. Yes, I read, critique, light edit, make/request revisions. It's a very personal small agency."

Ⓝ ERIN MURPHY LITERARY AGENCY, P.O. Box 2519, Flagstaff AZ 86003-2519. (928)525-2056. Fax: (928)525-2480. E-mail: alwayserin@aol.com. **Contact:** Erin Murphy. Considers both new and established writers, by referral or personal contact (such as conferences) only. Estab. 1999. Member of SCBWI. Represents 40 clients. 80% of clients are new/previously unpublished writers. 100% of material handled is books of young readers.

insider report

Arizona-based editor-turned-agent's insights on the industry

Erin Murphy, the former editor-in-chief of Northland Publishing, never imagined she would become a literary agent. But looking back, she says agenting is what she first thought editing would be: working closely with authors, forming career-long relationships, learning and growing together, focusing on the words. And as an agent, she says she can take more risks, take on projects that she thinks break new ground, and advocate with editors she respects. Murphy works out of Flagstaff, Arizona. That fact of geography forced her into a steep learning curve when it came to working with New York publishing houses, but she believes that in the long run her persistence and "smarts" will open more doors to her than anything else—she apparently has plenty of both.

Erin Murphy

Some writers are hesitant to sign up with an agent who works outside New York. How do you respond to that?

I don't think it matters anymore where your office is. A majority of my correspondence with editors is handled by e-mail, and another large chunk by phone. Editors are busy people. Unless they're well established, they don't have time for long lunches with agents—and as a newer agent, I'm reaching out to up-and-comers. I do meet editors at conferences and conventions, and I make trips to New York to develop contacts there, but who cares where I am, as long as editors look forward to getting my packages in the mail?

How does a writer best approach you or another agent?

I want to know that writers have been working hard, establishing contacts, attending conferences, and getting involved in critique groups. In general, I don't think a writer should contact an agent without a referral or connection. If a writer hasn't gotten out there enough to have met agents at conferences or met other writers who know agents, she's not ready for an agent. Being part of the world of writing for children is what takes a writer to a new level and gets her ready to be published. Children's writers form a unique community. They look at each other's work and help each other improve and learn, so a referral from another writer means a lot to me.

What should a writer include in a cover letter to an agent?

The writer should say whether she belongs to SCBWI and list published works and awards. She should briefly describe what she has available to market. If there are more than three or four projects, it's usually best to keep it quick—title, genre, age group. If she has relationships with particular editors, I like to know. If she's worked with other agents, I like to know why those relationships ended. All writers say they've been writing since they could pick up a pencil, so I like to know how long a potential client has been *serious* about writing. It's nice when I can pick up on a writer's confidence and personality, and if she's opinionated about what she wants from an agent, that's good to know too—no sense in my reading further if her needs and my style don't match up.

Do you think a children's book writer can make a living at writing?
It happens, although rarely, and it seems to happen in one of two ways—writing one thing consistently and well, or writing a bit of everything. It helps if writers supplement their writing income with school visits, conference stints, and teaching about writing, but I tell my clients not to quit their day jobs. Inspiration comes from life, not from being holed up in a garret writing. If writers don't do anything but write, the well will run dry.

Who publishes a book better—the independent houses or the New York conglomerates?
If a book has a high profile on a larger house's list, it generally gets more attention from stores and the media, and can go on to sell large numbers of copies and stay in print a long time—and can bring prestige to the writer. Big houses also do more with subsidiary rights than small houses. Small houses, which rarely have bestsellers and have to depend more on the backlist for continued sales, generally keep their books in print longer, even if they have a lower profile.

Personally, I'd rather take a lower advance up front and get a royalty check sooner from an established, respected smaller house, and have a better chance of a book selling over the long haul.

Of course, there are no guarantees that anything will sell, much less over the long haul. All of publishing is a gamble. Sometimes it's better to take a big risk, and sometimes it's better to go for the sure thing. What increases the odds is making a good match of author and book to editor and house—and an editor's passion for a manuscript can make all the difference, regardless of the company's size.

Are first-time authors stuck with boilerplate contracts?
Just remember that the worst the publisher can say is no. If you've done your homework and know what's standard in a boilerplate contract, you won't be thought foolish for negotiating. And if you know what's important to you going into a contract negotiation, you can usually come away with it, within reason.

For example, if you grant all subsidiary rights to a publisher, but you have a mechanism for finding some of these sales yourself, ask if you can get a higher percentage if you bring a buyer to the publisher and the deal goes through. But, remember, it's better to include rights in a publisher's contract than to retain them and do nothing with them. Big publishers have whole departments of people who do nothing but sell subsidiary rights, and you'll make more money from your portion of those sales than you would from not selling them at all.

How would you like to see the industry change?
I'm not much on mulling where the future may take us. For example, there's been so much talk about the way superstores have ruined the industry. Although I miss many independent stores that are now out of business, I think their demise is the result of a change driven as much by buyers' and readers' needs as anything else. If it's a bad change, things will come back around, or at least moderate. Just a couple of years ago, people were fretting about the ways

electronic books would change things for the worse, and readers essentially spoke up and said they liked paper books. Now e-companies and e-imprints are going under right and left. Things happen for the best in the long run.

What are your suggestions to an author who is trying to market her first book?
One thing to remember is that you're trying to get people to *buy* books, not give away all your free copies. It's important to get that professional mindset. Charge for presentations—schools expect to pay for them. Charge for books—you're not made of money! If you have a list of publications where you'd like your book to go for review or promotion, ask your publisher's publicity department to send the books out, or provide you with free review copies. As long as you're savvy and flexible, and not trying to send books to inappropriate places, the publicity department should be willing to work with you. Save your free copies for yourself and loved ones. They're treasures, after all.

What do established writers seem to be doing right when it comes to managing their careers?
Established writers who continue to evolve in their work and continue to be published success-fully seem to stay connected to a peer writing group. They don't believe they're experts who have all the answers—they're still looking for feedback and criticism. They're involved in the living, breathing world of writing.

What are your criteria for a great client?
Friend and professional, blended together. Someone I can respect and who respects me. If they can make me laugh—a bonus!
—Anna Olswanger

● Prior to opening her agency, Erin Murphy was editor-in-chief at Northland Publishing/Rising Moon.
Represents: Fiction, nonfiction, picture books, middle grade, young adult.
How to Contact: Query with SASE. Considers simultaneous queries. Responds in 1 month to queries; 3 months to mss. Returns material only with SASE. Obtains clients through recommendations from others or conferences.
Terms: Agent receives 15% commission on domestic sales; 20% on foreign sales. Offers written contract. 30 days notice must be given to terminate contract.

THE NORMA-LEWIS AGENCY, 311 W. 43rd St., Suite 602, New York NY 10036. (212)664-0807. **Contact:** Norma Liebert. Currently accepting new clients. Estab. 1980. 50% of clients are new/previously unpublished writers. Specializes in juvenile books (pre-school to high school).
Represents: 60% juvenile books. Considers: nonfiction, fiction, picture books, middle grade, young adult, artwork, ms/illustration packages.
How to Contact: Accepts queries by mail only. Prefers to be only reader. Responds in 6 weeks. Returns materials only with SASE.
Terms: Agent receives 15% commission on domestic sales; 20% on foreign sales.

STERNIG & BYRNE LITERARY AGENCY, 3209 S. 55th St., Milwaukee WI 53219-4433. (414)328-8034. Fax: (414)328-8034. E-mail: jackbyrne@aol.com. **Contact:** Jack Byrne.
● Not currently accepting submissions.

SCOTT TREIMEL NY, 434 Lafayette St., New York NY 10003. (212)505-8353. Fax: (212)505-0664. **Contact:** Scott Treimel. Estab. 1995. Represents 33 clients. 10% of clients are new/unpublished writers. Specializes in children's books, all genres: tightly focused segments of the trade and, to a lesser extent, educational markets. Member AAR, Author's Guild, SCBWI.

● Prior to opening his agency, Treimel was an assistant to Marilyn E. Marlow of Curtis Brown; a rights agent for Scholastic, Inc.; a book packager and rights agent for United Feature Syndicate; the founding director of Warner Bros. Worldwide Publishing, a freelance editor; and a rights consultant for HarperCollins Children's Books.

Represents: 100% juvenile books. Considers all juvenile fiction and most nonfiction areas. No religious books.

How to Contact: Query with SASE. For picture books, send entire ms (no more than 2). Does not accept queries by fax or e-mail. No multiple submissions. Requires "90-day exclusivity on all submissions." Replies to submissions only with SASE, otherwise discards.

Needs: Interested in seeing picture book author-illustrators, first chapter books, middle-grade fiction and teen fiction. Obtains most clients through recommendations. Prefers published authors and illustrators.

Terms: Agent receives 15-20% commission on domestic sales; 20-25% on foreign sales. Offers verbal or written contract, binding on a "contract-by-contract basis." Charges for photocopying, overnight/express postage, messengers and books ordered for subsidiary rights sales.

Tips: Attends Society of Children's Book Writers & Illustrators Conferences, participates in panel discussions. Sold 20 titles in the last year. Do not pitch: let your work speak for itself. Offers editorial guidance selectively, if extensive charges higher commission.

WECKSLER-INCOMCO, 170 West End Ave., New York NY 10023. (212)787-2239. Fax: (212)496-7035. **Contact:** Sally Wecksler. Estab. 1971. Represents 25 clients. 50% of clients are new/previously unpublished writers. "However, I prefer writers who have had something in print." Specializes in nonfiction with illustrations (photos and art).

● Prior to becoming an agent, Wecksler was an editor at *Publishers Weekly*; publisher with the international department of R.R. Bowker; and international director at Baker & Taylor.

Member Agents: Joann Amparan (general, children's books), S. Wecksler (general, foreign rights/co-editions, fiction, illustrated books, children's books).

Represents: 25% juvenile books. Considers: nonfiction, fiction, picture books.

How to Contact: Query with outline plus 3 sample chapters. Include brief bio. Responds in 1 month to queries; 2 months to mss.

Needs: Actively seeking "illustrated books for adults or children with beautiful photos or artwork." Does not want to receive "science fiction or books with violence." Obtains new clients through recommendations from others and solicitations.

Terms: Agent receives 15% commission on domestic sales; 20% on foreign sales. Offers written contract, binding for 3 years.

Tips: "Make sure a SASE is enclosed. Send three chapters and outline, clearly typed or word processed manuscript, double-spaced, written with punctuation and grammar in approved style. *We do not like to receive presentations by fax.*"

WRITERS HOUSE, 21 W. 26th St., New York NY 10010. (212)685-2400. Fax: (212)685-1781. Estab. 1974. Member of AAR. Represents 280 clients. 50% of clients were new/unpublished writers. Specializes in all types of popular fiction and nonfiction. No scholarly, professional, poetry or screenplays.

Member Agents: Amy Berkower (major juvenile authors); Merrilee Heifetz (quality children's fiction); Susan Cohen, Jodi Reamer (juvenile and young adult fiction and nonfiction); Steven Malk (quality YA fiction and picture books); Robin Rue (YA fiction).

Represents: 35% juvenile books. Considers: nonfiction, fiction, picture books, young adult.

How to Contact: Query. Responds in 1 month on queries.

Needs: Obtains new clients through recommendations from others.

Terms: Agent receives 15% commission on domestic sales; 20% on foreign sales. Offers written contract, binding for 1 year.

Tips: "Do not send manuscripts. Write a compelling letter. If you do, we'll ask to see your work."

**FOR EXPLANATIONS OF THESE SYMBOLS,
SEE THE INSIDE FRONT AND BACK COVERS OF THIS BOOK**

WRITERS HOUSE, (West Coast Office), 3368 Governor Dr., #224F, San Diego CA 92122. (858)678-8767. Fax: (858)678-8530. **Contact:** Steven Malk.
- See Writers House listing above for more information.
Represents: Nonfiction, fiction, picture books, young adult.

N WYLIE-MERRICK LITERARY AGENCY, 1138 S. Webster St., Kokomo IN 46902. (765)459-8258, or (765)457-3783. E-mail: smartin@wylie-merrick.com or rbrown@wylie-merrick.com. Website: wylie-merrick.com. **Contact:** Sharene Martin or Robert Brown. Seeking both new and established writers. Estab. 1999. Signatory of SCBWI. Represents 6 clients. 50% of clients are new/previously unpublished writers. 60% of material handled is books of young readers. Staff includes Sharene Martin (picture books, middle-grade and young adult novels), Robert Brown (young adult novels).
- Prior to opening their agency, Sharene Martin worked as an English teacher, grades 8-adult; writer; and educational technology consultant. Robert Brown worked as an engineer; dance instructor; and writer.
Represents: Considers fiction, nonfiction, picture books, middle grade, young adult. "We are very focused on representing quality literature; our agency represents a true passion for 'good reads.' We work closely with our clients to develop their potential to the greatest extent possible. If we request a writer's work, we try to give him/her a critique and some suggestions on improving its marketability even if we don't represent it." Actively seeking genre fiction: mystery, science fiction/fantasy; novels depicting strong relationships, romance, sports, and/or Christian themes. Not looking for poetry.
How to Contact: For novels submit first 10 pages and synopsis; submit entire ms for picture books. Consider simultaneous queries and submissions. Responds in 1 month to queries; 3 months to mss. Returns material only with SASE. Obtains clients through recommendations from others, queries/solicitations, conferences.
Recent Sales: Sold 1 book for young readers in the last year.
Terms: Agent receives 15% commission on domestic sales; 20% on foreign sales. Offers written contract binding on all sales even after canceled. 10 days notice must be given to terminate contract.
Writers' Conferences: Attended SCBWI Conference in Los Angeles CA August, 2002; will attend Aspiring Authors Conference in Plymouth IN (local high school event ONLY) April, 2003.
Tips: "We are a small, low-key agency that works closely with its clients. We do edit some material for clients (no charge) and request revisions as needed. We are excited about the projects we represent, and we enjoy working with our authors to develop great literature for children and young adults."

ART REPS

ARTISTS INTERNATIONAL, 17 Wheaton Rd., Marbledale CT 06791. (860)868-6655. Fax: (860)868-1272. E-mail: artsitnl@javanet.com. Website: www.artistsintl.com. **Contact:** Michael Brodie. Commercial illustration representative. Estab. 1970. Represents 20 illustrators. Specializes in children's books. Markets include: design firms; editorial/magazines; licensing.
Handles: Illustration.
Terms: Rep receives 30% commission. No geographic restrictions. Advertising costs are split: 70% paid by talent; 30% paid by representative.
How to Contact: For first contact, send slides, photocopies and SASE. Responds in 1 week.
Tips: Obtains new talent through recommendations from others, solicitation, conferences, *Literary Market Place*, etc. "SAE with example of your work; no résumés please."

ASCIUTTO ART REPS., INC., 1712 E. Butler Circle, Chandler AZ 85225. (480)899-0600. Fax: (480)899-3636. E-mail: Aartreps@aol.com. **Contact:** Mary Anne Asciutto. Children's illustration representative. Estab. 1980. Member of SPAR, Society of Illustrators. Represents 12 illustrators. 99% of artwork handled is children's book illustration. Specializes in children's illustration for books, magazines, posters, packaging, etc. Markets include: publishing/packaging/advertising.
- Asciutto is now representing children's book writers as well as illustrators.
Handles: Stories and illustration for children only.
Recent Sales: *Bats*, illustrated by Henderson (Boyd's Mill's Press).
Terms: Rep receives 25% commission. No geographic restrictions. Advertising costs are split: 75% paid by talent; 25% paid by representative. For promotional purposes, talent should provide "prints (color) or originals within an $8\frac{1}{2} \times 11$ size format."
How to Contact: Send printed materials, tearsheets, photocopies and/or ms in a SASE. Responds in 2 weeks. After initial contact, send appropriate materials if requested. Portfolio should include original art on paper, tearsheets, photocopies or color prints of most recent work. If accepted, materials will remain for assembly.

Tips: In obtaining representation "be sure to connect with an agent who handles the kind of accounts you (the artist/writer) *want*."

CAROL BANCROFT & FRIENDS, 121 Dodgingtown Rd., P.O. Box 266, Bethel CT 06801. (203)748-4823 or (800)720-7020. Fax: (203)748-4581. E-mail: artists@carolbancroft.com. Website: www.carolbancroft.com. **Owner:** Carol Bancroft. Illustration representative for children's publishing. Estab. 1972. Member of SPAR, Society of Illustrators, Graphic Artists Guild, SCBWI. Represents 40 illustrators. Specializes in illustration for children's publishing—text and trade; any children's-related material. Clients include Scholastic, Houghton Mifflin, HarperCollins, Dutton, Harcourt Brace.
Handles: Illustration for children of all ages. Seeking multicultural and fine artists.
Terms: Rep receives 25-30% commission. Advertising costs are split: 75% paid by talent; 25% paid by representative. For promotional purposes, talent must provide "laser copies (not slides), tearsheets, promo pieces, good color photocopies, etc.; 6 pieces or more is best; narrative scenes and children interacting." Advertises in *RSVP, Picture Book, Directory of Illustration*.
How to Contact: Send 2-3 samples by e-mail only and include website address."

SHERYL BERANBAUM, 75 Scenic Dr., Warwick RI 02886. (401)737-8591. Fax: (401)739-5189. E-mail: sheryl@beranbaum.com. Website: www.beranbaum.com. Commercial illustration representative. Estab. 1985. Member of Graphic Artists Guild. Represents 15 illustrators. 75% of artwork handled is children's book illustration. Currently open to illustrators seeking representation. Open to both new and established illustrators. Submission guidelines available by phone.
Handles: Illustration.
Recent Sales: Books by Albert Molnar (Harcourt, Simon & Schuster); Beth Buffington (Harcourt, Houghton Mifflin); John Kastner (Harcourt). "My illustrators are diversified and their work comes from a variety of the industry's audiences."
Terms: Rep receives 30% commission. Charges marketing plan fee or web only fee. Offers written contract. Advertising costs are split: 75% paid by illustrators; 25% paid by rep. Requires Itoya portfolio; postcards only for promotion. Advertises in *Creative Black Book*.
How to Contact: For first contact, send direct mail flier/brochure, tearsheets, photocopies. Responds only if interested. Portfolio should include photocopies.

SAM BRODY, ARTISTS & PHOTOGRAPHERS REPRESENTATIVE & CONSULTANT, 77 Winfield St., Apt. 4, E. Norwalk CT 06855-2138. Phone/fax: (203)854-0805 (for fax, add 999). E-mail: sambrody@bigplanet.com. **Contact:** Sam Brody. Commercial illustration and photography representative and broker. Estab. 1948. Member of SPAR. Represents 4 illustrators, 3 photographers, 2 designers. Markets include: advertising agencies; corporations/client direct; design firms; editorial/magazines; publishing/books; sales/promotion firms.
Handles: Consultant.
Terms: Agent receives 30% commission. Exclusive area representation is required. For promotional purposes, talent must provide back-up advertising material, i.e., cards (reprints—*Workbook*, etc.) and self-promos.
How to Contact: For first contact, send bio, direct mail flier/brochure, tearsheets. Reports in 3 days or within 1 day if interested. After initial contact, call for appointment or drop off or mail in appropriate materials for review. Portfolio should include tearsheets, slides, photographs. Obtains new talent through recommendations from others, solicitation.
Tips: Considers "past performance for clients that I check with and whether I like the work performed."

PEMA BROWNE LTD., P.O. Box 4063, N. Hollywood CA 91617. (818)340-4302. Fax: (914)985-7635. **Contact:** Pema Browne or Perry Browne. Estab. 1966. Represents 10 illustrators. Specializes in general commercial. Markets include: all publishing areas; children's picture books; collector plates and dolls; advertising agencies. Clients include HarperCollins, Thomas Nelson, Bantam Doubleday Dell, Nelson/Word, Hyperion, Putnam. Client list available upon request.
Handles: Illustration. Looking for "professional and unique" talent.
Terms: Rep receives 30% commission. Exclusive area representation is required. For promotional purposes, talent must provide color mailers to distribute. Representative pays mailing costs on promotion mailings.
How to Contact: For first contact, send query letter, direct mail flier/brochure and SASE. If interested will ask to mail appropriate materials for review. Portfolios should include tearsheets and transparencies or good color photocopies, plus SASE. Obtains new talent through recommendations and interviews (portfolio review).

Tips: "We are doing more publishing—all types—less advertising." Looks for "continuity of illustration and dedication to work."

N CATUGEAU: ARTIST AGENT, 110 Rising Ridge Rd., Ridgefield CT 06877. (203)438-7307. Fax: (203)984-1993. E-mail: catartrep@aol.com. Website: www.CATugeau.com. **Owner:** Chris Tugeau. Children's publishing—trade, mass market, educational. Estab. 1994. Member of SPAR, SCBWI, Graphic Artists Guild. Represents 35 illustrators. 100% of artwork handled is children's book illustration. Staff includes Chris Tugeau, owner.
Handles: Illustration.
Terms: Rep receives 25% commission. "Artists responsible for providing samples for portfolios, promotional books and mailings." Exclusive representation required. Offers written contract. Advertises in *Picturebook*, *RSVP*, *Directory of Illustration*.
How to Contact: For first contact, send SASE, direct mail flier/brochure, photocopies. Responds ASAP. Portfolio should include tearsheets, photocopies. Finds illustrators through recommendations from others, conferences, personal search. Do not e-mail samples. No CDs!
Tips: "Do research, look at artists' websites, talk to other artists—make sure you're comfortable with personality of rep. Be professional yourself . . . know what you do best and be prepared to give rep what they need to present you!"

CORNELL & McCARTHY, LLC, 2-D Cross Hwy., Westport CT 06880. (203)454-4210. Fax: (203)454-4258. E-mail: cmartreps@aol.com. Website: www.cornellandmccarthy.com. **Contact:** Merial Cornell. Children's book illustration representatives. Estab. 1989. Member of SCBWI and Graphic Artists Guild. Represents 30 illustrators. Specializes in children's books: trade, mass market, educational.
Handles: Illustration.
Terms: Rep receives 25% commission. Advertising costs are split: 75% paid by talent; 25% paid by representative. For promotional purposes, talent must provide 10-12 strong portfolio pieces relating to children's publishing.
How to Contact: For first contact, send query letter, direct mail flier/brochure, tearsheets, photocopies and SASE. Responds in 1 month. Obtains new talent through recommendations, solicitation, conferences.
Tips: "Work hard on your portfolio."

N DIMENSION, 1500 McAndrew Rd. W, #217, Burnsville MN 55337. (952)892-8474. Fax: (952)892-1722. E-mail: jkoltes@dimensioncreative.com. Website: www.dimensioncreative.com. **Contact:** Joanne Koltes. Commercial illustration representataive. Estab. 1982. Member of MN Book Builder. Represents 12 illustrators. 45% of artwork handled is children's book illustration. Staff includes Joanne Koltes.
Terms: Advertises in *Picturebook*.
How to Contact: Responds only if interested.

DWYER & O'GRADY, INC., P.O. Box 239, Lempster NH 03605. (603)863-9347. Fax: (603)863-9346. **Contact:** Elizabeth O'Grady. Agents for children's picture book artists and writers. Estab. 1990. Member of Society of Illustrators, SCBWI, ABA. Represents 12 illustrators and 6 writers. Staff includes Elizabeth O'Grady, Jeffrey Dwyer. Specializes in children's picture books (middle grade and young adult). Markets include: publishing/books, audio/film.
• Dwyer & O'Grady is currently not accepting new clients.
Handles: Illustrators and writers of children's books.
Terms: Receives 15% commission domestic, 20% foreign. Additional fees are negotiable. Exclusive representation is required (world rights). Advertising costs are paid by representative. For promotional purposes, talent must provide both color slides and prints of at least 20 sample illustrations depicting the figure with facial expression.

N PAT HACKETT/ARTIST REP, 7014 N. Mercer Way, Mercer Island WA 98040. (206)447-1600. Fax: (206)447-0739. Website: www.PatHackett.com. **Contact:** Pat Hackett. Commercial illustration representative. Estab. 1979. Member of Graphic Artists Guild. Represents 12 illustrators. 10% of artwork handled is children's book illustration. Currently open to illustrators seeking representation. Open to both new and established illustrators.
Handles: Illustration. Looking for illustrators with unique, strong, salable style.
Recent Sales: Represents Bryan Ballinger, Kooch Campbell, Jonathan Combs, Eldon Doty, Martin French.
Terms: Rep receives 25-33% commission. Advertising costs are split: 75% paid by illustrators; 25% paid by rep. Illustrator must provide portfolios (2-3) and promotional pieces. Advertises in *Picturebook*, *Workbook*.

How to Contact: For first contact, send query letter, tearsheets, SASE, direct mail flier/brochure. Responds only if interested. Wait for response. Portfolio should include tearsheets; lasers OK. Finds illustrators through recommendations from others, queries/solicitations.
Tips: Send query plus 1-2 samples, either by regular mail or e-mail. I don't have time to visit websites at first contact.

HANNAH REPRESENTS, 14431 Ventura Blvd., #108, Sherman Oaks CA 91423. (818)378-1644. E-mail: hannahrepresents@yahoo.com. **Contact:** Hannah Robinson. Literary representative for illustrators. Estab. 1997. Represents 8 illustrators. 100% of artwork handled is children's book illustration. Looking for established illustrators only.
Handles: Manuscript/illustration packates. Looking for illustrators with book already under contract.
Terms: Rep receives 15% commission. Offers written contract. Advertises in *Picturebook*.
How to Contact: For first contact, send SASE and tearsheets. Responds only if interested. Call to schedule an appointment. Portfolio should include photocopies. Finds illustrators through recommendations from others, conferences, queries/solicitations, international.
Tips: Present a carefully developed range of characterization illustrations that are world-class enough to equal those in the best children's books.

HK PORTFOLIO, 666 Greenwich St., New York NY 10014. (212)675-5719. E-mail: harriet@hkportfolio .com. Website: www.hkportfolio.com. **Contact:** Harriet Kasak or Mela Bolinao. Commercial illustration representative. Estab. 1986. Member of SPAR, Society of Illustrators and Graphic Artists Guild. Represents 43 illustrators. Specializes in illustration for juvenile markets. Markets include: advertising agencies; editorial/magazines; publishing/books.
Handles: Illustration.
Recent Sales: *What's That Noise*, illustrated by Paul Mersel (Candlewick); *The Secret of the Great Houdini*, illustrated by Leonid Gore (Simon & Schuster); *My Last Chance Brother*, illustrated by Jack E. Davis (Dutton).
Terms: Rep receives 25% commission. No geographic restrictions. Advertising costs are split: 75% paid by talent; 25% paid by representative. Advertises in *Picturebook* and *Workbook*.
How to Contact: No geographic restrictions. For first contact, send query letter, direct mail flier/brochure, tearsheets, slides, photographs or photocopies and SASE. Responds in 1 week. After initial contact, send in appropriate materials for review. Portfolio should include tearsheets, slides, photographs or photocopies.
Tips: Leans toward highly individual personal styles.

KIRCHOFF/WOHLBERG, ARTISTS' REPRESENTATION DIVISION, 866 United Nations Plaza, #525, New York NY 10017. (212)644-2020. Fax: (212)223-4387. Director of Operations: John R. Whitman. Estab. 1930. Member of SPAR, Society of Illustrators, AIGA, Association of American Publishers, Bookbuilders of Boston, New York Bookbinders' Guild. Represents over 50 illustrators. **Artist's Representative:** Elizabeth Ford. Specializes in juvenile and young adult trade books and textbooks. Markets include: publishing/books.
Handles: Illustration and photography (juvenile and young adult).
Terms: Rep receives 25% commission. Exclusive representation to book publishers is usually required. Advertising costs paid by representative ("for all Kirchoff/Wohlberg advertisements only"). "We will make transparencies from portfolio samples; keep some original work on file." Advertises in *American Showcase*, *Art Directors' Index*, *Society of Illustrators Annual*, children's book issues of *Publishers Weekly*.
How to Contact: Please send all correspondence to the attention of Elizabeth Ford. For first contact, send query letter, "any materials artists feel are appropriate." Responds in 6 weeks. "We will contact you for additional materials." Portfolios should include "whatever artists feel best represents their work. We like to see children's illustration in any style."

N LEVY CREATIVE MANAGEMENT, 300 E. 46th St., Suite 8E, New York NY 10017. (212)687-6465. Fax: (212)661-4839. E-mail: info@levycreative.com. Website: www.levycreative.com. **Contact:** Sari Levy. Commercial illustration representative. Estab. 1998. Member of Society of Illustrators, Graphic

---

A SELF-ADDRESSED, STAMPED ENVELOPE (SASE) should always be included with submissions within your own country. When sending material to other countries, include a self-addressed envelope (SAE) and International Reply Coupons (IRCs).

Artists Guild, Art Directors Club. Represents 13 illustrators. 30% of artwork handled is children's book illustration. Currently open to illustrators seeking representation. Open to both new and established illustrators. Submission guidelines available on website.

Handles: Illustration, ms/illustration packages.

Recent Sales: Represents David Cooper, Max Gafe, Liz Lomax, Oren Sherman.

Terms: Rep receives 25% commission. Exclusive representation required. Offers written contract. Advertising costs are split: 75% paid by illustrators; 25% paid by rep. Advertises in *Picturebook*, *American Showcase*, *Workbook*, *Alternative Pick Contact*.

How to Contact: For first contact, send tearsheets, photocopies, SASE, direct mail flier/brochure. "See website for submission guidelines." We will contact only if interested. Portfolio should include professionally presented materials. Finds illustrators through recommendations from others, word of mouth, competitions.

LINDGREN & SMITH, 250 W. 57th St., #521, New York NY 10107. (212)397-7330. Fax: (212)397-7334. E-mail: tricia@lindgrensmith.com. Website: www.lindgrensmith.com. **Contact:** Pat Lindgren, Piper Smith, Tricia Weber. Illustration representative. Estab. 1984. Member of SCBWI. Markets include children's books, advertising agencies; corporations; design firms; editorial; publishing.

Handles: Illustration.

Recent Sales: *Wolf Who Cried Boy*, by Steven Salerno, illustrator (Dutton); *The Christmas Treasury*, by Valerie Sokolova, illustrator (Golden).

Terms: Exclusive representation is required. Advertises in *American Showcase*, *The Workbook*, *The Black Book* and *Picturebook*.

How to Contact: For first contact, send direct mail flier, photocopies or postcard. "We will respond by mail or phone—if interested. For response include SASE."

Tips: "Check to see if your work seems appropriate for the group. We only represent experienced artists who have been professionals for some time."

MARLENA AGENCY, INC., 145 Witherspoon St., Princeton NJ 08542. (609)252-9405. Fax: (609)252-1949. E-mail: marzena@bellatlantic.net. Website: www.marlenaagency.com. Commercial illustration represenative. Estab. 1990. Member of Society of Illustrators. Represents 25 illustrators. Staff includes Marlena Torzecka, Greta T'Jonck, Ella Lupo. Currently open to illustrators seeking representation. Open to both new and established illustrators. Submission guidelines available for #10 SASE.

Handles: Illustration.

Recent Sales: *Pebble Soup*, by Marc Monqeau (Rigby); *Sees Behind Trees*, by Linda Helton (Harcourt Brace & Company); *New Orleans band*, by Marc Monqeau (Scott Foresman); and *My cat*, by Linda Helton (Scholastic). Represents Marc Mongeau, Gerard Dubois, Linda Helton, Cyril Cabry, Martin Jarrie, Serge Bloch and Ferrucio Sardella.

Terms: Exclusive representation required. Offers written contract. Advertising costs are split: 70% paid by illustrator; 30% paid by rep. Requires printed portfolios, transparencies, direct mail piece (such as postcards) printed samples. Advertises in *Picturebook*, *American Showcase*, *Creative Black Book*, *Workbook*.

How to Contact: For first contact, send tearsheets, photocopies. Responds only if interested. Drop off or mail portfolio, photocopies. Portfolio should include tearsheets, photocopies. Finds illustrators through queries/solicitations, magazines and graphic design.

Tips: "Be creative and persistent."

NACHREINER BOIE ART FACTORY, 925 Elm Grove Rd., Elm Grove WI 53122. (262)785-1940. Fax: (262)785-1611. E-mail: nbart@execpc.com. Website: www.expecpc.com/artfactory. **Contact:** Tom Stocki. Commercial illustration representative. Estab. 1978. Represents 9 illustrators. 10% of artwork handled is children's book illustration. Currently open to illustrators seeking representation. Open to both new and established illustrators.

Handles: Illustration.

Recent Sales: Represents Tom Buchs, Tom Nachreiner, Todd Dakins, Linda Godfrey, Larry Mikec, Bill Scott, Amanda Aquino, Gary Shea.

Terms: Rep receives 25-30% commission. Offers written contract. Advertising costs are split: 75% paid by illustrators; 25% paid by rep. "We try to mail samples of all our illustrators at one time and we try to update our website; so we ask the illustrators to keep up with new samples." Advertises in *Picturebook*, *Workbook*.

How to Contact: For first contact, send query letter, tearsheets. Responds only if interested. Call to schedule an appointment. Portfolio should include tearsheets. Finds illustrators through queries/solicitations.

Tips: "Have a unique style."

 REMEN-WILLIS DESIGN GROUP, 2964 Colton Rd., Pebble Beach CA 93953. (831)655-1407. Fax: (831)655-1408. E-mail: AnnRWillis@aol. Website: www.Picture-book.com. Childrens' book illustration trade/education. Estab. 1984. Member of SCBWI. Represents 15 illustrators. 100% of artwork handled is children's book illustration.
Recent Sales: List of illustrators represented available upon request.
Terms: Rep receives 20% commission. Offers written contract. Advertising costs are split: 50% paid by illustrators; 50% paid by rep. Illustrator must provide small precise portfolio for promotion. Advertises in *Picturebook, Workbook.*
How to Contact: For first contact, send tearsheets, photocopies. Responds in 1 week. To set up an interview or portfolio review mail portfolio. Portfolio should include tearsheets, photocopies.
Tips: Send samples of only the type of work you are interested in receiving. Check out rep's forte first.

RENAISSANCE HOUSE, 9400 Lloydcrest Dr., Beverly Hills CA 90210. (800)547-5113. Fax: (310)358-5282. E-mail: info@renaissancehouse.net. Website: www.renaissancehouse.net. **Contact:** Raquel Benatar. Children's, educational, travel and advertising rep. Estab. 1991. Represents 60 illustrators. 95% of artwork handled is children's book illustration. Currently open to illustrators seeking representation. Open to both new and established illustrators.
Handles: Illustration, photography.
Recent Sales: Pablo Torrecilla (Hampton Brown); Ana Lopez (Scholastic); Ruth Araceli (Houghton Mifflin). Represents Vivi Escriva, Ruth Araceli, Pablo Torrecilla, Adrian Rubio, Ana Lopez.
Terms: Rep receives 40% commission. Exclusive representation required. Illustrators must provide scans of illustrations. Advertises in *Picturebook, Directory of Illustration,* on website and *Catalog of Illustrators* (Spanish language).
How to Contact: For first contact send tearsheets. Responds in 2 weeks. Call to schedule an appointment or e-mail. Portfolio should include tearsheets. Finds illustrators through recommendations from others, conferences.

S.I. INTERNATIONAL, 43 E. 19th St., New York NY 10003. (212)254-4996. Fax: (212)995-0911. E-mail: info@si-i.com. Website: www.si-i.com. Commercial illustration representative. Estab. 1983. Member of SPAR, Graphic Artists Guild. Represents 50 illustrators. Specializes in license characters, educational publishing and children's illustration, digital art and design, mass market paperbacks. Markets include design firms; publishing/books; sales/promotion firms; licensing firms; digital art and design firms.
Handles: Illustration. Looking for artists "who have the ability to do children's illustration and to do license characters either digitally or "reflectively."
Terms: Rep receives 25-30% commission. Advertising costs are split: 70% paid by talent; 30% paid by representative. "Contact agency for details. Must have mailer." Advertises in *Picturebook.*
How to Contact: For first contact, send query letter, tearsheets. Reports in 3 weeks. After initial contact, write for appointment to show portfolio of tearsheets, slides.

✅ GWEN WALTERS ARTIST REPRESENTATIVE, 269 Ridgeview Dr., Palm Beach FL 33480. (781)235-8658. E-mail: artincgw@aol. Website: www.gwenWaltersartrep.com. Commercial illustration representative. Estab. 1976. Represents 18 illustrators. 90% of artwork handled is children's book illustration. Currently open to illustrators seeking representation. Looking for established illustrators only.
Handles: Illustration.
Recent Sales: Sells to "All major book publishers."
Terms: Rep receives 30% commission. Artist needs to supply all promo material. Offers written contract. Advertising costs are split: 70% paid by illustrator; 30% paid by rep. Advertises in *Picturebook, RSVP, Directory of Illustration.*
How to Contact: For first contact, send tearsheets. Responds only if interested. Finds illustrators through recommendations from others.
Tips: "Go out and get some first-hand experience. Learn to tell yourself to understand the way the market works."

● **SPECIAL COMMENTS** by the editors of *Children's Writer's & Illustrator's Market* are set off by a bullet.

N: WILKINSON STUDIOS, LLC, 901 W. Jackson Blvd., Suite 201, Chicago IL 60607. (312)226-0007. Fax: (312)226-0404. E-mail: chris@wilkinsonstudios.com. Website: www.wilkinsonstudios.com. Illustrator's representative for publishing. Estab. 1999. Member of SCBWI, Graphic Artists Guild. Represents more than 50 illustrators. 100% of artwork handled is children's book illustrtion. Staff includes Christine Wilkinson, president; Lisa O'Hara, vice president; and support staff including project managers, image specialists and artist/client relations. Currently open to illustrators seeking representation. Open to both new and established illustrators.

Handles: Illustration.

Terms: Standard commission "within industry standards." Marketing costs "are assessed on an annual basis and split between artist and agent." Exclusive representation required within the publishing industry. "We also work with artists on a project-by-project basis." Offers written contract. "We work with artists to develop promotional pieces and portfolios. Advertises in *Picturebook*, *Directory of Illustration*.

How to Contact: For first contact, send tearsheets, photocopies, SASE or e-mail. Responds only if interested. Portfolio should include tearsheets, photocopies. Finds illustrators through recommendations from others, queries/solicitations, conferences.

Tips: "Sending samples that are appropriate for the children's trade and educational market including children in typical situations, and a variety of ethnicities. Animals, more complex scenes, and character continuity are also considered."

N: DEBORAH WOLFE LTD., 731 N. 24th St., Philadelphia PA 19130. (215)232-6666. Fax: (215)232-6585. E-mail: dwolfetd@artistrep.com. Website: www.illustrationOnline.biz. **Contact:** Deborah Wolfe. Commercial illustration representative. Estab. 1978. Member of Graphic Artist Guild. Represents 30 illustrators. Currently open to illustrators seeking representation.

Handles: Illustration.

Terms: Rep receives 25% commission. Exclusive representation required. Offers written contract. Advertising costs are split: 75% paid by illustrators; 25% paid by rep. Advertises in *Picturebook*, *American Showcase*, *Directory of Illustration*, *The Workbook*.

How to Contact: Responds in 2 weeks. Portfolio should include "anything except originals." Finds illustrators through queries/solicitations.

Clubs & Organizations

Contacts made through organizations such as the ones listed in this section can be quite beneficial for children's writers and illustrators. Professional organizations provide numerous educational, business and legal services in the form of newsletters, workshops or seminars. Organizations can provide tips about how to be a more successful writer or artist, as well as what types of business records to keep, health and life insurance coverage to carry and competitions to consider.

An added benefit of belonging to an organization is the opportunity to network with those who have similar interests, creating a support system. As in any business, knowing the right people can often help your career, and important contacts can be made through your peers. Membership in a writer's or artist's organization also shows publishers you're serious about your craft. This provides no guarantee your work will be published, but it gives you an added dimension of credibility and professionalism.

Some of the organizations listed here welcome anyone with an interest, while others are only open to published writers and professional artists. Organizations such as the Society of Children's Book Writers and Illustrators (SCBWI, www.scbwi.org) have varying levels of membership. SCBWI offers associate membership to those with no publishing credits, and full membership to those who have had work for children published. International organizations such as SCBWI also have regional chapters throughout the U.S. and the world. Write or call for more information regarding any group that sounds interesting, or check the websites of the many organizations that list them. Be sure to get information about local chapters, membership qualifications and services offered.

Information on organizations listed in the previous edition but not included in this edition of *Children's Writer's & Illustrator's Market* may be found in the General Index.

AMERICAN ALLIANCE FOR THEATRE & EDUCATION, Theatre Department, Arizona State University, Box 872002, Tempe AZ 85287-2002. (480)965-6064. Fax: (480)965-5351. E-mail: aate.info@asu.edu. Website: www.aate.com. **Administrative Director:** Christy M. Taylor. Purpose of organization: to promote standards of excellence in theatre and drama education. "We achieve this by assimilating quality practices in theater and theater education, connecting artists, educators, researchers and scholars with each other, and by providing opportunities for our members to learn, exchange and diversify their work, their audiences and their perspectives." Membership cost: $110 annually for individual in US and Canada, $160 annually for organization, $60 annually for students, $70 annually for retired people; add $30 outside Canada and US. Annual conference. Newsletter published quarterly (on website only). Contests held for unpublished play reading project and annual awards in various categories. Awards plaque and stickers for published playbooks. Publishes list of unpublished plays deemed worthy of performance in newsletter and press release and staged readings at conference.
How to Contact/Writers: Manuscripts should be 8-10 pages, or 2,000 words. Manuscripts may include lesson plans, interviews, Coda Essays, and reviews of computer software, books, and plays (as scripts or in performance). A three-sentence biographical statement should also be included with a SASE.

AMERICAN SCREENWRITERS ASSOCIATION, 269 Beverly Dr., Suite 2600, Beverly Hills CA 90212-3807. Phone/fax: (866)265-9091. Sponsors annual Selling to Hollywood scriptwriting conference in the Los Angeles area each August.

AMERICAN SOCIETY OF JOURNALISTS AND AUTHORS, 1501 Broadway, New York NY 10036. E-mail: staff@asja.org. Website: www.asja.org. **Executive Director:** Brett Harvey. Qualifications for membership: "Need to be a professional nonfiction writer. Refer to website for further qualifictions."

Membership cost: Application fee—$25; annual dues—$195. Group sponsors national conferences; monthly workshops in New York City. Workshops/conferences open to nonmembers. Publishes a newsletter for members that provides confidential information for nonfiction writers.

ARIZONA AUTHORS ASSOCIATION, P.O. Box 87857, Phoenix AZ 85080-7857. Fax: (623)780-0468. E-mail: info@azauthors.com. Website: www.azauthors.com. **President:** Vijaya Schartz. Purpose of organization: to offer professional, educational and social opportunities to writers and authors, and serve as a network. Members must be authors, writers working toward publication, agents, publishers, publicists, printers, illustrators, etc. Membership cost: $45/year writers; $30/year students; $60/year other professionals in publishing industry. Holds regular workshops and meetings. Publishes bimonthly newsletter and Arizona Literary Magazine. Sponsors Annual Literary Contest in poetry, essays, short stories, novels, and published books with cash prizes and awards bestowed at a public banquet in Phoenix. Winning entries are also published or advertised in the *Arizona Literary Magazine*. Send SASE or view website for guidelines.

ASSITEJ/USA, % Steve Bianchi, 724 Second Ave. S., Nashville TN 37210. (615)254-5719. Fax: (615)254-3255. E-mail: usassitej@aol.com. Website: www.assitej-usa.org. Purpose of organization: to promote theater for children and young people by linking professional theaters and artists together; sponsoring national, international and regional conferences and providing publications and information. Also serves as US Center for International Association of Theatre for Children and Young People. Different levels of membership include: organizations, individuals, students, retirees, libraries. *TYA Today* includes original articles, reviews and works of criticism and theory, all of interest to theater practitioners (included with membership). Publishes journal that focuses on information on field in US and abroad.

THE AUTHORS GUILD, 31 E. 28th St., 10th Floor, New York NY 10016. (212)563-5904. Fax: (212)564-8363. E-mail: staff@authorsguild.org. Website: www.authorsguild.org. **Executive Director:** Paul Aiken. Purpose of organization: to offer services and materials intended to help authors with the business and legal aspects of their work, including contract problems, copyright matters, freedom of expression and taxation. Guild has 8,000 members. Qualifications for membership: Must be book author published by an established American publisher within 7 years or any author who has had 3 works (fiction or nonfiction) published by a magazine or magazines of general circulation in the last 18 months. Associate membership also available. Annual dues: $90. Different levels of membership include: associate membership with all rights except voting available to an author who has a firm contract offer or is currently negotiating a royalty contract from an established American publisher. "The Guild offers free contract reviews to its members. The Guild conducts several symposia each year at which experts provide information, offer advice and answer questions on subjects of interest and concern to authors. Typical subjects have been the rights of privacy and publicity, libel, wills and estates, taxation, copyright, editors and editing, the art of interviewing, standards of criticism and book reviewing. Transcripts of these symposia are published and circulated to members. The *Authors Guild Bulletin*, a quarterly journal, contains articles on matters of interest to writers, reports of Guild activities, contract surveys, advice on problem clauses in contracts, transcripts of Guild and League symposia and information on a variety of professional topics. Subscription included in the cost of the annual dues."

⚹ ⚹ CANADIAN SOCIETY OF CHILDREN'S AUTHORS, ILLUSTRATORS AND PER-FORMERS, (CANSCAIP), Northern District Library, Lower Level, 40 Orchard View Blvd., Toronto, Ontario M4R 1B9 Canada. (416)515-1559. Fax: (416)515-7022. E-mail: office@canscaip.org. Website: www.cansaip.org. **Office Manager:** Lena Coakley. Purpose of organization: development of Canadian children's culture and support for authors, illustrators and performers working in this field. Qualifications for membership: Members—professionals who have been published (not self-published) or have paid public performances/records/tapes to their credit. Friends—share interest in field of children's culture. Membership cost: $60 (members dues), $25 (friends dues), $30 (institution dues). Sponsors workshops/conferences. Publishes newsletter: includes profiles of members; news round-up of members' activities countrywide; market news; news on awards, grants, etc; columns related to professional concerns.

LEWIS CARROLL SOCIETY OF NORTH AMERICA, P.O. Box 204, Napa CA 94559. E-mail: hedgehog@napanet.net. Website: www.lewiscarroll.org/lcsna.html. **Secretary:** Cindy Watter. "We are an organization of Carroll admirers of all ages and interests and a center for Carroll studies." Qualifications for membership: "An interest in Lewis Carroll and a simple love for Alice (or even the Snark)." Membership cost: $20/year. There is also a contributing membership of $50. Publishes a quarterly newsletter.

THE CHILDREN'S BOOK COUNCIL, INC., 12 W. 37th St., 2nd Floor, New York NY 10018. (212)966-1990. Fax: (212)966-2073. E-mail: info@cbcbooks.org. Website: www.cbcbooks.org. **President:**

Paula Quint. Purpose of organization: "A nonprofit trade association of children's and young adult publishers and packagers, CBC promotes the enjoyment of books for children and young adults and works with national and international organizations to that end. The CBC has sponsored National Children's Book Week since 1945 and Young People's Poetry Week since 1999." Qualifications for membership: US trade publishers and packagers of children's and young adult books and related literary materials are eligible for membership. Publishers wishing to join should e-mail membership@cbcbooks.org or contact the CBC for dues information." Sponsors workshops and seminars. Publishes a newsletter with articles about children's books and publishing and listings of free or inexpensive materials available from member publishers. Individuals wishing to receive mailings from the CBC (semi-annual newsletter *CBC Features* with articles of interest to people working with children and books and materials brochures) may be placed on CBC's mailing list for a one-time-only fee of $60. Sells reading encouragement graphics and informational materials suitable for libraries, teachers, booksellers, parents, and others working with children.

FLORIDA FREELANCE WRITERS ASSOCIATION, Cassell Network of Writers, P.O. Box A, North Stratford NH 03590. (603)922-8338. Fax: (603)922-8339. E-mail: danakcnw@ncia.net. Website: www.writers-editors.com. **Executive Director:** Dana K. Cassell. Purpose of organization: To act as a link between Florida writers and buyers of the written word; to help writers run more effective communications businesses. Qualifications for membership: "None. We provide a variety of services and information, some for beginners and some for established pros." Membership cost: $90/year. Publishes a newsletter focusing on market news, business news, how-to tips for the serious writer. Non-member subscription: $39—does not include Florida section—includes national edition only. Annual *Directory of Florida Markets* included in FFWA newsletter section and on disk. Publishes annual *Guide to CNW/Florida Writers*, which is distributed to editors around the country. Sponsors contest: annual deadline March 15. Guidelines available fall of each year and on website. Categories: juvenile, adult nonfiction, adult fiction and poetry. Awards include cash for top prizes, certificate for others. Contest open to non-members.

GRAPHIC ARTISTS GUILD, 90 John St., Suite 403, New York NY 10038. (800)500-2672. E-mail: membership@gag.org. Website: www.gag.org. **Executive Director:** Steven Schubert, CAE. Purpose of organization: "to promote and protect the economic interests of member artists. It is committed to improving conditions for all creators of graphic arts and raising standards for the entire industry." Qualification for full membership: 50% of income derived from the creation of artwork. Associate members include those in allied fields, students and retirees. Initiation fee: $25. Full memberships $130, $175, $230, $290; student membership $55/year. Associate membership $140/year. Publishes *Graphic Artists Guild Handbook, Pricing and Ethical Guidelines* (free to members, $34.95 retail) and bimonthly *Guild News* (free to members, $12 to non-members). "The Guild UAW Local 3030 is a national union that embraces all creators of graphic arts intended for presentation as originals or reproductions at all levels of skill and expertise. The long-range goals of the Guild are: to educate graphic artists and their clients about ethical and fair business practices; to educate graphic artists about emerging trends and technologies impacting the industry; to offer programs and services that anticipate and respond to the needs of our members, helping them prosper and enhancing their health and security, to advocate for the interests of our members in the legislative, judicial and regulatory arenas; to assure that our members are recognized financially and professionally for the value they provide; to be responsible stewards for our members by building an organization that works efficiently on their behalf."

HORROR WRITERS ASSOCIATION, P.O. Box 50577, Palo Alto CA 94303. E-mail: hwa@horror.org. Website: www.horror.org. **Office Manager:** Nancy Etchemendy. Purpose of organization: To encourage pubic interest in horror and dark fantasy and to provide networking and career tools for members. Qualifications for membership: Anyone who can demonstrate a serious interest in horror may join as an affiliate. Any non-writing professional in the horror field may join as an associate. (Booksellers, editors, agents, librarians, etc.) To qualify for full active membership, you must be a published, professional writer of horror. Open to students as affiliates, if unpublished in professional venues. Membership cost: $55 annually in North America; $65 annually elsewhere. Holds annual Stoker Awards Weekend and HWA Business Meet-

FOR EXPLANATIONS OF THESE SYMBOLS,
SEE THE INSIDE FRONT AND BACK COVERS OF THIS BOOK

ing. Publishes monthly newsletter focusing on market news, industry news, HWA business for members. Sponsors awards. We give the Bram Stoker Awards for superior achievement in horror annually. Awards include a handmade Stoker trophy designed by sculptor Stephen Kirk. Awards open to non-members.

INTERNATIONAL READING ASSOCIATION, 800 Barksdale Rd., Newark DE 19714-8139. (302)731-1600 ext. 293. Fax: (302)731-1057. E-mail: jbutler@reading.org. Website: www.reading.org. **Public Information Associate:** Janet Butler. Purpose of organization: "Formed in 1956, the International Reading Association seeks to promote high levels of literacy for all by improving the quality of reading instruction through studying the reading process and teaching techniques; serving as a clearinghouse for the dissemination of reading research through conferences, journals, and other publications; and actively encouraging the lifetime reading habit. Its goals include professional development; enhance and improve professional development, advocacy, partnerships, research and global literacy development. **Open to students.** Basic membership: $30. Sponsors annual convention. Publishes a newsletter called "Reading Today." Sponsors a number of awards and fellowships. Visit the IRA website for more information on membership, conventions and awards.

THE INTERNATIONAL WOMEN'S WRITING GUILD, P.O. Box 810, Gracie Station, New York NY 10028. (212)737-7536. **Executive Director and Founder:** Hannelore Hahn. IWWG is "a network for the personal and professional empowerment of women through writing." Qualifications: open to any woman connected to the written word regardless of professional portfolio. Membership cost: $45 annually. "IWWG sponsors several annual conferences a year in all areas of the US. The major conference is held in August of each year at Skidmore College in Saratoga Springs NY. It is a week-long conference attracting over 500 women internationally." Also publishes a 32-page newsletter, *Network*, 6 times/year; offers health insurance at group rates, referrals to literary agents.

⊞ LITERARY MANAGERS AND DRAMATURGS OF THE AMERICAS, P.O. Box 728, Village Station, New York NY 10014. E-mail: lmda@lmda,org. Website: www.lmda.org. LMDA is a not-for-profit service organization for the professions of literary management and dramaturgy. Student Membership: $20/ year. Open to students in dramaturgy, performing arts and literature programs, or related disciplines. Proof of student status required. Includes national conference, New Dramaturg activities, local symposia, job phone and select membership meetings. Active Membership: $45/year. Open to full-time and part-time professionals working in the fields of literary management and dramaturgy. All privileges and services including voting rights and eligibility for office. Associate Membership: $35/year. Open to all performing arts professionals and academics, as well as others interested in the field. Includes national conference, local symposia and select membership meetings. Institutional Membership: $100/year. Open to theaters, universities, and other organizations. Includes all privileges and services except voting rights and eligibility for office. Publishes a newsletter featuring articles on literary management, dramaturgy, LMDA program updates and other articles of interest.

THE NATIONAL LEAGUE OF AMERICAN PEN WOMEN, 1300 17th St. N.W., Washington D.C. 20036-1973. (202)785-1997. Fax: (202)452-6868. E-mail: nlapw1@juno.com. Website: members.aol.com/ penwomen/pen.htm. **President:** Dr. Bernice Strand Reid. Purpose of organization: to promote professional work in art, letters, and music since 1897. Qualifications for membership: An applicant must show "proof of sale" in each chosen category—art, letters, and music. Membership cost: $40 ($10 processing fee and $30 National dues); Annual fees—$30 plus Branch/State dues. Different levels of membership include: Active, Associate, International Affiliate, Members-at-Large, Honorary Members (in one or more of the following classifications: Art, Letters, and Music). Holds workshops/conferences. Publishes magazine 6 times a year titled *The Pen Woman*. Sponsors various contests in areas of Art, Letters, and Music. Awards made at Biennial Convention. Biannual scholarships awarded to non-Pen Women for mature women. Awards include cash prizes—up to $1,000. Specialized contests open to non-members.

PEN AMERICAN CENTER, 568 Broadway, New York NY 10012. (212)334-1660. Fax: (212)334-2181. E-mail: jm@pen.org. Website: www.pen.org. Purpose of organization: "To foster understanding among men and women of letters in all countries. International PEN is the only worldwide organization of writers and the chief voice of the literary community. Members of PEN work for freedom of expression wherever it has been endangered." Qualifications for membership: "The standard qualification for a writer to join PEN is that he or she must have published, in the United States, two or more books of a literary character, or one book generally acclaimed to be of exceptional distinction. Editors who have demonstrated commitment to excellence in their profession (generally construed as five years' service in book editing), translators who have published at least two book-length literary translations, and playwrights whose works have been professionally produced, are eligible for membership." An application form is available upon request from PEN Headquarters in New York. Candidates for membership should be nominated by 2 current members of PEN. Inquiries about membership should be directed to the PEN Membership Committee. Friends of PEN is also open to writers who may not yet meet the general PEN membership requirements. PEN sponsors public events at PEN Headquarters in New York, and at the branch offices in Boston, Chicago, New Orleans, San Francisco and Portland, Oregon. They include tributes by contemporary writers to classic American writers, dialogues with visiting foreign writers, symposia that bring public attention to problems of censorship and that address current issues of writing in the United States, and readings that introduce beginning writers to the public. PEN's wide variety of literary programming reflects current literary interests and provides informal occasions for writers to meet each other and to welcome those with an interest in literature. Events are all open to the public and are usually free of charge. The Children's Book Authors' Committee sponsors biannual public events focusing on the art of writing for children and young adults and on the diversity of literature for juvenile readers. The PEN/Phyllis Naylor Working Writer Fellowship was established in 2001 to assist a North American author of fiction for children or young adults. Pamphlets and brochures all free upon request. Sponsors several competitions per year. Monetary awards range from $2,000-20,000.

PUPPETEERS OF AMERICA, INC., P.O. Box 29417, Parma OH 44129-0417. (888)568-6235. Fax: (440)843-7867. E-mail: pofajoin@aol.com. Website: www.puppeteers.org. **Membership Officer:** Joyce and Chuck Berty. Purpose of organization: to promote the art of puppetry as a means of communications and as a performing art. Qualifications for membership: interest in the art form. Membership cost: single adult, $40; youth member, $20 (6-17 years of age); full-time college student, $25; retiree, $25 (65 years of age); family, $60; couple, $50. Membership includes a bimonthly newsletter (*Playboard*). Discounts for workshops/conferences, access to the Audio Visual Library & Consultants in many areas of Puppetry. *The Puppetry Journal*, a quarterly periodical, provides news about puppeteers, puppet theaters, exhibitions, touring companies, technical tips, new products, new books, films, television, and events sponsored by the Chartered Guilds in each of the 8 P of A regions. *The Puppetry Journal* is the only publication in the United States dedicated to puppetry in the United States. Subscription: $35 (libraries only). The Puppeteers of America sponsors an annual National Day of Puppetry the last Saturday in April.

SOCIETY OF CHILDREN'S BOOK WRITERS AND ILLUSTRATORS, 8271 Beverly Blvd., Los Angeles CA 90048. (323)782-1010. E-mail: info@scbwi.org (autoresponse). Website: www.scbwi.org. **President:** Stephen Mooser. Executive Director: Lin Oliver. Chairperson, Board of Directors: Sue Alexander. Purpose of organization: to assist writers and illustrators working or interested in the field. Qualifications for membership: an interest in children's literature and illustration. Membership cost: $50/year. Plus one time $10 initiation fee. Different levels of membership include: full membership—published authors/illustrators; associate membership—unpublished writers/illustrators. Holds 100 events (workshops/conferences) worldwide each year. Open to nonmembers. Publishes a newsletter focusing on writing and illustrating children's books. Sponsors grants for writers and illustrators who are members.

SOCIETY OF MIDLAND AUTHORS, % SMA, P.O. 10419, Chicago IL 60610-0419. E-mail: DCWN 66@aol.com. Website: www.midlandauthors.com. **Membership Secretary:** David Cowan. Purpose of organization: create closer association among writers of the Middle West; stimulate creative literary effort; maintain collection of members' works; encourage interest in reading and literature by cooperating with other educational and cultural agencies. Qualifications for membership: author or co-author of a book demonstrating literary style and published by a recognized publisher and be identified through residence with Illinois, Indiana, Iowa, Kansas, Michigan, Minnesota, Missouri, Nebraska, North Dakota, Ohio, South Dakota or Wisconsin. Membership cost: $35/year dues. Different levels of membership include: regular—published book authors; associate, nonvoting—not published as above but having some connection with literature, such as librarians, teachers, publishers and editors. Program meetings at Cliff Dwellers, 200 S. Michigan Ave., Borg-Warner Bldg. Chicago, held 5 times a year, featuring authors, publishers, editors or the like individually or on panels. Usually second Tuesday of October, November, February, March and April. Also holds annual awards dinner at Cliff Dwellers, 200 S. Michigan Ave., Chicago, in May. Publishes a newsletter focusing on news of members and general items of interest to writers. Non-member subscription: $5. Sponsors contests. "Annual awards in six categories, given at annual dinner in May. Monetary awards for books published which premiered professionally in previous calendar year. Send SASE to

---

VISIT OUR WEBSITES at www.writersmarket.com and www.writersdigest.com, for helpful articles, hot new markets, daily market updates, writers' guidelines and much more.

contact person for details." Categories include adult fiction, adult nonfiction, juvenile fiction, juvenile nonfiction, poetry, biography. No picture books. Contest open to non-members. Deadline for contest: January 30.

SOCIETY OF SOUTHWESTERN AUTHORS, P.O. Box 30355, Tucson AZ 85751-0355. Fax: (520)296-5562. E-mail: wporter202@aol.com. Website: www.azstarnet.com/nonprofit/ssa. **President:** Penny Porter. Purpose of organization: to promote fellowship among members of the writing profession, to recognize members' achievements, to stimulate further achievement, and to assist persons seeking to become professional writers. Qualifications for membership: proof of publication of a book, articles, TV screenplay, etc. Membership cost: $25 initiation plus $20/year dues. The Society of Southwestern Authors has annual 2-day Writers' Conference held the next to last weekend in January (check website for updated information). Publishes a bimonthly newsletter, *The Write Word*, about members' activities, achievements, and up to the minute trends in publishing and marketing. Yearly writing contest open to all writers. Applications are available in September. Send SASE to the P.O. Box, Attn: Contest.

☑ **TEXT AND ACADEMIC AUTHORS ASSOCIATION**, University of South Florida, 140 Seventh Ave., St. Petersburg FL 33701. (727)553-1195. E-mail: taa@bayflash.stpt.usf.edu. Website: www.taao nline.net. **President:** Michael Sullivan. Purpose of organization: to address the professional concerns of text and academic authors, to protect the interests of creators of intellectual property at all levels, and support efforts to enforce copyright protection. Qualifications for membership: all authors and prospective authors are welcome. Membership cost: $30 first year; $75 per year following years. Workshops/conferences: June each year. Newsletter focuses on all areas of interest to text authors.

WESTERN WRITERS OF AMERICA, INC., 1012 Fair St., Franklin TN 37064-2718. (615)791-1444. Fax: (615)791-1444. E-mail: candywwa@aol.com or tncrutch@aol.com. Website: www.westernwriters.o rg. **Secretary/Treasurer:** James A. Crutchfield. **Open to students.** Purpose of organization: to further all types of literature that pertains to the American West. Membership requirements: must be a *published* author of Western material. Membership cost: $75/year ($90 foreign). Different levels of membership include: Active and Associate—the two vary upon number of books published. Holds annual conference. The 2003 conference will be held in Helena, MT. Publishes bimonthly magazine focusing on western literature, market trends, book reviews, news of members, etc. Non-members may subscribe for $30 ($50 foreign). Sponsors contests. Spur awards given annually for a variety of types of writing. Awards include plaque, certificate, publicity. Contest open to nonmembers.

🅽 **WRITERS OF KERN**, P.O. Box 6694, Bakersfield CA 93386-6694. (661)399-0423. Open to published writers and any person interested in writing. Dues: $45/year, $20 for students. Types of memberships: professional, writers with published work; associate—writers working toward publication, affiliate—beginners and students. Monthly meetings held on the third Saturday of every month. Bi- or tri-annual writers' workshops, with speakers who are authors, agents, etc., on topics pertaining to writing; critique groups for several fiction genres, nonfiction, journalism and screenwriting which meet bimonthly. Members receive a monthly newsletter with marketing tips, conferences and contests; access to club library; discount to annual CWC conference.

Conferences & Workshops

Writers and illustrators eager to expand their knowledge of the children's publishing industry should consider attending one of the many conferences and workshops held each year. Whether you're a novice or seasoned professional, conferences and workshops are great places to pick up information on a variety of topics and network with experts in the publishing industry, as well as your peers.

Listings in this section provide details about what conference and workshop courses are offered, where and when they are held, and the costs. Some of the national writing and art organizations also offer regional workshops throughout the year. Write or call for information.

Writers can find listings of more than 1,200 conferences (searchable by type, location and date) at The Writer's Digest/Shaw Guides Directory to Writers' Conferences, Seminars and Workshops—www.writersdigest.com/conferences.

Members of the Society of Children's Book Writers and Illustrators can find information on conferences in national and local SCBWI newsletters. Nonmembers may attend SCBWI events as well. SCBWI conferences are listed in the beginning of this section under a separate subheading. For information on SCBWI's annual national conferences, contact them at (323)782-1010 or check their website for a complete calendar of national and regional events (www.scbwi.org).

Information on conferences listed in the previous edition but not this edition of *Children's Writer's & Illustrator's Market* may be found in the General Index.

SCBWI CONFERENCES

SCBWI; ANNUAL CONFERENCES ON WRITING AND ILLUSTRATING FOR CHILDREN, 8271 Beverly Blvd., Los Angeles CA 90048. (323)782-1010. Fax: (323)782-1892. E-mail: scbwi@scbwi.org. Website: www.scbwi.org. **Conference Director:** Lin Oliver. Writer and illustrator workshops geared toward all levels. **Open to students.** Covers all aspects of children's book and magazine publishing—the novel, illustration techniques, marketing, etc. Annual conferences held in August in Los Angeles and in New York in February. Write for more information or visit website.

N SCBWI—ARIZONA; ANNUAL EDITORS DAY, (formerly Society of Children's Book Writers and Illustrators—Arizona Writers Day), 735 W. Pine St., Tucson AZ 85704. (520)544-2650. E-mail: desertmorn@aol.com. Regional Advisor: Dawn Dixon. **Open to Students.** Editors are invited to speak to book and illustration needs. Workshop held in Phoenix. Usually includes 2-3 book publishers, Q&A sessions included. Registration limited to 100. Usually has 75-85 participants. Cost of workshop: $80-90. Information available on SCBWI website; registration begins in February.

N SCBWI—ARIZONA; WORKING WRITERS RETREAT, 735 W. Pine St., Tucson AZ. (520)544-2650. E-mail: desertmorn@aol.com. **Regional Advisor:** Dawn Dixon. **Open to SCBWI members.** Annual fall hands-on workshop for writers with works-in-progress. Workshop held in Prescott. Presenters include 2-3 editors. Q&A sessions included. Registration limited to 25. Cost of workshop: $265-295. Information available on SCBWI website; registration begins in August.

SCBWI—CANADA; ANNUAL CONFERENCE, 130 Wren St., Dunrobin, Ontario K0A 1T0 Canada. E-mail: webinfo@SCBWIcanada.org or noreen@SCBWIcanada.org. Website: www.scbwicanada.org. **Contact:** Lizann Flatt or Noreen Violetta. Writer and illustrator conference geared toward all levels. Offers speakers forums, book sale, portfolio displays, one-on-one critiques and a silent auction. Annual conference held in May. Write above address for brochure or e-mail for more information or visit website.

SCBWI—CAROLINAS; ANNUAL FALL CONFERENCE. (919)967-2549. Fax: (919)929-6643. E-mail: eld513@earthlink.net. **Contact:** Frances A. Davis, regional advisor. Most recent conference was held September 27-28, 2002 at the Village Inn in Clemmons, NC, and geared toward picture books, writing for middle grade, and young adults. Speakers included Paula Danziger, Harold Underdown (editor), and Scott Treimel (agent). Fee: $60 for SCBWI members, $65 for NCWN and SCWN members, and $70 for nonmembers. Critiques for writers, illustration portfolios displayed. Conference open to adult students.

SCBWI—FLORIDA CONFERENCE, 2158 Portland Ave., Wellington FL 33414. (561)798-4824. E-mail: barcafer@aol.com. **Florida Regional Advisor:** Barbara Casey. Writer and illustrator workshops geared toward beginner, intermediate, advanced and professional levels. Subjects to be announced. Workshop dates and location to be announced. Write or e-mail for more information.

SCBWI—HOFSTRA UNIVERSITY CHILDREN'S LITERATURE CONFERENCE, 250 Hofstra University, U.C.C.E., Hempstead NY 11549. (516)463-5016. Fax: (516)463-4833. E-mail: marionflomenhaft@hofstra.edu. Website: www.hofstra.edu/writers. **Writers/Illustrators Contact:** Marion Flomenhaft, director, Liberal Arts Studies. Writer and illustrator workshops geared toward all levels. Emphasizes: fiction, nonfiction, poetry, submission procedures, picture books. Workshops will be held April 12, 2003. Length of each session: 1 hour. Cost of workshop: approximately $80; includes 2 workshops, reception, lunch, 2 general sessions, and panel discussion with guest speakers and a critiquing of randomly selected first-manuscript pages submitted by registrants. Write for more information. Co-sponsored by Society of Children's Book Writers & Illustrators.

SCBWI—HOUSTON CONFERENCE, 7730 Highland Farms, Houston TX 77095. (281)855-9561. E-mail: phoebe5@pdq.net. Website: www.scbwi-houston.org. **Conference Co-Chair:** Melanie Chrismer. Writer and illustrator workshops geared toward all levels. Critiques available. Annual conference. "Writing Off into an Illustrated Sunset." Conference held October 31-November 3, 2003. Other Events: Editors "Open House held in early 2003. Indian Paintbrush Writing Retreat held May 1-4, 2003. For cost and information check website, event, or contact page.

SCBWI—INDIANA; SPRING & FALL WRITERS' AND ILLUSTRATORS' CONFERENCE, 934 Fayette St., Indianapolis IN 46202. E-mail: inscwbwi@hotmail.com. **Conference Director:** Sara Murray-Plumer. Writer and illustrator workshops geared toward all levels. Three conferences in April (Crowne Point, Indiana), June (Indianapolis Children's Museum), and September (Terre Haute, Indiana). Cost of workshop includes meal and workshops. Write or e-mail for more information.

N **SCBWI—IOWA CONFERENCE**, 1462 Olde Freeport Place, Bettendorf IA 52722-7001. (563)359-0337. Iowa SCBWI **Regional Advisor:** Connie Heckert. Writer workshops geared toward all levels. "Usually speakers include one to two acquiring book editors who discuss the needs of their publishing house and manuscripts that caught their attention. Also, we usually have several published Iowa authors discussing specific genres and/or topics like promotion, marketing, school visits, etc." Annual conference. Iowa has 1 or 2 conferences a year, usually in May and September or October. Cost of conference includes lunch and refreshments: usually about $60-75; less for SCBWI members. Individual critique costs $30 extra. Work must be submitted in advance.

✓ **SCBWI—METRO NEW YORK; PROFESSIONAL SERIES**, P.O. Box 646, New York NY 10116-0646. (718)937-6810, ext. 1. E-mail: scwi_metrony@yahoo.com. Website: www.scbwi.org/regions/nymetro. **Regional Advisors:** Vicky Shiefman and Nancy Lewis. Writer and illustrator workshops geared toward all levels. **Open to students.** The Metro New York Professional Series meets the second Tuesday of each month, from October to June, 7-9 p.m., at Teachers and Writers Collaborative, 5 Union Square West (14/15 streets), 7th floor. See website for details and registration information. Cost of workshop: $12 for SCBWI members; $15 for nonmembers. "We feature an informal, almost intimate evening with coffee, cookies, and top editors, art directors, agents, publicity and marketing people, librarians, reviewers and more."

SCBWI—MICHIGAN; ANNUAL RETREAT, E-mail: lannrhugh@provide.net or lisawtoo@yahoo.com. Website: www.kidbooklink.org. **Event Chair:** Lisa Wroble. Writer and illustrator workshops geared toward intermediate and advanced levels. Program focus: the craft of writing. Features peer facilitated critique groups, creativity, motivation and professional issues. Retreat held October 4-6, 2002 in Gull Lake (near Battle Creek and Kalamazoo). Registration limited. Cost of retreat: approximately $229 for members, $249 for nonmembers; includes meals, lodging, linens and tuition. Write or e-mail for additional information.

SCBWI—MIDSOUTH CONFERENCE, P.O. Box 120061, Nashville TN 37212. (615)646-4527 or (615)315-9683. E-mail: cmoonwriter@aol.com or jmamenta1@aol.com. **Conference Directors:** Candace Moonshower and Joanne Mamenta. Writer workshops geared toward all levels. Illustrator workshops geared toward beginner and intermediate levels. **Open to Students.** Previous workshop topics have included Monkey Girl: The History of a Manuscript, Illustraight Talk, All My Writing Secrets in 60 seconds, Promoting Yourself, A Beginner's Guide to Getting Published, Writing for the Older Child, Stone Soup: The Making of a Picture Book, Introduction to Magazine Illustration. There are also opportunities for ms and portfolio critiques, which may be formed at the conference. Conference held April 26, 2003. Speakers include working authors, illustrators, editors, and others. Cost of conference: $65 SCBWI members; $70 nonmembers; ms critiques extra. Manuscripts for critique must be typed, double-spaced, and submitted in advance with payment. Portfolios are brought to the conference, but reservations for critique time and payment must be made in advance.

SCBWI—MISSOURI; CHILDREN'S WRITER'S CONFERENCE, St. Charles County Community College, P.O. Box 76975, 103 CEAC, St. Peters MO 63376-0975. (314)213-8000 ext. 4108. E-mail: suebe@cyberedge.net. **SCBWI MO Regional Advisor:** Sue Bradford Edwards. Writer and illustrator conference geared toward all levels. **Open to students.** Speakers include editors, writers and other professionals, mainly from the Midwest. Topics vary from year to year, but each conference offers sessions for both writers and illustrators as well as for newcomers and published writers. Previous topics included: "What Happens When Your Manuscript is Accepted" by Dawn Weinstock, editor; "Writing—Hobby or Vocation?" by Chris Kelleher; "Mother Time Gives Advice: Perspectives from a 25 Year Veteran" by Judith Mathews, editor; "Don't Be a Starving Writer" by Vicki Berger Erwin, author; and "Words & Pictures: History in the Making," by author-illustrator Cheryl Harness. Annual conference held in early November. For exact date, see SCBWI website: www.SCBWI.org. Registration limited to 50-70. Cost of conference includes one day workshop (8 a.m. to 5 p.m.) plus lunch. Write for more information.

SCBWI—NEW JERSEY; ANNUAL SPRING CONFERENCE, E-mail: NewJerseySCBWI@hotmail.com. **New Jersey SCBWI Regional Advisor:** Susan Heyboer O'Keefe. Writer workshops geared toward beginner and intermediate levels. SCBWI members are preferred since this is a very limited enrollment. This conference brings in several editors from top houses to speak to small groups of about 10-12 on their editorial likes and dislikes, as well as their houses' general submissions procedures. In the daylong conference, attendees are able to sit in on three such sessions. The lunch break also includes a First Pages panel of all the editors commenting on a random selection, and after the conference, attendees who arranged and paid for it participate in a separate one-on-one critique with an editor. Conference traditionally held at Seton Hall University, South Orange, New Jersey. E-mail for more information or see www.scbwi.org/event.htm.

SCBWI—NEW MEXICO; FALL RETREAT. E-mail: Kelitchman@yahoo.com. Retreat held in October at Hummingbird Music Camp in the Jemez Mountains of New Mexico. E-mail for more information or check calendar on SCBWI's website (www.scbwi.org).

SCBWI—NEW YORK; CONFERENCE FOR CHILDREN'S BOOK ILLUSTRATORS & AUTHOR/ILLUSTRATORS, 32 Hillside Ave., Monsey NY 10952. (845)356-7273. **Conference Chair:** Frieda Gates. Held April 28, 2003. Registration limited to 80 portfolios shown out of 125 conferees. Portfolios are not judged—first come—first served. Cost of conference: with portfolio—$95, members, $100 others; without portfolio—$60 members, $70 others; $50 additional for 30-minute portfolio evaluation; $25 additional for 15-minute book dummy evaluation. Call to receive a flier. "In addition to an exciting program of speakers, this conference provides a unique opportunity for illustrators and author/illustrators to have their portfolios reviewed by scores of art buyers and agents from the publishing and allied industries. Art buyers admitted free. Our reputation for exhibiting high-quality work of both new and established children's book illustrators, plus the ease of examining such an abundance of portfolios, has resulted in a large number of productive contacts between buyers and illustrators."

MARKET CONDITIONS are constantly changing! If you're still using this book and it is 2004 or later, buy the newest edition of *Children's Writer's & Illustrator's Market* at your favorite bookstore or order directly from Writer's Digest Books (800)448-0915.

SCBWI—NORCAL (SAN FRANCISCO/SOUTH); RETREAT AT ASILOMAR. Website: www.sc bwinorca.org. **Regional Advisor:** Jim Averbeck. While we welcome "not-yet-published" writers and illustrators, lectures and workshops are geared toward professionals and those striving to become professional. Program topics cover aspects of writing or illustrating picture books to young adult novels. Past speakers include editors, art directors, published authors and illustrators. Annual conference, generally held last weekend in February; Friday evening through Sunday lunch. Registration limited to 100. Most rooms shared with one other person. Additional charge for single when available. Desks available in most rooms. All rooms have private baths. Conference center is set in wooded campus on Asilomar Beach in Pacific Grove, California. Approximate cost: $265 for SCBWI members, $315 for nonmembers; includes shared room, 6 meals, ice breaker party and all conference activities. Vegetarian meals available. One full scholarship is available to SCBWI members. Registration opens at the end of September and the conference sells out very quickly. A waiting list is formed. "Coming together for shared meals and activities builds a strong feeling of community among the speakers and conferees. For more information, including exact costs and dates visit our website in September."

SCBWI—OREGON CONFERENCES, E-mail: robink@rio.com. Website: http://users.rio.com/robink/ scbwi.html. **Regional Advisor:** Robin Koontz. Writer and illustrator workshops and presentations geared toward all levels. "We invite editors, agents, authors, illustrators and others in the business of writing and illustrating for children. They present lectures, workshops and critiques." Annual retreat and conference. Two events per year: Working Writers and Illustrators Retreat: Retreat held Thursday-Sunday the 2nd weekend in October. Cost of retreat: $200-350 (depending on length); includes double occupancy and all meals; Spring Conference: Held in the Portland area (1-day event in May); cost: about $60, includes continental breakfast and lunch. Registration limited to 100 for the conference and 50 for the retreat.

SCBWI—POCONO MOUNTAINS RETREAT, E-mail: arlnb52@yahoo.com or lkiernan@tacsol utions.com. Website: www.scbwiepa.org. **Co-Regional Advisors:** Arlette Braman and Laurie Krauss Kiernan. Workshop held April 4-6, 2003 at Sterling Inn, Sterling PA. Faculty addresses writing illustration, and publishing. Registration limited to 75. Cost of workshop: about $350; includes tuition, room and board. For information e-mail or visit website for registration materials.

SCBWI—ROCKY MOUNTAIN; 2002 EVENTS. Website: www.rmcscbwi.org/events.html. **Regional Advisor:** Phyllis Cahill. SCBWI Rocky Mountain chapter will offer these events in 2003: Spring Workshop, April 5, Golden, Colorado; Summer Retreat, July 18-20, Colorado Springs, Colorado; Fall Conference, September (date to be determined), Golden, Colorado. For more information check website.

SCBWI—SOUTHERN BREEZE; SPRINGMINGLE '03, P.O. Box 26282, Birmingham AL 35260. E-mail: joanbroerman@home.com. Website: members.home.net/southernbreeze. Regional Advisor: Joan Broerman. Writer and illustrator workshops geared toward intermediate, advanced and professional levels. **Open to college students.** All sessions pertain specifically to the production and support of quality children's literature. Annual conference held in one of the three states comprising the Southern Breeze region. Registration limited to 60. Cost of conference: $100 for members; $110 for nonmembers; includes Saturday lunch and Saturday banquet. Breakfast is complimentary for hotel guests. Pre-registration is necessary. Write for more information or visit our website. "Springmingle will be held in Gulf Shores, Alabama, February 22-24. Speakers include author Larry Dave Brimner, illustrator Karen Stormer Brooks, Paula Morrow (*Ladybug*, *Babybug*), Alison Keehn, (Barefoot Books)."

SCBWI—UTAH/SOUTHERN IDAHO, E-mail: utidscbwi@juno.com. Website: members.aol. com/kimorchid/utahscbw.htm. **Regional Advisor:** Cathi Chipman. Writer workshops geared toward all levels. Illustrator workshops geared toward beginners and intermediate. **Open to students.** Conference held March 21-22, 2003. Write or e-mail for more information.

SCBWI—VENTURA/SANTA BARBARA; FALL CONFERENCE, P.O. Box 941389, Simi Valley CA 93094-1389. (805)581-1906. E-mail: alexisinca@aol.com. Website: www.scbwisocal-org/calendar. **Regional Advisor:** Alexis O'Neill. Writers conference geared toward all levels. "We invite editors, authors and author/illustrators and agents. We have had speakers on the picture book, middle grade, YA, magazine and photo essay books. Fiction and nonfiction are covered." Conference held October 25, 2003. Scheduled at California Lutheran University in Thousand Oaks, California in cooperation with the School of Education. Cost of conference $65; includes all sessions and lunch. E-mail for more information.

SCBWI—VENTURA/SANTA BARBARA; PROFESSIONAL RETREAT FOR CHILDREN'S AUTHORS AND ILLUSTRATORS, P.O. Box 941389, Simi Valley CA 93094-1389.

(805)581-1906. E-mail: AlexisInCA@aol.com. Website: www.scbwisocal.org. Open to published children's authors and illustrators. Dates: March 7-9, 2003. Location: Historic Mission Santa Barbara. Focus: "Presenting Yourself: Coaching for School Visits and Public Appearances." Learn how to increase your income by sharpening your public presentations. Personal coaching in a nonthreatening atmosphere featured. Also includes how to use media effectively, create school-friendly supplemental materials, and develop successful PR packages. Write for information on fees.

SCBWI—WISCONSIN; FALL RETREAT FOR WORKING WRITERS, 15255 Turnberry Dr., Brookfield WI 53005. (262)783-4890. E-mail: aangel@aol.com. **Co-Regional Advisor:** Ann Angel. Writer and illustrator conference geared toward all levels. All our sessions pertain to children's writing/illustration. Faculty addresses writing/illustrating/publishing. Annual conference held October 3-5, 2003 in Racine, WI. Registration limited to 70. Bedrooms have desks/conference center has small rooms—can be used to draw/write. Program has free time scheduled in. Cost of conference: $285; includes program, meals, lodging. Write for more information. "We usually offer individual critique of manuscripts with faculty—$40 extra."

OTHER CONFERENCES

Many conferences and workshops included here focus on children's writing or illustrating and related business issues. Others appeal to a broader base of writers or artists, but still provide information that can be useful in creating material for children. Illustrators may be interested in painting and drawing workshops, for example, while writers can learn about techniques and meet editors and agents at general writing conferences. For more information visit the websites listed or contact conference coordinator.

AMERICAN CHRISTIAN WRITERS CONFERENCE, P.O. Box 110390, Nashville TN 37222-0390. 1(800)21-WRITE or (615)834-0450. Fax: (615)834-7736. E-mail: detroitwriters@aol.com. Website: www. ACWriters.com. **Director:** Reg Forder. Writer and illustrator workshops geared toward beginner, intermediate and advanced levels. Classes offered include: fiction, nonfiction, poetry, photography, music, etc. Workshops held in 3 dozen US cities. Call or write for a complete schedule of conferences. 75 minutes. Maximum class size: 30 (approximate). Cost of conference: $99, 1-day session; $169, 2-day session (discount given if paid 30 days in advance) includes tuition only.

[N] ANNUAL MIDWEST POETS AND WRITERS CONFERENCE, P.O. Box 23100, Detroit MI 48223. (313)897-2551. Fax: (248)557-2606. E-mail: detroitwriters@aol.com. Website: www.blackarts-literature.org. **Director:** Heather Buchanan. Writer and illustrator workshops geared toward beginner, intermediate and advanced levels. **Open to students.** Includes sessions on writing for children and writing for young adults. Annual conference. Conference usually held the last weekend of August or 1st weekend of September. Cost of workshop: $150 (early registration); $175 (late registration); includes admission to opening reception, admission to all workshops, closing ceremony. Write for more information. "Individual manuscript critiques available for additional fee; manuscript must be submitted prior to conference."

[N] AUTUMN AUTHORS' AFFAIR . . . A WRITER'S RENDEZVOUS, 1507 Burnham Ave., Calumet City IL 60409. (708)862-9797. E-mail: exchbook@aol.com. **President:** Nancy McCann. Writer workshops geared toward beginner, intermediate, advanced levels. **Open to students.** Sessions include children/teen/young adult writing, mysteries, romantic suspense, romance, nonfiction, etc. Annual workshop. Workshops held October 18-20, 2002. Cost of workshop: $75 for 1 day, $125 for weekend, includes meals, workshops, speeches, gifts. Write for more information.

BUTLER UNIVERSITY CHILDREN'S LITERATURE CONFERENCE, 4600 Sunset Drive, Indianapolis IN 46208. (317)940-9861. Fax: (317)940-9644. E-mail: nminnick@butler.edu. **Contact:** Norman Minnick. Writer and illustrator conference geared toward intermediate level. **Open to college students.** Annual conference held the last Saturday of the month of January each year. Includes sessions such as Creating the Children's Picture Book, and Nuts and Bolts for Beginning Writers. Registration limited to 350. Cost of conference: $85; includes meals, registration, 3 plenary addresses, 2 workshops, book signing, reception and conference bookstore. Write for more information. "The conference is geared toward three groups: teachers, librarians and writers/illustrators."

[N] CAPE COD WRITER'S CONFERENCE, Cape Cod Writer's Center, P.O. Box 186, Barnstable MA 02630. (508)375-0516. Fax: (508)362-2718. E-mail: ccwc@capecod.net. Website: www.capecod.net/

writers. Writer conference and workshops geared toward beginner, intermediate and professional levels. **Open to students.** "We hold a young writer's workshop at our annual conference each summer for writers ages 12-16. 40th annual conference held third week in August on Cape Cod. Cost of conference includes $60 to register; $90 first course. Other courses $80. Manuscript evaluations and faculty conferences available.

CAT WRITERS ASSOCIATION ANNUAL WRITERS CONFERENCE, 22841 Orchid Creek Lane, Lake Forest CA 92630. (949)454-1368. Fax: (949)454-0134. E-mail: franshaw1@juno.com. Website: www.catwriters.org. **President:** Amy D. Shojai. Writer workshops geared toward beginner, intermediate, advanced and professional levels. Illustrator workshops geared toward intermediate, advanced and professional levels. **Open to students.** Annual workshop. Workshop held in November. Cost of workshop: approximately $100 for nonmembers; includes 9-10 seminars, 2 receptions, 1 banquet, 1 breakfast, press pass to other events, interviews with editors and book signing/art sale event. Conference information becomes available in June/July prior to event, and is posted on the website (including registration material). Seminars held/co-sponsored with the Dog Writers Association (We often receive queries from publishers seeking illustrators or writers for particular book/article projects—these are passed on to CWA members).

☑ **CELEBRATION OF CHILDREN'S LITERATURE**, Montgomery College, 51 Mannakee St., Workforce Development and Continuing Education, Rockville MD 20850. (240)683-2589. Fax: (240)683-1890. E-mail: ssonner@mc.cc.md.us. **Senior Program Director:** Sandra Sonner. Writer and illustrator workshops offered in conjunction with Montgomery County Public Schools, Montgomery County Public Libraries, Children's Book Guild and other local organizations is geared toward all levels. **Open to students.** Past topics included The Publisher's Perspective, Successful Picture Book Design, The Oral Tradition in Children's Literature, The Best and Worst Children's Books, Websites for Children, The Pleasures of Nonfiction and The Book as Art. Annual workshop. Will be held April 26, 2003. Registration limited to 200. Art display facilities, continuing education classrooms and large auditorium. Cost of workshop: approximately $75; includes workshops, box lunch and coffee. Contact Montgomery College for more information.

CHATTANOOGA CONFERENCE ON SOUTHERN LITERATURE, P.O. Box 4203, Chattanooga TN 37405-0203. (423)267-1218. Fax: (423)267-1018. E-mail: srobinson@artsedcouncil.org. Website: www.artsedcouncil.org. **Executive Director:** Susan Robinson. **Open to students.** Conference is geared toward readers. No workshops are held. Biennial conference. Conference held April 24-26 2003. Registration limited to first 1,000 people. Cost of conference: $50. Write for more information. "The Chattanooga Conference on Southern Literature is a conference that celebrates literature of the South. Panel discussions, readings, music, food and art are featured."

[N] CHILDREN'S AUTHORS' BOOTCAMP, P.O. Box 231, Allenspark CO 80510 (303)747-1014. E-mail: CABootcamp@aol.com. Website: www.WeMakeWriters.com. **Contact:** Linda Arms White. Writer workshops geared toward beginner and intermediate levels. "Children Authors' Bootcamp provides two full, information-packed days on the fundamentals of writing fiction for children. The workshop covers developing strong, unique characters; well-constructed plots; believable dialogue; seamless description and pacing; point of view; editing your own work; marketing your manuscripts to publishers, and more. Each day also includes in-class writing exercises and small group activities." Workshop held 6-7 times/year at various locations throughout the United States. Bootcamps are generally held in March, April, June, September, October and November. Please check our website for upcoming dates and locations. Maximum size is 55; average workshop has 40-50 participants. Cost of workshop: $239. Tuition for both Saturday and Sunday (9:00 a.m. to 4:30 p.m.); morning and afternoon snacks; lunch; handout packet.

[N] CHILDREN'S BOOK CONFERENCE, Portland State University Haystack Program, P.O. Box 1491, Portland OR 97207 (503)725-4186. Fax: (503)725-4840. E-mail: snydere@pdx.edu. Website: www.haystack.pdx.edu. **Contact:** Elizabeth Snyder, program coordinator. Writer and illustrator workshops geared toward beginner and intermediate levels. **Open to students.** Topics covered include Assembling a Portfolio, Every Picture Tells a Story, The Business of Illustrating, Making a Good Impression, Making a Dummy, Retelling Folk Literature, Finding Your Voice, Where Have All the Stories Gone?, How to Succeed in Children's Publishing Today. Annual workshop. Workshop held July 21-25, 2003. Cost of workshop: $415—noncredit; $435—3 university credits individual ms/portfolio reviews for an additional fee. Write for more information. Linda Zuckerman, editor, coordinates conference and collects knowledgeable and engaging presenters every year. The 4th annual conference takes place on the Oregon coast (Cannon Beach). Haystack Program is in its 34th year on the sparkling Oregon coast. University credit available.

CHILDREN'S LITERATURE CONFERENCE, 250 Hofstra University, U.C.C.E., Hempstead NY 11549. (516)463-5242. Fax: (516)463-4833. E-mail: uccelibarts@hofstra.edu. Website: www.hofstra.edu (under "Academics/Continuing Education"). Writers/Illustrators **Contact:** Marion Flomenhaft, director, Liberal Arts Studies. Writer and illustrator workshops geared toward all levels. Emphasizes: fiction, nonfiction, poetry, submission procedures, picture books. Workshops will be held April 12, 2003. Length of each session: 1 hour. Cost of workshop: approximately $80; includes 2 workshops, reception, lunch, 2 general sessions, and panel discussion with guest speakers and critiquing of randomly selected first-manuscript pages submitted by registrants. Write for more information. Co-sponsored by Society of Children's Book Writers & Illustrators.

COLLEGE OF NEW JERSEY WRITERS CONFERENCE, Dept. of English, The College of New Jersey, P.O. Box 7718, Ewing NJ 08628-0718. (609)771-3254. Fax: (609)637-5112. E-mail: write@tcnj.e du. **Director:** Jean Hollander. Writer workshop geared toward all levels. **Open to students.** Sessions at 2000 workshop included "Literature for the Young," taught by Nancy Hinkel, assistant editor, Knopf and Crown Books for Young Readers. Annual conference held in April. Cost: $50-80 ($25 and up for students); includes admission to all talks, panels and readings. Workshops are $10 each.

THE COLUMBUS WRITERS CONFERENCE, P.O. Box 20548, Columbus OH 43220-0176. (614)451-3075. Fax: (614)451-0174. E-mail: angelapl28@aol.com. Website: www.creativevista.com. **Director:** Angela Palazzolo. Sessions geared toward all levels. "The conference offers a wide variety of topics and has included writing in the following markets: children's, young adult, screenwriting, historical fiction, humor, suspense, science fiction/fantasy, travel, educational and greeting card. Other topics have included writing the novel, the short story, the nonfiction book; playwriting; finding and working with an agent; independent publishing; book reviewing; technical writing; and time management for writers. Specific sessions that have pertained to children: children's writing, children's markets, young adult and publishing children's poetry and stories. Annual conference. Conference held in September. Cost of full conference: $189 for early registration (includes a day-and-a-half of sessions, Friday night dinner program, open mic sessions, Saturday continental breakfast, lunch and refreshments); $209 regular registration. Saturday only: $154 for early registration; $139 regular registration. Friday night dinner program is $38; $70 early registration for Friday afternoon sessions, $85 for regular registration. Call, e-mail or write for more information.

PETER DAVIDSON'S HOW TO WRITE A CHILDREN'S PICTURE BOOK SEMINAR, 982 S. Emerald Hills Dr., P.O. Box 497, Arnolds Park IA 51331-0497. E-mail: Peterdavidson@mchsi.com. **Seminar Presenter:** Peter Davidson. "This seminar is for anyone interested in writing and/or illustrating children's picture books. Beginners and experienced writers alike are welcome." **Open to students.** *How to Write a Children's Picture Book* is a one-day seminar devoted to principles and techniques of writing and illustrating children's picture books. Topics include Definition of a Picture Book, Picture Book Sizes, Developing an Idea, Plotting the Book, Writing the Book, Illustrating the Book, Typing the Manuscript, Copyrighting Your Work, Marketing Your Manuscript and Contract Terms. Seminars are presented year-round at community colleges. Even-numbered years, presents seminars in Minnesota, Iowa, Nebraska, Kansas, Colorado and Wyoming. Odd-numbered years, presents seminars in Illinois, Minnesota, Iowa, South Dakota, Missouri, Arkansas and Tennessee (write for a schedule). One day, 9 a.m.-4 p.m. Cost of workshop: varies from $40-59, depending on location; includes approximately 35 pages of handouts. Write for more information.

N: DUKE CREATIVE WRITER'S WORKSHOP, Box 90702, Room 203, The Bishop's House, Durham NC 27708. (919)684-2827. Fax: (919)681-8235. E-mail: kprice@mail.duke.edu. Website: www.learn more.duke.edu. **Director:** Kim Price. Writer workshops geared toward intermediate to advanced levels. The Creative Writer's Workshop allows each participant to explore creative writing in-depth with the instructor of their choice. Each instructor focuses on a particular style or area of creative writing; for example, Short Fiction, Personal Narrative, Playwriting, Poetry and others. Annual workshop. Every summer there is one 2-week session in July. Registration limited to 40. All participants have access to University facilities including computer clusters, libraries and classrooms. Costs for 2002 were $1,375 for this 2-week residential session. This cost includes room, board, activity and course expenses, special events and meals, and 1 camper T-shirt. Interested participants are requested to send a sample of their writing and a letter of introduction prior to registration. Write or call for more information.

FIRST NOVEL FEST, P.O. Box 18612, Milwaukee WI 53218-0612. (414)463-2301. Fax: (414)463-5032. E-mail: books@gardeniapress.com. Website: www.gardeniapress.com. **Senior Editor:** Bob Collins. **President:** Elizabeth Collins. Writer workshops geared toward beginner. **Open to students.** Emphasizes story writing of book-length work for children of all ages, including young adult. Annual conference. Workshop held in October. Cost of workshop: changes depending on location of conference. Cost includes agent appointments, ms consultation, banquet and more.

FLORIDA CHRISTIAN WRITERS CONFERENCE, 2344 Armour Ct., Titusville FL 32780. (321)269-5831. Fax: (321)264-0037. E-mail: dwilson@digital.net. Website: www.flwriters.org. **Conference Director:** Billie Wilson. Writer workshops geared toward all levels. **Open to students.** "We offer 50 one-hour workshops and 6 six-hour classes. Approximately 24 of these are for the children's genre: Seeing Through the Eyes of an Artist; Characters . . . Inside and Out; Seeing Through the Eyes of a Child; Picture Book Toolbox; and CD-ROM & Interactive Books for Children. Annual workshop held each February. We have 30 publishers and publications represented by editors teaching workshops and reading manuscripts from the conferees. The conference is limited to 200 people. Usually workshops are limited to 25-30. Advanced or professional workshops are by invitation only via submitted application." Cost of workshop: $500; includes food, lodging, tuition and ms critiques and editor review of your ms. Write for more information.

GOD USES INK CONFERENCE, M.I.P. Box 487, Markham, Ontario L3R 3R1 Canada. (905)471-1447. Fax: (905)471-6912. E-mail: info@thewordguild.com. Website: www.thewordguild.com. Estab. 1984. Annual conference for writers who are Christian. Hosted by The Word Guild, an association of Canadian writers and editors who are Christian. The Word Guild seeks to connect, develop, and promote its members. Keynote speaker, continuing classes, workshops, panels, editor appointments, reading times, critiques, and more. For all levels of writers from beginner to professional. Held at a retreat center in Guelph ON. June 12-14, 2003. Conference is open to anyone.

THE HEIGHTS WRITER'S CONFERENCE, Sponsored by Writer's World Press, 35 N. Chillicothe Rd. #D, Aurora OH 44202-8741. (330)562-6667. Fax: (330)562-1216. E-mail: writersworld@juno.com. **Conference Director:** Lavern Hall. This conference is on hiatus, but the conference director welcomes inquiries on future events.

HIGHLAND SUMMER CONFERENCE, Box 7014, Radford University, Radford VA 24142-7014. (540)831-5366. Fax: (540)831-5004. E-mail: jasbury@radford.edu. Website: www.radford.edu/~arsc. **Director:** Grace Toney Edwards. **Assistant to the Director:** Jo Ann Asbury. **Open to students.** Writer workshops geared toward beginner, intermediate and advanced levels. Emphasizes Appalachian literature, culture and heritage. Annual workshop. Workshop held first 2 weeks in June annually. Registration limited to 20. Writing facilities available: computer center. Cost of workshop: Regular tuition (housing/meals extra). Must be registered student or special status student. E-mail, fax or call for more information. Past visiting authors include: Wilma Dykeman, Sue Ellen Bridgers, George Ella Lyon, Lou Kassem.

HIGHLIGHTS FOUNDATION WRITERS WORKSHOP AT BOYDS MILLS, Dept. CWF, 814 Court St., Honesdale PA 18431. (570)253-1192. Fax: (570)253-0179. E-mail: maewain@highlightsfoundation.org. Website: www.highlightsfoundation.org. **Contact:** Maggie Ewain. Writer workshops geared toward those interested in writing for children; intermediate and advanced levels. Classes offered include: Nonfiction Research, Word Play: Poetry for Children, Writing from the Heart, Heart of the Novel. Spring/ Fall workshops. Workshops held in March, April, May, June, September, October, November, 2003 at home of the Founders, Boyds Mills, PA. Workshops limited to 14. Cost of workshops range from $795 and up. Cost of workshop includes tuition, meals, conference supplies and housing. Call for availablility and pricing. Call for more information or visit the website.

HIGHLIGHTS FOUNDATION WRITERS WORKSHOP AT CHAUTAUQUA, Dept. CWL, 814 Court St., Honesdale PA 18431. (570)253-1192. Fax: (570)253-0179. E-mail: maewain@highlightsfoundation.org. Website: www.highlightsfoundation.org. **Contact:** Maggie Ewain. Writer workshops geared toward those interested in writing for children; beginner, intermediate and advanced levels. Classes offered include: Children's Poetry; Book Promotion; Autobiographical Writing. Annual workshop. Workshops held July 12-19, 2003 and July 17-24, 2004 at Chautauqua Institution, Chautauqua, NY. Registration limited to 100/ class. Cost of workshop: $1,485; includes tuition, meals, conference supplies. Cost does not include housing. Call for availability and pricing. Scholarships are available for first-time attendees. Call for more information or visit the website.

HOFSTRA UNIVERSITY SUMMER WRITERS' CONFERENCE, 250 Hofstra University, UCCE, Hempstead NY 11549. (516)463-5016. Fax: (516)463-4833. E-mail: uccelibarts@hofstra.edu. Director, **Liberal Arts Studies:** Marion Flamenhaft. Writer workshops geared toward all levels. Classes offered include fiction, nonfiction, poetry, children's literature, stage/screenwriting and other genres. Children's writing faculty has included Pam Conrad, Johanna Hurwitz, Tor Seidler and Jane Zalben, with Maurice Sendak once appearing as guest speaker. Annual workshop. Workshops held for 2 weeks July 8-19, 2002. Each workshop meets for 2½ hours daily for a total of 25 hours. Students can register for 2 workshops, schedule an individual conference with the writer/instructor and submit a short ms (less than 10 pages) for critique. Enrollees may register as certificate students or credit students. Cost of workshop: noncredit students' enrollment fee is approximately $425; 2-credit student enrollment fee is approximately $1,100/ workshop undergraduate and graduate (2 credits); $2,100 undergraduate and graduate (4-credits). On-campus accommodations for the sessions are available for approximately $350/person for the 2-week conference. Students may attend any of the ancillary activities, a private conference, special programs and social events.

N KARITOS, 1116 State St. B21, Lemont IL 60439 E-mail: editor@karitos.com. Website: www.karitos.c om. **Managing Editor:** Chris Wave. **Director:** Bob Hay. Writer and illustrator workshops geared toward beginner, intermediate and advanced levels. **Open to students.** Children's writing workshops are not scheduled every year; check website. Annual workshop. Conference held in Chicago, Illinois in June. Illustrators fall under visual artists category and are scheduled separately for workshops. Cost of workshop: $40 for the entire conference Thursday night through Saturday night. Writers wishing to submit for consideration in *Karitos Review* should submit via website anytime from August to April prior to conference.

✓ KENTUCKY WOMEN WRITERS CONFERENCE, P.O. Box 1042, Lexington KY 40588-1042. (859)254-4175. Fax: (859)281-1151. E-mail: kywwc@hotmail.com. Website: www.carnegieliteracy.org. **Contact:** Brenda Weber. Writer workshops geared toward beginner, intermediate and advanced levels. **Open to students.** Past sessions have included "writing for young adults" with Gloria Velasquez, author of *Tommy Stands Alone*; a variety of workshops with children's writer George Ella Lyon, Anne Shelby, Pat Mora and other women writers such as Maya Angelou, Alice Walker, Joy Harjo, Barbara Kingsolver, Lee Smith and a host of others. Annual conference. Cost of conference: $80-150; includes all conference registration, some meals, some performances. Write for more information.

LEAGUE OF UTAH WRITERS' ROUNDUP, 4621 W. Harman Dr., West Valley City, Utah Valley City UT 84120. (801)964-0861. Fax: (801)964-0937. E-mail: crofts@numucom.com. Website: www.luwrit e.tripod.com. **Membership Chairman:** Dorothy Crofts. Writer workshops geared toward beginner, intermediate, advanced. **Open to students.** "We have included an 'Illustrations' category in our annual contest." Annual workshop. Workshop held 3rd weekend of September 2002. Registration limited to approximately 400. Our conference is held at the Hilton Hotel. Cost of workshop: $125 for members/$160 for nonmembers; includes 4 meals, all workshops, all general sessions, a syllabus of all handout materials and a conference packet. "When requesting information, please provide an e-mail address and/or fax number."

MANHATTANVILLE WRITERS' WEEK, Manhattanville College, 2900 Purchase St., Purchase NY 10577-2103. (914)694-3425. Fax: (914)694-3488. E-mail: rdowd@mville.edu. Website: www.gps.mville.e du. **Dean, School of Graduate & Professional Studies:** Ruth Dowd. Writer workshops geared toward beginner, intermediate and advanced levels. **Open to students.** Writers' week offers a special workshop for writers interested in children's/young adult writing. We have featured such workshop leaders as: Patricia Gauch, Richard Peck, Elizabeth Winthrop and Janet Lisle. Annual workshop held last week in June. Length of each session: one week. Cost of workshop: $560 (non-credit); includes a full week of writing activities, 5-day workshop on children's literature, lectures, readings, sessions with editors and agents, etc. Workshop may be taken for 2 graduate credits. Write for more information.

MARITIME WRITERS' WORKSHOP, Department Extension & Summer Session, P.O. Box 4400, University of New Brunswick, Fredericton, New Brunswick E3B 5A3 Canada, Phone/fax: (506)474-1144. E-mail: k4jc@unb.ca. Website: unb.ca/extend/writers/. **Coordinator:** Rhona Sawlor. Week-long workshop on writing for children, general approach, dealing with submitted material, geared to all levels and held in July. Annual workshop. 3 hours/day. Group workshop plus individual conferences, public readings, etc. Registration limited to 10/class. Cost of workshop: $350 tuition; meals and accommodations extra. Room and board on campus is approximately $280 for meals and a single room for the week. 10-20 ms pages due before conference (deadline announced). Scholarships available.

N MENDOCINO COAST WRITERS CONFERENCE, College of the Redwoods, 1211 Del Mar Dr., Ft. Bragg CA 95437. (707)961-6248. E-mail: mcwc@jps.net. Website: www.mcwc.com. **Registrar:** Jan Boyd. Writing workshops geared toward beginner, intermediate and advanced levels. Annual conference in its 14th year. This year's conference will take place June 5-7, 2003. Registration limited to 99.

Conference is held on the campus of College of Redwoods. Cost of conference (early registration): $250-315, includes Friday and Saturday lecture sessions; 2 social events; 2 lunches; 2 breakfasts; 1 dinner; editor/agent panels. $315 includes all of the above plus Thursday intensive workshops (choice of one) in poetry, fiction, nonfiction, screen and YA/children's. After April 2003 price increases to $300/350. "What we offer for children's writers varies from year to year."

N **MID MISSISSIPPI RIVER WRITER'S CONFERENCE**, John Wood Community College, 1301 S. 48th St., Quincy IL 62305. (217)641-4903. Fax: (217)228-9483. **Contact:** Sherry Sparks. Speakers talk on a variety of topics including children's writing, poetry, fiction, songwriting. The college also sponsors a writing contest open to the entire area for poetry, fiction and nonfiction. In addition, the college sponsors writing workshops, readings, speakers, a humanities series, a photography show in spring, and an art competition in the fall.

MIDLAND WRITERS CONFERENCE, Grace A. Dow Memorial Library, 1710 W. St. Andrews, Midland MI 48640-2698. (517)837-3435. Fax: (517)837-3468. E-mail: ajarvis@midland-mi.org. Website: www.midland-mi.org/gracedowlibrary. **Conference Chair:** Ann Jarvis. **Open to students.** Writer and illustrator workshops geared toward all levels. "Each year, we offer a topic of interest to writers of children's literature. Last year, Shirley Nietzel "What I've Learned From Rejection" was the agenda. Classes offered include: catching the attention of an editor, writing poetry, Christian fiction, memoirs, and writing your family history. Annual workshop. Workshops held usually second Saturday in June. Length of each session: concurrently, 4 1-hour sessions repeated in the afternoon. Maximum class size: 50. "We are a public library." Cost of workshop: $60; $50 seniors and students; includes choice of workshops and the keynote speech given by a prominent author (last year Homer Hickam). Write for more information.

MIDWEST WRITERS WORKSHOP, Department of Journalism, Ball State University, Muncie IN 47306. (765)282-1055. Fax: (765)285-7997. **Director:** Earl L. Conn. Writer workshops geared toward intermediate level. Topics include most genres. Past workshop presenters include Joyce Carol Oates, James Alexander Thom, Bill Brashler and Richard Lederer. Workshop also includes ms evaluation and a writing contest. Annual workshop. Workshop will be held July 24-26, 2003. Registration tentatively limited to 125. Most meals included. Offers scholarships. Write for more information.

MISSOURI WRITERS' GUILD 86th STATE CONVENTION, P.O. Box 22506, Kansas City MO 64113-0506. (816)361-1281. E-mail: eblivingsfun@hotmail.com. **State President:** Jane Simmons. Writer and illustrator workshops geared to all levels. **Open to students.** Annual workshop. Workshop held late April or early May each year. Cost of workshop: $56.

N **MOONDANCE INTERNATIONAL FILM FESTIVAL**, 970 Ninth St., Boulder CO 80302. (303)545-0202. E-mail: moondanceff@aol.com. Website: www.moondancefilmfestival.com. **Executive Director:** Elizabeth English. **Director:** Tara Allgood. Sessions include screenwriting, playwriting, short stories, film making (feature, documentary, short, animation), TV and video filmmaking, writing for TV (MOW, sitcoms, drama), writing for animation, adaptation to screenplays (novels and short stories). Annual workshop and film festival held May 15-18, 2003. Cost of workshops, seminars, panels, pitch session: $100 each. Check website for more information and registration forms. "The competition deadline for entries is October 1, 2002. Entry forms are on website.

MOUNT HERMON CHRISTIAN WRITERS CONFERENCE, Mount Hermon Christian Conference Center, P.O. Box 413, Mount Hermon CA 95041-0413. (831)335-4466. Fax: (831)335-9413. E-mail: rachel w@mhcamps.org. Website: www.mounthermon.org. **Director of Adult Ministries:** David R. Talbott. Writer workshops geared toward all levels. Open to students over 16 years. Emphasizes religious writing for children via books, articles; Sunday school curriculum; marketing. Classes offered include: Suitable Style for Children; Everything You Need to Know to Write and Market Your Children's Book; Take-Home Papers for Children. Workshops held annually over Palm Sunday weekend: April 11-15, 2003 and April 6-10, 2004. Length of each session: 5-day residential conferences held annually. Registration limited 45/class, but most are 10-15. Conference center with hotel-style accommodations. Cost of workshop: $650-950 variable; includes tuition, resource notebook, refreshment breaks, full room and board for 13 meals and 4 nights. Write or e-mail for more information or call toll-free to 1-888-MH-CAMPS.

NEW JERSEY SOCIETY OF CHRISTIAN WRITERS FALL SEMINAR, P.O. Box 405, Millville NJ 08332-0405. (856)327-1231. Fax: (856)327-0291. E-mail: daystar405@aol.com. Website: www.njscw.c om. **Founder/Director:** Dr. Mary Ann Diorio. Writer workshops geared toward beginner, intermediate.

Open to students. Annual workshop. Workshop held first Saturday in November. Cost of workshop: $75 includes lunch; $65 does not include lunch. Write for more information. "We have one guest speaker per conference—usually 30-50 attendees."

NORTH CAROLINA WRITERS' NETWORK FALL CONFERENCE, P.O. Box 954, Carrboro NC 27510-0954. (919)967-9540. Fax: (919)929-0535. E-mail: mail@ncwriters.org. Website: www.ncwriter s.org. **Program and Services Director:** Janet Wheaton. Writer workshops geared toward beginner, intermediate, advanced and professional levels. **Open to students.** "We offer workshops and critique sessions in a variety of genres: fiction, poetry, children's. Past young adult and children's writing classes included: 'Everybody's Got a Story to Tell—or Write!' with Eleanora Tate; 'Writing Young Adult Fiction' with Sarah Dessen and 'Writing for Children' with Carole Boston Weatherford." Annual conference. Conference held November 15-17, 2003 in Durham, NC. Readings done by Josephine Humphreys, Lee Smith and others. Cost of workshop: approximately $200/NCWN members, $225/nonmembers; includes workshops, panel discussions, round table discussions, social activities and 2 meals. "Cost does not include fee for critique sessions or accommodations."

OAKLAND UNIVERISTY WRITER'S CONFERENCE, 221 Varner Hall, Oakland University, Rochester MI 48309-4401. (248)370-3125. Fax: (248)370-4280. E-mail: gjboddy@oakland.edu. Website: www.oakland.edu/contin-ed/writersconf. **Program Director:** Gloria J. Boddy. Writer and illustrator conference geared toward beginner, intermediate, advanced and professional levels. **Open to Students.** Two-day conference featuring one-day writer retreats, ms critiques, hands-on workshops on Friday and a choie of 32 presentations on Saturday. Offers sessions in Children's Poetry, Marketing a Children's Book Manuscript, Writing Nonfiction for Teens. Annual conference. Conference held October 18, 19, 2002. Cost of conference: $95 one-day writer retreat, $58 hands-on workshop, $68 ms critique, $95 Saturday program with keynote speaker, Judity Piercy. Write or call for more information.

OHIO KENTUCKY INDIANA CHILDREN'S LITERATURE CONFERENCE, % Greater Cincinnati Library Consortium (GCLC), 2181 Victory Parkway, Suite 214, Cincinnati OH 45206-2855. (513)751-4422. Fax: (513)751-0463. E-mail: gclc@gclc-lib.org. Website: www.gclc-lib.org. **Staff Development Coordinator:** Judy Malone. Writer and illustrator conference geared toward all levels. **Open to students.** Annual conference. Emphasizes multicultural literature for children and young adults. Conference held annually in November. Contact GCLC for more information. Registration limited to 250. Cost of conference: $50; includes registration/attendance at all workshop sessions, Tri-state Authors and Illustrators of Childrens Books Directory, continental breakfast, lunch, author/illustrator signings. E-mail or write for more information.

OUTDOOR WRITERS ASSOCIATION OF AMERICA ANNUAL CONFERENCE, 158 Lower Georges Valley Rd., Spring Mills PA 16875. (814)364-9557. Fax: (814)364-9558. E-mail: cking4owaa@cs com. **Meeting Planner:** Eileen King. Writer workshops geared toward all levels. Annual workshop. Workshop held in June. Cost of workshop: $175; includes attendance at all workshops and most meals. Attendees must have prior approval from Executive Director before attendance is permitted. Write for more information.

PHOTOGRAPHY: A DIVERSE FOCUS, 610 W. Poplar St., #4, Zionsville IN 46077-1220. Phone/fax: (317)873-0738. E-mail: charlenefaris@hotmail.com. **Director:** Charlene Faris. Writer and illustrator workshops geared to beginners. "Conferences focus primarily on children's photography; also literature and illustration. Annual conferences are held very often throughout year." Registration is not limited, but "sessions are generally small." Cost of conference: $200 (2 days), $100 (1 day). "Inquiries with a SASE only will receive information on seminars."

ROBERT QUACKENBUSH'S CHILDREN'S BOOK WRITING AND ILLUSTRATING WORKSHOP, 460 E. 79th St., New York NY 10021-1443. Phone/fax: (212)861-2761. E-mail: rqstudios

@aol.com. (E-mail inquirers please include mailing address). Website: www.rquackenbush.com. **Contact:** Robert Quackenbush. Writer and illustrator workshops geared toward all levels. **Open to students.** Five-day extensive workshop on writing and illustrating books for children, emphasizes picture books from start to finish. Also covered is writing fiction and nonfiction for middle grades and young adults, if that is the attendees' interest. Current trends in illustration are also covered. This July workshop is a full 5-day (9 a.m.-4 p.m) extensive course. Next workshop July 8-12, 2002. Registration limited to 10/class. Writing and/or art facilities available; work on the premises; art supply store nearby. Cost of workshop: $650 for instruction. Cost of workshop includes instruction in preparation of a ms and/or book dummy ready to submit to publishers. Class limited to 10 members. Attendees are responsible for arranging their own hotel and meals, although suggestions are given on request for places to stay and eat. "This unique workshop, held annually since 1982, provides the opportunity to work with Robert Quackenbush, a prolific author and illustrator of children's books with more than 170 fiction and nonfiction books for young readers to his credit, including mysteries, biographies and song-books. The workshop attracts both professional and beginning writers and artists of different ages from all over the world." Recommended by Foder's *Great American Learning Vacations*.

ROCKY MOUNTAIN RETREATS FOR WRITERS & ARTISTS, 81 Cree Court, Lyons CO 80540. (303)823-0530. E-mail: deborah@indra.com. Website: www.expressionretreats.com. **Director:** Deborah DeBord. Writers and illustrator workshops geared to all levels. **Open to students.** Includes information on releasing creative energy, identifying strengths and interests, balancing busy lives, marketing creative works. Monthly conference. Registration limited to 4 per session. Writing studio, weaving studio, private facilities available. Cost of workshop: $1,099/week; includes room, meals, materials, instruction. "Treat yourself to a week of mountain air, sun, and personal expression. Flourish with the opportunity for sustained work punctuated by structured experiences designed to release the artist's creative energies. Relax over candlelit gourmet meals followed by fireside discussions of the day's efforts. Discover the rhythm of filling the artistic well and drawing on its abundant resources."

SAGE HILL WRITING EXPERIENCE, Writing Children's & Young Adult Fiction Workshop, Box 1731, Saskatoon, Saskatchewan S7K 3S1 Canada. Phone/fax: (306)652-7395. E-mail: sage.hill @sasktel.net. Website: www.lights.com/sagehill. **Executive Director:** Steven Ross Smith. Writer conference geared toward intermediate level. **Open to students.** This program occurs every 2 or 3 years, but the Sage Hill Conference is annual. Conference held July 25-August 5. Registration limited to 6 participants for this program, and to 37 for full program. Cost of conference: $775; includes instruction, meals, accommodation. Require ms samples prior to registration. Write for more information.

SAN DIEGO STATE UNIVERSITY WRITERS' CONFERENCE, The College of Extended Studies, Gateway Center: Room 2503, San Diego CA 92182-1920. (619)594-2517. Fax: (619)594-8566. E-mail: extended.std@sdsu.edu. Website: www.ces.sdsu.edu. **Conference Facilitator:** Paula Pierce. Writer workshops geared toward beginner, intermediate and advanced levels. Emphasizes nonfiction, fiction, screenwriting, advanced novel writing; includes sessions specific to writing and illustrating for children. Workshops offered by children's editors, agents and writers. Workshops held third weekend in January each year. Registration limited. Cost of workshop: approximately $280. Write for more information or see our home page at the above website.

SOCIETY OF SOUTHWESTERN AUTHORS' WRANGLING WITH WRITING, P.O. Box 30355, Tucson AZ 85751-0355. (520)546-9382. Fax: (520)296-0409. E-mail: wporter202@aol.com or apatrillo@earthlink.net. Website: www.azstarnet.com/nonprofit/ssa. **Conference Director:** Penny Porter. Writer workshops geared toward all levels. "Limited scholarships available." Sessions include Writing and Publishing the Young Adult Novel, What Agents Want to See in a Children's Book, Writing Books for Young Children. "We always have several children's book editors and agents interested in meeting with children's writers." Annual workshop held January 19-20, 2001; January 18-19, 2002; January 24-25, 2003 (usually MLK weekend). Registration limited to 500—usually 300-400 people attend. Hotel rooms have dataports for internet access. Tucson has many art galleries. Tentative cost: $250 non-members, $220 for SSA members; includes 3 meals and 2 continental breakfasts, all workshop sessions—individual appointments with agents and editors are extra. Hotel accommodations are not included. Some editors and agents like to see mss prior to the conference; information about requirements is in the brochure. If you want a portfolio of artwork critiqued, please contact us directly, and we'll try to accommodate you. Write for more information. SSA has put on this conference for over 25 years now. It's hands-on, it's friendly, and every year writers sell their mss.

SOUTH COAST WRITERS CONFERENCE, P.O. Box 590, 29392 Ellensburg Ave., Gold Beach OR 97444. (541)247-2741. Fax: (541-247-6247. E-mail: scwc@southwestern.cc.or.us. **Coordinator:** Janet Pretti. Writer workshops geared toward beginner, intermediate levels. **Open to students.** Include fiction, nonfiction, nuts and bolts, poetry, feature writing, children's writing, publishing. From 2001—Archetypes & Ideas in Children's Writing, How I Sold My Babies into Bondage for Fun & Profit (Making a living as a children's writer); from 1999—Children Have Language . . . Listen, Writing & Selling a Children's Book. Annual workshop. Workshop held February 14-15, 2003, Friday and Saturday of President's day weekend in February. Registration limited to 25-30 students/workshop. Cost of workshop: $45 before January 31, $55 after; includes Friday night author's reading and book signing, Saturday conference, choice of 4 workshop sessions, Saturday evening writers' circle (networking and critique). Write for more information. "We also have two six-hour workshops Friday for more intensive writing exercises. The cost is an additional $25."

N SPLIT ROCK ARTS PROGRAM, University of Minnesota, 360 Coffey Hall, 1420 Eckles Ave., St. Paul MN 55108-6084. (612)625-8100. Fax: (612)624-6210. E-mail: srap@cce.umn.edu. Writing workshops including poetry, stories, memoirs, novels and personal essays geared toward intermediate, advanced and professional levels. Workshops begin in July for 5 weeks. Optional college credits available. Registration limited to 16 per workshop. Workshops held on the University of Minnesota-Duluth campus. Cost of workshop: $485; includes tuition and fees. On-campus apartments and residence hall housing available. Complete catalogs available in March. Call or e-mail anytime to be put on mailing list or check out website for complete workshop offerings. Some workshops fill very early.

N ✵ SUNSHINE COAST FESTIVAL OF THE WRITTEN ARTS, P.O. Box 2299, Sechelt, British Columbia V0N-3A0 Canada. (604)885-9631, 1-800-565-9631. Fax: (604)885-3967. E-mail: info@writersf estival.ca. Website: www.writersfestival.ca. **Festival Producer:** Gail Bull. Writer and illustrator workshops geared toward professional level. **Open to Students.** Annual literary festival held August 7-10, 2003. Writers-in-residence workshops. Pavilion seating 500 per event. Festival pass $175; individual events $12. Writer's workshops are 3 days. Fee schedule available upon request.

N ✵ SURREY WRITER'S CONFERENCE, Guilford Continuing Education, 10707 146th St., Surrey, British Columbia U3R IT5 Canada. (604)589-2221. Fax: (604)588-9286. Website: www.surreywritersc onference.bc.ca. **Coordinator:** Russ Nixon. Writer and illustrator workshops geared toward beginners, intermediate and advanced levels. Topics include marketing, children's agents and editors. Annual Conference. Conference held October 17-19, 2003. Cost of conference includes all events for 3 days and most meals. Check our website for more information.

TAOS SUMMER WRITERS' CONFERENCE, University of New Mexico, Humanities 255, Albuquerque NM 87131. (505)277.6248. Fax: (505)277-5573. E-mail: swarner@unm.edu. Website: www.unm.edu/ ~taosconf. **Director:** Sharon Oard Warner. Writing workshops geared toward all levels. **Open to students.** Must be 18 years old. "Our conference offers both weekend and week-long conferences, not only in children's writing, but also adult fiction (novel, short story), creative nonfiction, poetry and screenwriting." Annual conference held July 12-18, 2003—(usually 3rd week of July). Maximum of 12 people per workshop. Usually 5 weekend workshops and 8- or 10-week-long workshops. "We provide an on-site computer room." Cost of conference: approximately $485/weeklong; $235/weekend; includes tuition, opening and closing night dinner, all the readings by instructors, Wednesday night entertainment. Lodging and meals extra but we offer a reduced rate at the Sagebrush Inn in Taos, Comfort Suites; breakfast included. Write for more information.

THE 21ST CENTURY WRITER'S GET-A-WAY, 625 Schuring, Suite B, Portage MI 49024-5106. (616)232-2100. Fax: (309)694-1153. E-mail: jfriendspub@aol.com. Website: justfriendspublishing.com. **Public Relations Manager:** John Williams. Workshops geared toward new aspiring authors. Sessions offered include "Marketing Strategies For The 21st Century." **Open to students.** In this workshop our workshop facilitator brings the latest information on how to jumpstart your book including information on software for graphic arts designs. Workshop held twice a year, April 25 and August 9, 2003. This event will be held at Brook Lodge-MSU in Augusta, Michigan near Kalamazoo. Cost of workshop: $125. The fee includes: 4 workshops, a writing clinic, continental breakfast, lunch, and a notebook. Write for a full-color brochure.

N UMKC/WRITERS PLACE WRITERS WORKSHOPS, University of Missouri—Kansas City, 5100 Rockhill Rd., 215 55B, Kansas City MO 64110-2499. (816)235-2736. Fax: (816)235-5279. E-mail:

seatons@umkc.edu. **Continuing Education:** Sharon Seaton. Writer workshops geared toward intermediate, advanced and professional levels. Workshops open to students and community. Semi-annual workshops. Workshops held in fall and spring. Cost of workshop varies. Write for more information.

UNIVERSITY OF THE NATIONS SCHOOL OF WRITING AND WRITERS WORKSHOPS, P.O. Box 1380 YWAM Woodcrest Lindale TX 75771-1380. (903)882-WOOD [9663]. Fax: (903)882-1161. E-mail: info@ymamwoodcrest.com. Website: www.ywamwoodcrest.com. **Director of Training:** Pamela Warren. Writer workshops geared toward beginner, intermediate, advanced levels. **Open to students.** Workshops held September 26 to December 17, 2002. Workshops held various weeks during that time. Cost for workshop: $20 registration fee (nonrefundable) plus $175 tuition per week (the 1st week) plus $175/week if staying on our campus. ($125 tuition each additional week.). $175 tuition/week covers lectures, critique groups, hands-on-training. $175 if staying at our campus includes food and housing. Students may make own arrangements for lodging and meals. If you want college credit for the workshop or are taking the entire 12-week school of writing, you must have completed the University of the Nations Discipleship Training School first. Otherwise no requirements for workshop students. Write for more information. Although we are associated with the Youth with A Mission missionary group we welcome inquiries from all interested parties–not just missionaries.

THE VICTORIA SCHOOL OF WRITING, P.O. Box 8152, Victoria, British Columbia V8W 3R8 Canada. (250)595-3000. E-mail: vicwrite@islandnet.com. Website: www.islandnet.com/vicwrite. **Director:** Ruth Slavin. Writer conference geared toward intermediate level. In the 2003 conference there may be 1 workshop on writing for children and young adults. Annual conference. Workshop third week of July. Registration limited to 12/workshop. Conference includes close mentoring from established writers. Cost of conference: $575 (Canada); includes tuition and some meals. To attend, submit 3-10 pages of writing samples. Write for more information.

VIRGINIA FESTIVAL OF THE BOOK, 145 Ednam Dr., Charlottesville VA 22903. (434)924-6890. Fax: (434)296-4714. Website: www.vabook.org. **Program Director:** Nancy Damon. **Open to Students.** Readings, panel discussions, presentations and workshops by author and book-related professional for children and adults. Most programs are free and open to the public. Held March 19-23, 2003 in Charlottesville. See website for more information.

WASHINGTON CHRISTIAN WRITERS WORKSHOPS/RETREATS, (formerly Seattle Christian Writers Conference), sponsored by Writers Information Network, P.O. Box 11337, Bainbridge Island WA 98110. (206)842-9103. Fax: (206)842-0536. E-mail: writersinfonetwork@juno.com. Website: www.bluejaypub.com/win. **Director:** Elaine Wright Colvin. Writer workshops geared toward all levels. Conference open to students. Past conferences have featured subjects such as 'Making It to the Top as a Children's Book Author,' featuring Debbie Trafton O'Neal. Check website for future dates and locations. Write for more information and to be added to mailing list.

WESLEYAN WRITERS CONFERENCE, Wesleyan University, Middletown CT 06459. (860)685-3604. Fax: (860)685-2441. E-mail: agreene@wesleyan.edu. Website: www.wesleyan.edu/writing/conferen. html. **Director:** Anne Greene. Writer workshops geared toward all levels. "This conference is useful for writers interested in how to structure a story, poem or nonfiction piece. Although we don't always offer classes in writing for children, the advice about structuring a piece is useful for writers of any sort, no matter who their audience is." Classes in the novel, short story, fiction techniques, poetry, journalism and literary nonfiction. Guest speakers and panels offer discussion of fiction, poetry, reviewing, editing and publishing. Individual ms consultations available. Conference held annually the last week in June. Length of each session: 6 days. "Usually, there are 100 participants at the Conference." Classrooms, meals, lodging and word processing facilities available on campus. Cost of workshop: tuition—$530, room—$120, meals (required of all participants)—$190. "Anyone may register; people who want financial aid must submit their work and be selected by scholarship judges." Call for a brochure or look on the web at address above.

WHIDBEY ISLAND WRITERS' CONFERENCE, P.O. box 1289, Langley WA 98260. (360)331-6714. E-mail: writers@whidbey.com. Website: www.whidbey.com/writers. Director: Celeste Mergens. Writer and illustrator workshops geared toward beginner, intermediate and advanced levels. **Open to students**. Topics include "Writing for Children," "Writing in a Bunny Eat Bunny World," "The Art of Revision." Annual conference in March. Registration limited to 275. Cost of conference: $325; includes all workshops and events, 2 receptions, activities and daily luncheons. Those who register before September 1st get an early-bird discount rate of just $275. Volunteers who commit to work 8-10 hours either before, during, or after the conference may receive the volunteer discount rate of $180."For writing consultations participants pay $35 for 20 minutes to submit the first five pages of a chapter book, youth novel or entire picture book idea with a written 1-page synopsis." Write, e-mail or check website for more information. "This is a uniquely personable weekend that is designed to be highly interactive." 2003 Children's Presenters are Bruce Coville, Paula Danziger, Michael Stearns and Kirby Larson.

WILLAMETTE WRITERS ANNUAL WRITERS CONFERENCE, 9045 SW Barbur Blvd., Suite 5A, Portland OR 97219. (503)452-1592. Fax: (503)452-0372. E-mail: williamettewriters.com. Website: www.willamettewriters.com. **Office Manager:** Bill Johnson. Writer workshops geared toward all levels. Emphasizes all areas of writing, including children's and young adult. Opportunities to meet one-on-one with leading literary agents and editors. Workshops held in August. Cost of conference: $285; includes membership.

✔ **TENNESSEE WILLIAMS/NEW ORLEANS LITERARY FESTIVAL**, 938 Lafayette St., Suite 308, New Orleans LA 70113. (504)581-1144. Fax: (504)523-3680. E-mail: info@tennessee@williams.net. Website: www.tennesseewilliams.net. **Executive Director:** Shannon Stover. Writer workshops geared toward beginner, intermediate levels. **Open to students.** Annual workshop. Workshop held March 26-30, 2003. Master classes are limited in size to 100—all other panels offered have no cap. Cost of workshop: prices range from $15-45. Write for more information. "We are a literary festival and may occasionally offer panels/classes on children's writing and/or illustration, but this is not done every year."

WISCONSIN REGIONAL WRITER'S ASSOCIATION, INC., Spring and Fall Conferences, 510 W. Sunset Ave., Appleton WI 54911-1139. (920)734-3724. E-mail: info@wrwa.net. Website: www.wrwa.net. **Contact:** Donna Potrykus, vice president. Estab. 1948. Annual. Conferences held in May and September are dedicated to self-improvement through speakers, workshops and presentations. Topics and speakers vary with each event. Average attendance: 100-150. We honor all genres of writing. Spring conference is a one-day event that features speakers and awards for two contests (humor writing and feature article writing). Fall conference is a two-day event featuring the Jade Ring Banquet and awards for six genre categories. Spring 2002: Holiday Inn—Manitowoc, WI. Agents and editors participate in each conference. Cost of workshop: $40-75. Provides a list of area hotels or lodging options. "We negotiate special rates at each facility. A block of rooms is set aside for a specific time period." Award winners receive a certificate and a cash prize. First Place winners of the Jade Ring contest receive a jade ring. Must be a member to enter all contests. For brochure call, write, e-mail or visit our website.

WRITE ON THE SOUND WRITERS CONFERENCE, 700 Main St., Edmonds WA 98020-3032. (425)771-0228. Fax: (425)771-0253. E-mail: wots@ci.edmonds.wa.us. Website: www.ci.edmonds.wa.us. **Cultural Resources Coordinator:** Frances Chapin. Writer workshops geared toward beginner, intermediate, advanced and professional levels with some sessions on writing for children. Annual conference held in Edmonds on Puget Sound on the first weekend in October with 2 full days of a variety of lectures and workshops." Registration limited to 200. Cost of workshop: approximately $60/day, or $99 for the weekend, includes 4 workshops daily plus one ticket to keynote lecture. Brochures are mailed in August. Attendees must preregister. Write, e-mail or call for brochure. Writing contest for conference participants.

WRITERS' LEAGUE OF TEXAS WORKSHOP SERIES, 1501 W. Fifth St., Suite E-2, Austin TX 78703. (512)499-8914. Fax: (512)499-0441. E-mail: awl@writersleague.org. Website: www.writersleague.org. **Executive Director:** Stephanie Sheppard. Writer and illustrator workshops and conferences geared toward adults. Annual conferences. Classes are held during the week, and workshops are held on Saturdays during March, April, May, September, October and November. Annual Teddy Children's Book Award of $1,000 presented each fall to book published from June 1 to May 1. Write for more information.

WRITE-TO-PUBLISH CONFERENCE, 9731 N. Fox Glen Dr., #6F, Niles IL 60714-4222. (847)296-3964. Fax: (847)296-0754. E-mail: lin@wtpublish.com. Website: www.WTPublish.com. **Director:** Lin Johnson. Writer workshops geared toward all levels. **Open to students.** Conference is focused for the Christian market and includes classes on writing for children. Annual conference held June 4-7, 2003. Cost of conference: $350; includes conference and banquet. For information, call (847)299-4755 or e-mail brochure@wtpublish.com. Conference takes place at Wheaton College in the Chicago area.

Ⓝ **WRITING CHILDREN'S FICTION**, Rice University, Houston TX 77005. (713)348-4803. Fax: (713)348-5213. E-mail: scs@rice.edu. Website: www.scs.rice.edu. **Contact:** School of Continuing Studies. Weekly evening children's writing courses and workshops geared toward all levels held in fall and spring semesters. Topics include issues in children's publishing, censorship, multiculturalism, dealing with sensitive subjects, submissions/formatting, the journal as resource, the markets—finding your niche, working with an editor, the agent/author connection, the role of research, and contract negotiation. Contact Rice Continuing Studies for current information on course offerings.

WRITING FOR CHILDREN: A Conference for Teachers, Parents, Writers & Illustrators, 933 Hamlet St., Columbus OH 43201-3595. (614)291-8644. E-mail: writingforchildren@mail.com. Website: www.sjms.net/conf. **Development Director:** Jim Mengel. Writer and illustrator workshops geared toward beginner, intermediate and advanced levels. **Open to students.** Annual workshop. Workshop held Saturday, March 22, 2003. Registration limited to 140. Cost of workshop: $105; $55 full-time college or high school students; $10 late fee if registering after February 28, 2003. $40 additional charge for ms or portfolio evaluations; includes attendance, lunch, continental breakfast, snacks. Manuscript and portfolio evaluation require pre-registration (call Jim Mengel). Manuscripts and/or portfolios to be evaluated must be submitted by February 12, 2003. "Event will be at the Crowne Plaza in downtown Columbus, OH and will be an all-day affair with two keynote speakers."

N WRITING FOR CHILDREN AND CHILDREN'S BOOK ILLUSTRATION WITH JOAN CAVANAUGH, Taos Institute of Arts, 108 Civic Plaza Dr., Taos NM 87571. (505)758-2793. E-mail: tia@taosnet.com. Website: www.tiataos.com. **Curriculum Director:** Susan Mihalic. Workshops geared toward beginner, intermediate and advanced levels. Open to students over 18. Workshops take place March-October 2002. Check website for dates. Registration limited to 12. All classroom needs are accommodated, but students buy/bring materials, computers, etc. Cost: $395 plus $40 registration fee.

✓ WRITING FOR YOUNG READERS WORKSHOP, Brigham Young University, 348 Harman Bldg., Provo UT 84602-1532. (801)378-2568. Fax: (801)378-8165. Website: http://ce.byu.edu/cw/writing. **Coordinator:** Susan Overstreet. Writer workshops geared toward all levels. **Open to students.** Offers workshops on picture books, book-lengh fiction (novels) and general writing. Annual workshop. Workshop held July 15-18, 2002. Registration limited to 125 people. Computer lab, library, conference rooms available. Cost of workshop: $389 includes workshop fees, concluding banquet, access to facilities. "Workshoppers are expected to bring a manuscript-in-process." Write for more information.

Contests, Awards & Grants

Publication is not the only way to get your work recognized. Contests and awards can also be great ways to gain recognition in the industry. Grants, offered by organizations like SCBWI, offer monetary recognition to writers, giving them more financial freedom as they work on projects.

When considering contests or applying for grants, be sure to study guidelines and requirements. Regard entry deadlines as gospel and follow the rules to the letter.

Note that some contests require nominations. For published authors and illustrators, competitions provide an excellent way to promote your work. Your publisher may not be aware of local competitions such as state-sponsored awards—if your book is eligible, have the appropriate person at your publishing company nominate or enter your work for consideration.

To select potential contests and grants, read through the listings that interest you, then send for more information about the types of written or illustrated material considered and other important details. A number of contests offer information through websites given in their listings.

If you are interested in knowing who has received certain awards in the past, check your local library or bookstores or consult *Children's Books: Awards & Prizes*, compiled and edited by the Children's Book Council (www.cbcbooks.org). Many bookstores have special sections for books that are Caldecott and Newbery Medal winners. Visit these websites for more information on award-winning children's books: The Caldecott—www.ala.org/alsc/caldecott.html; The Newbery—www.ala.org/alsc/newbery.html; The Coretta Scott King Award—www.ala.org/srrt/csking; The Michael L. Printz Award—www.ala.org/yalsa/printz; The Boston Globe-Horn Book Award—www.hbook.com/bghb.html; The Golden Kite Award—www.scbwi.org/goldkite.htm.

Information on contests listed in the previous edition but not included in this edition of *Children's Writer's & Illustrator's Market* **may be found in the General Index.**

JANE ADDAMS CHILDREN'S BOOK AWARDS, Jane Addams Peace Association, Inc./Women's International League for Peace and Freedom. 777 United Nations Plaza, New York NY 10017. (212)682-8830. Fax: (212)286-8211. E-mail: japa@igc.apc.org. Website: www.educationwisc.edu/ccbc/public/jaddams.htm. **Award Director:** Ginny Moore Kruse. Submit entries to: Ginny Moore Kruse. "Two copies of published books (in previous year only)" Address: 1708 Regent St. Madison WI 53705. Annual award. Estab. 1953. Previously published submissions only. Submissions made by author, author's agent, a person or group, submitted by the publisher. Must be published January 1-December 31 of preceding year. Deadline for entries: January 1 each year. SASE for contest rules and entry forms but better to check website. Awards cash and certificate $1,000 to winners (awards are for longer book, shorter book) and $500 each to Honor Book winners—(split between author and illustrator, if necessary). Judging by national committee from various N.S. regions (all are members of W.I.L.P.F.).

AIM Magazine Short Story Contest, P.O. Box 1174, Maywood IL 60153-8174. (773)874-6184. **Contest Directors:** Ruth Apilado, Mark Boone. Annual contest. **Open to students.** Estab. 1983. Purpose of contest: "We solicit stories with lasting social significance proving that people from different racial/ethnic backgrounds are more alike than they are different." Unpublished submissions only. Deadline for entries: August 15. SASE for contest rules and entry forms. SASE for return of work. No entry fee. Awards $100. Judging by editors. Contest open to everyone. Winning entry published in fall issue of *AIM*. Subscription rate $12/year. Single copy $4.50.

ALCUIN CITATION AWARD, The Alcuin Society, P.O. Box 3216, Vancouver, British Columbia V6B 3X8 Canada. (604)985-2758. Fax: (604)985-1091. E-mail: jrainer@shaw.ca. Website: www.alcuinsociety.com. Annual award. Estab. 1983. **Open to students.** Purpose of contest: Alcuin Citations are awarded annually for excellence in Canadian book design. Previously published submissions only, "in the year prior to the Awards Invitation to enter; i.e., 1996 awards went to books published in 1995." Submissions made by the author, publishers and designers. Deadline for entries: March 15. SASE. Entry fee is $10 per book. Awards certificate. Judging by professionals and those experienced in the field of book design. Requirements for entrants: Winners are selected from books designed and published in Canada. Awards are presented annually at the Annual General Meeting of the Alcuin Society held in late May or early June each year.

AMERICA & ME ESSAY CONTEST, Farm Bureau Insurance, Box 30400, 7373 W. Saginaw, Lansing MI 48909-7900. (517)323-7000. Fax: (517)323-6615. E-mail: lfedewa@fbinsmi.com. Website: farmbureau insurance-mi.co. **Contest Coordinator:** Lisa Fedewa. Annual contest. **Open to students.** Estab. 1968. Purpose of the contest: to give Michigan 8th graders the opportunity to express their thoughts/feelings on America and their roles in America. Unpublished submissions only. Deadline for entries: mid-November. SASE for contest rules and entry forms. "We have a school mailing list. Any school located in Michigan is eligible to participate." Entries not returned. No entry fee. Awards savings bonds and plaques for state top ten ($500-1,000), certificates and plaques for top 3 winners from each school. Each school may submit up to 10 essays for judging. Judging by home office employee volunteers. Requirements for entrants: "Participants must work through their schools or our agents' sponsoring schools. No individual submissions will be accepted. Top ten essays and excerpts from other essays are published in booklet form following the contest. State capitol/schools receive copies."

AMERICAN ASSOCIATION OF UNIVERSITY WOMEN, NORTH CAROLINA DIVISION, AWARD IN JUVENILE LITERATURE, North Carolina Literary and Historical Association, 4610 Mail Service Center, Raleigh NC 27699-4610. (919)733-9375. Fax: (919)733-8807. **Award Coordinator:** Michael Hill. Annual award. Purpose of award: to recognize the year's best work of juvenile literature by a North Carolina author. Book must be published during the year ending June 30 of the year of publication. Submissions made by author, author's agent or publisher. Deadline for entries: July 15. SASE for contest rules. Awards a cup to the winner and winner's name inscribed on a plaque displayed within the North Carolina Office of Archives and History. Judging by Board of Award selected by sponsoring organization. Requirements for entrants: Author must have maintained either legal residence or actual physical residence, or a combination of both, in the State of North Carolina for three years immediately preceding the close of the contest period.

AMERICAS AWARD, Consortium of Latin American Studies Programs (CLASP), CLASP Committee on Teaching and Outreach, % Center for Latin American and Caribbean Studies, University of Wisconsin-Milwaukee, P.O. Box 413, Milwaukee WI 53201. (414)229-5986. Fax: (414)229-2879. E-mail: jkline@uw m.edu. Website: www.uwm.edu/Dept/CLACS/outreach_americas.html. **Coordinator:** Julie Kline. Annual award. Estab. 1993. Purpose of contest: "Up to two awards are given each spring in recognition of U.S. published works (from the previous year) of fiction, poetry, folklore or selected nonfiction (from picture books to works for young adults) in English or Spanish which authentically and engagingly relate to Latin America, the Caribbean, or to Latinos in the United States. By both combining and linking the "Americas," the intent is to reach beyond geographic borders, as well as multicultural-international boundaries, focusing instead upon cultural heritages within the hemisphere." Previously published submissions only. Submissions open to anyone with an interest in the theme of the award. Deadline for entries: January 15. SASE for contest rules and any committee changes. Awards $500 cash prize, plaque and a formal presentation at the Library of Congress, Washington DC. Judging by a review committee consisting of individuals in teaching, library work, outreach and children's literature specialists.

AMHA LITERARY CONTEST, American Morgan Horse Association Youth, P.O. Box 960, Shelburne VT 05482. (802)985-4944. E-mail: info@morganhorse.com. Website: www.morganhorse.com. Annual contest. Open to students under 21. Purpose of contest: "to award youth creativity." The contest includes categories for both poetry and essays. Unpublished submissions only. Submissions made by author. Deadline for entries: October 1. SASE for contest rules and entry forms. No entry fee. Awards $25 cash and ribbons to up to 5th place. "Winning entry will be published in *AMHA News and Morgan Sales Network*, a monthly publication."

N AMHA MORGAN ART CONTEST, American Morgan Horse Association, Box 960, Shelburne VT 05482. (802)985-4944. Fax: (802)985-8897. E-mail: info@morganhorse.com. Website: www.morganh orse.com. Annual contest. The art contest consists of two categories: Morgan art (pencil sketches, oils, water colors, paintbrush), Morgan specialty pieces (sculptures, carvings). Unpublished submissions only. Deadline for entries: October 1. Contest rules and entry forms available for SASE. Entries not returned.

Entry fee is $5. Awards $50 first prize in 2 divisions (for adults) and AMHA gift certificates to top 6 places (for children). Judging by *The Morgan Horse* magazine staff. "All work submitted becomes property of The American Morgan Horse Association. Selected works may be used for promotional purposes by the AMHA." Requirements for entrants: "We consider all work submitted." Works displayed at the annual convention and the AMHA headquarters; published in *AMAHA News* and *Morgan Sales Network* and in color in the *Morgan Horse Magazine* (TMHA). The contest divisions consist of Junior (to age 17), Senior (18 and over) and Professional (commercial artists). Each art piece must have its own application form and its own entry fee. Matting is optional.

HANS CHRISTIAN ANDERSEN AWARD, IBBY International Board on Books for Young People, Nonnenweg 12, Postfach, CH-4003 Basel Switzerland. Phone: (004161)272 29 17. Fax: (004161)272 27 57. E-mail: lbby@eye.ch. Website: www.ibby.org. **Executive Director:** Leena Maissen. Award offered every two years. Purpose of award: A Hans Christian Andersen Medal shall be awarded every two years by the International Board on Books for Young People (IBBY) to an author and to an illustrator, living at the time of the nomination, who by the outstanding value of their work are judged to have made a lasting contribution to literature for children and young people. The complete works of the author and of the illustrator will be taken into consideration in awarding the medal, which will be accompanied by a diploma. Previously published titles only. Submissions are nominated by National Sections of IBBY in good standing. The National Sections select the candidates. The Hans Christian Andersen Award, named after Denmark's famous storyteller, is the highest international recognition given to an author and an illustrator of children's books. The Author's Award has been given since 1956, the Illustrator's Award since 1966. The Andersen Award is often called the "Little Nobel Prize." Her Majesty Queen Margrethe of Denmark is the Patron of the Hans Christian Andersen Awards. The Hans Christian Andersen Jury judges the books submitted for medals according to literary and artistic criteria. The awards are presented at the biennial congresses of IBBY.

ARTS RECOGNITION AND TALENT SEARCH (ARTS), National Foundation for Advancement in the Arts, 800 Brickell Ave., Suite 500, Miami FL 33131. (305)377-1140. Fax: (305)377-1149. E-mail: nfaa@nfaa.org. Website: www.ARTSaward.org. **Contact:** Lisanne Norton. **Open to students**/high school seniors or 17- and 18-year-olds. Annual award. Estab. 1981. "Created to recognize and reward outstanding accomplishment in dance, music, jazz, theater, photography, film and video, visual arts and/or writing. Arts Recognition and Talent Search (ARTS) is an innovative national program of the National Foundation for Advancement in the Arts (NFAA). Established in 1981, ARTS touches the lives of gifted young people across the country, providing financial support, scholarships and goal-oriented artistic, educational and career opportunities. Each year, from a pool of more than 8,000 applicants, an average of 500 ARTS awardees are chosen for NFAA support by panels of distinguished artists and educators. Deadline for entries: June 1 and October 1. Entry fee is $30/40. Fee waivers available based on need. Awards $100-3,000—unrestricted cash grants. Judging by a panel of authors and educators recognized in the field. Rights to submitted/winning material: NFAA/ARTS retains the right to duplicate work in an anthology or in Foundation literature unless otherwise specified by the artist. Requirements for entrants: Artists must be high school seniors or, if not enrolled in high school, must be 17 or 18 years old. Applicants must be US citizens or residents, unless applying in jazz. Works will be published in an anthology distributed during ARTS Week, the final adjudication phase which takes place in Miami. NFAA will invite 40% of artists to participate in "ARTS Week 2003," in January in Miami-Dade County, Florida. ARTS Week is a once-in-a-lifetime experience consisting of performances, master classes, workshops, readings, exhibits, and enrichment activities with renowned artists and arts educators. All expenses are paid by NFAA, including airfare, hotel, meals and ground transportation.

ASPCA CHILDREN'S ESSAY CONTEST, American Society for the Prevention of Cruelty to Animals, 424 E. 92nd St., New York NY 10028-6804. (212)876-7700. Fax: (212)860-3435. E-mail: education@aspca .org. Website: www.aspca.org. **Contest Manager:** Miriam Ramos. Submit entries to: Miriam Ramos, manager, education programs, humane education. **Open to students.** Annual contest. Estab. 1990. An essay contest for students in grades 1-6. Unpublished submissions only. Submissions made by author, parent, teacher. Deadline for entries: December 16, 2003. SASE for contest rules and entry forms. Prizes vary, could include books, magazine subscriptions, T-shirts. Judging by ASPCA staff. Requirements for entrants: Open to all students in grades 1-6, must be student's own writing. Prizes are given for winning individuals and their classrooms. Judging in 2 categories, Grades 1-3 and Grades 4-6.

THE ASPCA HENRY BERGH CHILDREN'S BOOK AWARD, The American Society For the Prevention of Cruelty to Animals, 424 E. 92nd St., New York NY 10128-6804. (212)876-7700, ext. 4409. Fax: (212)860-3435. E-mail: education@aspca.org. Website: www.aspca.org. **Award Manager:** Miriam

Ramos. Submit entries to: Miriam Ramos, manager of education programs, humane education. Competition open to adults. Annual award. Estab. 2000. Purpose of contest: To honor outstanding children's literature that fosters empathy and compassion for all living things. Awards presented to authors. Previously published submissions only. Submissions made by author or author's agent. Must be published January 2002-December 2002. Deadline for entries: October 31, 2002. SASE for contest rules and entry forms. Awards foil seals, plaque, certificate. Judging by professionals in animal welfare and children's literature. Requirements for entrants: Open to children's literature about animals and/or the environment published in 2002. Includes fiction, nonfiction and poetry in 3 categories: Companion Animals, Ecology and Environment and Humane Heroes.

ATLANTIC WRITING COMPETITION, Writer's Federation of Nova Scotia, 1113 Marginal Rd., Halifax, Nova Scotia B3H 4P7 Canada. (902)423-8116. Fax: (902)422-0881. E-mail: talk@writers.ns .ca/competitions. Website: www.writers.ns.cacompetitions. Annual contest. Purpose is to encourage emerging writers in Atlantic Canada to explore their talents by sending unpublished work to any of five categories: novel, short story, poetry, writing for children or magazine article. Unpublished submissions only. Only open to residents of Atlantic Canada who are unpublished in category they enter. Visit website for more information.

BAKER'S PLAYS HIGH SCHOOL PLAYWRITING CONTEST, Baker's Plays, P.O. Box 6992222, Quincy MA 02269-9222. Fax: (617)745-9891. E-mail: editor@bakersplays.com. Website: www.bakersplays.c om. **Contest Director:** Kurt Gombar. Annual contest. Estab. 1990. Purpose of the contest: to acknowledge playwrights at the high school level and to insure the future of American theater. Unpublished submissions only. Postmark deadline: January 30, 2002. Notification: May. SASE for contest rules and entry forms. No entry fee. Awards $500 to the first place playwright and Baker's Plays will publish the play; $250 to the second place playwright with an honorable mention; and $100 to the third place playwright with an honorable mention in the series. Judged anonymously. **Open to any high school student.** Plays must be accompanied by the signature of a sponsoring high school drama or English teacher, and it is recommended that the play receive a production or a public reading prior to the submission. "Please include a SAE with priority postage." Teachers must not submit student's work. The first place playwright will have their play published in an acting edition the September following the contest. The work will be described in the Baker's Plays Catalogue, which is distributed to 50,000 prospective producing organizations.

BAY AREA BOOK REVIEWER'S ASSOCIATION (BABRA), %*Poetry Flash*, 1450 Fourth St., #4, Berkeley CA 94710. (510)525-5476. Fax: (510)525-6752. E-mail: babra@poetryflash.org. Website: www.poetryflash.org. **Contact:** Joyce Jenkins. Annual award for outstanding book in children's literature, open to books published in the current calendar year by Northern California authors. Annual award. Estab. 1981. "BABRA presents annual awards to Bay Area (northern California) authors annually in fiction, nonfiction, poetry and children's literature. Purpose is to encourage writers and stimulate interest in books and reading." Previously published books only. Must be published the calendar year prior to spring awards ceremony. Submissions nominated by publishers; author or agent could also nominate published work. Deadline for entries: December. No entry forms. Send 3 copies of the book to attention: Babra. No entry fee. Awards $100 honorarium and award certificate. Judging by voting members of the Bay Area Book Reviewer's Association. Books that reach the "finals" (usually 3-5 per category) displayed at annual award ceremonies (spring). Nominated books are displayed and sold at BABRA's annual awards ceremonies in the spring of each year; the winner is asked to read at the San Francisco Public Library's Main Branch.

JOHN AND PATRICIA BEATTY AWARD, California Library Association, 717 20th Street, Suite 200, Sacramento CA 95814. (916)447-8541. Fax: (916)447-8394. E-mail: info@cla-net.org. Website: www. cla-net.org. **Executive Director:** Susan Negreen. Annual award. Estab. 1987. Purpose of award: "The purpose of the John and Patricia Beatty Award is to encourage the writing of quality children's books highlighting California, its culture, heritage and/or future." Previously published submissions only. Submissions made by the author, author's agent or review copies sent by publisher. The award is given to the author of a children's book published the preceding year. Deadline for entries: Submissions may be made January-December. Contact CLA Executive Director who will liaison with Beatty Award Committee. Awards cash prize of $500 and an engraved plaque. Judging by a 5-member selection committee appointed by the president of the California Library Association. Requirements for entrants: "Any children's or young adult book set in California and published in the U.S. during the calendar year preceding the presentation of the award is eligible for consideration. This includes works of fiction as well as nonfiction for children and young people of all ages. Reprints and compilations are not eligible. The California setting must be depicted authentically and must serve as an integral focus for the book." Winning selection is announced through press release during National Library Week in April. Author is presented with award at annual California Library Association Conference in November.

THE IRMA S. AND JAMES H. BLACK BOOK AWARD, Bank Street College of Education, 610 W. 112th St., New York NY 10025-1898. (212)875-4450. Fax: (212)875-4558. E-mail: lindag@bnkst.edu. Website: http://streetcat.bnkst.edu/html/isb.html. **Contact:** Linda Greengrass. Annual award. Estab. 1972. Purpose of award: "The award is given each spring for a book for young children, published in the previous year, for excellence of both text and illustrations." Entries must have been published during the previous calendar year (between January '02 and December '02 for 2002 award). Deadline for entries: December 15th. "Publishers submit books to us by sending them here to me at the Bank Street Library. Authors may ask their publishers to submit their books. Out of these, three to five books are chosen by a committee of older children and children's literature professionals. These books are then presented to children in selected second, third and fourth grade classes here and at a few other cooperating schools on the East Coast. These children are the final judges who pick the actual award. A scroll (one each for the author and illustrator, if they're different) with the recipient's name and a gold seal designed by Maurice Sendak are awarded in May."

BOOK OF THE YEAR FOR CHILDREN, Canadian Library Association, 328 Frank St., Ottawa, Ontario K2P 0X8 Canada. (613)232-9625. Fax: (613)563-9895. Website: www.cla.ca. **Contact:** Chairperson, Canadian Association of Children's Librarians. Annual award. Estab. 1947. "The main purpose of the award is to encourage writing and publishing in Canada of good books for children up to and including age 14. If, in any year, no book is deemed to be of award calibre, the award shall not be made that year. To merit consideration, the book must have been published in Canada and its author must be a Canadian citizen or a permanent resident of Canada." Previously published submissions only; must be published between January 1 and December 1 of the previous year. Deadline for entries: January 1. SASE for award rules. Entries not returned. No entry fee. Awards a medal. Judging by committee of members of the Canadian Association of Children's Librarians. Requirements for entrants: Contest open only to Canadian authors or residents of Canada. Winning books are on display at CLA headquarters.

THE BOSTON GLOBE-HORN BOOK AWARDS, The Boston Globe & The Horn Book, Inc., The Horn Book, 56 Roland St., Suite 200, Boston MA 02129. (617)628-0225. Fax: (617)628-0882. E-mail: info@hbook.com. Website: www.hbook.com/bghb.shtml. Annual award. Estab. 1967. Purpose of award: "to reward literary excellence in children's and young adult books. Awards are for picture books, nonfiction and fiction. Up to two honor books may be chosen for each category." Books must be published between June 1, 2002 and May 31, 2003. Deadline for entries: May 15, 2003. "Publishers usually submit books. Award winners receive $500 and silver engraved bowl, honor book winners receive a silver plate." Judging by 3 judges involved in children's book field. *The Horn Book Magazine* publishes speeches given at awards ceremonies. The book must have been published in the U.S."

ANN ARLYS BOWLER POETRY CONTEST, *Read* Magazine, 200 First Stamford Place, P.O. Box 120023, Stamford CT 06912-0023. (203)705-3406. Fax: (203)705-1661. E-mail: jkroll@weeklyreader.c om. Website: www.weeklyreader.com/read.html. **Contest Director:** Jennifer Kroll. Annual contest. Estab. 1988. Purpose of the contest: to reward young-adult poets (grades 6-12). Unpublished submissions only. Submissions made by the author or nominated by a person or group of people. Entry form must include signature of teacher, parent or guardian, and student verifying originality. Maximum number of submissions per student: three poems. Deadline for entries: January 15. SASE for contest rules and entry forms. No entry fee. Awards 6 winners $100 each, medal of honor and publication in *Read*. Semifinalists receive $50 each. Judging by *Read* and *Weekly Reader* editors and teachers. Requirements for entrants: the material must be original. Winning entries will be published in an issue of *Read*.

BRANT POINT PRIZE, What's Inside Press, P.O. Box 18203, Beverly Hills CA 90209. (800)269-7757. Fax: (800)856-2160. E-mail: bpp@whatsinsidepress.com. Website: www.whatsinsidepress.com. and www.brantpointprize.com. Submit entries to: Brant Point Prize. **Open to students.** Annual contest. Estab. 1999. Purpose of contest: To recognize excellence in unpublished children's writing and provide opportunities to get published. Unpublished submissions only. Submissions made by author. Deadline for entries: August. SASE for contest rules and entry forms. Entry fee is $10 fully tax-deductible donation to children's charity. Awards publishing contract. Other prizes include Tiffany & Co. pens, money, T-shirts. Judging panel changes every year. Includes previous year's winner. Rights to winning material acquired. Contest is open to everyone.

⚡ ANN CONNOR BRIMER AWARD, Nova Scotia Library Association, P.O. Box 36036, Halifax, Nova Scotia B3J 3S9 Canada. (902)490-5875. Fax: (902)490-5893. **Award Director:** Heather MacKenzie. Annual award. Estab. 1991. Purpose of the contest: to recognize excellence in writing. Given to an author of a children's book who resides in Atlantic Canada. Previously published submissions only. Submissions made by the author's agent or nominated by a person or group of people. Must be published in previous year. Deadline for entries: November 15. SASE for contest rules and entry forms. No entry fee. Awards $1,000. Judging by a selection committee. Requirements for entrants: Book must be intended for children up to age 15; in print and readily available; fiction or nonfiction except textbooks.

✅ BYLINE MAGAZINE CONTESTS, P.O. Box 5240, Edmond OK 73083-5240. E-mail: mpreston@b ylinemag.com. Website: www.bylinemag.com. **Contest Director:** Marcia Preston. **Open to adults.** Purpose of contest: *ByLine* runs 4 contests a month on many topics to encourage and motivate writers. Past topics include first chapter of a novel, children's fiction, children's poem, nonfiction for children, personal essay, general short stories, valentine or love poem, etc. Send SASE for contest flier with topic list and rules, or see website. Unpublished submissions only. Submissions made by the author. "We do not publish the contests' winning entries, just the names of the winners." SASE for contest rules. Entry fee is $3-4. Awards cash prizes for first, second and third place. Amounts vary. Judging by qualified writers or editors. List of winners will appear in magazine.

✅ BYLINE MAGAZINE STUDENT PAGE, P.O. Box 5240, Edmond OK 73083-5240. (405)348-5591. Website: www.bylinemag.com. **Contest Director:** Marcia Preston, publisher. **Open to students.** Estab. 1981. "We offer writing contests for students in grades 1-12 on a monthly basis, September through May, with cash prizes and publication of top entries." Previously unpublished submissions only. "This is not a market for illustration." Deadline for entries varies. "Entry fee usually $1." Awards cash and publication. Judging by qualified editors and writers. "We publish top entries in student contests. Winners' list published in magazine dated 2 months past deadline." Send SASE for details.

RANDOLPH CALDECOTT MEDAL, Association for Library Service to Children, Division of the American Library Association, 50 E. Huron, Chicago IL 60611. (312)280-2163. Website: www.ala.org/alsc/caldecott.html. **Executive Director:** Malore I. Brown. Annual award. Estab. 1938. Purpose of the award: to honor the artist of the most distinguished picture book for children published in the US (Illustrator must be US citizen or resident.) Must be published year preceding award. Deadline for entries: December. SASE for award rules. Entries not returned. No entry fee. "Medal given at ALA Annual Conference during the Newbery/Caldecott Banquet."

CALIFORNIA YOUNG PLAYWRIGHTS CONTEST, Playwrights Project, 450 B St., Suite 1020, San Diego CA 92101. (619)239-8222. Fax: (619)239-8225. E-mail: write@playwrightsproject.com. Website: www.playwrightsproject.com. **Director:** Deborah Salzer. **Open to Californians under age 19.** Annual contest. Estab. 1985. "Our organization and the contest is designed to nurture promising young writers. We hope to develop playwrights and audiences for live theater. We also teach playwriting." Submissions required to be unpublished and not produced professionally. Submissions made by the author. Deadline for entries: April 1. SASE for contest rules and entry form. No entry fee. Award is professional productions of 3-5 short plays each year, participation of the writers in the entire production process, with a royalty awarded. Judging by professionals in the theater community, a committee of 5-7; changes somewhat each year. Works performed in San Diego at the Cassius Carter Centre Stage of the Globe Theatres. Writers submitting scripts of 10 or more pages receive a detailed script evaluation letter.

ℕ RAYMOND CARVER SHORT STORY CONTEST, English Dept. Humboldt State University, Arcata CA 95521-8299. (707)826-5946, ext. 1. Fax: (707)826-5939. E-mail: carver@humboldt.edu. Submit entries to Student Coordinator. **Open to students**, US citizens and writers living in the US. Annual contest. Estab. 1982. Unpublished submissions only. Submissions made by author. Send 2 copies of each story. Author's name and contact information must appear on separate cover sheet only. Deadline for entries: January 10, 2003. SASE for contest rules and entry forms. Entry fee is $10/story. Awards $1,000 1st place and publication in TOYON; $500 2nd place and honorable mention in TOYON; 3rd place honorable mention. Judges change every year. For a sample copy in TOYON, send a separate $5 check to the above address.

CHILDREN'S BOOK AWARD, Federation of Children's Book Groups. The Old Malt House, Aldbourne Marlborough, Wiltshire SN8 2DW England. 01672 540629. Fax: 1672 541280. E-mail: marianneade y@aol.com. **Coordinator:** Marianne Adey. Purpose of the award: "The C.B.A. is an annual prize for the best children's book of the year judged by the children themselves." Categories: (I) books for younger children, (II) books for younger readers, (III) books for older readers. Estab. 1980. Works must be published in the United Kingdom. Deadline for entries: December 31. SASE for rules and entry forms. Entries not returned. Awards "a magnificent silver and oak trophy worth over $6,000 and a portfolio of children's work." Silver dishes to each category winner. Judging by children. Requirements for entrants: Work must be fiction and published in the UK during the current year (poetry is ineligible). Work will be published in current "Pick of the Year" publication.

CHILDREN'S WRITER WRITING CONTESTS, 93 Long Ridge Rd., West Redding CT 06896-1124. (203)792-8600. Fax: (203)792-8406. Contest offered twice per year by *Children's Writer*, the monthly newsletter of writing and publishing trends. Purpose of the award: To promote higher quality children's literature. "Each contest has its own theme. Any original unpublished piece, not accepted by any publisher at the time of submission, is eligible." Submissions made by the author. Deadline for entries: Last weekday in February and October. "We charge a $10 entry fee for nonsubscribers only, which is applicable against a subscription to *Children's Writer*." Awards 1st place—$250 or $500, a certificate and publication in *Children's Writer*; 2nd place—$100 or $250, and certificate; 3rd-5th places—$50 or $100 and certificates. To obtain the rules and theme for the current contest send a SASE to *Children's Writer* at the above address. Put "Contest Request" in the lower left of your envelope. Judging by a panel of 4 selected from the staff of the Institute of Children's Literature. "We acquire First North American Serial Rights (to print the winner in *Children's Writer*), after which all rights revert to author." Open to any writer. Entries are judged on age targeting, originality, quality of writing and, for nonfiction, how well the information is conveyed and accuracy. "Submit clear photocopies only, not originals; submission will *not* be returned. Manuscripts should be typed double-spaced. No pieces containing violence or derogatory, racist or sexist language or situations will be accepted, at the sole discretion of the judges."

CHILDREN'S WRITERS FICTION CONTEST, Stepping Stones, P.O. Box 8863, Springfield MO 65801-8863. (417)863-7369. E-mail: verwil@alumni.pace.edu. **Coordinator:** V.R. Williams. Annual contest. Estab. 1993. Purpose of contest: to promote writing for children by giving children's writers an opportunity to submit work in competition. Unpublished submissions only. Submissions made by the author. Deadline for entries: July 31. SASE for contest rules and entry forms. Entry fee is $8. Awards cash prize, certificate and publication in chapbook; certificates for Honorable Mention. Judging by Goodin, Williams and Goodwin. First rights to winning material acquired or purchased. Requirements for entrants: Work must be suitable for children and no longer than 1,500 words. "Send SASE for list of winners."

MR. CHRISTIE'S BOOK AWARD® PROGRAM, Christie Brown & Co., Division of Nabisco Ltd, 95 Moatfield Dr., Don Mills, Ontario M3B 3L6 Canada. (416)441-5238. Fax: (416)441-5328. E-mail: pamela.singh@kraft.com. **Coordinator:** Pamela Singh. Competition is open to Canadian citizens, landed immigrants and students. Books must be published in Canada the previous year. Annual award. Estab. 1989. Purpose of award: "to reward excellence in the writing and illustration of Canadian children's books in both official languages and honor those authors and illustrators who, with their words and pictures, create the magic that sparks children's imaginations." Contest includes three categories: Best Book for 7 and under; 8-11; and 12 and up. Write for more information. Awards $7,500 annually in each of the English and French categories. Requirements for entrants: must have published children's literature in the previous calendar year written and/or illustrated by a Canadian citizen or landed immigrant.

COLORADO BOOK AWARDS, Colorado Center for the Book, 2123 Downing St., Denver CO 80205. (303)839-8320. Fax: (303)839-8319. E-mail: ccftb@compuserve.com. Website: www.coloradobook.org. **Award Director:** Christiane Citron. Annual award. Estab. 1993. Previously published submissions only. Submissions are made by the author, author's agent, nominated by a person or group of people. Requires Colorado residency by authors. Deadline for entries: January 15, 2003. SASE for contest rules and entry forms. Entry fee is $45. Awards $250 and plaque. Judging by a panel of literary agents, booksellers and librarians. Please note, we *also* have an annual competition for illustrators to design a poster and associated graphics for our Book Festival. The date varies. Inquiries are welcomed.

THE COMMONWEALTH CLUB'S BOOK AWARDS CONTEST, The Commonwealth Club of California, 595 Market St., San Francisco CA 94105. (415)597-4846. Fax: (415)597-6729. E-mail: blane@commonwealthclub.org. Website: www.commonwealthclub.org/bookawards. **Attn:** Barbara Blane. Chief Executive Officer: Gloria Duffy. Annual contest. Estab. 1932. Purpose of contest: the encouragement and production of literature in California. Juvenile category included. Previously published submission; must be published from January 1 to December 31, previous to contest year. Deadline for entries: January 31. SASE for contest rules and entry forms. No entry fee. Awards gold and silver medals. Judging by the Book

Awards Jury. The contest is only open to California writers/illustrators (must have been resident of California when ms was accepted for publication). "The award winners will be honored at the Annual Book Awards Program." Winning entries are displayed at awards program and advertised in newsletter.

CRICKET LEAGUE, *Cricket*, P.O. Box 300, 315 Fifth St., Peru IL 61354. (815)224-5803. Website: www.cricketmag.com. Address entries to: Cricket League. Monthly. Estab. 1973. "The purpose of Cricket League contests is to encourage creativity and give young people an opportunity to express themselves in writing, drawing, painting or photography. There is a contest each month. Possible categories include story, poetry, or art. Each contest relates to a *specific theme* described in each *Cricket* issue's Cricket League page. Signature verifying originality, age and address of entrant required and permission to publish. Entries which do not relate to the current month's theme cannot be considered." Unpublished submissions only. Deadline for entries: the 25th of each month. Cricket League rules, contest theme, and submission deadline information can be found in the current issue of *Cricket* and via website. "We prefer that children who enter the contests subscribe to the magazine or that they read *Cricket* in their school or library." No entry fee. Awards certificate suitable for framing and children's books or art/writing supplies. Judging by *Cricket* editors. Obtains right to print prizewinning entries in magazine. Refer to contest rules in current *Cricket* issue. Winning entries are published on the Cricket League pages in the *Cricket* magazine 3 months subsequent to the issue in which the contest was announced. Current theme, rules, and prizewinning entries also posted on the website.

DELACORTE PRESS PRIZE FOR A FIRST YOUNG ADULT NOVEL, Delacorte Press, Books for Young Readers Department, 1540 Broadway, New York NY 10036. (212)782-9000. Fax: (212)302-7985. Website: www.randomhouse.com/kids/submit. Annual award. Estab. 1982. Purpose of award: to encourage the writing of contemporary young adult fiction. Previously unpublished submissions only. Manuscripts sent to Delacorte Press may not be submitted to other publishers while under consideration for the prize. "Entries must be submitted between October 1 and New Year's Day. The real deadline is a December 31 postmark. Early entries are appreciated." SASE for award rules. No entry fee. Awards a $1,500 cash prize and a $6,000 advance against royalties for world rights on a hardcover and paperback book contract. Contest results will be announced in late Spring 2003. Works published in an upcoming Delacorte Press, an imprint of Random House, Inc., Books for Young Readers list. Judged by the editors of the Books for Young Readers Department of Delacorte Press. Requirements for entrants: The writer must be American or Canadian and must *not* have previously published a young adult novel but may have published anything else. Foreign-language mss and translations and mss submitted to a previous Delacorte Press are not eligible. Send SASE for new guidelines. Guidelines are also available on our website.

MARGARET A. EDWARDS AWARD, 50 East Huron St., Chicago IL 60611-2795. (312)280-4390 or (800)545-2433. Fax: (312)664-7459. E-mail: yalsa@ala.org. Website: www.ala.org/yalsa. Annual award administered by the Young Adult Library Services Association (YALSA) of the American Library Association (ALA) and sponsored by *School Library Journal* magazine. Purpose of award: "ALA's Young Adult Library Services Association (YALSA), on behalf of librarians who work with young adults in all types of libraries, will give recognition to those authors whose book or books have provided young adults with a window through which they can view their world and which will help them to grow and to understand themselves and their role in relationships, society and the world." Previously published submissions only. Submissions are nominated by young adult librarians and teenagers. Must be published five years before date of award. SASE for award rules and entry forms. No entry fee. Judging by members of the Young Adult Library Services Association. Deadline for entry: June 1. "The award will be given annually to an author whose book or books, over a period of time, have been accepted by young adults as an authentic voice that continues to illuminate their experiences and emotions, giving insight into their lives. The book or books should enable them to understand themselves, the world in which they live, and their relationship with others and with society. The book or books must be in print at the time of the nomination."

DOROTHY CANFIELD FISHER CHILDREN'S BOOK AWARD, Vermont Department of Libraries, % Northeast Regional Library, 23 Tilton Rd., St. Johnsbury VT 05819. (802)828-3261. Fax: (802)828-2199. E-mail: ggreene@dol.state.vt.us. Website: www.dol.state.vt.us. **Chair:** Sally Margolis. Annual award. Estab. 1957. Purpose of the award: to encourage Vermont children to become enthusiastic and discriminating readers by providing them with books of good quality by living American authors published in the current year. Deadline for entries: December of year book was published. SASE for award rules and entry forms. No entry fee. Awards a scroll presented to the winning author at an award ceremony. Judging is by the children grades 4-8. They vote for their favorite book. Requirements for entrants: "Titles must be original work, published in the United States, and be appropriate to children in grades 4 through 8. The book must be copyrighted in the current year. It must be written by an American author living in the U.S."

FLICKER TALE CHILDREN'S BOOK AWARD, Flicker Tale Award Committee, North Dakota Library Association, Bismarck Public Library, 515 N. Fifth St., Bismarck ND 58501. (701)222-6412. Fax: (701)221-6854. **Contact:** Marvia Boettcher. Estab. 1979. Purpose of award: to give children across the state of North Dakota a chance to vote for their book of choice from a nominated list of 10: 5 in the picture book category; 5 in the juvenile category. Also, to promote awareness of quality literature for children. Previously published submissions only. Submissions nominated by librarians and teachers across the state of North Dakota. Awards a plaque from North Dakota Library Association and banquet dinner. Judging by children in North Dakota. Entry deadline in June.

FLORIDA STATE WRITING COMPETITION, Florida Freelance Writers Association, P.O. Box A, North Stratford NH 03590. (603)922-8338. Fax: (603)922-8339. E-mail: danakcnw@ncia.net. Website: www.writers-editors.com. **Executive Director:** Dana K. Cassell. Annual contest. Estab. 1984. Categories include children's literature (length appropriate to age category). Entry fee is $5 (members), $10 (nonmembers) or $10-20 for entries longer than 3,000 words. Awards $100 first prize, $75 second prize, $50 third prize, certificates for honorable mentions. Judging by teachers, editors and published authors. Judging criteria: interest and readability within age group, writing style and mechanics, originality, salability. Deadline: March 15. For copy of official entry form, send #10 SASE or visit website. List of 1999-2002 winners on website.

FOR A GOOD TIME THEATRE COMPANY'S ANNUAL SCRIPT CONTEST, For A Good Time Theatre Company, P.O. Box 5421, Saginaw MI 48603-0421. (989)753-3861. Fax: (989)753-5890. E-mail: theatreco@aol.com. **Contest Director:** Lee-Perry Belleau, artistic director. Annual contest. Estab. 1997. Purpose of contest: To award top-notch playwrights in theater for young audiences with a production by a critically acclaimed regional theater company. Unpublished submissions only. Submissions made by author or by author's agent. Deadline for entries: May 1 (postmark). SASE for contest rules and entry forms. Entry fee is $10. Awards production of the winning script; cash award of $1,000 and a videotape of the produced script. Judging by For A Good Time Theatre's staff dramaturg (prescreening). Screening is then done by the producer. Final judging is done by the artistic director. Acquires regional production rights for the year of the contest. Plays must be 50 minutes long; must be a musical (composed music is not necessary, just song lyrics); written for multiple characters played by three actors, with roles for men and women. Other criteria, such as subject matter, varies from year to year. Send SASE for details.

DON FREEMAN MEMORIAL GRANT-IN-AID, Society of Children's Book Writers and Illustrators, 8271 Beverly Blvd., Los Angeles CA 90048. E-mail: scbwi@scbwi.org. Website: www.scbwi.org. Estab. 1974. Purpose of award: to "enable picture book artists to further their understanding, training and work in the picture book genre." Applications and prepared materials will be accepted between January 15 and February 15. Grant awarded and announced on June 15. SASE for award rules and entry forms. SASE for return of entries. No entry fee. Annually awards one grant of $1,500 and one runner-up grant of $500. "The grant-in-aid is available to both full and associate members of the SCBWI who, as artists, seriously intend to make picture books their chief contribution to the field of children's literature."

AMELIA FRANCES HOWARD GIBBON AWARD FOR ILLUSTRATION, Canadian Library Association, 328 Frank St., Ottawa, Ontario K2P 0X8 Canada. (613)232-9625. Website: www.cla.ca. **Contact:** Chairperson, Canadian Association of Children's Librarians. Annual award. Estab. 1971. Purpose of the award: "to honor excellence in the illustration of children's book(s) in Canada. To merit consideration the book must have been published in Canada and its illustrator must be a Canadian citizen or a permanent resident of Canada." Previously published submissions only; must be published between January 1 and December 31 of the previous year. Deadline for entries: January 1. SASE for award rules. Entries not returned. No entry fee. Awards a medal. Judging by selection committee of members of Canadian Association of Children's Librarians. Requirements for entrants: illustrator must be Canadian or Canadian resident. Winning books are on display at CLA Headquarters.

GOLD MEDALLION BOOK AWARDS, Evangelical Christian Publishers Association, 1969 East Broadway Rd., Suite Two, Tempe AZ 85282. (480)966-3998. Fax: (480)966-1944. E-mail: dross@ecpa.org. Website: www.ecpa.org. **President:** Doug Ross. Annual award. Estab. 1978. Categories include Preschool Children's Books, Elementary Children's Books, Youth Books. "All entries must be evangelical in nature and cannot be contrary to ECPA's Statement of Faith (stated in official rules)." Deadlines for entries: December 1. Guidelines available annually in October. SASE for award rules and entry form. "The work must be submitted by the publisher." Entry fee is $300 for nonmembers. Awards a Gold Medallion plaque.

[N] GOLDEN ARCHER AWARD, Wisconsin Educational Media Association, 1300 Industrial Dr., Fennimore WI 53809. Website: www.wemaonline.org. **Award Director:** Annette R. Smith. **Open to students.** Annual award. Estab. 1974. Purpose of award: to encourage young readers to become better acquainted with quality literature written expressly for them, to broaden students' awareness of reading and literature as life-long pleasure and to honor favorite books and their authors. Previously published submissions only. Submissions nominated by Wisconsin students. No entry fee. Three awards are given—one in each of 3 categories, Primary, Intermediate and Middle/Junior High.

GOLDEN KITE AWARDS, Society of Children's Book Writers and Illustrators, 8271 Beverly Blvd., Los Angeles CA 90048. (323)782-1010. E-mail: scbwi@scbwi.org. Website: www.scbwi.org. **Coordinators:** Ruby Guerrero and Mercedes Coats. Annual award. Estab. 1973. "The works chosen will be those that the judges feel exhibit excellence in writing, and in the case of the picture-illustrated books—in illustration, and genuinely appeal to the interests and concerns of children. For the fiction and nonfiction awards, original works and single-author collections of stories or poems of which at least half are new and never before published in book form are eligible—anthologies and translations are not. For the picture-illustration awards, the art or photographs must be original works (the texts—which may be fiction or nonfiction—may be original, public domain or previously published). Deadline for entries: December 15. SASE for award rules. No entry fee. Awards statuettes and plaques. The panel of judges will consist of professional authors, illustrators, editors or agents." Requirements for entrants: "must be a member of SCBWI." Winning books will be displayed at national conference in August. Books to be entered, as well as further inquiries, should be submitted to: The Society of Children's Book Writers and Illustrators, above address.

[N] AURAND HARRIS MEMORIAL PLAYWRITING AWARD, The New England Theatre Conference, Northeastern University, 360 Huntington Ave., Boston MA 02115. Website: www.netconline.org/harris.htm. Annual award. Estab. 1997. Unpublished submissions only. Submissions by author. Deadline for entries: May 1. Handling fee is $20; no fee to current members of New England Theatre Conference. Awards 2 cash prizes: First prize of $1,000 and second prize of $500. Judging by a panel of judges named by the NETC Executive Board. Playwrights living outside of New England may participate by joining NETC. No scripts will be returned. Winners notified by mail.

[✓] HIGHLIGHTS FOR CHILDREN FICTION CONTEST, 803 Church St., Honesdale PA 18431-1895. (570)253-1080. Fax: (570)251-7847. Manuscripts should be addressed to Fiction Contest. Editor: Christine French Clark. Annual contest. Estab. 1980. Purpose of the contest: to stimulate interest in writing for children and reward and recognize excellence. Unpublished submissions only. Deadline for entries: February 28; entries accepted after January 1 only. SASE for contest rules and return of entries. No entry fee. Awards 3 prizes of $1,000 each in cash and a pewter bowl (or, at the winner's election, attendance at the Highlights Foundation Writers Workshop at Chautauqua). Judging by *Highlights* editors. Winning pieces are purchased for the cash prize of $1,000 and published in *Highlights*; other entries are considered for purchase. Requirements for entrants: open to any writer. Winners announced in June. Length up to 800 words. Stories for beginning readers should not exceed 400 words. Stories should be consistent with *Highlights* editorial requirements. No violence, crime or derogatory humor. Send SASE for guidelines. 2003 theme: " 'Stories About Friendship.' We are seeking all types of stories: humor, world cultures, adventure—within the theme of learning to get along with others."

HRC'S ANNUAL PLAYWRITING CONTEST, Hudson River Classics, Inc., P.O. Box 940, Hudson NY 12534. (518)828-0175. Fax: (518)828-1480. E-mail: jangrice2002@yahoo.com. **President:** Jan M. Grice. Annual contest. Estab. 1992. Hudson River Classics is a not-for-profit professional theater company dedicated to the advancement of performing in the Hudson River Valley area through reading of plays and providing opportunities for new playwrights. Unpublished submissions only. Submissions made by author and by the author's agent. Deadline for entries: May 1st. SASE for contest rules and entry forms. Entry fee is $5. Awards $500 cash plus concert reading by professional actors. Judging by panel selected by Board of Directors. Requirements for entrants: Entrants must live in the northeastern US.

[✓] INFORMATION BOOK AWARD, Children's Literature Roundtables of Canada, Dept. of Language Education, University of British Columbia, 2125 Main Mall, Vancouver, British Columbia V6T 1Z4 Canada. (604)822-5788. Fax: (604)922-1666. E-mail: aprilg@direct.ca. Website: www.library.ubc.ca/edlib/table/index.html. **Award Directors:** April Gill and Dr. Ron Jobe. Annual contest. Estab. 1987. Purpose of contest: The Information Book Award recognizes excellence in the writing of information books for young people from 5 to 15 years. It is awarded to the book that arouses interest, stimulates curiosity, captures the imagination, and fosters concern for the world around us. The award's aim is to recognize excellence

"WE WANT TO PUBLISH YOUR WORK."

Completely UPDATED Each Year

CHILDREN'S WRITER'S & ILLUSTRATOR'S MARKET

800+ EDITORS AND ART DIRECTORS WHO WANT YOUR WORK

● "I RECOMMEND THIS BOOK TO ANYONE SERIOUS ABOUT GETTING PUBLISHED. IT'S THE CHILDREN'S WRITER'S BIBLE."
—Allyn Johnson, Editorial director, Harcourt Children's Books

● Complete submission guidelines, contact names, and payment info

You would give anything to hear an editor speak those six magic words. So you work hard for weeks, months, even years to make that happen. You create a brilliant piece of work and a knock-out presentation, but there's still one vital step to ensure publication. You still need to submit your work to the right buyers. With rapid changes in the publishing industry it's not always easy to know who those buyers are. That's why each year thousands of writers, just like you, turn to the most current edition of this indispensable market guide.

Keep ahead of the changes by ordering *2004 Children's Writer's & Illustrator's Market* today! You'll save the frustration of getting manuscripts returned in the mail stamped MOVED: ADDRESS UNKNOWN, and of NOT submitting your work to new listings because you don't know they exist. All you have to do to order next year's edition — at this year's price — is complete the attached order card and return it with your payment. Lock in the 2003 price for 2004 — order today!

2004 Children's Writer's & Illustrator's Market will be published and ready for shipment in November 2003.

Turn Over for More Great Books to Help You Get Published!

Get Your Children's Stories Published
with Help from These Writer's Digest Books!

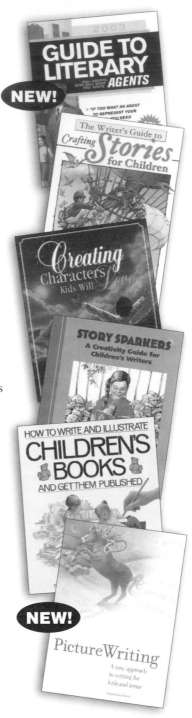

2003 Guide to Literary Agents
Your search for powerful representation and the perfect writer's contract begins here. Find the right agent to get your fiction, nonfiction or screenplay into the hands of the publishers who can make your dreams come true! With 100% updated listings of 570+ agents who sell what you write.
#10811-K/$23.99/400p/pb

The Writer's Guide to Crafting Stories for Children
This unique guide offers detailed information and an in-depth examination of storytelling and story structure. Using worksheets, exercises and checklists you'll discover how to capture and keep a young reader's attention, whether your topic is fact or fiction.
#10762-K/$16.99/192p/pb

Creating Characters Kids Will Love
Learn to develop vivid characters that come to life on the page and engage children. Includes characterization exercises, observation techniques and memory builders for incorporating experiences from your own childhood.
#10669-K/$16.99/208p/pb

Story Sparkers:
A Creativity Guide for Children's Writers
Fire up your imagination! These easy-to-apply techniques will give your creativity a refreshing boost. You'll learn how to assess each new idea and use it to its fullest potential. Includes a guide to determine which formats will best showcase your ideas.
#10700-K/$16.99/208p/pb

How to Write and Illustrate Children's Books
And Get Them Published
Advice and insider tips from some of the finest talents in children's publishing are collected in this must-have guide for success in writing and illustrating in the children's market. You'll find inspiring and insightful instruction from experts in the field to help you get your work published.
#10694-K/$19.99/144p/pb

Picture Writing:
A new approach to writing for kids and teens
Learn to create evocative characters, setting and plots fueled by the power of vivid description. You'll discover how to optimize the five senses, and how to recognize what type of descriptive words work best for various age groups.
#10755-K/$16.99/224p/pb
Will be shipped when available in December 2002

◀ **Books are available at your local bookstore, or directly from the publisher using the Order Card on the reverse.**

in Canadian publishing of nonfiction for children. Previously published submissions only. Submissions nominated by a person or group of people. Work must have been published the calendar year previous to the award being given. Send SASE for contest rules. Certificates are awarded to the author and illustrator, and they share a cash prize of $500 (Canadian). Judging by members of the children's literature roundtables of Canada. In consultation with children's bookstores across Canada, a national committee based in Vancouver sends out a selective list of over 20 titles representing the best of the information books from the preceding year. The Roundtables consider this preliminary list and send back their recommendations, resulting in 5-7 finalists. The Roundtables make time at their Fall meetings to discuss the finalists and vote on their choices, which are collated into one vote per Roundtable (the winner is announced in November for Canada's Book Week). The award is granted at the Serendipity Children's Literature Conference held in February in Vancouver British Columbia.

INSIGHT WRITING CONTEST, *Insight Magazine*, 55 W. Oak Ridge Dr., Hagerstown MD 21740-7390. E-mail: insight@rhpa.org. Website: www.insightmagazine.org. **Open to students.** Annual contest. Unpublished submissions only. Submissions made by author. Deadline for entries: June 1, 2002. SASE for contest rules and entry forms. Awards First prizes, $100-250; second prizes, $75-200; third prizes, $50-150. Winning entries will be published in *Insight*. Contest includes three catagories: Student Short Story, General Short Story and Student Poetry. You must be age 21 or under to enter the student catagories. Entries must include cover sheet form available with SASE or on website.

IRA CHILDREN'S BOOK AWARDS, International Reading Association, 800 Barksdale Rd., P.O. Box 8139, Newark DE 19714-8139. (302)731-1600. Fax: (302)731-1057. E-mail: exec@reading.org. Website: www.reading.org. Open to adults. Annual award. Awards are given for an author's first or second published book for fiction and nonfiction in three categories: primary (ages preschool-8), intermediate (ages 9-13), and young adult (ages 14-17). This award is intended for newly published authors who show unusual promise in the children's book field. Deadline for entries: November 1. Awards $500. For guidelines write or e-mail.

JOSEPH HENRY JACKSON AND JAMES D. PHELAN LITERARY AWARDS, sponsored by The San Francisco Foundation. Administered by Intersection for the Arts. 446 Valencia St., San Francisco CA 94103. (415)626-2787. Fax: (415)626-1636. E-mail: info@theintersection.org. Submit entries to Awards Coordinator. **Open to Students**. Annual award. Estab. 1937. Purpose of award: to encourage young writers for an unpublished manuscript-in-progress. Submissions must be unpublished. Submissions made by author. Deadline for entry: January 31. SASE for contest rules and entry forms. Judging by established peers. All applicants must be 20-35 years of age. Applicants for the Henry Jackson Award must be residents of northern California or Nevada for 3 consecutive years immediately prior to the January 31 deadline. Applicants for the James D. Phelan awards must have been born in California but need not be current residents.

☑ **THE EZRA JACK KEATS NEW WRITER AND NEW ILLUSTRATOR AWARD**, (formerly The Ezra Jack Keats New Writer Award), Ezra Jack Keats Foundation/Administered by The Office of Children's Services, the New York Public Library, 455 Fifth Ave., New York NY 10016. (212)340-0906. Fax: (212)340-0988. E-mail: mtice@nypl.org. **Program Coordinator:** Margaret Tice. **Open to students.** Annual award. Purpose of the award: "The award will be given to a promising new writer of picture books for children. Selection criteria include books for children (ages nine and under) that reflect the tradition of Ezra Jack Keats. These books portray: the universal qualities of childhood, strong and supportive family and adult relationships, the multicultural nature of our world." Submissions made by the author, by the author's agent or nominated by a person or group of people. Must be published in the preceding year. Deadline for entries: mid-December. SASE for contest rules and entry forms. No entry fee. Awards $1,000 coupled with Ezra Jack Keats Silver Medal. Judging by a panel of experts. "The author should have published no more than five books. Entries are judged on the outstanding features of the text, complemented by illustrations. Candidates need not be both author and illustrator. Entries should carry a 2002 copyright (for the 2003 award)." Winning books and authors to be presented at reception at The New York Public Library.

N EZRA JACK KEATS/KERLAN COLLECTION MEMORIAL FELLOWSHIP, University of Minnesota, 113 Elmer L. Andersen Library, 222 21st Ave. S., Minneapolis MN 55455. (612)624-4576. Fax: (612)625-5525. E-mail: clrc@tc.umn.edu. Website: http://special.lib.umn.edu/clrc/. Competition open to adults. Offered annually. Deadline for entries: May 1, 2003. Send request with SASE (6×9 or 9×12 envelope), including 60¢ postage. The Ezra Jack Keats/Kerlan Collection Memorial Fellowship from the Ezra Jack Keats Foundation will provide $1,500 to a "talented writer and/or illustrator of children's books who wishes to use the Kerlan Collection for the furtherance of his or her artistic development. Special consideration will be given to someone who would find it difficult to finance the visit to the Kerlan Collection." The fellowship winner will receive transportation and per diem. Judging by the Kerlan Award Committee—3 representatives from the University of Minnesota faculty, one from the Kerlan Friends, and one from the Minnesota Library Association.

KENTUCKY BLUEGRASS AWARD, Northern Kentucky University & Kentucky Reading Association, % Jennifer Smith, Steely Library, Northern Kentucky University, Highland Heights KY 41099. (859)572-6620. Fax: (859)572-5390. E-mail: smithjen@nku.edu. Website: www.kyreading.org. **Award Directors:** Jennifer Smith. Submit entries to: Jennifer Smith. Annual award. Estab. 1983. Purpose of award: to promote readership among young children and young adolescents. Also to recognize exceptional creative efforts of authors and illustrators. Previously published submissions only. Submissions made by author, made by author's agent, nominated by teachers or librarians. Must be published no more than 3 years prior to the award year. Deadline for entries: March 15. Contest rules and entry forms are available from the website. No entry fee. Awards a framed certificate and invitation to be recognized at the annual luncheon of the Kentucky Bluegrass Award. Judging by children who participate through their schools or libraries. "Books are reviewed by a panel of teachers and librarians before they are placed on a Master List for the year. These books must have been published within a three year period prior to the review. Winners are chosen from this list of pre-selected books. Books are divided into four divisions, K-2, 3-5, 6-8, 9-12 grades. Winners are chosen by children who either read the books or have the books read to them. Children from the entire state of Kentucky are involved in the selection of the annual winners for each of the divisions."

Ⓝ CORETTA SCOTT KING AWARD, Coretta Scott King Task Force, Social Responsibility Round Table, American Library Association, 50 E. Huron St., Chicago IL 60611. Website: www.ala.org/srrt/csking. "The Coretta Scott King Award is an annual award for books (1 for text and 1 for illustration) that convey the spirit of brotherhood espoused by M.L. King, Jr.—and also speak to the Black experience—for young people. There is an award jury of children's librarians that judges the books—reviewing over the year—and making a decision in January. A copy of an entry must be sent to each juror by December 1st of the juried year. Acquire jury list from ALA Office for Literary Services at (312)280-4294 or olos@ala.org. Awards breakfast held on Tuesday morning during A.L.A. Annual Conference. See schedule at www.ALA.org.

ANNE SPENCER LINDBERGH PRIZE IN CHILDREN'S LITERATURE, The Charles A. and Anne Morrow Lindbergh Foundation, % Lindbergh Foundation, 2150 Third Ave., Suite 310, Anoka MN 55303. (763)576-1596. Fax: (763)576-1664. E-mail: info@lindberghfoundation.org. Website: www.lindberghfoundation.org. Competition open to adults. Contest is offered every 2 years. Estab. 1996. Purpose of contest: To recognize the children's fantasy novel judged to be the best published in the English language during the 2-year period. Prize program honors Anne Spencer Lindbergh, author of a number of acclaimed juvenile fantasies, who died in late 1993 at the age of 53. Previously published submissions only. Submissions made by author, author's agent or publishers. Must be published between January 1 of odd numbered years and December 31 of even numbered years. Deadline for entries: November 1 of even numbered years. Entry fee is $25. Awards $5,000 to author of winning book. Judging by panel drawn from writers, editors, librarians and teachers prominent in the field of children's literature. Requirements for entrants: Open to all authors of children's fantasy novels published during the 2-year period. Entries must include 4 copies of books submitted. Winner announced in January.

LONGMEADOW JOURNAL LITERARY COMPETITION, % Rita and Robert Morton, 6750 N. Longmeadow, Lincolnwood IL 60712. (312)726-9789. Fax: (312)726-9772. **Contest Directors:** Rita and Robert Morton. Competition open to students (anyone age 10-19). Held annually and published every year. Estab. 1986. Purpose of contest: to encourage the young to write. Submissions are made by the author, made by the author's agent, nominated by a person or group of people, by teachers, librarians or parents. Deadline for entries: June 30. SASE. No entry fee. Awards first place, $175; second place, $100; and five prizes of $50. Judging by Rita Morton and Robert Morton. Works are published every year and are distributed to teachers and librarians and interested parties at no charge.

Ⓝ LOUISE LOUIS/EMILY F. BOURNE STUDENT POETRY AWARD, Poetry Society of America, 15 Gramercy Park, New York NY 10003-1705. (212)254-9628. Fax: (212)673-2352. E-mail: brett@poetrysociety.org. Website: www.poetrysociety.org. **Contact:** Award Director. **Open to students.** Annual award. Purpose of the award: award is for the best unpublished poem by a high or preparatory school student (grades 9-12) from the US and its territories. Unpublished submissions only. Deadline for entries: Oct. 1 to Dec. 21. SASE for award rules and entry forms. Entries not returned. "High schools can send an unlimited number of submissions with one entry per individual student for a flat fee of $10." Award: $250. Judging by a professional poet. Requirements for entrants: Award open to all high school and preparatory students from the US and its territories. School attended, as well as name and address, should be noted. PSA submission guidelines must be followed. These are printed in our fall calendar and are readily available if those interested send us a SASE. Line limit: none. "The award-winning poem will be included in a sheaf of poems that will be part of the program at the award ceremony and sent to all PSA members."

MAGAZINE MERIT AWARDS, Society of Children's Book Writers and Illustrators, 8271 Beverly Blvd., Los Angeles CA 90048. Fax: (323)782-1010. Website: www.scbwi.org. **Award Coordinator:** Dorothy Leon. Annual award. Estab. 1988. Purpose of the award: "to recognize outstanding original magazine work for young people published during that year and having been written or illustrated by members of SCBWI." Previously published submissions only. Entries must be submitted between January 31 and December 15 of the year of publication. For brochure (rules) write Award Coordinator. No entry fee. Must be a SCBWI member. Awards plaques and honor certificates for each of the 3 categories (fiction, nonfiction, illustration). Judging by a magazine editor and two "full" SCBWI members. "All magazine work for young people by an SCBWI member—writer, artist or photographer—is eligible during the year of original publication. In the case of co-authored work, both authors must be SCBWI members. Members must submit their own work." Requirements for entrants: 4 copies each of the published work and proof of publication (may be contents page) showing the name of the magazine and the date of issue. The SCBWI is a professional organization of writers and illustrators and others interested in children's literature. Membership is open to the general public at large.

MILKWEED PRIZE FOR CHILDREN'S LITERATURE, Milkweed Editions, 1011 Washington Ave. S., Suite 300, Minneapolis MN 55415-1246. (612)332-3192. Fax: (612)215-2550. E-mail: editor@milkwee d.org. Website: www.milkweed.org. **Award Director:** Emilie Buchwald, publisher/editor. Annual award. Estab. 1993. Purpose of the award: to find an outstanding literary novel for readers ages 8-13 and encourage writers to turn their attention to readers in this age group. Unpublished submissions only "in book form." Must send SASE for award guidelines. The prize is awarded to the best work for children ages 8-13 that Milkweed agrees to publish in a calendar year by a writer not previously published by Milkweed. The Prize consists of a $5,000 advance against royalties agreed to at the time of acceptance. Submissions must follow our usual children's guidelines.

MINNESOTA BOOK AWARDS, Minnesota Center for the Book, 987 E. Ivy Ave., St. Paul MN 55106-2046. (651)774-0105, ext. 111. Fax: (651)774-0205. E-mail: paul@minnesotahumanities.org. Website: www.minnesotahumanities.org. **Award Director:** Paul Druckman. Submit entries to: Paul Druckman, director, Minnesota Center for the Book. Annual award. Estab. 1988. Purpose of contest: To recognize and honor achievement by members of Minnesota's book community. Previously published submissions only. Submissions made by publisher, author or author's agent. Fee for some categories. Work must hold 2002 copyright. Deadline for entries: December 31, 2002. Awards to winners and finalists, some cash. Judging by members of Minnesota's book community: booksellers, librarians, teachers and scholars, writers, reviewers and publishers. Requirements for entrants: Author must be a Minnesotan. The Minnesota Book Awards includes over 20 award categories for children and young adult fiction and nonfiction titles and designs.

MYTHOPOEIC FANTASY AWARD FOR CHILDREN'S LITERATURE, The Mythopoeic Society, P.O. Box 320486, San Francisco CA 94132-0486. E-mail: cmfarrell@earthlink.net. Website: www.mythsoc. org. **Award Director:** Eleanor M. Farrell. Annual award. Estab. 1992 (previous to 1992, a single Mythopoeic Fantasy Award was given to either adult or children's books). Previously published submissions only. Submissions nominated. Must be published previous calendar year. Deadline for entries: February 28. Awards statuette. Judging by committee members of Mythopoeic Society. Requirements for entrants: books only; nominations are made by Mythopoeic Society members.

NATIONAL CHILDREN'S THEATRE FESTIVAL, Actor's Playhouse at the Miracle Theatre, 280 Miracle Mile, Coral Gables FL 33134. (305)444-9293. Fax: (305)444-4181. Website: www.actorsplayhouse .org. **Director:** Earl Maulding. **Open to Students**. Annual contest. Estab. 1994. Purpose of contest: to bring together the excitement of the theater arts and the magic of young audiences through the creation of new musical works and children's plays and to create a venue for playwrights/composers to showcase their artistic products. Submissions must be unpublished. Submissions are made by author or author's agent.

Deadline for entries: August 1, 2002. SASE for contest rules and entry forms or online at www.actorsplayho use.org. Entry fee is $10. Awards: first prize of $500 plus production. Final judges are of national reputation. Past judges include Joseph Robinette, Moses Goldberg and Luis Santeiro.

NATIONAL PEACE ESSAY CONTEST, United States Institute of Peace, 1200 17th St. NW, Washington DC 20036. (202)429-3854. Fax: (202)429-6063. E-mail: essay_contest@usip.org. Website: www.usip.o rg. Annual contest. Estab. 1987. "The contest gives students the opportunity to do valuable research, writing and thinking on a topic of importance to international peace and conflict resolution. Teaching guides are available for teachers who allow the contest to be used as a classroom assignment." Deadline for entries is January 22, 2003 "Interested students, teachers and others may write or call to receive free contest kits. Please do not include SASE." No entry fee. State Level Awards are $1000 college scholarships. National winners are selected from among the 1st place state winners. National winners receive scholarships in the following amounts: first place $10,000; second $5,000; third $2,500. Judging is conducted by education professionals from across the country and by the Board of Directors of the United States Institute of Peace. "All submissions become property of the U.S. Institute of Peace to use at its discretion and without royalty or any limitation. Students grades 9-12 in the U.S., its territories and overseas schools may submit essays for review by completing the application process. U.S. citizenship required for students attending overseas schools. National winning essays will be published by the U.S. Institute of Peace."

NATIONAL WRITERS ASSOCIATION NONFICTION CONTEST, 3140 S. Peoria, Suite 295, Aurora CO 80014. (303)841-0246. **Executive Director:** Sandy Whelchel. Annual contest. Estab. 1971. Purpose of contest: "to encourage writers in this creative form and to recognize those who excel in nonfiction writing." Submissions made by author. Deadline for entries: December 31. SASE for contest rules and entry forms. Entry fee is $18. Awards three cash prizes; choice of books; Honorable Mention Certificate. "Two people read each entry; third party picks three top winners from top five." Judging sheets sent if entry accompanied by SASE. Condensed version of 1st place published in *Authorship*.

NATIONAL WRITERS ASSOCIATION SHORT STORY CONTEST, 3140 S. Peoria, Suite 295, Aurora CO 80014. (303)841-0246. **Executive Director:** Sandy Whelchel. Annual contest. Estab. 1971. Purpose of contest: "To encourage writers in this creative form and to recognize those who excel in fiction writing." Submissions made by the author. Deadline for entries: July 1. SASE for contest rules and entry forms. Entry fee is $15. Awards 3 cash prizes, choice of books and certificates for Honorable Mentions. Judging by "two people read each entry; third person picks top three winners." Judging sheet copies available for SASE. First place published in *Authorship* Magazine.

THE NENE AWARD, Hawaii State Library, 478 S. King St., Honolulu HI 96813. (808)586-3510. Fax: (808)586-3584. E-mail: hslear@netra.lib.state.hi.us. Estab. 1964. "The Nene Award was designed to help the children of Hawaii become acquainted with the best contemporary writers of fiction, become aware of the qualities that make a good book and choose the best rather than the mediocre." Previously published submissions only. Books must have been copyrighted not more than 6 years prior to presentation of award. Work is nominated. Ballots are usually due around the beginning of March. Awards Koa plaque. Judging by the children of Hawaii in grades 4-6. Requirements for entrants: books must be fiction, written by a living author, copyrighted not more than 6 years ago and suitable for children in grades 4, 5 and 6. Current and past winners are displayed in all participating school and public libraries. The award winner is announced in April.

NEW ENGLAND BOOK AWARDS, New England Booksellers Association, 1770 Massachusetts Ave., Suite 332, Cambridge MA 02140. (617)576-3070. Fax: (617)576-3091. E-mail: neba@neba.org. Website: newenglandbooks.org. **Award Director:** Mayre Plunkett. Annual award. Estab. 1990. Purpose of award: "to promote New England authors who have produced a body of work that stands as a significant contribution to New England's culture and is deserving of wider recognition." Previously published submissions only. Submissions made by New England booksellers; publishers. "Award given to authors 'body of work'

**FOR EXPLANATIONS OF THESE SYMBOLS,
SEE THE INSIDE FRONT AND BACK COVERS OF THIS BOOK**

not a specific book." Entries must be still in print and available. SASE for contest rules and entry forms. No entry fee. Judging by NEBA membership. Requirements for entrants: Author/illustrator must live in New England. Submit written nominations only; actual books should not be sent. Member bookstores receive materials to display winners' books.

NEW VOICES AWARD, Lee & Low Books, 95 Madison Ave., New York NY 10016. (212)779-4400. Fax: (212)532-6035. E-mail: info@leeandlow.com. Website: www.leeandlow.com. **Executive Editor:** Louise May. **Open to students and adults.** Annual award. Estab. 2000. Purpose of contest: Lee & Low Books is one of the few publishing companies owned by people of color. We have published over 50 first-time writers and illustrators. Titles include *In Daddy's Arms I Am Tall: African Americans Celebrating Fathers*, winner of the 1998 Coretta Scott King Illustrator Award; *Passage to Freedom: The Sugihara Story*, an American Library Association Notable Book; and *Crazy Horse's Vision*, a Bank Street College Children's Book of the Year. Submissions made by author. Deadline for entries: September 30. SASE for contest rules. No entry fee. Awards New Voices Award—$1,000 prize and a publication contract along with an advance on royalties; New Voices Honor Award—$500 prize. Judging by Lee & Low editors. Restrictions of media for illustrators: The author must be a writer of color who is a resident of the US and who has not previously published a children's picture book. For additional information, send SASE, call for entries or visit Lee & Low's website.

JOHN NEWBERY MEDAL AWARD, Association for Library Service to Children, Division of the American Library Association, 50 E. Huron, Chicago IL 60611. E-mail: alsc@ala.org. Website: www.ala. org/alsc/newbery.html. (312)280-2163. **Executive Director, ALSC:** Malore Brown. Annual award. Estab. 1922. Purpose of award: to recognize the most distinguished contribution to American children's literature published in the US. Previously published submissions only; must be published prior to year award is given. Deadline for entries: December 31. SASE for award rules. Entries not returned. No entry fee. Medal awarded at Caldecott/Newbery banquet during annual conference. Judging by Newbery Award Selection Committee.

[N] THE NOMA AWARD FOR PUBLISHING IN AFRICA, Kodansha Ltd., P.O. Box 128, Witney, Oxon OX8 5XU England. 44-1993-775235. Fax: 44-1993-709265. E-mail: maryljay@aol.com. **Secretary to the Managing Committee:** Mary Jay. Annual award. Estab. 1979. Purpose of award: to encourage publications of works by African writers and scholars in Africa, instead of abroad, as is still too often the case at present. Books in the following categories are eligible: scholarly or academic, books for children, literature and creative writing, including fiction, drama and poetry. Previously published submissions only. 2002 award given for book published in 2001. Deadline for entries: end of February 2002. Submissions must be made through publishers. Conditions of entry and submission forms are available from the secretariat. Entries not returned. No entry fee. Awards $10,000. Judging by the Managing Committee (jury): African scholars and book experts and representatives of the international book community. Chairman: Walter Bgoya. Requirements for entrants: Author must be African, and book must be published in Africa. "Winning titles are displayed at appropriate international book events."

[✓] NORTH AMERICAN INTERNATIONAL AUTO SHOW HIGH SCHOOL POSTER CONTEST, (formerly North American International Auto Show Short Story and High School Poster Contest), Detroit Auto Dealers Association, 1900 W. Big Beaver Rd., Troy MI 48084-3531. (248)643-0250. Fax: (248)283-5160. E-mail: sherp@dada.org. Website: www.naias.com. **Contact:** Sandy Herp. **Open to students.** Annual contest. Submissions made by the author and illustrator. Contact DADA for contest rules and entry forms or retrieve rules from website. No entry fee. Awards in the High School Poster Contest are as follows: Chairman's Award, Best Theme, Best Use of Color, Best Use of Graphics, Most Creative, and Designer's Best of Show. A winner will be chosen in each category from grades 9, 10, 11 and 12. Each winner in each grade from each category will win $250. The winner of the Chairman's Award will receive $1,000. Entries will be judged by an independent panel of recognized representatives of the art community. Entrants must be Michigan high school students enrolled in grades 9-12. Junior high students in 9th grade are also eligible. Winners will be announced during the North American International Auto Show in January and may be published in the *Auto Show Program* at the sole discretion of the D.A.D.A. "No shared work please."

OHIOANA BOOK AWARDS, Ohioana Library Association, 274 E. First Ave., Suite 300, Columbus OH 43201. (614)466-3831. Fax: (614)728-6974. E-mail: ohioana@sloma.state.oh.us. Website: www.oplin.l ib.oh.us/OHIOANA/. **Director:** Linda R. Hengst. Annual award. "The Ohioana Book Awards are given to books of outstanding literary quality. Purpose of contest: to provide recognition and encouragement to Ohio writers and to promote the work of Ohio writers. Up to six are given each year. Awards may be given in the following categories: fiction, nonfiction, children's literature, poetry and books about Ohio or an Ohioan. Books must be received by the Ohioana Library during the calendar year prior to the year the award is given and must have a copyright date within the last two calendar years." Deadline for entries: December 31. SASE for award rules and entry forms. No entry fee. Winners receive citation and glass sculpture. "Any book that has been written or edited by a person born in Ohio or who has lived in Ohio for at least five years" is eligible. The Ohioana Library Association also awards the "Ohioana Book Award in the category of juvenile books." Send SASE for more information.

OKLAHOMA BOOK AWARDS, Oklahoma Center for the Book, 200 NE 18th, Oklahoma City OK 73105. (405)521-2502. Fax: (405)525-7804. E-mail: gcarlile@oltn.odl.state.ok.us. Website: www.odl.state.ok.us/ocb. **Executive Director:** Glenda Carlile. Annual award. Estab. 1989. Purpose of award: "to honor Oklahoma writers and books about our state." Previously published submissions only. Submissions made by the author, author's agent, or entered by a person or group of people, including the publisher. Must be published during the calendar year preceding the award. Awards are presented to best books in fiction, nonfiction, children's, design and illustration, and poetry books about Oklahoma or books written by an author who was born, is living or has lived in Oklahoma. Deadline for entries: early January. SASE for award rules and entry forms. No entry fee. Awards a medal—no cash prize. Judging by a panel of 5 people for each category—a librarian, a working writer in the genre, booksellers, editors, etc. Requirements for entrants: author must be an Oklahoma native, resident, former resident or have written a book with Oklahoma theme. Winner will be announced at banquet in Oklahoma City. The Arrell Gibson Lifetime Achievement Award is also presented each year to an Oklahoma author for a body of work.

ONCE UPON A WORLD CHILDREN'S BOOK AWARD, Simon Wiesenthal Center's Museum of Tolerance Library and Archives, 1399 S. Roxbury Dr., Los Angeles CA 90035-4709. (310)772-7605. Fax: (310)772-7628. E-mail: library@wiesenthal.net or aklein@wiesenthal.net. **Award Director:** Adaire J. Klein. Submit entries to: Adaire J. Klein, Director of Library and Archival Services. Annual award. Estab. 1996. Previously published submissions only. Submissions made by publishers, author or by author's agent. Must be published January-December of previous year. Deadline for entries: March 31, 2003. SASE for contest rules and entry forms. Awards $1,000 and plaque. Judging by 3 independent judges familiar with children's literature. Award open to any writer with work in English language on subject of tolerance, diversity, and social justice for children 6-10 years old. Award is presented in October. Book Seal available from the library. 2002 winner: *Freedom Summer*, by Deborah Wiles, illustrated by Jerome Lagarrigue (NY:/Atheneum Books for Young Readers, Simon & Schuster 2001).

ORBIS PICTUS AWARD FOR OUTSTANDING NONFICTION FOR CHILDREN, The National Council of Teachers of English, 1111 W. Kenyon Rd., Urbana IL 61801-1096. (217)328-3870, ext. 3603. **Chair, NCTE Committee on the Orbis Pictus Award for Outstanding Nonfiction for Children:** Carolyn Lott, University of Montana, Missoula. Annual award. Estab. 1989. Purpose of award: to honor outstanding nonfiction works for children. Previously published submissions only. Submissions made by author, author's agent, by a person or group of people. Must be published January 1-December 31 of contest year. Deadline for entries: November 30. Call for award information. No entry fee. Awards a plaque given at the NCTE Elementary Section Luncheon at the NCTE Annual Convention in November. Judging by a committee.

THE ORIGINAL ART, Society of Illustrators, 128 E. 63rd St., New York NY 10021-7303. (212)838-2560. Fax: (212)838-2561. E-mail: si1901@aol.com. Website: www.societyillustrators.org. Annual contest. Estab. 1981. Purpose of contest: to celebrate the fine art of children's book illustration. Previously published submissions only. Deadline for entries: August 20. Request "call for entries" to receive contest rules and entry forms. Entry fee is $20/book. Judging by seven professional artists and editors. Works will be displayed at the Society of Illustrators Museum of American Illustration in New York City October-November annually. Medals awarded.

HELEN KEATING OTT AWARD FOR OUTSTANDING CONTRIBUTION TO CHILDREN'S LITERATURE, Church and Synagogue Library Association, P.O. Box 19357, Portland OR 97280-0357. (503)244-6919. Fax: (503)977-3734. E-mail: csla@worldaccessnet.com. Website: www.worldaccessnet.com/~csla. **Chair of Committee:** Barbara Graham. Annual award. Estab. 1980. "This award is given to a person or organization that has made a significant contribution to promoting high moral and ethical values through children's literature." Deadline for entries: April 1. "Recipient is honored in July during the conference." Awards certificate of recognition and a conference package consisting of all meals, day of awards banquet, two nights' housing and a complimentary 1 year membership. "A nomination for an award may be made by anyone. It should include the name, address and telephone number of the nominee, plus the church or synagogue relationship where appropriate. Nominations of an organization should include the name of a contact person. A detailed description of the reasons for the nomination should be given, accompanied by documentary evidence of accomplishment. The person(s) making the nomination should give his/her name, address and telephone number and a brief explanation of his/her knowledge of the nominee's accomplishments. Elements of creativity and innovation will be given high priority by the judges."

PATERSON PRIZE FOR BOOKS FOR YOUNG PEOPLE, Poetry Center at Passaic County Community College, One College Blvd., Paterson NJ 07505-1179. (973)684-6555. Fax: (973)523-6085. E-mail: mgillan@pccc.cc.nj.us. Website: www.pccc.cc.nj.us/poetry. **Director:** Maria Mazziotti Gillan. Estab. 1996. Part of the Poetry Center's mission is "to recognize excellence in books for young people." Previously published submissions only. Submissions made by author, author's agent or publisher. Must be published between January 1, 2002-December 31, 2002. Deadline for entries: March 15, 2003. SASE for contest rules and entry forms or visit website. Awards $500 for the author in either of 3 categories: PreK-Grade 3; Grades 4-6, Grades 7-12. Judging by a professional writer selected by the Poetry Center. Contest is open to any writer/illustrator.

PENNSYLVANIA YOUNG READERS' CHOICE AWARDS PROGRAM, Pennsylvania School Librarians Association, 148 S. Bethelehem Pike, Ambler PA 19002-5822. (215)643-5048. Fax: (215)628-8441. E-mail: bellavance@erols.com. **Coordinator:** Jean B. Bellavance. Annual award. Estab. 1991. Submissions nominated by a person or group. Must be published within 5 years of the award—for example, for 2003-2004 books published 1999 to present. Deadline for entries: September 1. SASE for contest rules and entry forms. No entry fee. Framed certificate to winning authors. Judging by children of Pennsylvania (they vote). Requirements for entrants: currently living in North America. Reader's Choice Award is to promote reading of quality books by young people in the Commonwealth of Pennsylvania, to promote teacher and librarian involvement in children's literature, and to honor authors whose work has been recognized by the children of Pennsylvania. Three awards are given, one for each of the following grade level divisions: K-3, 3-6, 6-8.

PEN/PHYLLIS NAYLOR WORKING WRITER FELLOWSHIP, PEN, 568 Broadway, New York NY 10012. (212)334-1660. Fax: (212)334-2181. E-mail: jm@pen.org. Website: www.pen.org. Submit entries to: John Morrone. (Must have published 2 books to be eligible). Annual contest. Estab. 2001. To support writers with a financial need and recognize work of high literary caliber. Unpublished submissions only. Submissions nominated. Deadline for entries: January 14, 2002. Awards $5,000. Upon nomination by an editor or fellow writer, a panel of judges will select the winning book. Open to a writer of children's or young adult fiction in financial need, who has published at least two books, and no more than three during the past ten years.

PLEASE TOUCH MUSEUM® BOOK AWARD, Please Touch Museum, 210 N. 21st St., Philadelphia PA 19103-1001. (215)963-0667. Fax: (215)963-0424. E-mail: marketing@pleasetouchmuseum.org. Website: www.pleasetouchmuseum.org. **Open to students.** Annual award. Estab. 1985. Purpose of the award: "to recognize and encourage the publication of books for young children by American authors that are of the highest quality and will aid them in enjoying the process of learning through books. Awarded to two picture books that are particularly imaginative and effective in exploring a concept or concepts, one for children age three and younger, and one for children ages four-seven. To be eligible for consideration a book must: (1) Explore and clarify an idea for young children. This could include the concept of numbers, colors, shapes, sizes, senses, feelings, etc. There is no limitation as to format. (2) Be distinguished in both text and illustration. (3) Be published within the last year by an American publisher. (4) Be by an American author and/or illustrator." Deadline for entries: (submissions may be made throughout the year). SASE for award rules and entry forms. No entry fee. Judging by selected jury of children's literature experts, librarians and early childhood educators. Education store purchases books for selling at Book Award Ceremony and throughout the year. Autographing sessions may be held at Please Touch Museum, and at Philadelphia's Early Childhood Education Conference.

POCKETS MAGAZINE FICTION CONTEST, *Pockets Magazine*, The Upper Room, P.O. Box 340004, Nashville TN 37203-0004. (615)340-7333. Fax: (615)340-7267. (Do not send submissions via fax.) E-mail: pockets@upperroom.org. Website: www.upperroom.org/pockets. **Contact:** Lynn W. Gilliam, associate editor. The purpose of the contest is to "find new freelance writers for the magazine." Annual competition for short stories. Award: $1,000 and publication in *Pockets*. Competition receives 600 submissions. Judged by *Pockets* editors and editors of other Upper Room publications. Guidelines available upon request and SASE or on website. No entry fee. No entry form. Note on envelope and first sheet: Fiction

Contest. Submissions must be postmarked between March 1 and August 15 of the current year. Former winners may not enter. Unpublished submissions welcome. Word length: 1,000-1,600 words. Awards $1,000 and publication. Judging by *Pockets'* editors and 3 other editors of other Upper Room publications. Winner notiied November 1. All other submissions returned if accompanied by SASE.

MICHAEL L. PRINTZ AWARD, Young Adult Library Services Association, Division of the American Library Association, 50 E. Huron, Chicago IL 60611. Website: www.ala.org/yalsa/printz. The Michael L. Printz Award is an award for a book that exemplifies literary excellence in young adult literature. It is named for a Topeka, Kansas school librarian who was a long-time active member of the Young Adult Library Services Association. It will be selected annually by an award committee that can also name as many as 4 honor books. The award-winning book can be fiction, non-fiction, poetry or an anthology, and can be a work of joint authorship or editorship. The books must be published between January 1 and December 31 of the preceding year and be designated by its publisher as being either a young adult book or one published for the age range that YALSA defines as young adult, e.g. ages 12 through 18. The deadline for both committee and field nominations will be December 1.

PRIX ALVINE-BELISLE, Association pour l'avancement des sciences et des techniques de la documentation (ASTED) Inc., 3414 Avenue Du Parc, Bureau 202, Montreal, Québec H2X 2H5 Canada. (514)281-5012. Fax: (514)281-8219. E-mail: info@asted.org. **Award President:** Micheline Patton. Award open to children's book editors. Annual award. Estab. 1974. Purpose of contest: To recognize the best children's book published in French in Canada. Previously published submissions only. Submissions made by publishing house. Must be published the year before award. Deadline for entries: June 1. Awards $500. Judging by librarians jury.

TOMÁS RIVERA MEXICAN AMERICAN CHILDREN'S BOOK AWARD, Southwest Texas State University, EDU, 601 University Dr., San Marcos TX 78666-4613. (512)245-2357. Fax: (512)245-7911. E-mail: jb23@academia.swt.edu. **Award Director:** Dr. Jennifer Battle. Competition open to adults. Annual contest. Estab. 1995. Purpose of award: "To encourage authors, illustrators and publishers to produce books that authentically reflect the lives of Mexican American children and young adults in the United States." Previously published submissions only. Submissions made by "any interested individual or publishing company." Must be published during the year of consideration. Deadline for entries: February 1 post publication year. Contact Dr. Jennifer Battle for nomination forms, or send copy of book. No entry fee. Awards $3,000 per book. Judging of nominations by a regional committee, national committee judges finalists. Annual ceremony honoring the book and author/illustrator is held during Hispanic Heritage Month at Southwest Texas State University.

SASKATCHEWAN BOOK AWARDS: CHILDREN'S LITERATURE, Saskatchewan Book Awards, Box 1921, Regina, Saskatchewan S4P 3E1 Canada. (306)569-1585. Fax: (306)569-4187. E-mail: director@bookawards.sk.ca. Website: www.bookawards.sk.ca. **Award Director:** Joyce Wells. **Open to Saskatchewan authors.** Annual award. Estab. 1995. Purpose of contest: to celebrate Saskatchewan books and authors and to promote their work. Previously published submissions only. Submissions made by author, author's agent or publisher by September 15. SASE for contest rules and entry forms. Entry fee is $15 (Canadian). Awards $1,500 (Canadian). Judging by two children's literature authors outside of Saskatchewan. Requirements for entrants: Must be Saskatchewan resident; book must have ISBN number; book must have been published within the last year. Award-winning book will appear on TV talk shows and be pictured on bookmarks distributed to libraries, schools and bookstores in Saskatchewan.

SEVENTEEN FICTION CONTEST, 1440 Broadway, 13th Floor, New York NY 10018. Annual contest. Estab. 1945. Unpublished submissions only. Deadline for entries: April 30. SASE for contest rules and entry forms; contest rules also published in December issue of *Seventeen*. Entries not returned. Submissions accepted by mail only. No entry fee. Awards cash prize and possible publication in *Seventeen*. Judging by "inhouse panel of editors, external readers." If 1st, 2nd or 3rd prize, acquires first North American rights for piece to be published. Requirements for entrants: "Our annual fiction contest is open to anyone between the ages of 13 and 21 who submit on or before April 30. Submit only original fiction that has not been published in any form other than in school publications. Stories should be between 1,500 and 3,000 words in length (6-12 pages). All manuscripts must be typed double-spaced on a single side of paper. Submit as many original stories as you like, but each story must include your full name, address, birth date, e-mail address, and signature in the top right-hand corner of the first page. Your signature on submission will constitute your acceptance of the contest rules."

☑ **SHUBERT FENDRICH MEMORIAL PLAYWRITING CONTEST**, Pioneer Drama Service, Inc., P.O. Box 4267, Englewood CO 80155-4267. Fax: (303)779-4315. E-mail: editors@pioneerdrama.com. Website: www.pioneerdrama.com. **Director:** Lori Conary. Annual contest. **Open to students.** Estab. 1990. Purpose of the contest: "to encourage the development of quality theatrical material for educational and family theater." Previously unpublished submissions only. Deadline for entries: March 1. SASE for contest rules and guidelines. No entry fee. Cover letter must accompany all submissions. Awards $1,000 royalty advance and publication. Upon receipt of signed contracts, plays will be published and made available in our next catalog. Judging by editors. All rights acquired with acceptance of contract for publication. Restrictions for entrants: Any writers currently published by Pioneer Drama Service are not eligible.

SKIPPING STONES YOUTH HONOR AWARDS, *Skipping Stones*, P.O. Box 3939, Eugene OR 97403-0939. (541)342-4956. E-mail: skipping@efn.org. Website: www.efn.org/~skipping. Annual award. Purpose of contest: "to recognize youth, 7 to 17, for their contributions to multicultural awareness, nature and ecology, social issues, peace and nonviolence. Also to promote creativity, self-esteem and writing skills and to recognize important work being done by youth organizations." Submissions made by the author. The theme for 2002 is "Internet's Impact on Multicultural Issues." Deadline for entries: June 20. SASE for contest rules. Entries must include certificate of originality by a parent and/or teacher and background information on the author written by the author. Entry fee is $3. Judging by *Skipping Stones*' staff. "Up to ten awards are given in three categories: (1) Compositions—(essays, poems, short stories, songs, travelogues, etc.) should be typed (double-spaced) or neatly handwritten. Fiction or nonfiction should be limited to 750 words; poems to 30 lines. Non-English writings are also welcome. (2) Artwork— (drawings, cartoons, paintings or photo essays with captions) should have the artist's name, age and address on the back of each page. Send the originals with SASE. Black & white photos are especially welcome. Limit: 8 pieces. (3) Youth Organizations—Tell us how your club or group works to: (a) preserve the nature and ecology in your area, (b) enhance the quality of life for low-income, minority or disabled or (c) improve racial or cultural harmony in your school or community. Use the same format as for compositions." The winners are published in the September-October issue of *Skipping Stones*. The winners also receive "Honor certificates, five books and a subscription. Everyone who enters the contest receives the March-April issue featuring Youth Awards.

KAY SNOW WRITERS' CONTEST, Williamette Writers, 9045 SW Barbur Blvd. #5A, Portland OR 97219-4027. (503)452-1592. Fax: (503)452-0372. E-mail: wilwrite@teleport.com. Website: www.willamet tewriters.com. **Contest Director:** Elizabeth Shannon. Annual contest. **Open to students.** Purpose of contest: "to encourage beginning and established writers to continue the craft." Unpublished, original submissions only. Submissions made by the author. Deadline for entries: May 15. SASE for contest rules and entry forms. Entry fee is $10, Williamette Writers' members; $15, nonmembers, free for student writers grades 1-12. Awards cash prize of $300 per category (fiction, nonfiction, juvenile, poetry, script writing), $50 for students in three divisions: 1-5, 6-8, 9-12. "Judges are anonymous."

N] SOCIETY OF MIDLAND AUTHORS AWARDS, Society of Midland Authors, P.O. Box 10419, Chicago IL 60610-0419. E-mail: writercc@aol.com. Website: www.midlandauthors.com. **Open to students.** Annual award. Estab. 1915. Purpose of award: "to stimulate creative literary effort, one of the goals of the Society. There are six categories, including children's fiction, children's nonfiction, adult fiction and nonfiction, biography and poetry." Previously published submissions only. Submissions made by the author or publisher. Must be published during calendar year previous to deadline. Deadline for entries: March 1. SASE for award rules and entry forms or check website. No entry fee. Awards plaque given at annual dinner, cash ($300). Judging by panel (reviewers, university faculty, writers, librarians) of 3 per category. Author must be currently residing in the Midlands, i.e., Illinois, Indiana, Iowa, Kansas, Michigan, Minnesota, Missouri, Nebraska, North Dakota, South Dakota, Ohio or Wisconsin.

GEORGE G. STONE CENTER FOR CHILDREN'S BOOKS RECOGNITION OF MERIT AWARD, George G. Stone Center for Children's Books, Claremont Graduate University, 131 E. 10th St., Claremont CA 91711-6188. (909)607-3670. **Award Director:** Doty Hale. Annual award. Estab. 1965. Purpose of the award: to recognize an author or illustrator of a children's book or a body of work exhibiting the "power to please and expand the awareness of children and teachers as they have shared the book in their classrooms." Previously published submissions only. SASE for award rules and entry forms. Entries not returned. No entry fee. Awards a scroll. Judging by a committee of teachers, professors of children's literature and librarians. Requirements for entrants: Nominations are made by students, teachers, professors and librarians. Award made at annual Claremont Reading Conference in spring (March).

SUGARMAN FAMILY AWARD FOR JEWISH CHILDREN'S LITERATURE, District of Columbia Jewish Community Center, 1529 16th St. N.W., Washington DC 20036. (202)518-9400. Fax: (202)518-9420. E-mail: brett@jcc.org. **Award Director:** Brett Rodgers. **Open to students.** Biannual award. Estab. 1994. Purpose of contest: to enrich all children's appreciation of Jewish culture and to inspire writers and illustrators for children. Newly published submissions only. Submissions are made by the author, made by the author's agent. Must be published January-December of year previous to award year. Deadline: May 30, 2003. SASE for entry deadlines, award rules and entry forms. Entry fee is $25. Award at least $750. Judging by a panel of three judges—a librarian, a children's bookstore owner and a reviewer of books. Requirements for entrants: must live in the United States. Work displayed at the D.C. Jewish Community Center Library. Presentation of awards—October 2003.

SWW ANNUAL CONTEST, SouthWest Writers, 8200 Mountain Rd. NE, Suite 106, Albuquerque NM 87110. (505)265-9485. Fax: (505)265-9483. E-mail: SWriters@aol.com. Website: www.southwestwriters.org. Submit entries to: Contest Chair. Annual contest. Estab. 1982. Purpose of contest: to encourage writers of all genres. Previously unpublished submissions only. Submissions made by author. Deadline for entries: May 1, 2002. SASE for contest rules and entry forms. Entry fee. Award consists of cash prizes in each of over 15 categories. Judging by national editors and agents. Official entry form is required.

THE TORONTO BOOK AWARDS, City of Toronto, 100 Queen St. W, 10th Floor, West Tower, Toronto, Ontario M5H 2N2 Canada. (416)392-8191. Fax: (416)392-1247. E-mail: bkurmey@city.toronto.on.ca. Submit entries to: Bev Kurmey, protocol consultant. Annual award. Estab. 1974. Recognizes books of literary or artistic merit that are evocative of Toronto. Submissions made by author, author's agent or nominated by a person or group. Must be published the calendar year prior to the award year. Deadline for entries: last day of February annually. SASE for contest rules and entry forms. Awards $15,000 in prize money. Judging by committee.

TREASURE STATE AWARD, Missoula Public Library, Missoula County Schools, Montana Library Assoc., 301 E. Main, Missoula MT 59802. (406)721-2005. Fax: (406)728-5900. E-mail: bammon@missoula.lib.mt.us. Website: www.missoula.lib.mt.us. **Award Directors:** Bette Ammon and Carole Monlux. Annual award. Estab. 1990. Purpose of the award: Children in grades K-3 read or listen to a ballot of 5 picture books and vote on their favorite. Previously published submissions only. Submissions made by author, nominated by a person or group of people—children, librarians, teachers. Must be published in previous 5 years to voting year. Deadline for entries: March 20. SASE for contest rules and entry forms. No entry fee. Awards a plaque or sculpture. Judging by popular vote by Montana children grades K-3.

VEGETARIAN ESSAY CONTEST, The Vegetarian Resource Group, P.O. Box 1463, Baltimore MD 21203. (410)366-VEGE. Fax: (410)366-8804. E-mail: vrg@vrg.org. Website: www.vrg.org. Address to Vegetarian Essay Contest. Annual contest. Estab. 1985. Purpose of contest: to promote vegetarianism in young people. Unpublished submissions only. Deadline for entries: May 1 of each year. SASE for contest rules and entry forms. No entry fee. Awards $50 savings bond. Judging by awards committee. Acquires right for The Vegetarian Resource Group to reprint essays. Requirements for entrants: age 18 and under. Winning works may be published in *Vegetarian Journal*, instructional materials for students. "Submit 2-3 page essay on any aspect of vegetarianism, which is the abstinence of meat, fish and fowl. Entrants can base paper on interviewing, research or personal opinion. Need not be vegetarian to enter."

VFW VOICE OF DEMOCRACY, Veterans of Foreign Wars of the U.S., 406 W. 34th St., Kansas City MO 64111. (816)968-1117. Fax: (816)968-1149. Website: www.vfw.org. **Open to students.** Annual contest. Estab. 1960. Purpose of contest: to give high school students the opportunity to voice their opinions about their responsibility to our country and to convey those opinions via the broadcast media to all of America. Deadline for entries: November 1st. No entry fee. Winners receive awards ranging from $1,000-25,000. Requirements for entrants: "Ninth-twelfth grade students in public, parochial, private and home schools are eligible to compete. Former first place state winners are not eligible to compete again. Contact your participating high school teacher, counselor or your local VFW Post to enter."

VSA (VERY SPECIAL ARTS) PLAYWRIGHT DISCOVERY PROGRAM, (formerly Very Special Arts Playwright Discovery), VSA, 1300 Connecticut Ave., NW, Suite 700, Washington DC 20036. (202)628-2800 or 1-800-933-8721. TTY: (202)737-0645. Fax: (202)737-0725. E-mail: playwright@vsarts.org. Website: www.vsarts.org. Annual contest. Estab. 1984. "All scripts must document the experience of living with a disability." Unpublished submissions only. Deadline for entries: May 1, 2003. Write to Playwright Discovery Program Manager for contest rules and entry forms. No entries returned. No entry fee. Judging by Artists Selection Committee. Entrants must be students, grades 6-12. "Script will be selected for production at The John F. Kennedy Center for the Performing Arts, Washington DC. The winning play(s) is presented each fall."

☑ **WASHINGTON POST/CHILDREN'S BOOK GUILD AWARD FOR NONFICTION**, E-mail: theguild@childrensbookguild.org. Website: www.childrensbookguild.org. **President:** Laura Krauss Melmed, 2002-2003. Annual award. Estab. 1977. Purpose of award: "to honor an author or illustrator whose total work has contributed significantly to the quality of nonficiton for children." Award includes a cash prize and an engraved crystal paperweight. Judging by a jury of Children's Book Guild librarians and authors and a *Washington Post* book critic. "One doesn't enter. One is selected. Authors and publishers mistakenly send us books. Our jury annually selects one author for the award."

WE ARE WRITERS, TOO!, Creative With Words Publications, P.O. Box 223226, Carmel CA 93922. Fax: (831)655-8627. E-mail: cwwpub@usa.net. Website: members.tripod.com/CreativeWithWords. **Contest Director:** Brigitta Geltrich. Four times a year (April, May, June, September). Estab. 1975. Purpose of award: to further creative writing in children. Unpublished submissions only. Can submit year round on any topic. Deadlines for entries: year round. SASE for contest rules and entry forms. SASE for return of entries "if not accepted." No entry fee. Awards publication in an anthology, on website if winning poem, and a free copy for "Best of the Month." Judging by selected guest editors and educators. Contest open to children only (up to and including 19 years old). Writer should request contest rules. SASE with all correspondence. Age of child and home address must be stated and ms must be verified of its authenticity. Each story or poem must have a title. Creative with Words Publications (CWW) publishes the top 100-120 mss submitted to the contest CWW also publishes anthologies on various themes throughout the year to which young writers may submit. Request theme list, include SASE, or visit our website. "Website offers special contests to young writers with prizes."

WESTERN HERITAGE AWARDS, National Cowboy and Western Heritage Museum, 1700 NE 63rd St., Oklahoma City OK 73111-7997. (405)478-2250. Fax: (405)478-4714. E-mail: editor@nationalcowboy museum.org. Website: www.nationalcowboymuseum.org. **Director of Public Relations:** Lynda Haller. Annual award. Estab. 1961. Purpose of award: The WHA are presented annually to encourage the accurate and artistic telling of great stories of the West through 15 categories of western literature, television, film and music; including fiction, nonfiction, children's books and poetry. Previously published submissions only; must be published the calendar year before the awards are presented. Deadline for literary entries: November 30. Deadline for film, music and television entries: December 31. Entries not returned. Entry fee is $35/entry. Awards a Wrangler bronze sculpture designed by famed western artist, John Free. Judging by a panel of judges selected each year with distinction in various fields of western art and heritage. Requirements for entrants: The material must pertain to the development or preservation of the West, either from a historical or contemporary viewpoint. Literary entries must have been published between December 1 and November 30 of calendar year. Film, music, or television entries must have been released or aired between January 1 and December 31 of calendar year of entry. Works recognized during special awards ceremonies held annually at the museum. There is an autograph party preceding the awards. Awards ceremonies are sometimes broadcast.

JACKIE WHITE MEMORIAL NATIONAL CHILDREN'S PLAY WRITING CONTEST, Columbia Entertainment Company, 309 Parkade Blvd., Columbia MO 65202-1447. (573)874-5628. **Contest Director:** Betsy Phillips. **Open to students.** Annual contest. Estab. 1988. Purpose of contest: to find good plays for over 20 theater school students, grades 8-9, to perform in CEC's theater school and to encourage writing production of large cast scripts suitable for production in theater schools. Previously unpublished submissions only. Submissions made by author. Deadline for entries: June 1. SASE for contest rules and entry forms. Entry fee is $10. Awards $250, production of play, travel expenses to come see production. Judging by board members of CEC and at least one theater school parent. Play is performed during the following season. 2003 winner to be presented during CEC's 2003-04 season. We reserve the right to award 1st place and prize monies without a production. All submissions will be read by at least three readers. Author will receive a written evaluation of the script.

LAURA INGALLS WILDER AWARD, Association for Library Service to Children, Division of the American Library Association, 50 E. Huron, Chicago IL 60611. (312)280-2163. E-mail: alsc@ala.org. Website: www.ala.org/alsc. Interim **Executive Director:** Malore Brown. Award offered every 2 years. Purpose of the award: to recognize an author or illustrator whose books, published in the US, have over a period of years made a substantial and lasting contribution to children's literature. Awards a medal presented at banquet during annual conference. Judging by Wilder Award Selection Committee.

☒ PAUL A. WITTY OUTSTANDING LITERATURE AWARD, International Reading Association, Special Interest Group, Reading for Gifted and Creative Learning, School of Education, P.O. Box 297900, Fort Worth TX 76129. (817)921-7660. Fax: (817)257-7480. E-mail: c.block@tcu.edu. **Award Director:** Dr. Cathy Collins Block. Annual award. Estab. 1979. Categories of entries: poetry/prose at elementary, junior high and senior high levels. Unpublished submissions only. Deadline for entries: February 1. SASE for award rules and entry forms. SASE for return of entries. No entry fee. Awards $25 and plaque, also certificates of merit. Judging by 2 committees for screening and awarding. Works will be published in International Reading Association publications. "The elementary students' entries must be legible and may not exceed 1,000 words. Secondary students' prose entries should be typed and may exceed 1,000 words if necessary. At both elementary and secondary levels, if poetry is entered, a set of five poems must be submitted. All entries and requests for applications must include a self-addressed, stamped envelope."

PAUL A. WITTY SHORT STORY AWARD, International Reading Association, P.O. Box 8139, 800 Barksdale Rd., Newark DE 19714-8139. (302)731-1600. E-mail: exec@reading.org. Website: www.reading .org. The entry must be an original short story appearing in a young children's periodical for the first time during 2001. The short story should serve as a literary standard that encourages young readers to read periodicals. Deadline for entries: The entry must have been published for the first time in the eligibility year; the short story must be submitted during the calendar year of publication. Anyone wishing to nominate a short story should send it to the designated Paul A. Witty Short Award Subcommittee Chair by December 1. Send SASE for guidelines. Award is $1,000 and recognition at the annual IRA Convention.

WOMEN IN THE ARTS ANNUAL CONTESTS, Women In The Arts, P.O. Box 2907, Decatur IL 62524-2907. (217)872-0811. Submit entries to Vice President. **Open to students.** Annual contest. Estab. 1995. Purpose of contest: to encourage beginning writers, as well as published professionals, by offering a contest for well-written material in plays, fiction, essay and poetry. Submissions made by author. Deadline for entries: November 1 annually. SASE for contest rules and entry forms. Entry fee is $2/item. Prize consists of $30 1st place; $25 2nd place; $15 3rd place. Send SASE for complete rules.

ALICE LOUISE WOOD OHIOANA AWARD FOR CHILDREN'S LITERATURE, Ohioana Library Association, 274 E. First Ave., Suite 300, Columbus OH 43201. (614)466-3831. Fax: (614)728-6974. E-mail: ohioana@sloma.state.oh.us. Website: www.oplin.lib.oh.us/OHIOANA/. **Director:** Linda R. Hengst. Annual award. Estab. 1991. Purpose of award: "to recognize an Ohio author whose body of work has made, and continues to make a significant contribution to literature for children or young adults." SASE for award rules and entry forms. Award: $1,000. Requirements for entrants: "must have been born in Ohio, or lived in Ohio for a minimum of five years; established a distinguished publishing record of books for children and young people; body of work has made, and continues to make, a significant contribution to the literature for young people; through whose work as a writer, teacher, administrator, or through community service, interest in children's literature has been encouraged and children have become involved with reading."

☑ CARTER G. WOODSON BOOK AWARD, National Council for the Social Studies, 8555 16th St., Suite 500, Silver Spring MD 20910. (301)588-1800, ext. 114. Fax: (301)588-2049. E-mail: excellence@ ncss.org. Website: www.socialstudies./awards. **Contact:** Manager of Recognition Programs. Annual award, named after Carter G. Woodson (1875-1950), a distinguished African-American historian, educator and social activist. Purpose of contest: to recognize nonfiction books relating to ethnic minorities and authors of such books. NCSS established the Carter G. Woodson Book Awards for the most distinguished social science books appropriate for young readers which depict ethnicity in the United States. This award is intended to "encourage the writing, publishing, and dissemination of outstanding social studies books for young readers which treat topics related to ethnic minorities and race relations sensitively and accurately." Submissions must be previously published made by publishers because copies of the book must be supplied to each member of the selection committee and NCSS headquarters. Eligible books must be published in the year preceding the year in which award is given, i.e., 1997 for 1998 award. The contact deadline is November 1. Rules, criteria and requirements are available at www.ncss.org/awards and are mailed to various publishers in December. Publishers that would like to be added to this mailing list should e-mail or mail their request to the contact information listed above, attention: Carter G. Woodson. No entry fee. Award consists of: a commemorative gift, annual conference presentation, and an announcement published in NCSS periodicals and forwarded to national and Council affiliated media. The publisher, author and illustrator receive written notification of the committee decision. Reviews of award-winning books and "honor books" are published in the NCSS official journal, *Social Education*. The award is presented at the NCSS Annual Conference in November. Judging by committee of social studies educators (teachers, curriculum supervisors and specialists, college/university professors, teacher educators—with a specific interest in multicultural education and the use of literature in social studies instruction) appointed from the NCSS membership at large.

WORK-IN-PROGRESS GRANTS, Society of Children's Book Writers and Illustrators, 8271 Beverly Blvd., Los Angeles CA 90048. Fax: (323)782-1892. E-mail: scbwi@scbwi.org. Website: www.scbwi.org. Annual award. "The SCBWI Work-in-Progress Grants have been established to assist children's book writers in the completion of a specific project." Five categories: (1) General Work-in-Progress Grant. (2) Grant for a Contemporary Novel for Young People. (3) Nonfiction Research Grant. (4) Grant for a Work Whose Author Has Never Had a Book Published. (5) Grant for a Picture Book Writer. Requests for applications may be made beginning October 1. Completed applications accepted February 1-April 1 of each year. SASE for applications for grants. In any year, an applicant may apply for any of the grants except the one awarded for a work whose author has never had a book published. (The recipient of this grant will be chosen from entries in all categories.) Five grants of $1,500 will be awarded annually. Runner-up grants of $500 (one in each category) will also be awarded. "The grants are available to both full and associate members of the SCBWI. They are not available for projects on which there are already contracts." Previous recipients not eligible to apply.

WRITER'S INT'L FORUM CONTESTS, Bristol Services Int'l., P.O. Box 2109, Sequim MA 98382. Website: www.bristolservicesintl.com. Estab. 1997. Purpose to inspire excellence in the traditional short story format and for tightly focused essays. "In fiction we like identifiable characters, strong storylines, and crisp, fresh endings. Open to all ages." SASE or see website to determine if a contest is currently open. Only send a ms if an open contest is listed at website. Read past winning mss online. Judging by Bristol Services Int'l. staff.

WRITING CONFERENCE WRITING CONTESTS, The Writing Conference, Inc., P.O. Box 664, Ottawa KS 66067. Phone/fax: (785)242-1995. E-mail: jbushman@writingconference.com. Website: www.writingconference.com. **Contest Director:** John H. Bushman. **Open to students.** Annual contest. Estab. 1988. Purpose of contest: to further writing by students with awards for narration, exposition and poetry at the elementary, middle school and high school levels. Unpublished submissions only. Submissions made by the author or teacher. Deadline for entries: January 8. SASE for contest rules and entry form or consult website. No entry fee. Awards plaque and publication of winning entry in *The Writers' Slate*, March issue. Judging by a panel of teachers. Requirements for entrants: must be enrolled in school—K-12th grade.

WRITING FOR CHILDREN COMPETITION, The Writers Union of Canada, 40 Wellington St. E., 3rd Floor, Toronto, Ontario M5E 1C7 Canada. (416)703-8982, ext. 223. Fax: (416)504-7656. E-mail: projects@writersunion.ca. Website: www.writersunion.ca. **Contest Director:** Caroline Sin. Submit entries to: Caroline Sin, projects manager. **Open to students.** Annual contest. Estab. 1997. Purpose of contest: to discover, encourage and promote new writers of children's literature. Unpublished submissions only. Submissions made by author. Deadline for entries: April 23, 2003. Entry fee is $15. Awards $1,500 and submission of winner and finalists to 3 publishers of children's books. Judging by members of the Writers Union of Canada (all published writers with at least one book). Requirements for entrants: Open only to writers; illustrated books do not qualify.

YEARBOOK EXCELLENCE CONTEST, *Quill and Scroll*, School of Journalism, University of Iowa, Iowa City IA 52242-1528. (319)335-5795. Fax: (319)335-5210. E-mail: quill-scroll@uiowa.edu. Website: www.uiowa.edu/~quill-sc. **Executive Director:** Richard Johns. **Open to students.** Annual contest. Estab. 1987. Purpose of contest: to recognize and reward student journalists for their work in yearbooks and to provide student winners an opportunity to apply for a scholarship to be used freshman year in college for students planning to major in journalism. Previously published submissions only. Submissions made by the author or school yearbook adviser. Must be published between November 1, 2001 and November 1, 2002. Deadline for entries: November 1. SASE for contest rules and entry form. Entry fee is $2 per entry. Awards National Gold Key; sweepstakes winners receive plaque; seniors eligible for scholarships. Judging by various judges. Winning entries may be published in *Quill and Scroll* magazine.

YOUNG ADULT CANADIAN BOOK AWARD, The Canadian Library Association, 328 Frank St., Ottawa, Ontario K2P 0X8 Canada. (613)232-9625. Fax: (613)563-9895. Website: www.cla.ca. **Contact:** Committee Chair. Annual award. Estab. 1981. Purpose of award: "to recognize the author of an outstanding English-language Canadian book which appeals to young adults between the ages of 13 and 18 that was published the preceding calendar year. Information is available upon request. We approach publishers, also send news releases to various journals, i.e., *Quill & Quire*." Entries are not returned. No entry fee. Awards a leather-bound book. Requirement for entrants: must be a work of fiction (novel or short stories), the title must be a Canadian publication in either hardcover or paperback, and the author must be a Canadian citizen or landed immigrant. Award given at the Canadian Library Association Conference.

☑ **YOUNG READER'S CHOICE AWARD**, Pacific Northwest Library Association, 3738 W. Central, Missoula MT 59804. (406)542-4055. Fax: (406)543-5358. E-mail: monlux@montana.com. Website: www. PNLA.org. **Award Director:** Carole Monlux, chair YRCA. "This award is not for unsolicited books—the short list for this award is nominated by students, teachers and librarians and it is only for students in the Pacific Northwest to vote on the winner." YRCA is intended to be a Book Award chosen by students—not adults. It is the oldest children's choice award in US and Canada. Previously published submissions only (the titles are 3 years old when voted upon). Submissions nominated by a person or group in the Pacific Northwest. Deadline for entries: Febraury 1—Pacific Northwest nominations only. SASE for contest rules and entry forms. Awards medal made of Idaho silver, depicting eagle and salmon in northwest. Native American symbols. Judging by students in Pacific Northwest.

Helpful Books & Publications

The editor of *Children's Writer's & Illustrator's Market* suggests the following books and periodicals to keep you informed on writing and illustrating techniques, trends in the field, business issues, industry news and changes, and additional markets.

BOOKS

AN AUTHOR'S GUIDE TO CHILDREN'S BOOK PROMOTION, by Susan Salzman Raab, 345 Millwood Rd., Chappaqua NY 10514. (914)241-2117. E-mail: info@raabassociates.com. Website: www.raabassociates.com/authors.htm.

THE BUSINESS OF WRITING FOR CHILDREN, by Aaron Shepard, Shepard Publications. Website: www.aaronshep.com/kidwriter/Business.html. Available on www.amazon.com.

☑ **CHILDREN'S WRITER GUIDE**, (annual), The Institute of Children's Literature, 93 Long Ridge Rd., West Redding CT 06896-0811. (800)443-6078. Website: www.writersbookstore.com.

☑ **CHILDREN'S WRITER'S REFERENCE**, by Berthe Amoss and Eric Suben, Writer's Digest Books, 4700 E. Galbraith Rd., Cincinnati OH 45236. (800)448-0915. Website: www.writersdigest.com.

☑ **CHILDREN'S WRITER'S WORD BOOK**, by Alijandra Mogilner, Writer's Digest Books, 4700 E. Galbraith Rd., Cincinnati OH 45236. (800)448-0915. Website: www.writersdigest.com.

THE COMPLETE IDIOT'S GUIDE® TO PUBLISHING CHILDREN'S BOOKS, by Harold D. Underdown and Lynne Rominger, Alpha Books, 201 W. 103rd St., Indianapolis IN 46290. Website: www.idiotsguides.com.

☑ **CREATING CHARACTERS KIDS WILL LOVE**, by Elaine Marie Alphin, Writer's Digest Books, 4700 E. Galbraith Rd., Cincinnati OH 45236. (800)448-0915. Website: www.writersdigest.com.

☑ **FORMATTING & SUBMITTING YOUR MANUSCRIPT**, by Jack and Glenda Neff, Don Prues and the editors of *Writer's Market*, Writer's Digest Books, 4700 E. Galbraith Rd., Cincinnati OH 45236. (800)448-0915. Website: www.writersdigest.com.

☑ **GUIDE TO LITERARY AGENTS**, (annual) edited by Rachel Vater, Writer's Digest Books, 4700 E. Galbraith Rd., Cincinnati OH 45236. (800)448-0915. Website: www.writersdigest.com.

HOW TO PROMOTE YOUR CHILDREN'S BOOK: A SURVIVAL GUIDE, by Evelyn Gallardo, Primate Production, P.O. Box 3038, Manhattan Beach CA 90266, Website: www.evegallardo.com/promote.html.

HOW TO WRITE A CHILDREN'S BOOK & GET IT PUBLISHED, by Barbara Seuling, Charles Scribner's Sons, 1230 Avenue of the Americas, New York NY 10020. (212)702-2000.

☑ **HOW TO WRITE AND ILLUSTRATE CHILDREN'S BOOKS AND GET THEM PUBLISHED**, edited by Treld Pelkey Bicknell and Felicity Trottman, Writer's Digest Books, 4700 E. Galbraith Rd., Cincinnati OH 45236. (800)448-0915. Website: www.writersdigest.com.

☑ **HOW TO WRITE ATTENTION-GRABBING QUERY & COVER LETTERS**, by John Wood, Writer's Digest Books, 4700 E. Galbraith Rd., Cincinnati OH 45236. (800)448-0915. Website: www.writersdigest.com.

IT'S A BUNNY-EAT-BUNNY WORLD: A Writer's Guide to Surviving and Thriving in Today's Competitive Children's Book Market, by Olga Litowinsky, 435 Hudson St., New York NY 10014. (212)727-8300. Website: www.walkerbooks.com.

☒ **PICTURE WRITING: A New Approach to Writing for Kids and Teens**, by Anastasia Suen, Writer's Digest Books, 4700 E. Galbraith Rd., Cincinnati OH 45236. (800)448-0915. Website: www.writersdigest.com.

☑ **STORY SPARKERS: A Creativity Guide for Children's Writers**, by Marcia Thornton Jones and Debbie Dadey, Writer's Digest Books, 4700 E. Galbraith Rd., Cincinnati OH 45236. (800)448-0915. Website: www.writersdigest.com.

A TEEN'S GUIDE TO GETTING PUBLISHED, by Danielle Dunn & Jessica Dunn, Prufrock Press, P.O. Box 8813, Waco TX 76714-8813. (800)998-2208.

☑ **THE WRITER'S ESSENTIAL DESK REFERENCE**, Second Edition, Writer's Digest Books, 4700 E. Galbraith Rd., Cincinnati OH 45236. (800)448-0915. Website: www.writersdigest.com.

☑ **THE WRITER'S GUIDE TO CRAFTING STORIES FOR CHILDREN**, by Nancy Lamb, Writer's Digest Books, 4700 E. Galbraith Rd., Cincinnati OH 45236. (800)448-0915. Website: www.writersdigest.com.

☑ **WRITING AND ILLUSTRATING CHILDREN'S BOOKS FOR PUBLICATION: Two Perspectives**, by Berthe Amoss and Eric Suben, Writer's Digest Books, 4700 E. Galbraith Rd., Cincinnati OH 45236. (800)448-0915. Website: www.writersdigest.com.

WRITING BOOKS FOR YOUNG PEOPLE, Second Edition, by James Cross Giblin, The Writer, Inc., 120 Boylston St., Boston MA 02116-4615. (617)423-3157.

☑ **WRITING FOR CHILDREN & TEENAGERS**, Third Edition, by Lee Wyndham and Arnold Madison, Writer's Digest Books, 4700 E. Galbraith Rd., Cincinnati OH 45236. (800)448-0915. Website: www.writersdigest.com.

WRITING WITH PICTURES: How to Write and Illustrate Children's Books, by Uri Shulevitz, Watson-Guptill Publications, 1515 Broadway, New York NY 10036. (212)764-7300.

☑ **YOU CAN WRITE CHILDREN'S BOOKS**, by Tracey E. Dils, Writer's Digest Books, 4700 E. Galbraith Rd., Cincinnati OH 45236. (800)448-0915. Website: www.writersdigest.com.

☑ **THE YOUNG WRITER'S GUIDE TO GETTING PUBLISHED**, by Kathy Henderson, Writer's Digest Books, 4700 E. Galbraith Rd., Cincinnati OH 45236. (800)448-0915. Website: www.writersdigest.com.

PUBLICATIONS

BOOK LINKS: Connecting Books, Libraries and Classrooms, editor Laura Tillotson, American Library Association, 50 E. Huron St., Chicago IL 60611. (800)545-2433. Website: www.ala.org/BookLinks. *Magazine published 6 times a year (September-July) for the purpose of connecting books, libraries and classrooms. Features articles on specific topics followed by bibliographies recommending books for further information. Subscription: $25.95/year.*

CHILDREN'S BOOK INSIDER, editor Laura Backes, 901 Columbia Rd., Ft. Collins CO 80525-1838. (970)495-0056 or (800)807-1916. E-mail: mail@write4kids.com. Website: www.write4kids.com. *Monthly newsletter covering markets, techniques and trends in children's publishing. Subscription: $29.95/year. Official update source for* Children's Writer's & Illustrator's Market, *featuring quarterly lists of changes and updates to listings in CWIM.*

CHILDREN'S WRITER, editor Susan Tierney, The Institute of Children's Literature, 95 Long Ridge Rd., West Redding CT 06896-0811. (800)443-6078. Website: www.childrenswriter.com. *Monthly newsletter of writing and publishing trends in the children's field. Subscription: $26/year; special introductory rate: $15.*

☑ **THE FIVE OWLS**, editor Dr. Mark West, 2000 Sheridan Ave. S., Minneapolis MN 55405. (612)377-2004. Website: www.fiveowls.com. *Bimonthly newsletter for readers personally and professionally involved in children's literature. Subscription: $35/year.*

THE HORN BOOK MAGAZINE, editor-in-chief Roger Sutton, The Horn Book Inc., 56 Roland St., Suite 200, Boston MA 02129. (800)325-1170. E-mail: info@hbook.com. E-mail: jlorder@jhu.edu. Website: www.hbook.com. *Bimonthly guide to the children's book world including views on the industry and reviews of the latest books. Subscription: special introductory rate: $29.95.*

THE LION AND THE UNICORN: A Critical Journal of Children's Literature, editors Jack Zipes and Louisa Smith, The Johns Hopkins University Press, P.O. Box 19966, Baltimore MD 21211-0966. (800)548-1784 or (410)516-6987. E-mail: jlorder@jhu.edu. Website: www.press.jhu.edu/press/journals/uni/uni.html. *Magazine published 3 times a year serving as a forum for discussion of children's literature featuring interviews with authors, editors and experts in the field. Subscription: $26.50/year.*

ONCE UPON A TIME, editor Audrey Baird, 553 Winston Court, St. Paul MN 55118. (651)457-6223. Fax: (651)457-9565. Website: http://members.aol.com/OUATMAG/. *Quarterly support magazine for children's writers and illustrators and those interested in children's literature. Subscription: $25/year.*

☑ **PUBLISHERS WEEKLY**, editor-in-chief Nora Rawlinson, Reed Business Information, a division of Reed Elsevier Inc., 360 Park Ave. S., New York NY 10010. (800)278-2991. Website: www.publishersweekly.com. *Weekly trade publication covering all aspects of the publishing industry; includes coverage of the children's field and spring and fall issues devoted solely to children's books. Subscription: $189/year. Available on newsstands for $4/issue. (Special issues are higher in price.)*

☑ **RIVERBANK REVIEW of books for young readers**, editor Martha Davis Beck, 1624 Harmon Place, Suite 305, Minneapolis MN 55403. (615)486-5690. E-mail: mail@riverbankreview.com. Website: www.riverbankreview.com. *Quarterly publication exploring the world of children's literature including book reviews, articles and essays. Subscription: $22.95/year.*

SOCIETY OF CHILDREN'S BOOK WRITERS AND ILLUSTRATORS BULLETIN, editors Stephen Mooser and Lin Oliver, SCBWI, 8271 Beverly Blvd., Los Angeles CA 90048. (323)782-1010. Website: www.scbwi.org/pubs.htm. *Bimonthly newsletter of SCBWI covering news of interest to members. Subscription with $60/year membership.*

Useful Online Resources

The editors of *Children's Writer's & Illustrator's Market* suggest the following websites to keep you informed on writing and illustrating techniques, trends in the field, business issues, industry news and changes, and additional markets.

AMAZON.COM: www.amazon.com
Calling itself "A bookstore too big for the physical world," Amazon.com has more than 3 million books available on their website at discounted prices, plus a personal notification service of new releases, reader reviews, bestseller and suggested book information.

Ⓝ AMERICA WRITES FOR KIDS: usawrites4kids.drury.edu/
Lists book authors by state along with interviews, profiles and writing tips.

Ⓝ ARTLEX ART DICTIONARY: www.artlex.com
Art dictionary with more than 3,200 terms

ASSOCIATION FOR LIBRARY SERVICE TO CHILDREN: www.ala.org/alsc/awards.html
This site provides links to information about Newbery, Caldecott, Coretta Scott King and Michael L. Printz Awards as well as a host of other awards for notable children's books.

AUTHORS AND ILLUSTRATORS FOR CHILDREN WEBRING: www.webring.org/cgi-bin/webring?ring=aicwebring;list
Here you'll find a list of link of sites of interest to children's writers and illustrators or created by them.

THE AUTHORS GUILD ONLINE: www.authorsguild.org/
The website of The Authors Guild offers articles and columns dealing with contract issues, copyright, electronic rights and other legal issues of concern to writers.

BARNES & NOBLE ONLINE: www.bn.com
The world's largest bookstore chain's website contains 600,000 in-stock titles at discount prices as well as personalized recommendations, online events with authors and book forum access for members.

BOOKWIRE: www.bookwire.com
A gateway to finding information about publishers, booksellers, libraries, authors, reviews and awards. Also offers frequently asked publishing questions and answers, a calendar of events, a mailing list and other helpful resources.

CANADIAN CHILDREN'S BOOK CENTRE: www.bookcentre.ca
The site for the CCBC includes profiles of illustrators and authors, information on recent books, a calendar of upcoming events, information on CCBC publications, and tips from Canadian children's authors.

Ⓝ CANADIAN SOCIETY OF CHILDREN'S AUTHORS, ILLUSTRATORS AND PERFORMERS: www.canscaip.org
This organization promotes all aspects of Children's writing, illustration and performance.

THE CHILDREN'S BOOK COUNCIL: www.cbcbooks.org/
This site includes a complete list of CBC members with addresses, names and descriptions of what each publishes, and links to publishers' websites. Also offers previews of upcoming titles from members; articles from CBC Features, *the Council's newsletter; and their catalog.*

Ⓝ CHILDREN'S LITERATURE: www.childrenslit.com
Offers book reviews, lists of conferences, searchable database, links to over 1,000 author/illustrator websites and much more.

CHILDREN'S LITERATURE WEB GUIDE: www.ucalgary.ca/~dkbrown/index.html
This site includes stories, poetry, resource lists, lists of conferences, links to book reviews, lists of awards (international), and information on books from classic to contemporary.

CHILDREN'S WRITING SUPERSITE: www.write4kids.com
This site (formerly Children's Writers Resource Center) includes highlights from the newsletter Children's Book Insider; *definitions of publishing terms; answers to frequently asked questions; information on trends; information on small presses; a research center for Web information; and a catalog of material available from* CBI.

THE COLOSSAL DIRECTORY OF CHILDREN'S PUBLISHERS ONLINE: (formerly Children's Publishers' Submission Guidelines) www.signaleader.com/childrens-writers/
This site features links to websites of children's publishers and magazines and includes information on which publishers offer submission guidelines online.

THE DRAWING BOARD: http://members.aol.com/thedrawing
This site for illustrators features articles, interviews, links and resources for illustrators from all fields.

EDITOR & PUBLISHER: www.mediainfo.com
The Internet source for Editor & Publisher, *this site provides up-to-date industry news, with other opportunities such as a research area and bookstore, a calendar of events and classifieds.*

N IMAGINARY LANDS: www.imaginarylands.org
A fun site with links to websites about picture books, learning tools and children's literature.

N INTERNATIONAL BOARD ON BOOKS FOR YOUNG PEOPLE: www.ibby.org
Founded in Switzerland in 1953, IBBY is a nonprofit that seeks to encourage the creation and distribution of quality children's literature. They cooperate with children's organizations and children's book institutions around the world.

INTERNATIONAL READING ASSOCIATION: www.reading.org
This website includes articles; book lists; event, conference and convention information; and an online bookstore.

N NATIONAL WRITERS UNION: www.nwu.org
The union for freelance writers in U.S. Markets. The NWU offers contract advice, greviance assistance, health and liability insurance and much more.

ONCE UPON A TIME: http://members.aol.com/OUATMAG
This companion site to Once Upon A Time *magazine offers excerpts from recent articles, notes for prospective contributors, and information about OUAT's 11 regular columnists.*

PICTUREBOOK: www.picture-book.com
This site brought to you by Picturebook sourcebook offers tons of links for illustrators, portfolio searching, and news, and offers a listserv, bulletin board and chatroom.

PUBLISHERS' CATALOGUES HOME PAGE: www.lights.com/publisher/index.html
A mammoth link collection of more than 6,000 publishers around the world arranged geographically. This site is one of the most comprehensive directories of publishers on the Internet.

PUBLISHERS WEEKLY CHILDREN'S FEATURES: www.publishersweekly.com/childrensindex.asp
This is a direct link to Publishers Weekly *articles relating to children's publishing and authors.*

THE PURPLE CRAYON: www.underdown.org
Editor Harold Underdown's site includes articles on trends, business, and cover letters and queries as well as interviews with editors and answers to frequently asked questions. He also includes links to a number of other sites helpful to writers and excerpts from his book The Complete Idiot's Guide to Publishing Children's Books.

SLANTVILLE: www.slantville.com/
An online artists community, this site includes a yellow pages for artists, frequently asked questions and a library offering information on a number of issues of interest to illustrators. This is a great site to visit to view artists' portfolios.

SOCIETY OF CHILDREN'S BOOK WRITERS AND ILLUSTRATORS: www.scbwi.org
This recently redesigned site includes information on awards and grants available to SCBWI members, a calendar of events listed by date and region, a list of publications available to members, and a site map for easy navigation. Balan welcomes suggestions for the site from visitors.

THE SOCIETY OF ILLUSTRATORS: www.societyillustrators.org
Since 1901, this organization has been working to promote the interest of professional illustrators. Information on exhibitions, career advice, and many other links provided.

UNITED STATES POSTAL SERVICE: www.usps.gov/welcome.htm
Offers domestic and International postage rate calculator, stamp ordering, zip code look up, express mail tracking and more.

VERLA KAY'S WEBSITE: www.verlakay.com
Author Verla Kay's website features writer's tips, articles, a schedules of online workshops (with transcripts of past workshops), a good news board and helpful links.

WRITERSDIGEST.COM: www.writersdigest.com
Brought to you by Writer's Digest *magazine and* Writer's Market, *this site features a hot list, conference listings, markets of the day, and a searchable database of more than 1,500 writer's guidelines.*

WRITERSMARKET.COM: www.writersmarket.com
This gateway to the Writer's Market *online edition offers market news, FAQs, tips, featured markets and web resources, a free newsletter, and more.*

N WRITING-WORLD.COM: www.writing-world.com/children
Site features reams of advice, links and offers a free bi-weekly newsletter.

Glossary

AAR. Association of Authors' Representatives.

ABA. American Booksellers Association.

ABC. Association of Booksellers for Children.

Advance. A sum of money a publisher pays a writer or illustrator prior to the publication of a book. It is usually paid in installments, such as one half on signing the contract; one half on delivery of a complete and satisfactory manuscript. The advance is paid against the royalty money that will be earned by the book.

ALA. American Library Association.

All rights. The rights contracted to a publisher permitting the use of material anywhere and in any form, including movie and book club sales, without additional payment to the creator. (See Answers to All Your Questions About All-Rights Contracts, page 20.)

Anthology. A collection of selected writings by various authors or gatherings of works by one author.

Anthropomorphization. The act of attributing human form and personality to things not human (such as animals).

ASAP. As soon as possible.

Assignment. An editor or art director asks a writer, illustrator or photographer to produce a specific piece for an agreed-upon fee.

B&W. Black & white.

Backlist. A publisher's list of books not published during the current season but still in print.

Biennially. Occurring once every 2 years.

Bimonthly. Occurring once every 2 months.

Biweekly. Occurring once every 2 weeks.

Book packager. A company that draws all elements of a book together, from the initial concept to writing and marketing strategies, then sells the book package to a book publisher and/or movie producer. Also known as book producer or book developer.

Book proposal. Package submitted to a publisher for consideration usually consisting of a synopsis, outline and sample chapters. (See Before Your First Sale, page 8; and The Nonfiction Proposal: Put Your Best Foot Forward, page 66.)

Business-size envelope. Also known as a #10 envelope. The standard size used in sending business correspondence.

Camera-ready. Refers to art that is completely prepared for copy camera platemaking.

Caption. A description of the subject matter of an illustration or photograph; photo captions include persons' names where appropriate. Also called cutline.

Clean-copy. A manuscript free of errors and needing no editing; it is ready for typesetting.

Clips. Samples, usually from newspapers or magazines, of a writer's published work.

Concept books. Books that deal with ideas, concepts and large-scale problems, promoting an understanding of what's happening in a child's world. Most prevalent are alphabet and counting books, but also includes books dealing with specific concerns facing young people (such as divorce, birth of a sibling, friendship or moving).

Contract. A written agreement stating the rights to be purchased by an editor, art director or producer and the amount of payment the writer, illustrator or photographer will receive for that sale. (See The Business of Writing & Illustrating, page 13.)

Contributor's copies. The magazine issues sent to an author, illustrator or photographer in which her work appears.

Co-op publisher. A publisher that shares production costs with an author, but, unlike subsidy publishers, handles all marketing and distribution. An author receives a high percentage of royalties until her initial investment is recouped, then standard royalties. (*Children's Writer's & Illustrator's Market* does not include co-op publishers.)

Copy. The actual written material of a manuscript.

Copyediting. Editing a manuscript for grammar usage, spelling, punctuation and general style.

Copyright. A means to legally protect an author's/illustrator's/photographer's work. This can be shown by writing ©, the creator's name, and year of work's creation. (See The Business of Writing & Illustrating, page 13.)

Cover letter. A brief letter, accompanying a complete manuscript, especially useful if responding to an editor's request for a manuscript. May also accompany a book proposal. (See Before Your First Sale, page 8.)

Cutline. See caption.

Disk. A round, flat magnetic plate on which computer data may be stored.

Division. An unincorporated branch of a company.

Dummy. A loose mock-up of a book showing placement of text and artwork.

Electronic submission. A submission of material by modem or on computer disk.

E-mail. Electronic mail. Messages sent from one computer to another via a modem or computer network.

Final draft. The last version of a polished manuscript ready for submission to an editor.

First North American serial rights. The right to publish material in a periodical for the first time, in the United States or Canada. (See The Business of Writing & Illustrating, page 13.)

F&G's. Folded and gathered sheets. An early, not-yet-bound copy of a picture book.

Flat fee. A one-time payment.

Galleys. The first typeset version of a manuscript that has not yet been divided into pages.

Genre. A formulaic type of fiction, such as horror, mystery, romance, science fiction or western.

Glossy. A photograph with a shiny surface as opposed to one with a non-shiny matte finish.

Gouache. Opaque watercolor with an appreciable film thickness and an actual paint layer.

Halftone. Reproduction of a continuous tone illustration with the image formed by dots produced by a camera lens screen.

Hard copy. The printed copy of a computer's output.

Hardware. All the mechanically-integrated components of a computer that are not software—circuit boards, transistors and the machines that are the actual computer.

Hi-Lo. High interest, low reading level.

Home page. The first page of a website.

IBBY. International Board on Books for Young People.

Imprint. Name applied to a publisher's specific line of books.

Internet. A worldwide network of computers that offers access to a wide variety of electronic resources.

IRA. International Reading Association.

IRC. International Reply Coupon. Sold at the post office to enclose with text or artwork sent to a recipient outside your own country to cover postage costs when replying or returning work.

Keyline. Identification of the positions of illustrations and copy for the printer.

Layout. Arrangement of illustrations, photographs, text and headlines for printed material.

Line drawing. Illustration done with pencil or ink using no wash or other shading.

Mass market books. Paperback books directed toward an extremely large audience sold in supermarkets, drugstores, airports, newsstands, online retailers, and bookstores.

Mechanicals. Paste-up or preparation of work for printing.

Middle grade or mid-grade. See middle reader.

Middle reader. The general classification of books written for readers approximately ages 9-11. Also called middle grade.

Modem. A small electrical box that plugs into the serial card of a computer, used to transmit data from one computer to another, usually via telephone lines.

Ms (mss). Manuscript(s).

Multiple submissions. See simultaneous submissions.

NCTE. National Council of Teachers of English.

One-time rights. Permission to publish a story in periodical or book form one time only. (See The Business of Writing & Illustrating, page 13.)

Outline. A summary of a book's contents; often in the form of chapter headings with a descriptive sentence or two under each heading to show the scope of the book.

Package sale. The sale of a manuscript and illustrations/photos as a "package" paid for with one check.

Payment on acceptance. The writer, artist or photographer is paid for her work at the time the editor or art director decides to buy it.

Payment on publication. The writer, artist or photographer is paid for her work when it is published.

Photostat. Black & white copies produced by an inexpensive photographic process using paper negatives; only line values are held with accuracy. Also called stat.

Picture book. A type of book aimed at preschoolers to 8-year-olds that tells a story using a combination of text and artwork, or artwork only.

Print. An impression pulled from an original plate, stone, block, screen or negative; also a positive made from a photographic negative.

Proofreading. Reading text to correct typographical errors.

Query. A letter to an editor or agent designed to capture interest in an article or book you have written or propose to write. (See Before Your First Sale, page 8.)

Reading fee. Money charged by some agents and publishers to read a submitted manuscript. (*Children's Writer's & Illustrator's Market* does not include operations that charge reading fees.)

Reprint rights. Permission to print an already published work whose first rights have been sold to another magazine or book publisher. (See The Business of Writing & Illustrating, page 13.)

Response time. The average length of time it takes an editor or art director to accept or reject a query or submission and inform the creator of the decision.

Rights. The bundle of permissions offered to an editor or art director in exchange for printing a manuscript, artwork or photographs. (See The Business of Writing & Illustrating, page 13.)

Rough draft. A manuscript that has not been checked for errors in grammar, punctuation, spelling or content.

Roughs. Preliminary sketches or drawings.

Royalty. An agreed percentage paid by a publisher to a writer, illustrator or photographer for each copy of her work sold.

SAE. Self-addressed envelope.

SASE. Self-addressed, stamped envelope.

SCBWI. The Society of Children's Book Writers and Illustrators. (See listing in Clubs & Organizations section.)

Second serial rights. Permission for the reprinting of a work in another periodical after its first publication in book or magazine form. (See The Business of Writing & Illustrating, page 13.)

Semiannual. Occurring every 6 months or twice a year.

Semimonthly. Occurring twice a month.

Semiweekly. Occurring twice a week.

Serial rights. The rights given by an author to a publisher to print a piece in one or more periodicals. (See The Business of Writing & Illustrating, page 13.)

Simultaneous submissions. Queries or proposals sent to several publishers at the same time. Also called multiple submissions. (See Before Your First Sale, page 8.)

Slant. The approach to a story or piece of artwork that will appeal to readers of a particular publication.

Slush pile. Editors' term for their collections of unsolicited manuscripts.

Software. Programs and related documentation for use with a computer.

Solicited manuscript. Material that an editor has asked for or agreed to consider before being sent by a writer.

SPAR. Society of Photographers and Artists Representatives.

Speculation (spec). Creating a piece with no assurance from an editor or art director that it will be purchased or any reimbursements for material or labor paid.

Stat. See photostat.

Subsidiary rights. All rights other than book publishing rights included in a book contract, such as paperback, book club and movie rights. (See The Business of Writing & Illustrating, page 13.)

Subsidy publisher. A book publisher that charges the author for the cost of typesetting, printing and promoting a book. Also called a vanity publisher. (*Children's Writer's & Illustrator's Market* does not include subsidy publishers.)

Synopsis. A brief summary of a story or novel. Usually a page to a page and a half, single-spaced, if part of a book proposal.

Tabloid. Publication printed on an ordinary newspaper page turned sideways and folded in half.

Tearsheet. Page from a magazine or newspaper containing your printed art, story, article, poem or photo.

Thumbnail. A rough layout in miniature.

Trade books. Books sold in bookstores and through online retailers, aimed at a smaller audience than mass market books, and printed in smaller quantities by publishers.

Transparencies. Positive color slides; not color prints.

Unsolicited manuscript. Material sent without an editor's or art director's request.

Vanity publisher. See subsidy publisher.

Word processor. A computer that produces typewritten copy via automated text-editing, storage and transmission capabilities.

World Wide Web. An Internet resource that utilizes hypertext to access information. It also supports formatted text, illustrations and sounds, depending on the user's computer capabilities.

Work-for-hire. An arrangement between a writer, illustrator or photographer and a company under which the company retains complete control of the work's copyright. (See The Business of Writing & Illustrating, page 13.)

YA. See young adult.

Young adult. The general classification of books written for readers approximately ages 12-18. Often referred to as YA.

Young reader. The general classification of books written for readers approximately ages 5-8.

Age-Level Index

This index lists book and magazine publishers by the age-groups for which they publish. Use it to locate appropriate markets for your work, then carefully read the listings and follow the guidelines of each publisher. Use this index in conjunction with the Subject Index to further narrow your list of markets. **Picture Books** and **Picture-Oriented Material** are for preschoolers to 8-year-olds; **Young Readers** are for 5- to 8-year-olds; **Middle Readers** are for 9- to 11-year-olds; and **Young Adults** are for ages 12 and up.

BOOK PUBLISHERS

Young Readers

AGE-LEVEL INDEX

Middle Readers

Young Adult/Teen

AGE-LEVEL INDEX

MAGAZINES

Picture-Oriented Material

Young Readers

Middle Readers

Young Adult/Teen

Subject Index

This index lists book and magazine publishers by the fiction and nonfiction subject area in which they publish. Use it to locate appropriate markets for your work, then carefully read the listings and follow the guidelines of each publisher. Use this index in conjunction with Age-Level Index to further narrow your list of markets.

BOOK PUBLISHERS: FICTION

Adventure

Animal

Anthology

Concept

Contemporary

DISCOVER A WORLD OF WRITING SUCCESS

Are you ready to be praised, published, and paid for your writing? It's time to invest in your future with *Writer's Digest*! Beginners and experienced writers alike have been enjoying *Writer's Digest*, the world's leading magazine for writers, for more than 80 years — and it keeps getting better! Each issue is brimming with:

- Inspiration from writers who have been in your shoes
- Detailed info on the latest contests, conferences, markets, and opportunities in every genre
- Tools of the trade, including reviews of the latest writing software and hardware
- Writing prompts and exercises to overcome writer's block and rekindle your creative spark
- Expert tips, techniques, and advice to help you get published
- And so much more!

That's a lot to look forward to every month. Let *Writer's Digest* put you on the road to writing success!

NO RISK!
Send No Money Now!

☐ **Yes!** Please rush me my 2 FREE issues of *Writer's Digest* — the world's leading magazine for writers. If I like what I read, I'll get a full year's subscription (12 issues, including the 2 free issues) for only $19.96. That's 67% off the newsstand rate! If I'm not completely happy, I'll write "cancel" on your invoice, return it and owe nothing. The 2 FREE issues are mine to keep, no matter what!

Name_____

Address_____

City_____

State_____ZIP_____

Annual newsstand rate is $59.88. Orders outside the U.S. will be billed an additional $10 (includes GST/HST in Canada.) Please allow 4-6 weeks for first-issue delivery.

www.writersdigest.com

T6NM1

Get 2 FREE TRIAL ISSUES of Writer's® Digest

Packed with creative inspiration, advice, and tips to guide you on the road to success, *Writer's Digest* will offer you everything you need to take your writing to the next level! You'll discover how to:

- Create dynamic characters and page-turning plots
- Submit query letters that publishers won't be able to refuse
- Find the right agent or editor for you
- Make it out of the slush-pile and into the hands of the right publisher
- Write award-winning contest entries
- And more!

See for yourself by ordering your 2 FREE trial issues today!

Fantasy

Folktales

Health

Suspense/Mystery

BOOK PUBLISHERS: NONFICTION

Activity Books

SUBJECT INDEX

MAGAZINES: FICTION

MAGAZINES: NONFICTION

Poetry Index

This index lists markets that are open to poetry submissions, and is divided into book publishers and magazines. It's important to carefully read the listings and follow the guidelines of each publisher to which you submit.

Photography Index

This index lists markets that buy photos from freelancers, and is divided into book publishers, magazines and greeting cards. It's important to carefully read the listings and follow the guidelines of each publisher to which you submit.

GREETING CARDS

General Index

Market listings that appeared in the 2002 edition of *Children's Writer's & Illustrator's Market* but do not appear in this edition are identified with a two-letter code explaining why the listing was omitted: **(NR)**—No (or late) Response to Listing Request; **(NS)**—Not Currently Accepting Submissions; **(OB)**—Out of Business; **(RR)**—Removed by Request.

Market listings that appeared in the 2002 *Children's Writer's & Illustrator's Market*, but do not appear in this edition are identified with a two-letter code explaining why the listing was omitted: (NR)—No (or late) Response to Listing Request; (NS)—Not Currently Accepting Submissions; (OB)—Out of Business; (RR)—Removed by Request.

GENERAL INDEX

GENERAL INDEX